Dictionary of
Black African Civilization

This dictionary was written with the assistance of

Pierre Alexandre
Hélène Balfet
Genevieve Calame-Griaule
Georges Condominas
Jacqueline Delange
Ariane Deluze
Marguerite Dupire
Igor de Garine
Jean Herniaux

Pierre Ichac
Jean-Paul Lebeuf
Michel Leiris
Raymond Mauny
Paul Mercier
Henri Moniot
Denise Paulme
André Schaeffner
Claude Tardits

Dictionary of Black African Civilization

Georges Balandier
Jacques Maquet

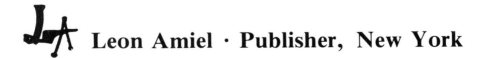

Leon Amiel · Publisher, New York

Copyright © 1974 by Leon Amiel · Publisher, New York.

Picture research and captions by **Nathalie Noël.**

Translated from the French by **Lady (Mariska Caroline) Peck, Bettina Wadia** and **Peninah Neimark**.

PRINTED IN THE UNITED STATES OF AMERICA BY GANIS AND HARRIS, NEW YORK

Library of Congress Cataloging in Publication Data
Main entry under title:

Dictionary of Black African civilization.

   Translation of Dictionnaire des civilisations
africaines.
   1. Africa, Sub-Saharan—Civilization—Dictionaries.
I. Balandier, Georges   II. Maquet, Jacques
Jérome Pierre, 1919-
DT352.4.D5213   916.7'03'03   72-85389
ISBN 0-8148-0480-2

Translator's Note

In preparing this translation, we have attempted to update the original, 1968 French edition of *Dictionaire des Civilisations Africaines* on a limited basis. Names of independent nations have been changed, where necessary, to conform to current usage, and in several instances we have updated articles to reflect current events and new archeological data. However, none of the tribal population or agricultural production figures have been revised.

For the translation of the names of tribes and ethnic groups, we have generally followed George Peter Murdock's *Africa: Its Peoples and Their Culture History* (New York: McGraw-Hill, 1959). For the names of Bantu tribes, however, we have conformed to the common American and British practice of using the Bantu personal plural prefix *Ba*; e.g., "Baluba" rather than "Luba."

On behalf of my co-translators, Lady (Mariska C.) Peck and the late Bettina Wadia, I want to thank William Fagg C.M.G. for the assistance he gave them in the course of the translation of various portions of the book. I also want to thank Glorya Cohen, who proofread the galleys, for her numerous helpful comments, Jerry Burstein for his handsome layout of the English edition and Roy Jensen for his careful handling of all aspects of the production of this book.

PENINAH NEIMARK

Preface

The continent of Africa is no longer on the fringe of the known world; a trip there is no longer a voyage into the dark unknown. Its peoples and their cultural wealth were separated from the course of history for too long, and now they have been summoned to rejoin it. Its civilizations are changing and are becoming creative once again; with a new found strength they are stimulating the soul and the mind of Africa. Its peoples are struggling to become a part of the modern world without losing the values and ways that are an integral part of that soul and mind. This rebirth has made Africa topical and has piqued our curiosity. Today, Africa is more misunderstood than it is exotic.

This book is an attempt by French Africanists to dissipate that misunderstanding. It is an epitome of the knowledge scattered throughout the rapidly accumulating quantity of works on Africa. In addition, it is a synthesis of the authors' experiences with the peoples of Africa, for their experience is not purely academic; they are also fieldworkers.

It covers the civilizations and black African societies in all their variety and individuality, but it does not offer a complete list of tribes and ethnic groups; this would have turned the dictionary into an unenlightening inventory. We have had to select the outstanding and most representative of the great cultural regions, but at the same time we have tried to give an idea of their variety in a number of articles on individual tribes in addition to discussions of general subjects. This will decrease, if not eliminate, the risk of sinning by omission. In the overall picture of black Africa, a profound affinity unites the many in the one; in the "dissemblances" are many resemblances.

The dictionary form has the advantage of helping the reader to find a term or a subject or it may simply stimulate his interest. Discovery and unexpected meaningful encounter may be his as he browses through its pages: *Taboos*, for example, is juxtaposed with *Theater*, *Sacrifice* with *Sahara*. There is an intellectual challenge in its apparent incongruity. The reader who has time can build up a more thorough body of information by systematically following the cross-references from one subject to another.

The *Dictionary of Black African Civilization* satisfies this curiosity through the principles that have guided the choice of articles. The main outlines of African geography are described in it as well as the basic features that give a unique character to its landscape. The landmarks of its history have been plotted to remind us of a fact that has been neglected for too long: the roots of African history have penetrated deep down through the centuries, with a complexity of human endeavor and vicissitude equal to that of the histories which are familiar to us. The principal purpose of this book is to focus attention on the creative life and history of Africa as displayed in its culture, techniques and extraordinarily varied social relationships. The arts, liberally illustrated by photographs of products from the artistic centers, are a reminder of the rich contribution made by the black African to the museums of our cities and our minds. Accounts of traditional oral literature help to give a more exact idea of the African mind, which is also reflected in its cultural diversity, ranging from craft techniques to physical postures and significant movements, myths and ritual practices. This kaleidoscope of everyday life is set in the framework of several articles on social and political structures.

The African himself has not been lost in the alphabetical classification of the dictionary form. He is everywhere present, as much in his symbolic activities as in his work and in his games, as much in his links with tradition as in his march toward the future. Thus, this book is a modest encyclopedia of the black African world and a contribution toward the building of a fuller humanism for today.

GEORGES BALANDIER
JACQUES MAQUET

NOTE: The articles are signed with the initials of their authors.

Dictionary of
Black African Civilization

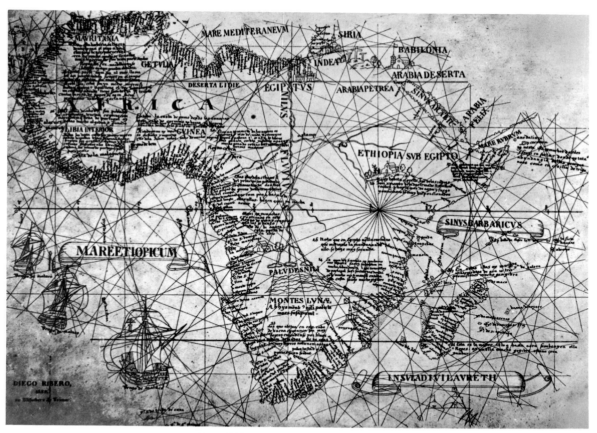

Map of Africa by Diego Ribero (1529) *Photo: Viollet, Roger.*

ADORNMENT. In Africa, as in Oceania and Indonesia, it is the men who wear the brightest and most splendid adornments. During the dance that culminates the great festival which brings together the scattered tribes of the Fulani Bororo of the Niger River region, the young men, covered with jewelry and makeup, appear smiling before the girls, who have to choose the most handsome among them; the dance itself bears some resemblance to the rivalry between the males of a herd in the rutting season. Among the Koniagi of Guinea, only the young men have the privilege of wearing huge crests on their heads, like those of gallinaceous birds, which are symbols of power and beauty.

In several societies, adornments and body markings are arranged in an actual system of signs that almost constitutes a language. Like all languages, it has no meaning outside the framework of fixed and generally accepted conventions. Ornaments are rarely without social significance, which prescribes their use by some and prohibits it to others. In most African societies, a little girl, a marriageable young girl, a young mother, a woman who has lost a child and a widow are distinguished by different hairstyles and are not entitled to the same ornaments. A single plait across her head is all that a little Bambara girl keeps of her hair, and, when she is older, it will be arranged into two plaits on either side of her head. The Kikuyu woman of East Africa shows that she is married by shaving her entire head except for a tuft of hair on the nape. In other parts of Africa, a married woman keeps only an oval patch of hair, which is carefully marked out above her forehead. When her first child is born, a Herero woman of South-West Africa wears a diadem of iron beads mounted on leather. As soon as a Diola woman of Portuguese Guinea realizes that she is pregnant, she exchanges her belt of glass beads for a girdle decorated with grass and fruit. Widows are considered impure everywhere and forced into retirement; their heads are shaved, and they have to dress in a special way during the period of their widowhood.

Adornment tends more to sharpen the differences between the sexes than to efface them; the loincloth, for instance, seems designed to attract attention to the part of the body that it covers. Another motive affecting the choice of adornment is the desire to

1

Loin cover of wrought iron decorated with beads. Kirdi of northern Cameroun. *Photo: Hoa-Qui.*

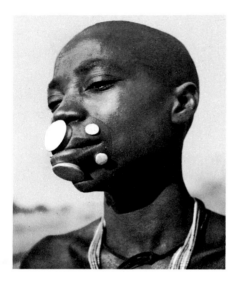

Kirdi woman wearing quartz labrets. Cameroun. *Photo: Hoa-Qui.*

Fulani woman with her hair in the style appropriate for a young mother. Fouta Djallon region, Guinea. *Photo: Musée de l'Homme.*

protect the orifices of the body from dangerous contacts, especially from evil exhalations and supernatural dangers. The lip disc fulfills the dual purpose of adornment and protection. The process of preparing the lip for a disc involves piercing the upper or lower lip with a stem of grass or millet; a disc of stone, wood or metal is eventually inserted in the lip. The extremes to which this very common practice is carried by the Sara women of Chad, with their enormously distended lips, are well known. The Lobi of Upper Volta perform the operation when the child is four or five years old. A woman pierces the child's lip quickly with a thorn about an inch long. The thorn is taken out on the third day and replaced by a piece of straw, which is changed each morning. The wound takes about a week to heal, after which larger and larger grass stems are inserted to increase the hole until the opening is ready to receive a disc of wood or polished quartz, which is never more than an inch wide in this society.

The belt of blue beads, porcelain or glass, which every little girl throughout most of Africa is given as soon as she begins to walk, is again both ornament and talisman. She wears this, her first ornament, nearly all her life. The young girl expects her parents and her boyfriends to increase the length of her belt. A girl's first loincloth, made of a length of cotton with the ends falling free, is slipped into the belt when she is about five or six. The clicking, as she walks, of the beads hidden under her skirt is supposed to arouse male desire. Concealment is the purpose of clothing, but the main function of adornment is to excite desire and admiration. (See also *Basketry; Beads; Birds; Body; Body Painting; Calabashes; Clothing; Combs; Jewelry; Kirdi; Prayer; Scarification.*) D.P.

AFRICA. When Rome destroyed Carthage, she made the conquered territories into a province that she called *Africa,* a word derived from *Afri,* the name of a group of people about whom little is known. The province covered only the northeastern part of present-day Tunisia. After Rome had extended her control over the Maghrib, Caesar created a new province, *Africa Nova* ("New Africa"), to the west of the original province of Africa, which was then designated *Africa Vetus* ("Old Africa"), and the two provinces were united to form the Africa of the early Roman Empire, called *Africa Proconsularis,* after its system of administration. Roughly, it comprised Tunisia, a fairly small strip of eastern Algeria and Tripolitania.

Around the time of the administrative reorganizations of the late Empire and the

Left: Young Daza woman adorning herself. Chad. Photo: Pierre Ichac.
Right: Koniagi dancer. Guinea. Photo: Hoa-Qui.

Byzantine period, Islam inherited the use of the term "Africa." At first a vague concept, *Ifriqiya* soon came to denote the same Tunisian nucleus slightly expanded into eastern Algeria. These were the limits of the Aghlabite Emirate of the ninth century.

While the connotation of the term "Africa" has broadened, the connotations of two other terms of classical origin have become more limited. "Libya" originally signified the entire continent, as Ionian geographers imagined it to be, bordered on the west by the Nile. The Romans called all the white African peoples "Libyans," and all the dark-skinned peoples were "Ethiopians" ("people with burnt faces"). The term "Ethiopian" consequently included those who today are distinguished, sometimes incorrectly, from the "true" blacks under the generally unsatisfactory name of "Hamites."

In the late fifteenth and early sixteenth centuries, the name "Africa" began to denote the entire continent instead of being applied, as it was when its meaning was first widened, only to Mediterranean and white Africa, in contrast to "Ethiopia," the land of the blacks. For a long time, the name "Ethiopia" had a much broader meaning, although it was concurrently applied to Abyssinia only. The word has survived in its widest sense— meaning "blacks and black Africa"—in classical and biblical contexts. "Ethiopiques," the title of a poem by Léopold Senghor, and also the name of the Ethiopian church—founded in South Africa in 1892 as a reaction against the churches of missionaries and white people's use of the word "African"— are examples of its more recent currency. (See also *European Discovery of Black Africa; Race.*)   H.M.

AFRICANITY. Those with a superficial knowledge of black Africa see it as a monolithic culture in which everyone lives, feels and thinks alike; those who know it better stress the diversity of languages, customs and local traditions; and those who know it really well detect beneath the diversity a large cultural unity as broad and as typical as the culture of the civilizations termed Western

Adorned woman. Dapango region, Togo. *Photo: Hoa- Qui.*

European, Islamic and Indian. The cultural unity of the diverse African peoples—the sum of all the component parts that give the various societies of traditional Africa their common characteristics—is known as Africanity. A catalogue of these common elements covers every aspect of culture: production techniques (cultivation of burnt-over land); economics (teamwork in collective fields); politics (decisions reached unanimously rather than by majority vote); kinship (the vital significance of heredity); family (polygamy); religion (ancestor worship); philosophy (the idea of a single life force underlying all living things); and art (the expressionist representation of the concept of man). These are, of course, only a few examples of Africanity.

The explanation of the cultural unity of black Africa is not to be found in some vague, common, racial origin or some mysterious black soul. Basic to Africanity are the similar physical and human conditions, such as poor and unprofitable soil and living in small communities, which produced similar technical, social and psychological adaptations. Secondly, the cultural unity can be explained by the innumerable reciprocal influences on African tribes during their

continual migrations in the interior of this vast area. The fact that Africa south of the Sahara remained isolated and cut off from the mainstream of world development up to the end of the nineteenth century explains how Africanism has kept its original and specific character down to modern times. (See also *Agriculture; Art, African; Culture; Family; Kinship; Migrations; Music; Negritude; Philosophy; Religion.*)   J.M.

AFRO-AMERICANS and AFRICAN INFLUENCE IN THE AMERICAS. See *Hares; Hausa; Heroes; Literature, Written; Music; Pan-Africanism; Pipes; Rattles; Slave Trade; Spiders; Stories; Thumb Pianos; Voodoo; Xylophones; Yoruba.*

AGE GROUPS. In all African societies, an individual's age, as much as the generation to which he belongs, determines his position, rights and duties. The process of growing older is solemnized in various ceremonies. The aged can accede to positions of authority only in societies without established political hierarchies. Certain kinds of knowledge should be acquired only at a specified age, for if acquired before, it is of no advantage to the possessor. Learning is always a form of initiation, and initiation ceremonies are linked to distinct phases of life. In a number of societies, this principle is applied very comprehensively: the men—the women less frequently or organized with more flexibility —are grouped according to their age. Individuals pass from one age group to another, or the entire group moves from one stage to the next, accompanied by rituals and complicated instruction. These groups have economic, military, political and religious functions which are often of greatest importance in the so-called egalitarian communities with no formal government.

Sometimes the age groups control all social activity. Among the Nyakyusa, in the region of Lake Nyasa, a person is considered to be in "good company" only when he is with members of his own age group. These groups are the bases of the villages: they originate in the children's camps that are in charge of the herds; as soon as the eldest children in the group reach manhood, the camp becomes fixed and permanent; when they marry, it becomes an independent village that will later receive its headman from the community to which it originally belonged. New Nyakyusan villages are constantly being formed in this way. This, however, is a very extreme case.

It is more usual for the young men to live, from the time they reach puberty until they are married, in a community of young men their own age, separated from their families, whom they will join again later; this occurs among the Masai of Kenya. Generally, members of these age groups get together again only on special occasions.

The groups, especially those of adolescents and young adults, play a particularly prominent part in the organization of labor. One group, or a combination of groups, works for the village community, the heads of families who ask for help or their future fathers-in-law to whom payment is due for their brides or mistresses. Older age groups are exempt from this work, sometimes as soon as the members are married, for now they are citizens who have a say in village affairs; later on, they will manage the village affairs. In this way, the entire structure of authority can be based on age groups. In Benin, the Edo villages had three age groups: the first was composed of adolescents and young men, who were wholly engaged in work; the second was a unit of young adults, who acted as warriors and police and performed certain extremely arduous tasks; and the third formed the village council and tribunal. The oldest man, the oldest of the third group, was the village chief. The first two groups also had their chiefs, but they were responsible to the village chief. In pastoral societies, the military significance of age groups tended to be dominant. Among the Masai, a new age group was constituted with a circumcision ceremony every seven or eight years. Thus, young men from adolescence to their early thirties formed two age groups. The two groups were specially trained as warriors. They lived together in one house and organized raids on cattle and other possessions which enriched the group and enhanced its prestige. They did not marry until all the members reached thirty; at that point the group dispersed, but even then they retained strong ties of brotherhood based, as always, on the rituals they had experienced together.

The system of age groups also provides a method of establishing the passing of time. The groups could be permanent, each having its own name, and the individual would slip from one group to another, leaving his place empty for a newcomer. In the absence of exact information about the age of individuals, periodic initiations establish the individual's personal chronology. In some communities, there are a limited number of groups, each with a permanent name, and the passage of time is encompassed by a circle round which the society endlessly rotates as the younger members fill the places in each group left vacant by their elders. The groups could also be flexible and keep pace with their members as they grew up. In this case, each group chooses its name when it is constituted, and the succession of one group after another, carefully preserved in tribal memory, serves as the basis for the community's chronology and fixes the date of events. The Masai can recall their history for a century and a half in this way. These are only the most common and simplest conceptions of the passage of time in a society. Sometimes the movement in time of age groups, or of a series of groups, coincided roughly with a generation and was accompanied by physical displacement as well; after a certain age, people went to live in a sector of the village that older people had left uninhabited when they died. (See also *Armies; Bambara; Circumcision; Education; Excision; Initiation; Kikuyu; Law; Royalty; Widows; Zulus.*)   P.M.

AGRICULTURE. Most African peoples have been engaged in agriculture for a long time. Hunting and food-gathering now contribute little to the diet of Africans other than such marginal groups as the Pygmies of the great forest and the Bushmen of the southern deserts. Most pastoral peoples farm in addition to their other activities or live together with farmers, either by sharing the land or by dominating them, as is frequently the case in the region of the Great Lakes. But however

Masai initiation dance. Tanzania. *Photo: Hoa-Qui.*

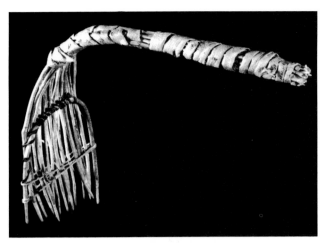

Rake for gathering wild *Gramineae*. Zaghawa. Chad. Musée de l'Homme. *Photo: R. Pasquino.*

remote the preagricultural era may be, it has rarely been obliterated, much less forgotten. The Bashilele of Zaire now scarcely depend on hunting for their livelihood, but it is still the basis of all their social and religious life. The Palaeonegrid Somba of northern Dahomey developed advanced farming techniques at an even earlier date than the Bashilele, but this does not prevent them from expressing as part of their rites and beliefs the particular problems of hunters as well. And in many legends, agriculture as well as metallurgy is either a dazzling revelation of civilizing gods and heroes or a pattern of behavior for mortals to follow. In Dahomey, Lissa, the god of heaven, carrying Gtu, god of the forge, makes the first clearings by furrowing the world. In the country of the Dogon, the ancestral blacksmith, after descending from heaven, immediately marks out the first field and sows the seed he brought with him. Elsewhere, as is the case with the Balamba of the Zambezi Valley, the sister of the ancestor obtains the first seeds by means of a theft that is celebrated in ritual. They are all echoes that perpetuate man's amazement at the new powers he has gained from a technological revolution.

Work on the land has always remained as sacred as the land itself. Work and ritual are inseparable. The ritual element is at least as important as the functional one and is a condition of the laborer's efficiency. This helps to explain the conservatism and the relative stagnation of agricultural methods; the teaching of the gods can only be modified with prudence. This has not prevented the adoption over a period of centuries of new forms of cultivation, however, even though old practices that had become marginal were retained and endowed with the deepest re-

ligious significance. For example, fonio (a type of cereal) has begun to be cultivated by some Sudanese tribes, and millet by several communities in the region of Guinea. Similarly, the religious factor has not prevented increasing flexibility in the division of labor between men and women, which was based on the idea of a connection between the fertility of women and the fecundity of the soil. The solemn ritual of agricultural work, however, has not been altered. Among the Yoruba and the Mossi, the king ushered in the new year by marking the first furrow. Everywhere the choice and preparation of plots of land, sowing, hoeing and harvesting are occasions for ceremonies. If it is not the priest of the earth who gives the sign for work to begin, it is the head of the extended family. Before sowing time, grain is offered to the gods or ancestors, in whose skulls a portion of the seeds are sometimes kept, and later they will be offered the first fruits of the harvest before anyone else may touch them.

Agricultural methods are not always as poor as they appear. In the most elementary systems there are only three tools: a digging stick, which is a relic from the days of food-gathering, and, more frequently, a short-handled hoe and a long-handled spade. Since black Africans have no plows (plows are unknown in traditional black Africa outside Ethiopia), they can only scratch the surface of the earth; but in regions where the topsoil is shallow and light, this is as much a safeguard of the land as a hindrance to its development. Admittedly, productivity is low, and the farming period is too short. In the dry tropical zone, farming is possible only for three or four months of the year; in other areas there is a loss of productivity because no use is made of wind or water power nor of wheeled vehicles or animals for transportation, and also because much time is spent in preparing and transporting food. There is certainly no lack of space, but it is often wasted through extensive cultivation that takes up far more room than the climate warrants. In the tropics, for example, waste areas of bush are burnt merely to fertilize a few fields with the ashes, and in the equatorial region the fields are sometimes only stripped, a system not much more advanced than food-gathering.

Despite these serious shortcomings, however, there are a number of ingenious farming methods. Both indigenous and imported plants are profitably used. African farmers have been able to develop numerous strains: 37 varieties of rice in West Africa and 14 of fonio; 45 varieties of yam have been developed in central Africa, each precisely classified with a different harvesting time and a different taste. It has therefore been possible to extend the productive season, even if in the dry tropical zone it is difficult to bridge the gap between the two harvests. Planned rotation of crops and mixed cultivation, instead of letting land lie fallow for a long period when it is exhausted, as was done formerly, have permitted far better use to be made of the land.

The next stage in technical development is intensive farming, and this is practiced in Africa. In the valleys of the Senegal and the Niger, flooded land is cultivated as the water subsides and supplements the extensive cultivation of the dry plateaus. Permanent gardens exist in the humid land of the Congo Basin. In the most populated part of the Benin coast, intensive market gardening is practiced beneath the shadow of the palm groves. In lower Guinea, an efficient rice cultivation has flourished since the de-salination of the mangrove swamps. Most important of all, the multitude of Pal-aeonegrid peoples have learned how best to utilize the limited and often stony ground: the slopes are worked; erosion is kept in check; the ground is fertilized with compost and human and animal manure and is sometimes irrigated; and a wide variety of plants are cultivated—all of which is made easier, admittedly, by a favorable climate.

A pertinent question is: How much does African agriculture owe to local enterprise and how much to foreign imports? The large number of cultivated plants imported into Africa from abroad is a fact of prime importance. Many plants of American origin were introduced from the fifteenth century onward by the Portuguese: corn, cassava, sweet potatoes, peanuts, fruits—pineapple, avocado, guava—tomatoes and pimento. Today, some of these form the basic diet of many people. In preceding centuries, many plants originating in Asia Minor and Southeast Asia entered black Africa by way of the Sahara or the coast of the Indian Ocean: rice, yams, beans, Angolan peas and taro. One sometimes wonders what Africans lived on before they acquired all these plants. The fact is that one plant often replaced another of the same kind or added to the range of cultivated varieties. These imports were integrated into an agriculture that was already old, rich and thoroughly African in origin. There seem to have been two principal areas of agricultural development: West and East Africa. West Africa was without doubt the more important; it developed the cultivation of rice and a savanna agriculture based on cereals—fonio, millet, sorghum—and fostered the cultivation of many other crops—voandzeia,

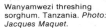
Wanyamwezi threshing sorghum. Tanzania. *Photo: Jacques Maquet.*

Dance for the fertility of the earth. Kirdi of northern Cameroun. *Photo: Hoa-Qui.*

yams, sesame, the shea tree and the oil palm. East Africa, which includes Ethiopia, produced mainly—with the exception of one cereal, eleusine—subsidiary crops; of these, coffee is comparatively important. Many African peoples are still primarily sustained by these traditional crops.

Native African plants and those of foreign origin gradually intermixed, dispersed and spread great distances across the entire continent. The people whom they reached selected them according to the techniques at their disposal and their suitability to the climate and soil. The regions where these crops were cultivated corresponded with some of the major farming areas. Study of basic crop cultivation reveals a major regional division. The agriculture of the tropical savannas, which depends on there being a rainy season, is based on cereals— millet, sorghum, fonio in West Africa, and eleusine in East Africa; corn, yams, cassava and peanuts can be added to these. In the forest regions and humid equatorial zones, permanent agriculture depends on root crops—yams, cassava and taro—or corn or bananas; vegetables, condiments, oil plants and others can, of course, be added to these. In modern Africa, export products such as cocoa, coffee, peanuts and cotton consume an increasing part of working time, sometimes at the expense of growing essential foodstuffs. (See also *Bateke; Calendars; Cassava; Civilization; Dance; Diet; Dogon; Feudalism; Fruit; Granaries; Hunger; Industry; Migrations; Millet; Palaeonegrids; Peanuts; Rain; Rice; Sahara Desert; Vegetables; Work.*)   P.M.

AKSUM. The capital city of Aksum, in the Tigre Delta, and its kingdom, which stretched from the Tigre to the port of Adulis on the Red Sea, were established between the middle of the first and the middle of the second centuries A.D. A flourishing civilization had existed in this region for six centuries, with cities and a political organization of which we know nothing. A few classical texts, local inscriptions in Greek, Geez and southern Arabic, and coins throw some light on the royal dynasties and their history and show how the country established relations with the political, economic and cultural life of the East. Aksum seems to have developed at first to the west of its present site, on the slopes and at the foot of the hill of Beta Giorgis, at Dar'o Addit Kilte. Between the middle of the third and the fourth centuries, when the vitality of the kingdom was reflected in its activities abroad, the construction of hydraulic works and the minting of gold coins, the site of the capital moved to the east of its present position, on damp soil. On an imposing terrace between the peaks of Beta Giorgis and Mai-Ooho, the Aksumites erected their famous monolithic steles of granite. One which is still standing measures over 75 feet, and the tallest reached over 108 feet. Seven of them are carved like the facade of a

Stele at Aksum, Ethiopia.
Photo: Rapho, Michaud.

multistoried house with doors, windows, beams and so on. Nothing is known about these monuments, but it is thought that they may be funerary steles. There is a stone table at the foot of each one with a cavity for offerings. After the king of Aksum had been converted to Christianity in the middle of the fourth century, the center of the city gravitated more to the south. The present cathedral is built on the ancient site of the principal Christian quarter. The coinage, which was then in bronze and silver, gilt bronze and gold leaf, reflected the prosperity of the city till the middle of the sixth century, while the architecture—notably the palace and tombs, named after Caleb and Gabra Masqal—remained just as splendid. But after King Caleb, the economic and political decadence of the kingdom set in. Toward the end of the eighth century, the city seems to have been abandoned by its most prominent citizens; the disorders and destruction of the tenth century completed its downfall. Although its glory had passed, it remained a holy city and as late as 1872 provided the setting for the coronation of the emperor of Ethiopia. (See also *Arabs in East Africa; Ethiopia; Meroe.*) H.M.

ALLADA. The kingdom of Allada was known to Europeans in the seventeenth and eighteenth centuries as Ardres, Ardrah or Great Ardrah. It only covered a small part of the modern Republic of Dahomey, but it was historically of great importance. It was from Allada that, after a war of succession, the founders of the kingdoms of Dahomey and Porto Novo set out. The ruling dynasty in Allada, the Agassuvi or "Children of Agassu," themselves had migrated from the west, from within the present boundaries of Togo and Dahomey, possibly in the fifteenth century. This region was the seat of the kingdom of Tado, which tradition links with the kingdom of the Yoruba; the legend says that the creator of the world divided it between two brothers, one of whom reigned over Ife and the other over Tado. Little is known of Tado, which seems to have suffered from frequent wars of succession. One of these wars can be traced in the legend of Agassu the panther, the founder of the Allada dynasty. The story relates that one of the daughters of the king of Tado, while walking in the forest, was seduced by a panther. She bore a son of remarkable strength, whose descendants laid claim to the throne. When their claims were rejected, they tried to seize it by force. They were defeated and fled eastward, where they founded the kingdom of Allada.

In the seventeenth century, Allada enjoyed a brief period of glory. At that time, the king controlled a vital staging post on the slave route leading from the north to the port of Ouidah, and he grew rich on the proceeds. European trading depots sprang up in his realms, and French Capuchin monks tried to convert the people. A prince was baptized with Louis XIV as godfather. A catechism, written in the Ardrah language, is one of the oldest documents in existence on the languages of this part of Africa. The kingdom collapsed in the eighteenth century. Those Agassuvi who had fled northwards took their revenge. In 1724 the king of Dahomey conquered Allada in the course of an expedition to Ouidah, which fell to him some years later. After this, Allada was no more than a religious center of the Agassuvi. The king of Dahomey, and later his successor, had to go there at the time of his coronation to have the ancestral "marks of the panther," scars cut on his face, which none of his subjects were permitted to see. (See also *Dahomey; Migrations.*) P.M.

ALMORAVIDS. The Almoravids were a Muslim Berber dynasty who came from Adrar in Mauritania. They ruled the Sudanese western Sahara, Morocco and Spain from 1050 to about 1147. The chief of the Gudala Berbers, Yahya ibn-Ibrahim, made the pilgrimage to Mecca about 1048 and brought the preacher Abdallah ibn-Yasin back with him. They withdrew to an island off the Mauritanian or Senegalese coast (possibly Tidra) to meditate and gather a military force. Several followers joined them, and there they founded a sort of *ribat,* or fortified monastery, whence the name Almoravids (*al-murabitum,* "the people of the ribat").

Under their chief Yahya ibn-Umar, who had as an advisor ibn-Yasin, they united the country and the Sanhadja tribes, such as the Lamtuna and Gudala, and brought back "orthodoxy," which included some hardly commendable practices. Then they attacked the caravan city of Sidjulmassa and sacked Awdaghast (the ruins of Tegdaoust excavated by the University of Dakar), the last dependency of the animist kingdom of Ghana (1055). They pursued their successful campaign into Morocco, where Yahya ibn-Umar died (1055). His brother and successor, Abu Bakr ibn-Umar, conquered the Maghrib (1056-1058), and during the course of this campaign ibn-Yasin died.

After disagreements had arisen in the desert between the Lamtuna and Massufa, Abu Bakr returned south and left his repudiated wife Zainab and his cousin Yusuf ibn-Tashfin to govern Morocco (about

1060). When he returned to Morocco, Yusuf, on the advice of Zainab, made it clear to Abu Bakr that he ought to return to the desert. Abu Bakr acquiesced. After this, there were two Almoravid empires: the northern one, governed by Yusuf, which eventually covered an enormous territory from the Sahara to the Ebro River in Spain, and the southern empire, under Abu Bakr.

Abu Bakr conquered Ghana in 1076 and converted the inhabitants by force to Islam. The Soninke and other Sudanese tribes were also Islamized. But Abu Bakr's empire was short-lived; he was killed in a campaign against the Soninke of the Tagant and his empire collapsed with him in 1087.

The Almoravids of the south are responsible for bringing Islam to the Sarakole and other Sudanese tribes; they are equally responsible for the destruction of the secular, animistic kingdom of Ghana. (See also *Ghana; Islam.*)   R.M.

ALTARS. Direct contact between man and his gods is rare. He needs a material bond, an altar, which is usually an object made by man for the purpose of capturing the power of gods. The altar may be the sole habitat of a divinity or may comprise only one of his multiple manifestations. On the altar, either in secret or before the assembled faithful, the priest makes his offerings and sacrifices and offers up prayers. The gods, who are

attached to an altar by rituals, come to feed there, and men often communicate with them. As a rule, the altar as such has no value; it can be replaced on condition that the power contained in it is correctly transferred to another structure with an appropriate ritual. New altars can also be set up from already existing ones with similar rites of transfer. Deviations are possible, and there are all sorts of gradations from altars to objects with protective powers—magic talismans and fetishes, which can be procured from people who know how to make them and which can act by themselves. The altar, even when placed in full view of everyone, always has a special officiating priest who alone may use it. Altars are sometimes hidden in secluded parts of dwellings, under granaries or in simple structures that serve as temples, and then only priests have access to them, unless they can be moved and taken out for the performance of a rite.

The structures and shapes of altars are infinitely varied. Sometimes they are natural objects, such as stones or trees on which sacrifices are offered. More often they are fabricated objects whose exteriors conceal a core of elements, such as leaves, animal organs, earth or stones, which associate myths with a particular god and bind to the god by countless links. The elements are put in a basket, pot or calabash, hidden in a

Family altar at the gravesite where ancestors are buried. Dekun-Afio, Dahomey. *Photo: Documentation française.*

bench or clay cone or incorporated into a statue. The altars of ancestors include this whole variety of forms. The altar may be the tomb itself or, as in the ancient kingdom of Benin, the shriveled body of the dead man around which clay has been molded or, as with the Fang of Gabon and many other peoples, the exhumed skull. It may also be something that was linked to the dead person's life: the seat or throne of the Ashanti, for example, may hold one of his souls. It could also be one of a large variety of objects with which he was associated by ritual: the pottery of the Dogon of Mali and the Kotoko of Chad; the clay cone of the Kabre of Togo; the stone of the Somba of Dahomey; the pole of the Sara of Chad; the iron rod with a tray on top on which statuettes and ornaments epitomize the devices and express the personality of an ancestor of the Fon of Dahomey. Nothing, not even the outward appearance of the altar, has meaningless decoration; but many altars, if they are statues or masks or if they are crowned or surrounded by statues or finely worked objects, are works of art. (See also *Architecture; Ashanti; Baule; Dogon; Fetishes; Funerals; Ijo; Kissi; Priests; Religion; Sacrifice; Sculpture, Stone.*) P.M.

AMAZONS. In most African societies, woman is the giver of life, associated with all the symbolism of fecundity and peace, and may not shed blood; she may neither offer sacrifices nor take part in war. There are, however, exceptions. The most striking and best known was in Dahomey. In this kingdom, women acted as warriors beginning in the eighteenth century, and perhaps even earlier. Traditions about their origin differ. The first Amazons may have been elephant hunters whom King Ouegbadja, struck by their skill and courage, began to enlist in the middle of the seventeenth century, or they may have been women dressed as soldiers by the conqueror Agadja, fifty years later, to swell the ranks of his meager army and impress the enemy. In any case, they are mentioned with amazement by the first European travelers, to whom their martial qualities instantly suggested the name Amazons. In stories and in drawings of them, Dahoman reality and Greek mythology were intermingled, like the purely fictitious idea that they cut off their right breasts in order to draw bows more easily. But, like the legendary Amazons, the warrior women of Dahomey were sworn to chastity, at least during the period of their service. They lived in the enclosure of the palace and were carefully supervised. They were reminded by their chiefs that they were "men, not women," and anyone who forgot that was condemned to death with her accomplice. At first, they were only ceremonial troops; then they became the personal bodyguard of the king; and finally, from the middle of the nineteenth century, they were made the elite units of the Dahoman army. They were armed with guns, sabers, short pikes with razor-sharp blades, and organized into regiments with their own uniforms, insignia and women officers. When the Yoruba town of Abeokuta was first attacked, it seems that they were 6,000 strong. Their exploits in this unhappy war probably surpassed those of the men. The women soldiers fought their last battles against French troops in 1890 and 1892, when their spirit, endurance, courage and "incredible ferocity" in the fight astonished their conquerors. (See also *Dahomey*.) P.M.

ANCESTORS. Our museums have many African statues representing ancestors. For a long time, we took them to be gods—

AMAZONES   BEHANZIN   AMAZONES

King Behanzin attended by Amazons. Colored print.

Shambala ancestor. Tanzania. Wood. Sammlung für Völkerkunde, University of Zurich. *Photo: Eva Stoll.*

and prosperity, a fixed point of reference; he lives in the memory of his descendants and in the family ritual in which he receives regular invocations and daily offerings of a little food and drink. The statues are an integral part of this worship.

In these statues we can perceive the image that the Africans had of their forebears. They saw them as strong and powerful. Although less than lifesize—the statues are usually no more than three feet high—they convey a monumentality and intense vitality. This is due to certain formal characteristics: frontality, verticality, symmetry of the left and right sides, the solidity of the base, the broken line of the limbs and the shape of the eyes. Some of these features are due to the limitations of the materials and the techniques employed by the sculptor. He begins with a cylindrical form, a branch or a tree

Bura ancestor. Nigeria. Wood. British Museum. *Museum photo.*

"fetishes" (from the Portuguese word *feitiço* meaning "fabricated," "artificial") worshiped by the simple people who had fashioned them. Admittedly, not every African statue representing a human being is an ancestral figure; some are substitutes for a dead child, others are used for prophecy or magic. Ancestors appear frequently in the sculpture of the agricultural peoples of the Atlantic and equatorial forests, where the main artistic centers are found that created the Negro art that so amazed the cubists at the beginning of this century. This emphasis on the theme of the ancestor in classical statuary reflects a basic fact about the nature of African existence: each African is what he is and has what he has as a member of a family—that is, as the descendant of an ancestor. This ancestor is the source of life trunk, which he whittles away, reducing and shaping the wood with his adz and knife. Consequently, the figures tend to be stiff and symmetrical, but this is not the whole explanation. The angle of knees and elbows, which suggests restrained movement, the treatment of the lines of the face, which, unlike the masks, portray peace and dignity, are not determined by the material or by the tool; they could have been quite different. In this integration of lines, planes and volumes in ancestral statues, we can perceive the calm strength of lineage. Had African artists wanted to express the concept of ancestral relationship, they would not have set about it in any other way. Their statues do not represent a particular ancestor, but *the* Ancestor. They have tried neither to portray an individual, nor to describe a social group through physical characteristics or particular ornaments, nor even to represent the visual image of a man or woman. Through conscious distortion of proportions they have expressed a mental image. Their sculptures are, in the strict sense of the word, abstractions; by rejecting the individual qualities, they have achieved the idea of Ancestor. What was important to the African, with the obvious exception of chiefs and kings, was to feel that he belonged to *some* line, not a *particular* line.

Ancestors were always represented naked —adult nudity was extremely rare in African tradition—and their sexual organs were carved realistically. Although some parts of the body were lightly traced or omitted entirely, breasts and vulva, penis and testicles were nearly always there and often enlarged. This sexuality, while openly displayed, is very austere. It conjures up less the joys of love than the burgeoning of fertility. It is a reminder that the Ancestor, man or woman, is the origin of many generations, that his descendants are strong because they are numerous, and that they are responsible for the continuation of the line. The same things that are expressed by these statues of ancestors—the calm strength of the founder of the family, the importance of the principle of descent, the values of virility and fertility—can also be detected in the ritual worship that is paid to them, in oral traditions about their exploits, their interventions in the life of their descendants, as revealed by the soothsayer. These converging facts combine to demonstrate the impact upon daily life of ideas about ancestors and the origin of such ideas. They are not fortuitous; they are the outward expression, formulated by the collective mind, of a very real experience among people for whom life would be impossible without

Sikasingo ancestor. Zaire. Wood. Musée royal de l'Afrique centrale, Tervuren. *Photo: Jacques Verroust.*

the solidarity of the family tree. (See also *Altars; Art, African; Art, Negro; Bull-Roarers; Clan; Divinities; Dreams; Fauna; Funerals; Genealogy; Heads; Heaven; Kinship; Legends; Lineage; Person; Religion; Sculpture, Stone; Sculpture, Wood; Spirits and Genii; Villages; Zimbabwe.*)
J.M.

Bahutu cattle-raiser.
Rwanda.
Photo: Jacques Maquet.

ANIMAL HUSBANDRY. According to former theories of evolutionary development, the domestication and raising of animals to meet human needs was supposed to be an earlier stage of development than agriculture. In Africa, the two new production techniques of the Neolithic revolution—agriculture and animal husbandry—have been closely associated ever since their introduction to the continent. Brought from Asia Minor, they penetrated Egypt in the fifth millennium B.C. From that period onward, all kinds of domestic animals lived in Africa, both small, such as goats, sheep and pigs, and large, such as the Mediterranean long-horned cattle. During the second millennium B.C., the zebu, or humped ox, arrived, and the dromedary, horse and donkey came at the beginning of the Christian era. Despite this association of agriculture and animal husbandry, some societies have been entirely or mainly pastoral. Their economy was based on the possession of large animals, for example, the Fulani in the Sudan region, the Galla of Ethiopia, the Luo of the Nilotic marshes, the Bahima of the high plateau between the Great Lakes and the Hottentots in the southern savanna. As this list shows, many regions of Africa were suitable for raising livestock —all the regions, in fact, with extensive grasslands and water supplies lasting through the dry season that were free of the tsetse fly and sleeping sickness. As land was not prepared especially for grazing and there was no stabling of animals, a large area was

Fulani herdsmen near
Abéché, Chad.
Photo: Hoa-Qui.

needed for each animal, and the seasonal movement of herds between grazing grounds was inevitable. These two characteristics of animal husbandry were reflected in social organization: animal husbandry limited the density and the sedentariness of populations that lived by it. A pastoral society cannot be concentrated in a small space, and at least part of its population must be temporarily nomadic.

Despite these limitations, animal husbandry was a technique of production which, under African conditions, was markedly different from, and more advantageous than, agriculture. A herd, however large, did not require much man power. Its upkeep and development needed only a few experts in selection and in the occasional attention that the animals required and some cowherds capable of finding pastures during the dry season. In traditional Africa, the land was rarely irrigated or fertilized; the soil was poor and yielded only what the farmer's hard work could extract from it. On the other hand, an animal itself produced its own return in the form of milk and blood, meat and leather. It was natural capital. Unlike our capital, money, its productivity did not depend on an economic system, but on its inherent natural qualities.

The herd was a permanent possession. It did not die and did not wear out. Even if its produce was not "capitalized," but rather consumed, it existed indefinitely and multiplied. Land, by contrast, once it ceased to be worked, lost all its usefulness. The herd was a mobile means of production. If the group managing it had to emigrate, as frequently happened in Africa, it could do this without loss or diminution of its principal source of subsistence, or indeed its only source, since it was possible to live entirely on the herd. Some nomadic Bahima still do this. They milk their animals, bleed them and live daily on a mixture of milk and blood, and their clothes are made of leather. The Dje in Kenya do the same; their young men, cut off completely from their villages, have to look after their herds for long periods of time. The advantages of animal husbandry were obvious in societies that were exclusively or principally pastoral. Even when it fulfilled a secondary function, which was far more common in Africa, domesticated animals were considered a sign of privilege and prestige. This paradox is more apparent than real, for in these societies, the herd was also a genuine form of wealth, whereas the soil, although indispensable, was not. (See also *Camels; Cattle; Cows; Goats; Great Lakes; Horses; Meat; Savanna; Work.*)   J.M.

ANTELOPES. The best-known sculptures of the Bambara are their antelopes. The rhythmical treatment of the headdress carved in wood, the extraordinary variations in size, type and style so that no two specimens are alike, have made them desirable items for collectors of Negro art. Unlike many African statues and in contrast to other Bambara sculptures, they give a gay and carefree impression. These headdresses belong to the societies of young men that are found in every Bambara village. Although no longer children, young men are not considered members of adult society and must work for the community. These groups of workers use the antelope-topped headdresses in the dances that take place just before the rains or before laying out a new field during the dry season. Two men, their bodies disguised in plant fibers and wearing straw bonnets with antelope sculptures attached to them, accompany the workers to the field and watch over them. Back in the village, men in antelope costume dance in pairs, representing male and female, to drums before the entire village. When two neighboring villages have a race to complete the hoeing of a field, it is the privilege of the victor to put on the costume and perform the ritual.

The carved antelope, called *chi wara* ("wild animal"), commemorates a fabulous being, half man, half animal, who taught men agriculture. Chi wara, the son of Earth and a snake, from the moment of birth used his claws and a pointed stick, which he held in his hands, to dig the soil; wild nature was made fit for man's use. Men followed Chi wara's example; but as the corn became more abundant, they began to waste it. Chi wara, disappointed in them, buried himself in the earth; so, having lost him, they carved a mask in his memory.

The *chi wara* headdress recalls the legend of the tireless worker, and the people who wear these masks are the keenest and fastest workers on the land. The male and female, both impersonated by a man, dance together and must never be separated. Anyone who tried to come between them would be killed instantly. The two dancers leap, jump, turn and lean on two sticks in order to imitate the motion of antelopes. The dance is supposed to be the propitiation of the earth spirits who have been disturbed by human activities such as putting animals to flight by burning underbrush. It is a magic fertility rite as well.

Antelope sculptures can be divided into three main types, each one associated with a quite clearly defined area of Bambara country. The best-known style is that of the vertical antelopes, which is found in the east

Chi wara mask; vertical style. Bambara. Mali. Wood. Pierre Vérité Collection, Paris. Photo: Ina Bandy.

more naturalistic than the vertical antelopes, as their hoofs, bodies, heads and horns are in better proportion. In some, the head is carved separately and attached to the body with metal clips. The third and most abstract style of work comes from around Bougouni, in the southwest. There again, the sculptor stresses the mane and horns but the curves and angles are so stylized that it is often difficult to identify the original model. The antelope is mounted on the back of a lizard, a tortoise or some other crawling creature. Sometimes, too, the animal has a small, human figure standing on top, whose outlines correspond with the lines of the horns and ears. It has been suggested that these stylistic differences could be explained by the different species of antelope, but the diversity of styles is great enough to show quite clearly that this is not the real reason. The explanation is far more likely to be found in the gradual development of a tradition that gave the artist both a starting point and a stimulus for his imagination. (See also *Art, African; Bambara; Masks*.)

D.P.

APPLIQUÉ WORK. The most refined products of the appliqué technique come from Dahomey. Cutout patterns, made of materials in contrasting colors, are sewn on a solid-colored fabric base. (This method was employed in the Middle Ages in Europe, for example, in the famous *Bayeux* tapestry.) It was a royal art, practiced in the capital of Dahomey by only a few families who specialized in it. The finished products were reserved for the king and for those dignitaries who were allowed to use them. The art is still practiced today, but it is now commercialized and accessible to everyone. Funeral hangings for ritual use, commemorating the life of the departed, are still made, and decorative panels and cushions are now manufactured as well. The most remarkable works are the hangings that used to decorate royal palaces. The background is black, white or gold, decorated with motifs in vivid colors, with red, blue and yellow predominating. They depict royal names, sentences pronounced by the king at his accession and on great occasions during his reign, particularly military occasions. Thus, Dakodounou might be represented by a flint and steel and its case: "The flint and steel will not go into its case; it is torn"; Ouegbadja by a fish and bow-net: "The fish that escapes the net will not enter it again"; Guezo by a little bird with red wings: "Cardinals will not set the bush on fire." These were mottoes describing either the enemy's impotence, resistance to all foreign domination or the

of the country, from Sikasso to Koutiala and Segou. Body and hoofs are reduced to a minimum, but the sculptor elongates the neck, muzzle and horns. The males boast an abundant mane; the females, with their slender necks, carry their young on their backs, like all African mothers. The second type is that of the horizontal antelopes, which are created in the neighborhood of Bamako. They are generally smaller and invincibility of the king. An entire pictorial language developed in this fashion. Royal emblems such as thrones, *recados* and sabers were added, then battle scenes were depicted in stylized form with rarely more than two figures. These hangings provide a more complete account of royal exploits than the briefer records presented by the bas-reliefs in painted clay, the *recados* and the portable altars. Every year, new tapestries were made for royal ceremonial occasions. Appliqué work was also used for other things as well: parasols for the king and his dignitaries, regimental banners, uniform hats, the hammocks in which the king was carried and his sandals were all decorated in this fashion. It is said that maps of the districts where a campaign was being planned were put together in the same way, based on intelligence reports by the king's spies. Unfortunately, not a single example has been preserved. (See also *Dahomey; Recados.*)　　　　P.M.

ARAB CHRONICLERS. The Arab chroniclers al-Fazari, al-Masudi, ibn-al-Faqih, al-Yaqubi, ibn-Hawqal, al-Bakri, Edrissi (al-Idrisi), al-Biruni, Yakub al-Rumi, Abu 'l-Fida, al-Umari, ibn-Batuta, al-Makrizi, ibn-Khaldun, ibn-al-Wardi, Hazan ibn-Muhammed al-Wazzani (known as Johannes Leo Africanus) and many others are the source of almost all we know of the Sudanese and east coast history from the ninth to the seventeenth century. Even though nearly all of them led active and sometimes turbulent lives, Saint-Exupéry's distinction between travelers and geographers can be applied to them, despite the fact that the latter were generally historians as well and nearly all were well traveled.

Three "travelers" are outstanding. Al-Masudi (d. 956) gives a fairly enthusiastic picture of the wealth of the east coast in his *Fields of Gold,* as the title suggests. Ibn-Batuta (1304-1377), a phlegmatic Moroccan, who traveled all over the Islamic world from the Atlantic Ocean through Malaya to China, provides an account of Mali in its heyday. His meticulous and prudish style is reminiscent of certain Victorian explorers. Leo Africanus (1459-c. 1550), a Moor from Granada, was captured by Italian privateers in 1519 and temporarily converted to Christianity (he returned to die on Muslim soil). His *Description of Africa: The Third Part of the World,* written in Latin and translated into racy French by Jean Temporal (1556), offers a mixture of direct observation and second-hand information about Africa Minor, the Sahara and the Sudan that was regarded as authoritative until the eighteenth century.

Appliqué work. Meviaso, god of thunder, overcoming the Nabe. Fon. Dahomey. Musée de l'Homme, Paris. *Museum photo.*

The "geographers" relied on other people's accounts with varying success, depending on whether they got their information from travelers or simply drew upon the accounts of earlier authors. It is impossible to mention them all or even the works of those listed here. Most of the information provided by al-Yaqubi (c. 897), ibn-al-Faqih (tenth century), Yakub al-Rumi (1179-1229), al-Makrizi (1364-1442) and ibn-al-Wardi (c. 1457) concerns Nubia, Ethiopia and the east coast. Al-Fazari (eighth century), al-Bakri (c. 1094), al-Umari (fourteenth century) and ibn-Khaldun (1332-1406) deal with West Africa and the Sahara; the first of these authors furnishes the oldest and most complete information on Ghana. Ibn-Hawqal (eleventh century), al-Biruni (973-1048), al-Idrisi (1100-1166) and Abu 'l-Fida (1273-1331) wrote general histories and geographical works embracing all the knowledge of the world of their time. The most remarkable work in this last group is that of al-Idrisi, a Moroccan by birth and geographer to King Roger of Sicily. He wrote the *Geographia Nubiensis* and the historical and general

Title page of *Description de l'Afrique: Tierce Partie du Monde*, by Leo Africanus, translated into French by Jean Temporal (Lyon, 1556).

Title page of *De Geographia Universali*, by al-Idrisi (Rome, 1592).

geographical atlas known as the *Book of Roger*.

There are also a number of black Africans who wrote in Arabic, but most of their works have, unfortunately, been lost. The best known are the Songhai Mahmud al-Kati (1468-c. 1530), author of the *Tariqa el-*

Fettash, which was continued until 1665 by his son, his grandson and Ahmad Baba (c. 1627), whose work we know only through Abdarrahman as-Sadi, author of the *Tariqa as-Sudan* that was completed in 1655. Closer to our time, there are the Fulani and Tukulor writers of the nineteenth century, of whom the most prominent are the conquerors Osman and Abdallah dan Fodio, Ahmadu Bello and the author of the *Life of el-Hadj Umar*, Ahmadu Ali Tyam. Other works by composite and anonymous writers include the *Tadhkirat an Nisyan,* written by the cadis of Timbuktu and Djenne when they were under Arma domination (1590-1750) and the Bornu and Kano chronicles. (See also *Bow, Musical; European Discovery; Ghana; Hausa; Islam; Mali; Sudan; Xylophones.*)
P.M.

ARABS IN EAST AFRICA. Commerce between Arabia Felix and Africa across the Red Sea and the Gulf of Aden goes back to classical times; there is evidence of this both in the Bible and in the works of Herodotus. South of Cape Guardafui, on the coast of Azania (the Kenya and Tanzania of today), the traffic depended on the monsoon season. The Greek merchant Hippalos commented on this traffic in 45 B.C., but Arabs and Indians had probably followed the same route long before. The Yemenites controlled the greater part of the trade with Rome, which prospered until the third century A.D. These commercial relationships did not lead to any form of permanent settlement, although the Himyarite rulers of Arabia claimed some sort of suzerainty over the Azanian coast. From the third to the seventh century, the decline of Rome, the wars between the Ethiopians of Aksum and the Yemenites and the invasion of the coast by the Hamites and the Bantu from the interior endangered or interrupted this trade.

The Arabs began to establish themselves in Africa in the seventh century, after the decline of Aksum. The first were Muslims, evicted from Arabia at the time of the Hegira, followed by groups who had rebelled against Islam. The latter traversed the continent as far as Chad, where they became the forebears of the Shuwa, present-day "black Arabs." With the triumph of Islam, two different kinds of settlers appeared. Those from within the continent spread from Egypt along the Nile Valley but were held up until the sixteenth century by the resistance of the Christian kingdoms of Nubia. The maritime settlers spread along the coast as far as the Mozambique Channel. The latter group was the more important. It created the Zanguebar Empire, which was, in fact, a federation of mercantile city-states, mainly established on the coastal islands from Socotra to the Comoros. Their principal coastal towns and islands were Mogadishu (Somaliland), Mombasa, Lamu and the island of Pemba (Kenya), Zanzibar, Dar es Salaam and Kilwa (Tanzania) and Sofala (Mozambique). Kilwa exercised a doubtful authority over these treasure-houses which until the end of the fifteenth century maintained a lively trade with the Middle East, India, Malaya and China, exporting gold, ivory, rhinoceros horns and especially slaves, and importing cloth, weapons and pottery. The Arabs did not attempt to penetrate the interior but, in the immediate hinterland, intermarriage with the Bantu living on the coast produced the Islamic black Arabic civilization of the Swahili (from the Arabic word *sahil,* "coast"). Until the nineteenth century, these black Arabs were invaluable intermediaries with the people of the interior.

From the fifteenth to the seventeenth century there was fierce rivalry in the Indian Ocean between the Arabs and the Portuguese. Portuguese power reached its zenith at the end of the sixteenth century but collapsed in 1698 when the Arabs, under the Imam of Oman, retook Mombasa, Pemba and Kilwa. A century passed before coastal trade regained its former prosperity. From the eighteenth century onward, the Arabs began to penetrate the interior in earnest, looking for ivory and slaves, who carried the ivory as far as the Nile Valley or to the coast. This penetration started first from Sennar on the upper Nile and then from the coastal ports. In 1832 Seyyid Said, the Imam of Muscat, settled in Zanzibar, which under him and his successors became the principal slave port and the main supplier of cloves on the east coast. From Khartoum or the Indian Ocean ports, the slave traders thrust steadily toward the Great Lakes, then to the Congo. On the trade routes, they built chains of fortified posts (Tabora, Ujiji, Nyangwe), which were surrounded by agricultural colonies for supplying the caravans. At the end of the nineteenth century, they clashed with the British and the French in the region of Chad, with the British and the Portuguese on the Nyasa, and with the Belgians to the east of the Congo and in Katanga. By 1860, particularly after the travels of Schweinfurth and Livingstone, Arab slave trading aroused the indignation of European antislavery societies. Its repression was used to justify colonial penetration in central and East Africa, especially after 1885. By the end of the century, Arab influence in the interior had been practically wiped out, although small colonies of Arab traders still existed in the towns in Uganda, Kenya and Tanzania. On the coast, Zanzibar, a British protec-

torate, was still governed by an Arab aristocracy, supported by a Swahili bourgeoisie. Independence brought serious political and social tension between the Muslims and the non-Muslim Bantu immigrants from the interior.

Arab cultural influence has been much less important in East Africa, except on the coast, than in the Sudan. There has been hardly any attempt to convert the Bantu population to Islam, a conversion which would, strictly speaking, have constituted an obstacle to slave trading. Among the Swahili, on the other hand, the Shafi'ite Muslims are solidly established, while almost half the words in literary Swahili are Arabic. (See also *Ethiopia; Gold; Iron; Islam; Ivory; Nile; Slave Trade; Towns and Cities.*)　P.A.

ARCHITECTURE. Although there is a wealth of plastic art in Africa, the architecture leaves a general impression of poverty and impermanence. However, there are a great variety of architectural forms which are often well adapted to climate and terrain, and there is evidence of some brilliant ideas. The inadequacies of traditional techniques are largely responsible for the architectural poverty. Furthermore, the height and proportions of the buildings are

Musgu building. Cameroun.
Photo: Hoa-Qui.

Koniagi hut. Guinea. *Photo:
Hoa-Qui.*

generally weak, and the clay and plants with which they are constructed have no durability. Clay buildings can last, of course (the Sudanese mosques, built in the Middle Ages, are proof of this); but they require constant maintenance, even in a dry climate. Also, palaces cannot long survive the collapse of dynasties and political institutions. Stone alone withstands centuries of neglect, but stone was rare in many regions, as well as hard and difficult to handle where advanced techniques were nonexistent. It was mostly used in its natural state: erected stones in Senegambia, cattle enclosures in southeastern Africa and foundations for ramparts or dwellings in several parts of the African savanna. There are exceptions, however, and they are the most interesting remains in existence of ancient architecture; for example, the small, square structures of the Lobi on the Ivory Coast, whose builders and functions are alike unknown, and especially the monumental constructions in Rhodesia (the best known are at Zimbabwe), whose African origin is now no longer disputed. The walls of the latter, the tallest of which reach a height of nearly thirty-three feet, are made of blocks of stone cut to shape and laid without mortar. The earliest may date from the fourteenth century. This type of work

Mosque. Douentza, Mali.
Photo: Hoa-Qui.

demanded genuine skills. Elsewhere, however, such skills were less necessary, and the techniques remained simple, despite a certain ingenuity, examples of which will be given further on. Sudanese towns like Timbuktu were almost unique in having guilds of stonemasons.

The basic building techniques of the Africans were derived either from pottery or from basketry. The first technique is common in the tropical zone. The walls are made of successive layers of clay, each one applied as the one beneath dries. A fine example can be seen in the cupola huts of the Musgu in Cameroun, fluted with buttresses on which the workers perch as the building rises and which lessen the contraction of the clay as it dries. The second technique is prevalent in the equatorial zone but is not limited to it. Here the most rudimentary structures are to be found, like the shelters of the Pygmies, made of branches pressed into the ground, then bent down, interwoven and covered with leaves. The use of nothing but plant material—such as boughs, bamboo, palm ribs and fronds, lianas, raffia and banana leaves—for walls and roofs produces some highly complicated structures that are not necessarily less durable than clay buildings. Sometimes lightness is the most desirable quality in a dwelling, as in the transportable wattle huts of the Koniagi of northwest Guinea. The two main building methods are often combined: sometimes the walls are made of mud over a framework of plant material, and sometimes, of course, a roof of plant material is placed on top of mud walls.

The variety of forms is considerable, but they can be reduced to four main types. In the first type, the walls tend to be built as a single unit (in the other three types, they are separate units); a notable example is the beehive hut of the pastoral cultures. The most curious of these is the tunnel-hut of the Masai in eastern Africa. The huts of the second type are square or rectangular, with a gabled or pitched roof or one made in four sections. It is common in the wet zones and can be seen in its most elaborate form in the Benin region. Thirdly, there are the round huts with conical roofs of the savanna country. A center pillar permits a larger span, and the huts are sometimes surrounded by broad verandas, like the mosques and houses of chiefs built by the Fulani of Guinea. The fourth type is a square or round hut with a flat roof, found in the dry areas of the Sudan, which can be elaborated into huge buildings and multistoried houses. The medieval trading towns like Djenne, Kano and Timbuktu possess some remarkable examples of this type of building. Generally the individual "huts" are only elements of an architectural whole. Multiplied, in a greater or lesser number of forms and sizes, they constitute the house. This includes an organized open area—part of which is built upon, often with granaries in the center— that is enclosed by a wall or by straw matting which connects the huts. Almost the entire daily routine is carried on in the open air, between the buildings or around them. The huts vary in size and sometimes in shape, according to whether they function as bedrooms, entrances, kitchens for wet days, shrines and so on. In some regions, houses are built as single compact structures, and some ingenuity is required to solve the resulting technical problems. The Yoruba and the Edo of Benin built large rectangular houses in which the rooms opened onto one

Somba dwelling. Dahomey.
Photo: Rapho, Philippe Billère.

Hut of a Bamileke chief of the Bafoussam tribe. Cameroun. *Photo: Hoa-Qui.*

or more courtyards with a pool and a broad veranda. They had ingenious systems for circulating air between ceiling and roof and for draining the water out of the pools through underground pipes. The Somba of northern Dahomey built small "fortresses" with round turrets surrounding a stepped terrace, where most of the activities of daily life took place. Stairwells, gutters and sometimes a fireplace and chimney are to be found in these houses.

Only these kinds of domestic architecture existed among many African peoples, but specialized types were developed by others. Military architecture was usually simple, consisting of trenches, ramparts made of earth, heaped stones or stakes gathered together and bound. But sometimes it was more complex, as, for example, the watchtowers of the Fang, guarding the outer limits of the villages, or the towers of the Yoruba, with sentrywalks to protect the town gates. Royal buildings were often distinguished only by their superior size and decoration. The palaces of the Bamileke chiefs, which consist of groups of buildings shaped like tall mushrooms on square bases, are a remarkable example. The posts supporting the enormous round roof, the thresholds, the doorposts and lintels are covered with carvings. However, palaces were sometimes built in a special style. One in particular has often been described with amazement and wonder: the palace of the Benin kings, with its profusely decorated galleries and majestic halls. African religious architecture is poor. The only exceptional religious structures were built by the peoples of the West African savanna, who were converted to Islam at an early date. Their massive mosques in the "Sudanese" style, like those at Djenne, Gao and Timbuktu, have heavy minarets and thick buttresses ending in domes, studded with beams projecting from the brickwork. The fact is that there are no buildings designed as meetingplaces for the African faithful. Altars are placed in the open air or under a simple shelter, or set in a corner of the house or under the granary. Structurally, the only distinguishing features of temples, when they do exist, are a roof reaching almost to the ground and a low entrance through which the priests crawl. However, the decoration of altars and temples—mural paintings, bas-reliefs modeled in clay and painted, and carved poles—is distinctive. The rare architectural complexes designed for religious purposes, such as the "monasteries" of Dahomey in which the initiated live during their long retreat, are hardly distinguishable in form from ordinary dwellings. (See also *Bamileke; Basketry; Benin; Dwellings; Granaries; Pottery; Towns and Cities; Zimbabwe.*)   P.M.

ARMIES. African peoples, like every group, resort to war as an extreme political measure, but they seldom glorify the violence it engenders. Still less do they deify it, with the exception of the people of Benin, who have sculpted and honored the god of war and iron, called Ogun or Gun. They distinguish between internal war (limited and regulated conflicts, or feuds) and external war (conflicts of aggression against foreign peoples for material gain: to capture prisoners for slaves or cattle to enrich their herds). The Nuer of the southern Sudan make a distinction between three different levels of waging war: a clash within the tribe,

which is settled by arbitration; limited warfare in the form of intertribal cattle raiding; and a state of permanent mistrust and war with non-Nuers. This last version of war exists in Africa, but territorial gain is seldom the motive. War is waged in order to dominate, take prisoners and accumulate riches. Religion was also a cause, as in the case of the jihads, which did so much to expand and strengthen Islam. One of the most famous of these religious wars ended in 1804 when Osman dan Fodio won his victory and founded the modern Hausa states.

Some tribes regard war and hunting as supreme trials to prove the real quality of a man. They are a test of his strength and an initiation into courageous activities. This is the belief of the Bete of the Ivory Coast, who forbid any man to take part in military expeditions before he is thirty. Women are excluded from their company as soon as preparations for war begin. The warriors are isolated in an enclosure, where they rejoice with dancing and the firing of their guns. The women may only rejoin the men at the feast to celebrate victory and reconciliation with the vanquished. War is waged according to strict rules: the attacker gives advance warning to his adversary, the attack is halted the moment the village is stormed and compensation is paid for the dead by those responsible. War is kept under strict control, and its purpose is never the annihilation of opponents.

Warrior. Benin. Nigeria. Bronze. Private Collection. *Photo: Viollet, Roger.*

Horseman. Lower Niger, Nigeria. Bronze. Pitt Rivers Museum, Farnham, Dorset, England. *Photo: Walter Dräyer.*

Mada warriors. *Photo: Documentation française.*

In societies organized as sovereign states, the arts of war were often highly developed. Ancient chroniclers imply this in their accounts of the kingdom of Kongo, where they allude to defense works, particularly those of the capital, which had a permanent garrison. They describe the troops and their positions on the battlefield, the martial sounds employed to instill courage and give the soldiers orders and the strategy employed to provoke a decisive battle. They describe the weapons in use from early times and then modified under Portuguese influence: bows, clubs, daggers, lances and assegais, small axes, shields of bark or leather and, from the sixteenth century on, firearms. On many occasions, forces numbering from 20,000 to 30,000 men were assembled. Military operations demanded not only arms and material equipment but also ritual training and special conditioning of both soldiers and the civilian population. The place reserved for ceremonial, ritual and magic—which were always present in armies and all human enterprises in Africa where death was involved—still left much scope for the arts of war.

In east-central Africa, military states proliferated; for example, in the state of the Balunda, where political and military hierarchies overlapped and the rulers forged an empire because tradition required that

they be victorious in battle; and in Rwanda, where each new king created a new army and the profession of soldier was the privilege of the aristocracy. In the Chad region, too, kingdoms were founded that commanded powerful armies and, in particular, magnificently caparisoned cavalry. The most typical of all these military states was created in the land of the Zulus by Chaka, the black Napoleon, in about 1820. There, the army was the foundation of the nation; tribal forces supported the chiefs in the provinces, and regiments based on age groups protected the king. In a sense, the country was a fortress, the ruler being primarily a commander-in-chief and only secondarily the "father of the people." His justification was that of all military reformers—that he wanted to transform weapons of power into instruments of progress. (See also *Amazons; Balunda; Horses; Islam; Kongo; Rwanda; Songhai; Weapons; Zulus.*)   G.B.

ART. See *Appliqué Work; Art, African; Art, Negro; Art, Styles of; Basketry; Body Painting; Painting, Modern; Painting, Mural; Pottery; Rock Art; Sculpture, Stone; Sculpture, Wood; Weaving.*

ART, AFRICAN. The African artist, whether sculptor or dancer, painter or singer, is motivated primarily by a ritual purpose. His art is linked to his religious beliefs, which are the source of all his powers of expression. There is a universal belief in a vital force, of which the unique, invisible god-creator is the ultimate repository. This god delegated his original power to his sons, who animate the forest, the bush and rivers. By degrees, a fraction of this power was bestowed on the tribal ancestors, the heroes of myth and legend. Animals, trees and even rocks share in this great, nameless force. Since it can diminish, it must be maintained by means of ceremonies and acts performed in the common interest by those who are specially designated for this purpose. The god alone can bestow rain, harvest, wives, children, life itself. But an African will never address himself directly to the object of his entreaties; he must have an intermediary, and who is better qualified than a revered ancestor? The ancestor, invoked with prayers and offerings, answers his descendants and appears for a brief moment to give life to the statue carved in his image.

Nearly all the statues of ancestors possess a markedly static quality. They embody the calm and the solemnity of the dead in the other world. The human figure is carved in one piece; the simplified forms are designed symmetrically, to be viewed from the front and with the vertical axis serving as a unifying element. The figure is generally standing, sometimes seated, but seldom squatting. The impression of calm is not incompatible with a controlled strength, emanating from the rhythm of the lines and the brilliance of the polished wood, whose surfaces reflect light. Dignity and detachment are the dominant features of these statues. They are worshiped, and a descendant would never sell a statue that is still the object of his prayers and veneration. When a family becomes extinct, the worship disappears with the worshipers and the statue is abandoned.

Masks representing spirits are used to conjure up magical forces. It is impossible to describe the effect produced by the masked dancer as he jumps, leaps and crouches to the beat of drums, bells and horns. No one can approach him with impunity; he is inviolable and invulnerable. A mask, as long as it does not recall an ancestor, must be as dynamic as possible. Everything that may seem exaggerated—the acute angles, prominent volumes, violent colors and accessories—is calculated to inspire fear. Masks are invariably part of the accouterments of secret societies (secret, that is, as far as women are concerned) which control politics and administer justice for the entire community. Such societies act in the name of the ancestors and spirits who created them and who are embodied in the masks. The masks are their executive agents, and they punish every breach of custom. From time to time, they set upon women who no longer go in fear of their fathers or husbands and who must be reminded to obey and not defy established order.

Fetishes draw their powers from people's belief in magic. A buffalo horn retains the power of the buffalo; a water animal can bring water with its promise of fertility; the writhing of the snake evokes a lightning flash across the sky. There are many such magical associations, and they vary from one society to another. Among the bric-a-brac of the fetishist, such as horns, powders and shapeless, meticulously bound packets, there is very little of artistic importance. However, magical elements are sometimes embodied in statues, such as those of the Bakongo. The magical statue, baring its teeth, flashing its eyes and holding a lance or dagger in its clenched fist, acts as a bodyguard or sentry at the entrance to a dwelling. Its appearance represents its aggressive character and dual role as protector and, occasionally, avenger.

It is only where a central political authority has been established that we find court art. Its function is to glorify the sovereign and his circle. The king had a monopoly on precious materials such as

Masked Bobo dancers. Upper Volta. *Photo: Hoa-Qui.*

Mbembe statue. Zaire or Uganda. Wood. Museum für Völkerkunde, Berlin. *Photo: Jacques Verroust.*

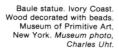

Baule statue. Ivory Coast. Wood decorated with beads. Museum of Primitive Art, New York. *Museum photo, Charles Uht.*

gold, ivory, bronze, pearls and cornelian; he alone had the right to wear embroidered clothes, and the craftsmen were attached to him personally and to a few of the highest dignitaries.

The African artist finds his inspiration in nature, but he does not copy it. The proportions that he gives the human body are deliberately arbitrary. The head, as the center of the life force, is generally exaggerated (one-quarter of the whole, whereas in reality it is only one-sixth). The torso is long. The legs are solidly planted, separated and often bent; the aim is to indicate their function as supports for the body and also to balance the massive head. The legs may even be omitted completely, the general effect being more important than a realistic rendering.

It is possible to find works of art in Africa that show some correspondence to trends in Western art such as the baroque or naturalistic movements, but tracing such similarities can be nothing more than an amusing diversion for the amateur. Only two of the most striking styles will be discussed here: cubism and naturalism. African "cubism" could have arisen as a technical consequence of using the adz, the sculptor's chief tool. The artist starts with a tree trunk, whose shape is still discernible in the finished work. The statue is a mass, composed of rigid forms without detail or superfluous decoration; the different parts of the body become spheres, cones or cylinders. Nevertheless, the overall effect is rhythmic and harmonious. Some "cubist" statues represent ancestors. Others —such as the *ejiri* of the Ijo, the fetishes of the Basonge and the funerary figures of the Bakota, whose function is to ward off evil influences from the baskets containing the relics of ancestors—embody supernatural forces. In European cubism, the replacement of natural curves by intersecting and superimposed planes and the treatment of every form as though it could be seen from several angles at once reflect an intellectual revolution. There is no equivalent for such a view of the world among African artists. They are not trying to explode a tidy and orderly whole; their aim, in so far as it is capable of explanation, is to offer a synthetic view. Similarities between works of such different origins imply no identity of purpose, inspiration or content.

In Africa, the "realistic" or "naturalistic" style, on the other hand, stresses curves, consequently emphasizing the organic nature and vitality of the work. But it does not copy nature any more than "cubism" does, because each essential or significant feature is emphasized or exaggerated.

Hairstyle, eyes and lips are treated in the finest detail; the torso is bulky; not even the nails are forgotten. The completed work resembles the model without slavishly imitating it. The planes merge harmoniously into one another; form and content agree perfectly. Less symbolism is involved in lifelike art, best described as "humanist," in which the figures no longer represent gods and spirits, but their devotees, both male and female. Where such art exists, as among the Baule and the Yoruba, there is a good chance for its survival. Round the mouth of the Congo River, where European influence made itself felt at a very early date, "naturalism" has been respected for so long that it has declined into academicism. "Realism" also found a form of expression in court art. To glorify the divinity of a king, the artist resorted to "naturalism," but nothing prevented him from giving free rein to his imagination and his taste for decoration. He was looking for spectacular effects and could add imposing weight to a royal portrait.

"Cubism" and "realism" have no precise geographical limits. Both styles can coexist in the same society and sometimes in the works of the same artist. African art can in no sense be called naive. It is the art of societies with more than a thousand years of history behind them, of which we know almost nothing. Lacking such knowledge, it is impossible for the expert to trace its evolution or to find the precise conditions that encouraged the development of a particular art form. The most that can be said is that court art, with its tendency toward "realism," developed in states with a centralized authority and that Islam, whose impact was strongest in the savanna belt, influenced artists in the direction of abstract and geometric forms, without completely prohibiting all human or animal representations.

A love of ornamentation prompts artists to decorate the simplest works with painted or carved motifs. It is natural for Europeans to describe these motifs as geometric; actually, they are often symbolic. Scarification—which may be done for tribal or for aesthetic reasons—the plumage of birds, fish scales and the markings of wild beasts are all indicated by dotted lines, stripes, triangles, rectangles, circles and spirals. An artist may also borrow foreign motifs and endow them with a significance based on his own beliefs. Strapwork, for instance, may be of Islamic origin. It is difficult for the uninitiated to say whether the ornamentation in any given example is symbolic or merely decorative. (See also *Altars; Ancestors; Architecture; Art, Styles of; Bakuba; Beads; Fetishes; Masks; Scarification; Sculpture, Stone; Yoruba.*) D.P.

ART, NEGRO. Negro art is a Western invention. It came into existence at the beginning of the present century, when some artists, of whom Vlaminck claimed to have been the first, "discovered" travel souvenirs —statues and masks brought back by explorers and sailors and left on wine merchants' counters and in junk-dealers' stalls at the Paris flea market. At that time, ethnographic museums already existed in nearly every capital—Vlaminck and Derain knew the galleries of the old Trocadero area of Paris well—but their curators, who were scholarly men, regarded the objects entrusted to their care simply as pieces of evidence about daily life, dance accessories or barbaric idols. It had not yet occurred to anyone that a "fetish" might also be a work of art. The movement that led the fauves and future cubists to interest themselves in the blacks was a revolt comparable to that which had impelled their elders to look toward the Far East and had drawn Gauguin to Polynesia. It was a rebellion against the dominance of academism, a rebellion above all against the vanishing forms of impressionism. However, there was one important difference between the discovery of Negro art and the discovery of Far Eastern art. Once Chinese or Japanese works were introduced into the West, no one ever denied

Basonge mask. Zaire. Painted wood. Tropen Museum, Amsterdam. *Museum photo.*

Anyang mask crest.
Cameroun. Wood.
Städtisches Museum für
Völkerkunde, Frankfurt.
Museum photo.

Head by Picasso. 1907.
Painting. Private Collection,
Paris.

Head by Modigliani. About
1912. Stone. Tate Gallery.

that really understanding these works,
knowing how their creators viewed the world
and what they wanted to convey, could be of
interest to people. "Savage" art (a description that for a long time lumped
together the sculptures of Africa with those
of Oceania), however, was not conceived of
as being of such interest. Vlaminck made fun

of attempts to classify African works, as he
did of all systematic study. Both he and
Derain were at the same time interested not
only in black African works but also in
images d'Épinal (popular prints) and in
advertisements for different brands of
chicory. Epithets such as "primitive,"
"barbaric" and "naive" stimulated the
imaginations of artists and art lovers who
cared little about the exact origin and still
less about the basic purpose of each object.
One of the first real enthusiasts was
Guillaume Apollinaire, who immediately
placed his forceful pen at the service of the
new aesthetics. He loved this art for its
rejection of natural proportions, which he
saw as a deliberate creation of mystery, and
he also found in it the same naivety that he
detected in the work of Rousseau, the
Douanier.

It would not be true to say that Negro art
had a direct influence on fauve or cubist
painting, but it is true that the study of
African statues and masks accustomed first
the artists and then the public to seeing art
forms where no one had ever looked for them
before. The general public caught the craze
in the years immediately after the First
World War. The first exhibition in Paris of
sculpture from Africa and Oceania took
place in May 1919, at the Devambez Gallery.
At the same time, jazz, which claimed to be
of African origin although it came from
America, captivated the musical world. For

a long time experts on and admirers of Negro art looked on each other with suspicion. However, knowledge of African societies was progressing, and systematic investigation was bringing to light the complexities of their institutions and rituals. Today the reconciliation is complete. No one would now dispute the fact that to know the name of a mask or the function of a statue or to understand the significance of an antelope's mane with its interplay of arabesques adds to our pleasure. One must be grateful to the specialists for their efforts, clumsy as they may sometimes have been, to pick out the distinctive characteristics of different styles, enabling art lovers to better appreciate the willingness of true artists to both abide by rules and take liberties with them. (See also *Ancestors; Fetishes; Sculpture, Wood.)* D.P.

Detail of a Nimba mask. Baga. Guinea. Wood. Georges Salles Collection, Paris. *Photo: Jacques Verroust.*

ART, STYLES OF. A specialist can tell from the style of a work of art which tribe produced it and where it came from. Sculptural form depends on the relations of lines and surfaces and on the proportions of the masses: the elongated masks of the Guro, the concave faces and statues of the Balega, the horns on the Bambara antelope crests, the symmetrical limbs of Senufo figures, the long necks of the carved women of the Bena Lulua, the lozenge shape of Bakota reliquaries, the pointed breasts of Bakongo mother-and-child statues, the regular striations on Basonge masks, the angle of the knees in Baluba sculptures, the curving lines of Baule statues. The styles persist because they are a part of a master's instruction to his apprentices. They learn the techniques of their craft (how to choose the most suitable wood; how to handle an adz, a gouge and a knife), what the common subjects are (for royal statues, headrests, *recados*) and how to treat them—that is, the style. Like all artists, Africans take their predecessors' works, not nature, as their models. Each one, of course, reinterprets the forms of traditional sculpture according to his personal talents, and the work of certain great artists is easily recognizable. Nevertheless, style is the formal expression of the community. Its permanence in every workshop and artistic center belies the romantic and surrealist conceptions of the "primitive" artist. He expresses neither a spontaneous, unique personality, as the romantics assert, nor an individual's irrational, oneiric world, as the surrealists believe. It is within the narrow limits of a stylistic tradition that the sculptor creates.

The styles are many and varied in African plastic arts. Attempts have been made to correlate them with the physical en-

Basonge mask. Zaire. Painted wood. Roland Penrose Collection, London. *Photo: Jacques Verroust.*

vironments in which they were created. The savanna is supposed to have fashioned a symbolist style and the forest a realistic style; or again, a concave style has been associated with the kingdoms of central Africa. The search for a correspondence between styles and ecological or sociological variables is not entirely useless, but it is difficult, because the styles seem to be independent of physical and social conditions. For example, the Fang and Bakota are neighbors, live in the same

Mbala mother and child. Zaire. Wood. Etnografisch Museum, Antwerp. *Museum photo, Verhoft.*

Bakota reliquary figure. Gabon. Wood, brass and copper. Charles Ratton Collection, Paris. *Photo: Charles Ratton.*

Fang reliquary head. Gabon. Wood. Princess Gourielli Collection. *Photo: Eliot Elisofon.*

natural surroundings and preserve the bones of the dead in baskets guarded by statues; yet the styles of these statues are completely different. (See also individual tribes.) J.M.

ASHANTI. The Ashanti, who number about 1 million, inhabit the central area of Ghana. Their origin is obscure. One theory has it that they came from the territory between Senegal and Niger and were one of the peoples who were dispersed after the fall of the ancient empire of Ghana. Although this is a debatable theory, the Gold Coast nationalists endorsed it when the question of naming their country arose after independence had been granted. The Ashanti suddenly appear in history toward the end of the seventeenth century. At the beginning of the eighteenth century, King Osei Tutu founded the capital, Kumasi, and unified the state into a loose but effective organization. Each province, district and village mirrored the central administration on a smaller scale while keeping a large measure of autonomy; Ashanti, in fact, has been described as a federation. It was formerly a military kingdom, which conquered its northern neighbors and harassed the others. It put up a vigorous resistance to colonial penetration, attacking British dependencies as far as the coast, and was only subjugated toward the end of the nineteenth century after two bloody wars. Even in 1900 a violent uprising resulted in the British governor's being besieged in Kumasi. Despite the discovery of a new source of wealth in the peaceful pursuit of growing cocoa, the Ashanti have lost none of their pride and individuality.

Ancestor worship was rigorously practiced, and royal ancestors were naturally the most important subjects of veneration. The Ashanti believed that the souls of ancestors inhabited their seats. The king had a special seat, a golden throne sent down to the founder of the kingdom from above when heaven was rent open during a thunderstorm. This throne was the pledge of his power, the repository of the souls of the Ashanti people, the symbol of their unity and permanence as well as their national altar. Later it was also the cause of bitter and violent misunderstandings with the colonizers. The Ashanti also worshiped Nyamye, the god of heaven and creator of all things, for whom they built temples, and a host of minor divinities with special characteristics, each associated with a particular place, such as a river. They had a complex idea of the human individual. The principal elements were blood from the mother; *ntoro,* the vital force, from the father; and *okra,* breath. Blood was the essential element: the line of descent was matrilineal, and children belonged to the mother's clan. Even so, women did not play a dominant part in every situation. The queen mother took part in state and provincial politics, in the choice of the king and chieftains; she attended councils, and in religious matters, it was said that her seat was more powerful than that of the king.

The Ashanti kingdom was the hinterland of the Gold Coast as it was known to early travelers. Having failed to reach the great gold-bearing lands of the upper Niger, which brought wealth to the empires of Ghana and Mali, the Portuguese, followed by other Europeans, were content to remain on the coast. From the end of the fifteenth century onward, gold was exchanged in the coastal fortresses for slaves from Benin and, later, for arms, gunpowder, alcohol and textiles, when the slave trade extended to the Americas. Europeans had no direct contact with the interior. It was not until the beginning of the nineteenth century that the Ashanti capital received its first visitors. They were dazzled by the brilliance of a court where gold glittered on all the furniture and garments. It is true that they sometimes mistook the gold leaf on carved wood for solid gold, but this did not diminish its importance, and the perfection of its metalwork is the striking feature of this culture.

The Ashanti rarely worked in wood. There are no wooden masks or statues except for the strange fertility dolls with cylindrical bodies, short arms projecting like those of a cross and flat, circular or rectangular heads, whose shape has been compared to some Egyptian mirrors. Metal was supreme: it was worked by the lost-wax process, embossed or modeled in thin leaf over a wooden core. Molten gold was used to make necklaces, pendants, bracelets, rings and ornaments for headdresses and for belts and gold masks. The most famous of these is the one made for King Kofi Kakari at the beginning of the nineteenth century. The mask was a very realistic and expressive image of a vanquished enemy and was attached to the throne of the king. Walking sticks, sword hilts and parasol decorations were plated with metal.

Among the best-known works in bronze are the weights for weighing gold powder, and there are some remarkable collections of these weights. Their shapes are extremely varied: some are simple plates with geometric designs, including the swastika; others are figures modeled in the round and sometimes mounted on a base. The most common figures are of animals: insects, fish, snakes, birds and antelopes. Models of various objects also appear, such as stools, musical instruments, tools and weapons. Then there are human figures, scenes from daily life and some that illustrate proverbs

Ashanti funerary sculpture. Ghana. Terracotta. British Museum. *Photo: Jacques Verroust.*

An Ashanti *akua'ba* or fertility doll. Ghana. Wood. Musée de l'Homme, Paris. *Photo: Eliot Elisofon.*

and mottoes. These small objects, only a few inches in size, with their harmonious proportions, vigorous expression and sometimes surprising sense of humor, reflect in microcosm the knowledge and wisdom of a people. Bronze was also used to make *kuduo.* These were receptacles with a lid, in

the form of a vase, cup or box, decorated
with geometric designs and motifs in bas-
relief, or, like the weights, illustrating
proverbs and mottoes in the round. The
offerings to the *ntoro* were placed in these
containers, and the *kuduo* were then put in
the graves of their owners and filled with
gold powder and beads. Today they are used
for nonreligious purposes. There have
undoubtedly been many external influences
on Ashanti art and culture: Egypt has
already been mentioned in connection with
the fertility dolls; the decoration of the
kuduo suggests Hispano-Moorish art; and
the complicated weighing system for gold is
very similar to several systems used in India.
(See also *Baule; Blood; Divinities; Dreams;
Games; Gold; Household Furnishings; Slave
Trade.*) P.M.

AZANDE. The name Azande (singular,
Zande) has been given to the group of
peoples called "Nyam Nyam" by explorers of
the last century. This group, which lives on
the edge of the great forest, straddling Sudan, the Republic of Central Africa and
Zaire, comprises the Azande themselves, the
Abandiya, the Nzakara and the Mangbetu.
They all have the same racial composition:
Awro, who were either aboriginals or early
arrivals and who form the lower class, and
Ambomu, later invaders who dominated and
reorganized the Awro and who form the
ruling class. The Ambomu seem to have
come from the north, possibly Chad, in three
successive waves in the fifteenth, seventeenth
and eighteenth centuries. The royal chronicles, collected about 1875, record fifteen

generations. The Azande have never formed
a state that remained unified over long
periods. Their history is more a succession of
temporary supremacies, when overlords established themselves, followed by periods of
disintegration, after the deaths of overlords.
At the time of the European conquest, this
had ended in the coexistence of a number of
kingdoms of varying importance.

The "Nyam Nyam" acquired from the first
explorers and the Arab slave traders a reputation for cannibalism, which, as always,
seems to have been exaggerated. Cannibalism appears to have been the privilege
of the royal clan of the Avungura and to have
been practiced less for gastronomic than for
social reasons.

Nevertheless, the same sources, especially
Schweinfurth, recognized the general superiority of Zande culture over that of the

Nyam Nyam hamlet on the banks of the Diamvonou. Illustration from *Im Herzen von Afrika*, by G. Schweinfurth (1874).

neighboring tribes, particularly in music, poetry, arts and metalwork. It was this superiority that enabled the Azande to resist the Egyptian slave trade. They became the Egyptians' principal suppliers of slaves, whereby they vastly enriched themselves and almost completely depopulated neighboring territories in the process.

Their society was based on patrilineal descent and was divided into loosely knit, exogamous clans, with the clans of the Awro, or common people, corresponding to the conquered tribes. The royal clan of the Avungura was not required to observe the rule of exogamy, and incest, even between brother and sister, was sometimes practiced in the ruling families. This privilege did not extend to the invading Ambomu clans. The kings were always Avungura, but provincial governors and military chiefs could be Ambomu. The Avungura clan, as a matter of fact, symbolized the essence of the Zande nation and was, consequently, in many ways above the law. One of the principal prerogatives of the Avungura chiefs, which had political and judicial effects but was essentially connected with magic, was the control of the soothsayers, who organized the trials by ordeal to unmask sorcerers. A belief in sorcery was implied in nearly all social relationships, since the Azande considered that all the misfortunes and accidents of life were due to conscious or unconscious ill will, displayed in the long-range action of a physical substance, *mangu,* which could be found in an autopsy of the organs of a sorcerer. Apart from the Avungura, anyone was open to the suspicion of sorcery and subject to an ordeal before the soothsayer of a chief. If he was found guilty, the sorcerer was generally condemned to compensate the victim and made to pay a fine to the chief in spearheads, throwing knives, women and valuable merchandise. Black magic, called *menzere,* was different from sorcery in as much as it was not "natural" and could even attack the Avungura.

The decline of the Azande, particularly the true Azande, was due to colonization, which put a stop to the slave trade and introduced sleeping sickness. Their population had already dwindled critically by the end of World War II and has been further reduced by the massacres following the independence of Sudan and the Republic of Zaire. The Azande, steeped in the glory of their past, which is still extolled today in their lively poetry, and often contemptuous of their neighbors, have paid a heavy price for their disdain of Khartoum, Kinshasa and Stanleyville. Many have had to take refuge in the Central African Republic. (See also *Sorcery.*)   P.A.

BAGA. The Baga group includes the Landuma, the Nalu and the Baga themselves. They occupy the swampy coastal region of the Republic of Guinea as far inland as Conakry, that is, the southern part of the Low Coast—so called because it is impossible to tell from the air where the land begins and the water ends under the foliage

Azande statue. Zaire. Wood. Rhodes National Gallery, Salisbury. *Museum photo.*

Nimba, goddess of fertility. Baga mask. Guinea. Wood and plant fibers. Georges Salles Collection, Paris. Photo: William Fagg.

presence of "Bagoes" along the seaboard. This marshland was probably always a refuge for people coming from all over the area, and the movement continues. The Susu are gradually invading the villages along the edge of the palm groves; the Fula abandon the mountains between rainy seasons and drive their herds, badly in need of salt, down toward land that is still damp.

Many young Baga are leaving their villages for nearby townships, where they hope to escape the tyrannical control of their elders. Those who stay are giving up their own language and speaking Susu. Some have converted to Islam, others to Christianity. They forsake their own customs and hardly know about *Simo,* a secret society whose activities René Caillé reported more than a century ago. The *Simo* made its presence felt after the rice harvest. Threshing the grain was a joyous occasion, and masked initiates would dance around family relics that were protected by an *elek*—the head of a horned animal or a bird with a very long beak on which small horns containing powders with magical properties were fixed. Like all masked societies in Africa, the *Simo* also took part in the burial service of its members.

Baga sculptures are prized by collectors and have disappeared today from the villages, whose inhabitants no longer celebrate the ceremonies of their fathers. In these ceremonies, they used what may be the largest mask known in Africa, called *nimba. Nimba* represents the goddess of fertility. Her great bust, with its narrow face, hooked nose and flat chin, is worn on the head of a dancer, whose body is completely hidden under a huge raffia cloak. His eyes are level with two holes pierced between the breasts. Another huge mask is the *bansonyi,* which is connected with the ceremonies of male initiations. It consists of a painted and indented pole, ending in a triangular, human face and a strip of calico floating in the wind. The pole and the framework beneath it are over eighteen feet high. Among the Baga Fore, the emergence of the young initiates was celebrated by dancing with two similar poles, representing husband and wife, each the champion of half the village; the two halves of the village would challenge each other to a real duel. In the land of the Nalu, the *banda* mask is a long, stylized crocodile's head, painted in several colors and having antelope horns, human eyes and a human nose. It is carried horizontally on one's head and can measure more than five feet in length. It associates man with the two great complementary elements of water and forest and was greatly feared. Other types of Baga

of mangroves. The coastline is indented by the estuaries of numerous rivers that flow down from the nearby Fouta Djallon Mountains. A paradise for mosquitoes and crabs, this unhealthful region is extremely rich agriculturally. The rice fields of the Baga are polders reclaimed from the less watery zones, where the inhabitants cultivate the rice on ridges by a highly ingenious method of transplanting. Their main implement is a spade, which may be over eight feet long. Its blade is shaped like an oar and is attached to the handle by splicing it to the pointed end of the shaft. A danger threatening these lands is the silting up of the coastline.

According to what the natives themselves say, their arrival in this area dates back only a few generations. However, the first Portuguese travelers at the end of the sixteenth century had already reported the sculpture include drums, supported by figures in the same style as the *nimba,* multicolored mask crests in the form of birds, free-standing sculptures and panels of carved wood, whose main subject is the bird that "lives in the marshes and eats little fish." (See also *Societies, Secret.*)   D.P.

BAHUTU. See *Rwanda.*

BAJOKWE. This tribe has been called by forty-seven different names, and only an experienced linguist can recognize the same root in the names Chokwe, Chiboque and Makioko. Today, they number about 600,000 persons, divided into several groups in the savanna, stretching south of the equatorial forest in a region where the present frontiers of Angola, Zambia and Zaire meet. A century and a half ago, the Bajokwe occupied only a limited territory near the sources of the Kasai and the Kwango. Their rapid expansion has been due to an enterprising use of the possibilities of hunting, trading and pillaging. They exported the products of food-gathering and hunting—honey, wax and ivory—to distant regions, notably to the west to the land of the Ovimbundu, two weeks' march away. They obtained firearms in exchange, which enabled them to expand both their business transactions and their power. They attacked caravans and villages, taking prisoners and selling them as slaves, or small bands established themselves on fresh hunting grounds, situated between the villages of farmers. They would recognize the authority of the village chiefs for a certain time; then, when a conflict broke out, the Bajokwe's superior arms enabled them to subject the people who had accepted their presence. The subjected tribes were rapidly assimilated: the Bajokwe sold the men as slaves and kept the women, whose children by them were Bajokwe. Finally, the Bajokwe seized the capital of the Balunda, which had been the center of such a brilliant kingdom.

Slave trading, pillaging and conquest did not exhaust the energies of the Bajokwe. These seminomads were excellent blacksmiths and exceptional sculptors in wood. Although they had no unifying political organization, they were divided into chiefdoms, where a refined, sometimes mannered court art was able to develop in rich and vital surroundings. With their enterprising and open-minded attitude, they assimilated some European influences and reinterpreted them in their own manner. The thrones of chiefs are based on the form of sixteenth-century European chairs, but the rungs are decorated with scenes from

Bajokwe statue. Angola. Wood. Museum für Völkerkunde, Berlin. *Photo: Hélène Adant.*

Detail of a Bajokwe chair. Angola. Wood. Musée royal de l'Afrique centrale, Tervuren. *Photo: Jacques Maquet.*

Bajokwe mask. Angola.
Wood. Musée royal de
l'Afrique centrale, Tervuren.
Photo: Eliot Elisofon.

BAKOTA. The Bakota, or Kota, are not a homogeneous people. They appear to be a number of tribes which, during the course of their migrations, banded together under pressure from the Fang and are related through the customs and cultural systems that they evolved in common. They came from the upper Ogooué River and straddle the frontiers of the Republic of Congo and Gabon. Theirs is a village society based on lineage and secret societies. The most important of these is the *Mungala,* an all-male society responsible for the initiation of adolescents, which confers virility upon them. The *Mungala* is active in everyday life, keeping the peace and protecting plantations, and in events that affect the entire community, such as funerals. *Mungala* originally designated a masked person. It signified a very large mask, about six and a half feet high, supported by two initiates; whitened matting, palm tufts and a bunch of leaves suggested the outline of an animal. In recent times, the mask has become distinct from the society and has gained independence, which gives its proprietor some personal advantages.

The Bakota live in the heart of a country in which masks have multiplied, undergone transformations and followed some unexpected lines of migration. In one place, the mask is a flimsy object, lasting only as long as a ceremony. In another, it is merely a form of painting used to change the appearance of the actor. Elsewhere, it becomes a grotesque figure or appears unpredictably as white faces with features reminiscent of the Orient, which have been generally attributed to Mpongwe sculptors. As personifications of forces, spirits of the dead and legendary characters, these masks are ubiquitous. They travel along roads trodden by men as well as along imaginative paths.

Bakota art is one of the most famous types of Negro art. Abstract forms are mastered, masses flattened out, surfaces and lines fall into a taut composition. Like their neighbors, especially the Fang, the Bakota preserve the relics of their distinguished dead in baskets watched over by a "guardian." The "guardian" is an image which is always highly stylized and relies entirely on the face to make an impact: its body is merely a support, often carved in a lozenge shape to suggest arms and legs; its face is a flat wooden oval, flanked by two wings and surmounted by a crescent moon lying horizontally; its eyes and nose are portrayed in very low relief and the mouth is sometimes omitted. The technique concentrates on the importance of the surfaces, which symbolize the different elements of the human face and

everyday village life, the feet are caryatids or atlantes in a typically Bajokwe style and the back may be shaped as a female figure leaning slightly backwards, as in the very fine chief's seat in the Musée de Tervuren. The decoration offers another example of borrowing that is not imitation; the cruciform strapwork so often reproduced on the fronts of masks, everyday objects and jewelry, originated in the cross of the Portuguese Order of Christ. The Bajokwe sculptors shared the universal African repugnance toward the individual portrait (any head carved by a Bajokwe is a convincing proof that the artist did not try to reproduce a human face), but the sculptors of masks took as their models "women with comely foreheads." They reproduced the actual proportions and sometimes the tattooing. European influence may explain this use of a model. It is certainly present in wooden objects that are assembled, as in the chairs, because this is completely alien to the traditional technique of carving the whole object from a single block of wood. These influences, however, were not forced on the Bajokwe artists; it was they who chose the elements that they could integrate into their sculptural tradition to offer new possibilities without destroying it. It has been an undoubted success; the Bajokwe style is extremely original and has an unforgettable appeal. (See also *Balunda; Breasts; Combs; Granaries; Headrests; Masks.*)   J.M.

BAKONGO. See *Kongo.*

Bakota reliquary figure. Wood covered with leather. Private Collection. *Photo: Giraudon.*

Bakota reliquary figure. Gabon. Wood covered with copper leaf and wire. Paul Tishman Collection, New York. *Photo: Musée de l'Homme.*

body. The wood is actually covered with copper, brass or iron. Planes, colors and the technical effects produced by hammering, embossing, cutting into narrow strips and engraving all show a masterly treatment of metal. There are many variations on the same theme. Some images have a convex forehead; in others it is concave. Some sculptures are in low relief, which permits some modeling of the face, while others are almost entirely two-dimensional. Most of these figures have one face, but others, which are supposed to be the oldest, have two. Bakota tradition contrasts these Janus faces, called *mbulu-viti,* with the ordinary statues, the *mbulu-ngulu,* and declares that the double face is necessary "in order to eat different foods." Bakota art has an exceptional power of expression. It is both fascinating and disturbing, because the secret of its success remains hidden. Picasso wanted to penetrate the mystery, and in 1907 he painted a series of variations on *mbulu* images. (See also *Art, African; Art, Styles of; Societies, Secret.*)   G.B.

BAKUBA. Rarely has art reflected social values as perfectly as that of the Bakuba. Their famous royal statues demonstrate the importance and antiquity of the institution of monarchy in this society of the southern savanna, which is typical of the granary civilization. Shamba Bolongongo, the ninety-third sovereign of the Bakuba, reigned from 1600 to 1620. If his statue, now in the British Museum, was made in his lifetime, it is one of the oldest African wood sculptures that we possess. But it is not the sole extant example of early Bakuba sculpture, for the effigies of several of Shamba's successors have been preserved. These statues in the round, which vary in height from between about twelve to thirty inches, are not portraits. Each monarch is identified not by his individual features,

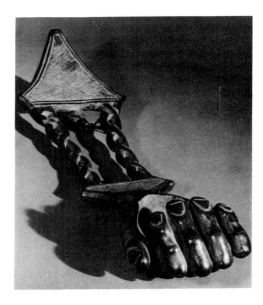

Bakuba spoon. Zaire.
Sculpted wood. Musée royal
de l'Afrique centrale,
Tervuren. *Museum photo.*

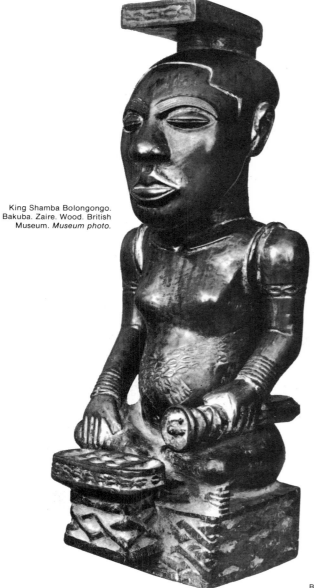

King Shamba Bolongongo.
Bakuba. Zaire. Wood. British
Museum. *Museum photo.*

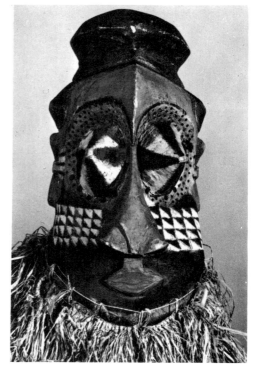

Bakuba mask. Zaire. Wood.
Musée royal de l'Afrique
centrale, Tervuren.
Museum photo.

which the sculptors have evidently not tried to reproduce, but by an emblem, in high relief on the base, that typifies one of the most characteristic achievements of his reign. The Bakuba, who live in Zaire and today number around 75,000, were organized into several chiefdoms that recognized the supremacy of the chief of the Mbala, the *Nyimi,* to whom they paid tribute. Despite the federal character of the Bakuba kingdom, also known as Bushongo, the king established extensive personal authority and, in particular, the power of life and death over his subjects. The royal statues express the greatness of the kings and their desire to be known by name to posterity.

King Shamba was supposed to have said, according to oral tradition, that he had ordered his image carved so that his successors would remember him and his laws. Monarchy is the source of history, and when the written word is lacking, statuary can replace it.

Traditional Bakuba art has produced other works which are also a significant reflection of their social structure. Their drinking vessels for palm wine are well known. They are made of wood in the shape of a hollow head whose features are stylized in the same way as the faces of the kings. Cosmetic boxes, pipe bowls, headrests, drums and chairs originating in Bakuba country are common in our museums. In contrast to other African sculptors who carve in wood, Bakuba craftsmen make objects for everyday use whose practical purposes are clearly subordinated to their aesthetic significance. This is expressed in the careful decoration covering every surface of the object. The motifs are either linear geometric figures repeated with slight variations or the human face, which is stereotyped and at the same time naturalistic in aspect. The high finish of these objects, which show no trace of toolmarks, is quite remarkable. The exuberant decoration and the refinement of these utensils for everyday use transform them into objects of luxury and prestige, worthy of the Bakuba aristocracy. And a large court indeed lived in Mushenge, the capital. All the chiefs of the kingdom were obliged to spend long periods in attendance on the sovereign, during which time they acted as councillors and judges, while dignitaries and servants of the state helped the king in his administration. All these titled persons formed a privileged minority which had become hereditary and hence formed the nobility. The revenue they obtained from taxation enabled them to employ professional sculptors, which explains the high quality of their work. The common people had to be content with cups and boxes of cruder workmanship but similar in style. This is why the court art and the popular art of the Bakuba are indistinguishable in form.

The same emphasis on decoration, with the same patterns, is found in the "Kasai velvets," lovely materials in which blacks, beiges and red-browns are perfectly harmonized. Bakuba ironwork has produced some finely worked tools and ceremonial weapons as well as real arms, such as throwing knives with four blades, simple and elegant in design but formidable weapons of war. (See also *Basketry; Granaries; Headrests; Mottoes; Polygamy.*)   J.M.

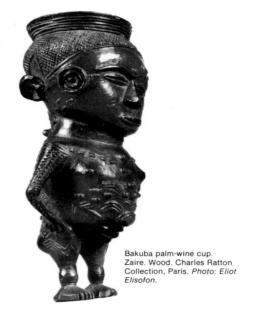

Bakuba palm-wine cup. Zaire. Wood. Charles Ratton Collection, Paris. *Photo: Eliot Elisofon.*

BALEGA. The Balega live in the eastern extremity of the rain forest in the equatorial belt, where it is suddenly interrupted by the Great Lakes. They are scattered in clearings cut out with considerable effort from the dense vegetation, which regrows ceaselessly. This isolated, deprived tribe has created one of the most vigorous and "modern" artistic styles of black Africa. It has been called "cubist" because of its way of conceptualizing the human face by inscribing it within a lozenge and analyzing the body in a few simple masses with straight lines and bare planes. It also suggests surrealism in its daring foreshortenings (a head on a leg, a trunk supported by two limbs that are both arms and legs) and German expressionism in some of its violent gestures with huge hands thrown high above the head.

Ivory is the material most often used by the Balega sculptors; wood is very rarely employed. Consequently, their work is limited in size and consists of narrow masks and statuettes. A concave style predominates in carved faces: the eyebrows, cheekbones and lower lip are carved around a hollow in which the eyes, nose and mouth are set in relief. Henri Lavachery placed great emphasis on this treatment of the human face and suggested dividing all Negro statuary into two main styles: the convex and the concave. Balega sculpture offers an excellent example of the potentialities of the concave form. The statues are very massive and the torso and limbs are heavy. The eyes are either cowries —a rather rare shell, since it is used for money—inserted into the ivory or wood, or

Statuette of the *Bwami* society of the Balega. Zaire. Ivory. Musée de l'Homme, Paris. *Museum photo.*

they are carved in the form of cowries. A point in a circle is a common motif on Balega sculpture. This motif is common throughout the world, but in Africa, according to Frans Olbrechts, it is a sign of Muslim influence.

Balega figurines and masks are associated with a society of initiates, the *Bwami*. The society provides a strong structure uniting the small Balega groups, which are separated from each other in a vast region where nature is a formidable obstacle to communication. It takes the place of a political organization and helps to give them a tribal consciousness. The *Bwami* society is essential to the cohesion of the tribe, and it also provides the stimulus for a variety of activities, including dancing, adornment and sculpture. The members of the *Bwami* are organized into a complex hierarchy: five grades for men and three for women. The masks and statuettes are the insignia of these grades. As the passage from one grade to another depends not only on ritual trials but also on ostentatious spending, these insignia are a real indication of the social status and personal prestige of their owners. (See also *Race; Spoons.*)   J.M.

BALUBA. The Baluba live midway between the oceans, in the central region of the vast savanna extending to the south of the equatorial forest. In the course of four centuries, from the beginning of the six-

teenth to the end of the nineteenth, the Baluba created kingdoms that dominated, in some periods, a considerable area between the Kasai River and Lake Tanganyika. The man who was believed by the Baluba to be the founder of their kingdom was called Kongolo. He was probably Basonge by origin and established his capital at Mwibele, near Lake Boya. Although the Basonge are patrilineal, it was Kalala, the son of Kongolo's sister, who succeeded him as the result of a conflict between the two men. Kalala conquered several neighboring chiefdoms, and this was the beginning of Baluba history, according to their oral tradition.

Baluba unity was cultural rather than political. There were centralized kingdoms, but they were never rigidly established, and two or more sometimes co-existed. This political organization, which remained fluid within its structure, was well adapted to the physical and economic conditions of the savanna. The basic unit was the chiefdom, which comprised several villages. A group of chiefdoms constituted a province, and the provinces together formed the kingdom. The authorities at each level depended on the king, but many of the chiefs were actually hereditary. The principal link between

Baluba mask. Zaire. Wood.
Musée royal de l'Afrique
centrale, Tervuren.
Museum photo.

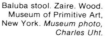

Baluba stool. Zaire. Wood.
Museum of Primitive Art,
New York. *Museum photo,
Charles Uht.*

chiefdoms, or provinces, and the central government was the payment of tribute. Whenever royal power was on the wane, remote chiefdoms and provinces ceased sending taxes to the capital and part of the kingdom seceded, sometimes only temporarily. The king and important chiefs had to be descendants of Kongolo or Kalala because, in order to govern, it was essential to possess *bulopwe,* the power of command, which only heredity could transmit.

Frans Olbrechts took the main stylistic features of Zaire sculpture, which he defined as "a mass of small morphological details," and then divided Zaire into five principal stylistic regions. The fact that one of them was called the Baluba region indicates the artistic importance of this powerful people. Amplitude of form is the most obvious characteristic of Baluba style: the heads, faces, breasts, and bellies are all fully rounded. As in other societies that have aristocratic castes—the aristocracy is made up of those among the Baluba who hold *bulopwe*—the careful finish of the sculptures shows the professional touch. Hairstyle and scarification are delineated in the finest detail. Another feature of the Baluba sculpture is the high proportion of statues of women. The female ancestors of the clans are carved on the walking sticks of the chiefs; stools and headrests are supported by caryatids, and quivers and pipes are decorated with female figures. This may be a manifestation of the matrilineal descent recognized by the Baluba. There is no homogeneity of style in the Baluba area. Olbrechts distinguished several regional substyles, including the substyle of a particular workshop, that of Buli, from which ten works are now in European museums. The proportion of head to body in Buli figures differs from most other Baluba sculpture. The face is angular, with an elongated profile, thin nose, pointed chin and protruding cheeks. There is nothing fleshy about the body; the arms are slender, the thighs thin, the breasts tiny and the buttocks flattened. Evidently, it was possible for a sculptor working in the depths of Baluba country to modify the formal conventions of its sculpture substantially and to maintain, in relation to his native traditions, a detachment comparable to that claimed by artists of the West. (See also *Balunda; Bena Lulua; Granaries; Headrests; Royalty.*) J.M.

BALUNDA. The Balunda are probably descended from the same parent group as the Baluba. A short while after the Baluba kingdom was established in the sixteenth

Seat of a Baluba chief by the School of Buli. Zaire. Wood. Museum für Völkerkunde, Berlin. *Photo: Jacques Verroust.*

century, a few men broke away from the ruling class of the new state and established themselves as rulers of a chiefdom that already existed to the west of their former home. A legendary adaptation of these facts offers an explanation of the conquest and a justification of the authority of the conquerors' successors: In an obscure village, the chief's two sons behaved very badly toward their father. He therefore decided to disinherit them and to delegate his authority to his daughter. At this point, a son of the Baluba king appeared, married the chief's daughter and became king. Thus began the Balunda kingdom. This legendary version clearly indicates that the new state originated in a Baluba conquest and that succession was matrilineal. The Balunda very quickly established not only their own identity, but also their power over the people of the savanna, which spreads from ocean to ocean, south of the equatorial forest; Balunda influence was felt from the Kwango River to the Zambia plateau. Balunda did not create a unified kingdom as such; the king, the *Mwata Yamvu,* allowed the different cultural and even political structures to remain, as long as tribute money—a symbol of submission and a source of revenue—was duly paid. Itinerant functionaries called *kakwata,* accompanied by soldiers, constantly toured the various provinces to collect taxes. This system of administration involved the rapid movement of military police over long distances; neither terrain nor vegetation presented serious obstacles. The Balunda empire was far from being monolithic, which is why the maps where present-day historians have tried to locate it are so unsatisfactory; the names Balunda, Baluba and Bajokwe recur in several places, and the outlines of the territories concerned are seldom marked. These problems of cartography reflect two important characteristics of savanna states. First, the subjected tribes persistently retained their identity, and payment of taxes did not generally imply cultural assimilation. Second, the bond of tribute-paying was extremely tenuous. Only a shift in the balance of political power against the king was required for some remote district to stop payment; there were instances, too, of chieftains effectively defending themselves against the tax collectors and creating permanent enclaves in "the Empire."

The Baluba origin of the Balunda is reflected in their plastic art. Frans Olbrechts believed Balunda traditional art to be a substyle of the Baluba region and ascribed to it the following characteristics: the eye is indicated in relief in the hollow of a large almond-shaped socket; the spine is clearly marked by a groove; important persons are often portrayed wearing headdresses in the shape of miters, higher in front than at the back; genre scenes occur frequently; zoomorphic themes abound; and the work of Balunda sculptors tends to be somewhat precious. These particularities of style make it possible to identify Balunda art in museum collections; but they should not obscure the many similarities among the sculptures of southern savanna societies. From the kingdom of Kongo to the Babembe chiefdoms, plastic art expresses the aristocratic foundations of granary civilization, made possible by the economic overproduction symbolized by the granaries: the power of chiefs and kings, who appropriated part of this surplus for themselves by means of taxation, and the wealth of the noble castes, who enjoyed the privileges of life at the king's court or helped him to administer his subjects. Balunda sculpture, like all the savanna arts, represents the same prosperity and aristocratic tastes. (See also *Armies; Bajokwe; Baluba; Granaries; Headrests; Royalty.*)   J.M.

BAMBARA. The Bambara, or Banmana, belong to the Mande group, which constitutes the major part of the population of the present-day Republic of Mali. Among the Mande, it was the Bambara who put up the strongest resistance to Islam, and "the infidels" is the name still given them by their Islamic neighbors. The land they inhabit extends from the upper reaches of the Senegal River to those of the Niger, and from the Sahel in the north to the Ivory Coast in the south. There are about 1 million settled Bambara, to which must be added an unknown number of *navetanes,* or migrant workers, who travel to and fro looking for temporary work in Guinea, Senegal, the Ivory Coast and Ghana.

The Bambara made their first appearance in history in the seventeenth century. The legend explaining their origins tells of two brothers who came from the east and managed to cross the Niger near Segou on the back of an enormous catfish, which earned them the nickname of *Kulubali,* meaning "no boat." The good brother, Baramangolo, stayed there to become the founder of the kingdom of Segou. Niangolo, the bad brother, killed their benefactor, then waged war further west and founded the dynasty of the chiefs of Kaarta. In reality, it seems that the Fulani cavalry took advantage of the chaos caused by the collapse of the Songhai empire and invaded the region. They organized the anarchic Bambara and established the two kingdoms of Segou and Kaarta. Mamari (Biton) Kulibali (c. 1660-1710) was their greatest king. He conquered his neighbors and unified all the Bambara of the Niger Valley. The Scottish traveler Mungo Park, who reached the Niger in 1799, wrote admiringly of the kingdom and its capital, Segou: "Sego, the capital of Bambarra . . . consists, properly speaking, of four distinct towns; two on the northern bank of the Niger, called Sego Korro and Sego Boo; and two on the southern bank, called Sego Soo Korro and Sego See Korro. They are all surrounded with high mud walls; the houses are built of clay, of a square form with flat roofs; some of them have two storeys, and many of them are whitewashed. Besides these buildings, Moorish mosques are seen in every quarter; and the streets, though narrow, are broad enough for every useful purpose, in a country where wheel-carriages are entirely unknown. From the best inquiries I could make, I have reason to believe the Sego contains altogether about thirty thousand inhabitants. The King of Bambarra constantly resides at Sego See Korro; he employs a great many slaves in conveying people over the river, and the money they receive (though the fare is only ten cowrie shells for each individual) furnishes a considerable revenue to the king in the course of a year. . . . The view of this

Statue of a Bambara ancestor. Mali. Wood. Pierre Vérité Collection, Paris. Photo: Eliot Elisofon.

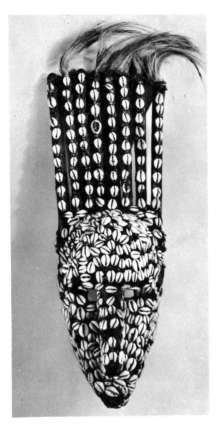

Ntomo mask. Bambara. Mali. Wood and cowries. Musée de l'Homme, Paris. *Museum photo.*

extensive city; the numerous canoes upon the river; the crowded population, and the cultivated state of the surrounding country formed altogether a prospect of civilisation and magnificence, which I little expected to find in the bosom of Africa" (*Travels in the Interior of Africa*).

The political history of the Bambara was checkered until in 1854 the Tukulor conqueror el-Hadj Umar tried to impose the Muslim faith upon them. They resisted, but it was too late. Only the intervention of Archinard's French troops delivered Segou and its Bambara inhabitants from the yoke of el-Hadj Umar's son, Ahmadu. Bambara society only rarely and temporarily achieved an organized and centralized structure. The term "empire" meant little more than the influence of a powerful and respected family on those who accepted its sovereignty. Domination in Africa has always meant domination over men and not over the territories they inhabit.

The Bambara are men of the hoe rather than of the sword, cultivators of millet rather than the arts of war, whose traditional institutions are fiercely preserved. The real social entity is the large united clan, consisting of a number of families whose heads claim descent from a common ancestor. All the family heads obey the chief of the village, whose duty it is to dispense justice and organize religious festivals and initiations. He is the descendant and representative of the founder of the village. He alone can fulfill the functions of his ancestor and deal with the chief of the earth spirits, ensuring that he is properly worshiped and that the land is well cultivated.

Animal figure from the sanctuary of the *Kono* society of initiates. Bambara. Mali. Clay. Musée de l'Homme, Paris. *Museum photo.*

When they emerge from childhood, the males form age groups. An age group that has taken part in the same ceremony of circumcision is called a *flambolo;* three *flambolos* compose a *flanton,* or age group. Thus, Bambara society is made up of a certain number of *flantons,* which together comprise the entire male population. Wherever he goes, a Bambara will always find companions of his age group who will house him and help him in remembrance of having undergone their ordeal at the same time.

Worship may be a personal or a family affair, or it may be common to the whole village. It is organized by six societies, the *Dyo,* whose aim is to preserve the spiritual strength of its members: the *Ntomo, Komo, Nama, Kono, Chi wara* and *Kore.* Their order is that of the successive initiations an individual must undergo for his complete fulfillment. The instruction given by these societies, their dogmas, symbols and rituals, are linked to a cosmological theory and mythology that permeate all religious thought and conduct. Initiation and religious practices are kept secret, at least from women and children, but the rituals are accompanied by public ceremonies which everyone attends. It is for these ceremonies that the Bambara carve masks and statues. Each society uses its own traditional forms, which are repeated with variations for all objects having a similar purpose. The meaning of their decoration is understood only by the members of the group, or is accepted without understanding, if its meaning has been lost.

The most frequently used sacred objects are the *boli.* These are made of a bizarre collection of odds and ends, pieces of wood, roots, horns, claws and beaks of birds, which symbolize different parts of the universe and are covered with a thick, black crust, the blood of sacrificial victims. The *boli* are the altars of the *Komo,* the most important of the secret societies. The name denotes at the same time all members of the society living or dead, their sanctuary, their altars, the head of the society and the mask. The *Komo* intervenes at every point in the life of its members: birth, initiation, death and ancestor worship. It plays an important part in agricultural rites, and the head of the *Komo,* who is always a blacksmith, judges all cases of serious crime. While the *Komo* honors ancestors and the *Nama* protects witch doctors, the *Kono* is specially charged with maintaining order and neighborly relations. Its home is in the middle of the village. Its masks resemble those of the *Komo,* but they are bigger and less ornate.

Kore is the god of vegetation, harvests and increase in general, whose name is borne by the age group responsible for the fertility of the fields. He is offered prayers for rain in rites that take place in a sacred grove at the end of the dry season, when the spirits descend to accept their offerings. The god is honored by a procession whose members are divided into eight sections, each wearing an animal mask; the *kore duga* rides a stick and plays the part of a clown in the procession. *Ntomo* is the society of small boys up to the age of circumcision. Children gain admittance to it by offering a chicken for a great feast that takes place at harvest time. During the dry season, the *Ntomo* mask goes begging to the villagers for the millet which will then be shared and eaten together. The *Ntomo* society protects its members against illness and all evil influences and decides how the common tasks will be shared. The antelopes, the best known of the Bambara sculptures, are closely associated with the *Chi wara,* the society of young men. The range of Bambara art extends from almost pure abstraction to comparative realism and is one of the most important in all Africa. (See also *Adornment; Antelopes; Societies, Secret.*)   D.P.

BAMILEKE. The Bamileke, who now number about 700,000, occupy a relatively small area in the central highlands of Cameroun, to which they were driven by their Bamum conquerors. There they organized themselves under chieftains. Political power, vested in the chief, his dignitaries and his bodyguard, was strengthened by various religious and military societies.

This extremely hierarchical structure was reflected in their sculptures, which were produced in great numbers by excellent artists. As soon as the chief was enthroned, he gave orders not only for his own image to be made, but also for that of whichever of his wives had first given birth to a daughter. These statues were not portraits intended to reproduce individual features, but images that retain only the essential and significant attributes pertaining to the high, social functions of the chieftain. In these statues the sovereign often held a skull in one hand and a battle-knife in the other. The skull of his ancestor, which was considered the seat of his survival, was, in fact, carefully preserved in a calabash that was richly decorated with imported beads and had a long neck ending in the likeness of an animal's head. His wife was portrayed in a respectful attitude, holding her right hand on her pubis and her left in front of her mouth. The statues were displayed beneath the porch of the chief's

Chi wara dance headdress. Bambara. Mali. Wood. Musée de l'Homme, Paris. *Museum photo.*

house, next to those of his predecessors. These were venerated, but as they were inadequately sheltered from the weather, they slowly disintegrated, providing a parallel, no doubt unintentional, between the slowly fading memory of a once powerful chief and the neglect of his image. These statues of earlier rulers, progressively consigned to oblivion by more recent ones and all of them eclipsed by that of the reigning chief, were collected under the exterior colonnade of the impressive dwelling of the present holder of authority. They were there to confirm the legitimacy of his power, to mark his close relationship with the guardian spirits of his ancestors and to assure the continuity of the chiefdom.

Another sculpted object that symbolizes power and constantly renews it is the high-backed throne, also constructed for the accession of a new chief. It is a most impressive object, carved in wood, minutely covered with beads sewn onto closely fitting material. The seat is supported by a carving in the form of a woman or an animal, and the back is the figure of an ancestor. This imposing seat bestows power and life on its occupant. Like the statues of former chiefs, these thrones are kept and exhibited on certain occasions. The rank of members of different societies is established by the chairs to which they have a right; the decoration and the number of feet indicate the class to which the initiate belongs.

This concern with rank and its outward manifestations seems to penetrate deeply into Bamileke life. Their houses, which have the cubic shape characteristic of forest dwellings but are surmounted by thatched, conical roofs characteristic of savanna huts, indicate the social standing of the occupant. Only dignitaries are allowed to have carved doorjambs, lintels and thresholds, or to set up decorated posts, which appear to support the roof but have no useful architectural function. Even the amazing beds, carved from a single block of wood, may be decorated with certain designs only if the social standing of the owner permits it.

Societies were equipped with dance masks, which had long, hooked noses, obliquely set eyes, fat cheeks and bulging foreheads, closely resembling the work of the Bamum. On the other hand, the faces carved on ivory bracelets, trumpets, goblets and small statues are like those of the Balega, in the concave style, in which the eyes, nose and mouth stand out in relief from the flat surface. Bamileke statuary and decoration portrayed a wealth of human forms such as

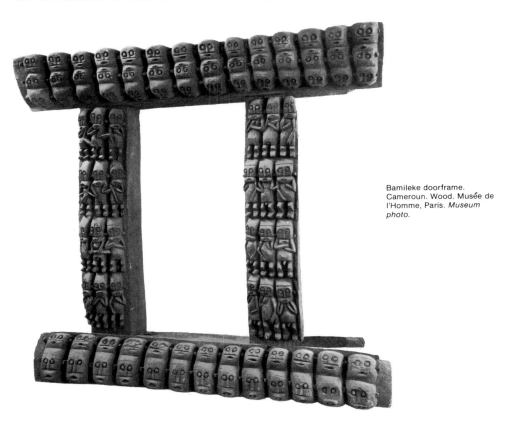

Bamileke doorframe. Cameroun. Wood. Musée de l'Homme, Paris. *Museum photo.*

Bamileke chief's throne from the Nsaw district. Cameroun. Wood and beads. *Photo: Giraudon.*

prisoners, either crouching or bound in chains, and ancestral couples with exaggerated sexual organs, and animals such as elephants with atrophied trunks, spotted panthers, spiraling serpents, chameleons with curling tails and buffalo with stylized horns, which were most harmoniously incorporated in the double-gong ritual. As in many other societies, the Bamileke appreciate aesthetic values not only for themselves, but also for the social prestige that their possession bestows. (See also *Architecture; Bamum; Clothing; Dwellings; Heaven; Ordeal; Royalty; Scarification; Societies, Secret; Twins.*)   J.M.

BAMUM. Bamum taste tends toward dramatization through the gigantic and has not always escaped the charge of vulgarity. How-

ever, this may be a strictly Western impression created by the enormous, chubby cheeked, hilarious masks, which we associate with carnivals and caricatures. The Bamum, who came from the north as conquerors, established themselves two or three hundred years ago in the high savanna of the Cameroun. They drove back some of the Bamileke toward the western mountains, where they still live today, subjugated those who remained and adopted their language and other elements of their culture. Foumban, the capital, became the center of a strong and unified kingdom. In the nineteenth century the Bamum clashed with the Muslim Fulani.

Njoya the Great, the sixteenth king of the Bamum, whose reign in Foumban began in 1895, was an exceptional man. In order to suppress a conspiracy which threatened him, he appealed for support to the Fulani, despite the fact that they were his hereditary enemies. When he was victorious through their help, he decided, like Constantine, that military efficacy was proof of religious truth and was converted to Islam. In 1902, the German colonial conquest convinced him of the strength of Christianity, and he destroyed his mosque. In 1915, the Germans left the Cameroun, and he was reconverted to Islam, but before long his interest in Christianity revived with the arrival of French Protestant missionaries. These successive conversions stimulated his creative spirit; he founded a new religion and wrote a book, a condensation of passages from the Koran and the Bible.

This remarkable king's fertile intellect found expression in many spheres. As a child, he saw some old books in Arabic, realized the importance of writing and tried to create a written language of his own. From characters submitted to him at his request by leading citizens, he developed seven alphabets, each one progressively simplified. The seventh comprised eighty-three characters, which transliterate the sounds of the language spoken by the Bamum. This alphabet was taught in a royal school, and the scribes trained there were attached to the law courts and recorded the verdicts. In addition to being clerks to the courts, they were ethnographers, who questioned the elders and recorded the edicts of Bamum law, recollections of past events, methods of healing and geography. Njoya compiled a history of his people, based on these documents, wrote a treatise on medical practices and drew a map of the kingdom.

Near his palace, a huge, two-story edifice, he built a museum to preserve examples of Bamum sculpture. The tradition of modeling is as old as the kingdom of Foumban itself; a terracotta statuette was found on the site of the first royal residence. Bamum society, though reduced in numbers (it used to be about 80,000), was rich and stratified. It included a group of professional artisans who were expert in delicate and costly techniques. They produced metal objects, especially small copper masks, by the lost-wax process. The sculptors who carved in wood were also professionals. They made furniture, chairs, bed feet and, what is rare in Africa, architectural elements, such as lintels and doorjambs, poles for roof supports, as well as statues and masks. These objects bear a close stylistic resemblance to the work of the craftsmen in other societies of the Cameroun savanna, especially the Bamileke. Their decoration is inspired by animals, such as two-headed snakes, spiders, buffaloes and rams, and is given geometric form. The profane character of their masks, with blown out cheeks, is surprising because it is so rare in Africa. Although the influence of Islam could not suppress entirely all representation of the human figure, it may have managed to divorce these forms from all sacred significance. (See also *Bamileke; Buffalo; Islam; Pipes; Spiders; Writing*.)   J.M.

BANTU. *Ba-ntu* means "the men." This term, originally used only to describe a linguistic group, has come to denote also a group of men with similar physical characteristics and a way of life imposed by their particular agricultural practices. Criteria of language, race and culture have consequently been mixed and confused at the expense of scientific exactitude. The desire for clarification has had remarkable results. The linguist Joseph Greenberg has distinguished a linguistic group called Negero-Congolese, which covers a large part of the continent from Daker in the west to Mombasa in the east, and to the Cape of Good Hope in the south. This group comprises fourteen linguistic subgroups, one of which, called "central," corresponds to the Bantu languages. This approach eliminates the term "Bantu," even in the context where it is most relevant.

The comparative unity of Bantu languages has long been recognized. The first Portuguese travelers noticed that the people of Angola in the west could communicate with those of Mozambique in the east. Missionaries, who began traveling in central Africa in the sixteenth century, also observed the close relationship of the spoken languages. In 1860, W. H. Bleck suggested giving the name Bantu to all languages that used the term *mu-ntu* for "man" (plural: *ba-ntu*) or corresponding words. In 1899, C. Meinhof published a comparative study of the phonetics of these languages. This linguistic

kinship led to the discovery of a cultural unity and a common approach to life. In 1945, in a study which attracted much attention, P. Tempels asserted the existence of a

Throne of King Njoya. Bamum. Cameroun. Wood and beads. Museum für Völkerkunde, Berlin. *Museum photo.*

Bamum mask. Cameroun. Wood. British Museum. *Photo: Jacques Verroust.*

Bantu "philosophy," which he expounded, illustrated and defended. A dynamic metaphysic and a sort of vitalism are revealed in the course of his study. He provided the key to this implicit philosophy: the "idea of *force*" takes the place of the "idea of *being*." The whole culture is devoted to the defense and strengthening of forces in the struggle against their loss or capture. Every hierarchy is based upon the degree of "vital force" at each level. Although this theory has been contested and is, indeed, contestable, its application to Bantu thought nevertheless opens up interesting avenues of reflection upon black African humanism. (See also *Arabs in East Africa; Education; Genealogy; Great Lakes; Hottentots; Islam; Pygmies; Rock Art; Tribute; Zulus.*) G.B.

BAPENDE. In the vast savanna zone, stretching from one ocean to the other, south of the dense rain forests of the equatorial belt, there were countless migrations of peoples and displacements of groups. The resulting contacts and reciprocal cultural borrowings gradually built up a common background and cultural unity. Some oral traditions of the Bapende recorded between 1930 and 1950 have preserved the memory of these long and fruitful wanderings: "Our

Bapende roof statue. Zaire. Wood. Musée royal de l'Afrique centrale, Tervuren. *Museum photo.*

ancestors, who came from the Zambezi, arrived at the great sea at Luanda," which meant that they crossed more than half the continent from east to west. "They were warriors and hunters, but did not know iron. One day Bembo Kalamba, the blacksmith, came to us and taught us how to cast and forge iron, and also to weave and make pots. His wife, Ngombe, was chief, and she taught us cattle breeding and farming. Our ancestors asked to marry all Ngombe's daughters, and they became the founder-mothers of the Bapende clans." A large statue of a woman is still placed on the ridge of the dwelling of the chief of the Kasai Bapende.

The essentials are all here in the concision of a legendary epitome: the transition from a food-gathering economy to agriculture and the origin of the matrilineal principle. The blacksmith was elected king, or *ngola,* and his state became Angola. They lived peacefully on the Atlantic coast among the banana plantations and near the salt marshes until, at the end of the fifteenth century, the Portuguese disembarked from a ship "with white sails, dazzling like a knife." The people of Angola thought that the Portuguese were spirits returned from the dead and tried to drive them back to the sea, but they spat fire. They brought corn and cassava, peanuts and tobacco. However, in 1512, they carried 300 slaves back to Lisbon. And so began the traffic that divided Angola against itself, because the king raided his own villages to sell slaves to the Portuguese. In 1520, the Portuguese penetrated the hinterland in search of the legendary mountains of silver, but, as one of them wrote, "Why need we look for mines of gold and silver? The best and richest of mines is the mine of slaves, where we draw up quantities of pieces of India." (The pieces of India were slaves nearly six feet tall with no physical defects.) After initially retreating as far as Pungu a Ndongo, groups of the *ngola*'s subjects fled even further into the interior to escape capture. After wandering around in the savanna, they settled in two regions, Kwango and Kasai, where they are living at the present time. Their neighbors call them the Bapende.

The Bapende carve few statues, but produce a great many masks. The masks that we are familiar with have a very consistent style; this holds true for both the "real" masks—those worn over the head—and the miniature masks—those hung around the neck. The former are carved of wood; the latter are carved in ivory, bone or wood or cast in lead, copper or brass. The triangle is the dominant shape used for both. The whole face can be inscribed in a triangle; the upper eyelid is lowered to form a V; the continuous line of the eyebrows, carved in relief from the forehead, forms a broad, obtuse angle over the nose, which is slightly retroussé and, again, triangular when it is observed full-face. The mouth is often half-open, showing pointed teeth. Some writers have taken these serious, expressionless faces to be the images of dead men; they have described the cheeks as emaciated and sunken, the cheekbones prominent, the nose pinched and the mouth twisted. This interpretation is acceptable, but not the only one possible. The masks were worn in dances that celebrated the end of the initiation period for a group of boys. The jewel masks were the insignia of the initiated and also ensured a magical protection for those who wore them. (See also *Blacksmiths*.)   J.M.

BASKETRY. Traditional African cultures, like most preindustrial groups, use basketry for a variety of purposes. The raw materials grow everywhere, although their abundance and variety differ from one natural environment to another. The forest regions, which furnish bark, lianas, palms and bamboo, are the richest source of the requisite materials, while the savanna provides the stems of grasses and dwarf palms. The relative abundance of plant materials in one area compared to another does much to explain its widespread use by any given group, but a group's way of life is a particularly vital factor. Therefore, before examining craft techniques, we will take a look at the principal uses of African basketwork. One of its most important purposes is to provide protection from the weather in the form of dwellings. It would be interesting to have a detailed study, by regions, of comparative methods of constructing enclosures or walls of houses, of making roofs shaped like huge conical baskets or mats, which are as easily put on as taken off the frames of transportable huts, or of fashioning interior screens, wall coverings and places for relaxation. A further point of interest would be a comparison between houses built of basketwork and those made of mud bricks or stone, or the relationship between building in basketry and the construction of flat panels, such as matting, designed for subsequent installation. A great deal of basketry has a personal use—for clothing or adornment, for example. There is a very great variety of headdresses, loin-cloths, aprons, penis shields, as well as of combs and accessories such as wrist- and anklebands, which are made in large quantities by, for instance, young Massa in northern Cameroun. The dividing line

Bwaka basket. Zaire. Musée de l'Homme. Paris. *Museum photo.*

Basketry fire fan. Massa. Chad. *Photo: Viollet, Roger.*

between clothing, strictly speaking, and ornaments for personal or ritual use is often vague. Such ritual articles are known in many regions. Among them are masks made partially or wholly of basketwork—various combinations that cover the chest or the entire body—found in Angola, and rattles used in dances. Braided shields seem to be found mainly in the forest regions, sometimes in conjunction with basketwork quivers, particularly in the Congo. But the majority of the objects that are of interest to us are containers, a general term covering objects with a great variety of uses. There are containers for transporting things—cases, panniers (which are uncommon in regions where loads are usually carried on the head), hampers and satchels of all shapes and sizes —and there are storage containers, which range from very small boxes to immense baskets that serve as granaries and are raised above the ground on platforms and pro-

Small Batusi basket. Rwanda. Musée royal de l'Afrique centrale, Tervuren. *Museum photo.*

fairly stiff materials provide the necessary strength. The process of *using superimposed stakes* held together by plant stalks is often employed either to give double strength to flat surfaces or rigidity and delicacy to objects requiring these qualities. In the group of products made by this technique, the broadest range of decorative effects—whether obtained from the materials needed for the process or by the use of strands in alternating colors—is to be found in objects created in the Congo: boxes and little baskets, some of which are virtually embroidered work. The "square with three elements" and a number of other variants, including one with broad hexagonal meshes that has been frequently, but inaccurately, described as typically Oriental, are found in the same area of Africa. The technique of *placing together two identically plaited mats* is almost as important. This technique can employ, besides straight weaving, two types of weaving that take advantage of the properties of bias working: a diagonal basketry, used especially for sieves and filters by the Central Bantu and inhabitants of the Chad region, in which the elasticity of the bias stretch is useful; and basketry in which the cavity of the basket is formed by drawing the outside edges of a square, flat surface within a somewhat rigid rim. Examples of this last technique are found in the east, west and south. *True weaving* may be done according to the linen formula (1/1) or in many combinations of twill or even, as among the Bakuba in Zaire, with a complicated satin weave that makes clever use of contrasting colors.

Coiled basketwork is less varied, but it is found nearly everywhere. It can be categorized according to the material and stitches used. An original and homogeneous style of basketry, found particularly in the upper Zambezi region, employs fairly tough fibers with twisted strands. It is used to make receptacles that have necks ending in reversed lips, which are fitted with flat lids. These receptacles are decorated with geometric and figurative motifs picked out with black strands on a particularly finely worked background. Coiled and sewn basketwork that uses grass stems is far more common. The material is fragile but is made rigid and compact by gathering it into sheaves and sewing the successive coils tightly together. The appearance can be varied by means of slight differences in techniques. The framework may be coarse or very fine; it may be visible or concealed by the coiling of broad or narrow strands closely pressed together, with either well-spaced or overlapping stitches, which are sometimes arranged with

tected by a vast roof. Although many are of openwork weave, suited only for containing solids, others are very closely worked and coiled in shape, specially designed to contain liquids. Good examples of the latter exist in Chad, Rwanda and even Ethiopia, where they hold milk used for ritual purposes. Others again are used as sieves or filters. Finally, there are a number of implements used for trapping, notably a large variety of traps and snares, which take the form of baskets fitted with blocking devices to prevent escape, and contraptions shaped like truncated cones open at both ends and used to catch fish or other creatures by hand in shallow waters.

There is also a great diversity in manufacturing techniques, and this diversity of methods is found not only between regions but also within a single culture. There is no major type of basket-making, or even significant variation, that does not figure somewhere or other on the African continent. The Pygmies alone, for example, provide specimens of every known method of manufacture. *Wattled basketry,* employing woven or twisted stalks, is used mainly for everyday purposes and includes baskets, filters and traps; upright stakes of perfect regularity between one row and the next, particularly in work sewn with split stitching. Coiled basketry includes objects made of long, braided strips sewn edge to edge. Finally, there are two uncommon types, in which coiled frames are held in place by pliant strands put in position beforehand, which serve as the binding to hold it firm; these strands may be woven, as in West Africa, or corded, as in the southeast.

This brief article gives only a cursory description of the clearly defined characteristics of some of the varieties of basketry mentioned. In central and eastern Sudan, for example, a wealth of decorative effects is obtained by the interplay of color against a uniform background of sewn coiled work, whereas in the area of the Great Lakes, the same technique, accompanied by an extremely careful finish, has produced a restrained elegance in a number of admirable works. The latter area, which is also known for its remarkably fine corded basketry, is preeminent among those regions that have made basketry one of the arts of Africa and have given African basketry an acknowledged place among the triumphs of the art of weaving. (See also *Combs; Flora; Granaries; Kongo; Massa; Palaeonegrids; Rattles; Traps; Weapons; Weaving.*) H.B.

BATEKE. Bateke or Teke are the names that foreigners have given the inhabitants of the plateaus to the north of Brazzaville on both banks of the Congo River; they call themselves Tyo. Their present population is about 75,000. There was a Bateke kingdom at the end of the fifteenth century, when the Portuguese arrived at the mouth of the Zaire River (the old name of the Congo River). In the course of their history, the Bateke were often at war with the neighboring states of Kongo and Loango. At the beginning of the seventeenth century, the Bateke took advantage of the slave trade between Africa and America, which had begun at least a century earlier, and supplied slaves to the coastal kingdom of Loango, which sold them to the European traders. They also took up tobacco growing for commercial purposes and, at about the same period, corn, introduced from America, replaced millet as their staple food. Two centuries later, there were further changes: corn was replaced by cassava, and while the slave trade fell off, the trade in meat and fish, acquired by hunting and fishing, began to develop. It is not often that we have such precise historical information about important changes in the way of life of an African people.

In 1880, King Makoko signed a treaty

Basketry platecover. Hausa. Nigeria. Musée de l'Homme, Paris. *Museum photo.*

presented to him near his capital of Mbe by Pierre Savorgnan de Brazza, which placed his country under the protection of France. As a consequence of the growth of Brazzaville in the colony of the middle Congo, the frontier between the traditional territories of the Bateke and the Kongo moved a little toward the north, to the disadvantage of the former. Since independence, the Bateke have taken only a limited part in the political life of the Republic of Congo.

The attachment of the Bateke to tradition can be seen in their sculpture. As late as 1965, they were still making statues for boys in the plateau villages. These were carved at the birth of a boy and protected him till puberty, when they lost their power and became profane objects. They were not made by professionals but by a talented villager, and so their quality is very uneven. The cylindrical trunk is barely trimmed; the limbs are roughly carved; and there is a helmet on the head. The face bears the regular scarification of the Bateke and ends with a short spade beard. The best of these statues are worthy of a place among the great works of African sculpture. (See also *Masks; Scarification; Weapons.*) J.M.

BATUSI. See *Rwanda.*

BAULE. The Baule, who number about 500,000, occupy the savanna region in the central part of the Ivory Coast, which penetrates like a wedge into the coastal forest. They form one of the principal ethnic groups in the Ivory Coast, and their dynamic nature has led them to play an important part in the economic and political life of the country. The Baule are of mixed racial origin. In the eighteenth century, they were formed into a

Bateke reliquary statue. Republic of the Congo. Wood. Jacques Maquet Collection. *Photo: Jacques Maquet.*

unified people by a minor tribe of conquering invaders from the east, whose customs and social structure they never fully assimilated. These invaders were the Ashanti. Under Queen Aura Poku—a sister of a pretender to the throne who was defeated when King Osei Tutu, founder of the Ashanti kingdom, ascended the throne—they left their land in order to join small groups of their compatriots who were already living beyond the Comoe River. The river crossing was a great undertaking and was achieved only by the sacrifice of one of Aura Poku's children.

The kingdom survived until the arrival of the French. An aristocracy established itself, but the ancient social customs of the subjugated people persisted. The political organization of the Baule was not as sound as that of the Ashanti, nor was their military prowess so brilliant. While the broad outlines of their recent history are known, the earlier period has been the subject of several different theories, some of which involve the Akan group—the Ashanti, the Anyi and others. M. Delafosse thought that he was able to detect the "imprint of the legislators of Thebes and Memphis" in Baule sculpture, their royal insignia, their conception of the human soul and many other aspects of their culture; according to him, the

Ivory Coast was the end of a long trail along which Egyptian influence had traveled.

In politics and religion, the Baule have retained part of their Ashanti heritage. In the arts, they enriched and elaborated it with borrowings from the people of their new country, which they assimilated with remarkable skill. Their treatment of wood is as refined as their metalwork. The territory they occupied was the center of a great synthesizing art that influenced all the neighboring peoples. It formed a transition between the more geometric tendencies of the north and subtler, often more detailed volumes of the Benin culture. As everywhere else in Africa, it was largely religious and sometimes court art. But the extent of the decoration on the most ordinary objects, such as combs, hairpins, pulleys for weaving and stools, suggests that it was done purely for aesthetic pleasure. Baule metalwork is very similar to that of the Ashanti. Their weights for measuring gold dust are nearly identical, and they used gold in the same way in their jewelry, their large masks, which they covered with gold foil, and their small masks cast by the lost-wax process. Besides objects in current use, there is a great variety of wood sculpture. Doors are carved in bas-relief depicting human or animal figures such as elephants, crocodiles, fish and birds, which

Baule receptacle for divination with mice. Ivory Coast. Wood and pottery. Musée de l'Homme, Paris. *Museum photo.*

symbolize the history of a family or the royal line. Sometimes the masks are abstract, like the circular masks in which only the cylindrical eyes project. Usually these are carved in the form of animals, like the stylized bull mask that is painted white and red, or of human faces with rounded foreheads, semi-circular eyebrows, half-closed eyes, thin noses in low relief and mouths that are either slits or rectangular projections placed very low on the face. These human masks are sometimes surmounted by small animals such as birds facing each other. The statuettes, most of which are images of the dead and are placed over altars, are very delicate. The face, hands, feet and scarification are treated in great detail; the hair is often given particular attention; the arms are pressed against the body; and the legs are slightly parted. Some of these figures are seated on chairs. In addition, there are cylindrical vessels used for divination with mice. Divination was performed by interpreting the way small sticks lay when they were scattered by mice that had been specially fattened and kept in a cage for this purpose. These receptacles are decorated in bas-relief or flanked by a statue of a seated man. In all these objects, the delicacy and elegance of style are remarkable. (See also *Ashanti; Bronze; Guro; Jewelry; Legends; Migrations; Spoons; Weights.*)   P.M.

BAYAKA. It seems that every rich, well-administered kingdom felt itself threatened at some period of its history by barbarian people wandering near its frontiers. In the sixteenth century, it was the Jaga who were the barbarians menacing the Kongo kings. They had a reputation for being savages, cannibals and invincible. In fact, in 1528, they took São Salvador, the capital of the Kongo, pillaged it and took several prisoners, even from among the nobles, and sold them as slaves. The king, Affonso I, managed to escape and asked for help from the Portuguese to drive away the invaders. They supplied assistance, but it took two years. We do not know exactly where these Jaga came from, but they were probably less turbulent and disorderly than the Congolese and Portuguese thought, since they founded a number of states to the east of the kingdom of Kongo. One of these, situated between the Kwango and Wamba rivers, was called Bayaka of the Kwango.

The Bayaka sculptors carved masks and statues. Most of these pieces have a curious feature: the nose is disproportionately large and retroussé, which, together with the protruding ears, makes the face look rather

Baule mask. Ivory Coast. Wood. Charles Ratton Collection, Paris. *Photo: Charles Ratton.*

Bayaka comb. Zaire. Wood. Musée royal de l'Afrique centrale, Tervuren. *Museum photo.*

Bayaka statue. Zaire. Wood. Musée royal de l'Afrique centrale, Tervuren. *Museum photo.*

Young Danagla woman
adorned with beads. Chad.
Photo: Hoa-Qui.

Young Banda initiate
adorned with beads.
Republic of Central Africa.
Photo: Hoa-Qui.

comical. The masks are helmet-masks, and on the crests are carved animals, figures and even entire scenes. They have a didactic purpose: they are used during the initiation of boys to help illustrate the instruction and to help them remember it. Faces with re-troussé noses also decorate everyday objects such as combs, headrests and batons. Huge masks in quite a different style are used for the rites of passage from adolescence to maturity. Called *kakungu* and worn by the initiation masters, they are an impressive, striking sight because of their size (the face can be almost three feet long), their color-fulness (they are painted black, white and red), their high relief, which creates a play of shadows, and their closed eyes. Male and female statues are also used during the initiation retreat. Nearly all Bayaka art is concerned with the initiation of boys, and circumcision figures as one of the chief elements of initiation. The extreme im-portance in this tribe of a man's coming of age may indicate the high value the Bayaka once set on conquest and warfare.   J.M.

BEADS. The term "aggry" (stones) is cur-rently applied to all ancient beads found in western Africa, whether made of stone or glass, but particularly to the beautiful, blue, elongated beads found on the coast of Guinea. These famous "stones" are men-tioned in texts dating back to the beginning of the sixteenth century, shortly after the Portuguese discovered the coast. Whether used for women's hair ornaments, gorgets, necklaces or bracelets, the aggry of the seventeenth century was cut by artisans of the kingdom of Benin and displayed on every plaque and statue. From there, trade of the beads gradually spread until they reached the coast of present-day Ghana and the Ivory Coast. In the eighteenth century, when Benin began to decline, the supply became more scarce and then stopped altogether. The Africans, in order to obtain these prized articles of adornment, then dug up the sites of ancient villages and abandoned tombs. The demand was such that imitations in paste, glass and pottery soon appeared. Since their exact source was forgotten, the collection of aggry ceased a long time ago. Their origin is still not certain. At one time it was thought that they came from a purplish-blue coral, *Allopora subviolacea,* which grows in shallow water only off the rocky coasts of Cameroun and the island of São Tomé. This theory has now been discredited.

Besides the highly prized blue aggry beads, Africans have always valued jewels of hard stone such as quartz, chalcedony or cor-nelian and of paste. Quartz is worked in many parts of Africa. A piece larger than the desired finished ornament is roughly shaped with a hammer and then wedged into a groove in a small stick. The craftsman takes the stick in both hands and, pressing it down on a hard, moistened stone, slides the stick up and down, thus gradually wearing the quartz away. Cornelian has been used in Egypt since the predynastic period. Museums in Algeria and Tunisia today preserve beads found in Neolithic Saharan tombs, and similar ones are still traded in Nigerian and Sudanese markets. From the Middle Ages onward, Cambay, on the west coast of India, has held the monopoly of cornelian, and its beads have covered enormous distances in their travels. The sovereign of Benin used to distribute necklaces of "red stones" as a sign of distinction to the dignitaries of his court. Since the middle of the nineteenth century, there has been only one place in Europe, Idar-Oberstein in the Rhineland, which has manufactured objects in cornelian.

As to paste beads, Venice—which has produced them since the fifth century and for a long time withheld the secret of their production—and Czechoslovakia continue to send large quantities every year to West Africa. Artisans still exist today, at least in Mauritania and Nigeria, who recut stone, glass and even broken bottle ends and from them fashion beads in the shape of cylinders, prisms, cubes, spheres, cones and ellipses. (See also *Adornment; Combs; Dolls; Gold; Heads; Headrests; Jewelry; Ivory.*)   D.P.

BELLS. The type of bell most frequently found in Africa is made of iron. Usually, a sheet of iron is folded to form two valves whose vertical sides are pressed together and sometimes soldered. The base is generally oval. Bells may also be made from tubes split all along their lengths and then resemble slightly opened pea pods. Bells are hardly ever hung, but whether they are fixed or swinging, it is the outer side that is struck to produce the sound. The clapper is made of an iron rod, or a small wooden stick held in the hand or a thick iron ring slipped over the thumb or middle finger. The use of a freely moving clapper inside the bell suggests European influence. This is certainly true of some bells in Benin, which are made of bronze and are round or square in shape. A bell can produce two different sounds of different pitch if either the valves are of different thicknesses or the instrument is composed of two bells of different sizes joined on top with a curved handle or even soldered together, one on top of the other. Iron bells are almost exclusively for ritual

use, mainly during initiation ceremonies. The sound is a protection against evil spirits and consequently accompanies the new initiates when they emerge or rings out during funerals. The custodian of the bell, the "bellman," is the artisan who made it or a dignitary somewhat on the fringe of society. It is important to distinguish between the holding of the bell in the right and left hands: one is the sign of the great initiated, or indeed the magician; the other marks the eldest in an age group. Only two instances are known when bells are handled by women: either, as in the Malinke lands, when professional women musicians accompany their chants with the beating of the instrument or when female relations of a dead or newly circumcised person take over instruments that are ordinarily played by men. There are also various types of bells and handbells carved in wood. All have several clappers on the inside that clash against each other as well as against the sides. In the Congo, wooden handbells are decorated and shaped either like small hourglasses or round boxes from which the clappers emerge like the legs of a tortoise. (See also *Bronze; Dance; Hunting; Music; Rattles; Xylophones.*)   A.S.

BENA LULUA. Traditional societies are commonly supposed to be static and unchanging from time immemorial, but Bena Lulua history refutes this common notion. The Bena Lulua were perfectly aware of their tribal identity in 1959, for it was as Bena Lulua that they embarked on a war against the Baluba of Kasai. Yet seventy-five years earlier, there were no Bena Lulua. The Baluba fleeing from the Arab slave trade took refuge in large numbers in the outposts that the Belgians had just set up and were there called Bena Lulua, "the Lulua River people." (Lulua is the name of a river that crosses a Baluba region.)

Culturally, the Bena Lulua, who today number nearly 500,000 and live between the Kasai and Sankuru rivers, are obviously very closely linked to the Baluba. Their sculpture, however, has a style all its own. It is rare for traditional African sculpture to be described as graceful, but this is a quality that the Western eye immediately appreciates in most of the statuettes of Bena Lulua women. These statues, with faces thrust slightly forward and long necks, are covered with decorations in high relief representing scarification. The lavishness and amount of decoration in relation to the size of the body show that it is intended as ornamentation of the statue and is not copied from a living model. The lines are often curved and circular, especially around the navel, which

Iron bell without a clapper; the handle is carved wood. Gabon. Musée de l'Homme, Paris. *Museum photo.*

Bronze bell. Benin, Nigeria. *Photo: Louis Carré.*

Small hemp mortar. Bena Lulua. Zaire. Wood. Musée de l'Homme, Paris. *Museum photo.*

Bena Lulua drum. Zaire. Wood. Museum für Völkerkunde, Berlin. *Photo: Jacques Verroust.*

protrudes more than the breasts. Masculine figures have the same strong umbilical protuberance. According to local interpretation, the circular theme is a reminder that the Bena Lulua are river people, because the concentric circles suggest the ripples formed by a stone thrown into the water. These statues, of which the largest are about thirty inches high, are protective. Some were carried into battle by warriors, others were kept near children during the first years of their lives and given the same care—baths in tepid water and massages with palm oil. This attention gave them their beautiful patina, which they still retain. (See also *Baluba; Headrests.*)   J.M.

BENIN. Very little is known about the first state founded by the Bini, or Edo, to the west of the Niger Delta. The history of the kingdom of Benin can be traced back only as far as the setting up of a new dynasty founded by a Yoruba prince whom the Edo, tired of a long period of anarchy, had invited from the fabulous city of Ife. This probably happened in the thirteenth century. The expansion of the Benin kingdom and the development of its culture, enriched by Yoruba influence, began toward the end of the fourteenth century. A century later, the Portuguese found it a flourishing state. In the sixteenth century, the kingdom reached its greatest extent, covering an area stretching from the border of the present Republic of Dahomey to the further side of the Niger Delta. Its population at that time is unknown. Today the Edo and related tribes number about 500,000. The influence of Benin culture spread far beyond the conquered or dependent regions to the neighboring areas of the Ibo in the east and the Igala in the northeast. Here their social and political systems and the forms and techniques of their art spread far and wide through the prestige and power of Benin.

The kingdom of Benin was one of the first states on the Guinea Coast to establish diplomatic relations with a European power, Portugal, at the end of the fifteenth century. A representative of the king of Benin traveled to Lisbon and returned bearing "rich gifts" and "holy and Catholic counsel." A Portuguese mission was established in "Great Benin" (Benin City), the capital, and missionaries soon followed it. The king received them warmly and promptly took them with him to his wars. Each party had its ulterior motives. The king himself wanted to make use not only of the new weapons the Portuguese had brought with them, but also of the spiritual power of the foreign priests. The king of Portugal, on his side, wanted to

convert the pagans and also to buy slaves, which his powerful ally could presumably supply in great numbers. Churches were quickly built, princes and dignitaries were converted, but the enterprise was abandoned in the eighteenth century. All that survived of Christianity were faint traces in traditional Benin religion and, according to some authorities, crucifixion as a form of torture and punishment. The slave trade itself continued until the nineteenth century. In Benin, slave trading existed in its original form, before the traffic was directed to the Americas. The Portuguese bought slaves for twelve or fifteen copper bracelets a head and transported them to São Jorge da Mina, in present-day Ghana, where they were exchanged for gold. The region between the Niger and Volta was for a long time called either the Benin Coast or the Slave Coast.

Commercial relations with Europeans—first the Portuguese, then the Dutch, British and French—were organized in great detail and controlled by royal authority. They flourished until the last quarter of the nineteenth century. At this time, the king of Benin was confronted by a new set of demands from the whites, this time in the guise of morality: the abolition of the slave trade, slavery and human sacrifice. He sensed the danger of foreign domination and closed his borders to all foreign enterprise. But before many years had passed, the king, robed in white, adorned with coral and supported by two dignitaries, was to scrape his forehead three times on the ground before the representative of the victorious British. During the four centuries leading up to 1897, many descriptions of the kingdom of Benin were published. Some of them written toward the end of this period were contemptuous or ironical, but generally they were full of admiration. The word "fascination" is used by one of the last British traders to visit independent Benin. What impressed Europeans most was the art and the profusion of beautiful things throughout the capital and the royal palaces as well as the organization of the state, "the most powerful kingdom in Guinea and that which most closely resembles a European monarchy."

The king was the head of a rather highly centralized state, "the Chief of the world of the living and the world of the dead," both man and god. According to a widespread African conception of divine royalty, the belief was that he neither ate, drank nor slept. It was also said that he did not die. No one could address him directly, and he never appeared in public without his head, chest, arms and ankles covered with heavy ropes of coral. Under the weight of these ornaments,

Horseman. Benin. Nigeria. Bronze. British Museum. *Photo: Eliot Elisofon.*

Dwarf. Benin. Nigeria. Bronze. Museum für Völkerkunde, Vienna. *Photo: Eliot Elisofon.*

he could not walk without support; he was immobile, hieratic, unreal. He only rarely left his palace, and then only with great ceremony. An English traveler of the sixteenth century said, "the veneration accorded to him is such that if we offered as much to our Saviour we should avert from our heads many torments that we merit daily because of our sins and our godlessness."

The palace, where every king added his own buildings to those of his predecessors, was without any doubt one of the finest achievements of African architecture. According to O. Dapper, it occupied as much space as the town of Haarlem, and its "galleries were as wide as those of the Amsterdam Stock Exchange." The galleries were supported by wooden pillars covered with bronze bas-reliefs. The doors, made of carved wood, were overlaid with fine brass leaf, molded to the sculpture. Bronze heads and sculptures were lavishly displayed on altars, in audience chambers and on roofs. There were also many objects of carved ivory. The palace in its full splendor was a

town within a town, where thousands of people lived, either associated with or serving the king. Great Benin was immense. Its ramparts were said to be fifteen miles long. The streets were wide and straight. The houses, built around a central court with an impluvium, were well kept, at least in times of peace; a Dutch author once said that they were polished and shone like mirrors. In arrangement, the town faced the palace, and this dualism was reflected in the social and political organization. The great dignitaries, apart from those who formed the college that was responsible for appointing the king, were divided into chiefs of the palace and chiefs of the town. They represented the peerage and held the highest titles. These titles were mainly nonhereditary, and everyone, except slaves, could aspire to them. They were grouped according to complicated hierarchies, and anyone with the approval of the king and his lords could slowly rise within these hierarchies. The bearers of titles were divided into orders, and their most influential members made up the

Female figure. Benin.
Nigeria. Bronze. Museum
für Völkerkunde, Berlin.
Photo: Giraudon.

Head of a princess. Benin.
Nigeria. Bronze. *Photo: Louis
Carré.*

Head of a young man. Benin.
Nigeria. Bronze. *Photo:
Louis Carré.*

king's council or were charged with administrative or military responsibilities. The king was dependent on them and, despite his divinity, did not enjoy absolute power.

Benin art was above all a royal art. In particular, bronze objects cast by the lost-wax process such as statuettes, stylized heads, some of which served as supports for carved elephant tusks, and bas-reliefs representing historical events were reserved for the king's ritual and everyday use. Although the technique came from Ife, Benin developed its own, less austere, style, a "baroque" style in the words of William Fagg. Besides the art of casting bronze, terracotta modeling also appears to have been taken over from Ife, although few traces of it are left. There is even less wood sculpture, for in 1897, during the British punitive expedition, the capital was burned. The wood may have been covered with brass, copper or even silver or gold foil; this technique, although known in other parts of Africa, was employed most skillfully in Benin and Dahomey. Ivory was also worked with outstanding virtuosity; among the varied objects produced were complete elephant tusks decorated either with basketry, weaving or matting or with rows of figures that have suggested a form of pictorial writing to some people, masks encrusted with metal, small bells, boxes, statuettes, bracelets, batons and latches. Different styles appeared, ranging from "romanesque" simplicity through classical restraint to baroque exuberance. Weaving and embroidery, whose products were exported from the sixteenth to the eighteenth centuries, should be added to these art forms, as well as numerous minor crafts such as calabash engraving and sculpture on coconuts. The groups of artists or artisans were controlled by the king. Some were managed by his delegates, others by titleholders who were equally dependent on him. Each district in the town specialized in a particular craft and had its own special obligations to the king. There were districts of blacksmiths, bronze casters, sculptors in wood and ivory, drum makers, leather workers and weavers. This system was already decaying in the nineteenth century and did not survive the European conquest, when artistic production ceased almost completely. (See also *Age Groups; Armies; Bronze; Christianity; Heads; Horns; Ife; Ijo; Ivory; Jewelry; Lost-Wax Process; Savanna; Towns and Cities; Weapons; Widows; Yoruba.*)   P.M.

BEVERAGES. Water, with all the problems it presents in arid zones and where the soil is too porous, is the most important drink. Very often the sources of water are biologically polluted (causing amebiasis or schistosomiasis, for example), or are infrequent or far from the villages. Cow's milk is available only in cattle-raising areas, and this is limited to regions where the tsetse fly is not present. It is drunk fresh or sour, generally at natural temperature, but its consumption is controlled by a number of taboos, many of them related to age and sex. Camel's milk is consumed in the same way in the Sahel region. Goat's milk is hardly drunk at all.

The most common of the fermented drinks is beer, which is obtained from the malt of millet, corn (*dolo* in Mali, *tyapalo* in Togo and Dahomey, *pombe* in East Africa), bananas or, more rarely, cassava. When it is filtered and not flavored with spices, it looks and tastes like cider. When unfiltered, it has the consistency of clear broth and has some nutritional value. The alcohol content is rarely higher than 5 percent. Brewing requires large amounts of grain, and it is sometimes prohibited, either by a traditional ban or by administrative action, during times of shortage before the harvest. Brewing is done by women, either individually for family consumption or as a group for

Female figure. Benin. Nigeria. Ivory. Paul Tishman Collection, New York. *Photo: Musée de l'Homme.*

important ceremonies in which the offering and exchange of beer plays an important part.

Wines are made from the sap of plants, notably sugarcane and palm trees. Palm wine, which varies in taste according to the type of palm tree, is obtained either by felling the tree or by tapping it just below its crown. When the liquid is fresh, it is white and both tart and slightly sweet at the same time; it is also somewhat laxative. Fermentation starts a few hours after the palm is tapped and produces a liquid with a maximum alcohol content of 3 or 4 percent. It is often strengthened by the addition of aromatic or aphrodisiac barks as well as Indian hemp, and it is usually prepared by men. Mead is drunk in some parts of Africa, mostly in the Sudanese region.

Distillation has been practiced at least since the nineteenth century. A must of bananas, yams, cassava or grain is fermented in rudimentary stills, such as gun barrels or bicycle frames, to produce beverages such as *sodabi, arki* and bush rum that have an alcohol content as high as 60 percent and contain a dangerous proportion of methyl alcohol.

Preparing millet beer.
Dogon. Mali.
Photo: Rapho, Scoupe.

Bahutu child drinking
banana beer through a straw.
Rwanda.
Photo: Jacques Maquet.

to flourish today. The most popular European drinks have been, in turn, rum from islands of the West Indies and then Dutch and English gin. Strong red wine, which was first imported in demijohns and then by tankers or in highly concentrated form is drunk almost exclusively in French Africa. Prosperous local breweries (Patrice Lumumba was a representative of one of them) now produce European-type beer as well as lemonade and various soft drinks, which are particularly popular in Muslim countries.

Alcoholism has become a social problem, made all the more serious because financial —and fiscal—interests are involved. It is generally easier to fight against clandestine distillation in villages than against large-scale importation. Some states have tried to combat this scourge, but with varying results. It appears that the need for alcohol is connected with the neuroses caused by the difficulties of adaptation to sudden and violent changes in social conditions. (See also *Bushmen; Cattle; Flora; Fruit; Funerals; Goats; Kalahari; Lions; Massa; Millet.*)

P.A.

European alcohol figured importantly in the slave trade and in barter. Although its sale was theoretically forbidden by the international convention of Berlin and Saint-Germain-en-Laye, the trade continues

BIRDS. Some regions of the African continent have hardly any mammals, but none are unpopulated by birds. A country stretching from the equator to the Sahel like Cameroun contains more than 750 species. Each climatic zone has its typical breeds.

There are hornbills, parrots and touracos in the forest regions. The Sudanese savanna abounds in many kinds of doves and pigeons and gallinaceous species such as partridge and guinea fowl. African rivers and marshes are filled with extraordinary numbers of waders and web-footed birds. Africans have rarely tried to domesticate wild birds for food, although a few guinea fowl and ducks that have been hatched from eggs taken from nests are to be seen. Nor are birds kept captive for show, as in South America and the Orient. Some scavenger birds, such as vultures, kites and marabou storks, live in contact with human beings and provide an efficient refuse-disposal service in the villages. Birds of prey take their toll of poultry, but the greatest enemy of African farmers is the millet-eating quelea, which does so much damage that helicopters and flamethrowers have recently been used to destroy them. Despite the many traps that have been devised to deal with them—snares, nooses of all kinds and lime-twigs—they still remain difficult to catch. It is only during drives made at the time of bush fires and during searches for their nests that many are caught.

Feathers of African hummingbirds, parrots and emerald starlings and the beaks of the great birds of prey are used for adornment. The Eton of Cameroun, the Bahamba in the Congo and the Mossi of Chad have very beautiful headdresses made up of feathers and beaks. There has been a lively trade in ostrich feathers throughout Africa. Africans—the Bajokwe, for instance —use the shells of ostrich eggs to make beads and other ornaments. Birds like the hornbill, bustard and crowned crane, which perform a courting ritual, have inspired some of the dances of the savanna peoples.

Birds are frequently portrayed in African plastic art. They may be very stylized, like the bustard placed as a talisman on the top of Mauritanian tents. Dogon masks are virtual bestiaries, portraying ostriches, storks, rock fowl, ducks, owls and hornbills. Most of these masks are surmounted by a sort of cross of Lorraine, which symbolizes the bustard and contains his soul. The Senufo carve wonderful free-standing sculptures of the hornbill, which, as in many other traditional societies, is associated with initiations. Oral literature in Africa is full of characters who, though they are really birds, behave like human beings: ravens, partridges, guinea fowl, doves, bustards and hornbills. In myths, a bird often appears as an incarnation of a spirit or dead ancestor. Spirits that devour the soul generally take the form of birds in order to steal the life force of human beings while they sleep. This

Guinea fowl. Fon. Dahomey. Silver leaf over a wooden core. Pierre Vérité Collection, Paris. *Photo: Giraudon.*

Bird. Wood. Ivory Coast. Private Collection. *Photo: Musée de l'Homme.*

is one of the reasons why the roofs of African dwellings are nearly always covered with thorns, ostrich eggs or bottles turned upside down to prevent night birds from perching.

Africans foretell the future by the flight and behavior of birds. They announce the change of seasons according to their migration and nesting. Because of their ability to fly, birds are supposed to be in regular contact with the world beyond; the Massa and Mussoi of Cameroun regard the bateleur eagle as the messenger of a celestial creator spirit and the jacana as that of the

spirit of the water. It is hard to tell any longer where reality ends and legend begins. The oxpecker and cattle egret warn men of the presence of antelopes; honey guides (small birds belonging to the woodpecker family) lead men to hollow trees in which wild bees have built their hives: they too may well be spirits and messengers of the forest. (See also *Baga; Fauna; Headrests; Hen; Mussoi; Pharmacopoeia; Senufo.*)   I.G.

Fulani hunter in the guise
of a calao. Chad.
Photo: Pierre Ichac.

Cranes in flight. Cameroun.
Photo: Hoa-Qui.

BLACKSMITHS. The blacksmith is the master of metal and fire, the "technician" who makes weapons for security and tools that are indispensable for all forms of production. In African societies, he is regarded as different from all other artisans; as his power links him with magic, he is always held in awe but not always honored. Some societies, the Senegalese, for example, segregate him within a caste. Others associate him with the culture-hero and give him high social status, as in the ancient Kongo. His position was never ordinary, because his craft was not considered to be one of the ordinary arts. The blacksmith was as much part of the world of myths as of human society. Among the Dogon of Mali and in a large part of West Africa, he is an ambivalent character, bound to the living and the dead, and an intermediary between them. Because of his close association with metals, which originate in the womb of mother earth, he is said to belong to the world above and the world below.

His craft has made him master of the four elements—air, earth, fire and water. It gives him a special place in the order of creation. According to one myth, he was the first created being who changed into man and tamed the souls of the cereals. The Dogon commonly believe that he is capable of transforming himself at will into the shape of all kinds of animals and plants. His tools have great cultural significance, especially the hammer, which is the symbol of all his work, and the forge, whose operation suggests the mechanism for producing human speech. His symbolic status makes the blacksmith as much a privileged figure in society as a master of tools; among the Dogon he is the chosen intermediary at the time of atonement for serious offenses and pleas for mercy from irate masters.

In central Africa, notably in the kingdoms of Kongo and Angola, the sovereign-founders of the state were sometimes described in legends as blacksmith-kings. As such, they were the first of all masters of the forge, and the working of metal has continued to be practiced by the "nobility." In the Congo, the blacksmith possesses an authority that ranks him with chiefs, priests and sorcerers, as his title of *nganga lufu* indicates. He is subject to a number of taboos; many special spiritual protectors are at his command; and he is capable of driving off insidious threats, just as the weapons he fashions repel enemies. His magic, which is needed by everyone, especially by holders of political power, is beneficial. His principal tools, the hammer and anvil, go back to mythical times and the first ancestors; they belong to the world of religion and the works of magic, and they figure among royal symbols. Moreover, the water of the forge and the air of the bellows are used to increase vitality and it is believed that they preserve health for a long time. A noble form of labor, a symbolic activity as well as a means of material creation, the production of metals is the meeting-point of the powers that work upon forces, men and things. The main centers of the production of iron and of metallurgy are located in East Africa. The presence of metallurgy was considered one of the favorable conditions for establishing a political state or military society, and as a consequence, the blacksmith enjoyed a superior position. The Kikuyu of Kenya still respect and fear him, for he can call down curses without redress. By using skills that are vital to economic life and power politics, he wields technocratic powers in a rudimentary form. (See also *Agriculture; Castes; Circumcision; Iron; Kikuyu; Kirdi; Kongo; Massa; Migrations; Sculpture, Wood; Towns and Cities; Weapons; Work.*)

G.B.

BLOOD. Blood, the supreme, vital fluid, is dangerously ambivalent; nothing else can be so tainted or so pure: it can completely defile and totally purify. This is why involuntary bloodshed is universally redeemed by the voluntary shedding of blood. Blood is one of the essential elements of the individual, but while it makes him an individual, it transcends him in the course of time through his lineage. Among the matrilineal Ashanti, it is the spirit of blood, *ntoro,* that links the individual to the paternal side of his family, and the transmission of the *ntoro* from father to son is undoubtedly related to the exchange of blood in pacts that bind the lineages of the pact-makers through the persons whose blood is exchanged. Female blood is particularly dangerous—the blood of menstruation even more so than that lost on defloration. As proof of nonpregnancy, the former is charged with a negative, anti-fertility power, while at the same time it is the positive sign of femininity. The young girl who is not yet a woman is, in terms of magic,

Bird. Decoration on a musical instrument. Benin. Nigeria. Bronze. *Photo: Louis Carré.*

Bahutu blacksmith. Rwanda. *Photo: Jacques Maquet.*

Collecting blood. Blood
mixed with milk is drunk by
Banyoro herdsmen. Uganda.
*Photo: Magnum,
George Rodger.*

neutral, whereas the woman who has passed the menopause and is no longer a woman, yet not a man, is potentially dangerous; however, she is qualified to assist as a midwife, since she has become neutral again, for she is assured against the dangers of monthly and obstetric bleeding. Animal blood is consumed or forbidden, as the case may be, for similar reasons: swallowing it has the effect of absorbing the qualities of the animal, but also of risking its vengeance. The Masai and other Nilotic tribes of East Africa draw off the blood from the jugular vein of the "lead cow," which is prompted more by a desire to create a quasisocial link between the herd and its masters and servants than to add protein to their diet. Finally, the collective and hereditary character of blood, as the bond uniting the members of a clan, explains why an accidental homicide involving bloodshed can be considered more serious in its ritual aspect than premeditated poisoning and sometimes worse than an act of sorcery. (See also *Ashanti; Body Painting; Circumcision; Funerals; Lineage; Sacrifice; Societies, Secret.*)   P.A.

BOBO. The country of the Bobo stretches from the environs of San in Mali to Bobo-Dioulasso in Upper Volta. Their population

is about 300,000 and is divided into several groups, each differing in language, customs and artistic production. The name "Bobo" originally applied to only one of these groups, the Bobe or Boboy; it was adopted in a slightly different form by their neighbors, the Malinke, and then used by Europeans to designate all these groups. The largest group, the Bwa, consists of almost 200,000 persons.

The Bobo are scattered in villages and were never organized into a large political unit, but they have all had the same history. They succeeded in maintaining their independence from the great neighboring empires of Mali and the Mossi, but the long period during which they lived side by side led to an interchange of numerous objects, institutions and beliefs such as *Do,* the society of masks that is active everywhere and gives the country a kind of unity. They all lead the same kind of life, which has been described as that of "a particularly pure type of Palaeonegrid farmer." Their agriculture is very carefully organized, with huge, regularly fertilized fields and terracing, in a successful effort to prevent erosion. The social organization everywhere was founded on grouping into districts and villages of large patriarchal families. Each village was practically independent and constituted an economic and political unit of the whole society governed by a chief, who was the head of the most ancient family, and a religious unit, which observed the complementary cults of the earth and *Do.*

The artistic production of the Bobo includes jewelry, brass figurines made by the lost-wax process and three- and four-legged stools with handles carved in human and animal forms. The most important art form is the mask of the *Do;* these masks are used in all the major agrarian and funeral ceremonies. The Bwa make them from fragile materials—straw and fiber—plaited into extremely stylized and relatively uniform shapes. There is much greater variety among the wooden masks of the Bobe, painted with colored, geometric designs and sometimes extended by a cloth embroidered with cowrie shells, which covered the shoulders of the dancer's fiber costume. The masks represent animals, birds, antelopes, buffalo and, less often, human beings. Some are more abstract than others; for example, the great mask that has a flat, circular face with geometric eyes and nose in slight relief, crowned by a large, prominent hooked beak, and, above the face, a high, thin plank pierced and decorated with checks, triangles and black, white and ocher herringbone patterns. With its balanced construction and rich decoration, it is outstanding among the

Bobo art forms. (See also *Divinities; Palaeonegrids; Savanna*.) P.M.

BODY. The body, which sustains the life force and the soul, is an aspect of the individual person. For the African, the body forms an entity, every part of which represents the whole; a few nail parings and hairs are enough to make an altar, which is then identified with the person from whom they came. But the body also comprises certain special organs where the life force is concentrated, and these command special attention: the head, sexual organs, heart, liver and blood. The skull is often an object of worship. During cannibalistic rites not just any part of the body was consumed. When human sacrifice was practiced, the body was cut up and the various fragments assigned to their appropriate divinities. These were, of course, exceptional practices, but the body was always the object of mythical interpretation. It is often regarded as a microcosm as well. The Dogon see it prefigured with its seven elements (the head, which counts as two, the four limbs and the sexual organs) in the primordial egg out of which the world emerged. The body could consequently be used as a model for buildings that had to be an image of the world—the house of the head of the family—or for the village itself, whose layout symbolizes a man lying on his right side in the act of procreation. For some tribes, every movement of the body has mythical overtones. Muscular trembling and unconscious movements can be interpreted by divination. Sexual intercourse exercises an influence on the universe, so it may not be practiced in certain places, for instance in the bush, where there is a danger that it might arouse the resentment of the powers of the earth, nor at certain times, such as before special ceremonies or during some phases of funerals. Every gesture of a man who is half-priest and half-divinity can be reflected in nature, and sometimes each movement has to follow strict rules. Even technical gestures, in some cases, when properly executed, express and strengthen world order.

The body is also the first object to be embellished, and there are tribes whose artistic ability is used in virtually no other way. Aspects of the body are altered to give it complete meaning, to integrate it into society and to protect it from dangers and disorders that threaten it. Initiations, leading to a new life, may involve circumcision, excision and the shaping or filing of incisor teeth. Some people, like the Mangbetu of the northeast Congo, elongate the skull from early childhood onwards. Earlobes, wings and

Bobo mask. Upper Volta. Painted wood. Pierre Vérité Collection, Paris. *Photo: Eliot Elisofon.*

Bobo mask. Upper Volta. Wood. Webster Plass Collection, British Museum. *Photo: Eliot Elisofon.*

Right: Young Ngere women who have been excised. Ivory Coast. Photo: Hugo Zemp.
Below: Makere woman. Zaire. Photo: Musée de l'Homme.

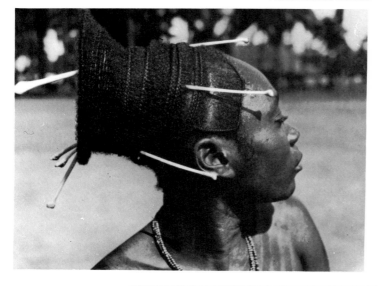

Woman from Maro, Chad.
Photo: Hoa-Qui.

septum of the nose and lips are pierced, and sometimes, as the skin expands progressively, larger wooden or stone discs are inserted, for example, to produce the enormous lips of the Sara women in Chad. It is still not clear whether the practice of piercing was part of an initiation ritual, but, in any case, it was done to protect particularly vulnerable body openings. Scarification of the skin often indicated a child's admission to society and could also signify special initiations or dedication to a divinity, as in Dahomey. The body also underwent modifications of a temporary nature in many regions of central Africa and Guinea: young initiates were painted all over with chalk and ocher or covered with symbolic designs, which were a substitute for masks and dance costumes. Although these transformations of the body had a primarily religious significance, they resulted in a form of decorative art. Although they always had other motives besides decoration, some of them, such as hairdressing, came to be used almost exclusively for adornment. Hair can be plaited or braided, shaved in places to set off the part of the hair arranged in a crest or in separately styled sections, built up on a frame of small sticks or fibers, or puffed out with a wig decorated with pendants. Sometimes, several long hairdressing sessions, with the head resting on the hairdresser's knees, are necessary for a particular style.

The hairstyle in the shape of a high helmet, worn by the aristocratic ladies of the Fulani of Guinea, is probably one of the most striking. (See also *Adornment; Blood; Body Painting; Breasts; Circumcision; Devination; Excision; Funerals; Heads; Initiation; Jewelry; Masks; Person; Scarification.*) P.M.

BODY PAINTING. On feast days, even currently, men and women anoint their arms, legs and entire bodies with palm oil or vegetable butter so that their black skins glisten with a special brilliance that is a sort of decoration in itself. To the reddish palm oil is often added a paste made from bark, which is also red. Inhabitants of central Africa keep their *nkula* powder in decorated wooden boxes, or they moisten the paste and mold it into the shape of a lizard or tortoise. Red is the symbol of life, health and joy. The bodies of young people, girls and boys, are dyed with *nkula* for the celebrations that mark their entry into adult life. Red powder is also put on the bodies of the sick to hasten their recovery, and it is rubbed on the bodies of the dead as a last mark of respect when preparing them for burial.

While red, the color of blood, signifies strength and life, white is often the color of the dead and of ghosts. White represents mourning and affliction among the living; as soon as a death is announced, women not only tear their clothing and ruffle their hair, but roll in mud and stain their faces with white streaks. However, white may also be purely decorative. To make white paint, clay is mixed with water and decanted. Before it is dry, it is kneaded into a ball as big as a fist, and water is added once more. The sticky paste is then traced onto the body with the fingers in regular patterns. At one time, the Basonge of Zaire held sacred dances for three nights running, at the beginning of the new moon; the women would dance and the men would look on, both with white circles around their eyes and white and red flames painted all over their bodies.

Strange though it may seem, black dye is also often used. The Mangbetu women in the Congo draw black designs on their bodies with dye made from the juice of the fruit of the gardenia. Their well-proportioned designs depict Maltese crosses, bees, flowers, straight and broken lines, ribbons and knots. This is all purely decorative. But much more frequently, color is meant to convey a message. During the period of retreat following their initiation, young Mandja in the Republic of Central Africa rub their bodies with crushed charcoal powder or with the sap of special roots in order to imitate warriors, who daub themselves with soot

Young Xosa initiates. Republic of South Africa. *Photo: Department of Information, Pretoria.*

Bakuba cosmetics box. Zaire. Wood. Musée de l'Homme, Paris. *Museum photo.*

when they set off on a campaign against a neighboring village. (Tacitus and Caesar described similar methods of intimidation among the Britons and the Teutonic tribes.) White, for the Mandja, is, on the contrary, the color of purification. Initiates, returning to the village, are no longer the same as when they set out; they have crossed a threshold of life; henceforth they are men. They too whiten their appearance with clay, drawing lines or points on their bodies, and some are even white from head to foot.

In addition, painting the face and skull may be a substitute for a mask. Among the Kissi of upper Guinea, who do not carve in wood and have no masks, the young men, emerging for the first time after undergoing the *toma* initiation, appear in Indian file, heads bent, their nude bodies completely whitened with chalk. However, one of them, chosen for his small stature, wears a fiber cloak down to his knees, which hides his arms, and his face and shaven skull are painted with red and white designs. "The mask" advances, knees bent, running right and left, shaking his shoulders to make the cloak quiver. He drags a rod along the ground, which inspires awe in his audience, for contact with it, so they say, will cause leprosy. (See also *Body; Cows; Scarification.*)   D.P.

BORNU. Bornu was a black Muslim empire which at the height of its power extended over all of northwestern Nigeria, northern Cameroun, western Chad as far as the Tibesti Mountains and the central Sahara reaching to the Fezzan. The Sefuwa dynasty, which reigned first at Kanem and then at Bornu from the tenth or eleventh to the nineteenth centuries, claimed Yemenite origin. It is more probable that it was founded by Berbers from the Sahara. In spite of its early conversion to Islam in the eleventh and twelfth centuries, its political organization remained black African in character. The sovereign, or *mai,* was a divine king, whose power was limited by protocol, supported by a queen mother. He enjoyed extensive privileges and a double hierarchy of dignitaries, one free, the other of slaves, who combined their duties at the court with those of provincial government. The Kanuri formed the dominant tribe and the one to which the sovereign belonged, but the other tribes in the empire, such as the Hausa, the Shuwa Arabs, the Fulani, the Mandara and the Kotoko, retained their chiefs, linked to the *mai* by a kind of personal bondage. Although theoretically subject to Koranic law, the Kanuri retained many black African characteristics that suggest a matrilineal organization which was not completely suppressed by Islam. Bornu reached its zenith in the sixteenth and seventeenth centuries when the *mai* Idris Alaoma extended his authority as far as Kano. The decline set in with the Fulani revolt, led by Osman dan Fodio toward 1800, and was followed by serious dynastic troubles. The usurpation of the throne by a Kanembu dynasty, then its conquest by the Sudanese slave trader Rabah, and finally its division into French, English and German colonies brought about the end of a once powerful state. (See also *Arab Chroniclers; Chad, Lake; Eunuchs; Hausa; Kanem; Sao.*)
P.A.

BOWS, MUSICAL. The bow, with its single string, is the most primitive stringed

Bodyguard of the Sheikh of Bornu. Bibliothèque nationale, Paris. *Library photo.*

instrument known to man. Its existence in Europe during the Paleolithic Age has been proved by engravings found in the grotto of the Trois-Frères in Ariège, and its appearance has been noted throughout Africa, from Senegal and Mali to the Cape of Good Hope. Its use was first mentioned among the Hottentots in the seventeenth century. A cord, usually made from a liana, is stretched between the two ends of a bow and is either plucked with a finger or struck with a small stick. The sound is amplified by a sounding board, which either is the mouth of the musician himself, who passes the string between his open lips, or is formed by half of a calabash tied to the string or to the wood of the bow and pressed against the musician's chest. The pitch is varied by changing the length of the string or the amount the mouth is opened. The notes it produces are harmonics of two basic notes about a tone apart, usually forming a pentatonic scale (Sol La Do Re Mi).

South Africa offers the greatest variety of musical bows. On some, the string is vibrated by scraping the bow, one side of which has a groove along part of its length. The *gura* of the Hottentots is an arc that has one end of the string tied to a feather or a blade of grass which is vibrated like a free reed by a musician inhaling and exhaling through his mouth. Ibn-Batuta, an Arab traveler of the fourteenth century, described how the king of Mali was greeted by his subjects by drawing and suddenly releasing the string of an ordinary bow. This tradition still exists in different parts of Africa like Upper Volta, northern Dahomey, Ghana and Ubangi. Here the wooden bow is used with a small sounding board or rattle attached; the rattle is set going by releasing the cord. In the Fouta Djallon Mountains and central Africa, traces have been found of an even older instrument, the earth bow, which was later taken to America by black African slaves. It is made by stretching a string between a flexible stick that has been driven into the ground and a strip of bark covering a trench that has been dug in the ground. The string is plucked with a small stick, scraped with a sliver of bamboo or rubbed with a resin-oiled hand. (See also *Calabashes; Drum Language; Harps; Music; Rock Art; Zithers*.)   A.S.

Girl playing a musical bow. Melmouth, Republic of South Africa. *Photo: South African Information Service, Pretoria.*

Man playing a musical bow. Ivory Coast. *Photo: Denise Paulme.*

BREASTS. The breasts of African women are usually conical in shape with a fingerlike nipple. In most traditional societies, where the accepted standards of beauty require an ample, deep bosom as a sign of fecundity, women go bare-breasted. The growth of the breasts that occurs at the onset of men-struation, along with the growth of pubic hair, is interpreted as a sign that a girl is nubile. In Africa, the erotic function of the breast is much less important than in Europe or America. To touch the nipple is not so much amorous stimulation as an invitation. In all African societies, breasts are the

Dogon "Young Girl" mask.
Mali. *Photo: Hoa-Qui.*

symbol of feminine fecundity. The Dogon and Bajokwe men who wear female masks dress up in brassieres stuffed with fruit to simulate breasts. Drums used by the women of northern Cameroun and Chad have two breasts as decoration. The tall furnaces of the Bajokwe and of the Kalanga of Katanga in Zaire, where iron "is born," are also decorated with breastlike ornaments. In mythology and traditional oral literature, the breast is the source of nourishment: the spirit that presides over the initiations of the Massa and Tuburi is portrayed as a female with numerous nipples which are sucked by neophytes about to be initiated.

One must note that in most rural African societies the breast is regarded as a strictly utilitarian appendage for feeding the young. Even pastoral tribes have been unable to devise a satisfactory technique for artificial feeding. If a mother's milk dries up while her child is still very young, the chances are that it will die, as she is only allowed to entrust it to a wet nurse who is a close relation. There are many traditional remedies for stimulating the secretion of milk, usually originating in magic by association.

Infants are fed on demand, and breast-feeding is usually continued for one to three years and, in some societies, even five. But the usual period is eighteen months, during which time the mother may be forbidden to have sexual relations. Indications of a new pregnancy generally entail the brutal weaning of the infant, who, in most cases, has not been given any supplementary nourishment while he was breast-fed and has not been properly conditioned to his new diet. After this, the child is forbidden the breast. He is either sent away to one of his grandmothers or aunts or made to feel disgusted by his mother's breast, which she does her best to turn into something repellent. The Wolof and Serer women in Senegal plaster their breasts with mud in which they stick hen feathers or spikes of millet, or else they coat the nipple with a bitter extract from the leaves of the baobab tree.

In traditional societies, the psychological trauma caused by weaning is frequently quite violent. The child, who is already suffering from undernourishment and lack of proteins caused by the poor quality of his mother's milk after prolonged feeding, is then suddenly introduced to food rich in carbohydrates and scarcely differing from the diet of adults. The new diet contains very little milk, but an effort is made to give children food that is considered easily masticated and digested, like pap made from millet, corn, ripe bananas and already chewed yams. Some tribes, including the Wolof of Senegal and the Bahutu in Rwanda, have developed baby foods based on sprouting cereals. Proteins such as meat and fish are not given until the child has its first four front teeth. Consequently, at an age when he has a great need of protein, between one and four years, his diet contains less protein than at any time during the rest of his life. In the worst cases, the child may develop symptoms of a nutritional disease called "kwashiorkor," which was first investigated in Ghana. The symptoms are a retarded growth, abnormal pigmentation of the skin and hair, and general edema, which may cause the child to die. Among some tribes of the rain forests, in Uganda, for example, this illness attacks 10 percent of the children in infancy. It is obvious that the brutal weaning and inadequate diet of young children are largely responsible for an infant mortality rate in rural African societies that is twenty-five times higher than the rate for children in Europe between the ages of one and four. (See also *Clothing; Excision.*)   I.G.

BRONZE. In its technical evolution, tropical Africa, with the exception of Nubia and Mauritania, never experienced the Bronze Age, but passed directly from the Stone Age to the Iron Age. (Iron has been used for the last 1,000 or 2,000 years, the length of time varying according to the region.) Bronze, as an alloy of nine parts

Wall plaque. Benin. Nigeria.
Louis Carré Collection, Paris.

copper to one part tin, was completely unknown. Moreover, there were few regions where both copper and tin were available; copper itself was often imported, and during the period of the slave trade, it was one of the principal media of barter on the Guinea Coast and particularly in Benin. As a matter of fact, the word "bronze" is commonly used in Africa to describe various alloys based on copper, zinc, lead and tin, mixed in varying proportions: the "bronze" bas-reliefs of Benin contain 84 percent copper, 8 percent lead and 2.5 percent tin. These alloys range from brass to metals that cannot be identified precisely. They are found most often in the area extending from Liberia to the Congo and from the Atlantic coast to the savanna and are always associated with the

Head from Ife. Nigeria.
Bronze. Ife Museum. *Photo:*
Walter Dräyer.

Detail of a Jebba statue.
Northern Nigeria. Bronze.
Collection of the Dagacin
(chief) of Jebba, Nigeria.
Photo: Walter Dräyer.

lost-wax process. There are two clearly defined centers of lost-wax casting: the Akan lands of the Ashanti and the Baule in the west; and the southern Nigerian country of the Nupe, the Yoruba and Benin in the east. The first is best known for its gold-measuring weights and very delicately worked vessels. The second was by far the most productive and brilliant. Both centers had a strong influence on their neighboring territories.

The oldest "bronze" sculptures, and those in the purest classical style, are the heads from Ife. Possibly, the art of bronze originated in Ife. It made its first known appearance further north, in Tada, on the shores of the middle Niger, with statues of classical proportions, the most famous of which is the figure of a crouching man, with his left leg on the ground and the right knee raised. The influence of Ife is here combined with that of Benin and is discernible in other statues. Forms of art borrowed from the Yoruba were, in fact, developed in the kingdom of Benin in a modified style, the development of which can be clearly traced. It is possible to distinguish one period from another and to discern in the composition of bas-reliefs, for example, evidence of experiments to make the relief as expressive as possible—a tendency that becomes more marked in the later plaques—and also to indicate, by the positioning of the persons and objects portrayed, an early approach toward the problem of perspective. It is no longer claimed that the Portuguese introduced the technique and art of bronze-making, but this does not exclude the possibility of European influence in the great period of Benin art, which began in the sixteenth century. There is evidence of this influence in the composition, the decoration and even the nature of objects such as the jugs made toward the end of this great era. A statuette of a rider carrying a lance and wearing a strange flat helmet and accompanied by a man holding the horse's bridle reminds one—incongruous as it may seem—of Don Quixote.

There is an immense variety in these works: plaques with bas-reliefs depicting the events and triumphs of each reign covered the pillars of the royal palaces; heads, sometimes hollowed out to act as bases for carved elephants' tusks, which were essential features of royal altars; statues of men or animals, alone or in groups; masks; pendants; handles of walking sticks; and vessels decorated in various ways. Not all of these objects were made in every period. The archaic period extends from the twelfth to the middle of the fourteenth centuries;

technically, it is close to Ife art, for example in the thin walls of some of its round bells. The ancient period extends to the early part of the sixteenth century; it produced heads which, like those from Ife, were apparently portraits and, similarly, are hollow and have very thin walls. The great period of the sixteenth and seventeenth centuries was the age of the bas-relief, which sometimes depicted Portuguese soldiers and merchants, but the king surrounded by his court was of course the central figure; and at the end of this period, the background decoration included landscapes and palaces. During the great period the heads became more massive, particularly those of women, which had peaked headdresses. In the second half of the seventeenth century, a certain amount of standardization made its appearance with heads, bas-reliefs and statues being mass-produced. Nevertheless, some very beautiful works stand out, like the stools supported by coiled snakes, animal sculptures and vessels in the shape of houses. A noticeable decline began in the eighteenth century, and cast work was steadily replaced by wood carving covered with metal. After these brilliant centuries, Benin art vanished, even before the kingdom crumbled under the impact of British colonization. But this heritage was preserved, and it was the sack of the conquered city that dispersed hundreds of masterpieces into European museums and private collections. (See also *Ashanti; Bells; Benin; Funerals; Heads; Ife; Iron; Lost-Wax Process; Sao; Spiders; Weapons; Weights; Yoruba.*) P.M.

BUFFALO. The buffalo is the biggest ruminant on the African continent. An animal with a liking for well-watered regions, its habitat extends from the Sahel region (from the 14° parallel to eastern Chad) to the equator. It is almost immune to the tsetse but suffers severely from outbreaks of rinderpest. The buffalo belongs to the bovine subgroup of the bovid family. Only the species *Syncerus* is found in Africa. Classification of African buffalo is difficult, for many variations in height, color and the shape of the horns can occur even among members of the same herd. In the plains of South Africa and region of the Great Lakes, the Cape buffalo (*Syncerus caffer caffer*) is found. The largest breed of buffalo, it can weigh as much as 1,800 pounds and have horns more than 40 inches long. The regions of the central African savanna are the home of the *Syncerus caffer oequinoxialis,* a smaller breed which weighs about 1,000 pounds. The forest buffalo (*Syncerus nanus nanus*) is small and black or reddish in color,

Bobo "buffalo" mask. Upper Volta. Painted wood and plant fibers. Rietberg Museum, Zurich. *Photo: Bernhard Moosbrugger.*

and its horns are no more than 30 inches long.

The buffalo is highly prized by the tribes that hunt it. The Pygmies hunt individual animals with arrows poisoned with strychnine or strophanthin. The Baya use traps that employ a slipknot. The Bathonga beat the buffaloes toward trenches fitted with pointed and poisoned stakes. The Mandja, the Guro and the Gagu use traps in which a poisoned assegai is suspended over a path so that it falls as the animal passes by. Although the buffalo is not often mentioned in African oral literature, it appears in numerous cave paintings in the Sahara and in South Africa. Among certain tribes like the Bathonga, the buffalo has been domesticated, which removes the need to perform purification rites and appease its spirit after it has been killed. Buffalo horns, richly decorated with anthropomorphic and geometric designs and used as goblets, are among the most characteristic objects of Bamum art in Cameroun. (See also *Fauna; Hunting; Rock Art.*) I.G.

BULL-ROARERS. The use of bull-roarers was first noticed in black Africa toward the

Buffalo hunt. Fon hanging. Dahomey. Musée de l'Homme, Paris. *Museum photo.*

through which a string is threaded, and the string rolls or unrolls itself depending upon whether the ends are pulled or released); a double reed, made from a millet stem, on a string (the skin of the millet stem is scooped out so as to leave two parallel blades which vibrate as the instrument is rotated like a bull-roarer); or a humming bow, which is also attached to a bit of string.

The use of true bull-roarers varies from tribe to tribe, but among most they are associated with the institution of masks or the rituals of male initiation. The Dogon consider the bull-roarer to be the masks' "little brother"; it is regarded as the voice of the masks, especially of the largest of them— the "mother of masks"—and, consequently, of the mythical snake which is represented on this mask. In a number of Dogon myths, the origins of the bull-roarer are connected with invention of masks, which are now emblems of the men's secret society. When one of the society's members dies, the instrument hums, or "weeps." The bull-roarer is also played during periods when new masks are made, and one of these masks precedes the second funeral ceremonies. In other regions, especially in the forest, the bull-roarer is played by the initiated who are responsible for instructing young men, and it rotates every day during the young men's retreat, either within the enclosure or at its edge, to warn women to keep away. Its humming is said to reproduce the voices of ancestors or spirits that haunt the forest. The instrument can also be an accessory of secret societies, as in southern Dahomey, where society members may play several of them of different sizes, either one after the other or in concert. One case has been reported of a magician who used a bull-roarer to heal the sick, in this case a baby girl. (See also *Societies, Secret.*)

A.S.

end of the last century, forty years after it had been discovered among the people of central Australia. Like the Australian instrument, the African bull-roarer is connected with secret rites: women, children and strangers are forbidden to look at it, and the noise it makes—apart from other effects—frightens them. A bull-roarer is usually a wooden board, generally ellipsoidal in shape, that is pierced at one end and has a string attached to the other. When it is swung in the air, it produces a characteristic humming, which to the initiated is the voice of ancestors and to the uninitiated is the roaring of a monstrous wild beast. Unlike Australian and New Guinean bull-roarers, the African instrument is not decorated with sculpture, engraving or painting and may be made from a rectangular or trapezoidal iron plate. The bull-roarer is sometimes confused with other rotating instruments whose whirring accompanies certain rites or with certain children's playthings, such as a sort of jack-in-the-box made from a fruit shell with a small disc cut out of it (the disc is pierced with two holes

BUSHMEN. The Bushmen (from the Dutch *Bosjeman*) are a non-Negroid people who found refuge in the Kalahari Desert. They are rapidly becoming extinct, and only a few thousand of them survive today. They average about five feet in height and have rather Mongoloid features—yellowish-brown skin, triangularly shaped face, prominent cheekbones, a caruncular fold and a lumbar mark at birth. They also have other physical peculiarities, such as steatopygia (a fatty development of the buttocks), iron-gray hair and a permanently semi-erect penis. Their prehistoric habitat must have covered all of the unforested area of eastern Africa as far as the Great Lakes and the Ethiopian mountain mass. They were driven into their South African retreat by the pastoral Hottentots, who were themselves probably harassed by the Bantu.

The Bushmen's social organization, which is based on their life as hunters, is very simple and may be a regression from an earlier, more elaborate structure. Their base is the area of their hunting grounds, which is well defined by the natural haunts of their prey. This area is inhabited by linguistically homogeneous groups of families, which form themselves into loosely knit groups for the duration of the hunting season and generally disperse as the difficult dry season begins. They have no chieftains, but an expert hunter, a famous witch doctor or a wise old man will be respected as a leader. There is a clear division of work between the men, who hunt, and the women, who do the food-gathering. This is not, however, a barrier to equality between the sexes, and the women enjoy a comparatively better position than do their black neighbors. Polygamy is rare, and morality is very strict. Adultery is strongly condemned, although there is no judicial system of punishment for it.

The cultural products of the Bushmen are very poor and do not appear to have changed since the Upper Paleolithic period. There is no metalwork, pottery or weaving, but they have adapted themselves in a remarkable fashion to desert life and are resourceful in their use of materials acquired from hunting and food-gathering. Their clothes, consisting of a slip and a cape, are made of skins treated with urine, and they make jewelry from the splinters of ostrich eggs. Containers are made from calabashes, the rinds of desert melons and ostrich eggs. They have no huts, and their only shelter is a hole in the ground or behind a screen of branches. Their principal weapons are bows and bone-tipped arrows, dipped in poisonous caterpillar juice. Hunting is the all-important activity of the Bushmen; the entire education of boys and most of their myths are centered around it. Gathering plants and small creatures such as insects and grubs provides a subsidiary source of food. In the dry season, the great problem is the lack of water; they obtain liquid either by drinking the juice of the desert melon or by sucking water up through a straw from shallow underground deposits or from the bellies of dead game.

In contrast to this material poverty, they have a comparatively rich intellectual culture. The Bushman languages are varied and highly complicated from every point of view; a preponderance of "clicks," or injective consonants, which are peculiar to southern Africa, is a notable characteristic of these languages. Until the end of the last century, their art comprised some very fine mural paintings, which are similar to those of the European Paleolithic period. The Bushmen possess a considerable knowledge of astronomy, anatomy, zoology and botany. Their rich mythology is woven around heroes who are half-human, half-animal, and the most important of whom is embodied in the praying mantis. Their religion appears to embrace a belief in one god, the creator, who was sacrificed, then reincarnated for the salvation of his creatures. Dances related to the movement of the stars are an essential part of several Bushman magic rituals connected with medicine and especially hunting. Their music includes freely improvised songs whose melancholy is perceptible even to strangers who do not understand the language.

Although some measures of protection have been taken by the South African, British and Portuguese administrations, the Bushmen appear to be doomed as a race, either through extinction or through fusion with their Bantu, Hottentot and Damara neighbors. Their hunting grounds, are shrinking because animal husbandry is becoming more widespread, and game is becoming rare as a result of the depredations of hunters and poachers, both black and white. The demographic prospects of the Bushmen are poor because they have a low birthrate and high infant mortality rate owing to their very difficult living conditions. Indeed, these "harmless people" have little chance of surviving the twentieth century. (See also *Calendars; Education; Fossils, Human; Hottentots; Hunting; Kalahari; Race; Rock Art; Scarification.*)

P.A.

Old Bushman woman.
Republic of South Africa.
Photo: *Musée de l'Homme.*

Calabash with pyrography decoration used at the conclusion of ritual festivals and dances. Bangangoulou. Angola. Musée de l'Homme, Paris. *Museum photo.*

Calabash decorated with basketry cord used as a funnel. Musée de l'Homme, Paris. *Museum photo, José Oster.*

Calabash with pyrography decoration used for marriage ceremonies. Bozo. Mali. Musée de l'Homme, Paris. *Museum photo.*

CALABASHES. The calabash, or bottle gourd, is the fruit of the calabash tree or vine. It is used throughout Africa for making containers, and in African culture, it is regarded as the preeminent container. According to Dahoman cosmology, for instance, the universe is a sphere consisting of two halves of a calabash—one half, holding the sky, is turned upside down and rests on the other, containing the waters and the earth, while the circle where the two halves are in contact is the horizon.

The calabash is picked when it is ripe and then left to decay in water. Its flesh is then taken out either by cutting the fruit in half or by making an opening in it, the size of which depends on the kind of utensil one wishes to produce. The woody rind, which hardens once it dries but is still easy to cut and work, is kept.

The fruit may be variously shaped: generally, it is round, but it can also be egg- or pear-shaped; more complex shapes can be produced by binding the fruit while it is growing to elongate or constrict it. The calabashes most frequently in use are hemispherical or completely round with a section cut away to form an opening. They serve as containers for grain, condiments, liquids and butter. Textiles, clothing and valuables are kept in the bigger ones.

Several other kinds of utensils and tools for everyday use, such as goblets, spoons and spatulas, are also made from calabashes. In addition, they are made into musical instruments of every shape and form: drums, fashioned from large calabashes turned upside down and struck with thin bundles of flexible sticks; pear-shaped clappers, filled with stones and covered with broad-meshed netting adorned with cowrie shells; and resonators, which are attached to xylophones, guitars and musical bows. They are also used to adorn the body: the Palaeonegrid peoples of West Africa use them as penis shields; some tribes in Chad use segments of calabashes shaped like handbells and attached to belts to serve as loincloths of sorts; and the Shilluk of eastern Africa carve crude masks out of them. And all over the continent, the calabashes are used either as amulets or vessels to contain magical preparations.

The calabash is also made into works of

art. It may be dyed with decoctions of leaves; its sides may be stitched with basketwork; or it may be engraved either with a red-hot iron or a knife, in which case the designs that encircle the calabash in bands are made to stand out on a light background. Some calabashes are decorated with simple geometric designs or stylized animal shapes. Elsewhere—in Dahomey, for example— these decorations may take the form of actual pictographic writing, and the calabashes are inscribed with proverbs, mottoes and messages of defiance, friendship or love. This form of elementary writing follows the same rules as the inscriptions in the appliqué work of Dahomey. (See also *Bows, Musical; Drums; Harps; Household Furnishings; Pipes; Rattles; Sistra; Spoons; Xylophones; Zithers.*) P.M.

CALENDARS. The measuring and reckoning of time combine astronomical, climatic and social factors in varying degrees, largely according to the religious or politico-religious systems of different societies. The moon and the seasons are the most common points of reference in Africa, but many stars are also used for calculations, especially in the dry savanna where the skies are bright and clear: the Pleiades, which are used almost everywhere, Orion, the Corona Australis, Cygnus and a number of single stars (the Dogon of Mali even know the companion of Sirius, which cannot be seen without powerful instruments). The pastoral people in the northeast and the Bushmen in the Kalahari Desert probably possess the most highly developed knowledge of stars.

The usual unit of time is the complete climatic cycle, consisting of a dry and a rainy season, divided into synodic months. Each of these months is named after the agricultural tasks that are performed during it (the "month of weeding," the "month of land clearance" or the "month of bush clearance"), or after the cycle of nature (the "month of calving," the "month of the flowering of such and such a tree," the "low-water month") or after ceremonies and rituals (the "month of funerals," the "month of betrothals"). In equatorial regions, where each season occurs twice a year, the normal unit consists of only six or seven synodic months—the *mbu* of the Fang, for example.

It is a curious fact that among most African peoples, the traditional year, like the Muslim year, consists of only twelve months instead of the thirteen lunar months that one would expect from an astronomical method of calculation. Some Africans correct this discrepancy by regarding two synodic months as a single agricultural or ritual

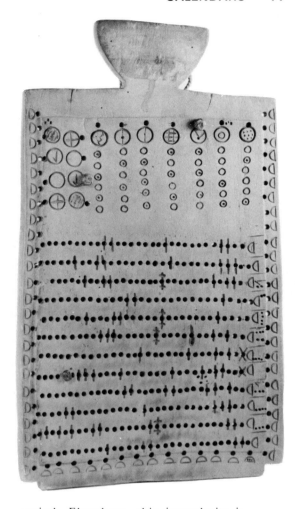

Calendar. Fon or Nago. Dahomey. Wood. Musée de l'Homme, Paris. *Museum photo.*

period. Elsewhere, this irregularity is corrected at the end of a cycle, depending on whether the year is calculated on a lunar or on a combined lunar and solar basis. The end of the cycle is celebrated by rituals of renewal and purification, which may be an explanation of the ceremonies performed by the Mande every forty years. On the whole, the disadvantages arising out of the discrepancies between the visible movements of the sun and the moon are often compensated by the fact that the reckoning in days is not always very precise, especially when the synodic month is the smallest unit. Some societies, however, use a smaller unit, namely a week, consisting of seven, six, four, three or five days (the six- and eight-day types are sometimes multiples of the unit based on three or four days), that follows the rhythm of their work and communal activities like markets. Two types may be combined, as in Togo and Dahomey, where the lunar month of twenty-eight days corresponds at the same time to four ritual weeks of seven days, as well as to seven market cycles of four days each. Further north, the Tem combine an agricultural calendar based on a month of five six-day weeks (corresponding to periodic markets) and a Muslim Hausa calendar based on lunar months and a seven-day week.

Days of the week may have names, as in the whole Kwa group, which extends from the Ivory Coast to Nigeria, or they may be reckoned by reference to the market or, among Muslims, to the great Friday prayer. Sunrise marks the beginning of the day for some tribes, but sunset is the more usual starting point. The day is not divided into hours, but into moments corresponding to daily activities like getting up, going to bed, eating and working, to extreme positions of the sun or to animal behavior; the Bulu of Cameroun call sunrise the "morning song" and the moment before sunset the "bath of the monkeys."

Dates are calculated in various ways, either by reference to social phenomena and periodic rituals such as initiations held at regular intervals, the creation and promotion of age groups and the mobilization and demobilization of "regiments" among the Ngoni; to special events such as eclipses, floods and epidemics; to important persons, for example, "during the reign of such and such a chief or administrator"; or to genealogies. These nonnumerical references are difficult to place in a European calendar, although on investigation they often prove extremely accurate. The Muslim calendar, introduced quite early into the western Sudan, furnishes exact dates from the end of the tenth century onward for societies strongly influenced by Islam and for some of their neighbors; however, it has no official standing today, since it was superseded by the Gregorian calendar, which is used even in states with a Muslim majority.   P.A.

CAMELS. The complete domestication of the dromedary probably took place in Arabia soon after 1500 B.C. Its use, which did not become general in Egypt until the Persian domination, about 500 B.C., was probably given added impetus by the connections established by the Ptolemies with both Cyrenaica and Meroe; but the dromedary must also have reached Nubia during the same period, as well as Ethiopia, at some unknown date, by means of the traffic across the Red Sea. It was from Meroe that it first penetrated deeply into Africa, according to the evidence of cave paintings of the Ennedi, the earliest of which apparently predate those of the Sahara and may date from the first century A.D. From Cyrenaica, the camel reached the eastern Maghrib, where it was known in the first century B.C. and was used for cultivation and transport in the coastal plains and oases from the second century A.D. Camels seem to have been common in Tripolitania during the late Roman Empire. Little is known about the later history of the animal. It is not clear whether the camel spread over the Sahara from the desert routes or from the borders of the Maghrib. Nomadic camel drivers must have existed before the caravan trade began and then provided it with animals and with experience in handling them. Aside from this, there is little information about dromedaries prior to the advent of Islam. Camels were apparently an important element in the life of the Sahara and the adjacent areas as well as in Somaliland; it is in this part of Africa that the real camel people, whose lives revolve around camel breeding, are to be found. The camel's principal importance is as a long-distance carrier between the Sahara, the Sahel and the Sudan, where it transports vital provisions, like salt, from one side of the desert to the other. Since a single camel can carry a load of up to 330 pounds and caravans consisted of hundreds and thousands of camels, they have rightly been

Camel. Rock painting. Tibesti, Chad. *Photo: Hoa-Qui.*

Girl sifting cassava flour.
Baya-Kara. Cameroun.
Photo: Musée de l'Homme.

compared to merchant ships. From the eighth century onward, their journeys have been an indispensable link between two worlds, which stimulated economic growth, trade and cultural exchange and made cities prosperous. The camel is one of the great figures of African history. It owes this fact to a mixture of rare biological characteristics, which do not, however, include the popular attribute of being able to stock up with water before a long day's journey. (See also *Beverages; Sahara; Salt; Sudan.*)　H.M.

CASSAVA. Cassava is American in origin. It was introduced to Africa in about the sixteenth century by Portuguese travelers and merchants. Today it is the principal diet of people living in and near the forest zones. The Ivory Coast produces 570,000 tons and Dahomey 750,000 tons yearly. In the countries of the savanna, it is cultivated on a fairly large scale; Senegal produces 160,000 tons and Niger 149,000 tons.

Africans prefer the various strains of bitter cassava because of their higher yield: 3,500 to 6,300 pounds for every acre, corresponding to about 770 pounds of flour per acre. Bitter cassava can only be made edible by soaking the roots for several days to remove its toxicity, then by peeling, washing and crushing it. This yields a paste that can be rolled into balls, wrapped in leaves and steamed. It can.also be dried in the sun and ground into flour. In West Africa, *gari,* a kind of finely granulated semolina, is obtained from the pulp of fermented cassava, which is first crushed, then sieved

and dried over a fire. The young leaves are eaten after boiling. They contain a little protein, vitamins A and C and the P.P. factor. The daily consumption of cassava reaches nearly 28 ounces per person in equatorial Africa, and it is also eaten in the savanna belt as an alternative to cereals. Farmers like it, as it is relatively easy to grow in almost any soil; it is resistant to locusts and can be harvested as and when it is needed. Most African towns are surrounded by fields of cassava. People eat cassava because it is filling and gives a feeling of satiety. However, it is a food that is rich in calories but poor in vitamins and minerals, containing less than seven grams of protein. Diets based on cassava are very unbalanced and need to be generously supplemented by meat, fish, eggs, milk and vegetables. It is in the areas where the most cassava is consumed that the incidence of kwashiorkor is highest. (See also *Agriculture; Beverages; Diet.*)　I.G.

CASTES. Descriptions of traditional West African societies contain frequent references to the caste organization of blacksmiths, leatherworkers and butchers. These bodies of artisans and certain other groups that participate in specialized activities—griots, for example—are socially distinct from other segments of the society to which they belong. Although they perform useful or indispensable functions for the community, they are nevertheless exiles within it, both envied and despised; their lives are those of people living in a ghetto. The men may marry only

Batusi master and his
Bahutu servant. Rwanda.
Photo: Jacques Maquet.

women belonging to their own guild and may hand down the technical and ritual knowledge of their trades only to their descendants. Such castes existed, for example, in Senegal among the Wolof and Serer and in Mali among the Bambara and Soninke. In a parallel and more fundamental sense, which is closer to the original meaning of the term as first applied to the elements of the Indian system of social stratification, the word "caste" is used to describe the broad social divisions in some kingdoms of the Great Lakes region in eastern Africa. Each of these societies comprises two or three strata which, like their geological counterparts, are superimposed one upon the other and form horizontal layers. These strata are hereditary: membership is by birth and for life, and the heirs inherit the same status. Instances of elevation to the next higher stratum are exceptional and are comparable to ennoblement. The strata are also endogamous —members must marry only within their caste—and a strict segregation is imposed for most activities; the castes neither eat nor dance together, nor do they dress alike. Each maintains its own subculture. These different characteristics turn the strata into separate, closed entities that can accurately be called "castes" (the term "classes" refers to open strata).

The castes in the Great Lakes region originated in war and conquest. The upper caste (the Bahima in the Uganda regions of Ankole, Bunyoro and Toro and the Batusi in Rwanda, Burundi and the Bua kingdoms) consists of descendants of nomadic pastoral warriors who invaded the region in small groups over a long period, probably extending from the thirteenth to the sixteenth century. They subjugated the indigenous peasants, who are the ancestors of the present inferior caste (the Iru under the Bahima, and Bahutu under the Batusi). In these instances, domination by conquest was institutionalized in an upper caste. The descendants of the invaders acquired and retained special privileges through the hierarchy of closed and hereditary strata: superior social power (in any social relationship between noble and peasant, the former can bring pressure to bear on the latter); a large share of the goods produced by the community as a whole (without cultivating any land themselves or contributing any economic equivalent, they had a wealth of consumer goods at their disposal); and a monopoly of political responsibility (although all members of the upper caste were not rulers, all rulers belonged to it).

During the colonial period, both Africans and Europeans who lived within the frontiers of dependent territories formed a group of people which, despite its artificial character, gradually became a genuine society. It was highly stratified: the dominant European minority (administrators, settlers, agents of industrial and commercial enterprises, missionaries) and the inferior African

Cattle. Rock painting.
Tintazarift, Tassili N'Ajjer.
Photo: Rapho, Lajoux.

majority formed two separate, closed, hierarchic castes. Relations between them could well be described by the preceding paragraph with scarcely a word changed. (See also *Blacksmiths; Cattle; Feudalism; Griots; Law; Royalty; Rwanda; Slavery; Villages.*)   J.M.

CATTLE. There are two kinds of domestic cattle in Africa: oxen similar to the European breeds and zebus (*Bos indicus*), which have humps on their backs. Zoological experts are agreed that the latter originated in India. Zebus are frequently portrayed in the rock paintings of Ennedi and Hoggar, but these can scarcely be from before the tenth century A.D. In earlier, prehistoric paintings and engravings, the cattle represented have no humps.

Thirty-six different types of cattle exist in Africa, and these are divided by specialists into various groups. Some of the more notable groups are: the humpless cattle of Mediterranean Africa and the Nile Valley; the zebus of the sub-Saharan region, the main types of which are the Adamawa, Azawak and Bororo; bulls with short horns, of which the Ndama is the best-known breed, found in the southern part of West Africa and in some of the highlands of central Africa; the humpless Kuri ox of Chad, which

has horns with a bulbous base that enable it to swim easily; a complex group comprising the cattle of the flood regions of the upper Nile and the South African Plateau, the best known being the Ankole; and the East African cattle, comprising the Angoni, Galla and the Afrikander zebus.

The cattle-rearing areas of Africa are found north of the equator between 8 and 17 North Latitude. The factors that limit development are the lack of water and feeding stuff in the north and the presence of the tsetse fly, the carrier of sleeping sickness, in the south. There are some indigenous breeds that are immune to the tsetse fly: the dwarf cattle of the mountains of northern Cameroun and Kordofan, the Lagoon breeds from the Ivory Coast, the Somra breed from Togo and, especially, the Ndama, which originated in Guinea.

In tropical Africa, there are 88 million heads of cattle to 164 million inhabitants, but the distribution of livestock is very uneven. A small group of tribes in the Sahel and savanna regions that specialize in cattle-raising hold more than three-quarters of the livestock. These tribes include some nomads, of which the Bororo of West Africa and the Fulani of Adamawa are good examples. The Nilotic population in Sudan (the Nuer, the Dinka and the Shilluk) and some tribes in

Ox from the Chad region.
Photo: Hoa-Qui.

Ethiopia, such as the Galla, practice a modified transhumance. In eastern and southern Africa, the pastoral tribes who have more or less settled have evolved aristocratic societies in which the owners of herds, for example the Batusi, form the dominant caste that rules over the agricultural population, the Bahutu. The pastoral tribes of southern Africa also include the Masai, the Kikuyu, the Awori of Kenya and Tanzania, the Ngoni of Malawi and the Herero of South-West Africa. In all these societies, cattle-raising dictates a way of life in which man is both a parasite and a servant of the livestock he owns. It is these societies that have given rise to the notion of a superiority complex in cattle-breeders. All economic, religious, aesthetic and social activities revolve around their herds. Their neighbors, who are settled agriculturists, hardly qualify as human beings. Several agricultural societies in the savanna regions also raise cattle, such as the Serer and Tukulor in Senegal, the agricultural Fulani in Guinea and Cameroun and some tribes in the plains of northern Cameroun and Chad.

The yield obtained from cattle in Africa is poor for two main reasons: first, in the eyes of their owners, the social, religious and aesthetic values of cattle far outweigh their economic importance; and second, most African breeds are indifferent producers of meat and milk. The fullest use cannot be made of the cattle because of the difficult climate. Milk is their main contribution to the diet. In the Sahel zone, the average daily consumption of milk is about 1,200 grams; it rises to a maximum in the rainy season and falls in March to less than 150 grams, for example, among the Fulani in Niger. The average daily consumption of the non-nomadic savanna peoples is about 200 grams. Further south, in the Guinean zone, tribes like the Lobi, Baule and Senufo do not drink milk regularly. African herdsmen do not make cheese; they drink fresh milk at milking time or, more often, curdled or sour milk with water added. Butter, made by churning milk in a gourd, sometimes with cow urine added, is used as often for a cosmetic as for nourishment.

The herd is regarded as capital on which the owner can draw to satisfy his social needs, but rarely to satisfy his appetite for meat. Apart from ceremonial occasions, cows are only slaughtered when on the point of death from sickness or age. The Nilotes and some tribes of southern Africa like the Masai often drink the blood of cows, which they obtain by bleeding live animals. Cattle hide is a choice material, often used by pastoral people in the construction of their dwellings. In the subdesert zone where there are few trees, dried cow dung is the principal fuel. Nomads like the Tuareg, Moors and Teda use the ox for transporting their goods and their wives.

There are two technical reasons for the underdevelopment of cattle-breeding in Africa. Primarily, it is owing to the low rate of growth of the herds (8 percent compared to 20 percent in Europe), but it is also the consequence of attitudes that are outside the sphere of economics. The Bororo nomads, for example, regard a herd not as a source of wealth, but as "a value in itself." The only real satisfaction they enjoy in their lives is in looking after their herds, appreciating their beauty, assessing how far the animals conform to traditional aesthetic standards and putting them through their paces during the various celebrations of tribal life. The main form of wealth is the herd, and the number of animals is more important than the physical condition. They are an outward sign of a man's riches in the eyes of the community and a prime factor in contracting a marriage. In all pastoral societies, cows form part of the gift offered by a man to his future father-in-law in exchange for a wife. The size of the bride-price varies from one society to another. Among Nilotic tribes, where there is one head of cattle to every person, the dowry used to be as much as forty to fifty head of cattle; now it is twenty cows. Among the Bororo, where there are sometimes five head of cattle to one person, it is only three to five animals. Among the Massa and Tuburi of northern Cameroun, where there is only one cow to every two inhabitants, the required bride-price is ten cows, which demands a considerable effort, in view of the fact that the son-in-law has to replace any of these animals that die after the transaction without breeding. In return, the father-in-law has to return all the bride-price animals if his daughter is sterile or dies without children. This parallel between the fertility of the cow and the wife, this desire to have offspring and the notion of an alliance maintained by a living bond have a profound bearing on the way herds are used in most African societies. In a number of pastoral societies, there exist systems of lending cattle which enable wealthy breeders to increase their social connections by lending their cows to less affluent individuals, who become obligated to the owners. The Musgu, Massa and Tuburi of northern Cameroun take milk cures: the men of the village, accompanied by their herds, withdraw to special camps; there they fatten themselves up on milk, in order to be in good physical condition for the festivities, which take place during the dry season. The pastoral Nuer rub ash on the backs of cows as a means of establishing contact with the world beyond.

Cattle are often dedicated to spirits or ancestors. These animals, or their progeny, provide the sacrifices for the cycle of religious ceremonies. Since an animal is hardly ever killed solely to be eaten, rural rites and festivities recording the different events of a lifetime—especially the return of the initiated and funerals—are occasions for a massive slaughter of cattle, when the various participating groups vie with each other in the lavishness with which they sacrifice their possessions. (See also *Animal Husbandry; Cows; Feudalism; Fulani; Goats; Hausa; Hottentots; Kirdi; Massa; Meat.*)   I.G.

CHAD, LAKE. Until the beginning of the nineteenth century, geographers believed in the existence of a great African river—the Niger or Abid Nile—that flowed from west to east, from Timbuktu across the lands of the Hausa, Bornu and Darfur toward Cairo and then joined the Nile. This river was believed to cross a vast expanse of water somewhere in the interior, the *Borno lacus, Bahar Sudan* or *Nigritic Sea,* which was compared in size to the Red Sea. Not until 1823 was the lake finally reached by the British, who—although its name, Chad, was well known in Europe—tried to rename it Lake Waterloo, but without success. Following this, its size was calculated correctly, and the numerous products, such as grain

A *kadeye,* made of papyrus stalks, on Lake Chad. *Photo: Pierre Ichac.*

Musgu dwellings. Chad.
Photo: Jean-Paul Lebeuf.

and salt, that were exchanged on its banks were mentioned in written accounts. The existence of a channel running northeastward, the Bahr el Ghazal, nevertheless gave rise to a belief, which persisted until the beginning of the twentieth century, that there might be a direct link between the Chari River and the Nile, the tributary joining the Nile in the neighborhood of Berber. During this period Lake Chad was considered for the first time as an extension of the Chari. Strangely enough, this geographical error tallies with a fact of another kind. We now know that the banks of the Bahr el Ghazal, which today is completely dry, were populated from a very early period. This is proved by the countless traces that have been discovered, such as stonework of Neolithic appearance and ceramics not unlike those of Ounianga and Khartoum. So there was indeed a connection with the Nile, but it was human and not geographical. The populations who lived along the Bahr el Ghazal abandoned it several centuries ago. They left the shifting, mosquito-infested and often insecure shores of the lake and headed south and east toward the banks of the Chari and the Logone.

In the fifteenth century at the latest, the islands and banks of the lake became the refuge of families of Sao origin, known as the Buduma and the Kuri. This settlement from the south was followed a hundred years later by the arrival on the northern banks of various groups, which included the Kanembu, who formed the majority, and the Kotoko, who came and mixed with the Buduma at the end of the nineteenth century. Besides being a haven for fugitives, the shores of the lake were throughout the centuries the scene of the seasonal gatherings of fishermen and hunters. This region was, however, always avoided by caravans, which followed routes much further to the north and one to the south, which is still used by pilgrims to Mecca.

The importance of Lake Chad in oral tradition and the fascination that it held for early travelers are equaled by the place it holds in the mythology of the area. Whether animists or Muslim, there is not one people for whom it is not an important place. The former claim it as their birthplace, and the latter believe that Noah's ark grounded on the rocks of Hadjer el Hamis. After the Treaty of Berlin, this region, which has attracted men since ancient times, became a point of attraction (but not of unity) for the nations of Europe—Germany, Britain and France—who considered its possession a trump card in the struggle for the domination of this part of Africa, and its waters were divided into geometric frontiers, which have been maintained by the newly independent African governments. The definition of the natural area of Lake Chad, which was given practical form by the creation of the Commission of the Chad Basin, has brought an end to the division of the lake in so far as scientific research is concerned; the interested states—Niger, Cameroun, Chad and the Republic of Central Africa—are carrying out joint programs of cartography, hydrology, agriculture, economics and the social sciences. (See also *European Discovery; Kanem; Nok; Sao; Sudan.*) J.-P.L.

CHAKA. The "Napoleon of the Bantu," Chaka (Shaka, or more correctly Ushaka-Zulu) was born in 1773, the illegitimate son of Senzangakona, chief of the Amazulu ("of the sky"), a Nguni clan, and Nandi, a woman of the Langeni clan. After a very unhappy childhood, he joined the service of Dingiswayo, chief of the Mtetwa clan, who was trying to federate the various clans of the Nguni complex under his authority. He attracted the chief's attention by his military qualities, and when Senzangakona died, contrary to custom, Dingiswayo forced the Amazulus to elect Chaka as chief (1816). Chaka gathered together the nucleus of an army, which included banished and proscribed men of various origins in addition to the members of his own clan. He gave them new arms and taught them new tactics—assegais for throwing were replaced by a short pike with a long iron head (*ixwa*) designed for hand-to-hand combat—and trained them with a Spartan discipline. He began attacking and subduing the neighboring clans and then incorporated the survivors into a new tribe, the Zulus. His power increased notably from 1818. After Dingiswayo had been killed by Zwide of the Ndwandwe clan—perhaps with Chaka's complicity—Chaka incorporated the Mtetwa into his own tribe, the Zulus, which then dominated all the southern Nguni. The basis of his power was a highly developed military organization with an administration, a postal service, regiments of women, an intelligence service and a special corps of magicians. He set out to construct a centralized state by destroying the old tribal structure with his usual practice of incorporation into the Zulus. In 1825, he made contact with the British and remained on good terms with them until his death, although they made him sign, without his knowledge, a treaty surrendering the region around the future town of Durban to them. At the height of his power, his authority extended over about 310,000 miles, covering present-day Natal, Lesotho, Swaziland and part of Cape Province and Mozambique, with a population that was probably about 1 million (the army numbered 50,000). After the death of his mother, in 1827, his authority, which was already arbitrary to the point of brutality, turned into the tyranny of a maniac. He was assassinated on September 22, 1828 by his brothers, Mhlangana and Dingaan, the latter of whom succeeded him, and his minister Mbopa, before he was able to make his projected alliance with the British, who, by supplying him with firearms, would have enabled him to extend his power over the northern Nguni.

Chaka had a striking personality which made contemporary British observers compare him to Napoleon, but he may have been sexually abnormal; although he had a large harem, he never married and had only one child. He seems to have shown, particularly in his attitude to sorcery, a marked rationalism, which appeared in the way he organized the Zulus. He was certainly not the bloodthirsty despot of legend before the death of his mother. The fact remains that his wars took a huge toll in human lives not only in battle, but also in the migrations they caused. The whole tribal structure of southern and central Africa as far as present-day Zambia was permanently altered. Chaka's life is the subject of a popular novel, *Chaka*, by the Basuto writer Thomas Mofolo. (See also *Armies; Literature, Written; Migrations; Zulus.*)   P.A.

CHRISTIANITY. In Acts 8:26 ff., the Apostle Philip, pioneer of hitchhiking and of missionary work in Africa, made one of the earliest converts to Christianity with an Ethiopian eunuch, minister to Queen Candace, who picked him up in her chariot on the way to Gaza. Candace was the name given to the rulers of the Nubian kingdom of Meroe. Nubia remained Christian until the beginning of the sixteenth century, when it finally collapsed before a Muslim invasion. Africa Minor was also converted by Saint Augustine at a very early date. It was torn apart by the struggle between Arians and orthodox Christians, but its conversion to Islam was only achieved in the eleventh century. After the Muslim invasions during the seventh to the eleventh centuries, European Christiandom had a vague knowledge of its African coreligionists in Prester John's empire, composed of Ethiopia and the Nubian kingdoms of the upper Nile. But when the Portuguese established relations at the beginning of the sixteenth century, all that Vasco da Gama could do, at the cost of his life, was to help the negus, Claude, to repel the Muslim invasion led by Mohammed Grañ (1542), allowing Ethiopia to remain Christian until today, the surviving witness to the expansion into Africa of the early Church.

In the fifteenth century, too, the Catholic Church tried, successfully at first, to take over. Caravels disembarked Portuguese, Flemish and Italian friars, mostly Ca-

Zulu dance in memory of Chaka. South Africa. *Photo: Rapho, Spencer.*

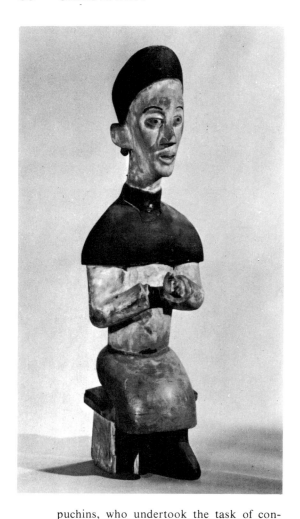

Missionary. Bakongo. Zaire. Painted wood. Musée royal de l'Afrique centrale, Tervuren. *Museum photo.*

Africa was closed to white people. The Bakongo rulers protested in vain to the Holy See, and some popes tried fruitlessly to reverse the current. The functions of the European priests left in Africa were soon limited to serving as chaplains at trading posts. The creation in 1622 of the Sacred Congregation for the Propagation of the Faith and the concentration of some orders on missionary work had little or no effect in Africa. The converts degenerated and disappeared, and Catholicism only left a few ethnographic traces such as the crucifixion of the condemned in Benin.

Protestantism began to expand in the seventeenth century among the Hottentots, or rather among the *bastaards* (half-breeds) on the fringe of the Dutch Huguenot colony on the Cape. The first serious attempts of Protestant missionaries to convert Africans began at the end of the eighteenth century and were linked to the social reform movement that accompanied the Baptist and Methodist revivals in England. They were associated with the antislavery campaign, as were the German, Swiss, French and American Protestant missions created in the first half of the nineteenth century. The competition of Protestants revived Catholic missionary activity in Africa; it led to the formation of new missionary orders, such as the Congregation of the Holy Ghost, the White Fathers and the Sociétés des Missions Africaines de Lyon, and to the sending out of new missions by the great orders. Religious rivalry too often led to political and international rivalry. Uganda was stained with blood during the struggle of the "French" and the "English," that is to say, by factions of the Baganda, who were converted either to Catholicism or Protestantism. Leopold II justified his action in the Congo to the Belgian public by appearing as the champion of the Catholic Church in the fight against heresy.

The results were spectacular. In 1962 there were more than 12 million Protestants and 15 million Catholics. The social—medical and educational—work of the missionaries often started sooner and was greater than that of the colonial administrations. Even if missionary penetration was often the prelude to colonial penetration, there are numerous cases of missionaries who were not under the sway of any colonial power—for example, French Catholics and Protestants in eastern and southern Africa, and American and Scandinavian Protestants in West Africa—and who began very early to keep their distance from the colonial administrations. From 1945 onward, moreover, missions adapted themselves to the tide of nation-

puchins, who undertook the task of converting the Africans living on the coast. They worked with both the chiefs and the people, and the first Bantu grammars were written at this time by and for the missionaries. They were particularly successful in the kingdoms of Benin and especially Kongo. The *mwanikongo* (emperor), Nzinga Bemba, was baptized in 1506 as Affonso I, and he acted as if he were a black Constantine or Clovis. One of his sons was enthroned as bishop of São Salvador in 1517. Churches sprang up all over the country, and the missionaries penetrated far into the interior without encountering much opposition, their only martyr being the Capuchin De Gheel. After the death of Affonso I in 1545, Christianity was expected to spread like wildfire all over central Africa, and European influence with it, but the development of the slave trade shattered these hopes. Missionary work slowed down—unless one includes the collective baptism of the cargoes of human flesh leaving Luanda—and the interior of

Funerary monument from an
area of Catholic influence.
Republic of the Congo.
Cement. *Photo: Viollet,
Mounicq.*

alism. While independent Protestant churches multiplied and joined the World Council of Churches, the Catholic Church progressively transferred episcopal seats to Africans (62 out of about 150 in 1962). Political emancipation was often preceded by ecclesiastical emancipation. Nonetheless, Christianity is the object of suspicion or is openly attacked by those who object to its links with Europe. Consequently, many African Christians have tried for several years to reinterpret their faith in an African cultural context. Definitive results have been achieved in sacred music, painting and sculpture. But the problem goes much deeper, and a complete liturgical and disciplinary reform, at least, has to be envisaged. (See also *Aksum; Bamum; Benin; Clothing; Emancipation of Women; Ethiopia; Gods; Islam; Kongo; Nile; Prayer.*)
P.A.

CIRCUMCISION. Circumcision is practiced in nearly all the main regions of Africa, but in most of them—the exceptions being the extreme east, west and south—societies which practice it live side by side with those which do not. The practice has rarely been dropped, as it was by the Swazi in South Africa, whose king suppressed it in 1875. During the last few centuries, it has been adopted more often than it has been stopped, and this is only partially the direct result of Muslim influence. Not even Christianity has managed to abolish it. It is said to have been introduced into certain countries at the request of the women, for example among various tribes in the Ubangi Valley and among the Azande. New meanings had to be attached to certain rituals when it was adopted, and this sometimes raised delicate problems of adaptation. The Yergum in the Benue Valley had to exempt families of chiefs from circumcision, owing to the risk of spoiling the harvests. Where circumcision is an ancient practice, its origin is unknown; it may have originated in the East or in a number of different places, considering the various ways in which it is performed— sometimes it is only a simple incision—and the different ages at which it is performed. In the myths about its origin, it is often linked to culture-heroes, who are frequently black-smiths, and in many communities it is the blacksmith who performs the operation. Circumcision of men is not necessarily accompanied by the excision of women, and the latter may occur alone, as among the Sara in Chad, but a number of tribes consider them to be complementary operations. The Dogon and Bambara, among other Sudanese tribes, believe that a human being is born as an incomplete pair of twins. A man therefore must be liberated by the

Ovimbundu being
circumcised. Angola. *Photo:
Musée de l'Homme, Leonar.*

Helmet of a circumcised
man. Banda. Republic of
Central Africa. Wood and
basketry. Musée de l'Homme.
Museum photo.

removal of the foreskin, where the female
spirits reside, and a woman by the removal of
the clitoris, inhabited by male spirits. Thus
circumcision is in itself an initiation, a kind
of transformation or confirmation. By
establishing the spirits of men, as the Dogon
believe, this operation, which may be

practiced on very young children, indicates
at least the possibility of entry into the adult
world and full membership in society.
Women and uncircumcised men are excluded from circumcision ceremonies; to
touch the blood of the circumcised may
sometimes make women sterile. Circumcision is a qualification for sexual intercourse and makes the wearing of clothes
compulsory. It also leads to many other
ceremonies. For the Dogon, it means
admission to the society of men and
participation in the making of masks. For
the Bambara, circumcision is a condition of
entry into the *Komo* society, which organizes
crucial religious activities. When circumcision is accompanied by going into retreat in
a camp in the bush, which is common in
southern Africa and western Sudan, it is the
time of the first social and religious
instruction, at least in sexual matters—since
this is the moment at which the ban on sexual
relations is lifted—and in genealogy—since
there must be a clear understanding of the
incestuous relationships that have to be
avoided. In exceptional cases, circumcision
does not mark the opening, but the conclusion of initiation ceremonies and is
preliminary to marriage rather than to free
sexual activity. This is the practice among
some of the Somba in Dahomey.

Boys are sometimes circumcised individually, but more often small groups of
children of about the same age who belong to
one family or one district are circumcised
together. When it is an integral part of the
ceremonies of transition from one age group
to another or of the composition of age
groups, it is performed upon all the children
or young people of a village or larger
community at the same time. By this means,
a larger fraternity is formed than the simple
brotherhood of the circumcised of the same
age group, which is almost universal. Among
the Masai in East Africa, for instance,
circumcision takes place every seven years
and is the solemn constitution of a group of
young people who later become a "regiment"
of warriors and live together before they are
separated through marriage, but without
ever breaking the profound bonds that unite
them and find expression in numerous forms
of mutual help. (See also *Excision; Initiation; Sistra; Societies, Secret.*)   P.M.

CITIES. See *Towns and Cities.*

CIVILIZATION. At the end of the nineteenth and the beginning of the twentieth
centuries, when people talked about "the
civilization of the peoples of Africa," it was
understood to be the act of civilizing them,
and not the sum of their ways of life and

thought. Europeans alone were then considered civilized. The rapid development of machinery, the prosperity of the industrial and commercial middle class and the establishment of vast colonial empires gave the Europe of that time an optimistic and intoxicated awareness of its power and progress. True civilization could only be European.

This calm self-satisfaction was unwittingly aided and abetted by the evolutionary ethnologists, who, trying to reconstruct the stages of social and cultural development, classified them in a series of growing complexity, beginning with the primitive stages and leading up to the higher levels. The three main levels were savagery, barbarism and civilization. Thus, perhaps without wishing to, the evolutionary school actually established a scale of values between these cultures and provided standards by which to judge them. A monotheistic religion, private property, monogamous families, Victorian morals, material wealth and academic art were some of the necessary components of civilization. Two world wars, economic crises and national crimes that were unthinkable half a century ago have put an end to the illusion of the West about the absolute superiority of its civilization. At the same time, theories of evolution have been replaced by other currents of thought that are much more concerned with understanding the functioning of a culture than allotting it a place on an ascending scale of values. As a result, the term "civilization" could be used without implying a moral judgment.

Civilization is the same kind of analytical and descriptive concept as culture. Exactly like a culture, a civilization is composed of man-made objects, modes of conduct based on established customs and, in general, a common way of life. But while a culture is the heritage of a clearly defined society, a civilization is not limited to a particular society. Thus, we speak of French culture and Western civilization, or Moroccan culture and the civilization of the Maghrib. Before the concept of civilization can serve a useful purpose, especially in the context of African studies, it needs closer analysis. The content of a civilization, which is independent of each individual society, is common and essential to several cultures and embraces several cultures derived from the same model. This naturally presupposes a theory of culture that will distinguish the essential from the inessential.

In sub-Saharan Africa, it is reckoned that there are almost a thousand identifiable societies, either kingdoms or tribes, each with its own name and its common heritage,

that is to say, culture. Grouping these cultures into civilizations can be effected at different levels; it can be done by trying to determine what factors are common and essential to all these societies, or to a large proportion of them, or to just a few. If the first of these approaches succeeds, then one may speak of African civilization. This single civilization is also equated with what is sometimes called "Africanism." Inside this single civilization, which is the largest, since it embraces all black African cultures, other, less generalized groups have been suggested to demarcate a small number of African civilizations. As an example, here is a breakdown of African civilization into six groups, according to methods of acquisition or production: (1) hunting and food-gathering; (2) forest agriculture, with root plants predominating; (3) agriculture in the savanna, with cereals and leguminous vegetables predominating; (4) animal husbandry and savanna-type agriculture; (5) use of material resources for artisan labor and external trade; (6) industrial production. Each of these systems of production is the foundation of an original culture, which is a small model of the civilization it defines. When seeking to demonstrate the similarities among only a few cultures, the term "civilization" is hardly ever used. Although one is covering the same ground, it is preferable to speak of cultural areas and to reserve the term "civilization" for much larger units. (See also *Culture*.)   J.M.

CLANS. The word "clan," which is so evocative of the old social structure of Scotland and Ireland, has been widely used by Africanists. Some have used it in its adjectival form to describe the society which they regarded as most typical of Africa. By "clan society" they meant a society based entirely on kinship and not at all on the ownership of land; it comprised neither government nor state, and its authorities wielded power not because they lived on a particular piece of land, but because they were descended from a particular Ancestor. Recent studies in political anthropology point to the conclusion that, while there are numerous kin groups who are an integral part of nearly all African societies, they very often coexist with a political authority that has the power to apply coercion. For this reason, Africanists no longer use the term "clan" as a general description of a type of society.

Today, the word "clan" describes one of the large groups into which a society is divided. These groups are based solely on kinship and are either matrilineal (the matriclan) or patrilineal (the patriclan). The

Clan sanctuary. Dogon. Mali.
Photo: Hoa-Qui.

they venerate the same totemic animal (however, this is not necessary, for some clans have no connection at all with any particular animal or plant). Membership in a clan generally has no matrimonial significance. The clan is not an exogamous group; that is to say, it does not insist that marriage must be with a nonmember. Certain clans, however, may have a mutual agreement to forbid or, contrariwise, to encourage intermarriage between their members. The clan illustrates less vividly than the lineage, but more vividly than the tribe, the fundamental importance of kinship, both in the daily life of Africa and in its social structure. (See also *Ancestors; Kinship; Languages, Secret; Lineage; Lions; Mottoes; Royalty; Taboos; Totemism.*) J.M.

CLOTHING. Tales told by the first missionaries to reach Africa in the last century have given the general public the impression that the majority of Africans are, or were, permanent nudists. In reality, total nudity of adults of both sexes occurs only among the Palaeonegrid tribes, including the Kabre of Togo, the Kirdi of Nigeria and Cameroun, the Sara of Chad and the Lobi and Birifor of the Ivory Coast and the Nilotic tribes, including the Nuer, the Shilluk and the Dinka. They are frequently neighbors of people who can only be described as "overdressed." A Fulani or Kanuri chief who is garbed in eight to ten boubous (robes), one on top of another, a flowing *sarwal* over one or two pairs of trousers, a coat and blankets, a turban on top of a tarboosh and with a veil covering the lower part of his face can hardly be described as a nudist. Nevertheless, temporary nudity for specific purposes is general. People undress completely for sleeping, bathing, working, playing and for some religious ceremonies.

Basically, clothing cannot be separated from adornment, which is associated with magical protection and fecundity. The so-called loincloth worn by many Palaeonegrid tribes draws attention to the sex of the wearer rather than hides it; it is intended to adorn the noble parts, noble because they are life-giving, and to protect them from supernatural dangers. The Somba of Dahomey wear their penis shields only outside the village, to protect themselves against the spirits of the bush, while the Lobi tie a string around their foreskin and fasten it to their waists. On the one hand, Kabre and Bamileke women remain nude in order to be able to absorb the fertile influences of the earth; on the other, Madjinngay and Fali women block their vaginas with corks, the visible part of which resembles a penis, for

clan should be clearly distinguished from the lineage not as a separate abstraction, but as a similar unit in a society that comprises groups representing different degrees of kinship. Unlike lineage, which changes continuously and cannot be traced further back than a few generations (normally five, six or seven), the clan is a stable group that exists and preserves its identity through many generations. The number of clans remains constant in a given society. Although a lineage cannot be regarded as a subdivision of a clan, a clan is, in fact, composed of members of related lineages. It is quite probable that the Ancestor of a particular clan was originally the head of a lineage and that his memory was kept alive despite rifts and fragmentation of that group.

The clan is a nominal group that lacks the internal organization necessary for strength and cohesion. Two people know they belong to the same clan when: (1) they claim the same Ancestor (even though they cannot trace the connection back to him through all the intervening generations, as in a lineage; in any case, the Ancestor may be mythical); (2) they are bound by the same taboos, such as that against eating a particular fruit; (3)

the same reason that Betyambe women emphasize their vulvas with red ribbons, namely to avert the absorption of hostile forces from the earth. The belt of beads tied around the waist has basically the same psychological connotation for African women as do transparent panties for their elegant European and American sisters.

Related to genital adornment are the covering for the buttocks and the loincloth-slip. In its simplest form, such a covering consists of a double bunch of leaves or a leather apron; it may also be a double apron or a band made of leather, beaten bark or fabric that goes between the legs. This type of garment is almost universal in Africa and is worn for all types of work—household chores, agricultural activities, hunting, etc. It has long remained the principal or sole garment of the ordinary people in all parts of Africa where clothes are worn. Two distinct general types of garment have developed from the loincloth: the dress that is sewn together, or partly sewn and partly draped, which is worn in Sudanese Africa; and the draped garment resembling a toga, which is worn in the area of Guinea and the rain forests and also by women in Sudanese Africa. Sewn garments may be Arabian in origin, even though the ample cut of Sudanese trousers differs from that of the *sarwal* worn in the Maghrib, and the boubou, cut like a dalmatic, differs even more from the floor-length, short-sleeved jellaba. Boubous and loose-fitting trousers are also worn by such non-Muslims as the Mossi, Gurma and Bambara.

Voluminous, draped clothes vary considerably from one region to another in material, color, shape and the manner of wearing them. Besides the Congolese "blankets" made of fig-tree bark or red-dyed raffia, there are the much more elaborate Sudanese capes made of bands of cotton or animal hair sewn together, whose designs indicate the owners' social status. Then there is the toga, or *kente,* worn from western Nigeria to the Ivory Coast and made of locally produced lamé (by the Yoruba and Akan) or cotton velvet (by the Nupe of the Ivory Coast), or even silk made from imported yarns and locally woven with gold (in Ghana, lower Togo, Dahomey and Nigeria). These clothes have long had a great social and ritual importance. Collecting them was a way of accumulating wealth and acquiring prestige: they formed parts of dowries; and a great many were buried and destroyed at funerals of notable citizens.

Christian and Islamic influence profoundly modified ideas of decency. Notions about the pudenda evidently varied greatly

Somba. Dahomey. *Photo: Hoa-Qui.*

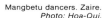

Mangbetu dancers. Zaire. *Photo: Hoa-Qui.*

between one society and another. Generally, among people who wore clothes, children remained naked until the age of puberty. At this stage, the vulva usually had to be concealed (the pubic hair of women was frequently removed), but the exposure of men's genital organs was more easily acceptable. Breasts did not need to be covered, except perhaps in the case of women of royal blood. Nearly a century had to pass before Christian missionaries discovered the perfectly moral and nonerotic character of this partial or total nudity. At the present time, governments of the newly independent states have adopted the same point of view. They endeavor, sometimes brutally, to compel all their nationals to dress "decently." They are impelled by a form of respect for human nature based on the stereotyped colonialist convention of "naked = savage; clothes = progress." Meanwhile, there are sound medical reasons for believing that clothing, and particularly such unsuitable clothing as military finery, may have very harmful effects on the general health of some peoples. (See also *Adornment; Basketry; Breasts; Bushmen;*

Fashion; Jewelry; Kirdi; Palaeonegrids; Weaving.)   P.A.

COLONIZATION. In the life of the people of black Africa, colonization was simultaneously a brief interlude, a common experience highly charged with emotion and a period that opened up Africa to the world and the world to Africa. In 1885, in the Treaty of Berlin, the European powers established the rules of the game for the partition of the interior of Africa: boundaries of spheres of influence, criteria of actual occupation, "treaties" with African authorities and "protection" offered by the national flag. In 1960, seventeen African states became independent, each one of which was the successor to a colonial regime. Although the independence movement, which began in 1956 with the independence of Sudan, continued after 1960, it reached its climax in that year: a greater number of young African nations won their independence in 1960 than in any other year. The seventy-five years from 1885 to 1960 constituted what may be considered the colonial interlude—an interlude because in many important respects

Tikar chiefs. Cameroun.
Photo: Documentation française.

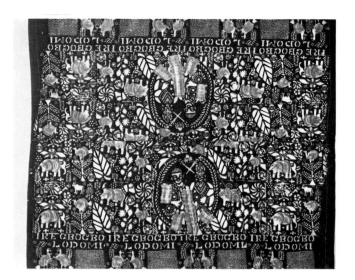

Batik loincloth printed
with indigo. Yoruba. Nigeria.
Musée de l'Homme, Paris.
Museum photo.

there was no break in the continuity of African life. Today, many Africans still work the land in the traditional way and mainly live off what they produce. Family and matrimonial institutions in villages and even towns are much as they were in the middle of the nineteenth century. In the guise of new syncretic forms of worship, traditional beliefs and practices remain very much alive, side by side with imported religions. Even in politics, where the colonial heritage was strongest, earlier habits make their presence felt in new institutions and give them fresh interpretations not envisaged by Europeans.

Now, only a few years after the end of the colonial regimes, it is clear that far fewer African traditions have been abolished than was previously thought. Nevertheless, the generations of Africans who lived during the colonial period were very deeply affected. There were great differences among the French, English, Belgian and Portuguese regimes, but they had one effect in common: the establishment of the European minority as a socially privileged class. The Europeans enjoyed a far higher standard of living than most Africans; they kept their own customs and habits, particularly in housing, food, dress and language; and they maintained segregation in daily life, social events and entertainment and marriage. Under the colonial economic system, Africans felt that they were exploited, as indeed they were. They were the unskilled workers and low-grade clerks, and they only had a modest share in the prosperity of undertakings whose purpose was to make large profits for foreign capital. Politically, they were "native subjects" of distant countries that never exported any part of their democratic

systems to Africa. The only duty of these subjects was to obey a hierarchy of civil servants, whose authority was derived solely from the governor, who was himself the representative of a European power. Not until the last years or months preceding independence did Africans have any part in the government of their own communities. To suffer colonial rule and then agitate for freedom from it was the almost simultaneous experience of nearly all the peoples of black Africa. This common experience is one of the constitutive factors of modern Pan-Africanism.

The psychological consequences of colonization were soon blurred and its real significance gradually became clear. Political and economic colonization in the nineteenth century put an end to the age-old isolation of black Africa. Admittedly, the periphery—the shores of the Indian and Atlantic oceans and the borders of the southern Sahara—had been frequented for at least 2,000 years by foreign sailors and traders—Greeks, Arabs, Indians and Europeans. But they had no need to penetrate the interior of the continent to obtain the luxury goods and slaves that they had come to seek. These "goods" were delivered to them in the ports and caravansaries. On the other hand, the commercial and industrial requirements of nineteenth-century Europe in Africa—raw materials, plentiful cheap labor and a vast market for its merchandise—required the effective occupation of vast areas, the building of an economic infrastructure and a permanent political presence. Once European expansion in Africa had gotten under way, it developed in totally unforseen ways: elementary, secondary and finally higher education were introduced; a growing minority of the population began to live in towns; there were African converts to Christian denominations; Africans began to be influenced by world ideologies. For the first time in its history, black Africa is no longer outside great cultural movements but is part of the world, not only as a receiver but also as a contributor. Besides labor and natural wealth, African music and sculpture since the colonial period have become part of the world's heritage. Future historians may well regard the inclusion of Africa in the worldwide traffic in goods and ideas as the most significant event of the colonial period. (See also *Christianity; Congo River; European Discovery; Education; Emancipation of Women; Fashion; Gold; Industry; Kongo; Law; Lion Men; Press; Rwanda; Slave Trade; Sports; Theater.*)   J.M.

COMBS. The broad-toothed comb, like the hairpin (which may serve as a head scratcher, among other things), is frequently used as an ornament. This is not surprising because hairstyling plays a major part in bodily adornment, which is so highly developed in all African societies whether they are agricultural, pastoral or urban. For both men and women, hair is virtually a material for building skillful structures, not only by styling the hair itself, but also by adding all kinds of jewelry. Men in particular use combs as ornaments. In the Ubangi Valley, Mandja hunters put combs made of vegetable fibers on one side of their closely cropped hair. The teeth of these combs, which are narrowly spaced, are bound together tightly with decorative netting to form a handle at the back of the comb. The combination of these bindings, either at the level of the handle or lower down (to provide additional decoration), gives each comb its originality. The handles of combs and the combs themselves are made from a variety of plants, such as bamboo, palm, palmyra and aloes. The decoration, which depends on the nature of the binding or basketry, may be obtained by superimposing coiled or split fibers, sometimes dyed black and red, on cloth. This type of comb is found among the Bakongo and Bajokwe in Angola. In addition, the Bajokwe have probably produced the greatest and richest variety of wooden combs. The backs of Bajokwe combs are decorated with geometric designs that may be surmounted by a small figure, a bust or the entire body, or again by a scene from daily life or familiar animals. Combs decorated with sculptured figures are also found in the Ivory Coast and the Congo. Combs—whether they are made of bone or ivory, are simple or decorated (with beads, bits of material in vivid color or braided string), or are intended for a functional purpose or as ornaments—may also have important symbolic significance. In the upper Ubangi Valley, among the Nzakara, a prospective bridegroom gives his future mother-in-law a comb as a pledge of a definite engagement when his fiancée is still only a child—long before the marriage can take place. (See also *Adornment; Basketry.*)   J.D.

CONGO RIVER. The Congo is such a powerful and impetuous river that the Portuguese navigators who discovered it in 1482 were unable to explore it. It thwarted their attempts to find a mysterious "central lake," but instead they discovered the splendid kingdom of Kongo. The Congo is the most powerful river on the continent of Africa and the second longest in the world. Its flow is more than double that of the Mississippi and four times that of the Mekong. The people who live on its banks regard it as divine; Léopold Sédar Senghor, the poet-president of Senegal, eulogized its majesty in a magnificent poem; and developmental engineers have estimated its colossal hydroelectric potential. Central Africa stretches around the Congo Basin. The river forms a complete system of natural water-

Bajokwe comb. Zaire. Carved wood. Musée royal de l'Afrique centrale, Tervuren. *Museum photo.*

Bajokwe comb. Zaire. Carved wood. Musée de l'Homme, Paris. *Museum photo.*

ways—which greatly aided communications and, hence, colonial occupation by settlers representing Leopold III of Belgium—and is like a great artery supplying central Africa. In spite of the awe and might of the river, there is a melancholy isolation about its grandeur. H. M. Stanley, the explorer, remarked upon its loneliness; on his way down to the coast during the last stages of his journey across Africa, he was moved by the "sadness" of the Congo, "abandoned by men, for no one stays to sing the praises of its brown majestic torrent." André Gide was also deeply impressed by the Stanley Pool, which spreads like a great lake between Kinshasa and Brazzaville: "The arm of the pool is cluttered with islands, whose banks merge with those of the river. Some of these islands are covered with bushes and low trees, others are sandy and low-lying and are covered unevenly by shaggy reeds. Huge eddies swirl and enliven the gray surface of the river. . . . There are crosscurrents, strange whirlpools and backwaters revealed by the drift of floating islands of grass, borne along by the currents." Long-stemmed papyrus grows on these islands as they drift along, and the water hyacinth spatters them with blazing color. The river was called "Nzadi" by the Bakongo, and the Portuguese rendering of this name was "Zaire." Today, we know the river by the name which the kingdom of Kongo bestowed upon it and made famous. (See also *Bateke; European Discovery; Kongo.*) G.B.

COWS. The Nuer used a great variety of terms to describe precisely the colors and shapes of the markings on their cows as well as the length and curves of their horns. Among the Longarim, another Nilotic tribe, each young warrior chose a "favorite bull" with which he mystically identified himself. In Rwanda, dithyrambic poems praise the strength and beauty of particular herds, or even of particular animals, each called by its own name; aristocratic women imitated the walk of cows and put jewels symbolizing cattle-raising on their diadems; girls, in their dances, imitated the long horns of the cattle by the movement of their arms. Among the Masai and in nearly all other pastoral societies, marriage payments were reckoned in head of cattle. The Luo women could not milk cows between puberty and the menopause. These practices and rules, more of which could be listed, show the key importance of cattle in the social and ritual life of African pastoral societies. Some travelers, reminded of the majestic long-horned cows in the Egyptian bas-reliefs and of the Egyptian god Apis or thinking of the

Congo River. *Photo: Hoa-Qui.*

splendidly useless cattle in India, have talked about African sacred cows. This interpretation is incorrect, because the cow is neither an object of worship nor a needless luxury in any African society.

If cattle seem to have no economic significance, it is because their use is appreciably different from that in the West. Europeans and Americans raise cattle in order to produce milk, meat, leather. They are bred and reared to give the largest yield at the best price. In Africa, these products (as well as blood for food and butter as a cosmetic) are, of course, used, but pastoral people needed them for their own consumption and not to sell to others. There is another, even more striking difference. It was most marked in stratified pastoral societies, such as those in the region of the Great Lakes. There, the king's subjects were divided between two social levels. The farmers, comprising from two-thirds to four-fifths of the populace, formed a large inferior caste, subordinate to a warrior and pastoral nobility. The members of the nobility were the sole owners of cattle. In order to have the right to one or a few cows, and so to enjoy their produce such as milk, blood and veal (but not heifers), a farmer supplied the owner with the produce of his fields and also worked for him. For the cattle owner, cows were virtually capital, and he exchanged the

Rwanda schoolgirls imitating the horns of cows. *Photo: Jacques Maquet.*

income from them against agricultural goods and services. Cattle therefore had an economic value, and a very high one at that; in Rwanda, the owner of a small herd of a dozen cattle could live from them, without working the land; whereas, if he sold his cows, which became possible after the introduction of money and markets during the colonial era, the price he received for his cattle was too small for him to obtain the same amount of goods and services.

The reasons for the overvaluation of cattle were not economic. In the first place, they conferred prestige (they were the almost exclusive possession of the superior caste and were a typically aristocratic possession); secondly, they were a unique source of wealth not requiring human labor (this was the fundamental difference between animal husbandry and the only other technique of production then known, agriculture). These are the two major reasons why cattle were so highly prized by the farmer. A further reason, which also explains why the farmer paid so much for cattle, is inherent in the feudal system: the farmer, having no power in a pastoral community, was at the mercy of the superior caste and needed the protection of a noble; protection was granted by a feudal agreement that included the transfer of cattle, though this was only one aspect of the transaction. (See also *Animal Husbandry; Beverages; Blood; Cattle; Diet; Feudalism.*)   J.M.

CULTURE. "He is to be envied for his good taste and the breadth of his culture." "It is sad that Provençal culture is disappearing." These two sentences illustrate different meanings of the term "culture." To what extent are they significant in an African context? In the traditional African villages there were open-minded and thoughtful men who had acquired a diversity and depth of knowledge not only through their own direct observation of nature and living beings, but because others had communicated it to them. In theory at least, the quality that makes a man cultivated is to be found in the spirit of enquiry, which impels him to adopt as his own the knowledge that others have already stored in their tradition. But can one be cultivated without books? The sum of knowledge gained by oral tradition in a single community is trifling compared with the mass of knowledge contained in the library of a reasonably well-educated man. Of course, it is merely a question of quantity, but we know that a large difference in quantity can amount to a difference in quality, which is precisely the case here.

In its second sense, culture is the common heritage of a society. It forms a unit, which at first glance seems to be disparate but on analysis turns out to be fairly coherent, comprised of: material objects, which assure the group its subsistence and daily needs; institutions, which coordinate the activities of the members; and a common way of life, which constitutes a certain conception of the world, a morality and the basis of an art. This unit, in its slow and continuous development, is transmitted to each member of the society by a process of education. Culture, in this sense of the word, is the key concept of anthropology, and there is no doubt that this concept is the most important contribution that this discipline has made to our knowledge of man and human society. Because it is universal, this concept of culture is naturally valid in Africa. It can even be said that culture in Africa, while no more important than elsewhere, is more homogeneous and therefore makes a deeper impression on the individual.

The domain of culture lies midway between that of human nature (in which all men are alike) and individuality (in which a man is different from all others); culture belongs to the area in which some men—those who share the same social heritage—are alike. Traditional African cultures were very homogeneous and offered few options. The young African on the threshold of manhood usually had only one way open to him: a single occupation, cultivating the land as his father had done before him; one group to join, that of the initiates of his own age group; one way of worship, that of his ancestors; one philosophy of life, that of his elders. It is in the wealth and fullness of this anthropological sense that the term "culture" is generally applied to Africa. (See also *Civilization; Ethnic Groups; Negritude; Pan-Africanism.*) J.M.

CUSH. See *Meroe.*

DAHOMEY. In the nineteenth century, Dahomey was one of the most famous states in West Africa and the most powerful on the Benin coast. Its beginnings, 200 years earlier, were modest. A group of fugitives from Allada came to live among the Guedevi, who may have been of Yoruba origin and who lived in the present-day region of Abomey. This first period was filled with village battles, resounding with invocations and challenges on a Homeric scale. The newcomers brought with them a new conception of political organization and a long-range goal. In the third generation, Abomey ("within the ramparts") was founded, and the kingdom was named Danhome ("in the belly of Dan"). Dan was a village chief who complained incessantly about the trespassing of the "people from Allada," saying, "Do they intend to build even in my belly?" The chief of the newcomers, Aho, taking him at his word, killed him and built his palace on Dan's tomb. Aho, also called Ouegbadja,

was the man who "made the country" and its military power. Less than fifty years later, Agadja seized Allada and Ouidah, reached the sea and took control of trade with Europe over a vital part of the Slave Coast. The "great plan" of the kings of Dahomey was fulfilled.

After this, wars were fought less for conquest than for slaves. Most of them were traded in Ouidah and transported by European ships to the Americas; the rest were allotted to royal plantations, distributed to dignitaries or to soldiers who had distinguished themselves in the field, or offered as sacrifices to honor royal ancestors. Dahomey's military power reached its zenith in the nineteenth century under King Guezo

Behanzin, king of Dahomey, in the form of a shark. Fon. Dahomey. Painted wood. Musée de l'Homme, Paris. *Museum photo.*

Glele, king of Dahomey, in the form of a lion. Fon. Dahomey. Painted wood. Musée de l'Homme, Paris. *Museum photo.*

Seat of a dignitary carved with figures from the court of the king of Dahomey at Kana. The king beneath his parasol is surrounded by his wives. Soldiers guard prisoners chained around the neck. Fon. Dahomey. Painted wood. Musée de l'Homme, Paris. *Museum photo.*

Gu, god of war and metallurgy. Fon. Dahomey. Iron. Musée de l'Homme, Paris. *Photo: Giraudon.*

and King Glele. Although it was out of all proportion to the population of the kingdom, which certainly was never more than 500,000, the army was very soundly organized and well supplied with firearms. Recruited on a system closely resembling conscription, the front-line troops numbered nearly 20,000 fighting men, of which a third, the Amazons, were women. Dahomey was dreaded by all its neighbors until 1850, when it clashed with an enemy more powerful than itself in its attack on the fortified and populous towns of the Yoruba. On that occasion, European observers described the impressive order of battle of the Dahoman regiments, with their uniforms and flags. The army was still vigorous, even after these setbacks, and it was this army that later put up the most organized resistance in the whole of West Africa to the French columns. In 1892 Abomey fell, and the king surrendered two years later. Thus ended one of the most solidly constructed and centralized states of the Guinea Coast.

In the kingdom of Dahomey, autonomy of villages and provinces, except at the borders, was reduced to a minimum. Royal control was firm. In principle, not even the construction of a temple or a monastery was done without the permission of the king. His subjects "belonged to him"; they were counted as "things of Dahomey" when he took a census. Their goods belonged to him, too, and it was by an act of grace that he passed them on to the natural heirs. Similarly, the fruits of their labor were his. Hence, there was strict control of the economy: a top official would decide each year which areas were to be cultivated and what crops were to be grown, and he would later supervise the delivery of compulsory contributions of produce. Foreign trade at Ouidah was strictly controlled, too, and the king's administrators laid down its terms. One of the numerous royal titles was "Master of Riches." Another was "Father of Life"; Dahomey, like its neighbors on the Benin Coast, regarded royalty as divine, but did so with greater moderation.

Although there was a "free" sector of artistic activity, such as wood sculpture for religious purposes and minor arts that included engraving on calabashes, art was mainly the work of groups of hereditary specialists who worked under the sole control of the king and for his profit, as in Benin. The most notable products of Dahoman art are statues and other wooden objects, sometimes decorated with metalwork or entirely covered with foil made of brass, silver or gold; brass statuettes cast by the lost-wax process; hangings and umbrellas decorated with appliqué work; fabrics; and painted clay bas-reliefs for the facades of the palaces. Most of the decorations celebrate a great event or convey— either directly or in the form of rebuses— royal mottoes, proverbs or declarations and may be considered a rudimentary form of writing. (See also *Allada; Amazons; Applique Work; Calabashes; Divinities; Lost-Wax Process; Mottoes; Priests; Recados; Slave Trade; Voodoo.*)　　　P.M.

DAN. The Dan live in the extreme west of the Ivory Coast, in the vicinity of Man and Danane, either in the savanna region or in the forest watered by the upper reaches of the Cavally, and also on the Liberian side of the border. They probably number about 150,000. In the south, the Dan are neighbors of the Ngere and the Wobe, whose institutions and way of life differ little from their own. However, while the latter speak languages of the Kru group and their horizons have always been bounded by the forest, the Dan language and traditions indicate that they originated in the savanna, and although the Dan masks fulfill nearly the same functions as those of the Ngere, their style is completely different. The Dan mask, with a high and slightly rounded forehead, a fine mouth and prominent cheekbones, is a relatively faithful reproduction of the human face. The men's masks have cylindrically shaped eyes, whereas women's masks have elongated eyes and are decorated with cowrie shells. The Dan sculptor is hardly concerned with producing a faithful image of his model: his aesthetic vision is closer to refined realism than to naturalism, and his sculpture possesses a classical purity and order. Dan masks are not, as was once believed, representations of spirits of ancestors, but incarnations of spirits of the bush; hence their fiber garments. Some masks watch over the boys while they are in camps during initiation. Others—those of singers, dancers and beggars—are mainly intended to entertain, although the fear inspired by their communication of the supernatural is never entirely absent. The importance of a Dan mask is in proportion to its size. The biggest and most impressive are the "Masks of Peace," whose function is to maintain order. Formerly their appearance among the fighters was enough to end hostilities between villages. Miniature masks, used as amulets, give protection to the wearers if kept under their garments and hidden from women's eyes; this is the same kind of protection as that emanating from the large masks, which are usually kept separately. (See also *Ngere.*)　　　D.P.

Large rice spoon. Detail. Wood and white iron. Dan. Ivory Coast. Paul Tishman Collection, New York. *Photo: Musée de l'Homme.*

Dan mask. Wood. Ivory Coast. Sammlung für Völkerkunde, University of Zurich. *Museum photo.*

DANCE. Dancing, which is perceptible in the very movements of the body when musicians play or when workers till the soil, is the art most closely linked to African life. Evidence of its existence dates from a very early period; it is represented on Egyptian monuments as well as on rock paintings in South Africa. Even in paintings of truly Egyptian dances, one finds the same positions, postures and gestures that are used in the contemporary dances of both East and West Africa, especially eastern Sudan, Rwanda, Dahomey and the frontiers of

Danagla women dancing.
Mongo, Chad. *Photo:
Hoa-Qui.*

"Goli" mask dancing. Baule.
Ivory Coast. *Photo: Hugo
Zemp.*

Dance costume of small
Kissi boys at the end of their
initiation. Guékédou, Guinea.
Photo: Hoa-Qui.

Guinea and Liberia. We do not know whether Egyptians and black Africans drew on a common source or whether the latter knew the dances performed in upper Egypt, which may gradually have spread as far as the Atlantic coast, as did certain types of musical instruments.

Just as choral music is more usual in Africa than solos or duets, so group dancing is more common than dancing solo or in pairs. The latter form is strictly secular, even when it occurs at the end of rituals, as, for instance, after funerals. In this case, it is performed by two men or by a man and a woman who face each other and leap in place without touching. Originally, this may have been a group dance in which two lines of men and women, facing each other, advanced until their bellies touched; examples of this occur in fecundity and fertility rites. The solo dance is rare. Its exhibitionist character counters the anonymity that is fundamental to dances in traditional societies, which are similar to masked dances except that the faces are uncovered. Women dancing in a line often detach themselves one by one, but all the solo parts are identical and no one is allowed to be a star. Convulsive dancing, which is found in different parts of Africa, would be an exception if it did not rapidly become group dancing in which spectators are encouraged to join. An element of simulation in these dances suggests the art of the comedian.

The only individual performance during a ritual is the dance of a mask, although generally several masks—either of the same type or each personifying a different being— "come out" at once. The masked man may limit himself to advancing a few steps and gesturing in a menacing way; at most he thrusts out his head or, if his neck is free, rotates it. His ample garments hide all other bodily movements. Thus, among the Dogon, masks surmounted by a double cross (*kanaga*) or by the emblem of a multistoried house (*sirige*) describe a complete circle while their wearers stand still. There has been a similar development in European ballet, in which a dancer's legs move only if they are visible—if they are bare or if the dancer is wearing trousers. However, African dance steps, whatever their elevation or direction, still have the characteristics of a walk, for the walk is the basis of African dancing. The gestures are conditioned by accessories such as ornaments or bells worn on the arms; or else, if the breasts are bare, the arms are held in fixed positions, forming geometric lines that accentuate the sculptural qualities of the dance. In fact, the dance may even be reduced to a procession of statues, for example, when a solemn conclusion to an initiation is desired.

The object of most dance groups, masked or unmasked, is to trace patterns on the ground. The choice of site is as important as the design of the pattern itself: for fertility

Mossi "red dancers."
Koudougou, Upper Volta.
Photo: Hoa-Qui.

Ngere girls dancing. Ivory Coast. *Photo: Hugo Zemp.*

Bateke men dancing. Fort Rousset, Republic of the Congo. *Photo: Hoa-Qui.*

rituals, the dancers tread a particular field, for example, the field of the patriarch. The dances of the newly initiated nearly always take place in an empty space on the edge of the village. During the funeral rites of a dignitary, the men of the village may invade the main open space to perform lengthy dances there. Dancers generally arrive in single file and may maintain this formation during the entire dance or divide into two parallel lines. The figures most frequently executed are a circle or a double circle. In the latter, men and women divide into two separate lines at a given moment, as in the sowing rites of the Dogon. Another dance performed by this tribe suggests a mythical snake, the avatar of the first ancestor. Dances before a hunt are almost exclusively male and are inspired either by the animals' gait or the methods employed in their capture, which are the origin of a wide variety of patterns and mimes. Animal dances feature performers on stilts who are invariably masked. Weapon dances, which are not necessarily war dances, often take place during funeral or fecundity rites, since a weapon can preserve as well as pursue the soul of the dead and may be a sexual symbol.

Less frequently, dancers of both sexes line up in several long lines, forming a mass that either moves slowly forward or stands still, and restrict themselves to a limited range of movements. In dances that are performed by men and women (and which are not unlike some Indonesian dances), the participants press closely against one another and move only their heads or arms. Similar dances are performed standing up; then, only a particular part of the body—such as the shoulders, belly or buttocks—is moved, or, on the contrary, different parts of the body are immobilized successively. One or more drums generally accompany dancers, the drummers either marching ahead of the dancers or facing them. Sometimes the dancers themselves, with bells tied to their limbs or by shaking sistra, provide the only musical accompaniment; then, gesture and movement are precisely synchronized. When, on the other hand, dances are performed to the rhythm of drums, there is a polyrhythmic complexity in the relationship between the music and the dancers' movements. (See also *Adornment; Drums; Funerals; Hunting; Masks; Music; Rattles; Sistra.*)   A.S.

DEATH. Africans, like all other people, find it difficult to understand why life ends without dignity and man is left a corpse. They too try to explain how death came to mankind, because for Africans, as in the Bible, death is not consistent with human nature; man was once immortal in the earthly paradise. In traditions as far removed from each other as those of the Dogon living at the bend of the Niger River and the Pygmies of the Ituri Forest is found the belief that originally men did not die. The event that introduced death, again as in the Bible, was a human error. In African mythology this error was not a sin, but a blunder, an oversight that resulted in a taboo not being respected, or, in some versions, even an act of charity that gave Death personified an opportunity to come among men.

These tentative explanations are as little satisfying to the mind as are those imagined in other civilizations, but the integration of death into a comprehensive conception of life appears successful in Africa. For in Africa, a human being is not regarded as completely detached from the total reality; clearly he is distinct from it, but, in contrast with the Western attitude, his identity is not asserted by emphasizing the distinction between himself and the world. In the African world view, the same vital force flows through all beings and completely unites men, animals, plants, even water and earth. This immense reality predates every human being, surrounds him while he lives and continues to exist after his death. The life of a man is an epiphenomenon, an existence that is secondary but part of true reality. Conceived of in this way, the death of an individual is not an ontological scandal, annihilating a being who is completely self-sufficient and has his own destiny. Rather, it is the progressive reabsorption into the world of one of its manifestations that was always deeply rooted in it; the death of a person is like the death of a tree. Survival after death is also of limited duration. It is viewed as a subterranean state in which the spirits of the dead lead a shadowy life resembling that of the living, but greatly diminished. In this twilight existence, the spirits of the dead are more or less supported by their descendants still on earth. As long as the living give them offerings and pay them homage, the dead continue to survive. But once they are neglected, they weaken and fade away. The dead can send sickness and troubles as reminders of their existence. To die without leaving descendants is a disaster. The African conception of survival conveys perfectly the melancholy statement that the dead exist only in the minds of the living and, once forgotten, cease to be.

If man's constant and total participation in the world enables him to rid death of its absurdity, it remains nonetheless a disturbing event for the living. When a member of a community dies, his death must first be explained. The cause is generally either witchcraft or the revenge of a man or a spirit. This does not mean that Africans deny that illness may cause death, as Westerners have sometimes supposed; rather, Africans recognize neither division nor incompatibility between what we call "natural" and "magical" causality. But is this so very different from the attitude of fervent Christians? For them, the death of a child is the result both of divine will and illness.

Now let us consider some of the ceremonies associated with death. Burial ceremonies differ throughout Africa, but their essential purpose is the same: to enable society to absorb this intrusion of the sacred into daily life. Death is made acceptable to society by declaring a limited period of mourning during which all ordinary activities are suspended, by insuring a new status for the dead through funeral ceremonies and by ending the time of mourning with festivities which clearly indicate the resumption of normal life.

To the universal themes—myths about the origin of death, beliefs concerning survival, ideas about mourning—Africa adds only a few variations. Africa shows more originality, at least in comparison with the West, in its philosophy of death. This philosophy is based on two existential experiences that are of profound and universal significance throughout black Africa: that of descent, whereby the individual is a link between generations, and that of the soil, whereby the farmer must adapt himself humbly to the forces of nature. In both situations, which can be experienced simultaneously, man has a relationship with an entity more real than himself. It is not surprising that man's position as a lineal descendant and as a farmer served as the model for the human condition. The African, who is never conscious of being an end in himself, accepts death as natural, for it does not pervert man's destiny. (See also *Ancestors; Dogon; Funerals; Myths; Philosophy; Spirits and Genii; Taboos.*) J.M.

DIET. Traditional African societies have found solutions for their nutritional problems that sometimes appear irrational to economists and dieticians. Nevertheless, they have proved adequate enough to enable these societies to exist until today, relying on rudimentary techniques and working poor soil. Rural societies are largely dependent for their food upon the natural resources of their environment and on their ability to exploit it. Research into nutrition conducted among nonnomadic African peoples has shown that there are two principal types of diets, with the type dependent upon the climatic zone in which the people live.

The farmers in the savanna belt have a diet based on cereals such as sorghum, millet or, occasionally, rice. Here, cultivated leguminous plants—peanuts, beans and chickpeas—are also eaten. Other vegetables and fruits like tomatoes, pimento, eggplant, marrow, guavas and mangoes are rare. Wild vegetables and fruits provide a useful supplement, but they are gathered only in the rainy season. The fat content of this diet comes from vegetable oils found in peanuts, sesame seeds and the fruit of the shea tree. Meat is usually available because most savanna peoples raise cattle and are in contact with pastoral peoples or, sometimes, river fishing peoples. This diet is fairly well balanced, but there are marked seasonal deficiencies of vitamins A and C, and a fall in caloric content during the rainy season. The length and gravity of this season, known as the "betweentime," varies greatly from one group to another. The Serer, Wolof, Tukulor, Bambara, Mossi, Bobo, Hausa and Tuburi are among the societies of this region

Woman doing her marketing.
Kisangani, Zaire. *Photo: Rapho, Hansen.*

whose nutritional problems have been studied.

The diet of the cultivators of the forest belt, such as the Ewe, Watyi, Guro, Yoruba, Fang, Eton and Kaeka is based on starchy foods including yams, taro, cassava, sweet potatoes and plantains. Cereals are almost nonexistent, and leguminous plants consist mainly of peanuts, and beans. Vegetables and fruits—some of which, like the fruit of the oil palm, are very rich in vitamin C—are abundant and are eaten all year round. On the other hand, food of animal origin is rare, because the tsetse fly prevents the raising of cattle. Difficulties of communication hamper distribution of fish. The caloric content of this diet is very adequate throughout the year. It causes no avitaminosis, but results in a permanent deficiency of animal protein.

Some specialists distinguish an intermediate dietary group, typical of the subforest zone (the Moba, Kabre, Mandja, Baya, and Banda). This group differs from the former because their diet is based on both tubers and cereals such as corn. Three other kinds of diets exist, and these also correspond with the way people live. The communities of fishermen that have been studied (including those on the coast of Senegal, the Ivory Coast and Ghana) have practiced a barter economy for a long time; their diet reflects that of the farmers of the climatic zone in which they live, but it is twice as rich in protein and calcium. Hunters and food-gatherers are disappearing and scarcely exist outside the great forests (the Pygmies) and the Kalahari Desert (the Bushmen and Hottentots). Their diet is varied, rich in vitamins and animal products of various kinds (rodents, lizards, snails and insects). It is subject to frequent fluctuations of quantity and quality because they keep no stocks and the supplies are irregular. Today, most of these societies live in symbiosis with their nonnomadic neighbors. The pastoral nomads were originally strictly dependent on their herds, drinking most of their milk and occasionally eating their meat. They often trade by barter with the settled farmers, who were once subject to them. It is paradoxical that the basic food of the Mauri and the Bororo should be millet rather than meat or milk, which may be their only resource at certain times of the year.

The problem of storing grain and tubers has, on the whole, been solved by African societies, but meat and fish are often eaten in such a state of decomposition that long habit must have inured the Africans to its dire consequences. The business of marketing and distributing food products has retained its individual or family character in rural Africa. Although famines, due to shortages of cereals and tubers, can be avoided, perishable products are only rarely made available to rural consumers.

Quite apart from material factors, diet is determined by numerous social patterns in which ideas concerning art, religion, magic and morality have a part. These cultural patterns embrace eating habits formed in infancy and are very deeply rooted. The frequency with which eating, famine, stealing food and characters like the Greedy Clown are mentioned in oral literature may reflect a fear of starvation coupled with the shock of weaning and the irregularities of food supply in rural societies. There are countless food taboos: permanent or temporary bans are imposed on certain foodstuffs or methods of preparation for particular persons or social groups. The best known are the totemic prohibitions, forbidding any group or individual to eat the meat of the animal whose name he bears and whose descendant he is supposed to be. Permanent prohibitions include, for instance, the eating of chickens and eggs by women in some societies. Some people with special functions —soothsayers and priests—may not eat the flesh of sacrificed animals. Temporary prohibitions often cover the crucial moments of life such as birth, initiation, pregnancy, breast-feeding, weaning and various illnesses.

Foods and meals often symbolize a reality beyond the act of eating; to eat sorghum in Chad or millet in Senegal is to absorb the "daily bread" dispensed by kindly gods. In social relationships, too, food customs are significant; for example, to offer a mother-in-law roast chicken during her visit is a public gesture indicating how attentive and prosperous her son-in-law is. In many African societies (for example, among the Dogon and Bambara), myths about the structure of the universe provide a complicated system of classification covering foodstuffs. In plain language, the gods and spirits of the African pantheons are associated with certain types of foods; these are the foods that they purvey and that they are also happy to accept in sacrifice. The impact of magico-religious beliefs on eating habits results in countless fine distinctions between secular and ritual food, between cooked and raw, grilled and boiled, unseasoned and salted, crops and herds, things hunted and things gathered. To serve food and eat is also to communicate with the spirit world through sacrifices and communal feasts. An example of this is found among the Mussoi, who, at the end of initiation ceremonies, invite the neophytes in the bush to eat dishes which until then they had thought were eaten by spirits.

Preparing a feast is a way of demonstrating rank, riches and prestige through the quality and abundance of food that is consumed or offered to guests. There is a sharp distinction between the food of the rich and that of the poor, between the ostentatious repast and the furtive snack when times are hard. Most major events of communal life—marriages, births, funerals —are accompanied by feasts whose ostentation borders on extravagance and which are public displays of the host's prosperity. Numerous factors in the current development of African society tend to eliminate differences between various dietary customs and to make the eating habits of urban black Africans more widespread among nonurban peoples. However, these changes are merely bringing about a modification in the symbolic content of the diet. In place of the traditional foodstuffs which were considered gifts of the gods, we find up-to-date foods, which are expensive and advertise the wealth of those who buy them. This background explains the craze for bleached rice, ready-made couscous, bread, stockfish, canned foods and alcohol, the heavy consumption of which is tending to become one of the principal signs of wealth. (See also *Breasts; Meals; Meat; Sacrifices; Taboos; Vegetables.*) I.G.

DIVINATION. Gods and powers of all kinds constantly make their presence felt in the world of men; there is no event in the life of an individual or the community that they

Small objects used in divination. Angola. Musée de l'Homme, Paris. *Museum photo.*

cannot affect. So men must be able to decipher the meaning of these manifestations correctly, and, when these meanings are wrongly interpreted, or not clearly expressed, or need confirmation, then the gods must be interrogated and consulted. This is done in various ways: by listening to an oracle, by observing the convulsions of an animal being sacrificed or by enforcing a trial by ordeal such as administering a poisonous substance that will distinguish the innocent from the guilty. Whatever method is adopted, interpretation is necessary, and this is sometimes very difficult. Most often, soothsaying, in the strict sense, is employed in order to discover the causes and the remedies necessary in a given situation. The diviner—"the man who speaks of hidden things," as many Sudanese people call him— knows precise techniques for asking questions and understanding the answers. Whether it is a matter of fixing the date of a ceremony so that it may take place without hindrance, choosing a king from among several claimants, deciding about a marriage or some other undertaking, embarking upon a journey or a warlike expedition, discovering the cause of death or an illness, obtaining news of an absent friend or finding out one's destiny in order to be able to conform to the powers that govern it, the soothsayer is always indispensable. In hierarchical societies, all the leading figures, and especially the king, had soothsayers attached to them, whom they consulted before taking any political action. Soothsayers in all societies were at the disposition of every person. The soothsayer, without having any authority himself, was a key figure in each group and was capable of influencing everything that happened.

The soothsayer had to know not only divining techniques, but also the myths and the vast body of legends on which the techniques were based. These gave him either stock answers to all basic questions or illustrations, with mythical overtones, of every situation in which a man could find himself. The missionary H. A. Junod, talking about soothsaying among the Thonga in southeastern Africa, said: "It is admirably suited to the needs of the natives because it corresponds to every element in their lives and photographs them, so to speak, in such a way that guidance and direction can be obtained in every possible situation." The diviner also had a good knowledge of men and their problems, which he acquired through observation and confidences he received. Among the best soothsayers, skill in divination was complemented by a profound intuitive sense.

Unless the diviner was in the service of the king, it was rare for him to practice his art fulltime. One could be a diviner by heredity. Usually, however, a young man who thought he had the necessary qualities of memory and perspicacity and wanted to go beyond the limited popular knowledge of divination would ask to be initiated by a soothsayer. But this initiation could take a long time, for, besides instruction, it entailed the collection of the equipment necessary for divination. Sometimes a pupil went from one master to another, but not all apprentices were capable of acquiring a complete knowledge of techniques and myths or, most important of all, had the necessary subtlety. Moreover, soothsayers varied in quality and reputation; some could only solve simple problems; most were both healers and magicians and treated their patients in the light of the answers they received.

African divining techniques are quite numerous. In the same society, several different techniques of varying complexity and refinement, which may be practiced by different specialists, are often used. The simplest method of all is that of the short straw, performed with the aid of small sticks. Many are more elaborate. Divination by examining an animal's entrails is most common in pastoral societies. Divination with the help of wild animals used to be practiced only by hunters, but it has sometimes survived the transformation of lifestyle of former hunting peoples. Interpretation of a pattern obtained by throwing a series of identical or different objects—which may be grain, pebbles, cowrie shells, small bones or palm nuts—is probably the most widely used method; it has elaborate forms, which sometimes merge into geomancy. There is also divination by observing reflections in water, muscular tremors, or unconscious movements of the body such as that of a hand holding a stick. The only type of divination that is almost unknown in Africa is astrological soothsaying. Complex forms of divination have led to the manufacture of all sorts of things—trays, cups, bells and sticks—that may be magnificent works of art if they are carved, like those found among the Venda of southeastern Africa and the Yoruba and neighboring tribes. Following are three examples of different divining systems taken from three contrasting regions.

The Dogon use the jackal for divining, and this method derives directly from one of their great myths. According to legend, the jackal is an avatar of the first creature, born of the god of heaven and of the earth. When the jackal rebelled and was confident of victory,

Divination by examining the orientation of the flame of a candle. Bahutu. Rwanda. *Photo: Jacques Maquet.*

it danced on the terrace of the sky and its paws left traces which spelled out the "First Word." Because it was the recipient of this First Word, it can reveal god's secrets. In the Dogon method, a divining table laid out in a complicated manner—each of its rectangles having a particular meaning—is covered with sand. In the evening, the sand is carefully smoothed and questions are asked by the soothsayer. Lured by bait set out by the soothsayer, the jackal comes at night, tramping on the sand spread over the divining table. The next morning, the soothsayer reads the traces left by the jackal's paws and gives his interpretation.

The Thonga and many other tribes in southeastern Africa practice divination with the aid of small bones, in a method that is only loosely connected with definite religious beliefs. The questioner throws bones and similar objects. By observing the exact position of each object (four positions—front, back, and sides—are possible), the frequency of each position in a series of throws, the direction in which the object points, the position of one object in relation to others, the diviner works out the answers to the questions put to him. The bones are taken both from domestic and wild animals: the former are meant to represent the inhabitants of the village, classed according to age and sex; the latter represent deities, different forces and special laws. Along with bones, shells (including cowrie shells) and stones may be thrown. The origin of each object and the circumstances under which it was obtained are significant. Together they form a picture of the world and the community. The consultant is represented by some personal possession, generally a necklace that is decorated with amulets.

Tray used in the divination cult of Fa. A portrait of the god is among the decorations. Yoruba. Dahomey. Wood. Paul Tishman Collection, New York. *Photo: Musée de l'Homme.*

Divination by sorting red and white beans into odd and even groups. Massa. Chad. *Photo: Pierre Ichac.*

Every situation in which a man may find himself is expressed by the distances separating these objects and the directions in which they point. Once the way is "open," the consultation can take a long time. The soothsayer gropes his way forward, occasionally retreating a bit, but gradually closing in on the revelation he is seeking. He very rarely gives up because the bones "do not wish to speak."

Geomancy is widespread in Sudanese Africa and further east; it is of eastern origin. Many tribes have developed it in special ways. Among the Yoruba and throughout the Benin region—where it is most commonly practiced—the most elaborate system has evolved. The diviner throws palm nuts rapidly from one hand to the other and, according to whether the left hand is finally holding one or two nuts, he draws one or two lines on the ground or on white powder spread on a tray. This is repeated eight times in order to obtain a pattern of eight signs. There are 256 possible combinations, the 16 principal patterns of which are symmetrical groupings and duplicates. These patterns are the *Du*—the signs of Fa (or fate), his "sons," and the forms of the words of the gods in his power. Each man is born under a sign of Fa, and the number of destinies possible for him is therefore limited. Through revelation, he can discover what his *Du* is and then worship it. In all consultation, his own *Du* must be reckoned with as well as the one that has just been drawn by chance. The *Du* of his country, his family, his father and the ancestor from whom he is descended must also be taken into account. The number of possible combinations is therefore enormous. The signs are only keys which open up a rich mythology in which Fa and the *Du,* either singly or in groups, are the actors. This mythology and the spiritual realities that it expresses or suggests are the sources of the answers that the diviner fashions and the advice he gives. (See also *Initiation; Ordeals; Sorcery; Spiders; Voodoo; Yoruba.*) P.M.

DIVINITIES. A complex and sometimes confusing hierarchy of powers extends from a host of petty spirits and genii and most recent ancestors to god the creator. The various powers may be regarded as simple intermediaries between the supreme god and men; they may also enjoy a large degree of independence, which is the criterion for divine status. But these divinities are not always clearly distinguishable in the multiform society of the other world of which they form a part. Sometimes they absorb the nature of the supreme god, as the sky gods Maw and Lissa have done in Dahomey, and real polytheism is established. They may be transformations of this god, like the gods of thunder and lightning of the Masai in East Africa. But no matter how specialized they may be or what role they play in governing the powers of the universe they may also be identified with ancestors. Each great Yoruba *orisha* appears to have been the divinity of one of the clans and its founding father before becoming the object of general worship because of the particular powers attributed to him. In East Africa, the great founder ancestors are frequently regrouped in a pantheon around the sky god or may even obscure him completely, as among the Shilluk of the upper Nile. Divinities also form part of the world of spirits and of powers that inhabit particular places. In principle, they are not connected with a certain spot, or are not any longer, but there are compromises and exceptions. A divinity, the earth god, for example, can absorb and then transcend his many different local manifestations, which were originally separate and individually named powers to which villages attached themselves.

The great cosmic deities who often figure in the drama of creation constitute the most important category. Heaven and Earth begot a son, Thunder, who later rebelled against his father and committed incest with his mother. This is the Ibibio myth of the three primary gods. Among many tribes, one or two water gods are added to this trio, and when these four great deities coexist, their hierarchy varies from one tribe to another. They are not always personified precisely; they are sometimes the elements, or else the elements are merely their dwelling place. In the Volta region, among others, Earth is sometimes the chief deity, but in any case its worship is important everywhere. The Bobo describe Earth as a hermaphrodite, the origin of all things. Elsewhere, it is the god of heaven who has generally made the earth fruitful. The worship of the earth is frequently associated with particular sacred places or with certain animals which are its messengers. Among the Bobo, the land priest is often the most important person in the community, the arbiter and the man of peace, because Earth detests murder. In the western Sudan, water is often the chief object of worship. Among the Bambara, Faro, the leading member of their cosmogony, took the form of water when he created life on earth. The Dogon Nommo has many aspects: he is the son of Heaven and Earth, the Ancestor, and the hero who brought civilization. The waters are his chosen element; he is manifested by them—in their currents, their reflections and their fish. In one of his aspects, Nommo is united with the divinities associated with atmospheric

phenomena. These occupy an important position among the tribes of eastern and southeastern Africa. The Bakamba and Suk of Kenya place a god of storms and one of rain on either side of the supreme god. Among all these people, the rainmaker is a central figure, and he sometimes wields political power.

Although they too rule the forces of nature, the deities of the more systematic polytheist religions have different characteristics. They often evolve from ancestral gods, and they are very numerous, but of varying importance. It is not possible to enumerate the *obosom* of the Ashanti or the *orisha* of the Yoruba. Because of affinities between some of them, they have gradually been grouped into families, families ruled by one of them or, more often, by a pair, and in which each deity has a particular, well-defined task. In the celestial pantheon of Dahomey, for example, one is the guardian of trees, others of animals, birds, or the home. Each family has some degree of independence from the other families, although they recognize each other and sometimes include each other's members. Each family has its own language, so that, in Dahomey, the god Legba and, among the Yoruba, the god Eshu, act as interpreters and messengers to prevent Olympus from turning into Babel.

Many African mythologies recount the adventures of gods—their conflicts, violence, ruses and loves. These adventures are made all the more complicated as a result of the fact that each great deity is often the result of a fusion of several deities with the same attributes. The pantheons have their clergy, temples and initiates who answer the call of the gods. Newcomers were always welcome. As in all polytheist religions, there are no jealous gods; new deities, new beliefs, introduced through migrations, wars and mixed marriages were accepted and quickly integrated. The Benin region, where polytheism flourishes as nowhere else in Africa, provides the best example of these prolific and fluid societies composed of divinities. (See also *Dreams; Fetishes; Gods; Heaven; Heroes; Spirits and Genii.*) P.M.

DOGON. The Dogon occupy the mountainous region called the Bandiagara Escarpment; this is the area southwest of the bend of the Niger River, in the Republic of Mali. According to the last census, there are 225,000 Dogon, and this is certainly a low estimate. Since 1931, their distinct and lively culture has been the object of detailed research by the Griaule expeditions. The Dogon claim common origin with the

Dogon religious statuette. Mali. Wood. Sir Jacob Epstein Collection, London. *Photo: Eliot Elisofon.*

Painting on stone of an antelope mask. Dogon-Pignari. Mali. Musée de l'Homme, Paris. *Photo: Giraudon.*

Baboon. Mask for a Dogon dance. Wood. Mali. Musée de l'Homme, Paris. *Photo: Eliot Elisofon.*

Mande tribes. However, the Dogon language, according to evidence provided by the latest research, belongs to the Voltaic group, although its relationship to other languages in the group seems to be fairly distant. The country is marked by a vast rocky plateau that ends abruptly in the southeast in a ridge about 125 miles long. The absence of permanent waterholes and the scarcity of arable land on the plateau and cliffs have forced the inhabitants to husband the soil carefully. They grow millet and some other cereals, raise small livestock and are excellent gardeners and tree growers. The recently developed cultivation of onions offers the only means of production for export.

The nucleus of society is formed by the extended family, grouped together under the authority of a patriarch. Each quarter of the village is composed of one or several large family houses, which contain the altars of the family's ancestors and are surrounded by the dwellings of other members of the group. Authority in the family hierarchy is exercised by the patriarch and in the village by a council of elders. The ultimate arbiter is the Hogon, the oldest man in a district and its religious leader. Filiation is patrilineal and residence is patrilocal.

The ambivalence of the human being, conceived as both male and female in body and psyche, produces a dualist vision of the universe. The great complementary opposites that are derived from this concept (life/death, order/disorder, night/day, humidity/drought) condition the whole cultural and material life of the Dogon. Emotion (female) and intellect (male), each possessing a positive and negative aspect, provide the four poles of self-identification. Upon these are superimposed the four poles of social organization: attachment to a totem and the maternal family, for the female element in the individual, and to the paternal family and the age group, for the male element in the individual. He is given four names, corresponding to these four divisions of society and to the relations that he has with each. Four poles are also found in the religious organization: the cult of the totem, the cult of Lebe or the earth-mother, the cult of the father-god Amma, and the cult of the Pale Fox, a mythical figure who is the incarnation of revolt and disorder and also of the emancipation of the individual from social conventions.

The creation myth plays an important part in this symbolic interpretation of the universe. Amma placed the seeds of future beings inside the first placenta, which was to become earth, but one of these beings emerged prematurely into the world and sowed disorder there. He was changed into a fox as a punishment and is in perpetual conflict with his twin, Nommo, who was sacrificed and resurrected to reorganize creation. Nommo represents fecundity and life triumphing over death, as well as man overcoming his destructive, Oedipal instincts and thereby becoming a responsible member of the community. The cult of the totem is dedicated to the different parts of Nommo's dismembered body, which are related to different animal and vegetable species, according to a network of symbolic correspondences that constitute the various categories of the universe.

Worship of the dead is an essential element of Dogon religion. The society of masks has a dominant position in funeral rites. Its principal aim is to assist in the transmission of part of the dead person's vital force to a child of his lineage, who will then offer his worship consisting mainly of libations whose purpose is to give him back a little life. Death thus fits into the Dogon perspective of resurrection and fecundity, which are the main preoccupations of this society whose dynamic force is directed toward the future and survival. (See also *Dreams; Masks; Myths; Philosophy; Priests; Religion; Societies, Secret.*)   G.C.-G.

DOLLS. Dolls and ritual figurines should not be confused. In many societies of initiates, the instruction given to the young neophytes includes the display of statuettes, made from a great variety of materials and

Dan dolls. Ivory Coast.
Pyrography on raffia;
earrings of copper wire; hair
of raffia fibers. *Photo: Musée
de l'Homme, Hugo Zemp.*

Basari doll. Senegal. Pottery
head; corncob body swathed
in cotton bands which are
held in place with red glass
bead ornaments; necklace
and earrings of aluminum.
Musée de l'Homme, Paris.
Museum photo.

with more or less elaborate techniques. Objects with a considerable didactic significance have been called "dolls" for a long time. In the same way, sculptures of the dead —chiefs, ancestors and tribal heroes, even divinities and spirits of special importance— used to be called indiscriminately dolls or fetishes. Admittedly, the dividing line between the ritual or magic figurines and the dolls that little girls play with is not always easily discernible. There are, for example, the *ibeji* of the Yoruba (Nigeria and Dahomey) and the *akua'ba* of the Ashanti (Ghana). The *ibeji*, a sculpture made when a twin dies (a pair of dead twins is represented by a pair of statuettes), is fed, clothed and tidied every day and is the family's substitute for a dead child. It is always carved realistically in wood, but with many stylistic variations. *Ibeji* may be very humorous, aesthetically sensitive and harmonious, severe or appealing, and many of them are beautifully modeled. An *akua'ba* is generally made of black wood with a fine patina. It consists of a broad flat disc on a long neck with rings and a cylindrical body with two small short arms and is nearly always legless. It is carried by women who want a child or by pregnant women in order, it is said, that "the

child may have a neck as long and a head as beautiful" as the doll. These two examples of the clothing, carrying and tending of a piece of sculpture very closely resemble playing with dolls.

Playing with a doll prepares the young girl for motherhood, but the doll is primarily a toy. Even the making of it, either by the child herself or by an elder sister or relative, is already a game requiring observation and manual skill. The many forms of this art of childhood range from the simple peeled corncob, found in Mali and Zambezi, to the wax doll, which is a real sculpture with delicate coils of wax threads imitating the crested hairstyle of a Fulani lady. In Senegal and Mali, corncobs, mutton bones, fruit such as guava and pomegranates, rolls of wax, rags, glass beads, pieces of wood and

Doll made by a little Kotoko girl. Cameroun. Wax. Musée de l'Homme, Paris. *Museum photo.*

stems of plants are all used and successfully combined: in one place, the outer leaves of an ear of corn are woven into plaits; in another, the tibia of a goat becomes a body and a fragment of bamboo tied across it suggests two outstretched arms; in yet another, a piece of yellow wax represents a nose and two balls of yellow wax form the breasts, which the artist finishes with two tips of black wax; elegant, long skirts are made from printed European fabrics, while head ornaments, necklaces, belts, eyes and sometimes even teeth are made from small glass beads. At the other end of the continent, in southern Africa, the most ingenious imitations of human beings are found in dolls made of leather, glasswork or fruits stuck together with resin. In Lesotho and particularly Botswana, multicolored beads are used to cover a body made of grass stems and fall from the head like braids; the clothing underneath is leather, and beads suggest all kinds of ornaments. In these dolls, as in many others in black Africa, small white beads portray eyes, nostrils and mouth. (See also *Games.*)   J.D.

DREAMS. Some Australian aborigines use one word to designate the mythical era, the totem and dreams. In thus associating the symbolism of time, the gods and the hidden being of man, they reveal their delicate understanding of the nature of dreams. Interpretations of myths and interpretations of dreams are arrived at through similar processes; both myths and dreams are means of communication with sacred things, and both furnish the instruments with which to "penetrate the mysteries by force." The dream is, in broad terms, a means of acquiring profound knowledge and knowledge of the future. Since classical times, it has also been viewed as serving a therapeutic function; the "therapists" of the Jordan Valley and the shores of the Dead Sea used dreams for this purpose.

African societies and civilizations evolved their theories of dreams and the key necessary to decipher them at an early stage. For the Dogon, dreams are "words" associated with their mythical fox; it is that "which comes out of the night," an intermediary of the dead; it is an obsessive riddle requiring interpretation; it is an inner monologue with a divinatory character. The Dogon know that dreams rise from the depths of the human being, from that level of instinct which is ill-controlled by reason and which they call "animal." They ascribe all forms of divination to dreams, except for that which is done by priests with prophetic gifts. Dreams are an expression of their

wishes for the future and their fear of trampling on the rights of Amma, the creator-god, who alone "has power over things to come."

Dreams often appear as the speech of ancestors, confined in subterranean haunts, transmitting their messages to their living descendants and thereby continuing to convey their criticisms and advice. If a dream is not sufficiently clear, the techniques of divination are employed to elucidate its meaning; the Thonga of southern Africa, for example, consult small bones for enlightenment. It is through the language of dreams that divinities and spirits, too, make their revelations and transmit their instructions about ritual practices, techniques or the use of new tools. The Kurumba of Upper Volta believe that it was a dream that taught Aguni, their ancestor, the use of the cleft ax, which has to be employed in sacrifices honoring a water spirit who is the dispenser of millet. Among the Sara of the central Chari Valley, it was through a recurrent dream that the "inventor" of the xylophone learned how to shape and use the instrument. A spirit taught him, in this way, all "the different rhythms" and how to tune "the thing." Sculptors of masks are inspired at times by the forms in which hidden powers appear to them in dreams. The diviner's skill is often enhanced by recourse to revelations that appear in dreams prior to a consultation. In the lands of the Banen in Cameroun, the diviner uses a powder obtained from bark to stimulate the visions that will haunt him in his sleep and give him the necessary guidance for future interpretations.

The majority of African tribes possess a "key to dreams," but the most systematic knowledge of this kind is found in areas influenced by Islam and reflects the science of the Arabic *mu'abbir.* The Wolof of Senegal use a very comprehensive table of dreams, which includes discussion of the elements, colors, animals, types of people and movements. The same precise details are given for the most propitious conditions under which to dream—the times of night (after midnight) and seasons of the year (April) and purified places—as well as for ablutions, formulas and prayers to stimulate dreams. These ritual requirements exclude the use of neither hallucinogenic drugs nor magic. The Wolof have developed a science of dreams which indicates their importance in daily life. This applies to all societies in which the limits of reality are imprecise and in which a person is responsible for the wandering of his soul while he is asleep. The Ashanti of Ghana are an outstanding example of people who believe in the overlapping of dreams and life; they condemn the dream of adultery in the same way that they condemn adultery itself. (See also *Spirits and Genii*.)　　　　G.B.

DRUM LANGUAGE. Out of all the different types of African sonic communication other than speech, it is drum language—the "bush telegraph," as it is commonly called—that has aroused the greatest interest. Even where it is not the only means of transmitting calls, alarm signals, commands and messages of every kind over small or large distances, it is found in a great variety of forms. It varies according to the subject and character of the information as well as according to the type of drum used (membrane drum, wooden drum with two lips or two tongues or xylophone drum with two or three bars) and, even more important, according to the number of instruments played and the number of drummers. Drum language is really a special kind of secret language: only initiated listeners can understand its meaning, which is conveyed by an irregular succession of drum beats. It may be based on the "tones" of the spoken language to the extent that these tones are distinguished by very marked contrasts in pitch or intensity; the melodic pattern arrived at in this way is arranged rhythmically, relying on the value of the musical notes—whether they are whole notes or fractional notes (half notes, quarter notes, eighth notes, etc.). Either two or three instruments of the same type but of different registers—low, medium or high—or a single drum that varies in sound or timbre according to where or how it is struck may be used. But when two men simultaneously beat a pair of wooden drums or even a single drum, as is done among tribes in upper Guinea, then each drummer may perform a distinct function, one transmitting the messages and the other beating out a continuous monotone, like a rapid metronome. The second drummer does not just keep the beat; the continuous drum roll has a timbre all its own and seems to be admired like certain percussive effects or the playing of glissandi on Western musical instruments. No one has sufficiently investigated the various reasons, practical or otherwise, for the use of drum language. Black people themselves speak of its early use in their domestic wars, but without distinguishing between communication by means of drums, whistles or trumpets. One of the first instruments European travelers described as probably capable of "conveying every meaning" (Pigafetta, *Regnum Congo,* 1598) had strings that were plucked and was

Banda drummers. Republic of Central Africa. *Photo: Viollet, Roger.*

vaguely designated by the term "lute." That an instrument could do this seemed highly improbable, and Cyrano de Bergerac, inspired by the tale, attributes this form of expression to the inhabitants of the moon. But since Bergerac's time, it has been discovered that the musical bow, the most primitive stringed instrument, is used to direct dance movements in initiation rituals held along the border between Guinea and Liberia. It was more or less in this region, and in the context of these initiation dances, that the wooden drum was discovered in the seventeenth century. The bow, the weapon used for hunting or war, has had almost equally widespread usage in Africa as a musical or sound-producing instrument. The music performed on it is based on one or two series of harmonic sounds that are distinguished and amplified, one at a time, by means of a sounding board, which is usually the human mouth. The wooden drum, the principal instrument used in the forest, symbolizes, above all, the secret rites that are practiced there. In the forest, initiation generally includes physical exercises, not unlike military training, and also includes displays of aggression, such as attacking villages or pillaging fields. Most of the standard drum messages, which novice boys learn to decode, represent proper nouns—to be more precise, the cognomens of "the forest"—or they give orders and direct movements, which are all things applicable to dancing as well as to military operations. Girls may be submitted to similar training during a period of retreat in the forest; they may form a dance group whose movements are controlled by the sounds of instruments that are either used exclusively by women or are in common use among both sexes, for example, rattles and bells. (See also *Drums; Mottoes; Music; Names.*)   A.S.

DRUMS. The term "drum" applies to two completely different types of instruments: drums without skins and drums over which one or two membranes are stretched. Among the former is the wooden or slit-drum (in German, *Schlitztrommel*), which is often wrongly called a gong or tomtom. It is found in Oceania, in southern and Southeast Asia and among American Indians, as well as in western and equatorial Africa. Its existence in Africa was first noted in the second half of the seventeenth century. The earliest references to it state that it was used in initiation rituals or for drum language, the same purposes for which it is employed today. Generally it is made of a cylindrical piece of wood, split lengthwise down one side and partly scooped out inside. The instrument is struck on either side of the orifice. There are two types of slit-drums: lip-drums and tongue-drums. In the former, the edges of the slit are straight and the two sides of the drum are not of the same thickness nor of the same curvature. In the latter, both sides of the slit have a rectangular projection that overhangs the cavity and is struck like the bars of a xylophone. When they are tuned to different pitches, the two tongues or lips produce sounds about a third or a quarter of a tone apart. Only lip-drums can be played in pairs or in groups of three, with a sound-range covering less than an octave (for example, those in upper Guinea and the Ubangi Valley). Drummed codes are based as much on contrasting sounds as on different combinations of rhythm. Wooden drums vary greatly in size: the smallest, which are portable, can be carried in the hands or hung on the backs of dancers and are no more than eight inches long; the largest may measure ten or more feet. Many are decorated; not only are they temporarily painted for rituals, but the sides may be carved, in high or low relief, with animals, human figures or geometric patterns. Sometimes a sculpture in the round projects from one end, as in the drums of Guinea, the Ivory Coast and Cameroun, or the entire instrument may be carved in the shape of an animal, like the wooden drums made in the Ubangi Valley in the form of cattle.

Two other types of instruments are related to the wooden drum: scrapers, made of wood or iron and shaped like the lip-drum except that the sides of the crack are cut in grooves which are scraped with a small stick or an iron rod (Mali); and xylophone drums, whose sides have several parallel cracks that separate from two to four bars resembling those of a xylophone and varying in length and width. These instruments are used in male initiation rituals in the forest in upper Guinea and northern Liberia.

In western Africa, Muslim tribes or those living near Islamic areas play what they call "water-drums," consisting of saucer-shaped calabashes floating in a vessel of water. They are beaten either with bare hands, with spoons (also made from calabashes) or with small sticks. This type of percussion

Yangere slit-drum. Republic of Central Africa. Wood. Musée de l'Homme, Paris. *Museum photo.*

instrument, which is known elsewhere in various forms, was originally used exclusively by women at the end of Ramadan or during the eclipse of the moon or to accompany dancers possessed by spirits. In southern Dahomey, its rhythm accompanies funeral songs. In Mali and Niger, half-calabashes, similarly inverted but placed on the ground, are played in groups of from three to eight exorcisors or griots.

One last type of drum without a membrane remains to be discussed. This is a drum made from a spherical clay vase. The neck opening of the vase is beaten with cowhide or a fan of palm leaves, and the body of the vase acts as the sounding chamber. The body is sometimes pierced with a second opening, which the player can close with his hand. This pot-drum is used in Dahomey as a funeral instrument and is also found among the Ibo in Nigeria. A large calabash is sometimes used instead of a ceramic vessel.

Membrane drums are found all over Africa. Tribes which do not make any themselves borrow them from neighbors for secular dances as well as for rituals. They vary in shape and in the way the skin is attached. Their variety is unequaled on any other continent. One-membrane drums are made either with a rectangular frame or with a cylindrical, truncated cone-shaped, ovoid or semicircular body that serves as a sounding chamber; the base may be open or closed. When the drum is cylindrical, the lower part may narrow and then widen to form a kind of stand or vase; otherwise, it rests on three or four feet. Two-membrane drums have bodies shaped like cylinders or truncated cones that sometimes bulge outward or contract midway, so that they look like hourglasses. The bodies of these drums are carved out of tree trunks, but there are membrane drums made of pottery and from the fruit of baobab and calabash trees. In Ethiopia, princely or royal kettledrums have bodies made of copper or silver. The single-skin instruments are the oldest drums in the world, with the exception of drums constructed on frames and kettledrums, and are purely African in origin. They are also very decorative compared with two-skin drums, which have no ornamentation at all, except south of the Congo River. Membrane drums are often used for religious purposes, and these drums can be immense. Some stand upright on the ground, like those in the Ivory Coast and Cameroun, while others, whose bodies, are shaped like cylindrical vases, are poised on top of a piece of sculpture or a tiered stand decorated with a variety of carvings, as in Guinea. In Gabon and the lower Congo region, the smallest

Conical cylinder drum mounted on a horse. Baga. Guinea. Painted wood. Musée de l'Homme, Paris. *Museum photo.*

drums are also set up in this manner. Sometimes, the sides of the support form a small recess enclosing figures that are carved in the round and painted.

The tension of the skin is obtained in various ways. If it is stuck or nailed to the edge of the body of the drum, the skin is restretched by warming it near a fire each time the drum is used. The same procedure is followed with drums whose skin is sewn on, is attached by "buttonholes" to pegs or is stretched with interlacing thongs or lianas that cover the body with either loose or tight meshwork. Two other methods of attaching the membrane allow for the tension to be controlled directly: the edge of the skin, having been rolled around a hoop, may be stretched either by pegs or by wedges driven home with a hammer. On instruments with two skins, the edges of the skins may also be attached to hoops; in this case, a thong going from one hoop to the other forms a pattern of *N*s, *W*s or *Y*s around the body. The skins are always fully stretched, and the pitch is determined by the size of the sounding board. Only small drums shaped like hourglasses have variable pitch; they are held

Baule vertical drum. Ivory Coast. Wood. Musée de l'Homme, Paris. *Photo: Sougez.*

under the armpit, and the arm presses on the thongs binding the two hoops.

Skins are beaten either with the palm, fist or fingertips of the hand or with straight or curved sticks. One end of a two-skin drum may be beaten with the hand and the other with a stick. Only the West African kettle-drum is beaten with a leather stick stuffed with cotton seed, which in earlier times may have been a mummified hand. Players of large instruments have to climb a rock, a scaffolding or a step carved in the body itself. Drums are often played in pairs of different sizes, or they can be arranged to form orchestras such as the royal orchestras in East Africa, which include up to fifteen drums of the same type whose pitches range from low to high.

Friction-drums are found in different parts of Africa. The skin may simply be rubbed with a small brush or set vibrating by a small stick pressed against it and rubbed with a wet or oiled hand; however, the more usual method is for a stem or cord, one end of which protrudes through a hole in the middle of the skin, to pass through the inside of the body and to be rubbed at the other end. Henry Balfour has suggested a connection between this kind of friction-drum and a blacksmith's bellows, which have been used in Africa since ancient Egyptian times. The sound produced is similar to that of the roaring of a wild beast, hence its common name of "leopard-drum." Generally, this instrument is kept hidden like the bull-roarer and, like it, used for initiation rituals. (See also *Calabashes; Dance; Drum Language; Music; Sculpture, Wood; Song; Work.*)
A.S.

DWELLINGS. African house construction is conditioned by material resources, social realities and economic systems, but African architecture, to a greater degree than that elsewhere, is governed by rules that correspond to a fixed religious reality and is the product of profound original thought. Within the limits of certain principal types of dwellings, each corresponding to a particular area, the appearance of houses varies greatly throughout the continent: the houses of the forest zones, the round dwellings and the vast buildings of the savanna, and the shelters of nomads and seminomads offer considerable diversity. The actual construction is the work of family groups. There are few specialized workmen, and the labor is divided among men, women and children. The only standard of measurement is the human body, which determines the dimensions and proportions of buildings.

Dwellings in the African forest regions are like those in Madagascar: they are rectangular, and their walls consist of a latticework frame, woven from plant materials such as small sticks, bamboo or reeds, coated with puddled clay. The roofs, which are gabled, have two or, occasionally, four surfaces and are made of wattling covered with folded palm leaves, raffia or sometimes sheets of bark. In certain regions—in Cameroun, among the Ndiki, for instance—the buildings may be quite large, but these are more than individual houses. They consist of a collection of dwellings sheltering several families; the rooms, which are separated by partitions, are shared with small family herds. The only real exceptions in the forest belt are the round structures with high pointed roofs found in Guinea and Liberia. One unusual architectural technique has been developed on the edge of the forest and savanna by the Bamileke of southwest Cameroun, who manage to construct square buildings surmounted by immense conical roofs.

On the other hand, dwellings in the savanna, which are of two basic types, display very great variety. One type is circular or, occasionally, oval, as among the Basuto, and has a pointed roof; the other comprises massive abodes that remind one of what is wrongly called "Arab architecture." Each type has a style of its own, and on the basic circle, the form of which determines both the shape of houses and their location, each tribe stamps its own personality. Walls are usually made of mud or puddled clay, rarely of stone; they support light roofs made of sticks and thatch, which are put together on the ground and then hoisted by hand when completed.

There are numerous dwellings that are only single units, with or without exterior granaries, such as those of the Baganda and Wakamba of Uganda, the Mossi of Upper Volta and the Walamba of Zambia. Oval buildings, likewise consisting of single units for each family, are found mainly among some Bantu and among the Ijebu in northern Nigeria; here, the roof forms a long, tapering appendage and the space inside it is divided into storerooms for grain. The finest of these houses are those of the Musgu in Chad. They are conical in shape and covered with uniform projections that serve as steps. No tool but the bare hands of the builders was used to make them. With their magnificent and harmonious facades, they are as much products of the potter's art as they are of architecture. It often happens, especially in agricultural areas, that a habitation is developed to such an extent that it comprises dozens of separate buildings, which only

Dogon cliff village. Mali.
Photo: Hoa-Qui.

Bamileke houses. Cameroun.
Photo: Hoa-Qui.

Senufo houses and
granaries. Ivory Coast.
Photo: Hugo Zemp.

Mossi dwelling. Upper Volta.
Photo: Hoa-Qui.

and cubic buildings are not often found side
by side, except among the Dogon of Mali
and the Kurumba of Upper Volta, where this
practice is common. The variation in size of
the houses of the savanna peoples is not
caused by class distinctions; it depends
basically on the size of the family groups,
who must adapt the number of shelters that
they build to the growth of their families, the
increase of their herds and the accumulation
of their grain.

The area that divides the savanna from the
Sahel is characterized by a distinct type of
architecture featuring vast edifices made of
puddled clay which are square or rectangular
in shape, often multistoried, surmounted by
terraces and built around large courtyards.
This type of architecture is found in
Timbuktu and Gao, Chad, northern Cameroun, the Hausa and Bornu territories, and
in the principalities of the Kotoko. Baked
brick is rare, except in Mauritania, where it
was brought by masons of North African
origin and is used only in some princely
houses in the ancient capitals of Ouara,
Birni-Ngazargamou, and Boum-Massenia.

The African dwelling has more than
geographical and social significance; it has
religious meaning as well. The life of the
individual and the group, in its material,
familial, social and spiritual aspects, unfolds
there in a setting whose living symbolism is
apparent every hour of every day, in every
part of the house and down to its smallest
details. The house, in black Africa, places
man into constant contact with the cosmos
to which he belongs and with which he
identifies himself. The human abode,
representing the earth, is in communication
with the heavens. The African house,
whether rustic or splendid, is the product of a
functional architecture in which art is based
on cosmological concepts and social systems; these concepts and systems require
artistic expression to develop within the
limits of symbolism that conveys the group's
world view. The rules of construction, which
were slowly elaborated by generations of
builders, have apparently not been changed
for centuries. Every detail of this exacting art
is dictated by traditions which the architect
respects; every aspect of the building has a
personal significance; every piece of material
is chosen carefully and worked according to
precise rules. Among other things, the lock
has considerable symbolic significance; it
may even "symbolize past love." Carefully
adapted to their settings and utilizing
available materials to greatest advantage,
African dwellings express, in various ways,
the daily requirements and social values of
family life. The African house makes the

rarely have direct communication with each
other; the vast family farms are then divided
into several circular enclosures, which
themselves form a circle or oval (for
example, among the Fali, the Matakam and
the Kapsiki of northern Cameroun). Round

individual aware of the universe, both visible and invisible, sacred and profane. Conceived of as a function of the cosmos, the residence, like the universe, is alive, and the activities that a man performs there maintain the order of the universe and keep it going. For this reason, architecture is the foremost art of black Africans, and their houses are works of art. The most gifted people give free rein to their talents by decorating walls with designs and compositions which, within the limits of strict rules, depend solely on the artist's inspiration. Settled agricultural tribes (such as the Fali), fishermen (such as the Musgu and Demsa), seminomads (such as the Bahima of Uganda) and former nomads (such as the Fulani) give only secondary consideration to the decorative effect when they trace traditional signs and pictures on the walls and even the floors of their dwellings; the primary purpose of these decorations is symbolic. African architecture supports a unique system of writing in which the houses are the archives of the society and record the main events of its tradition and history. The architect is always aware of the symbolic and social significance of his house; he knows how to conceive and construct his house so that nothing is left to chance, and he pays great attention to the most minor details. (See also *Architecture; Bamileke; Basketry; Household Furnishings; Massa; Painting, Mural; Sahara Desert; Yoruba; Zimbabwe.*)   J.-P.L.

EDUCATION. Traditional African education aimed at the harmonious integration of the individual into society in accord with his status, which was determined by such things as his sex, his rank at birth and the social standing of his parents. In societies in which competition was limited and where each man's role was determined by factors extraneous to personality, its primary purpose was to help individuals to adapt; the element of selection was only secondary and confined mainly to societies with complex economic and political systems. The child was taught the techniques necessary for individual and community life, as well as the nonmaterial aspects of the culture of the society.

The first stage of education until weaning (between eighteen months and three years) was, and still is, the mother's responsibility. After weaning, education differs for each sex and this difference is accentuated as the child gets older. Small boys and girls are educated first of all by their older brothers and sisters and then increasingly by adults of their own sex, first within the family circle, then in a broader sphere, which varies according to tribal customs but is always fairly extensive. Among the Bushmen of the Kalahari, all the adult members of the hunting band are responsible for the education of the children, each child being educated according to his sex and capabilities. In contrast to this, among many groups of West Africa, societies of initiates, for example the *Poro* of the Mande, are in charge of the education of the children. The children are taken from their families and sent to bush schools for periods which, in the old days, lasted as long

Bush school. Mouyondzi.
Republic of the Congo.
Photo: Rapho, L. Herschfriff.

as seven years. The Bantu in the southeast had an educational system grouped around the *impi,* or regiments, which were the foundation of the political and military structure of their society. In northern Kenya, each age group was responsible for the next. Without going into more details, one may say, generally speaking, that the organization of education, especially as far as men were concerned, ran parallel to the socio-political organization and was conditioned by it.

Educational systems comparable to American or European schools, in which the personnel was occupied solely with education, were almost unknown. The principal exceptions were the Koranic schools among Muslim tribes. However, there were a few specialists, some of whom taught as individuals and others as part of the general educational set-up. In the first category were certain experts—doctors, diviners, storytellers and hunters—who taught their trade for a fee to those who could afford to pay for their lessons. The second category included people with a particular competence in a certain sphere who were made responsible for initiating all the children of the group. Methods varied, beginning with initiation as a form of game and leading up to what was virtually an apprenticeship organized as lessons for the individual or group.

The subjects taught varied according to

Koranic school. Guinea.
Photo: Rapho, Bernheim.

sex and social standing. Generally they covered the basic skills, including war, love and cooking, as well as etiquette, historical and cosmological mythology, genealogy, common magical practices and often rhetoric and music, among other topics. In many tribes, education continued until adulthood for those who had the ability and means and who either wanted to specialize in an art or particular trade or wanted to attain the higher degrees of esoteric knowledge. Each phase of education usually ended with initiations or promotion rites, which could be very exacting. The introduction of European education has led to a marked decline in traditional education. Especially in regions where there are many schools, it has become weak, simplified and even distorted, but has never disappeared entirely. Colonial school systems left little or no room for instruction about African culture and traditions, and independence so far has not led to many changes. Here and there, however, are signs of reaction in favor of reviving some details of the old educational system. This tendency played an important part in the origins of the Kikuyu uprising in Kenya. But whatever the methods and programs, education is one of the major preoccupations of African governments as well as of a large proportion of their people. The problem to which no one has yet found a solution is that of how to reconcile the requirements of the modern world with the preservation of the cultural heritage of black Africa. (See also *Age Groups; Excision; Genealogy; Initiation; Kongo; Proverbs; Riddles; Societies, Secret; Sports; Towns and Cities; Wisdom.)*   P.A.

EGYPT. Did ancient Egypt have a particularly close relationship with black Africa? This is a reasonable question considering that writers have not failed to discover the stamp of Egyptian "influence" or "heritage" imprinted on different parts of the continent in both ancient and modern times; to find divinities, skills, sacred royalty and human groups transported from the shores of the Nile to the Gulf of Guinea or East Africa; to be struck by a family resemblance between certain thought patterns, beliefs or rituals of the land of the pharaohs and certain others which, only yesterday, were associated with particular black societies; to transform the ancient Egyptians into Negroid people and to attribute their civilization to the black genius. There is only one established fact in all this—an obsession with Egypt. Most of these suppositions sin grievously against both evidence and reason. The evidence that

Above: Fanyan woman
grinding millet. Chad.
Photo: Pierre Ichac.
Left: Grinding grain.
Egyptian sculpture. Cairo
Museum. *Photo: Pierre Ichac.*

these writers used as their starting points—
and to which they added a great deal—varies
in value. It consists mainly of resemblances
between institutions, ideas, languages,
techniques and representations of animal
and human figures, but also of some rare
finds of Egyptian and Nilotic objects in
distant places and of fragments from
traditions concerning the origins of certain
peoples. Some resemblances can only be
hasty impressions, and those which have
been examined in detail suggest that they
may result from entirely independent
developments made in response to similar
needs, environments or inspirations. There
are, however, a sufficient number of
meaningful similarities to indicate that the
problem of the relation between Egypt and
black Africa is both real and important. But
detecting such relationships throughout the
course of history is not the same as
identifying the exact content, import or
periods concerned, and still less does it solve
the problem of the form and means or
connecting links. No conclusions have really

been reached in this area, for studies are still
at the stage of cautious working hypotheses
and systematic research. Intermediaries, in
any case, must have played a major role. It is
quite clear, for example, that the Nilotic
Sudan was a very important staging post and
crossroads, and even the starting point of
several "influences." In fact, the evidence
implies that there were three areas involved
—Egypt, Nubia (Napata-Meroe) and the
interior of Africa—making the problem
twice as complex.

The history of Mesolithic, Neolithic and
predynastic Egypt cannot be separated from
that of a large part of the continent where
many of the tribes which intermingled on the
banks of the Nile originated. Egypt's very
early participation in a vast world of which
she was only one of several heirs may
account for some of the alleged relationships
with black communities far removed in time
and space. Later, at the time of the pharaohs,
Egyptian influence could have been absorbed and then spread extensively by the
surrounding pastoral civilizations. But the

only definite fact is that Egypt took direct action in Nubia—the land of the Cush. The Old, Middle and New Kingdoms extended their administrative, economic and cultural influences into Nubia, each kingdom penetrating deeper than the previous one. Nubia supplied manpower (for armies, police, etc.), riches and produce brought from the interior of Africa. In Nubia, the Egyptians subdued or were in close contact with African peoples, and the Nubian elite were marked by Egyptian influence. After each advance, the influence left behind by Egypt was stronger, but it was always greatest among the upper classes, and native culture survived among the common people. In the void left after each withdrawal, a native power would arise. During the dissolution of the New Kingdom, the House of Napata was in the ascendant, and it was this line of rulers that eventually became strong enough to conquer a chaotic Egypt and to become the Twenty-fifth Dynasty. Conscientiously, loyally and without foreign innovations, it administered the heritage of the pharaohs. Pushed back to its home territory, the empire of Napata-Meroe enjoyed many centuries of power alongside an Egypt that had become part of the Greco-Roman world. It was undoubtedly the most important channel for carrying Egyptian and Nilotic influences toward the west and southeast into Africa. There are also traces of later advances westward through the Nile-Chad savanna which brought elements first from Byzantine Egypt and then from the Christian kingdoms of Nubia. Still later, Muslim Egypt had economic, intellectual and even political connections with the Islamic states of the Sudan, but by then the nature and strength of its impact were negligible compared to that of the Maghrib.

This, in outline, is the context of the interplay of influences supposed to have existed between the Nile Valley and black Africa. Even if it were possible to establish the nature of the exchanges more precisely, we should still be careful not to overestimate their historical importance, since we know very little about the societies involved, and knowledge of the people concerned is essential to understanding why they have been influenced. A group of human beings accepts a technique, idea or belief, for example, only if the condition favorable to its adoption already exists in the group itself; conditions in the influenced society play as great a role as, and sometimes even a greater one than, the actual influences to which the society is subjected.

Ancient Egyptians were not Negroid, as Volney believed and as is maintained today by the Senegalese sheikh Anta Diop. Contemporary observations—for the basic population of the country has not changed noticeably—and the available evidence, such as skeletons from predynastic tombs, carved figures and written sources indicate, on the one hand, a great variety of skin colors and individual facial characteristics and, on the other, that the subjects of the pharaohs were regarded and regarded themselves as much more deeply tanned than most Mediterranean types, but different from the Nubians, who were darker, and from the northeast African type awkwardly called "Hamites," and different also from the true blacks, with whom they had particularly close contact during the New Kingdom. (See also *Baule; European Discovery; Ethiopia; Gold; Horses; Ife; Lost-Wax Process; Meroe; Nile; Pygmies; Slave Trade.*) H.M.

EKOI. The Ekoi, or Ejagham, who number about 100,000 including related tribes, live in southeastern Nigeria, between the Cross River and the Cameroun border. They are forest people and good hunters. The basis of their domestic economy is still tuber vegetables, cultivated with the hoe and almost entirely by the women. Children belong to the clans of their fathers, and dowries are relatively large. The system of government is based on the clan and the village. The Ekoi are known especially for their carved wooden heads covered with animal skins, which are among the most naturalistic works in all Africa. Like the Bambara antelopes, these sculptures are attached to basketwork bonnets, which are worn on the heads of participants in ceremonies. The wearer's face is hidden by a cowl, so that during the ceremony the mask dominates the gathering with its sinister presence. The teeth and eyes are represented by pieces of wood or metal. An almost demonic vitality emanates from the mask. This strange custom may have originated in headhunting practices; in early times, when the Ekoi returned from a raid, they would dance as they displayed the severed heads of their enemies. There are also numerous two-faced Janus heads, with the blackened face usually considered male and the whitened one female. According to other interpretations, the two faces represent the Sky-Father and Earth-Mother, respectively, or the Past and the Future. Both one- and two-faced sculptures may be surmounted by immense horns, a human figure or an animal. In addition, the Ekoi make human statues with mobile arms and legs. These sculptures are used in the secret society called *Egbo,* which is found under different names

King Taharqa. Egyptian. Bronze statuette. The Hermitage, Leningrad.

Etsiokum mask. Ekoi.
Nigeria. Wood. Museum für
Völkerkunde, Berlin. *Museum
photo, Karl H. Paulmann.*

Egbo mask. Ekoi. Nigeria.
Wood covered with skin.
Musée de l'Homme, Paris.
Photo: Giraudon.

throughout southern Nigeria and may have originated with the Ekoi. Among the Ekoi, the society has seven ranks, each with its own skin-covered "image"; according to some authorities, the skin may at one time have come from humans. (See also *Ibibio; Sculpture, Stone.*)   D.P.

ELEPHANTS. One can speak of an actual elephant culture in reference to India. There, the elephant has been domesticated for several thousands of years and is an inseparable feature of life; the elephant is also a part of the Hindu cosmogony, being the form taken by one of the Hindu deities. This is not the case in traditional Africa. Here, the relation between man and elephant has always been that of the hunter and the hunted. The elephant was a prey privileged, by its strength and intelligence, to become royal game as soon as any kingdom was created, for ivory belonged to the king. Among some tribes, it was believed that kings, when they died, sometimes changed into elephants, just as they sometimes changed into lions. The elephant still retains this symbolic and sacred quality in modern

Africa; in the Republic of Guinea, the elephant is the symbol of the ruling party.

The Greek writer Aelian related how a herd of sacred elephants with enormous tusks, which lived in a forest in the Atlas Mountains, was massacred by a king for the sake of the ivory. He was punished by an epidemic that decimated his people. Unfortunately, no texts or traditions exist that throw light on the significance of the elephants that are deeply engraved on some rock walls in the Moroccan Sahara and the Fezzan; very possibly, they had sacred significance.

According to a missionary of the heroic period, Father Trilles, the creator-god of the Negrillos of northern Gabon was supposed to have appeared in the guise of a white elephant and was so huge that he supported the sky on his shoulders. His voice was the thunder, and he was called Gor. When a hunter killed an elephant it was to this god that he had to offer the fat from under its right ear. This is the only instance in Africa of a divine elephant. All the rest of elephant lore is concerned with totemism, hunting magic or magic in general. Some African clans claim descent from an elephant, generally a female. There have been several instances in the forests of the Ivory Coast and Cameroun of an elephant that is dangerous or cannot be captured being regarded, by popular belief, as the reincarnation of a dead chief or possessed by an old man of the vicinity. The shot that wounds or kills the elephant simultaneously strikes down the old man, who is sitting outside his hut more than a mile away. Elsewhere, a man or woman has been recognized as the hereditary master of elephants, and his or her will alone has been sufficient to protect them from hunters.

Before the use of firearms and money became general, elephant-hunting was the monopoly of a few highly specialized tribes or of professional hunters who formed a society of initiates within the tribe. The Negrillos themselves are not all elephant hunters, but hunting rituals hold an important place in their society and include initiation, special tattoos, secret language, sacrifices for propitiation, divination and taboos. The hunter has magical power: he can make himself invisible; by spreading a little magical powder on the ground, he can make the elephant turn in its tracks. Once the

animal is killed, the hunters ask forgiveness for a necessary murder. "Our assegais went astray, O Father Elephant!" the Negrillos chanted, according to Father Trilles. Before they dismember it, the Babemba of Rhodesia extinguish a torch on its forehead. The nerves of its teeth are extracted out of sight of the initiated, and the chief of the tribe is given one of its tusks. Dances take place afterward to appease the spirit of the victim.

Traditional methods of hunting vary according to the region and tribe: trenches with magic bait; traps in which a liana, displaced by the animal, releases a harpoon weighted with a wooden block; mass hunts with fire, bows and poisoned arrows; and pursuit on horseback by Arab riders. The most audacious method is that practiced by some Negrillos, the Babinga on the borders of Cameroun and the Bambuti of the Ituri Forest. The tiny hunter, coated with elephant dung to cover his own smell, slips underneath the animal and thrusts an assegai with a broad point into its flank. He then has to follow the wounded animal, sometimes for days, until it dies. A special kind of assegai is also used to hamstring the elephant, which is then dispatched. As a result of the introduction of firearms, which

Elephant hunt. Rock engraving. Central Sahara. Photo: *Musée de l'Homme, Pierre Ichac.*

commercialized hunting and eliminated the religious factor, and the regulations passed by colonial governments, the occupation of elephant-hunting has developed in a curious way among some African tribes. An extreme example is noted among the Walangulo of Kenya. The Walangulo were traditional hunters whom the creation of national parks turned into dangerous poachers, but they are now official experts, controlled by the government, whose task is the methodical "cropping" of elephant herds in the valley of the Galana River, just beyond the limits of the famous Tsavo Park.

The politically organized states of Africa made the fullest use of the spoils taken from the elephant. They carved the ivory, fashioned shields and breastplates out of the skin and made membranes for royal drums out of the ears. Villagers who did not carry arms and traditionally relied on sacrifices to protect their crops, also found a use for such spoils: according to early writers, explorers discovered tusks being used as fences for cattle enclosures.

Despite its indisputable qualities, the African elephant has seldom been domesticated. The first people to domesticate it were non-Africans, who were following the Indian example; Livy described the drivers riding on the necks of .the Carthaginian elephants as "Indians." The first war elephants were used in the West toward the end of the fourth century B.C., by Alexander's successors. The Seleucids in Syria recruited their elephants in India. The Ptolemies, on the other hand, captured them in Africa, on the northern edge of present-day Ethiopia. In 269 B.C., Ptolemy Philadelphus created the port of Ptolemais Theron on the Red Sea for this purpose. Hannibal's elephants, and later those of the Romans, came from the region of the Chotts in Tunisia and the high Algerian plateaus. The elephants near the Red Sea, like those on the fringes of the Sahara, were the isolated remains of former herds, which were poorly nourished on semidesert vegetation. They were small and incapable of withstanding the large elephants imported from India by the Syrian kings. The elephants of Ptolemy Philopater demonstrated this inadequacy in 217, during the battle of Raphia, when they fled before those of Antiochus III and almost caused Ptolemy's defeat. The giant elephants, more than ten feet high, bred in central Africa, would have reversed the situation. The last African war elephants operated, it is said, in Arabia a few years before the birth of the Prophet Mohammed. "The Year of the Elephant," when a king of Ethiopia, riding upon an elephant, very nearly seized Mecca, is still graven in the memory of the Arabs. The only modern attempt to domesticate the animal took place in the Congo in 1899, under the initiative of King Leopold II of Belgium. The "elephant schools" of Api, then of Gangala na Bodio, trained more than a hundred animals for forest and agricultural work with a Congolese staff who were familiar with Indian methods. But the competition of machinery left such an uneconomic undertaking without a future. (See also *Fauna; Hunting; Ife; Ivory; Philosophy; Stories; Traps.*) P.I.

EMANCIPATION OF WOMEN.

The traditional status of women, including both their duties and their rights, varied considerably from one society to another, but could generally be described as a state of dependence. Whether as daughter or wife, a woman was nearly always legally dependent on a father figure or husband, even in cultures where custom granted her great liberty of behavior. Initially, colonization did not necessarily result in a lessening of this dependence. The changed nature of the customary dowry, which was now calculated in cash and tended to be a fixed sum, may, in some cases, have given marriages the appearance of a sale. But the same economic and monetary factors also had a reverse effect. On the Benin coast, for example, they permitted the Yoruba, Ge, Ga and Akan "middle women" to achieve, first, their independence, and then, a real economic ascendancy over the men. Most are still daughters or wives, but the increase in the number of adult women who are neither is striking. In traditional society, the bachelor girl, or spinster, was practically unknown, whereas, in modern society, the free woman is increasingly in evidence

The first of these emancipated women were often the mistresses of Europeans who used the generosity of their European lovers to redeem themselves, as it were, by paying their own dowries to their fathers, sometimes as part of fictitious marriages. Since then, the extension of European-style education has given more girls access to economic independence and at the same time, although perhaps not intentionally, has enabled them to choose to remain single. The work of Christian missions, especially the Protestant ones, has tended to propagate European-type marriage founded on free choice of husband and wife and a partnership between the two. Today, women's associations are being formed almost everywhere, sometimes based on ancient societies of initiates, but often organized with a modern religious,

African women voting.
Photo: Rapho,
Janine Niepce.

trade union or political framework. They all tend to end feminine dependence, and they sometimes encounter masculine resistance, which is not necessarily due to conservative or traditional factors. One significant result of these organizations is the increase in protests against "competition from white girls" who are the wives of African students they met in Europe. The origin of this complaint is much more social than racial. More and more, the contemporary African woman is insisting on her rights as an individual who is simultaneously part of African culture and in rebellion against it. (See also *Women*.) P.A.

EMBROIDERY. See *Appliqué Work*.

EPICS. The dictionary definition of an epic —"poetic composition, usually centered upon a hero, in which a series of great achievements or events is narrated continuously or at length in elevated style"—is precise, but it is incomplete when applied to Africa, where the epic, like other forms of literature, is "committed." The epic is more or less the historical equivalent of the cosmic myth, with which it is at times somewhat confused. Consequently, the oral epic is particularly common in African societies organized as states, where it relates the more or less supernatural accession to power of the ancestors of the ruling group; there are, for example, the dynastic epics of the royal castes in the kingdoms of the Great Lakes region, of which the best known are the dynastic poems of Rwanda, and the historical epics of the Keita and Toure clans in Mali. In these societies, the preservation and recital of such poems have often been entrusted to specialized castes of bards, such as the Sudanese griots and the *bwiru* of

Rwanda and Burundi. Epics are also found in less organized societies where there are victorious tribal groups; these works tell of the motives and history of the groups' migrations and conquests. There are, for example, the epics of the Fang-Bulu-Bane group in Cameroun and Gabon and of the Baluba branches in central and eastern Africa. Lastly, there are the written epics of Muslim peoples, partly inspired by Arabic epic poems, in which the supernatural element is concerned with the actions of Allah and the Prophet, and sometimes even the jinns, instead of ancestors or guiding heroes; examples of such poems are the Fulani and Hausa *gasidah* and the Swahili *utendi,* in which the Muslim coloring merely masks a far more ancient and purely black African tradition.

The epics are generally very long; their recitation, often intoned to the accompaniment of music and interrupted by songs, may take whole days or nights. The narrative nearly always refers back to the origin of the world (hence its confusion with cosmic myths) and goes up to the colonial period, sometimes even later. A certain amount of flexibility exists: there are examples of epics being revised to justify a usurpation or recent political claims. There are far fewer non-historical epics; indeed, it would be more correct to call these works "romances." There are also some modern historical epics which give popular versions of events following colonization, tales of uprisings against the colonizers and also of battles fought with them (the epic cycles of Dominik and of Von Hagen in Cameroun are examples of the latter), and these epics may have satirical overtones. (See also *Griots; Legends; Poetry*.) P.A.

ETHIOPIA. Ethiopia is a kind of mountain fortress, and its climate and vegetation are conditioned by the high altitude. As a result of its geographical position in Africa, Ethiopia has a unique character which history and numerous civilizations have never refuted. This uniqueness has not led to immobility—on the contrary, there have been profound upheavals—and still less has it led to uniformity. The first things that rightly come to mind in connection with the word "Ethiopia" are early Christianity, an ancient kingdom surviving the most terrible vicissitudes, and written literature; but these generalized associations should not veil the varied groups that had an impact upon the ethnic, linguistic and religious makeup of the country. Ethiopia is a real "museum of peoples." In addition to Amharic, the official and literary language today, and Geez, the language of classical and liturgical literature, there are many other major languages which are either Semitic, like Amharic and Geez, or Cushitic, as well as a number of minor tongues. The diversity of religions is comparable with the linguistic variety. Besides Christians and Muslims, who are historically and numerically of equal importance, there are the Falashas, who are pre-Talmudic Jews, and "pagans."

The history of ancient Ethiopia covers the shores of the Red Sea, the Eritrean Plateau and Tigre. There are traces of a civilization that already existed in this area in the fifth or fourth century B.C. It was strongly influenced by the brilliant civilizations of southern Arabia, but its distinct character is evident despite the borrowed elements. Nothing is known about the historical bases of these borrowings. It is no longer claimed that South Arabia made a preponderant ethnic contribution to Ethiopia, although there were some Sabaean settlements; nor is it claimed that it dominated the country politically and created the first kingdom; nor that Geez derives directly from Sabaean. This Ethiopian-Sabaean phase is attested to by inscriptions carved on buildings in the South Arabian tongue, by red luster ware and by sculptures in Haulti, such as statues of praying women and a throne in the form of a baldachin with bas-reliefs on the outside. Another, more complex phase, which seems to have lasted from the third century B.C. to the first century A.D., was marked by new elements in writing, pottery and building; Sabaean influence was more widely diffused; there were probably contacts with Meroe, Egypt and perhaps India; and evident signs of prosperity.

The kingdom of Aksum provides a frame for a more precise definition of the other two phases of early Ethiopian history: the pre-Christian period of Aksum (first century B.C. to mid-fourth century A.D.) and the Christian period (mid-fourth century to tenth century). With the emergence of Aksum, a distinctive style appeared that affirmed that this was a powerful civilization and showed little influence from abroad. The massive architecture was distinguished by rectangular, geometrically laid out buildings, constructed with very large blocks of stone and set on heavy foundations. The sculpture was limited to the carved bases of thrones and steles. Ceramic art featured elegant terracotta heads of women. The king of Aksum was converted to Christianity in the middle of the fourth century and the rest of the country within 200 years. Christianity came from Egypt (from the beginning the new Christian province was attached to the patriarchate of Alexandria, which, until 1950, would always appoint an Egyptian cleric to be its metropolitan), and above all from Syria. The religion was Monophysite (recognizing only one nature in Christ), and Ethiopia has always remained faithful to this doctrine. Soon the Bible, books for monks and tracts from the works of the Christian Fathers were translated from Greek into Geez. Churches and monasteries flourished, Christian symbols were adopted, but the style remained that of Aksum. The kingdom prospered until the sixth century. Aksum was allied to Byzantium for two reasons: to protect the Christians of Arabia and to maintain the maritime trade route with the Far East. It intervened in Arabia in about 520 A.D., but was driven out by the Persians, the enemy of both states, at the end of the century. The lightning onslaught of Islam, which redrew the whole map of the neighboring regions, accompanied Aksum's decline, isolation and loss of power.

Then followed the Dark Ages. Paralleling the loss of the coastal regions and of the Eritrean Plateau was the beginning of the great drive southward. This movement, which started in the north where Ethiopian civilization originated, was one of the invigorating features of the country's history until the twentieth century. It helped continually to renew the ethnic composition of the Abyssinian nucleus and made an appreciable impact upon Ethiopian culture.

Following the major crises of the tenth century, and while Muslim kingdoms surrounded it to the east and south, Ethiopia under the Zague kings (eleventh-thirteenth

Rock church of St. George. Thirteenth century. Lalibela, Ethiopia. *Photo: Rapho, R. Michaud.*

Castle of Gondar.
Seventeenth century.
Ethiopia. *Photo:*
T. Schneiders.

centuries) had its center in the province of Lasta. One of the Zague kings is credited with having built astonishing churches carved entirely out of living rock in the capital, Lalibela, which was named after him. Some of these rock churches—which were built mainly between the twelfth and the fifteenth centuries—rise up like monoliths in the open; others are underground or in grottoes. They retain the rectangular layout and several other features of the Aksumite style.

The Zague dynasty was overthrown in 1270 by the dynasty that is reigning today. According to tradition, this was a restoration of the line of Solomon; the new dynasty was supposed to be descended from Menelik, the son of Solomon and the Queen of Sheba, who was crowned king at Aksum. The legend about the origin of the Ethiopian royal family was related at the beginning of the fourteenth century in a composite work, the *Kebra nagast* ("Glory of Kings"), which became a propaganda weapon. We do not know how it came to be written. The fourteenth and fifteenth centuries belonged to a brilliant epoch. Great sovereigns, such as Amda Seyon (1314-1344) and Zara Yaqob (1434-1468), pursued a militant religious policy and continued to press toward the

south. Behind the combination of military and religious elements were national feeling and religious zeal aimed at converting the remaining pockets of paganism. Zara Yaqob fought against the heretics as much with force as with polemical theology. The main genres of Ethiopian literature developed with admirable vitality before they eventually became paralyzed by conventions. They included historical chronicles, sacred and profane poetry, hagiographies dedicated to the glory of saints, monks and kings, polemical and esoteric works, as well as a mass of translations of Arabic Christian works from Egypt.

The sixteenth century is full of drama and profound changes, The centuries-old struggle between the Christian kingdom and its Muslim neighbors culminated in mortal combat. From the kingdom of Adel, which centered on Harar and Zeila, the troops of the imam Ahmed Ibrahim (*Grañ*, "the left-handed"), filled with the spirit of a holy war, flooded over the entire Abyssinian Plateau in 1531. This marked the beginning of a terrible struggle between the two adversaries which greatly affected their destinies: it sowed destruction, insecurity and misery and was "the time of migration." Geez and Arabic literature bear witness to the fanaticism and misery of this bitter struggle, which was supported by the apologists of both sides. The Christian kingdom appeared doomed when salvation suddenly arrived in 1542 in the form of aid from a small Portuguese detachment, which brought a decisive victory. A little later, neither the Muslim nor the Christian Ethiopians, who were both exhausted by the war, were able to resist the powerful and repeated waves of the Galla, a people from the south. Their implantation profoundly modified the ethnic and cultural aspects of the southern and eastern parts of the country.

Latin Christianity, which had begun to penetrate Ethiopia in the fifteenth century, was actively represented by the Jesuits, who arrived somewhat later. They broadened the intellectual horizon of the court and the monasteries, while reviving theological controversies once again in a more acute form. A clever and subtle priest finally succeeded in converting the emperor Susenyos to the Roman Church, but the replacement of the priest unleashed latent opposition; the sovereign was forced to abdicate in 1632 and the Jesuits were expelled.

In a few generations, all this had brought profound changes to the country. For the following two centuries, Ethiopia returned to a weak and isolated state, although the products of its civilization were still fascinating. At the end of the Middle Ages, a new style church appeared, mainly in the southern and central parts of the country; it was round, with a thatched roof, but the central part was square. At the end of the sixteenth century, near Lake Tana, the kings built residences for themselves and created another style, which flourished for a long time in the form of churches and castles. Gondar became the capital during the seventeenth century, and the remains of its ancient splendor still exist. Profane and religious paintings, which decorated the buildings, developed similarly, both using simple lines and brilliant colors. This was also an age of regionalism and local authority. The slow assimilation of the Galla naturally affected the cohesion and nature of the kingdom. Increasingly, artificial religious quarrels divided the clergy. Political disintegration was at its worst from the end of the eighteenth century until about 1850. It was, in the Biblical phrase, the "time of judges." The rivalries of the rases, the great local princes, maintained the fiction of the sovereign king of Gondar.

In the middle of the nineteenth century, an adventurer of genius seized a large part of the country and, in 1855, had himself crowned

Guards of the King of Ethiopia. Folk painting. *Photo: Rapho, R. Michaud.*

emperor as Theodore II. This usurper revived Ethiopian traditions and ferociously imposed his authority and reforms. After his lamentable end, all the main elements of the nation's contemporary history were already present to confront the reinstated descendants of Solomon: John IV (1868-1889), Menelik (1889-1913) and the regent Ras Taffari, who became Emperor Haile Selassie. Reorganization and territorial expansion, the assimilation of heterogeneous peoples, the growth of central power and threats of foreign intervention were the major problems. Under Menelik, Ethiopia achieved unprecedented expansion toward the south, which justified the choice of Addis Ababa as a capital. Ethiopia was the only African country that succeeded in avoiding colonization (not counting the loss of Eritrea, which was recovered in 1952). However, in 1935-1936, she became the victim of Italian Fascist ambitions. Liberation came in 1941. Amharic became the literary language in the second half of the nineteenth century, and today literature, encouraged by the expansion of printing, is vital and varied. There is also a new and vigorous school of painting led by Afewerk Tekle. (See also *Africa; Aksum; Christianity; European Discovery; Great Lakes; Lions; Sistra; Slave Trade; Zar.*)   H.M.

ETHNIC GROUPS. Early European travelers to Africa were struck by the extreme diversity of its people. Crossing the continent, they came upon markedly different physical types, whose natural differences were frequently underlined by artificial deformities (such as the linear scarifications of the Bateke, the carving of the upper incisor teeth by the Azande, the elongation of the head by the Mangbetu, the incisions required for the wearing of lip ornaments by Somba women) accentuated by variations in clothing and jewelry, and made even more obvious by a multiplicity of languages and dialects. To give some order to this diversity, Europeans tried to distinguish separate groups, which they called "ethnos" or "ethnic groups." They conjured up "natural" groupings having fundamental similarities based on blood ties, roots in a certain territory and distant, obscure relationships and corresponding somewhat to the subspecies in the animal kingdom. This muddled concept, which was in keeping with the thinking of the late nineteenth century (biological evolution, romantic nationalism), did not long resist research that established that there were major differences between different types of anthropological organization including those based on race, language or culture. Each type of organization grouped different tribes, and the groupings rarely held up under investigation; if one were to superimpose maps based on these various kinds of groupings, none of the divisions would coincide. The term "ethnic group" was originally intended to mean "a people; a group of human beings who, for the most part, have a common culture but who are not necessarily united under the same political authority." It is in this sense that one can speak of the Mongo ethnic group being dispersed throughout the Congolese forest. In Europe the term "ethnos" was used mainly in referring to nonliterate peoples and took on pejorative overtones. J.M.

EUNUCHS. Several African kingdoms, especially in the Sudanese area reaching from the Nile Valley to the central Niger, employed eunuchs. Particular functions, most of which were ordinary, but some of which carried considerable political responsibility, were assigned to them. They could be thoroughly trusted because their personal and family ambitions were limited by their very nature. The origins of the eunuchs varied. Among the Hausa, for example, certain villages were obliged to supply a fixed number. Among the Mossi, the duty devolved on a particular group, composed perhaps of the descendants of slaves; but the king could also order certain captives or criminals, such as hardened thieves, to be emasculated. The operation

was performed by specialists who were under the direct control of the king. The Mossi surgeons were reputed to be very skillful, and apparently very few of their patients died by their hands. The king made a profit from the trade in eunuchs and sometimes sold them to distant lands (the French ambassador to Turkey was surprised to meet a Mossi eunuch in Istanbul in 1900).

The work undertaken by eunuchs was primarily domestic; it ranged from the extremely unpleasant, such as cleaning latrines, to the very noble, such as educating the royal children. The most important task was, of course, supervising the king's wives in the palace or in the villages where some of them lived. Eunuchs were trusted servants, and as such they guarded the treasury and the royal armories and acted as messengers with special responsibilities. The most highly placed palace officials were often eunuchs; among the Hausa, one of them would solemnly shut the doors once the king had retired to his room and would not open them again until the following morning. As trusted servants and advisers, the foremost political responsibilities were often reserved for them by right; this was customary among the Bagirmi, Hausa, and Mossi and in the kingdom of Bornu. Whether they were royal electors, ministers or military leaders, they seemed in comparison with other dignitaries to be the most reliable guarantors of the stability of the state. (See also *Mossi.*) P.M.

EUROPEAN DISCOVERY OF BLACK AFRICA. During much of the classical period knowledge of the interior of Africa was an Egyptian monopoly: most of the information about Africa that was recorded by Herodotus and the Greek geographers was obtained at second hand from Egyptian sources. The pharaohs had garrisons in Nubia and maintained commercial relations along the Nile Valley, probably as far as the Bahr el Ghazal. Their ships, or Phoenician ships chartered by them, sailed the Red Sea, and this trade continued under Roman rule. According to Herodotus, a Phoenician fleet, commissioned by the pharaoh Necho II, circumnavigated Africa in about 600 B.C., leaving through the Red Sea and returning via the Pillars of Hercules. The Carthaginians used to sail around the Moroccan coast, going about as far as the Draa River (but the famous text known as *Hanno's Periplus* is very likely a forgery). Other Carthaginians probably crossed the northern Sahara, although such voyages are known only through a few references in Herodotus. In effect, these were trade routes on which Carthage had a monopoly. When

Rome ruled over Africa Minor, military expeditions were dispatched along the Nile and beyond the frontier (the *limes*) as far as the oases of southern Morocco and Fezzan, and perhaps even to the Tibesti Mountains, but the results are only known in very vague and general terms. The most detailed and accurate accounts preserved of this period are found in the *Periplus of the Erythrean Sea,* a Greek-Alexandrian work written in the second century A.D., which gives a very good description of the coast as far as the approaches to Dar es Salaam. Greek and Levantine traders of this period knew about the Great Lakes and the central African mountains (the "Mountains of the Moon") apparently without having penetrated the interior themselves.

The fall of the Roman Empire and the Muslim invasion of Africa Minor caused all contact between Europe and Africa to be severed during the Middle Ages. The little that is known about Africa during this period comes via Spain, either from classical authors or from Jewish and Arab geographers. From the ninth century onward, Arab travelers constantly visited the Sudan, where Europeans could no longer venture (the voyage to Songhai of the Toulousian Anselme d'Yzalguier in the sixteenth century belongs to the realm of fiction).

Sea voyages along the Atlantic coast seem to have been resumed in the fourteenth century. The Canaries were rediscovered about 1336 by Lanzarote Malocelle, a Genoese, and the coasts were explored as far as Cape Bojador. The Norman Jean de Béthencourt conquered the Canaries be-

Priest carrying a cross on board a caravel. Dahomey. Bas-relief. *Photo: Musée de l'Homme.*

Illustration from *Missionary Travels and Researches in South Africa,* by David Livingstone (1857).

Fort Jesus. Mombasa, Kenya.
Photo: Jacques Maquet.

tween 1402 and 1406. The voyages made by sailors from Dieppe to the coast of Guinea in the fourteenth century are more than hypothetical. The great period of systematic exploration did not begin until the second third of the fifteenth century, under the initiative of the heir apparent of Portugal, Prince Henry the Navigator. With progress made in navigational methods and improved sailing ships, the caravels, Portuguese sailors would venture further each year: in 1434, Gilianes doubled Cape Bojador; Cape Blanc was reached in 1440 and Cape Verde in 1444; in 1456, Ca Da Mosto, a Venetian in the service of Portugal, landed in Gambia. In 1482 and 1485, Diogo Cam reached the Congo River; in 1487, Bartholomeu Dias doubled the Cape of Good Hope; and in 1498, Vasco da Gama explored the east coast and reached India from the Arab trading post of Malindi, on the coast of "Zanguebar."

During the first years of their connection with Africa, the Portuguese penetrated fairly deeply into the valleys of the Congo, the Cuanza and the Zambezi. The interior of Africa was soon closed to Europeans as a consequence of the slave trade. Until the end of the eighteenth century, the penetration of Africa was generally confined to some French surveys of Senegal and the progressive occupation of the hinterland of the Cape by Dutch and Huguenot settlers, beginning in 1652. After the great maritime explorations of the Pacific at the end of the eighteenth century, the interest of European philosophers, revivalists and pietist Protestants turned toward the mysteries of African geography, the sources of the Nile and the problems of the Niger. The era of geographical exploration had begun. The British, under the impetus of the Association for the Discovery of the Interior Parts of Africa, the forerunner of the Royal Geographical Society, later achieved special distinction.

The puzzle of the Niger, the "Nile of the Blacks" as it was called by Arab geographers, was solved by Mungo Park (1795-1797, 1805), Denham and Hugh Clapperton (1822-1827), the Frenchman René Caillé, who was the first explorer to come back alive from Timbuktu (1828) and Richard Lander, the erstwhile servant of Clapperton, who, in 1830, proved finally that the "Rivers of Oil" were really the Niger Delta. From 1850 to 1855, the German Heinrich Barth thoroughly explored all the western and central Sudan for the Royal Geographical Society. Further details were later added by Binger, Gentil, Monteil and Mizon, while two other German explorers, Gustav Nachtigal and the Balt George Schweinfurth, explored (1869-1875) the central and eastern Sudan, between Chad and the Nile.

The mystery of the source of the Nile was tackled simultaneously from Egypt, Ethiopia and the eastern coast: James Bruce (1768-1772) discovered the Blue Nile and explored Ethiopia; he was followed by the French, in the service of Mehemet Ali of Egypt, who explored upper Egypt and prepared the way for Schweinfurth and Sir Samuel Baker. Meanwhile, John Speke and James Grant, leaving from Zanzibar, reached Lake Victoria (1860-1863). "The spring of springs," Lake Tanganyika, was discovered by David Livingstone, although he was unaware of the fact, during his last journey (1866-1873), when he was found by Henry Morton Stanley, who spoke the famous words, "Dr. Livingstone, I presume?" Even if Livingstone confused the source of the Nile with that of the Congo, he remains the greatest explorer of southern and eastern Africa, which he crossed in every direction from 1841 until his death in 1873, achieving one of the first known journeys from ocean to ocean in 1853 to 1856. Stanley's greatest merit as a geographer was his journey across the continent through the Congo Valley from 1874 to 1877. The hinterland of Zanzibar had been discovered and explored (1847-1849) well before his time by the German missionaries Krapf and Rebmann, the first Europeans to see the snows of Kilimanjaro. Another German, Mauch, had explored (1860-1873) the interior of Mozambique. In 1900, Mauritania, the Libyan Sahara, the Kalahari and the Egyptian-Chad borders were the only large blank spaces left on the map of Africa. Colonization and the internal-combustion engine soon filled them, in. (See also *Arab Chroniclers; Chad, Lake; Great Lakes; Guinea; Hanno; Kongo; Sahara Desert; Slave Trade.*)   P.A.

EXCISION. The excision of women, which the myths of certain areas of Africa present as the exact counterpart of the circumcision of men, does not invariably accompany the practice of circumcision and is sometimes practiced independently. It is regarded as a means of making women more fertile. It can also, as among the Nankanse of Upper Volta and the Koniagi of Guinea, mark the beginning of a period of sexual liberty, but it was generally a form of preparation for marriage. It consists of the removal of the clitoris and sometimes of the labia minora, as among the Sara in Chad. The age at which the operation was performed varied greatly; it was usually performed on girls when they were very young or when they reached the age of puberty; much less frequently, it was performed on adult women, for example, among the Woaba in northern Dahomey. It was, like circumcision, an initiation rite, although it was rarely prolonged by complex ceremonies. The Koniagi, however, associated it with worship of the dead, and excision ceremonies were more important than those accompanying circumcision. The excised women spent a month in the bush.

The Sara enforced an even longer retreat. The Chaga of Kenya shut them up for three months, during which time they were systematically fattened, a custom also observed among the Ibibio in Nigeria, and simultaneously anointed with oil. Sexual and moral instruction was given during their retreat. Women's age groups, formed at the excision ceremonies, generally had less importance and less solid organization than those of men. In places where excision was not practiced, it was sometimes replaced by other rituals or operations. Several tribes in the Congo celebrated the first menstruation, which was followed by a period of retreat and instruction. The Hottentots enlarged the labia majora, forming what is known as the Hottentot apron. The Herero of South-West Africa made incisions under the breasts. All these practices had the same significance; they were rituals to celebrate puberty. (See also *Body; Circumcision; Guro; Kirdi; Rattles; Sistra; Women.*)   P.M.

EXPLORATION. See *European Discovery of Black Africa.*

FAMILY. It has not always been commonly accepted that the family existed as an institution in every African society. The evolutionists of the nineteenth century, who sometimes indulged in remarkable flights of fancy, thought that the human race was

Initiation exercises in the girls' camp of retreat the day after excision. Baya-Kara. Cameroun. *Photo: Musée de l'Homme.*

Rural family. Ndebele.
Republic of South Africa.
*Photo: Department of
Information, Pretoria.*

originally promiscuous and, consequently, the family did not exist as an institution. In another exercise of a priori reasoning, they thought that the African peoples were nearer to this state of nature than the civilized Europeans and that these vestiges of prehistoric practices explained customs such as matrilineal descent; since haphazard unions make it impossible to establish paternity, one can only determine affiliation by reference to the mother. These wild hypotheses were never confirmed by on-site investigations and have been abandoned today. They still persist in vague ideas about Africa being a paradise of sexual freedom.

Each African society recognizes and organizes the group that consists of a man, a woman and their young children; sociologists call this the "nuclear" or elementary family. The marriage ceremony at which this group originates brings the indispensable sanction of society to what would otherwise be nothing but a private arrangement without any status in the eyes of the law. In the urban environment of industrialized countries, the elementary family is the usual form of the institution. In Africa, two types of extensions are common: the extended family and the polynuclear family. In the extended family, parents and grandparents (particularly when one partner is dead), unmarried or widowed brothers and sisters, or nephews and nieces may temporarily or even permanently live with the nucleus of husband, wife and unmarried children. The presence of nieces and nephews is common in matrilineal societies, where the husband looks after the children of his sister and is responsible for their education, while his own children go to their mother's brother's house. It has just been noted that all the members of an extended family live together. In a village where the huts are very close to one another and where most activities of blood relatives are communal, living together means sharing food prepared for a common meal. Eating together is a sign of pooling everything that is produced; thus, the extended family forms a unit created for production as well as for consumption. The other type of extension, that of the polynuclear family, is the result of plural marriages. When a man marries several wives, he is the unique pivot of several elementary families. As a matter of fact, in Africa polygamy does not imply that all the wives and children share a single dwelling; the institution of the harem does not exist. Each wife, the communal husband and the children of that couple constitute a nuclear family, which cultivates its own fields and does its own cooking. This separation can be far-reaching. Among the aristocracy of Rwanda, each wife managed a household that included servants and dependents, herds and fields; the husband took his meals and spent the night with each of his wives in turn in strict order of rotation. This type of family organization clearly demonstrates the economic significance of African polygamy.

Whether extended, polynuclear or elementary, the African family forms the setting in which the newborn child progressively discovers the world. These first experiences, which psychologists consider so important in the forming of personality, are markedly different in the traditional African family and in the industrialized West. For a considerable amount of time—from birth until it can walk unaided—the child remains in close and constant contact with its mother, carried either on her back or hip, often with skin touching skin and hardly knowing the loneliness of the cradle; the mother is the source of warmth and food, affection and security. But when it is weaned, which occurs fairly late, usually between the ages of two and three, the child's universe rapidly expands outside the family. In the village there are many substitutes for parents, brothers and sisters. The infant has to take only a few steps in order to pass from the house of an uncle to that of an aunt, from the hut of one cousin to that of another, from one neighbor's dwelling to someone else's home. In the human world unfolding before the child, there are no strangers, and this experience of the friendly village, following that of the mother's back, causes the young African to have psychological security.

The two married partners are necessarily of two different lineages, because lineages are exogamous groups of relatives. The children of the couple also necessarily belong to only one of these two lineages—to that of the father, in a patrilineal system, or to that of the mother, in a matrilineal system. If these principles are strictly applied, either the father or the mother is considered an outsider by the children. When one considers the importance of descent in the life of the individual, one can understand that this situation has serious effects on the equilibrium of the family. The lineage, which depends on the family for the perpetuation of its ancestor's line, lays claim to the child. The matrimonial compensation provided by the husband's relatives at the time of marriage clearly establishes to whom the child belongs. It also indicates the overriding importance accorded to the mother, no matter which principle of descent is adopted, for, according to the laws of both patrilineal and matrilineal descent, the matrimonial compensation always goes in the same direction—that is, to the lineage of the future wife.

No one ever forgets that a wife represents fecundity. It is this quality that determines the status of the woman in the African family. A sterile wife is a disaster. The supreme importance of maternity is recognized in the masculine African society, which confers authority in the village and in the family upon men and which assigns to men the tasks that, no doubt, are appropriate to their sex but that also happen to be the most glamorous and least monotonous, tasks in which excellence is recognized and appreciated by the community. Without elaborating a doctrine of the inequality of the sexes, African men (among others) regard themselves as superior beings because of their strength, intelligence and wisdom, and they have organized their societies to conform with this self-confidence. Matrilineal systems are not matriarchies nor gynarchies. Even though the family's wealth, duties and possessions are transmitted through the female line, power lies in the hands of men; the position of the maternal uncle is proof of this.

The newly formed family usually lives close to the family of one of the two partners. This rule of locality, as sociologists call it, is more important than the principle of descent in determining the wife's well-being. When the newly married couple lives near the wife's parents, as in the matrilineal societies of the Babemba or Yao, the woman benefits from the support given her by the constant presence of her family. When the situation is reversed, as with the Bakongo, who are, in fact, also matrilineal, the wife is isolated in strange surroundings in which she may have difficulty in finding help. Even when the African family is polygamous or matrilineal (variants unknown in the West today), it assumes the universal functions of the family as an institution: sexual access confined to the partners, economic cooperation, procreation of children and their training on behalf of the community. (See also *Dwellings; Education; Lineage; Love; Marriage; Meals; Polygamy; Taboos; Tribute; Uncles; Work.*)   J.M.

FANG. The Fang (Pahouin or Pangwe) were, for a long time, a mobile and aggressive people, with a society and culture adapted to their mobility. Their social structure was much more dependent on the relationships of clans, lineages and families than on any ties with the territory they occupied. Their society was organized for war and placed the mature and virile man in a privileged position. The Fang had a number of types of secret societies for special functions: the *bieri* formed at initiation ceremonies and serving the worship of ancestors (*bieri* figures); the *Ngil,* which the community required for its welfare in moments of crisis; and the *Böyem,* which foiled the insidious practices of witch doctors.

The migrations of the Fang continued, in

Mask of the *Ngil* society. Fang. Gabon. Painted wood. Paul Tishman Collection, New York. *Photo: Musée de l'Homme.*

the direction of the coast of Gabon, until the early 1900s. Today, the Fang are a substantial people, numbering about 800,000, and occupy a territory covering about 70,000 square miles, which includes a large part of southern Cameroun, Equatorial Guinea and northern Gabon. They assimilated the various ethnic groups that lived in the areas they conquered and now comprise three principal groups: the Fang proper, the Bane and the Bulu. Most legends set their original habitat as far away, in the northeast; they describe the fauna of the savanna and "white men" who were masters at working iron and owners of horses. The legends give a symbolic version of the Fang arrival in the forest region, describing how migratory groups had to creep into the hole of an *adzap* tree, which became the symbol of physical and spiritual strength. The Fang are proud of their distant origins and have used them as a reason for their superiority and a justification for their supremacy. They subdued the surrounding country in wars (*oban*) and knew how to take economic advantage of these wars by seizing control of the key points and routes used in the slave trade. The Fang's neighbors found them terrifying. The first explorers regarded them as vigorous and "devoid of the vices of the coastal tribes." Europeans see them as the origina-

Reliquary statue. Fang. Gabon. Wood. Paul Tishman Collection, New York. *Photo: Musée de l'Homme.*

Reliquary head. Fang. Gabon. Wood and metal. Museum of Primitive Art, New York. *Museum photo, Charles Uht.*

tors of one of the most celebrated forms of Negro art.

The Fang, despite their restlessness, reached a high level of culture. Their traditions are rich, their esoteric knowledge is recorded and preserved by poet chroniclers and their many dances are spectacles as well as a form of mimed instruction. Their plastic art has a preeminent position in museums and the world of art. They evolved a form of statuary that has become famous for its hieratic stylization and its treatment of the face. The body of the statue is not particularly well executed; it is outlined roughly and includes only the most indispensable attributes, notably the designs of scarification. The face is set in an irregular oval. An immense forehead overshadows a nearly triangular face, all of whose features are incised or modeled on a concave surface. The eyes are closed and the mouth projects in a sort of mournful pout. An extremely simplified hairstyle envelops the whole head, suggesting a death mask. It has been said of Fang statuettes that they represent "the whole man" and that "naturalist painters or sculptors have never been able to achieve such a result." The most perfect of these works fully express the Fang conception of man and his destiny. They are the last frail testimony of a civilization swept away by the winds of change. (See also *Architecture; Funerals; Incest; Initiation; Lion Men; Masks; Mottoes; Sculpture, Wood; Widows; Writing.*)   G.B.

FASHION. Did precolonial African societies experience those variations in feminine attire that are reputed to be the joy of dressmakers and the despair of husbands? It is probable that the cosmopolitan and commercial societies of the Sudanese western Sahara, where materials were imported from the Maghrib and the East, and where there was an important center of textile production, did to a certain extent. It is less likely that non-Muslim societies—in which dress and adornment were, and sometimes still are, governed very strictly by custom and ritual—experienced such changes in fashion. What is certain is that in the eighteenth century De Boufflers compared the dress of the beautiful *signares* of Gorée to that of Parisian ladies. More sinister evidence is to be found in the reports of slave-ship captains, which periodically indicated changes in the tastes of their African suppliers of guinea cloth and other cotton materials. This trend was accelerated with the advent of colonization, possibly as a consequence of the need to find markets for European textiles. Even though at the old trading posts, clothing, particularly women's clothing, tended to maintain its original cut, it became more and more frequent for shopkeepers to periodically make fairly consistent changes based on unique innovative ideas. Tribes who went naked or wore very little adopted the Victorian mission dress and later copied European fashions. For men, European dress, often of military cut, and Muslim clothing, notably the Sudanese boubou and the kanzu of the east coast, began to be widely worn. Foreign fashions, whether European or Muslim, were adopted as a sign of prestige in contrast to the traditional costume. It was only after national independence that traditional dress regained favor with both sexes. The materials for these clothes are imported from Manchester, Lyons, Hamburg and Bombay. Their color, design and cut vary from one region to another, from one town to another and sometimes even from one political party to another. Thus, it has been observed that Nkrumah has replaced the Queen of England upon the backs of the ladies of Ghana. In the big towns and wealthy areas, not only dress but also hairstyles (especially since modern methods of straightening hair have been adopted), jewelry and accessories now change as quickly and freely as in Europe, since feminine fashion in Africa is often an original interpretation of current European and American fashion trends. In poor regions and rural areas, only the inexpensive details such as headcloths vary, and then they are copied from neighboring tribes rather than from Europe. (See also *Clothing; Jewelry.*)   P.A.

FAUNA. The popular image associated with Africa is of big-game hunting, immense herds of antelopes and zebras grazing freely at the foot of Mount Kilimanjaro under the indifferent gaze of sleek lions and leopards. Reality is somewhat different, but the savanna does provide the densest concentration of grazing animals in the whole world.

Africa is very rich in fauna. For instance there are 190 species of mammals and 750 species of birds to be counted in the Cameroun alone. There are 120 different reptiles in West Africa, and the continental shelf, which runs along the African coast from the Río de Oro to Nigeria, offers 600 species of fish. Each natural region has its own typical fauna. The desert and the subdesert zones abound in gazelles, addaxes, antelopes, jerboas, some snakes and insects that resist thirst. The number of species and the density of the animal population increase toward the tropical zone, where most of the

Young Bamako women. Mali.
Photo: Hoa-Qui.

Girls of the Fulani Bororo.
Cameroun. *Photo: Musée de l'Homme.*

Ram. Benin. Nigeria. Wood. Chicago Natural History Museum. *Museum photo.*

great antelopes and the great carnivores are to be found, as well as buffalo, elephants, hippopotamuses and many species of rodents, birds and reptiles. The animal life in the forests is more abundant than has often been made out, and it is not an accident that Pygmies, one of the few tribes in Africa that live by hunting alone, continue to live there. They can catch the bushbuck, of which there are dozens of varieties, many small carnivorous animals and rodents, birds such as the hornbill, the barbet, centropus and parrot. The great fauna in the forest consist of buffalo, elephants, wild boar, the bongo and last, but not least, the famous okapi. Some parts of African rivers, such as the central part of the Niger Delta and the lower course of the Chari, are among the richest sources of fish in the entire world. Fishing fleets come from Europe and even Japan to range over the African waters.

Traditional societies benefit in varying degrees from the animals that surround them. Only the Pygmies and Bushmen continue to derive an appreciable part of their subsistence from them. Hunting big game provides only an intermittent contribution to the larder; it is seasonal and takes the form of great drives after the undergrowth is burnt. It is more an opportunity for individuals to display their prowess and courage than for groups of people to improve their diet. Hunting small animals and collecting insects, reptiles and mollusks must seem the most systematic form of exploitation of wild fauna of the

earth. In accordance with the season and the population, traps are set up to catch birds; rodents and reptiles are routed out; snails, oysters, grasshoppers, stick insects and beetles are collected; tree trunks are split to facilitate the gathering of grubs; and at night torches are lit to attract winged termites. Honey is one of the few sweet items of nourishment available in Africa, and forest peoples seek it out, whereas those of the savanna practice beekeeping. Animal and bird skins are used for clothing, adornment and magic rites.

Among the factors which tend to widen the gap between rural societies and their animal environments are the sedentariness of groups, the mastery of production techniques such as those of agriculture, the population explosion and, more recently, the influence of urban blacks as models. The only incentives for acquiring an understanding of the fauna are the necessities of defending harvests from predators (birds, rodents and insects) and humans from harmful animals such as snakes and scorpions. Knowledge of the fauna has become the preserve of specialized individuals often provided with firearms and of socioprofessional groups, including the hunters of Mauritania, the Arabs of Salamat, Chad, the Lobi of Upper Volta, and the Dorobo trackers, who are serfs of the Masai. Only children and adolescents who spend most of their time in the bush looking after herds still hunt and gather small creatures in order to eat them; adults generally despise this type of animal.

Fishing communities, which have always had a high degree of technical skill and knowledge of the migrations and habits of fish, have not only retained their traditional skills, but have usually added to them by adopting new techniques. Of all the communities still living in a traditional environment, they are the ones that are the most thoroughly engaged in an exchange economy, which permits them to gain money and resources without impairing their way of life.

The animal world provides rural societies with an inexhaustible source of material for religious and artistic expression. Two kinds of classifications of animals seem to be employed within African religion and art: utilitarian and totemic. Utilitarian systems reflect the society's most primitive viewpoint: How the society can use the materials available. A distinction is made between useful and harmful animals, animals that can be eaten and those that cannot. Those that are of no material or other use are often described generically as "animal," "meat" or "bird." Those that can be used are given

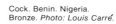
Cock. Benin. Nigeria.
Bronze. *Photo: Louis Carré.*

Hyena. Shilluk. Sudan. Clay
pipe. Eliot Elisofon
Collection, New York. *Photo:
Eliot Elisofon.*

Leopard. Benin. Nigeria.
Bronze. Museum of Primitive
Art, New York. *Photo:
Walter Dräyer.*

Small reptile and crocodile.
Weights for weighing gold
dust. Ashanti. Ghana. Brass.
Pierre Vérité Collection,
Paris. *Photo: Eliot Elisofon.*

Elephant. Baluba. Zaire.
Wood. Niedersächsisches
Landesmuseum, Hanover.
Museum photo.

precise names and are part of the community, whether their link with humanity consists in being eaten or whether it is nonmaterial and they are not eaten. Many tribes believe that the great beasts they hunt have human souls. This is the reason for purification and forgiveness rituals after their "murder." Some African societies have cosmological myths that set forth categories of beings in which plants and animals may be grouped together. Association of a human group with a particular breed of animal or of an individual with a single animal is common in Africa, and may take one of several forms. In totemic systems, human groups and animal species bear the same name; people are forbidden to eat their totemic animal; and marriage is prohibited within the group that carries an animal's name and is sometimes considered to be descended from it. Animal totems are found among the Baganda, who have more than forty of them, the Bantu of the Kavirondo Gulf, Kenya, and the Bamileke. A special association is often formed between an animal and a man after an unusual experience in which the animal has behaved like a human being. The animal is then promoted to the rank of guardian spirit and may become a totem. In some societies, such as the Hadjarai in Chad, a man with special qualities, generally a priest, is associated with lions. Further south, among the Sara and Mbai, there are secret societies of lion men, and the Mabale of the Congo have sects of leopard men whose members, sometimes disguised, are supposed to change into beasts of prey in

Leopard. Benin. Nigeria.
Bronze. *Photo: Louis Carré.*

order to punish their enemies. Divinities, spirits and ancestors have very often manifested themselves in the form of animals. They do not necessarily choose the biggest or most spectacular of the local beasts. There is nothing in the nature of animals as ordinary as spiders, toads, chameleons, geckos, nightjar, ants or catfish to make them figure in magic or religion; the connection can only be understood by reference to legends about tribal origins, which may be only fragmentary.

Oral African literature constantly portrays ambiguous creatures that may be either animal or human. This ambiguity and sharing of the animal in human nature and vice versa seem characteristic of traditional African thought. It is reflected in dances in which a man adopts the bearing of an animal and may wear its masks. Animals are sculpted in African art, especially by forest dwellers, and the animals painted on rocks of the Drakensberg Range in South Africa are admirably realistic. In both forms of art, the artist is very often trying to express this fusion of man and animal, this ambiguity between nature and culture. In the savanna, Bambara helmets decorated with stylized antelopes, Dogon masks (which depict nearly forty species of animals) and the masks of the Senufo, Kurumba and Guro show the same fusion. The increase in the number of firearms in Africa and the inadequate control of hunting may lead in a short while to the disappearance of much wildlife in Africa. (See also *Antelopes; Birds; Buffalo; Fishing; Hunting; Kalahari; Lions; Sahara Desert; Savanna; Spiders; Totemism; Traps; Weapons.*) I.G.

FETISHES. The word "fetish" is more popular than the word "idol," although both terms figure in many of the tales of early travelers. There is also an entire literature about Africa, some of it quite recent, that always speaks of fetishes rather than of divinities, of fetishists rather than of priests, and the term "fetishism" has often been used to describe all traditional religions. In texts fired with missionary fervor, which regard these religions as the work of the Devil, probably very often from force of habit or for want of a better description, this usage is disparaging. The word "fetish" originally described an object endowed with illusory powers. It derives from the Portuguese word *fetiço,* meaning "artificial," "fabricated" and, as a noun, "image" and "magic charm." Usage has gradually given it a broader range of referents, extending from simple talismen to altars and statues of divinities. Admittedly, African religions fabricated many

sacred objects, but a twofold misunderstanding arises from the common use of the word "fetish" to describe all of them: first, it prevents people from distinguishing between the very different categories to which these objects belong; and second, it makes people forget that these objects were usually viewed not as having power in

Magical figure. Bakongo. Republic of the Congo. Wood, iron blades and knives. Musée de l'Homme, Paris. *Museum photo.*

themselves, but as providing support for the powers with which they were endowed by means of ritual. Of course, any religion that uses sacred objects and images is strongly tempted to exaggerate their importance and to forget what they really are. L. Frobenius suggests that some African people yielded to this temptation during recent centuries under the influence of Europeans, who had already succumbed to it at an earlier date. As an example, he cites the Yoruba of Nigeria, in whose religion the "central core of the symbolism involving their gods" could be found "beneath a thick layer of ideas devoid of all interest, like a coating of mildew."

This "coating of impurity" is directly linked to the origin of the word "fetish" itself, which is not African but European. Horoscopes, charms and magic had considerable importance in the native land of the Portuguese conquerors of the west coast of Africa. An explanation of African fetishism is to be found in Europe: the Portuguese interpreted the religious practices they observed according to their own popular conceptions, and tribes who had been rendered more vulnerable by the social upheavals of slave trading could have been influenced by this interpretation. Of all the theories that propound a progressive corruption and degeneration of African religions, this is the most original. But it does not take account of all the facts.

Prior to modern times, Africans seem clearly to have made religious use of material objects as if they had power of their own. These objects certainly had more to do with magic than religion, but it is not always easy to draw a line between the two. It is quite certain that at the beginning these objects had to be singled out and consecrated by a magician, and, in practice, they appear to have been treated as if they had a virtue of their own. The term "fetish" can be accurately applied strictly to these objects. The word was apparently first applied to the *nkisi* of the Kongo Valley, and it can be considered an exact translation. The entire range of fetishes can be found in central Africa: stones, shells, animal horns filled with magic ingredients, reliquaries in the form of statuettes, in which a recess in the belly holds the required preparations, and statuettes studded with nails, which suggest the practice of witchcraft. In this region, however, the significance of the nails might be a relic of the arrival of Christianity at the end of the fifteenth century. Fetishes are objects that will ensure protection or perpetrate an act of aggression, sending sickness or death from afar on the chosen victim, and a magician, or anyone who has

obtained a fetish from a magician, can use it for these ends. As such, fetishes are very different from altars and statues, which enshrine divinities on whom the well-being of the whole community and the order of the world depend. (See also *Altars; Ancestors; Art, Negro; Dolls; Pharmacopoeia; Religion; Spirits and Genii.*)   P.M.

FEUDALISM. To find counts and barons, benefices and freeholds, or lieges and vassals in traditional Africa would be an abuse of comparative sociology. However, to examine the feudal system that existed in Europe between the ninth century and the end of the Middle Ages in search of a fundamental type of social relationship that could have developed elsewhere and at other periods is a legitimate exercise. It can throw light on the complex workings of certain African societies. The feudal relationship as an abstraction, reduced to its basic essentials, is born of an agreement between two persons of unequal status who promise each other reciprocal protection and service, in forms generally accepted by the society in which they live. This relationship, which is primordial, since it is independent of politics, family ties or class distinctions, is the focal point of some African institutions. It existed primarily in East Africa—in Ankole, Rwanda, Burundi and half a dozen small kingdoms of the Bua. In each case, it had a special name, which shows clearly that the members of these societies regarded it as something distinct from other kinds of social relations. In fact, feudalism as an aspect of African culture had a character all its own; it was feudalism based on cattle and not land. During the agreement ceremony, when one party asked for protection and offered his service in return, thereby becoming the dependent of the other, he was given one or perhaps several cows. The rich man, who by this gesture became the lord and master of the other, did not give the cattle as a present. He simply conveyed their holding—that is to say, the enjoyment of the usufruct—while he himself retained the ownership. Exactly like the land ceded in fief by the suzerain to the vassal, the cattle put at the disposal of the dependent performed a dual function: it was tangible proof of the agreement, and it gave the dependent an income, thereby enabling him to render the promised services. These services varied according to the caste of the dependent. If he was a noble, he helped his master by giving him advice, by carrying out delicate missions for him, by honoring him with his constant attendance wherever he went and by living near his residence. If he was a peasant, he paid his master his dues in kind, such as baskets of beans and sorghum or jugs of milk and banana beer, or he did manual work for him. Protection, the counterpart of these services, is impossible to describe in detail, because it consisted mainly of general assistance, which was given when it was necessary and on a scale left entirely to the discretion of the master. For instance, when a dependent was persecuted by a powerful man, or when, because of a bad harvest, he could not feed his family, or when he was not able to pay a marriage compensation, his master helped him.

Despite its being a personal agreement that was concerned with individual needs and problems, feudalism had important implications for society as a whole. In the first place, it strengthened the social power of the nobility, either by sealing caste solidarity with personal loyalty, when the feudal link united two members of the nobility (in Ankole such a link could only exist inside the superior caste), or by supporting caste solidarity by means of a link of personal dependence, when this link united members of different social strata (possible in Rwanda and Burundi and obligatory among the Bua). Secondly, feudalism maintained a certain cohesion in cases where caste distinctions could have led to a total breakdown of communication. Through the numerous links between the nobles and peasants, each dependent was symbolically associated with his master and benefited from his master's influence in the community if he were threatened by another noble. Finally, this network of feudal relationships had economic significance. Through its channels, agricultural produce went up from the peasant producers to the consumer of the pastoral class, whose capital, consisting of cattle, was put at the disposition of the farmers. But this two-way traffic was not of equal value; the flow of the produce of the soil was met by a mere trickle of pastoral products. The masters knew that the peasants could not do without their protection and made them pay dearly for it. (See also *Castes; Fulani; Rwanda; Sahara Desert.*)   J.M.

FISHING. Africa is relatively rich in fish, including those that live in salt, sweet and brackish water. Yet, many tribes that inhabit regions in which fish are very abundant are not greatly concerned with fishing. They often leave most of the fishing to tribes or tribal castes that specialize in it, such as the Sorko and Korangi of the Songhai province, the Bozo and Somono of the Mande group, peoples from the lagoon areas of the Ivory Coast and Nigeria, the Kotoko of the

Logone River region, the Batonga of Lake Nyasa and the Yakoma and Banziri of the Ubangi River region. Among many agricultural peoples, fishing is a useful supplementary activity often pursued by women, but some tribes, like the Fulani, object to fishing or, like the Masai, refuse even to eat fish. Deep-sea fishing is practiced only by the Swahili and Comoro islanders; the peoples of the Atlantic seaboard do not venture onto the high seas.

Fishing techniques vary. Fishing may be done with harpoons, eel prongs or, occasionally, bows and arrows. Or it may be done with nets such as seine or shank nets, handleless round or triangular shrimping nets to which special kinds of baskets are attached, oval fishing nets (used by the Demsa of Cameroun), triangular nets (used by the Kotoko) or standing nets that are attached to floats or stakes. The use of the cast net, which is probably of European origin and was first used on the lagoons of Ghana (by the Ge and Ga), has now spread all over West Africa. The dragnet, another importation, is found only in the form of a small bag net (used by the Kru and the Sherbro of Sierra Leone and Nigeria). Hooks are widely used as well as fishing rods, handlines, groundlines, trawls and trailing lines. Fishing traps, which are often very

Fishing with a net. Porto Novo, Dahomey. Photo: Service d'Information, Dahomey.

River fishing. Oum Hdjer, Chad. *Photo: Hoa-Qui.*

large and whose use may close off an entire river or lagoon, are very common. They include traps that employ trigger action, bag nets and standing nets, as well as bow nets. Fishing is also done by damming and, finally, by exhausting or poisoning fish with the aid of toxic plants (*Tephrosia*, for example).

The canoe is the most usual boat of the fishing tribes mentioned above. The Sorko are more interested in hunting hippopotamuses than fishing in the strict sense of the word. Some tribes, mainly agricultural ones, undertake large-scale seasonal fishing expeditions, which have a ritual rather than a utilitarian purpose (for example, the Mundang, Musgu and Tuburi of Cameroun and Chad).

Fish is eaten fresh only in the places where fish is actually caught. Most of the catch is preserved either by smoking or drying it in the sun. There is a large trade in smoked or dried fish, but African production is not sufficient to meet the demand and dried and salt cod have to be imported. Modern fisheries and canneries have been developed, for instance in Senegal and on the Ivory Coast and in ports of the Indian Ocean, but their produce does not always satisfy the demands of the local population, whose preference is for fish prepared in a traditional way as a spice or condiment rather than as a main dish. Whale and shark fishing have been undertaken on an industrial basis by European enterprises in African waters (there is a whaling station in Gabon and fisheries in Senegal), but without much success. There has been greater success with lobster and tuna, which are caught by European fishing fleets as far afield as Dakar and transported in refrigerated ships. (See also *Chad, Lake; Diet; Fauna; Kirdi; Massa; Sao; Savanna; Songhai; Traps; Weapons.*)

P.A.

FLORA. The vegetation zones of the African continent extend to two hemispheres and form bands running approximately parallel to the equator. First, there is the equatorial zone; this is the area of dense forests where very tall trees, growing close together but showing little homogeneity, rise above a thick undergrowth and where there are plants without chlorophyll. Near the tropics, the forest is thinner, the number of kinds of trees is more limited and the sparse undergrowth permits the development of Gramineae, or grasses. The tropical zone is the area of the savanna, where plants related to different types of ferns are the principal vegetation. In the subtropical zone, savanna grass takes its place and deciduous trees are gradually replaced by thornbushes, which disappear, in their turn, in the desert zones. Altitude and the availability of water determine the subtypes of vegetation: the forest range of the subtropical zone, the papyrus swamps of areas liable to flooding, the mangroves of the coastal equatorial zones and the mountain vegetation of eastern and southern Africa.

With the exception of the virgin forests, the original vegetation covering Africa has been modified everywhere by human activity. Selective felling of trees in cultivated zones has created man-made landscapes such as the park-forest of *Faidherbia albida* trees in the tropical zone stretching from Senegal to Lake Chad. Yearly bush fires, the stripping of land for agricultural purposes and overgrazing contribute alarmingly to the spread of arid zones which are useless to man.

The diet of traditional African societies is basically vegetarian and makes use of both wild and cultivated plants. Many of the plants cultivated today are of foreign origin: peanuts, corn, cassava, sweet potato and numerous fruits originated in tropical America; sesame, bananas, the jujube tree, sugarcane, coffee and some varieties of rice and beans are of Eastern or Far Eastern origin; and the coconut and the taro come from Oceania. Plants indigenous to Africa include the date palm, sorghum, oil palm, castor-oil plant, the chick-pea and some varieties of millet, eleusines, yams and gourds.

Rotproof and termite-proof wood is used for construction of frames for houses and granaries. Most of the masks in the savanna have been carved of fromager wood, which is easily worked and sufficiently light and solid to permit the creation of elaborate structures such as the tiered masks of the Dogon. The fibers used for basketry and ropework and for weaving come from grasses, the bark and leaves of wild trees, or from cultivated plants like the hibiscus, textile beans and cotton. Sorghum and palms are used to produce alcoholic beverages. Tobacco, kola nuts, Indian hemp (from which hashish is made) and kat (*Catha edulis*) are the principal stimulants.

No proper inventory exists as yet of the African plants used for magical or medicinal purposes. Cassia, kinkiliba and citronella are the best known. Some traditional poisons are included in the Western pharmacopoeia such as strophanthin, strychnines, the thorn apple, spurge and the Calabar bean. A kind of African mistletoe, the loranthus, has stirred the imagination of traditional societies, which attribute different magical properties to it, according to the tree it grows on.

Trees and plants are important in the mythology and religious practices of tradi-

tional societies. It is through the flora surrounding them that rural societies are made aware of the renewal of the seasons, the continuity of life and the blessings of the gods, who are the givers of harvests to men. Among the Dogon in the Sudan, the eight principal cultivated plants are believed to be made of the same substance as men and

Silk-cotton trees. *Photo: Hoa-Qui.*

Lobelia. *Photo: Jacques Maquet.*

Briers. *Photo: Jacques Maquet.*

instruments owe nothing to any other civilization, and nothing like them is found anywhere in North Africa. The flageolet, or fipple flute, was brought to North Africa by Islam but never really penetrated black Africa. Only the oblique flute used by Arabs, and also in Egypt, but at an earlier date, is found in several regions (among the Sara of Chad and in northern Dahomey, South Africa and Madagascar), but not necessarily as a result of Muslim influence. The oblique instrument played by the Zulu and Swazi, for example, is certainly of more ancient origin; furthermore, the sound is produced in a very primitive way, and only one note can be played on it. A palette made of shale, which was discovered in Egypt at Hierakonpolis, depicts an animal, probably a masked man, playing a long vertical flute. There is no trace of this instrument existing in the dynastic period, but it might well have survived in black Africa, at least in the form of large whistles, which were used until not so long ago. A few nose flutes exist. Reed pipes, or panpipes, seem to be unknown in Africa, although they are common on other continents. As a substitute for this row of pipes, a variety of tribes (in Abyssinia, East and South Africa and the Congo region) have orchestras of whistles or flutes in which each instrument is capable of producing one or two sounds; the instruments are played in turn in order to produce a continuous melodic line. There are references to orchestras composed of nine to twenty-six instruments, whose notes may span two to four octaves. As they play these instruments, the musicians move in Indian file and may even execute dance steps like those of whirling dervishes. The flute and whistle are used for profane purposes nearly everywhere in Africa, but this particular mode of playing them may be associated with hunting and fertility rites. (See also *Horns; Music.*) A.S.

enclosed in their collarbones. A baobab tree stained with libations is a common sight in West Africa. The societies of northern Cameroun perform their sacrifices on trees and plants which serve as the altars of the powers of the other world. The religious life of African civilizations is organized around agrarian rites associated with the principal plants that they cultivate, or the earliest to be harvested. The clearing of land, sowing, germination, weeding, harvesting, eating the first fruits or plants and garnering, in fact every agricultural activity, has to be accompanied by complicated rituals. (See also *Fruit; Savanna; Totemism; Vegetables.*) I.G.

FLUTES and WHISTLES. The flute should be clearly distinguished from the whistle; they are very different instruments. The latter can be made of various materials, such as wood, horn, soft stone, dried clay or white metal, and is far more widely distributed; it is held vertically; the mouthpiece, at the top end, can be straight, beveled or notched; pierced with holes along its sides and having a pipe that is either open or closed at the base, it can produce up to three notes. The flute, which is made either of large millet stems, reed or bamboo, is held horizontally and played like the transverse flute of Europe or Asia; it rarely has a range of more than five notes. These two types of

FOSSILS, HUMAN. The oldest human fossil was discovered in the earliest layer of the site at Olduvai Gorge, Tanzania, by Mary and L.S.B. Leakey, who called it *Homo habilis.* The culture of *Homo habilis* was characterized by roughly shaped stones, which were the first unquestionable traces of human activity and is known as the Oldowan Culture. *Homo habilis* was short and walked upright on feet that were not very different from present-day man's; but his hands were not developed, and his brain was distinctly smaller than ours. He was a hunter who lived at Olduvai nearly 2 million years ago and stayed there over a long period. The fossil found at Yayo, Chad, may have belonged to the same stage of evolution. Prior to this, various forms of Australopithecinae had been found in Africa; they belonged to the *Australopithecus* and *Paranthropus,* several fragments of which were found in South Africa. The *Zinjanthropus boisei,* which is classified in the latter genus, was discovered at Olduvai in the same layer as the *Homo habilis.* Australopithecinae can hardly be called men because, although they may have used stones and bones, they were not toolmakers.

A skull discovered in the second layer at Olduvai and bones discovered at Ternifine, Algeria, are associated with the Chelles-Acheul culture, which was more advanced than the Oldowan. Only a summary account has so far been given of the Chelles-Acheul Culture, but C. Arambourg, the discoverer of the bones, has shown that they are related to the *Homo erectus* of Asia.

At a later stage of the evolution of sub-Saharan Africa, creatures appeared who were like the Neanderthal men of Europe and Asia and belonged to the beginning of the Middle Stone Age or the period immediately preceding it. Their skulls were found at Broken Hill in Zambia *(Homo rhodesiensis),* at Hopefield near Saldanha Bay in South Africa (skulls very similar to those found at Broken Hill) and at Lake Eyasi, Tanzania (called *Africanthropus* by its discoverer); their mandibles were uncovered at Diredawa, Ethiopia, and in the Cave of Hearths at Makapansgat, South Africa. The mandible found at Kanjera, near Kanam, Kenya, and the skull at Singa, Sudan, may also have belonged to the same stage of evolution.

The final evolutionary stage was *Homo sapiens,* present-day man. During the last periods of the Stone Age, human beings related to present-day Khoisans (Bushmen and Hottentots) appeared in South Africa, but the earliest of them were taller and stronger than most later men; their remains resemble those found at Skildergat, Bambandyanalo, Mapungubwe, Zitzikam, Boskop and the Matjes River and some Hottentots today. D. Brothwell thinks that they may have been descended from the same stock as the Kanjera man of Kenya. The reduction in height and build of the Khoisan is a recent development. The Strong Khoisan man found at Florisbad, South Africa, has certain features that indicate he was a cross between the African Neanderthaloids and the Khoisans, and could even be classed among the Neanderthaloids.

In East Africa, the remains of the Stone Age *Homo sapiens* found in Gamble's Cave in Elemteita, Kenya, had a large skeleton, a long head with a thin nose and an orthogna-

Skull of Broken Hill Man *(Homo rhodesiensis).* South Africa. *Photo: Musée de l'Homme.*

thous face. These features were considered evidence of Europoid stock, but, in fact, they are also characteristic of the Batusi and Bahima of Rwanda, Burundi and Uganda, whose Europoid affinities have been disputed. The fossil remains which were thought, beyond any doubt, to be the ancestors of black Africans other than Khoisans and peoples related to the Batusi are reduced to little more than the Asselar man, found in the Sahara; but it is only a few thousand years old. The remote origins of the black race may be found, as Brothwell thought, in African types who were also ancestors of the Khoisans, for example, Kanjera man. Some special forms of evolution, like the development that produced the Pygmies, cannot be explained by any palaeontological remains today, partly because the nature of the soil where they took place is not conducive to fossilization. (See also *Olduvai Gorge; Race; Rock Art.*)

J.H.

FRUIT. In Africa, unlike in Europe and America, fruit is rarely eaten as part of a meal, so it is difficult to estimate exactly how much is actually consumed. Fruit, either cultivated or growing wild in the bush, is abundant in the equatorial zone, but less common in the Sudanese zone. Since various fruits ripen at various times of the year fruit helps to give variety to a monotonous diet. In some parts of Africa, eating fruit is almost regarded like taking a cure. Mangoes, for example, are devoured in large quantities at the end of the dry season by most tribes of West Africa. Desert and Sahel tribes gather every year in oases to take a date cure, which is an opportunity for merrymaking and enables groups that are normally scattered to maintain contact with each other.

Africans plant very few trees but have a certain respect for those that are useful to them. Apart from date palms, coconut palms, oil palms and banana and pineapple trees, which are cultivated on a commercial basis, trees whose fruit is intended for domestic consumption are given practically no attention at all. Many of the fruit trees that are common in Africa originated in tropical America, including the guava, papaya, annona, custard apple, alligator pear and cashew trees and the *Spondius mombin*. The jujube and mango trees may be of Eastern origin. Lemon is the only citrus fruit eaten in the Sudanese zone; oranges and grapefruit belong to more humid areas.

The uncultivated fruit most frequently gathered and used comes from the tamarind tree, the Barbary fig *(Opuntia)* and the desert date palm *(Balanites),* whose kernels produce an oil which is valued in Senegal. In Senegal, too, the baobab fruit is an important addition to the diet. Its pulp, when thinned with water, is called "milk of monkey bread" and is very rich in calcium and vitamin B_1. Dates are an important source of vitamin C, and the fruit of the oil palm contains a high proportion of vitamin A. The castor-oil plant, the cailcedra or

bastard mahogany and the shea tree *(Butyrospermum paradoxum),* the characteristic tree of the savanna, and the African locust *(Parkia)* are the principal source of fats for traditional societies. Shea butter and soumbala, which is made of the fermented fruit of the African locust, are condiments found in all markets in the bush.

It is impossible to describe in detail the wild fruit consumed in traditional African societies. Each group eats dozens of species: palm fruits, wild figs, tamarinds—a long list could be made. There are two kinds of wild fruit: the first is eaten by everyone and sometimes marketed; the second, and by far the larger category, is left to the children. Some fruits, such as the berries of the *Prunus mirobolant* and the tamarind, are picked and macerated in water; this gives the water a somewhat bitter flavor. The liquid is then drunk or is mixed with flour to make a gruel. Some other fruits, such as the *Faidherbia albida,* are used as fodder during the dry season. Most fruits are preserved by drying, like dates, or are pounded, like the pods of the tamarind and jujube trees. The kola nut is a stimulant eaten all over Africa. The tree grows in the Guinea region, and trade in kola nuts became one of the most extensive in the whole of traditional Africa. (See also *Diet; Vegetables.*)   I.G.

FULANI. It would be absurd to claim that a cultural unity exists among a population of about 6 million people, who speak the same language but are spread over the savanna belt and high plateau from Senegal to Chad. There is no proof either of the existence of two distinct groups, one made up of settled and Muslim communities—the black Fulani —and the other of pastoral and non-Muslim communities—the red Fulani. Both, in varying degrees, display certain morphologic and cultural characteristics that are the product of the impact or the amalgamation of contrasting civilizations of Mediterranean and Sudanese origin. Fulfulde, or Fulani, which is spoken by this people of mixed origin, is an African language that is generally considered as belonging to the western Atlantic group of Sudanese languages and as having a special affinity with Serer and Wolof. The history of the Fulani (or Peul) also began in the western Sudan region, in Senegambia. They began to disperse eastward in the eleventh century, and most of them settled and founded kingdoms, which were first pagan and later Muslim. Much has been written about the problem of their earliest origins, including some fanciful theories, but nothing worthy of being called "scientific."

Market. Ivory Coast. *Photo: Rapho, H. de Chatillon.*

Three great values govern the nomadic world: livestock, women and the power to command. The pastoral Fulani are pacific, hospitable and frugal, and they possess, according to the proverb, "plenty of oxen and restraint." The socio-political organization of these nomads resembles that of the Bedouin more closely than that of the pastoral societies of East Africa. It includes no military organization, age group system, initiation rituals or blood-price. The shepherd encampments, consisting of families who are seldom polygamous and rarely extend beyond brothers and their children, are constantly on the move to find pastures and water for their herds. They live on sour milk and millet, which they get by barter. They eat meat only at the end of ceremonies —in honor of a marriage or the assigning of a name *(gereol)*—which they all celebrate together with feasts of slaughtered cattle. The women do the milking and are entitled to the milk they draw. The custom of preheritage, in the form of cattle inherited from father to son, allows every man to acquire economic independence at a fairly early age. A migratory group, composed of agnate units whose members hypothetically belong to the same patrilineage, splits into smaller groups after establishing itself on new territory. Although each group is led by an independent leader, chosen by the adult men who follow him, the groups continue to cooperate and combine their encampments once a year for the great transhumance in the rainy season. Marriages, whether exogamous or endogamous in relation to the lineage and the agnate unit, are important in maintaining the balance of the various elements of the group and in its breakdown into smaller groups.

Where the Fulani have settled, they have developed many different ways of combining agriculture and cattle-raising, but have never achieved the balance found in societies with agricultural traditions, such as the Berbers and Serer. Many cultural traits have survived the transition from nomadic to settled life, such as living mostly with the father's group, the economic independence of the family and the absence, or minor importance, of the bride-price and even preference for certain types of marriages. The states created by fanatical Muslim Fulani were a kind of military theocracy with a graduated system of minor chieftains, headed by a superior authority who was constantly menaced by the rivalry of the great families that constituted the ranks of the dignitaries. These Muslim Fulani societies are very stratified and have a hierarchy based on serfdom. Most agricultural work, trade and crafts are in the hands of serfs or blacks, who belong to separate

Fulani Bororo. Niger. *Photo: Magnum, Marc Riboud.*

castes. Descent is patrilineal, but there is no worship of ancestors; divisions of the kin group follow the successive divisions of the land following inheritance, and each new group is responsible for the administration of its share. These patrilineal families are endogamous, like all Fulani societies, and the greater the strength of the patrilineal

Funerary statuette. Anyi.
Ivory Coast. Terracotta.
Christophe Tzara Collection,
Paris. *Photo: Hélène Adant.*

Grave in a Katanga village.
Zaire. *Photo:
Jacques Maquet.*

principle, the more pronounced is this exclusiveness. Islam has almost completely overlaid the remnants of any hypothetical pastoral religion, although research may still discover some traces. Non-Islamic rites and beliefs generally reflect more or less accurately the customs of African societies with whom these Fulani communities have continued to live. (See also *Arab Chroniclers; Bambara; Bamum; Bornu; Cattle; Clothing; Feudalism; Griots; Hausa; Islam; Lions; Migrations; Savanna; Sudan.*) M.D.

FUNERALS. The belief that the dead must be treated decorously and with great respect to prevent them from returning and taking revenge on the living is fundamental to the African approach to funerals. Legends of wandering, unhappy and dangerous souls abound in Africa. Only the most careful and detailed observance of funeral rites will ensure that the dead will leave their descendants and relations in peace and will enable the dead to be led painlessly to the final dwelling places between which their essence will be divided; these dwelling places are partially in the world of the gods and partially in the land of the living—on altars which are usually dedicated to the dead. The rites send the souls of the dead on their way (they are brought back later in a tamer form). These rites span a long period, extending from the pronouncement of death until the end of mourning, which finally installs the dead in their place among the ancestors who are recognized, propitiated, considered capable of transmitting to their descendants part of their vital force. Sometimes, the last ritual is postponed for a while so that the mourners can dispatch several dead at once. During the intervening time, the spirit of the dead often pursues some complicated wanderings through the world of the living.

Death has first to be ascertained beyond all doubt—the Edo in Benin wait several hours before lamenting the departed in the hope that a hesitant soul will join the body once more. Specialists for treating the dead are summoned. The word goes out to friends and relatives, each of whom will have to observe the conventions of every phase of the funeral, bringing gifts, sharing the remains of sacrifices, purging themselves of quarrels which divide them and, sometimes (as among the Bakongo), confronting each other in a gift exchanging ceremony. The body is exhibited in a courtyard or on a terrace, before a house or under a shelter, seated or lying, for a period of time depending on the man's importance in society. Since this could continue for several months among the Bakongo, it was necessary to envelop the body in the smoke of aromatic plants and provide a system for discharging body fluids. Sometimes the body received no treatment at all, but in many regions it was anointed with special preparations or preserved by smoking and then embalming, as among the Swazi in southern Africa, or embalmed and smoked at the same time and thus virtually mummified, as among numerous people in the central Sudan, the Songhai, Hausa and Jukun. Among the last group, only the kings were treated like this. As long as a dead body occupies a house, visitors are given food and drink, and a number of ceremonies take place. There are lamentations, panegyrics, offerings and dances miming his great deeds in the hunt or in war. Among the Somba in Dahomey, his sons make a symbolic attack upon the house; among the Dogon in Mali this is performed by the men's society.

No death is natural; therefore, in every case, its cause must be discovered before the body is laid in its grave. The Fang in Gabon used to perform an autopsy and examine the organs to try and find possible traces of sorcery. They also said that they could revive a dead person long enough for him to indicate who was responsible for his demise. A more common practice was to consult a soothsayer. Many Sudanese tribes questioned the corpse while it was being carried toward its grave. It answered these questions by imparting movements to the bearers, and these movements directed the bearers toward those who were responsible for the death. Rites of purification or expiation had to follow. Once the enquiry was over, the body could be put in its grave. Usually it was only enveloped in a mat, rug or skin; in the Chad region the body was put into an urn in a crouching position. The Bamangala and various tribes in the northern part of the Congo laid it in a wooden coffin carved in human shape, similar to Egyptian sarcophagi. The grave was dug in different shapes, according to the customs of different regions: it could be in the house itself or in a cemetery, by the roadside or at a crossroads; sometimes a watercourse served as a grave, water being the special domain of the dead; among several peoples of East Africa it was a tree. Personal possessions were often buried with the dead as presents; the Ashanti, for example, placed these in beautiful bronze funerary vessels. Sometimes an orifice would be made, through which libations or the blood of sacrifices could be poured. In many places, sacrifices were never made nor prayers offered at tombs, but only at altars where the ancestors were represented. Hunters covered graves with piles of stone;

Dance during funeral rites. Senufo. Ivory Coast. *Photo: Hoa-Qui.*

pastoral peoples, like the Nuer and Shilluk of the upper Nile, put on them the horns of the oxen which had been most closely connected with the dead person; and agricultural people marked graves by putting pottery on them. The Anyi of the Ivory Coast used a terracotta statuette or a pole, which was sometimes carved. But some people kept the burial place secret for fear of desecrators searching for magic substances.

There was no fixed period between burial and the end of mourning, which was in fact the most important part of the funeral rites. Its duration depended on the importance of the dead, his age, the age of his sons and his resources. Animals had to be sacrificed; there were gifts to be distributed to the participants; and food and beverages, including millet beer, had to be prepared in large quantities. This period could last twenty years, but generally it lasted several months or one year, during which time life slowed down and activities were diminished, at least in theory. Widows, and sometimes everyone, had to observe a number of taboos and to undergo certain rituals and restrictions: shaving of the head; letting clothes go unwashed; and, among some tribes like the Wakamba of Kenya, abstaining from sexual relations until the rites of purification. The funeral ceremonies lasted several days and were sometimes divided into different phases. Their complexity is indescribable. There were prayers, sacrifices and dances during which masks were often used; meals and drinking sessions followed in profusion. The altar of the dead man was set up, or he was appeased until it could be done; ceremonies of purification revitalized the living, who had been troubled and weakened by the intrusion of death.

The form and course of funerals, the place and circumstance of burial varied according to the age, sex and social position of the dead. The Ibo in Nigeria gave only old men tombs; the other dead were thrown into the bush. This is an extreme case, but throughout Africa those who died young were given only simple burial or none at all and were buried in a separate place. The rites for women, too, were often of the simplest, since female ancestors, with a few exceptions, are far less important. Societies that have castes treat their dead in different ways. The Wolof in Senegal inter everyone except griots, whose bodies are put inside trees. In many cases, sorcerers and victims of the wrath of gods were deprived of the general rites. On the other hand, priests, chiefs and kings received special honors with ceremonies appropriate to their rank, particularly kings, for a king's death could disturb the entire equilibrium of the community. "It is night," "the house is withered," they used to say in Dahomey when a king died. Life stopped until the king was laid in his tomb, no fires were lit, no water drawn from the well, no grain pounded, no meat eaten, no one washed, no one could sit on a chair. But at the same time, when the dark forces contained in the king were let loose, "moral laxity was given free rein.... Everyone could take his vengeance without fear of punishment" (A. Le Hérissé). Consequently, extremely powerful rites were essential to restore order in the world and in society. (See also *Bells; Body; Body Painting; Clothing; Dance; Death; Diet; Dogon; Drums; Gold; Religion; Senufo; Spirits and Genii; Widows.*)   P.M.

GAMES. Societies can be distinguished not only according to their basic methods of acquisition or production, but also according to the way they approach what J. Huizinga calls the "secular spirit of play." Games can be regarded as the products of institutions, and the institutions themselves can be viewed as games—especially in traditional African surroundings where social relationships are often put on show and, as it were, "produced." This interpretation is made even more plausible by the fact that children's games often contain an element of imitation or parody. In towns in Mali and Sudanese Guinea, children play a game of hide-and-seek that reenacts the

campaigns of the Samory Touré and his sofas. Young Wolof children in Saint-Louis, Senegal, amuse themselves by copying the sacred games of the Malinke, who live on the outskirts of the town, in particular the games of the *Komo* society of initiates, which they call *Koma*. The wealth of African inventiveness is just as evident in their games as in their arts. The two are never entirely distinct. The container for the game of twelve boxes, known in the Ivory Coast as *awele*, is carved out of special wood and is so meticulously and carefully made that it is really a work of art; it is said that even the gods play with it during the night. The dolls of the Ashanti of Ghana, known as *akua'ba*, serve three functions: primarily, they are used to protect pregnant women; secondly, they are playthings for little girls; and, finally, they are objects that delight admirers of Negro art. To go from magic to play to art merely requires changing the relationship between the object and the person using it.

It is impossible to make an inventory of African games. They are numerous and very varied. They tend to change with time, and some disappear completely. In some ways, they reflect the civilization that originates and disseminates them. Charles Béart has nevertheless written a monumental work that covers "the games of the peoples of western and equatorial Africa" and suggests a tentative classification of types of games. The toys and games usually associated with childhood are the cradle and the baby's rattle (not used as a plaything in many parts of Africa), hand and string games and dolls. Dolls are rarely simple toys; they are sometimes debased representations of gods, like those of the Grunshi of Upper Volta. As African children grow older, they display great skill in the construction of their own toys and keen powers of observation in their imitations of adult society. They build miniature villages and model inhabitants for them or use them as settings for their imitations of adult society. At a later stage, their ingenuity displays itself in search games that may involve magic: word games, mathematical games (using magic squares), games in which objects are hidden, craft games and so on.

Public competition is still the main incentive for participating in games. Each region has its special form of wrestling. It may be a rough, fierce bout decided by a single throw, as in Songhai lands, or it may extend over several rounds, as among the Wolof, or it may be in the form of a dance, as among the Fulani. Wrestling matches for children are found everywhere. They are taken seriously and sometimes are almost like a rite: in Louga, Senegal, the loser is regarded as "dead," undergoes a burial ceremony and is mourned for an entire month. African games also include games of chance, legerdemain, satirical parodies, competitions in making grimaces and musical entertainment involving dancing and singing.

Modern changes have, so to speak, upset all the rules of the game. The old wrestling bouts are being replaced by sporting contests. The magic of the traditional game is giving way to the magic of money, for which the new games are a pretext. But their inherited love of play has not yet been dissipated, and with the return of independence the African imagination has acquired new vigor. (See also *Bull-Roarers; Dolls; Proverbs; Rattles; Riddles; Sports; Xylophones*.)   G.B.

Two versions of the game of twelve boxes. *Left:* The game of "songo." Cameroun. *Below:* The Fanyan game of "yaro." Chad. *Photos: Pierre Ichac.*

Bagirmi doll. Chad. Wood. Charles Ratton Collection, Paris. *Photo Jean Roubier.*

Tuburi wrestling. Chad.
Photo: Pierre Ichac.

GENEALOGY. A knowledge of filiation is of prime importance in societies that are based entirely on kinship. As a result, genealogies play a major role almost all over Africa, particularly in the education of boys. The form, style and exact content of genealogies—and especially how far back they go—vary considerably, depending upon the nature of the social structures of different ethnic groups. In societies with a caste structure, where there are extreme social contrasts and a hierarchical political system, genealogies are the privilege of families of noble lineage and are rather like historical chronicles. Their preservation, recitation and transmission are therefore often entrusted to experts, who frequently enjoy a special status like that of medieval heralds—for example, the Wolof and Malinke genealogists, who are called griots, and the college of the *bwiru* in Rwanda. On the other hand, in less hierarchical societies, all free men must learn to keep their own genealogies, which tend to be merely simple pedigrees reaching back for a varying number of generations. In the Ewe city-states of Ghana and Togo and in the clan societies of the Bantu in the northwest, they go as far back as twenty generations, but they are often legendary and stereotyped beyond the twelfth. Among the Palaeonegrids of the Atakora Mountains in Togo and the Nigerian Plateau, eight generations is the limit. Descendants of prisoners and domestic slaves have a tendency today to attach their genealogies to those of the families of their old masters. This practice is allowed in some societies but frowned upon in many others. The recitation of genealogies plays a large part in social ceremonies; some tribes use it instead of greetings or formal introductions. The same word sometimes means "greeting," "genealogy" and "descent" (e.g., *sede* is used in this way by the Tem in Togo). From the religious point of view, this recitation may be considered as a kind of prayer or profession of faith if the genealogy links living people, through the chain of their forebears, to their founding Ancestor. (See also *Education; Griots; Heads; Royalty.*)   P.A.

GHANA. Ghana was the most ancient and one of the most powerful of the medieval black states. At the height of its power, the authority of its kings extended from the Sahara desert to the forest region, from the Atlantic Ocean to the bend of the Niger, covering the present-day territory of Mauritania, Senegal, western Mali and upper Guinea, but none of modern Ghana. The kingdom is said to have been founded in the fourth century A.D. by the Bafur, an unknown tribe. Until the eighth century, it was probably governed by a dynasty of Berber origin, which was overthrown in 790 by a Soninke king, Kaya Cisse, who founded the Sunkara dynasty. Ghana was neither the name of the kingdom nor of its capital, but merely one of the titles of the king—"chief warrior." His other names were *kaya maga* ("chief of the earth" or "chief of gold") and *tunka* ("king" or "prince"). The first capital, Koumbi Saleh, was originally in the Mauritanian Sahel, which was then more fertile than it is today. The site must have been changed several times. In one of its likely locations, more than 200 miles north of Bamako, between the Niger and Senegal rivers, archeologists have found the ruins of a city of 30,000 inhabitants, which may have been the commercial center of the capital. As a matter of fact, the capital was a twin city, with the commercial quarter, inhabited by foreigners and Muslims, separated from the royal residence, which was a town in itself.

Arab and Sudanese chroniclers never tired of describing the riches, power and ostentation of the *Kaya maga,* who was capable, according to al-Bakri (1067), of raising an army of 200,000 men. The same chroniclers describe Ghana as a black African monarchy ruled over by a divine king. The succession passed through the matrilineal line from the maternal uncle to his sister's son. The monarchy was distinguished by its regalia, including the sacred drums, and an organization that current ethnologists regard as very "modern." Ghana's power was based on trans-Saharan trade. Although gold mining was an occupation of the forest lands and not under their control, the sovereigns monopolized its export. The same was true of salt, which was extracted by the Saharan Berbers, who were vassals of Ghana, and was resold in the gold-bearing regions.

The ancient kingdom of Ghana was destroyed by the Almoravids, a Muslim Berber dynasty. In 1055, the Almoravids took Awdaghast, a vassal Berber kingdom and Ghana dependency on the eastern trans-Saharan route. In 1062, Ghana itself was attacked by the Almoravids under Abu Bakr ibn-Umar, who took the capital in 1076, aided perhaps by an uprising of the Muslim inhabitants, whose religion had always been tolerated by the sovereigns of Ghana. The Berbers, however, could not maintain their ascendancy, and their dominion collapsed with the death of Abu Bakr in 1087. The war made a desert of the Sahel region, stopped its trade and destroyed the cohesion of the Ghanan empire, because the border provinces became independent kingdoms. The most important of these was Susu, to the east of Ghana, which was governed by the Dyareso dynasty until 1180, then by the Kante. The second Kante king, Sumanguru Kante, succeeded in about 1220 in re-establishing the empire and even enlarged it by conquering the Mande in the southeast. This was its swan song. In 1235 the Malinke conqueror Sundiata Keita defeated Sumanguru, and in 1240 he seized the capital. He left Ghana, now reduced only to the Soninke territory, to subsist as a sort of protectorate of the Malinke empire, perhaps because of the prestige of the ancient Ghanan state. Another, and perhaps more likely, explanation for this relative respect for the fallen empire might be found in the interpretation of the traditional title *kaya maga* as "chief of the earth"; and the descendants of the original sovereigns maintained their ritual position despite the political domination of the new leadership. (See also *Almoravids; Arab Chroniclers; Gold; Islam; Mali; Markets; Migrations; Salt; Sudan.*)

P.A.

GOATS. The most common domestic animal on the African continent is the goat. There are two main types from which many breeds have developed. The Sahelan type is large, with a long body and an abundant coat that often resembles that of the long-haired sheep of the same region. The head is elongated, and the shape of the horns varies greatly. This type of goat (found in Niger, Egypt and the plains of northern Cameroun) weighs between forty and sixty pounds. Breeds of this type can walk long distances, are well adapted to drought and heat, are hardy and eat little. Goats of this type are even found in the Tibesti region of the Sahara. South of the Sahel, as far as the forests, there is a short type (the dwarf goat of Senegal and the Kirdi breed in Cameroun) that is low-built, short-haired and plump, weighing a maximum of about thirty pounds. Breeds of this type are well adapted to damp conditions, are hardy and are very prolific.

There are about 100 million goats in Africa. They are less numerous than sheep in the Sahel area but predominate elsewhere. They resist the tsetse fly better than cattle and are found in the heart of the equatorial forest, where there is reckoned to be one goat for every ten inhabitants, as against one for every two inhabitants in the Sudan region and one per person in the area south of the Sahara.

Goat's milk has much the same composition as that of cows. It is seldom drunk regularly except by simple herdsmen in the bush. There is a brisk trade in goats throughout Africa, and their sale is one of the most important sources of income for peasants. Goats provide most of the butcher's meat in traditional communities. In many societies they are part of the bride-price, which a man must give to the father of his future wife. They are often offered as sacrifices to ancestors and deities. Most of the Palaeonegrid peoples use goatskin to make men's loincloths. The Hausa in northern Nigeria and the Fulani in Cameroun, who excel in leatherwork, generally use goat- and sheepskins, most of which are marketed at Kano. (See also *Animal Husbandry; Sahara Desert.*)   I.G.

GODS. Having accused Africans of "superstition" and "idolatry," some missionary writers have gone to the opposite extreme and tried, in every possible way, to find in African thought a kind of intuitive knowledge of the principal Christian dogma. These two contradictory attitudes have rather obscured the problem of the concept, or concepts, of god in Africa, since even many lay researchers have shared this unconscious tendency either to attribute or to deny Africans particular elements of their own religious or philosophical beliefs.

An objective analysis of ethnographic literature shows that most black African religious systems accept the existence of a god who was the first creator. He is endowed with a personality and his own proper name, which does not exist in the plural and frequently resembles the root *nyama* or *liza* (which occurs throughout almost the whole of Africa). He is generally viewed as being human in form, although he is not human. He is the judge or supreme authority in the universe, the source of all strength and of all morality. Many myths relate how this god, who lived on earth among men at the creation, left them when they broke his commandments. He then became infinitely distant and transcendent; today, he is no longer accessible to man, which explains why relatively few prayers are addressed and sacrifices offered to him.

The details vary greatly between one ethnic cluster and another. The creator appears most frequently as a masculine element, often as the sun or a heavenly body. He can also be androgynous—he may be considered as two separate persons or as having two natures, perhaps asexual and feminine, in one person. Only rarely are there other gods on the same level as the creator-god; the nearest such gods are the mother-goddesses of the underworld in the Sudanese (the Yoruba and Kwa group and the Dogon and Volta group) cosmologies. On the other hand, African mythologies make frequent reference to either subordinate divinities, such as gods with special duties, or super-natural intermediaries between god and man, such as heroes or demigods, genii in the form of natural forces or spirits in the form of animals. Most of the customary rites are addressed to these divinities and inter-mediaries and to the shades of the departed. It is interesting to note that nowhere in Africa have Christian or Muslim mission-aries had any trouble in introducing their converts to the concept of a single god who is the creator, personal and all powerful, and that the modern, syncretic versions of Christianity and Islam that have developed in Africa have never called this concept into question. (See also *Altars; Divinities; Heaven; Heroes; Masks; Myths; Nile; Possession by Spirits; Prayer; Rain; Religion; Royalty; Sacrifice; Sculpture, Wood; Twins;* individual tribes.)   P.A.

GOLD. *Bilad as-Sudan,* "land of the blacks," was also called from earliest times "land of gold," the metal whose source remained mysterious. An inscription dating back to 2275 B.C. records how a servant of the pharaoh Pepi II went to the land of Cush —that is to say, to southern Nubia—and brought back gold, ivory, incense, a boomerang and even a Pygmy to amuse his master. The boomerang remained the throwing weapon of the river peoples living along the White Nile, upstream from Khartoum. To capture the Pygmy, the traveler may have sailed up the Bahr el Ghazal as far as the fringes of the Congolese forest. Anyway, he does not seem to have been the only one to have attempted such an adventure. In later periods, the Egyptians continued to show great interest in the interior. An Egyptian fortress of the Eleventh Dynasty has been found at Kerma, near Dongola, which was defended by a colonial garrison from a principality, said to be Cush, situated between the Third and the Fourth Cataracts. When, at the end of the second millennium B.C., the capital of Egypt was transferred to Thebes (present-day Luxor), all of Nubia was occupied by Egypt and thoroughly exploited by her. Its mines supplied forty tons of gold a year, an amount unequaled in worldwide production until the nineteenth century. The splendor of Tutankhamen's tomb is evidence of how

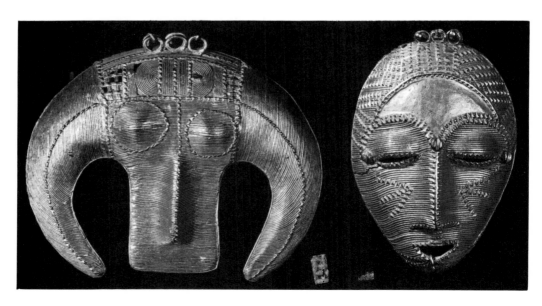

Baule gold ornaments. Ivory Coast. Musée de l'Institut français d'Afrique noire. *Photo: Giraudon.*

the precious metal poured into the country. Beyond Nubia, as the decline of Egypt became more pronounced during the first millennium B.C., the kingdom of Cush, whose capital was first at Napata and then at Meroe, grew stronger. It survived until the fourth century A.D. and continued to export the traditional riches of Africa: ivory, skins, ostrich feathers and slaves, and probably gold dust brought from regions as far away as the mountains of Ethiopia and the banks of the Niger.

After Rome replaced Egypt, the caravan routes changed, and West Africa, via the Maghrib and the Sahara, provided the civilized world with gold until the discovery of America. Two regions were exploited fairly rapidly: the Bambouk region, at the sources of the Gambia and the Faleme rivers; and the Boure district, around the upper reaches of the Niger River. Later on, traders ventured as far as the gold-bearing regions of the Lobi, the Ivory Coast and the Gold Coast (present-day Ghana). The mining methods were the same everywhere: the metal was found by sinking shafts in the alluviums covered with laterite, and it was extracted in this primitive fashion until recent times, producing four or five tons a year. As the deposits changed hands, the markets moved from Koumbi Saleh, the capital of ancient Ghana, to Niani, the capital of Mali, to Gao, the capital of the Songhai. According to the Arab chronicler al-Bakri, gold was used lavishly at the court of ancient Ghana: the king's horses were covered with gold caparisons, the swords of the pages were mounted in gold, and even the collars and bells of the dogs were gold. The pilgrimage to Mecca of the emperor Mansa Musa of Mali was celebrated with wild prodigality, and there was not a court official or public officer who did not receive a sum of money in gold. After he had passed through Cairo in 1324, the price of the precious metal fell and never recovered. Similarly, in 1495, Askia Mohammed, the greatest of the Songhai kings, distributed 3,000 pieces of gold in alms and to charitable foundations in Mecca.

Information about gold deposits was always secondhand until the nineteenth century; the prince who controlled them had every intention of keeping the secret of their exact location, and foreigners never went near them. Legends that circulated about gold and gold panners told how one kind of gold grew in the desert after the rains, and how another kind could be found throughout the year at particular spots in the form of roots: "In the country of Ghana, gold fields are planted in the sand, just like one plants carrots, and it is gathered at dawn."

Gold dust containers. Ashanti. Ghana. Musée de l'Homme, Paris. *Museum photo.*

According to another legend, the blacks who extracted the gold had very thick lips and were always rubbing salt on them to keep them from dropping off. The merchants who brought this salt, the story continued, did not see their customers, but left the salt in piles which the blacks later took away and replaced with gold. This is the silent trade that Herodotus mentioned. Gradually, the precious dust reached the great markets of the Sahel, where traders, who had come by caravan from the Maghrib, exchanged it for rock salt, which has always been prized in Africa (sea salt hardly traveled further inland than the Senegal) and also for copper, horses, fabrics, cowrie shells and beads of glass and stone. There were three great trade routes across the desert: the first linked Morocco to the country west of the mouth of the Niger; the second began in Tunisia and ended between Niger and Chad; and the third ran from Tripoli and Egypt to the Chad area. They were used until the end of the Middle Ages, when all trade across the Sahara ceased in the sixteenth century; the massacre of the Jewish colony of Tuat, the Moroccan invasion which ruined the Sudan and the hatred of the Christians brought overland communication between Europe and Africa south of the Sahara to a halt.

Land traffic was succeeded by sea travel. In 1475, after a Lisbon merchant had been granted a five-year monopoly of trade on the African coast beyond Cape Verde, the Portuguese sailors discovered a land where gold dust and nuggets were so abundant that they named it *Mina* (the Mine), or the Gold Coast. The gold came from Ashanti and the neighboring regions, because the other sources of production were too far away. It was an unexpected windfall at a time when Europe was suffering from a chronic shortage of gold caused not only by ruinous wars but also by expanding trade, especially with Asia, whose inhabitants did not care much for the products that the West could offer them. This was the background against which the fort of São Jorge da Mina was built in 1482 as an entrepôt for the Portuguese traders. The Portuguese were followed by the Dutch, and then the English (the first guineas were struck with gold from the Guinea Coast; hence their name). In the meanwhile, a far more profitable trade had begun—that of slaves, who were demanded by the plantations of the New World.

The Arab geographer al-Masudi, as early as the tenth century, described Sofala, which had been founded by the Arabs on the eastern coast of Africa as a trading post for the exchange of cloth and beads against gold from the interior. When the Portuguese had sailed around the Cape of Good Hope, they took possession of Sofala and established relations with Monomotapa, an empire that was said to extend from the Zambezi River to the Cape, and they tried in vain to gain access to its gold mines, just as Solomon had hoped to do according to those who identify Rhodesia with the biblical land of Ophir. The Portuguese founded trading posts in various places, where, as in São Jorge da Mina, they exchanged gold, ivory and slaves. But the trading posts were too isolated, and they declined rapidly. They had long since disappeared when, after the explorations of Livingstone, gold was discovered at Matabele in 1865, and Cecil Rhodes obtained the concession of all mining rights from King Lobengula, the distant successor of the ruler of Monomotapa.

Weights for weighing gold dust. Ashanti. Ghana. Brass. Pierre Vérité Collection, Paris. *Photo: Eliot Elisofon.*

The Africans used gold for jewelry but never for coinage. Gold remained the prerogative of the nobles and was concentrated in the hands of the sovereign. It was a sign of social distinction and was surrounded with religious associations. The gold that was worked into jewelry was a talisman as well as an ornament and was displayed on solemn occasions such as the enthronement of the chief, funerals, and marriages. It was never circulated for profane purposes among ordinary individuals, and foreigners were never allowed to approach its sources. This refusal was probably in part an indirect effect of the foreigners' attitude; the Africans were quick to realize that the Arabs and the whites were interested in the deposits and to goresee the consequences of their not being prevented from occupying the mines. (See also *Ashanti; Baule; Ghana; Jewelry; Lost-Wax Process; Mali; Markets; Monomotapa; Salt; Sudan; Towns and Cities; Weights.*)   D.P.

GRANARIES. Cereals—including sorghum, corn, rice and several varieties of millet—and legumes—such as peas and beans—are not stored in the upper parts of houses just under the roof, but in separate granaries. These granaries are made of wickerwork, often covered with clay, and set upon wooden supports that raise them off the ground. They are thus protected from the ravages of humidity and rodents. They are erected close to the homes of their owners, and their size indicates their owners' opulence and power. The stores contained in these granaries are not intended solely to feed the owners' families and provide seed for the following season; they also comprise the surplus left over from domestic consumption, and this makes up the largest portion of their contents. In the parts of Africa where farming techniques allow agricultural production to be above the subsistence level, societies display a greater complexity than that found among groups in areas where the family consumes everything it produces—for example, among hunters, isolated agricultural groups in clearings of the great equatorial forest and nomadic pastoral groups. Among these there is not, and there cannot be, either government or skilled craftsmen, nor is the population divided into rich and poor. A surplus of production is not only a sign of increased prosperity; it is also the dividing line between two types of social organization.

There are many granaries in the villages in the savanna belt, which extends from the Atlantic Ocean to the Indian Ocean, south of the fourth parallel (where the rain forests gradually thin out). The surplus contained in them has two major consequences: it permits specialized work, and it leads indirectly to political power for an upper class. Peasants with surplus agricultural produce can exchange it for tools, household utensils, raffia fabrics and carved objects, and the craftsmen who make these can specialize without having to grow their own food; one kind of possession can be exchanged for another. Societies in the savanna belt that can be distinguished by such an exchange of goods based on a surplus of agricultural products stored in granaries are considered to be part of a granary civilization. In some societies of this granary civilization, among the Bakuba, for example, the professional skill of the craftsman is visible in the delicate ornamentation and careful finish of luxury objects such as cups shaped like heads, cosmetic boxes, headrests, pipes and seats, which are common among the wealthy.

The producer with a surplus, however, was not always able to dispose of it in a fair exchange. Sometimes he had to give it up without compensation to his chieftain. It was the chieftain who owned the largest and best-filled granaries, because he was able to appropriate part of the surplus of all members of the community and consequently could devote himself entirely to the work of government. He could maintain a court and executive agents who made his authority effective by physical force. A permanent machinery for coercion was constituted—in other words, the state. No doubt, the territorial range of the power of chiefs was often quite limited, only extending over a few villages, but this power sometimes developed into vast hegemonies. There were some famous ones in the areas of the granary civilization: the great chiefdoms of the Ovimbundu and Babemba, the kingdoms of Kongo and of the Bajokwe, and the Baluba and Balunda empires. The art of these societies exalts the power of their rulers: royal statues in wood and stone, delicately worked scepters and staffs, ceremonial axes and adzes, all exist in great quantities in the southern savanna. Thus, the granaries, where the agricultural surplus is gathered, are both symbols and foundations of an African civilization in which we can discern the basic features of government, specialization, and the stratification of society. (See also *Architecture; Balunda; Flora; Peanuts; Vegetables.*)   J.M.

GREAT LAKES. The African Great Lakes are a group of six lakes formed by geological upheavals, in the latitude of the equator, that resulted in an arc of high ground where the great rain forest could not grow. The dense

Granary shutter. Dogon. Mali. Wood. Musée de l'Homme, Paris. *Photo: Sougez.*

Millet granaries in a village in Upper Volta. *Photo: Hoa-Qui.*

equatorial vegetation was stopped abruptly at its eastern end by the great rift which starts at Juba in the north and extends southward along the valley of the White Nile, through four of the Great Lakes—Albert, Edward, Kivu and Tanganyika—and then continues toward the south. The two other Great Lakes —Kyoga and Victoria—lie to the east of this fissure.

The six Great Lakes form the borders of a region of high plateaus, and this region between the lakes constitutes a homogeneous and primitive cultural area. These high plateaus are very suitable for human habitation. The western side of the massif, which is the watershed between the Nile and Congo basins, rises to nearly 10,000 feet. From this chain of peaks the land falls away toward the east (Lake Victoria is only 3,700 feet above sea level). Most of the plateau region is between 3,300 and 5,000 feet above sea level, and the annual rainfall varies from 30 to 60 inches. The natural vegetation is savanna grass, with scattered clumps of trees; along the rivers the grass is broken up by stretches of forest. This environment is suitable for agriculture and animal husbandry (it is, on the whole, free of the tsetse fly, which transmits sleeping sickness); and it is open country offering easy access to migrant peoples.

Migrants have come to this region in great numbers. The diversity of their origins accounts for the heterogeneity of the population, which is still very pronounced today. John Speke, who traveled to the lake area in the nineteenth century and was one of the first Western explorers of this region, was struck by the non-Negroid features of the ruling class. Speke's impression roused discussions that have gone on for a century about the "mysterious origin of Hamite shepherds." Since African peoples have always been on the move, problems of origin exist nearly everywhere on the continent. If a disproportionate amount of attention has been given to the problem of the origin of the "Hamites" and it has been treated as one of the great enigmas of history, it is only because the subject has drawn upon a more or less conscious racism. In fact, once analyzed, most of the arguments fall into the following pattern: because, in the lake area, some aspects of culture (such as a complex system of government) or some physical feature (such as the Roman profiles of Baganda nobles or the fine noses of the Bahima shepherds) is superior to what one normally expects of Africans, it follows that there must be a Caucasoid element in their racial origins.

On the evidence of the best and most recent works, a conjectural outline can be made of how this region came to be inhabited. Negrillo hunters were probably the first men to traverse the savanna and the high forests of the ridge between the Congo and the Nile. They were the remote ancestors

Batusi herdsman. Itombwe, Zaire. *Photo: Jacques Maquet.*

of a small minority who are still hunters but who also practice some crafts, such as pottery. Because intermarriage has modified some of their physical characteristics, they are described as "Pygmoid," rather than being called "Pygmies" or "Negrillos." The second group to penetrate the lake area was probably the Ethiopid shepherds (this is a more correct term than "Hamite," which refers to a language that is no longer spoken in this region). Whatever their distant origin may have been—either intermarriage of Caucasoid and Negroid peoples or an original primitive race distinct from either—they came in several waves. The first of these may have come very early, around 1000 B.C., while the more recent migrations—those of the Bachwezi, Batusi and Bahima—were probably later than the twelfth and thirteenth centuries A.D. The third group consisted of agricultural Bantu speakers, probably from the Congo Basin, who invaded the lake region during the first centuries A.D. They were numerous and their culture and race absorbed the Ethiopids, at least those who were already there before them. These Bantu speakers were the ancestors of the present rural population of the Great Lakes. The fourth group, the Nilotic shepherds, crossed the Victoria Nile, between Lakes Albert and Kyoga, toward the end of the fifteenth and the beginning of the sixteenth century. The Nilotes occupied only the northern half of the lake region, where they established powerful kingdoms whose dynasties have survived until today. If these theories are correct, the Caucasoid element in the mixed racial background of the lake areas is negligible, if it exists at all; at the most, it is a small part of the Ethiopid heritage. Since we know that there is no relation whatsoever between culture and race, this conclusion hardly matters; but as the question was raised, an answer had to be attempted. (See also *Castes; European Discovery; Iron; Kitara; Migrations; Rwanda; Savanna.*)   J.M.

GRIOTS. The word "griot" is derived either from the Portuguese word *criado* (servant) or from the French corruption of the Portuguese corruption of the Wolof word *gewel.* Throughout the western Sudan and part of the Guinean zone (among the Wolof, Serer, Fulani, Mande and Songhai, for example), the griots form a professional endogamous caste of specialists in the spoken word. They are to be found either at the courts of chiefs or established on their own in towns and villages, acting as storytellers, clowns, heralds, genealogists, musicians, oral reporters or paid flatterers or

Malinke griot with a "Kora" lute-harp. Mali. *Photo: Hugo Zemp.*

insulters. There is always something of the parasite about them, and they are simultaneously feared and despised. The internal organization of the caste varies in detail from one tribe to another. Sometimes it is homogeneous, sometimes divided into subcastes or lineages of specialists. Some griots have special family names, others take those of noble clans. However, their social and cultural standing is always ambiguous, and they are always set apart from the rest of society, like other professional castes (notably blacksmiths), although for different ritualistic reasons. Griots who composed history in the form of genealogies and royal musicians, as well as some clowns, could hold important positions at the courts of chiefs, becoming their advisers and wielding real political influence. Independent griots can acquire considerable wealth and reputation and a large following. They are nevertheless kept apart, rejected by farmers, free men and peasants alike. The paradox of their position is that, while they are considered as helots—noncitizens or slaves without masters—because of this very fact they enjoy almost complete freedom of expression, behavior and movement. They are bound neither by etiquette, nor by the community's rules of common law, nor by most religious taboos.

One of the main functions of the griot, male or female, is to sing the praise of free men. This is often done upon request—at a family feast, for example, or during an electoral campaign—but it can also be initiated by a griot who wants to virtually blackmail the object of his praises; the victim has to pay the griot to stop piling up his praises in order to avoid their becoming dangerous by somehow inflating the ego of the person praised or by attracting the attention of dangerous spirits or genii. In fact, whether the griot flatters or vituperates, it is almost impossible to refuse the griot his presents, so that he is often given them without even having to practice his art at all.

In present-day Africa, many griots make their living in professions that bear no relation to their traditional ministration of the spoken word; they are found in factories as well as universities. Nonetheless, they are still victims of the traditional social discrimination against them, although this has been illegal by the civil or penal code in several countries, such as Mali, Senegal and Guinea. The advent of Islam and Christianity have similarly made little difference; a gifted, well-educated griot may become a priest, a prefect or even a minister, but he has far less chance of marrying the daughter of a man not of his caste, no matter how poor that man may be.

The precise reasons for this discrimination are unknown. It is peculiar to societies in West Africa. In contrast, the "ministers of the spoken word"—genealogists, heralds and the like—among the Bantu of the northwest and the Great Lakes, and the royal orators or masters of languages of the Benin coast form a special, honored category. Historically, there is no evidence that the Sudanese griots were of a different ethnic background than the rest of the tribe, being descendants of either a conquered population or early prisoners of war. Explanations by Africans always relate to religion. A griot ancestor is nearly always accused of some serious pollution or of the breaking of a major taboo. This hereditary impurity is often contagious and can be transmitted in various ways, including sexual relations, even extramarital ones, with a member of the caste. In fact, a scientific explanation of the status of members of castes is possible only in the context of the overall structure of societies that have castes, and this structure is reflected in the cosmic myths of such societies. (See also *Castes; Drums; Epics; Funerals; Genealogy; Harps; Literature, Oral; Song.*)   P.A.

GUINEA. The name Guinea, which still figures today in the title of three African countries (Republic of Guinea, Republic of Equatorial Guinea and Portuguese Guinea) has had fluctuating fortunes. It has figured on maps since the middle of the fourteenth century, but its origin remains obscure. It has been suggested that "Guinea" is a form of "Djenne," the name of a town and a kingdom in the Niger Basin, which was probably founded in the eighth century and was famous for the enterprising spirit of its merchants, or that it might be a bad translation of "Ghana," the name of the oldest empire of the western Sudan. But these are only fortuitous resemblances, and the most likely source of the word is a borrowing by the Portuguese from the first African language they knew—that of the Berbers of Morocco. Strictly speaking, *Akal-n-Iguinawen* means the same thing in Berber as *Bilad as-Sudan* does in Arabic: "land of the blacks."

In modern geographical terms, Guinea designates the southern half of West Africa, corresponding to the forest region, while the northern half of West Africa, covered by the savanna, is known as the western Sudan. The expression "Guinea Coast" is used as a synonym for the great gulf carved out between Cape Palmas and the Gabon Estuary, following the coast as it swings around from east to south. Originally, however, the "land of the blacks" began at the Noun River—that is to say, at the latitude of the Canary Islands. The fifteenth-century historian Gomez Azurara may have been the first person to consider "Guinea" as existing south of the Senegal River. After this, the name covered an ever-growing expanse of newly discovered territory. Early European merchants retained the term "Guinea" to indicate the coast as a whole, but they used the names of the most typical products of each area in referring to particular parts of the coast. The Grain Coast, along the shores of Sierra Leone and Liberia, was named after the seeds produced in abundance by various plants related to the pepper tree and indiscriminately called "grains of paradise," "Guinea pepper seeds" and "melegueta pepper seeds." At the end of the eighteenth century, pepper from Southeast Asia replaced pepper from Guinea, but the name still remained as a reminder of the trade that created it. Next to the Grain Coast lay the Ivory Coast—called "Coast of Tusks" on a few ancient maps. Then followed the Gold Coast; this area, on gaining independence, took over the name of the most famous of all the medieval kingdoms of West Africa and became Ghana. The term "Slave Coast," which was applied to the southern part of the gulf, is a sufficient indication of the wretched cargoes that were loaded there into European ships to be transported to America. The Niger Delta was known for a long time as the Oil Rivers, an allusion to the palm oil that was available in vast quantities to foreign buyers all along the numerous branches of the river.

Besides being used to indicate a geographical area, the word "guinea" was also used for a long time to designate a coin. The first such coin was struck in London in 1663 by order of Charles II; it was minted from gold powder from the Guinea Coast, where forts had been built to stock slaves and the precious metal. The term "Guinea cloth" was employed up through the nineteenth century to designate a dark blue material that was used to make the ample garments worn by many Africans, especially peddlers (*dioula*); these people happily exchanged gold powder for calico dyed with indigo and made shiny with starch. (See also *Baga; Bambara; Beads; Benin; Bronze; European Discovery; Fruit; Ghana; Ivory; Migrations; Religion; Slave Trade.*) D.P.

GURO. The Guro, numbering about 110,000, occupy a territory in the interior of the Ivory Coast, between 6°30′ and 8° North Latitude and 5°25′ and 7° West Longitude. They are surrounded by the Bete in the west, the Gagu in the south, the Baule in the east and the Malinke in the north. Of Mande origin and speaking a Mande-fu language, the Guro penetrated the forest zone many centuries ago. A number of major tribes of the forest region emigrated eastward in the eighteenth century and got as far as the present-day city of Bouake, where they were driven back beyond the Bandama River by the Baule. Thus, half the Guro villages are situated in the forest and the other half in the savanna. The population density varies from 6.2 inhabitants per square mile in the forest zones to 103.6 inhabitants per square mile in the savanna, to the northeast. The Guro partly expelled and partly assimilated the small numbers of Gagu, Nwan, and Mwa tribes, but they themselves mixed with an appreciable number of Bete, Malinke and Baule.

It is fairly certain that the Guro transmitted the art of wood carving and weaving techniques to the Baule, who then reinterpreted them in their own style. While the Guro are best known as sculptors of masks, statuettes and pulleys for weaving, they are also outstanding singers. Women and men perform alternately during burials, funeral feasts and displays of the appropriate masks.

The Guro ethnic cluster consists of about forty tribes divided into territorial groupings that occupy several villages and undertake common duties mainly relating to military and economic affairs. The tribes generally consist of extended families that are patrilineal, of different origins and united by marriages. The villages are equally heterogeneous. The Guro have no chiefs, either hereditary or appointed; a council of elders resolves disputes at the family, village or tribal level. Warriors with temporary powers conduct wars, which they have often been responsible for starting. Mask societies perform social as well as religious functions; the best known are the *Gye,* the *Zamble* and the *Goli,* into which only men are initiated. In the northern part of the country only, young girls are excised and initiated into a women's society called *Kene.* These societies share the power of coercion and political control with the members of the *Gi, Vro* and *Yune* cults. Sacrifices are made to the village land by either the descendant of its first inhabitants, the oldest man, the person who is nearest in line of descent to the Ancestor or a person chosen by divination, but the performing of these sacrifices confers no special power on him. The same applies to the sacrifices that some families offer to a tree, a river or a rock.

A man who has become rich through traditional activities such as hunting, weaving, cultivating fields, commerce, forging iron or even war, and who controls a

Guro mask. Ivory Coast. Wood. Christophe Tzara Collection, Paris. *Photo: Ciccione.*

large number of dependents, including relations, kinsmen and clients, is called *migone* or *fwa,* "king" or "rich man." The generosity expected of the *migone* because of his position prevents him from accumulating excessive wealth. After his death, the costs of the funeral honors impoverish his family to such an extent that it is rare for the brother or son of a *migone* to be considered as one himself. Consequently, although this institution allows free expression to forceful personalities, it does not endanger the egalitarian character of Guro society. Wealth and authority are transmitted within an extended family that is patrilineal; they go from older brother to younger brother, then to the eldest of the next generation.

Great importance is, however, attached to relations with the maternal family. Nephews, who are sons of sisters (*yurugone*) are responsible for the burial of their maternal uncle; in exchange, they enjoy the privilege of taking what they want from his courtyard. The same *yurugone* are called before their uncle if his wife has committed adultery, and they have to kill the hen which is offered as a sacrifice to the earth in expiation. The maternal family serves as a refuge for anyone who is excluded, either voluntarily or involuntarily, from his paternal family. Even during wars, nephews from the opposing camps serve as ambassadors and mediators. In Guro marriages, the paternal relations of the future wife give one of their own

daughters or sisters to the family of the future husband, in exchange for clothes, animals and *bro* (the traditional iron money, now replaced by silver). The wife's parents have almost unlimited credit with the husband's parents, who have to give fresh presents each time a death occurs in the wife's family. In addition, the husband's family has no right of control over the children of his marriage unless his wife dies and her paternal relations have accepted a final contribution, "corpse money," which is the only thing that can put a final seal on the marriage. Under these conditions, the relations between husbands and wives are strained, relations between their respective families are hostile, and relations between maternal uncles and nephews with different fathers are ambiguous. The introduction of cash crops—coffee, cocoa and cotton—has led to an influx of money which, especially to the south of the Guro lands, is a further cause of instability in marriage. (See also *Art, Styles of; Buffalo; Diet.*) A.D.

HANNO. Hanno's voyage along the African coast, which is supposed to have taken place in the fifth century B.C., is described in a short Greek text known as *Hanno's Periplus.* According to this, the Carthaginian leader sailed with his fleet through the Pillars of Hercules and founded some colonies, the last on the island of Cerne. Further along the way, his expedition encountered a river full of crocodiles and hippopotamuses, and then savages, some of them timid and others performing terrifying music; on two occasions, the expedition came to an island in a lake on an island in a bay and a glowing mountain that spouted fire. Food ran short, so they went back to Carthage with the skins of three female monkeys.

Identifying places, people and animals mentioned in *Hanno's Periplus* while taking into account possible discrepancies, first, between events and the official version (which Hanno may have had inscribed in a temple), then, between this official version and the translation that the Greeks made and, finally, between the first Greek text and the two medieval manuscripts, which are the only versions that we possess, is a game in which the most subtle scholarship has been combined with the most astonishing liberties. But it is a hopeless undertaking. The strange and sketchy text is so inadequate that no identification carries conviction. It depends on the player whether the voyage ends in Gabon, in Guinea or at the Draa River. The location of Cerne fluctuates between the island of Gorée, just off the coast

Title page of *Hannonis Periplus* (Hanno's Periplus, 1661 edition). Bibliothèque nationale, Paris. *Library photo.*

of Dakar, and northern Morocco. The narrative gives no accurate account of the stages of a classical voyage, and it throws no additional light on any major problem such as Carthaginian trade or gold from the Sudan. Theories have been developed about these subjects from other data in order to elucidate the text, but such interest and substance as they possess owe nothing to it. From the point of view of the historians studying Gabon or Guinea, this little account may be important for establishing whether unknown visitors really set foot on their coasts one fine day to hunt chimpanzees or took fright at the sound of drums, but otherwise the *Periplus* game is probably quite futile. One may admire the seafaring skill of the ancients which enabled them, in ships powered only by oars, to traverse the Sahara coastal waters in the face of strong currents and trade winds. Archeology contradicts the story of the voyage and establishes that the Carthaginian presence on the Moroccan coasts was of uncertain date, but not particularly early, and that it was not very extensive. And analysis of the text has recently confirmed that it was a late literary exercise, compiled by shuffling elements from various sources. So a bogus problem can be laid to rest and the *Periplus* game shown to be a waste of time. (See also *European Discovery*.) H.M.

HARES. The hare or, more precisely, the *Lepus africanus,* which resembles the large white rabbit, is the principal character and hero of a cycle of morality tales that are widespread throughout the savanna regions of Africa. In the United States, the character, having crossed the Atlantic in slave ships, was transformed into Br'er Rabbit before ending up as the symbol for *Playboy* magazine. Among the Berbers and Bushmen he was changed into a jackal, and this is perhaps the source of the French Reynard the Fox. In the African forests his character is transferred to the land tortoise, which appears in American folk tales as Br'er Terrapin. In addition to being the source of Reynard the Fox, the hare may also have been the influence for Hugo's Gavroche, Rabelais's Panurge, and Tyl Eulenspiegel. Not very tough, not very honest, not heroic, he is, however, lively, mocking and crafty, with a roguishness that can be either spiteful or clever. His foil is the odious hyena—or, in the forest, the panther—whose faults balance his own and who represents sheer evil, violence without mercy or intelligence. But the hyena is not the only victim of Uncle (or Father or Brother, depending on family structures) Hare: all the mighty suffer—King

The "hare." Dogon mask. Mali. Painted wood. Musée des Arts africains et océaniens, Paris. *Photo: Hoa-Qui.*

Lion above all—as well as the weak, who are punished for their naivety. It is very rare that he finds anyone more cunning than himself, and even then his defeats are often caused by magic.

The stories about the hare display a remarkable basic homogeneity. Only relatively unimportant details vary from one tribe to another. It seems that their didactic significance concerns human nature in general rather than any particular form of social relationship. As a type, the hare is a trickster like Reynard and the coyote of the Plains Indians, but he only rarely intrudes onto the cosmic level, although he may sometimes count spirits or divinities among his victims. He nearly always performs on the human level, particularly on that of the common people, and those who listen to tales about this sympathetic and almost anarchic scamp tend to identify themselves with him. Stories about the hare may therefore be considered means of releasing psychological and social tensions. (See also *Heroes; Stories.*) P.A.

HARPS. The harp and the musical bow are the stringed instruments most frequently played in black Africa. By examining the many different types of harps, one can follow

Baule harp. Ivory Coast. Sculpted wood decorated with skin. Musée de l'Homme, Paris. *Museum photo.*

Multiple harps and bow harps have sounding boards made either of round calabashes with the tops sliced off or of rectangular wooden boxes. The sides may be engraved with geometric designs or surmounted by a human figure in high relief, as on the harps of the Ivory Coast, Gabon and the Congo. Harps of finer construction have boat-shaped bodies (northern Cameroun) or semiovoid bodies (Ubangi Valley) with curved sides, rather like our stringed instruments. The sounding boards of these are made of wood or, more often, of goat-, gazelle-, deer- or snakeskin. A circular sound hole is bored into the sounding board and may be covered with a thin membrane that modifies the sound of the strings, like the mute on a violin. Some harps in the Ubangi Valley are virtually statues of people: they stand on two legs; the rounded body forms the chest of the human figure; the sounding board forms the skin of the belly; and the neck is finished off with a small carved head.

The strings of African harps vary in number and may be made of vegetable fiber, twisted leather thongs or, occasionally, wire. Multiple harps have five to nine strings. Large bow harps mounted on calabashes have only three, and these sound like the strings of a double bass. Other harps usually have five or eight strings, not necessarily tuned to a heptatonic scale. There are two different ways of attaching the strings— knotting them around the neck of the instrument or winding them around pegs— but the two ways may be combined. It should be noted, however, that these delicate constructions of knots, rings and whorls are intended as much to beautify the instrument as to tune it. The tuning is somewhat haphazard and is rarely adjusted in the course of a performance, since the harp is used more to provide rhythmic accompaniment than melodic sound.

The lute harp, which is peculiar to West Africa, is a combination of the lute and the harp. Besides having a neck that is absolutely straight, it also has a high bridge erected on the surface of its sounding board. The sounding board is notched along its edges or pierced with two rows of holes, so that the strings are separated into two vertical rows. The knots around the neck are bound together by leather thongs. The largest of the lute harps, which are found in Casamance and in the Bissagos Islands, have between twenty-one and twenty-four strings. This is the type of instrument played by the famous griots in Senegal, Mali and Guinea.

Whatever its musical potential, the harp is primarily intended as a symbol of prestige. This is why it is used by diviners and

the evolution of the harp from the musical bow. The element to which the upper ends of the harp strings are attached forms a continuous curve whose arch may be more or less pronounced. In the multiple harp, flexible branches or flat strips of palm wood are simply juxtaposed, with a different length string stretched across each strip, and attached to the two ends. The bow harp, on the other hand, has an arched frame made of one piece of wood or ivory to which the strings are attached at different levels of the arch. This type of frame corresponds to the console of the European and the ancient Egyptian harp. The small ivory bow harp of the Azande is similar to the so-called shoulder harp represented on the monuments of the New Kingdom, and there is probably some connection between these two types of harps. However, the black African instrument is more ornamented, with the outer ends of the console or the pegs being carved to represent human heads.

magicians, by storytellers and griots and why chieftains keep one or more harpists in their service. (See also *Bows, Musical; Song; Zithers.*) A.S.

HAUSA. The Hausa, a group numbering between 6 and 8 million people, inhabit eastern Niger and the northwestern part of Nigeria, between 10°30′ and 14° North Latitude and 4° and 10° East Longitude. Ever since the Middle Ages their economy has been one of the most developed in Africa. In addition to intensive agriculture combined with the raising of horses and cattle, numerous crafts such as leatherworking, weaving and jewelry making were carried on by an outstanding group of urban craftsmen. These craftsmen formed the basis for the active and widespread trade carried on in association with Mande commercial enterprises. Hausa merchants are still active today in West Africa, and they may even be found along the Congo River and the Red Sea. Their language, which is the most common in West Africa, serves as a lingua franca among many other ethnic groups. In fact, in Cameroun the word "Hausa" has become the synonym for "Muslim Peddler," no matter what the person's racial origin.

The history of the Hausa lands is fairly well recorded as far back as the tenth century, thanks to the local chronicles (of which the most complete is the Kano Chronicle) and to the writings of Arab travelers such as ibn-Batuta and Leo Africanus. But the exact origin of the Hausa is still the subject of discussion. Their language has a close affinity with both the Hamito-Semitic family and the black African family. Physically, they are very varied, but on the whole they resemble the Sudanese blacks. Their culture has some features that have been attributed to palaeo-Mediterranean or Middle Eastern influences. It is probable that during the first millennium A.D. migrants from the east and north joined a people of Palaeonegrid origin and the first embryonic towns were formed by these migrants. Tradition relates the arrival in the middle of the tenth century of the hero Bayajidda (Abu Yazid), the son of the Sultan of Baghdad. He had been driven out by his father and so went and joined the court of the *mai* of Bornu, whose daughter he married. He fled from the court and left his pregnant wife at Biram, where she gave birth to a boy. He went on to the village of Queen Daura, which he freed from a snake-king who occupied the only spring in the land. The queen married him and gave him a slave girl as a concubine. He had one legitimate child by the queen, a son called Bawo.

Bawo's sons later became the chiefs of Kano, Rano, Katsina, Zazzau (Zaria), Gobir and Daura, which together with Biram constitute the seven Hausa states. By the slave girl he had a bastard, Karbogari, whose children founded "seven bastards" *(hausa bakwai)*— that is, the seven neighboring states: Kebbi, Zamfara, Gwari, Jukun (or Kororfawa), Yoruba, Nupe and Yauri. The Kano Chronicle relates, in a more rational account, that a blacksmith king-priest, Barbushe, welcomed some foreign horsemen, who some generations later became rulers of the country. Both of these versions confirm the theory of a mixed population, with the immigrants organizing the original inhabitants. The *hausa bakwai* never formed a great centralized state like the Hausa, but rather a loosely knit cultural and linguistic entity.

In the thirteenth century the Hausa were in the Malian sphere of influence, and it was from Mali that the first Muslim missionaries arrived in the fourteenth century. From the fifteenth to the seventeenth centuries, the Songhai and the Bornu both claimed sovereignty over the country. At the beginning of the nineteenth century, a highly educated Fulani Muslim from Gobir, Osman dan Fodio (the first Fulanis arrived between the fifteenth and sixteenth centuries), called a holy war against the Hausa sovereign, whom he accused of impiety. His son,

Hausa. Niger. *Photo: Hoa-Qui.*

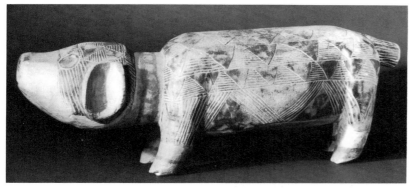

Ovambo headrest. South-
West Africa. Wood. Musée de
l'Homme, Paris.
Museum photo.

Baluba headrest. Zaire.
Wood. Webster Plass
Collection, British Museum.
Photo: Eliot Elisofon.

Mashona headrest with a
movable platform. Zambia.
Wood. Musée de l'Homme,
Paris. *Museum photo.*

Ahmadu Bello, combined all the northern part of the future Nigeria and Cameroun into the empire of Sokoto, which was destroyed in the course of European colonization.

The political organization of the Hausa was analogous to that of Bornu and underwent very little change at the hands of the Fulani emirs. It had at its head a sovereign who, though Muslim, retained many of the attributes of the sacred African kings. He was surrounded by a large court formed of ministers, slaves and eunuchs, an aristocracy composed of descendants of the ancient local pagan chiefs, peasants and free craftsmen, royal prisoners and tribute-paying dependents.

Although the country has, in theory, been Muslim since the fourteenth century, Islam was strictly practiced only in the large commercial towns (Kano, Sokoto, Katsina), while the pagan cults continued in the country. Even today, although conversion was vigorously carried out by Osman dan Fodio and his successors, some remnants of paganism survive, including the cult of genii *(bori)* and the chthonic and agrarian rites, which are performed particularly by tribes on the borders, such as the Mauri and the Maguzawa.

Hausanci is the language of northern Nigeria, where the Hausa and peoples assimilated with the Hausa form the political majority of the population, even though the aristocracy is Fulani. The commercial heritage of the Hausa has made them one of the most dynamic peoples of the central Sudan, especially on the economic level. Across the Atlantic, the descendants of the Hausa who were exported as slaves, even though outnumbered by the Yoruba, played an important role in the events leading to the Spartakist uprising in Brazil and Jamaica in the nineteenth century. (See also *Bornu; Goats; Jewelry; Poetry; Royalty; Slavery; Spirits and Genii; Sudan; Tribute; Women.*)
P.A.

HEADRESTS. A headrest usually consists of a more or less concave platform, carved from a single piece of wood, one or more supports and a base, which may be oval, circular, or rectangular. It makes a very comfortable piece of furniture on which to rest. When a person wants to sleep or take a siesta during the hottest part of the day, he or she places the back of his head on the half-moon shaped platform. Aged Dogon still use it in this way in the shade of their *toguna* (men's shelter). Like the backrest or the small stool, which is carried on journeys, the headrest is usually used in conjunction with the sleeping mat, but some headrests are permanently attached to beds. A map of the distribution of headrests in black Africa would show the greatest concentration to be in the east, from Ethiopia to the area south of the Zambezi, with a major zone further west that stretches into southern Zaire and Angola.

In Ethiopia and Somaliland headrests are usually made of soft wood. Peasants use simple rectangular blocks of wood with the top hollowed out, and they make these themselves. However, headrests owned by wealthy and important people are much more elaborately worked: the base is cylindrical, the underside of the platform is decorated with engraved geometric designs extending onto the thick upright supports which are sometimes carved out and may continue onto the base as well. The most elaborate are completely decorated with geometric designs of multicolored beads, which cover both the supports and the base.

In the upper Zambezi region, an area not noted for its wood carving, the richness and ingenuity of the decoration of the headrests is astonishing. It is probable that the influence of the decorative themes of the Bajokwe-Balunda cluster reached the Barotse Plain through groups who emigrated from Angola. The decorative sculpture of the support often consists of variations on the traditional motifs based on concentric circles and semicircles. The headrest is made of hard wood, its surface is often polished from use, and there is a certain preciousness about it. In Angola itself, there is a type of headrest that looks very much like a stool. It has a slightly concave platform on either a heavy, box-shaped or a double rectangular upright support and a flat, rectangular base. On the outer sides of the supports, one can recognize geometric designs of obvious Bajokwe origin, each with a specific meaning. The Bajokwe also have headrests shaped like birds, the head and tail of which form extensions of either end of the platform; the bent legs serve as supports and rest on the base.

In Zaire, among the Bakuba and Baluba (whose headrests have the same caryatid motif as the famous Katanga stools) and also among the Bena Lulua and Basonge, headrests are real masterpieces. They are said to be designed to protect complicated, fragile and carefully arranged hairdos during sleep, and their style has many of the characteristics of statuary. The most distinguished—those made of ivory by the Baluba and having platforms that rest on a female figure—indicate the social and political importance of the wife, particularly the first wife of the chief, for she is the guardian of all the material attributes of authority.

Headrests, whether they be magnificent wood sculptures like those of Kasai or simple flat stones like those of the Fali in northern Cameroun, possess, as do many other African objects, a wealth of different meanings. An eloquent example of this is the headrest of the Hogon (the spiritual leader of the Dogon in Mali); it has the mythological symbols of his people carved on it and when he dies is placed in his tomb. (See also *Bakuba; Baluba; Household Furnishings; Nile; Posture; Sculpture, Wood.*)   J.D.

HEADS. In Africa the head is a specially honored part of the body, the focal point of the vital force that is lodged in every man and every animal. The Dogon, who are very concerned with preserving and nourishing this force, dedicate one altar to the body and another to the head. A part of the Dogon's vital force is transferred to the altar when he offers a sacrifice on it. Consequently, his spirit drinks the blood of the future sacrifices that his father, and later he himself, spreads upon the altar. Thus, he increases his force under the best possible conditions. After the individual's death, these altars to the body and the head serve no further purpose and are destroyed. Rites such as these are not found everywhere. But it is the head, as the essential part of the body, that is usually sprinkled during ceremonies, and very often the heads of the dead are preserved.

Skull worship used to be widespread in Africa, the object of worship being either the skulls of ancestors or the skull of the king alone. The former type of cult was most common among the Bantu of northern and northeastern Africa. Among the Fang of Gabon and the Bulu, their kinsmen in the Cameroun, skulls were dyed and sometimes encrusted with beads or fragments of copper. Under the guardianship of the oldest member of the group, who acted as priest of the ancestors, they were then preserved in cylindrical baskets made of bark, with a statuette of the founder of the group on top. This was placed on an altar, but during migrations it was ceremoniously carried in procession and closely guarded, like the Ark of the Covenant. Each skull could be recognized and was familiar; one feature of ceremonial initiations of the young was to teach them how to distinguish skulls and how to place them in their exact genealogical order, starting with the founder, whose skull was the first to be put inside the basket. The exhumation of skulls, which took place some time after burial, was naturally accompanied by a complicated ritual. The latter type of cult, that of the king's skull, was observed in many regions, from the Zambezi and Congo rivers (for example, among the Baganda and the Banyoro in the Great Lakes region and among the Bajokwe of upper Kasai) as far as West Africa (in Dahomey a temple was

Head from Ife. Nigeria.
Bronze. Ife Museum, Nigeria.
Photo: Eliot Elisofon.

Head of a queen mother.
Benin. Nigeria. Bronze.
British Museum. *Photo:
Walter Dräyer.*

erected for the skull of each dead king; among the Temne of Sierra Leone, the king's skull was kept and worshiped by his successor until it was buried with him, thus assuring royal succession). The skull of the king was more than a simple relic; it represented one of the religious foundations for the country's unity. In Ife, in the kingdom of Benin, heads of kings were cast in bronze and put on people's altars.

Every head, every skull contained power. The skulls of animals killed in hunting were preserved and were often put on the walls of houses, where they were more than mere trophies, as well as on altars; they were used during hunting rituals. Warriors often tried to gain possession of the skulls of members of the enemy that had been killed in war; they attempted to get them at the time of the battle or they stole them, which led some tribes to keep the location of their tombs a secret. These skulls were built into the thrones of kings and into drums. In Dahomey they decorated the top of the palace walls and many of the objects, such as ceremonial swords, flywhisks and cups, that were part of the royal surroundings.

Some tribes, especially in central and eastern Nigeria, practiced headhunting as an important part of their social and religious life. It was essential to hold the skull of an enemy one had killed in order to be considered a grown man, to attain the position of an elder and take part in village affairs, or to acquire certain prestigious titles. Each tribe had a special store of heads: often these were the heads of members of conquering powers such as the House of the Fulani; sometimes they came from members of neighboring tribes and could be used in the exchange of skulls from various sources that took place when peace was made after hostilities with a particular neighbor. Headhunting could not take place indiscriminately; it was a trial, an initiation, and had to entail some risk. Men who had acquired their skulls through surprise attacks were often treated with contempt and sometimes the only skulls of value were those procured after the war trumpets had been formally sounded.

Some tribes practiced true skull worship, with skulls kept by priests and rites performed around the warrior and his trophy. Frequently, the warrior had to eat part of the flesh of the enemy he had killed, and sometimes, among the Ijo, for example, headhunting was part of a more important form of ritual cannibalism. In any case, skull worship included a long series of ceremonies culminating in the solemn presentation of the new initiate. (See also *Body; Household*

Furnishings; Ibibio; Ife; Ijo; Nok; Sculpture, Wood.)   P.M.

HEAVEN. The sky, which holds the stars, stores the rain and is the setting of storms, is viewed in Africa as a solid dome covering the earth until both meet at the horizon or as a ceiling protecting the earth. Many divinities or only a single one may live in it or be manifested by it. Divinities may be the focal point of religious beliefs or may instead be relegated to second place, and sometimes they are just about effaced by primordial ancestors, culture-heroes and demigods or by earth deities, who often intrude upon their domain by annexing the moon. When the supreme god, the creator, is not an abstract force imminent in all beings, he is a sky god or sometimes a sun god, as is indicated by the origin of his name in many societies. Often he is the only celestial power and controls all phenomena in the atmosphere. But he may have to fight against other gods, such as the gods of thunder and rain, as the Nandi of East Africa believe. When the supreme god engenders and controls a very specialized pantheon of sky gods, as in the rich polytheism of Dahomey, it is divided into a male figure and a female figure.

Heaven and earth are not always in opposition to one another. In many myths, creation is the result of their union. The Dogon believe that the supreme god, Amma, united himself with the earth after her excision, and she bore the principal actors in the drama of creation—the fox, who fomented disorder, and the water spirits, who organized the world. Much the same type of myth is found among the Ashanti, Yoruba and many other peoples in Africa and elsewhere. But the theme commonly associated with this type of myth in Egypt as well as in Oceania—namely, the forcible interruption of the union of Heaven and Earth, because this separation was necessary for the normal existence of earthly creatures—is found in black Africa only in vestigial remains of myths; for example, the sky used to be very low, but moved upward because women pounding grain would hit it with their pestles (Ivory Coast) or because men wiped their dirty hands on it (Togo). The tribes who have preserved these tales have forgotten their mythical significance and only see them as explanations of the remote character of a supreme god to whom no direct worship is rendered.

First ancestors, or at least the first ancestors of some tribes, often descended from heaven; sometimes they were banished from it. The Dogon's first ancestor came down to earth in an ark carrying animals,

plants and, above all, the seeds and skills which were to make human life possible. Among the Baule and many other peoples, the sons of Heaven came down in a cauldron or a hut, sliding down a chain or rope. Although it was in heaven that man began, it is much more rare in African belief that he should go there at the end. There are exceptions: in Dahomey, after death one of each person's souls joins the supreme god from which it emanated; similarly, the Dogon believe that the soul returns to the supreme god after a long journey; and the Herero of South Africa believe that the soul, when it returns to the supreme god, first crosses an abyss. But much more often the soul wanders toward the waters, as among the Bambara and Bamileke, or goes to the ends of the earth at sunset. In fact, the dead are simultaneously among the living and elsewhere, for a man has several souls, and these are dispersed when he dies; consequently, there cannot be, either in heaven or anywhere else, a true abode of the dead. (See also *Divinities; Myths; Religion.*) P.M.

HENS. "Long ago, the hen lived in the bush with the spirits of the dead, and the little bustard lived with men. The dead, who suffered from the cold, sent the hen to get fire from the living. She went, dawdling here and there. The bustard realized that the hen was a

Decoration painted with millet gruel on the outside of the Temple of the Binou of the Hyena: the moon, sun and scattered stars; a snake encircles the world on three sides. Dogon. Mali. *Photo: Musée de l'Homme.*

Hen eating an earthworm.
Cover of a cup. Ife, Nigeria.
Wood. Museum für
Völkerkunde, Berlin.
Museum photo.

Gu, god of metallurgy. Fon.
Dahomey. Brass. Charles
Ratton Collection, Paris.
Photo: Eliot Elisofon.

terrible messenger. Filled with pity, she took the fire from the yard where she lived and brought it to the dead. They kept the bustard and left the hen to men." This is how the Tupuri of Chad explain the domestication of the hen. Evidence indicates that the domesticated hen did not appear until late in Egyptian civilization.

Apart from the nomadic Bororo, the Pygmy hunters and the Bushmen, all traditional African societies raise chickens. Their number throughout the whole continent is estimated as 175 million. The physical characteristics of the common African chicken are fairly constant. It is a small bird with a slender body, weighing between one and two pounds, and with well-developed muscles. Its plumage is very varied today, but it often has red hackles, a black breast and tail, and a well-developed beak and comb, not unlike the Bankhiva cock in Asia, from which it is descended.

The hen develops slowly and is a poor egg-layer; but it is a good brooder, hardy and well able to look for food. Its owners give it little to eat. Some Sudanese tribes take hens to the fields at gleaning time, others feed brooding hens with termites, which are caught in special traps. Because of the number of predatory animals, all traditional societies build henhouses, either on the ground or on piles. Eggs are rarely eaten. They are difficult to collect and often lost because the hens live in semiliberty. Africans prefer eggs to be hatched rather than eaten; besides, eating eggs is often taboo. But the hen, more often

than other domestic animals, is the animal that is killed for a visitor or to be offered as a sacrifice to the powers beyond. Some sacrifices, even if they contain an element of communion, appear simply to be pretexts for a good meal. The methods of killing hens, their preparation and ritual consumption are infinitely varied. The introduction of European and American breeds, such as Sussex and Rhode Island hens, has produced some very successful crossbreeding with local strains. (See also *Animal Husbandry; Sacrifice.*)   I.G.

HEROES. The typical hero of classical Western culture was a mythical personage, often half-human, half-divine in origin, who was raised to the rank of demigod. He was either the archetype of a moral attribute (e.g., Hercules) or the founder of a society (e.g., Romulus). The latter type, the founder-hero, is more common in Africa than the former. A characteristic example is Nyikang, the founder of the Shilluk kingdom of the upper Nile (Sudan). Nyikang was the grandson of a man who descended from heaven and the son of a crocodile-woman.

He left his country after a quarrel with his half-brother, married a king's daughter and battled victoriously with the sun. He crossed the Bahr el Ghazal, as Moses had crossed the Red Sea, performed countless prodigies and finally vanished into immortality. Subsequent Shilluk kings were considered, to a certain extent, to be reincarnations of Nyikang, who himself is the symbol of Shilluk society. The kings are divine, and Nyikang is a supernatural being, not a god; he is more a mediator between the creator, the supreme god Juok, and the Shilluk people, and the reigning king and dynasty are his intermediaries.

Another very common type of hero is the culture- or teacher-hero, who has Promethean qualities and who teaches men new skills, sometimes even against the will of the supreme god or gods. An example of such a hero is the Fon *vodun* known as Gu (Ogun among the Yoruba), who is the patron of metallurgy and inventor of all crafts. He also is not imagined as a man, but as a minor divinity whose emblem is a sword that is simultaneously a tool. The dyadic creator Mawu-Lissa used this tool-weapon to put the world in order.

The most common examples of heroes who are the archetypes of moral and sometimes sociological tendencies are animals in fables, particularly the hare (the *Lepus africanus*). The hare is the star of a pan-African cycle, which is also found, in the form of Br'er Rabbit, among Afro-Americans and possibly as Reynard the Fox in Europe. The hare is a trickster, a hoaxer; he symbolizes craftiness, guile compensating for physical weakness, generally at the expense of the powerful (who are symbolized by other animals) and as a challenge to the established social order. In the stories of which he is the hero, there is an element of revolt, since those who listen identify themselves with the irreverent hare; but this is somehow neutralized by the comic side, and the story becomes an outlet for social tensions. (See also *Blacksmiths; Divinities; Hares; Heaven; Kikuyu; Kongo; Legends; Lions; Myths; Religion; Stories; Work.*)
P.A.

HORNS and TRUMPETS. The horn and the whistle are the most common wind instruments in Africa. There are two types of horns: the *vertical horn,* which has a mouthpiece at one end and is made either of a strip of rolled bark, a long fruit from a calabash tree, a hollowed trunk or branch of bamboo, or an iron, brass or copper tube; and the *transverse horn,* which is made of ox, buffalo or antelope horn or of ivory, wood

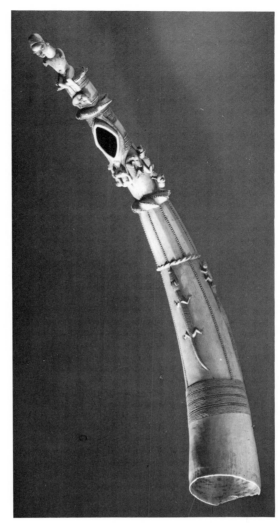

or, less commonly, bronze or iron and has a hole in its side that is sometimes provided with a lip. When the instrument is made of horn or ivory, the mouthpiece is usually located on the concave side, near the pointed tip, which may be pierced to act as a tone hole. With few exceptions, all horns are conical tubes. Most of them are constructed from a single, solid piece of material. However, there are *complex horns,* and these may be either vertical or transverse, that are made of two or three pieces of different materials joined together: one of them forms the tube itself; other pieces may be either an extension of the pipe or a sort of mouthpiece.

Transverse horns made of wood and ivory are decorated more often than those made of other materials. The mouthpiece is finely carved, the body is ornamented and the end nearest the mouthpiece is sculpted in the round. The upper parts of some wooden instruments are carved to represent masks (Mali) or human heads (equatorial Africa). The ivory horns of the Congo region are

Transverse horn. Yoruba. Carved ivory. Nigeria. Musée de l'Homme, Paris. *Museum photo.*

Badondo horn. Republic of the Congo. Wood. Etnografiska Museet, Göteborg. *Museum photo.*

engraved or carved with lozenges or cylinders in relief, while the tip is cut like a sawtooth or lancehead. The ivory horns of Benin are real works of art; human or animal figures are carved in relief on the bodies, and the tips are sometimes sculpted in the round with an anthropomorphic figure. They have been compared with medieval oliphants, or hunting horns, and sometimes assumed to be imitations of them, although oliphants always have terminal mouthpieces. The European origin of some oliphants that have been studied is questionable. However this may be, the ivorywork on the Benin horns reached a perfection unequaled in instruments made elsewhere.

The trumpet consists of a narrow metal tube, shaped like a conical cylinder, with a mouthpiece, also of metal, at one end. The only type of trumpet found in West Africa is seven or more feet in length and is made of several tubes, one inside the other. It was introduced with Islam and is still used in the sultanates of Niger, Chad, Nigeria and Cameroun. The trumpet is sometimes accompanied by the kettledrum, an instrument which, like the trumpet itself, is an insignia of power and is of Islamic origin. In Ethiopia, however, there is a long trumpet which may have come directly from Asia at an earlier period. The existence in East and South Africa, as far as Madagascar, of primitive trumpets with beveled mouthpieces or even with lateral mouthpieces suggests that this type of instrument had already appeared in a rudimentary form in several parts of the continent before the Arab invasion.

Horns and trumpets produce one or two sounds (with an interval of a fifth), seldom more. When they are played in a group, instruments of the same size are generally paired and played in unison, so that the scale range of the group depends on how many different sizes of instruments there are. There are instances when the same instrument plays two notes with an interval of about a tone, either because the African player, like the European horn player, covers the bell of the horn with his hand and lowers the note or alternately stops and opens the hole at the tip of the horn: the contrast between the two sounds can be used as the basis of a musical dialogue. Straight trumpets, made in a very rudimentary way, tend to be used as megaphones or voice disguisers. Similarly, in Gabon, small transverse horns of ivory have been converted into kazoos: the mouthpiece is covered with a membrane, and the musician mumbles or sings in front of the horn.

Both in lands influenced by Islam and in those that remained pagan, the horn was initially associated with the exercise of power. It was the instrument of the civil or religious chief and, as such, the instrument of public order, war or ritual—of activities associated with the well-being of the entire populace. Thus, among the horns used by the Dogon, there is one—and it is the only kind made of iron—that is attached to the person of the Hogon. It is sounded during his coronation, his funeral and at the annual festival of the sowing of seeds, over which he presides. In other regions, the chief has an orchestra of horns; it accompanies him on his tours and plays in ceremonies that he attends in person. If there is no chief, a particularly strong men's society, a confraternity responsible for the initiation of boys or a class of people—hunters or farmers—that supplies the food for the populace has one or more of these instruments. They are only played on prescribed occasions: at seasonal rites, during work in the field, on hunting expeditions, during the circumcision or initiation of males and at funerals. Private persons are allowed to own only small horns, just as they are allowed to keep whistles; shepherds and sorcerer-hunting diviners, for instance, often have a small horn. (See also *Hunting; Ivory; Music*.)   A.S.

HORSES. The domestic horse came to Africa via Egypt, at the time of the Hyksos kings. Their presence there is proved by skeletons at Buhen, one of which has been dated at about 1675 B.C. Figures of horses in works of art indicate that they were used during the New Kingdom; works from this period show horses drawing chariots, both

Horse. Crest of a dance headdress. Kurumba. Mali. Painted wood. Musée de l'Homme, Paris. *Museum photo.*

on parade and on the battlefield, and also mounted. They were ridden in the kingdom of Napata (seventh to sixth centuries B.C.) and horse-breeding and chariot-racing were carried on in Cyrenaica around 500 B.C. Herodotus described how the Garamantes of the Fezzan were equipped with battle chariots. These facts point to the two routes along which the horse was introduced: one from the Mediterranean coast to the Saharan hinterland, and the other along the Nile to the Chad savanna; but very little is known about the dates and stages of this double line of penetration into Africa.

The riders depicted on the rocks at Ennedi probably date from the beginning of the Christian era. Horses are also a common feature of the rock art of the central Sahara; but so little is known about these works, which are earlier than those at Ennedi and thus record another phase of the history of the domestication of the horse in Africa, that they have only a potential historical value. Horses harnessed to chariots are so common in the rock art along two routes—Morocco to Niger and Fezzan to Gao through Ahaggar—that the routes have even been referred to as the "chariot routes." Yet, these fragile, unsteady-looking vehicles—whose drivers, when they are depicted, are so precariously poised—seem quite unsuited to long journeys or useful loads and still less to serving as battle chariots. The suggestion that they were racing chariots raises the question of when and where. There is some foundation for the theories that they were either Roman or local, but these immediately raise further objections. It is not even certain that the pictures were intended to be realistic. Deductions from rock art are highly speculative, but it is certain that in classical times the packhorse was used on desert journeys near the Nile and in West Africa, where it carried a waterskin under its belly. During the historic period, the horse was used throughout an area that was bounded by the desert and the tsetse fly. Horses were imported from the East and the Maghrib. They were then highly prized animals, used as the proud mounts of kings and great men, in fantasias and processions and for war. Documentary sources mention the cavalry as a major feature of several Sudanese states and comment on the strength that it provided. Several of these states maintained heavy cavalry in which animals and their riders wore protective armor made of cloth, leather and metal. When the Dutch settled at the Cape, they imported horses from Java and then, in the eighteenth century, from America. (See also *Gold; Hausa; Mussoi; Rock Art.*)   H.M.

HOTTENTOTS. The Hottentots are a non-Negroid pastoral people living in South Africa. They are racially very mixed, and their numbers are declining rapidly; but when the Dutch came in the seventeenth century, the Hottentots inhabited all the Cape region, from which they had expelled the Bushmen. They resemble the Bushmen physically, although the Hottentots are bigger and more massively built (the Hottentot "apron" is an artificial aesthetic-erotic deformation of the labia and not a racial characteristic). They came from the northeast, like the Bushmen, but left remnant groups in Tanganyika and Kenya (Sandawe and Kindiga). Contrary to what was long believed, the Hottentot and the Bushman languages do not appear to be closely related; the grammatical structure of the Hottentot differs from that of the Bushman language. Common phonological and phonetic characteristics (the click sounds), which also occur among the neighboring Bantu, are probably features acquired or borrowed from Bushmen women whom they captured during migration. Intermarriage with the Dutch during the seventeenth and eighteenth centuries (all old Boer families have some Hottentot blood in their veins) produced mixed groups, like the Bastaards and Griqua. On the other hand, the Pygmoid Herero of southwestern Africa bear a resemblance to both the Hottentots and the Bushmen. It was often suggested that there was a Hamitic component in the ethnic makeup of the Hottentots, but this is strongly disputed today. They are most probably a very old, pre-Negroid race with a strong Bushmen admixture introduced at an early date.

Their principal economic and social activity is animal husbandry, which has important rituals associated with it. The fat-tailed sheep has almost entirely disappeared. Numerically, the most important type of cattle is the long-horned zebu, which is raised more for prestige than yield; there is a relationship between animal and cattleman that recalls that of the Masai in East Africa and of the Fulani in West Africa.

The old political organization, which was tribal, was completely destroyed by the Germans at the beginning of this century, when they suppressed the Nama uprising; the numbers of the Amraal tribe fell from 2,500 to 100 between 1880 and 1923. The displaced and dispersed tribes have no more chieftains. Only exogamic patriarchal clans survive. The chief is the oldest member of the oldest lineage, and he is only *primus inter pares* among the elders of the other lineages.

Hottentots. Engravings. Cabinet des Estampes, Bibliothèque nationale, Paris. *Library photo.*

Women enjoy many rights, notably in the choice of husbands. Engagements are the occasion for ritual displays of hostility, which culminate in real fisticuffs during the wedding night. It is thought that the Bushmen women, who were captured in large numbers at the time of the Hottentot invasion, introduced a whole system of beliefs centered on hunting and exactly parallel to those of the Bushmen. This system is combined with a mythology based on the sun and the weather (thunder god, primordial rainbow-snake), very like that of some Nilotic animal husbanders, as well as with an ancestor cult based on a national hero-ancestor (for example, Ts'ni-Kg'oab of the Nama). Their material culture is poor, but more modern than that of the Bushmen: basketry, pottery, primitive metallurgy, but no weaving.

After driving the Bushmen into the Kalahari Desert, the Hottentots found themselves caught, in their turn, between the Dutch and the Bantu, who confiscated their women and cattle and reduced the men to serfdom or slavery (all Bantu tribes in South Africa display a powerful Hottentot strain in their language and physical makeup). The Hottentots were more bellicose than their former victims and defended themselves very courageously. They suffered cruelly as a result; only a few tens of thousands remain, and demographically their situation is poor. As a final injustice, their name in English has become a synonym for "barbarous ugliness" and "ignoble savagery." And yet, the first colonizers of the Cape—until the decree of 1708 and even later—did not altogether despise the charms of Hottentot women. (See also *Animal Husbandry; Bushmen; Christianity; Diet; Excision; Fossils, Human; Migrations; Race; Rock Art.*) P.A.

HOUSEHOLD FURNISHINGS. The layout and furnishings of a dwelling should enable the inhabitants to rest during the day and at night, to prepare their meals, to arrange their material possessions, to have light and to keep warm (a minor consideration in tropical areas). Household furnishings are attributes of the way of life of a society. In Africa, the number of household articles varies from the extreme lack of possessions of the nomadic Bororo, who barely own a mat, to the profusion of objects and implements that are found in the palaces of the Sudan and the civilizations of the west-coast lagoons. Furniture is almost always decorated. The Bella, who are dependents of the Tuareg and are very poor, nevertheless

Baluba headrest. Zaire. Wood. Webster Plass Collection, British Museum. *Museum photo.*

Afo stool. Nigeria. Wood. Museum für Völkerkunde, Berlin. *Museum photo, Karl H. Paulmann.*

Bajokwe seat. Angola. Wood. Musée royal de l'Afrique centrale, Tervuren. *Photo: Jacques Maquet.*

own beautifully carved wooden tent pegs.

Sleeping arrangements are sometimes very ingenious. Among the Massa of northern Cameroun, the bed is an integral part of the house; it is made of mud and is shaped like a rectangle with its back to the wall. It is constructed with recesses in its base for storing objects, keeping small animals safe during the night and lighting fires for protection against the cold and mosquitos.

African beds generally have no mattresses; people sleep directly on a hard surface. Beds are made of many materials, but it seems that the hammock is unknown in Africa. Very often people sleep on mats on the floor. A smoothed and swept mat on the floor also makes a congenial setting for many of the family gatherings. Beds sometimes have headrests. The addition of a headrest is frequently dictated by considerations of a

Bakuba palm-wine cup.
Zaire. Wood. Musée royal de
l'Afrique centrale, Tervuren.
Museum photo.

Baga ceremonial table.
Guinea. Wood. Musée de
l'Homme, Paris.
Museum photo.

religious or social nature; the heads of some individuals in high authority (for example the Hogon, who is the high priest of the Dogon of Mali) must not touch the ground.

Chairs must enable people to fulfill several needs simultaneously: to rest comfortably, and also to raise themselves above the ground for magical reasons and to manifest their social rank. Among the Mossi of Chad, the members of societies possessed by spirits are not allowed to sit on the ground; they use logs from different kinds of trees, depending upon which spirit inhabits a particular kind of tree and which spirits they are possessed by. The chiefs of the Tuburi of Chad are always preceded by their portable chairs. Footstools developed rapidly into thrones, and in Dahomey they are the subject of a complex ritual. The manufacture of state stools among the Ashanti is carefully ruled by custom; each court dignitary owns one, and it is a symbol of the position he occupies. Many savanna tribes use seatsticks during rituals and dances. Chairs with a back are rare in traditional Africa, except for the admirably carved chairs of the Bajokwe. Copies of European-style lounge chairs and folding chairs make up part of the contemporary African household furniture. Tables, which serve a different function in Africa than they do in the West, are mostly used as movable shelves, while food is usually prepared and eaten on ground level.

Storage furniture has to protect its contents against rodents and insects, especially termites, and so wooden chests are rare, except among desert dwellers. The inhabitants of savanna and forest regions generally use receptacles of clay or pottery. "Wardrobes" often consist of stacked pots with calabashes for covers. Possessions are often raised above the ground by placing them on shelves that stand along the wall or are suspended on ropes or in nets that are hung either between the house walls or from the roof beams. People who live in huts generally use the thatched roof for putting away small objects. Very precious objects are always put in the thatch.

Houses are usually heated by an indoor fire, the smoke from which escapes through the chimneyless roof. Smoke is welcome in Africa because it keeps insects away. In traditional Africa, there was, until recently, no system of lighting that allowed work to be done after sunset, except for people living in the orbit of the Muslim world, who used oil lamps. At the very most, a fire of brushwood and millet twigs was lit in the enclosure to provide light for the evening meal. Nowadays, kerosene lamps and European furnishings, such as chairs, beds and china, are tending to become more common in traditional Africa. They indicate the wealth

Bamileke bed. Cameroun.
Carved wood. Musée de
l'Homme, Paris.
Museum photo.

Right: Bijogo receptacle. Portuguese Guinea. Wood. Statens Etnografiska Museum, Stockholm. *Museum photo.*
Left: Banana mortar. Dzem. Cameroun. Wood. Musée de l'Homme, Paris. *Museum photo.*

of their owner and sometimes, as in Senegal, are part of the dowry. (See also *Ashanti; Bajokwe; Basketry; Calabashes; Headrests; Massa; Posture; Pottery; Sculpture, Stone; Sculpture, Wood.*)   I.G.

HUNGER. The gap between population growth and food supply increase is tending to be enlarged in Africa as in the rest of the world. With a demographic growth of nearly 2 per cent per annum for the entire African continent, problems of hunger threaten to arise in the near future. The situation in Africa, however, is far from being as serious as in Asia. Famines in Africa are associated with historical events. They accompanied the creation of empires and, more recently, conquests: those of Samory Touré in West Africa, of Chaka in South Africa and of Rabah in central Africa. In traditional surroundings, armed conflict is nearly always accompanied by the burning of crops. The famines caused by the recent civil wars in Nigeria and Zaire are difficult for us to conceive of.

The agricultural and pastoral tribes on the southern border of the Sahara subsist in a precarious state, living at the mercy of drought and crop diseases. In the central Senegal Valley, the years 1879, 1895, 1903, 1914, 1926, 1927, 1932, 1935, 1942 and 1945 were marked by crop failures due to various causes: floods, droughts, plagues of quelea and locusts. The retreat of the monsoon rains from the southern Sahara, beginning in 1966, has resulted in ever-increasing famine in the lands of the Sahel. The frugality of the nomadic Teda is legendary, and they display endless ingenuity in preserving their small stocks of cereals. They even eat the ribs of palm leaves and date pits ground into flour to appease their hunger. Further south, in the Sudan region, the basic diet consists of cereals, which are harvested at the same time as industrial crops. Savanna communities then enjoy a period of plenty and merrymaking, which uses up some of their stocks of food and results in a period of shortage. This period of scarcity may last some weeks or months (as it did in Ghana, Nigeria and northern Togo in 1960, in Nyasaland—now Malawi—in 1959, in Kenya in 1960 and Somaliland in 1957 and 1960) and may become serious. It generally corresponds to the time for clearing the fields of weeds, and this is work that makes the greatest physical demands on the laborers. By picking edible plants that grow wild and by using the resources of improved marketing systems, rural people can subsist today, although it may be at the price of regularly running into debt, which is not unusual in the peanut areas of Senegal. Some tribes who choose to remain where the land is poor always live on

Cover of a Barotse dish. Zambia. Wood. Webster Plass Collection. British Museum. *Museum photo.*

the brink of famine despite the fact that they work very hard. This is true of some of the mountain people of northern Cameroun. In 1921 and 1931, the famine in the Mandara Mountains was so bad that the inhabitants traded their children to their Fulani neighbors for calabashes or millet. Among the Mofu, the caloric intake is 30 percent below the necessary minimum; deficiencies of vitamins A, C and B_2 are frequent; and consumption of animal proteins is less than five grams a day. Infant mortality before the age of four is 30 percent, and life expectancy at birth is twenty-four years.

Africa suffers from malnutrition more than anything else. Methods of food preparation that impair nutritional values and bad dietary habits are partly responsible. Although most ethnic groups manage to have a diet of sufficient caloric value, their food intake may still be short and not have sufficient amounts of certain elements that are essential for the development and protection of the human body. There are deficiencies in vitamins A, C, and B_2 in the savanna region and deficiencies of animal proteins and vitamin D in the forest zone. These shortages do not cause serious trouble to most of the adult population, although they do lower resistance to illness and

decrease the capacity to work. The consequences of nutritional deficiencies are infinitely more serious in what are known as the vulnerable groups: pregnant and nursing women and babies. In some parts of the forest zones, a heavy toll of infants is taken by kwashiorkor (a protein and vitamin deficiency syndrome), which strikes young children between birth and the age of four. Deficiencies of the PP factor, which causes pellagra among corn eaters, occur sporadically in Rhodesia, Malawi, South Africa and Mozambique. A deficiency of vitamin B_1, which causes beriberi, is almost nonexistent in Africa, but the growing demand for bleached rice may have serious consequences in the future. It is rare for scurvy to take a serious form in Africa, but the symptoms of vitamin C deficiency frequently appear in the savanna because not much fresh fruit and not many greens are eaten. And when greens are eaten, they are boiled for so long that most of the vitamin C is destroyed. The drying of leaves and vegetables in order to preserve them has the same effect. A deficiency of vitamin A occurs during the dry season all over the tropical zone, and many tribes have a name in the vernacular for it. It strikes traditional societies whose diet lacks milk, foods of

Hunter. Front and back views. Lower Niger, Nigeria. Bronze. British Museum. *Photos: Eliot Elisofon.*

animal origin such as fish and egg yolks, and fruit containing carotene (tomatoes, papayas, mangoes and peppers), but it is not found in forest zones where palm oil is regularly consumed. On the other hand, rickets, due to lack of vitamin D, occurs in the forest zones of Guinea and the Ivory Coast. There is often inadequate calcium in the diet, and lack of iodine causes endemic goiters in certain clearly defined areas: the Fouta Djallon Mountains, the land of the Sara in Chad, the mountains of Cameroun and the Abyssinian Plateau. Ariboflavinosis (deficiency of vitamin B$_2$) is quite widespread, due to lack of animal protein, particularly of milk.

The African diet is poor in proteins generally, and the percentage of animal protein in the daily diet is nearly always too low. Proteins are the material of which all the cells of living organisms are made; they build and preserve the human body, whose protein requirements are calculated as one gram per two pounds of weight for adults and two and a half grams per two pounds for children. Traditional African societies have sources of vegetable proteins (cereals and root crops), but for a balanced diet 25 to 30 percent of the protein ought to be of animal origin. Only fishermen and certain groups of animal husbanders who are willing to diminish their patrimony in order to eat have a diet that is rich in animal proteins. Savanna zones, where cereals and root crops form the basic diet and where the products of animal husbandry and fishing are readily available, seem to be better off than the forest zones. There, the tsetse fly prevents the raising of animals, and tuber vegetables, whose vegetable protein content is very low, provide the basic diet.

At the present time, the rural African is passing from a domestic economy to a market economy. His desire to adopt a way of life similar to that of urban societies often leads him to buy manufactured products or alcohol, which nowadays give him more prestige than buying foods that he himself no longer produces in sufficient quantities. Far from diminishing, the difficulty of maintaining an adequate standard of diet is tending to increase. The nutritional level of salaried workers in towns drops at the end of the month, because they no longer live in a food-producing economy and their incomes are poor and unwisely spent. Even when their salaries seem adequate, the desire to imitate a European way of life and the emancipation of women often lead them to give up their traditional, balanced but supposedly retrograde diet and adopt instead foods that are easy to prepare, such

as bleached rice, bread and canned foodstuffs, which are considered more advanced but whose nutritional value is often questionable. In the urban proletariat, formed of recent immigrants from the country without special qualifications or steady employment, cases of malnutrition and starvation have reached a level hitherto unknown in Africa. (See also *Diet; Meals; Meat; Salt.*) I.G.

HUNTING. No purely Negroid civilization is based exclusively on hunting and food-gathering. The only large groups of African hunters and gatherers are the Pygmies in the equatorial forests and the Bushmen in the Kalahari Desert, along with the groups related to them: the Dorobo, Sandawe and Kindiga of East Africa. Among the true blacks, hunting small game is a complementary activity practiced by men and children, while big-game hunting is more of a specialty reserved for experts, who often belong to societies that are both professional and ritual, or else for particular groups or subgroups, which are often endogamous, such as the Gow of the Songhai. This does not mean that all tribes are equally enthusiastic or skillful hunters: the Masai in Kenya, who have large herds of cattle, are passionate hunters of big game in contrast to their Kikuyu neighbors; on the other hand, the Baya farmers of the Republic of Central Africa hunt a great deal and much more successfully than the Fulani cattle-raisers in the same area.

Hunting techniques can be divided into two categories: those used by individuals and those used by groups. Individual methods include snaring by means of nooses, pits, sunken traps or nets; weapon throwing, using weapons such as assegais, knives or clubs; and shooting, using weapons such as modern rifles or flintlock guns, crossbows or slings. Group hunting techniques include driving the game into a net, to a line of marksmen or lancers, or to natural or artificial obstacles—such drives are carried out by means of fire, shouting and horn blowing, bell ringing, dogs or beaters—and coursing on foot, with or without dogs, or on horseback.

Big-game hunting is always dangerous, and therefore the hunter or hunters have to participate in a purification ritual before the hunt and often a ritual of reconciliation with the slaughtered game afterward. These rites are always in the form of propitiation or restitution ceremonies and are frequently similar to rites associated with military expeditions, usually taking the form of dances in which the various stages of the

Somba hunter. Dahomey.
*Photo: Documentation
française.*

hunt are mimed. Weaponmakers and special magicians occasionally join the ceremonies. Some types of hunting are a ritual in themselves—for example, the village group hunts of the Republic of Central Africa and Zaire and the lion hunt that concludes the ceremonial initiation into manhood of the young Masai in East Africa. The sharing of the game is governed by very strict rules which stipulate how the different pieces should be divided among the relatives and associates of the hunter. Furthermore, the chiefs have the right to special portions of certain game that might be considered "royal," especially elephants, lions, panthers, buffalo and some breeds of antelope.

The very strict ritual laws governing hunting and the quasi-religious monopoly that benefited certain groups and individuals helped, in earlier periods, to preserve game animals. The introduction of better weapons; hunting by European and Arab professionals, particularly the hunting of elephants and rhinoceros (rhinoceros horn, which was reputed to be a powerful aphrodisiac and a universal antidote derived from Chinese pharmacopoeia, was sold for almost its weight in gold); the state of peacefulness imposed by the colonial powers, which prevented hunting tribes from asserting their rights by force of arms; and finally the systematic and wholesale slaughter of game

in order to destroy centers infected by trypanosomes or to protect crops have all led to the rapid destruction of wildlife. The first protective measures date from the beginning of the twentieth century with the creation of Kruger Park in South Africa. Its example was gradually followed in all European colonies by the establishment of national parks and game reserves, and by enforcing more or less effective legislation concerning hunting and the protection of certain species. However, laws restricting freedom of hunting remain highly unpopular. Hunting tours and the safari business make a noticeable contribution to the economy of some countries, especially Kenya. Poaching for commercial purposes is rampant and all the more alarming because none of the meat of animals slaughtered for their skins is used to alleviate the protein deficiency that is a common feature of the African diet. For several years the International Union for the Protection of Nature has been considering a plan for creating natural ranches for large herbivorous animals. If it succeeds, this could save African fauna—and also hunting in Africa—as well as doubling or tripling the available supply of meat. (See also *Buffalo; Bushmen; Chad, Lake; Dance; Elephants; Fauna; Initiation; Lions; Meat; Migrations; Pygmies; Songhai; Taboos; Traps; Weapons.)*   P.A.

IBADAN. With 1 million inhabitants, Ibadan is the largest Yoruba city. Situated in southwestern Nigeria, it is also the largest of the African towns that existed before the colonial era, although it is not one of the oldest. Ibadan developed from a military camp, founded little more than a century ago, during the period of greatest upheaval in Yoruba history. The Fulani, having organized a powerful empire in northern Nigeria, extended their attack southward and, about 1830, after conquering the frontier areas of the Yoruba country, destroyed Oyo, the old Yoruba capital. The population fled in all directions, upsetting the balance between the Yoruba states and towns. Ibadan, which was the center of defensive activity against the Fulani invasion, attracted large numbers of warriors and refugees from all parts of the country. It formed the nucleus of a new state, which at various times recognized the suzerainty of the former king of Oyo, who had taken refuge further south, where he established a new capital and rapidly formed the most powerful army in the region. The end of precolonial Yoruba history is largely concerned with the struggles of Ibadan to impose its hegemony.

The city, originally founded on a group of seven hills, spread out over a large area and now includes a number of outlying districts, both traditional and modern. Ibadan came to dominate several minor towns, including Igangan and Iwo, and a territory containing scattered agricultural hamlets. Although Ibadan quickly became a center for trade and cottage industries, the majority of the inhabitants remained cultivators producing foodstuffs; but in recent times the cultivators have been gradually supplanted by cocoa plantations. Each family has a concession in town, and its fields may be as far as thirty miles away. Like nearly all Yoruba cities, Ibadan could be described as a country town. It follows a very ancient urban tradition and has shown its respect for the past by helping the reconstruction of Ife, a great part of which was destroyed in the civil war. But there are few impressive buildings in Ibadan, and some of the existing ones, such as the beautiful temple of Shango, have been seriously damaged by the recent construction of large avenues.

The organization of Ibadan was rudimentary and was not based on districts; each family gave its allegiance to a chief who was chosen on the basis of his age, wealth, lineage and popularity and these chiefs formed a town council. The president of the town council and his deputy, who was also the military leader, managed the business of the town. There was no king in Ibadan. (See also *Yoruba.*)   P.M.

IBIBIO. Ibibio is a generic name given to an entire group of neighboring tribes whose culture and language are related and who number, in all, more than 1 million inhabitants. The best known are the Efik, who live on the banks of the Cross River in southern Nigeria, and the Ibibio tribe itself, who live further east. These two tribes are fishermen, trading in fish and palm oil, while all the other tribes in the group are farmers. The skills of the Ibibio group are limited. They know very little about metallurgy, but they have developed a curious method of weaving raffia on a vertical frame.

The tribes are divided into autonomous units whose organization, founded on the clan and village, or groups of villages, is fairly loosely knit. Since there is no government, public order is maintained by the age groups and secret societies. There is sometimes a chieftain-priest, possibly modeled on Benin institutions. Masked members of the *Ekpo* society represent ancestors, who are especially involved in agrarian rites. The *Ekon* society was once the society of headhunters, but its recruitment is now based on wealth. The *Ekpe,* a society of lion men and leopard men taken over from the Ekoi, is more secret and more dangerous. Married women belong to the *Ebre* society, which performs agrarian rituals and controls the entire life of the women, but particularly the fattening of young girls in the period of preparation for marriage, when they are shut up in a hut, given vast quantities of food and not allowed to move.

Ibibio art, apart from the tall statues of ancestors made by the Oron of the Cross River estuary and the mural paintings of men and animals done by the Anang, who live to the northwest of the Oron, consists mainly of the masks of the *Ekpo* society. These comprise black masks, sometimes shaped like skulls, which are worn with costumes made of black fibers that cover the dancers; masks in vivid colors, with faces ornamented with horns or made to appear ravaged by leprosy; larger masks built up with a single standing figure surrounded by several less important seated figures; and masks in the form of a face surmounted by a sort of shelf decorated with statuettes. A marginal art form, the making of clay statues by some Ibibio uses techniques similar to those of the Ibo. One type of clay statue, with outstretched arms coiled about with snakes and elongated neck and breasts, bears a strange resemblance to Cretan figures. Can this be a survival, in one isolated area, of a remote

Oron statue. Ibibio. Nigeria. Wood. Nigerian Museum, Lagos. *Photo: Eliot Elisofon.*

Mask of the *Mau* society.
Ibo. Nigeria. Painted wood.
University Museum,
Philadelphia. *Museum photo.*

influence that has been obliterated else-where? (See also *Divinities; Excision; Societies, Secret.*)   P.M.

IBO. Nearly 8 million Ibo occupy the plateaus of eastern Nigeria on both sides of the lower Niger, and their population is one of the densest in Africa. There are sometimes over 2,500 inhabitants to the square mile. They live on moderately fertile land on which they cultivate yams or in forests which gradually give way to palm groves. The Ibo probably occupied this area at a very early date, but nothing is known of their history before the slave trade, which took a heavy toll of them. Since the Ibo never created a state, nor even a name to describe them-selves, their early history is merely a tissue of numerous village traditions, which are little more than legends, or tales about local events. We do know, however, that the Ibo in the west were subdued in the fifteenth century by the kings of neighboring Benin, which exercised a lasting influence upon them.

Ibo country consists of a multitude of villages or village groups, uniting some thousands or tens of thousands of in-habitants, all jealous of their independence; their language, beliefs and social or-ganization display countless local variations against a common background. However, commercial traffic and religious influences, particularly those of famous oracles, pre-vented the total isolation of village groups. In the villages, where there were no political leaders, decisions were taken unanimously by an assembly of all the men. But the real authority was shared in varying proportions by the priest of the earth, heads of family groups, who were the spokesmen and priests of the ancestor, and influential members of societies of titleholders. Every free man of good conduct who was capable of meeting the expenses entailed in acquiring rank or honorary titles could join these societies and rise in the hierarchy. Ibo society was characterized by democracy and religious sanctions, individualism and the glo-rification of personal success. The part played in modern times by the Ibo in the political and economic life of Nigeria shows how these traits persist.

Despite a certain technical poverty, the Ibo created a remarkable art, which is almost entirely religious in purpose. Its most unusual feature is a series of images of the earth goddess and other divinities, which are often larger than life-size, modeled in clay on a framework of palm fronds and painted black, red and brown. The same technique has been used to depict figures and scenes of everyday life. Their sculpture in wood is varied and suggests a number of influences. Protective statues (*ikenga*) are painted in vivid colors and may be more than 5 feet high. Sometimes they represent a single person, a horned man holding a human head in his hand, but they can also consist of several tiers of human and animal figures supporting round platforms, the whole surmounted with long horns. The masks of the *Mau* society, worn above long dancing robes, represent the dead ancestors, whose arrival among the living is announced by the sound of bull-roarers. They have skel-etonlike faces, painted white, with hollow eye sockets. The masks used in ceremonies to honor water spirits are probably copied from the masks of their Ijo neighbors and are very stylized representations of human beings, animals and fish. (See also *Benin; Drums; Funerals; Ijo; Societies, Secret; Twins.*)
                                    P.M.

IFE. Ife, the holy city of the Yoruba, first became known in Europe at the beginning of the century through its magnificent ancient bronzes. It was L. Frobenius who discovered

Oba of Ife. Nigeria. Brass. Ife
Museum, Nigeria. *Photo:
William Fagg.*

Ife mask. Nigeria. Copper.
Webster Plass Collection.
British Museum.
Photo: Eliot Elisofon.

Head from Ife. Nigeria.
Terracotta. Sir Adesaji
Aderemi Collection, Nigeria.
Photo: Walter Dräyer.

the first life-size bronze head, and now about
twenty bronze heads, probably dating from
before the thirteenth century, can be seen in
the museum at Ife. Technically, they are
nearly perfect: they are hollow, the bronze
shell is only a few millimeters thick, and they
have been retouched only very slightly. They
were cast by the lost-wax method and appear
to be portraits of kings or dignitaries which
were used during ceremonies commemorating the dead. Realistic portraits
with a classical serenity, they are remarkable
on a continent where stylization in various
guises predominates. The proportions are
exact, and the physiognomy is treated in the
greatest detail. Several of the faces are
decorated with narrow parallel lines that

Head from Ife. Nigeria. Terracotta. Private Collection, New York. *Photo: Brooklyn Museum.*

resemble the scarification employed for tribal identification today. Most of the heads are perforated around the skull, lips and chin, where hair, moustache and beard were probably attached, as they commonly are to masks in many regions of Africa. The art of bronze-casting died out in Ife, but was transmitted to the kingdom of Benin, where it underwent fresh development.

Not only the art of bronze-casting, but also the discovery during recent excavations of statues and chairs carved in stone are evidence of a great center of ancient civilization. Its origin remains obscure, although several theories have been put forward. Many writers on Africa have suggested a close relationship with classical Egypt. A comparison with the artistic techniques and forms of Nubia is justifiable. According to some historians, the Nubian influences, which were derived from the Hellenistic world, were only the culmination of a much earlier contact with the Mediterranean. E. F. Gautier thought that southern Nigeria was a "Carthaginian colony," and Carthage, while supplying itself with gold and tin from West Africa, introduced in exchange the techniques of casting bronze and making glass. For Frobenius, Ife is the Ophir mentioned in the Bible, where the Phoenicians went to look for gold for Solomon. He postulated a great empire of Ophir extending from present-day Ghana to the Niger Delta. He also identified this empire and the great cultural center with the mythical Atlantis. After seaborne contact with Ife had been lost, the memory of it survived in the Mediterranean area as a land that could only be reached after a long voyage beyond the Pillars of Hercules, where there were elephants, palm trees and fortresses covered with copper sheeting. All this corresponds with the reality of Benin. It was there that the Phoenicians took refuge and founded their last civilization after they had been driven out of the Mediterranean by Greek expansion. Even if one rejects this hypothesis as incapable of proof, the discussion remains open. But there is no doubt of the existence of a great center of civilization that exercised a far-reaching influence. Many tribes to the east, north and west of the Yoruba country took over gods, kings and arts from Ife. By the sixteenth century, the beginning of the historical period of which we have some knowledge, Ife was no longer the center of Yoruba political power. But Ife remained a holy city, and the king of Ife, "father" of all Yoruba kings, retained great religious prestige. The Portuguese who came to Benin heard of him at once, and one of them noted that the king

was venerated in exactly the same fashion as "the pope is with us." In Yoruba tradition, Ife is not only the capital of the original kingdom, but also the center of the earth, the place where the earth began to form as it rose from the sea, where the deity Odudua descended to become father (or mother) of men and was the first to reign in the town he founded. It was from Ife that his sons set out to found the other great Yoruba kingdoms, and for a long time their descendants returned to Ife to find indispensable confirmation of their royalty before being recognized as kings. (See also *Allada; Bronze; Heads; Lost-Wax Process; Pottery; Savanna; Sculpture, Stone; Towns and Cities; Yoruba.*)   P.M.

IJO. The Ijo, numbering 250,000, occupy the entire Niger Delta in close proximity to the Yoruba, the Edo from Benin, the Ibo and the Ibibio. They were probably driven back into this land of rain forests, mangroves, swamps, marshes and creeks by the first three of the above tribes when these tribes moved southward. The Ijo, who were exclusively fishermen and hunters, lived in isolation except when they bartered dried fish for yams with their neighbors. These were their only external contacts, because the main trade route of the lower Niger did not really penetrate their country. It has been suggested that some of their art forms, although technically inferior, were inspired by those of Benin.

The Ijo are very scattered and have never formed a kingdom. Membership of the elders, who directed the life of the villages, was attained by headhunting. It was accompanied by ritual cannibalism, when warriors, old men and women all ate the body of a fallen enemy. The skulls were preserved and worshiped in rituals in which only those who had killed an enemy could actively join, for participation consisted in carrying an enemy's skull during the dances. Besides this, there was an elaborate cult of ancestors and water spirits, the two being closely linked, that included masked dances in which both made their appearance.

There are two main art forms among the Ijo: the making of masks and "faces of the dead." Masks, which were used in the last-mentioned ritual and were worn above the costumes, thus hiding the dancer entirely, are schematic, with a flat triangular face, very elongated, with an overhanging forehead, cylindrically shaped eyes and a nose shaped like an upside-down T. Sometimes they have two faces, in which case the volumes are more emphatic, with cylindrical shapes predominating. Heads of ancestors that are part of the decorated screens which serve as altars are of the same style. These screens, which suggest a possible influence from Benin, consist of a rectangular piece of woven raffia in an upright wooden frame that is surmounted by heads of ancestors called the "faces of the dead," a term also used for the whole structure. The frame is covered with strange bas-reliefs, generally portraying a principal figure surrounded by attendants of much smaller size. These figures are not carved in one piece but in several; the head, trunk and limbs are tied together with raffia and appear to be articulated. The compositions of these "faces of the dead" often show remarkable balance. (See also *Art, African; Heads; Initiation.*)

P.M.

INCEST. Prohibition of incest is the first rule on which society is founded; it elevates the relationship between the sexes from crudity to culture; it governs the availability of women; and it determines the pattern of kin groups and of marriage. No society can remain unaware of it, since it is enforced by the most severe condemnation and penalties.

The theme of incest is often found in myths about the creation. The Dogon of Mali believe that the first beings created by Amma (god) were hermaphrodite twins. One of these twins typifies the disrupter of order in the world. The other twin appears in the guise of a savior who descended to earth with an ark containing men, animals and plants. The worst of the deeds of the rebellious brother was considered to be incest with the earth. It was evidently considered a violation of the laws that could bring back original chaos and is a significant indication of their recognition of the connection between disorder and incest. Incest, according to Dogon theory, is the cause of confusion between the generations, the destruction of basic social relationships and of the normal sequence of events, sterility, death, and the breakdown of civilization symbolized by the loss of the "true word."

All African societies, with a varying wealth of symbolism, have similar interpretations. To the Bakongo, incest is a crime; they hold it responsible for the most fearful calamities such as drought, famine, deadly illnesses, the barrenness of women and of the land. They consider it the instrument responsible for disrupting the order of nature and of man. Among the Fang in Gabon, incest is included in the ritual impurities and is indeed the principal one, because it is the cause of illness, sterility and countless crises in relations between human beings and between man and the universe. It calls for a

Funerary screen *(duen fobara)* used as an altar for dead members of the *Ekine* society. Ijo. Nigeria. Wood. British Museum. *Photo: William Fagg.*

complete procedure of collective expiation. Directed by a high initiate (*akum*), the men perform dances such as the *makuma,* which is prescribed for funeral rites, in order to counter the influence of death and of anything that might compromise fecundity.

In every African society, the laws of incest strictly define the categories of persons between whom sexual union and marriage are forbidden. Some criteria are based on kinship and alliance: prohibitions against relations between members of the class of "sires" and members of the class of children; between persons united by virtue of membership in a "fraternity," interpreted in a broad sense; and between certain relations by "alliance." And some criteria are based on membership in a lineage or clan: the Bakongo say "blood cannot be joined to the same blood," thus excluding marriage between persons of the same ancestral origin. The complex of taboos forms the foundation on which society and morality are built.

There are, however, certain circumstances in which incest is necessary to meet the requirements of a system of symbolism and ritual. The sovereign of traditional kingdoms was sometimes compelled to practice it, as in the Egypt of the pharaohs, where incestuous royal marriage was inspired by the mythical example of Osiris and Seth, in Madagascar and in various other parts of Africa, as well

Kariba Dam across the
Zambezi River. Rhodesia.
Photo: Jacques Maquet.

as in Peru and Polynesia. The most remarkable African version of incest occurred
in the vigorous states that developed in East
Africa (the kingdoms of Baganda, Banyoro
and Banyankole, for example). At his
enthronement the king was supposed to
perform an act that deviated from the norms
of society, thus proving the power of his
magic. This act was incest, which was
intended, among other things, to assert the
annulment of the old social order founded on
family relationships and the accession of a
new authority established for all and over all.
By this exceptional behavior, with its
overtones of magic, the king appeared as a
unique being who did not depend on men,
but on whom men depended. An early poem
from Rwanda echoes this: "The Sovereign
could never have a rival, he is the One and
Only, the Irreproachable." (See also *Azande;
Taboos; Uncles.*)   G.B.

INDIVIDUALITY. See *Person.*

INDUSTRY. It may appear strange that
this word should be listed in a dictionary of
African civilization. Industrial techniques
were certainly unknown in traditional Africa
and, compared to the industrialized countries, they hardly exist in modern Africa. In
order to understand the history of African
culture, however, it is necessary to offer some
consideration of industry. It is important, in
the first place, because it marks the border
between the traditional period and the
modern era. Normally, the initial phase of
colonization is considered the division
between them. This is a correct but superficial judgment, because colonial expansion
was both the consequence of European

industrialization and the origin of African
industrialization. As in the rest of the world,
the invention first of agriculture and then of
industry form the two great cultural revolu-
tions of African history. Each of these
production techniques represented an
enormous advance on its predecessor. The
return on human labor, the area of land
necessary to feed the community, and the
optimum population density reached a
critical threshold when the principal means
of subsistence changed from food-gathering
and hunting to domestic cultivation and
thence again to mechanical means of
production. In Africa, prehistory ends with
the discovery of agriculture, and the
traditional period extends from this point
until the introduction of industrial techniques. Here colonization began.

Industrial production entails the use of
powerful sources of energy to operate
complicated mechanical equipment, which
permits and requires manufacture in bulk on
a scale quite outside the scope of cottage
industry. When Europe was in the process of
industrialization in the nineteenth century,
this increase in manufactured goods created
various economic and social tensions, which
made the occupation of the African interior a
necessity, or at least very useful. Great
plantations of oil palms, rubber trees and
cotton plants supplied the raw materials
required by European industry, as did gold,
copper and tin mining. The infrastructure
that had to be built (ports, railways and
roads) and the new requirements of people
forced to participate in a monetary system
promised vast markets for European enterprises. For the good of Western industry,
Africa had to be colonized. Later, processing
plants and factories were established on site;
thus African industry was born under
colonial rule and the modern period began.

The civilization of this period may be
described as an industrial civilization, which
is the second reason for including "Industry"
in this dictionary. Admittedly, the Africa of
today is far from being industrialized. But, as
elsewhere, the adoption of this new method
of production has had repercussions on all
sectors of the life of the community. This
change in technique leaves no room for
certain traditional organizations: social,
such as tribes; political, such as chiefdoms;
or residential, such as temporary villages. It
weakens customs that are ill-adapted to the
new conditions, such as the solidarity of
kinship groups, polygamy and the worship
of ancestors. It tends toward structures that
suit it particularly well, like the nuclear
family and concentration in towns. Finally,
it imposes its own structures such as a single

homogeneous society molded from a large population, government institutions and bureaucratic administration. Even if industrial techniques, including the mechanization of agriculture, are only in the first stages of their development in black Africa, they are, nevertheless, already shaping, according to their own dynamism, the African civilization of tomorrow. (See also *Civilization; Colonization; Fishing.*)   J.M.

INITIATION. The term "initiation" is often used, on the principle that the part represents the whole, to designate the ceremonies and rites—usually the rites of passage—which mark the crucial stages of the whole process of initiation. It is an unfortunate use of the word, because there are rites of passage that are not preceded by any initiatory instruction, and there are forms of initiation devoid of ceremony or with only diffuse rites. And in other cases, the rite itself is an initiation. The object of initiation is to incorporate the initiate into a group or category of society of which he was previously not a member or was only a potential member.

In many ethnic groups, probably in the majority of them, initiation is part of the life cycle, especially at the beginning of adolescence and the coming of age for boys and at puberty, which is a brief prelude to marriage, for girls. The class of initiates often comprises an age group whose members differ in age by from three to seven years. Sometimes the variation is greater, either because there is a qualifying examination which some pass more easily than others or because of the expense, which may delay the admission of the poorest children. Once the candidates have been assembled, they may be isolated in a special bush school or in a sacred wood (as among the Mande of the western Sudan, the tribes in Upper Volta, the Fang, the Akan, etc.) or else grouped as a regiment or company (as among the Southern Bantu and the Nilo-Hamites). In these camps they receive their instruction in community matters (customs, genealogy, etiquette), professional training (for hunting, war) and sexual education. They are submitted to very strict discipline, with crude horseplay and tough physical ordeals that may prove fatal. The final rite of passage is often marked symbolic mutilation, such as circumcision, facial incisions, removal of a finger or toe joint, the filing or extraction of the incisors, and the like. It frequently symbolizes death followed by resurrection. The candidates, once accepted, change their names and, among the Moba of Togo and the Eastern Bantu, are supposed to forget the

past entirely, to the point of having to pretend to learn how to speak again. The secret character of initiations of this kind is completely relative. It is only kept secret from the young before initiation and from women, as regards masculine initiation, and vice versa. This type of initiation is primarily a kind of education designed to form a group of young people and integrate them into the

Transporting manganese by cable. Gabon. *Photo: Rapho, L. Herschfriff.*

Left: Young initiated Sara
girls. Chad. *Photo:*
Pierre Ichac.
Below: Initiation makeup.
Kenya. *Photo: Musée de*
l'Homme, J. Millot.

community. It may be a permanent feature,
in which case the cycle of initiations covers
the entire life of the individual and each
change of status is preceded by a new
initiation. Usually, however, it ends with
marriage. Among the Zulu, for example, the
stages were the following: adolescence
(puberty), manhood (joining a regiment),
and the age for marrying (leaving the
regiment). This pattern was common all over
East Africa. It suggests the form of an
hourglass: first, the children are scattered
around in their various families, then they
are channeled through the bush school or
regiment, and finally they are dispersed
again after marriage; but they always retain
the common bond of having belonged to the
same initiation group.

This type of initiation, which might be
called biosocial, also exists in West Africa,
but there it is more liable to be accompanied
by a network of optional initiations which
give access to the so-called secret societies, or
permit the initiated to mount one step higher
in the social hierarchy, or grant him the
privilege of performing certain magico-
religious practices (the three aspects are
often combined). Generally, after the
initiation that marks his entrance into
manhood or womanhood, each individual
has a choice among a number of more or less
compatible courses. Among the Fang, for
example, after passing through the national
initiation called "*so,*" a man could, if he had
the means, apply to join the *Ngil* (justice and
police), the Snakes (healers), or else a
profession such as minstrelsy or divination,
or he could join an illegal society, such as the
Ngbwel (sorcerers) or the *Ze Mimfaka*
("leopards"). In each case, he had to pay to
be admitted for instruction and undergo the
necessary trials. The eastern Kwa (the
Yoruba, Edo, Ijo, etc.) had a similar system
for admission to the guilds and for obtaining
honorific titles, as well as for admission to
certain cults of soothsaying and possession

by spirits. It should be noted that admission is not always voluntary. The Dahoman and Togolese "fetish convents" literally requisition little girls and young women and commit them to initiation at a later date; the same is done in Sierra Leone for some divisions of the *Poro* and its feminine counterpart, the *Bundu*. Initiation may also be brought about by illness: the sick person, who is looked after by the initiates of a particular cult, thereby becomes a member of their society and must complete his initiation as soon as he is healed (as among the Bantu in Zaire). This bears a slight resemblance to psychoanalysis and to the forms of some vows in the Catholic Church in Latin countries. Finally, it should be noted that black African Islam, on account of its sects or *tariqa*—both orthodox (Tidjaniya and Qadiriya, for example), and heretical (such as the Hamallists and Senegalese Murids)—has adopted a form of initiation, as have the schismatic churches and syncretic cults of Christian origin.

Initiations, especially those of the second, optional, type are just as significant for the individual as for the community. Individuals set out on the road to initiation in order to gain power or knowledge or both. At present, little is known to Westerners about instruction for initiation. It is always esoteric, consisting of a semantic explanation of the world on two or three levels of significance: the thing observed is first translated into a symbol, and the symbol itself is then translated, sometimes through several levels of meaning. The system of instruction is somewhat reminiscent of certain aspects of Zen. Seclusion in a sacred wood is hard to reconcile with preparation for a primary school diploma, and this irreconcilability alone is enough to explain why colonists and missionaries have thrust traditional forms of initiation into the background, but so far traditional initiation has been replaced more by catechism and sacraments than by an educational system and examinations. This partial or total disappearance of initiations and the accompanying rites of passage and integration into society has helped to disintegrate the structure both of tribes and the individual psyche. It is an interesting fact that many political movements, particularly those of an insurrectional nature (the Mau Mau of Kenya, the U.P.C. of Cameroun) have readopted forms and rituals resembling the old initiation ceremonies. Unfortunately, though, the intellectual and philosophical content of initiation training seems very often to have disappeared. (See also *Age Groups; Body; Bull-Roarers; Circumcision; Education; Excision; Hunting; Masks; Names; Ordeals; Scarification; Societies, Secret; Voodoo; Wisdom;* individual tribes.)

P.A.

Young Kapsiki initiates. Cameroun. *Photo: Pierre Ichac.*

IRON. Africa, south of the Sahara, passed directly from the Stone Age to the Iron Age. Unlike Europe it never had a Bronze Age or a Copper Age. Archeological research has been able to date the beginning of iron metallurgy in some places, but how this important transition from stone to iron actually happened remains conjectural. It may have been discovered independently; it may have begun in one or several places and spread with migrations and conquests; or again, the skill may have been acquired and passed on from person to person, a process facilitated by commercial exchanges. Metalwork demands a hotter fire than that required for domestic purposes, so a type of bellows that can produce sufficient heat for smelting and working a forge is indispensable for ironwork. Three African types are known, and these may be survivals of early ones: drum bellows, the type painted on Egyptian bas-reliefs and which are common in the west and south; Arabic bag bellows, which were introduced into Abyssinia by the Semitic conquerors, probably at the beginning of the Christian era; and the Asiatic piston bellows, which are used in Madagascar.

Egypt, which had imported iron objects for a long time, only started to work the metal in the sixth century B.C. Iron was worked in Meroe, the capital of Nubia, soon afterward, but not on an extensive scale before the fourth century B.C. In Nigeria, the people of Nok, famous for their terracotta heads, practiced metallurgy from the third century B.C. onward (if the carbon-14 date for the objects found on the site of Taruga, 280 B.C., can be taken as evidence). In the Great Lakes region, iron was introduced by a civilization whose culture covered a large area. The evidence for the beginning of iron metallurgy there is connected with the dimple-based pottery (so called because of the circular depression in the base) produced by these people and excavated just above the stratum containing the last chipped stones of the Stone Age. The pottery was made in a blast furnace that was also capable of smelting iron by a more refined technique than was known to the people of a later culture in the same region, whose furnaces were simple holes. One of these blast furnaces, discovered at Ndora, Burundi, has been dated about A.D. 250, with a margin of a hundred years. A layer of dimple-based pottery was also found in a rock shelter at Nsongezi, Uganda, and, as in Burundi, just above a layer of Stone Age remains. This pottery has been dated as belonging to the eleventh century A.D., which indicates that, at least in some places, the final stages of the Stone Age culture lasted a long time. In Zambia the introduction of iron also dates from the beginning of the Christian era. Here again, the presence of channeled-ware pottery, related to dimple-based pottery and likewise connected with the first indications of metalwork, provides evidence. The oldest known sites are those at Lusu and Machili on the upper Zambezi, which were used in the second century A.D. Further north, toward Kalambo Falls, the

Antelope and ox. Bakuba. Tanzania. Forged iron. Linden Museum, Stuttgart. *Museum photo.*

same pottery has been found in strata dating from the sixth to the sixteenth century. In Rhodesia the pottery known as "Gokomerian" was the work of the first metallurgists and dates from the second to the ninth century.

The conclusion to be drawn from all this evidence is that the Iron Age began early in the Christian era in the Great Lakes region, Zambia, Rhodesia and probably also to the south of the Congo Basin. This rapid diffusion over a vast territory has been linked by several scholars with the spread of the Bantu, and it could indeed be attributed to these invaders. The Iron Age expanded in various cultures, and relics of it have been preserved in the soil of Africa. Work in copper and gold developed with iron metallurgy. At Sanga, in present-day Katanga Province in Zaire, copper was fashioned by a rich and well-organized people, from the eighth century onward, into ornaments, chains and rings, and also into a cruciform coinage that is still in use today. More than 7,000 ancient gold and copper mines have been discovered in Rhodesia. It has not been possible to give them a precise date, but there are indications that they go back to the beginning of our era. They may have been exploited by the first Iron Age people, who furnished the traders of the east coast with these metals without using them themselves. During the eighth century the inhabitants of Ingombe Ilede, on the upper Zambezi, buried their dead with gold, copper and iron objects as well as shells from the Indian Ocean. These exchanges were not confined to the African continent. The Arab chroniclers of the twelfth century mention exports of iron ore from Africa to India. This trade produced lasting cultural exchanges; long before any European contacts, Africa borrowed some valuable ideas from Asian cultures, notably outrigger canoes, xylophones and banana trees. The arrival of the Portuguese put an end to these exchanges.

The techniques of metalworkers and blacksmiths have hardly changed throughout the centuries. Almost everywhere there is abundant ore on the surface. The iron is extracted by the Catalan method, that is, smelting at a low temperature. The furnaces, which are holes in the ground, or small towers up to ten feet high, are filled with a mixture of ore and charcoal. The heat of the fire, which is maintained by a ring of bellows placed all around the furnace which operates continuously for about two days, separates the bloom from the waste. This is then broken up and cut into pieces ready for forging.

The simplicity of the tools traditionally

Throwing knife used as currency. Yakoma. Republic of Central Africa. Forged iron. Musée de l'Homme, Paris. *Museum photo.*

used at the forge makes the beauty of the objects all the more astonishing. The blacksmith used a shaped stone or a heavy lump of iron as a sledgehammer. (In some regions this did not even have a handle, and one wonders how the workers protected their fingers from burns when they were only six inches away from the red-hot iron.) When this work was done, the iron mass was planted in the ground and served as a diminutive and unstable anvil for finer work with a lighter hammer. Among the Mungo in present-day Zaire, these iron hammers without handles had several striking surfaces of different sizes and could be used for several purposes. The surfaces were carefully maintained by the blacksmith, who chipped them periodically with the aid of a small adz in order to make them rough and less slippery. His tongs, which are indispensable for handling hot iron, might be just a simple cleft stick, but it was more often a bent iron bar or two pieces articulated to form a clamp. Sometimes, too, the object was manipulated quite simply by a temporary handle while it was being worked. The effect of tempering was known, at least empirically: blacksmiths kept water at hand, either in a wooden tub or in an earthenware pot into which they threw hot objects in order to harden them. These products were given a fine finish by cold chiseling, polishing, wiredrawing or other means, depending on the region in which they were worked. (See also *Bells; Blacksmiths; Kirdi; Kongo; Pottery; Sanga; Sao.*)   E.M.

ISLAM. There are more than 30 million Muslims in black Africa. About two-thirds of them live in what the Arab writers called *Bilad as-Sudan* ("land of the blacks")—that is to say, the immense stretch of steppe and savanna that extends from the Atlantic to the Nile Valley, bounded on the north by desert

Female figure. Bambara. Mali. End of a forged iron rod. Paul Tishman Collection, New York. *Photo: Musée de l'Homme.*

Mosque at Bobo-Dioulasso, Upper Volta. *Photo: Viollet, Roger.*

and on the south by dense forests. The rest are scattered over the archipelagoes and the coastal strip of the Indian Ocean (their name, Swahili, comes from the Arabic *sahil,* "coast") and in towns of West Africa. Broadly speaking, black African Islam covers almost all the Sudan but exists only in pockets or marginal fringes in Guinean and Bantu Africa. It penetrated the western Sudan via the Maghrib and the Saharan routes beginning at the end of the eighth century A.D. and spread by sea along the east coast from the ninth century onward. In the Nile Valley, its advance was halted by the Christian kingdoms of Nubia. The last of these, Aloa, fell in 1504, leaving Ethiopia as an island of Christianity south of the Sahara.

Sudanese Islam, the most important and the most typical of the Islamic forces in black Africa, acted, according to J. Richard-Molard, like a cyclical ferment in the political and cultural history of this part of Africa. Until the dawn of European colonization, it alternately expanded and contracted according to the growth and decay of the great imperial powers. In the second half of the eleventh century, the Almoravid Berber Muslims under Abu Bakr ibn-Umar destroyed the pagan empire of Ghana and converted the Tukulor and the Soninke. Toward 1230, the Soninke, under Sumanguru Kante, succeeded in reviving most of the destroyed empire, only to see it

collapse shortly thereafter under the hands of Sundiata Keita, founder of the Malinke dominion known as the Empire of Mali. This new empire reached the height of its power in the reign of Mansa Musa (1307-1332), who dazzled the Arab world by the ostentation of his pilgrimage to Mecca (1324-1326). Its decline, which began at the end of the fourteenth century under the assaults of the Mossi, Tuareg and Tekrur, ended with the victory of the Songhai in 1546. The Songhai empire, which began in the eighth century, had been Islamic since the eleventh century. It replaced the supremacy of Mali in the reign of the Khawarijite Si Ali Ber (1464-1492). Its zenith was reached under the Askia dynasty from 1495 to 1591, the date of the Battle of Tondibi in which the Moroccans crushed the Songhai army. The disorders that followed the Moroccan invasion made possible the pagan revival that accompanied Bambara supremacy. In the eighteenth century, it was the Tukulor and the Fulani who again took up the sword of Islam, first in Fouta Toro, with Abdelkader Toro, then in the Hausa confederation with Osman dan Fodio (1754-1812) and finally in upper Senegal with el-Hadj Umar (1797-1864). After this, the European presence was a factor to be taken into account; it gave the exploits of Samory Touré (1870-1898), although Touré had also declared a holy war, a completely different aspect, resembling in some ways the Mahdism (a fanatic Islamic movement) of the Nile and Somaliland.

The widespread propagation of Islam by these empires was superficial rather than profound. Conversion was a pretext for expansion and above all an instrument for creating or maintaining a certain amount of what could be described as political cohesion in order to transcend the racial divisions in the empires and the religious differences to which they gave rise. The central leadership and its representatives in the provinces—conquered chiefs, governors or underlings—were, or became, Muslim. The rural inhabitants continued to practice their traditional tribal religions while sometimes adopting an Islamic veneer. When the empires collapsed, isolated relics of Islam survived: Islam appeared as an attribute of a political chief of foreign origin as opposed to a landed chieftain or indigenous priest, or as an intertribal passport for traders on long journeys, or as a mark of a professional group forming a caste of its own. Even where the population as a whole did not renounce its religion, as for example among the Tukulor and Soninke, the cultural phenomenon of assimilation, of Negroization, which gave black African Islam a character very different from the Islam of the Mediterranean area, was to be observed. The black marabout—*alfa, mallam,* or *modibo*—scarcely differed from the magician or animist. The Islamic brotherhoods assumed the characteristics of societies of initiates. Outside the great market towns of the Sahel, where orthodoxy was maintained after a fashion because of its contact with North Africa, this Negroization led to a fragmentation by tribes and to syncretism, combining, for example, a cult of spirits (the *bori* of the Hausa and the *holley* of the Songhai) or the worship of ancestors (among the Kotokoli and Dagomba) with the surviving remnants of Muslim practices.

It may seem paradoxical that Islam made far more progress in the 50 or 100 years of colonial domination than during the 1,000 years that preceded the European penetration of black Africa. It is partly explained by the benevolence of the colonial authorities. Despite the fact that those who resisted the conquerors sometimes made use of Islam as a sort of ideology prior to nationalism (for example, Samory Touré and Mahdi Mohammed Ahmed in the Anglo-Egyptian Sudan), colonial administrators, as a matter of fact, often encouraged it because it was a more familiar religion and therefore easier to come to terms with than the tribal cults; its members were often already acquainted with writing, an indispensable feature of modern administration; and, lastly, it was mainly practiced by groups who were familiar with the structure of the state or rudimentary forms of it and who appeared more civilized than some of their animist neighbors. However, the most important factor affecting the progress of Islam during the colonial period was sociological. Colonization, by bringing about the disintegration and detribalization of the tribal societies, liberated the individual from former social restraints and simultaneously enabled Islam, which had become tribalized and Negroized, to recover its universal nature. And all this took place at a time when the Africans were seeking, consciously or not, to create new structures on a level of organization that would be able to meet the demands of the modern world and to attain a degree of social development superior to that of the societies that had disintegrated. Since Islam is a comprehensive system, like the tribal religions, and was already familiar and Africanized and not suffering from the social and cultural handicaps of Christianity, it benefited from these aspirations of the Africans, for it satisfied them quite well.

The most traditional and most Afri-

canized of current trends in Islam remains very much alive, although under constant attack: in the black African versions of some of the great Islamic sects, the local branches have sometimes turned to a form of anthropolatry in which the chief of a brotherhood is the focal point of worship. This is the practice of the Senegalese Murids, who are dissidents from the Qadiriya order and who have adopted a sort of agrarian socialism to the great benefit of their sheikh, the descendant of their founder Ahmadu Bamba. The same thing occurs among the dynasties of miracle-working marabouts, who sometimes claim, in rather arbitrary fashion, to belong to several brotherhoods at once and who nevertheless exercise considerable influence on local affairs in various parts of West Africa. A recent development has brought a reaction against the conformist political position of these marabouts, giving rise to brotherhoods that are animated by a spirit of social and political reform. The most famous is the Sudanese Hamallist brotherhood, a deviation from the Tidjaniya order of Mali, Niger and Senegal, whose members played an important part in the political struggles leading to independence. Today these reformed brotherhoods promulgate an African form of Islam that keeps its distance from the Arab world and emphasizes a native, black-African element in its manifestations and practices. Mahdism, famous for the part it played in Sudanese resistance to Anglo-Egyptian domination (1880-1899), has similar motives, but different aims. Instead of working for political and social reforms, it is evolving into a messianic and prophetic

Mosque at Ibadan University, Nigeria. *Photo: Jacques Maquet.*

movement preoccupied with doctrines of a second coming, similar to those of certain schismatic and syncretic movements of Christian origin. The belief in a Mahdi as a "prophet of the Last Days who, at the end of time, must overwhelm the world with justice as it has been overwhelmed with injustice" lends itself readily to the emergence of revolutionary movements with a religious and irrational basis and which reject the modern world rather than claim a share in it. This is a reaction that often develops in areas lacking economic resources, where the activity of the European authorities or that of the national government has been mainly political in character (e.g., Somalia and the semidesert of the Sudan).

In opposition to this deep-rooted form of Islam based on brotherhoods, two recent tendencies have emerged: one is modernist, similar in approach to the Young Turks, and the other is puritan and reformist. The modernists are African Muslims educated in Europe, much involved in modern politics and often influenced by Marxism. Some favor a kind of separation of church and state, while some envisage the use of Islam to support a nationalist ideology that is more political than religious. The puritan reformists, who share the nationalism of the modernists, are Africans of Arab culture—former pupils of North African universities or of local Arab schools (*mederseh*)—strongly influenced by the Wahhabi. They preach a return to the purity of early Islam and reject not only the innovations of European origin, but also the syncretic tendencies of black African Islamic practices. Both the modernists and the puritan reformists are opposed to brotherhoods, yet they tend to form societies not unlike these sects, so strongly does this propensity to form quasi-societies of initiates persist (it even appears in the running of political parties and trade unions). One final example of a recent phenomenon in African Islam is the activity of missionaries of Indian origin, Ismailians in East Africa and the Ahmadiyyah in the west, especially in Nigeria. These Indian missionaries use the same procedures as the Christian missionaries in converting animists or marginal Christians.

The most important cultural contribution of Islam to Africa is certainly writing. The only precolonial written works came from Muslim societies, whether written in Arabic (the Songhai chronicles such as the *Tariqa as-Sudan* and the *Tariqa el-Fettash*) or in an Arabic transliteration of a local language (Swahili, Hausa, Fulani, Malinke). Some genuine black African systems of writing,

such as that of the Bamum, have also been influenced by Arab writing. In other fields of culture, however, Muslim influence is either not so great or, at any rate, debatable. Sudanese architecture, for instance, is basically of local origin and was not, as was once thought, invented or imported by the Arab architect es-Saheli. Similarly, Sudanese dress is only Arab in certain details, such as the turban and chechia (cylindrical hat with a tassel), while the non-Muslim Mossi dress in almost the same way as their Islamized neighbors. Muslim cultural penetration is much less marked in East Africa than it is in West Africa. The Ibadite and Shafi'ite forms of Islam were confined almost entirely to Zanzibar, the neighboring islands and the adjacent coast. The Arab and Swahili slave traders who ravaged the interior as far as the Congo Valley made virtually no converts, except in the Lake Nyassa region among the Yao and to a limited degree in Uganda, where their proselytizing activities clashed with those of the Christian missions at the end of the nineteenth century. In the Nile Valley as well, the populations exploited by Sudanese slave traders resisted Islamization, except perhaps at the time of the Mahdist uprising, in so far as it was a revolt against the same slave traders.

Today Islam is making rapid progress even in the forest zones, which had once proved impenetrable to the Muslim cavalry. Although figures are unobtainable, observers agree that it is making more rapid and more significant progress than Christianity, some of whose followers it is luring away. The substantialness of this success suggests the emergence of a new black-African Muslim bloc which should eventually play an important part in the *'umma*, the world community of Islam, because of its size—the majority of the members of some international brotherhoods, such as the Tidjaniya, now live south of the Sahara—and because of the unique form of the religion that has resulted from Islam's adaptation to black Africa, that is, from Islam's Negroization. (See also *Almoravids; Arabs in East Africa; Bornu; Epics; Ethiopia; Fulani; Gods; Hausa; Initiation; Law; Mali; Prayer; Royalty; Song; Songhai; Sudan; Towns and Cities; Women; Writing.*)

P.A.

IVORY. From the earliest times until the beginning of the slave trade, ivory rivaled gold as the principal African export, transported by way of the Nile Valley and the Saharan routes. It resumed its importance in the nineteenth century, particularly in East

Above: Ivory warehouse. Tanzania. *Photo: Rapho, R. Michaud.*
Left: Pendant in the form of a mask. Benin. Nigeria. Ivory. Museum of Primitive Art, New York. *Museum photo, Charles Uht.*

Africa where the Arab slave traders were also elephant hunters. In southern Africa, the great white hunters such as Frederick C. Selous and Karamojo Bell were often the forerunners of the first colonists. By 1914 elephant hunting had reached such proportions that prices collapsed and the elephant disappeared from some areas, notably the savanna.

Whether worked or in its natural state, ivory was highly valued in all African societies. The tips were used as money, sometimes making up part of the "dowry," or hoarded as treasure. The so-called "elephant cemeteries" appear really to have been only the treasures of a few chiefs; these treasures were looted by adventurers who then invented a tale about elephant cemeteries in order to have a respectable explanation for their gains. In fact, the chiefs usually kept for themselves either all the ivory from the elephants killed on their land or else only one tusk from each of them, often the one which struck the ground when the elephant fell. Royal hunting horns made of ivory are found almost everywhere, often chiseled, sometimes fitted with a metal mouthpiece or decorated with beads and gold thread. Some of these horns, for example those of the Mossi and the emirates of Nigeria, were so heavy that it took two men to handle each of them, one to carry it and the other to blow it. They were used mainly in war or for great ceremonial occasions. In the region of the Great Lakes the feet of some royal thrones were made of tusks. Traditional sculpture in

ivory was common in certain selected areas along the coasts of Guinea and Benin, particularly among the Akan and Yoruba, and in Zaire, among the Baluba and the Basonge, for example. Some objects were carved in one piece, following the curvature of the tusk, while others, more substantial, were made of a number of separate pieces carved and fitted together. Ivory from the hippopotamus, which is much finer and harder than that from the elephant, was used only for small pieces. Many beautiful specimens of carved ivory are found in the Niger Valley, especially in Nigeria (among the Nupe and the Jukun, for example). Colonization had the effect of commercializing ivory sculpture for the benefit of the tourist trade: "caravans" of elephants holding each other by the tail or crocodiles grasping electric light bulbs in their jaws are to be found in the homes of retired ex-colonials from Glasgow to Ajaccio, who could buy them on every hotel terrace between Dakar and Mogadishu. (See also *Arabs in East Africa; Combs; Elephants; Harps; Headrests; Horns; Markets; Spoons.*) P.A.

JEWELRY. In the tropics there is no clear distinction between permanent bodily adornment, such as tattooing, scarification, filing of the teeth or elongation of the skull and putting on finery for feast days, nor between fine clothes and everyday attire. The Hausa of the Lake Chad area of Nigeria wear a lot of clothes because they want to have the

Yoruba horseman. Nigeria. Ivory. British Museum. *Photo: Service de documentation photographique des Musées nationaux.*

Fulani woman. Niger. *Photo: Hoa-Qui.*

Masai woman. Tanzania. *Photo: Musée de l'Homme.*

Breastplate from the mound at M'Banar Udyol kas, Senegal. Gold. Musée de l'Institut français d'Afrique noire. *Photo: Giraudon.*

the sun: panther-skin bonnets belong to princes, and the turban of the great Ashanti chief is embellished with gold ornaments.

Jewelry is usually worn on the neck, wrists, ankles and the vulnerable parts of the body, that is to say, the orifices; earrings or spikes are inserted into the earlobes and labrets into the lips. The beaded belt and the penis sheath both serve the same dual purpose—to attract attention and to avert all evil design. The little bell that is attached to a baby's ankle makes his whereabouts known, but primarily it serves to reinforce the power of the amulet around his neck and to keep at bay the unknown enemy who might attempt to kill the fragile child out of enmity toward his parents.

Besides being magic guardians, jewelry constitutes family treasure or is a mark of a newly won honor, or sometimes both. A Baule woman on her wedding day displays all the gold jewelry of her lineage. Thus adorned, she sets off, followed by her friends, on a round of visits. But on the day after this brief hour of triumph, she has to return all the treasures to the patriarch who looks after them. Every sister and cousin in the clan will in her turn display its splendor without ever keeping a piece for herself. Maternity means more than marriage to African women. At the birth of her first child, a Wolof woman is given a piece of jewelry, and on this occasion she is permitted to keep it. It is a silver bracelet which proclaims her new status to all the world and which she will use, by deftly moving her wrists, to keep her baby clean.

Priests, magicians, hunters and warriors all wear signs of their callings. Jewels speak a

varied, rich embroidery of their voluminous robes admired. In a hot country, dress is primarily a sign of power and secondarily of opulence. If clothes are to protect, it is a magical protection like that of jewelry. Nor does this protection always operate as one might expect. Sandals are not needed to protect tough skin from rough ground, but the sovereign could not go barefoot; he is the son of the Sun, and his tread would dry up the earth and scorch the harvest. A hat is a sign of authority rather than a shield from language that some do not understand, but all accept. On feast days an Attie girl in the southeastern Ivory Coast wears a necklace of leopard teeth when she dances and sings, and everyone knows that it is lent to her for this one occasion by her suitor; it is a sign of his importance, because leopard teeth are the mark of the outstanding member of an age group.

Jewelry can also be a sign of merit. The heavy high collars of cornelian beads that adorn the bronze heads from Benin were an honor conferred by the king for services rendered. This jewelry reverted to the king on the death of the man so honored, and the foolhardy man who wore such an insignia without authority was condemning himself to a disgraceful death. At the other extreme, there are modest little ornaments that anyone can wear and that deceive no one. Girls in Timbuktu who do not have finely worked pendants made of gold are satisfied with fake jewelry made of wax and decorated with straw, which at least suggests the color of the precious metal. (See also *Adornment; Baule; Beads; Bushmen; Combs; Fashion; Gold; Magic; Massa; Sanga; Weapons; Yoruba.*) D.P.

KALAHARI. Although South Africans choose to call the Kalahari the little Sahara, it is more of a semidesert steppe than a true desert. Most of the landscape consists of low dunes covered with tough, poor grass and thorny bushes (acacia, pseudo-cacti, euphorbiacae). The Kalahari covers about 350,000 square miles, its borders being roughly Lake Ngami and the Okovango River Valley (20° S.), the Nama and Damara Hills (19° E.), the Orange River (28° S.) and the Limpopo Basin (24° E.). It is a flat plateau with an average height of 3,000 feet and forms an enclosed basin that corresponds to a zone of high atmospheric pressure and is protected from the rain-bearing southeast winds by the Transvaal Massif. The average annual rainfall varies from five to ten inches (the north is the most humid region) in the form of a few heavy showers between October and March. The average temperature varies from 68° to 81° F., with a maximum of 88° F. and a minimum of 59° F. The main geological formations are alluviums, which are composed of sand, limestone and clay of the Tertiary and Quaternary periods, and hillocks, which have survived from earlier ages. There are no permanent watercourses, only shallow depressions in which temporary pools form and generally dry up at the beginning of winter (June). Animals and men must then slake their thirst from the

desert melon, a form of gourd which is the characteristic plant of the Kalahari. The fauna—consisting of ungulates, especially antelopes; carnivores, such as Cape hunting dogs; aardvarks; and ostriches—is much reduced today as a result of the excesses of white, black and Hottentot hunters and to

Fon bracelet. Dahomey. Bronze. Musée de l'Homme, Paris. *Museum photo.*

Fon bracelet. Dahomey. Silver. Musée de l'Homme, Paris. *Museum photo.*

Senufo ring. Dahomey. Copper. Musée de l'Homme, Paris. *Museum photo.*

the detriment of the Bushmen. The Bushmen have been driven back further and further into the most arid parts of the Kalahari by Hottentot cattlemen from the south and by Bantu (Herero and Tswana) from the north. If the potentialities for large-scale ranching in the steppe were developed, it would mean the complete disappearance of the Bushmen. This development has been delayed mainly because the Kalahari falls within the domain of several different administrations: South-West Africa (formerly German), the Republic of South Africa (the Cape province and Transvaal) and Botswana. (See also *Bushmen; European Discovery; Hottentots.*) P.A.

KANEM. Kanem was an ancient kingdom on the edge of the Sahara, extending from the Tibesti Mountains to the eastern shore of Lake Chad and covering much of the present-day Republic of Chad. Its history is closely associated with that of the kingdom of Bornu and the sultanate of Wadai. It was probably founded between the seventh and tenth centuries by the Zaghawa and was invaded in the eleventh century by the Teda of Tibesti, who converted it to Islam. In the thirteenth century the throne passed to a black dynasty, the Kanembu, which extended the frontiers of the kingdom as far as the borders of Tunisia and Egypt. In the fourteenth century the Bulala, a tribe from the southeast of present-day Chad, rebelled and drove out the reigning dynasty, whose members took refuge in the kingdom of Bornu. In the sixteenth century Kanem became a province of Bornu, causing a dispute between the kingdom of Bornu and Wadai that lasted until Kanem was allotted to France during the distribution of territories among the colonial powers. The population of present-day Chad comprises nomads of Arab and Teda stock, a sedentary black population, Muslim Kanembu cultivators, animist Dogara hunters and Kuri and Buduma fishermen, who lived around Lake Chad. The ancient political organization of the area disappeared in the nineteenth century, but the Bornu of Nigeria still lay claim to their old sovereignty over Kanem. (See also *Bornu; Sao.*) P.A.

KIKUYU. For several centuries, perhaps for 800 years, the Kikuyu (or Kuyu) have been known as an exceptional people. They occupy a mountainous region in Kenya that reaches as far as Nairobi and resembles an ocean of low hills. In this area they have created a distinctive, man-made landscape. It is heavily populated, for they number more than 1 million and have a population density of more than 200 to the square mile. They are tied to their land, because they believe the earth is the "mother of the tribe" and the means of communication with their ancestors.

Traditional Kikuyu society is a complex edifice which still maintains its vigorous culture. In his book *Facing Mount Kenya* (1938), Jomo Kenyatta described its principal components—clans, kinship groups and age groups that incorporate men, women and children. He made it clear that the unattached individual hardly exists, since he is associated with sorcerers, and that each Kikuyu is "above all the relative and fellow citizen of a great many people." There are nine principal clans; each of these is related to one of the nine daughters who constituted the progeny of the first couple. Kikuyu mythology describes these early times, as well as a period long ago when women imposed their government and laws on men. According to legend, the men succeeded in revolting against the women only by resorting to trickery; they then instituted masculine authority and polygamy, and the warrior became one of the principal figures for others to emulate. The warrior often appears in oral literature, sometimes in the shape of a young hero who overcomes the mighty ravagers of villages and herds, as, for example, the "Giant of the Great Water."

Initiation, associated with circumcision, turns adolescent Kikuyu into complete men (*mondo-morome*) and then into the young warriors. This is the point at which fathers turn over their weapons to their sons—a spear, a shield and a sword. The *mondo-morome,* whose education includes the military training, discipline and ceremonies appropriate for a warrior class, have a formidable spirit and swear that "If the skies threaten to crush us, we will keep them off with our spears." They have to prove their personal qualities on the battlefield. Later on, they can only join the council of "elder warriors" through their own merit, which alone will win them the approval of their companions. This military society gives a privileged place to the metalworker's art. The Kikuyu blacksmiths enjoy a high social standing and are respected because they make arms and tools, but they are also feared because they possess formidable power to invoke curses; they can "break a man" as they break a piece of red-hot iron. The Kikuyu have excellent potters, and some clans are specialists in the art of pottery-making. They also have craftsmen who are skilled in working and cutting skins and who still know how to make their traditional national dress.

British colonization dispossessed the farmers of part of their lands, while the warriors were reduced to inactivity by peaceful conditions. The Kikuyu reaction was vigorous and hostile. In the 1950s their resistance led to the formation of the revolutionary society known as the Mau Mau. The society stimulated political revolt in villages and moral revolt in the individual conscience. It bound its members by compelling oaths, mobilized the resources of magic, exploited certain aspects of traditional religion and combined rural revolt with incipient nationalism. It was far more than a simple flare-up of insurrection or a nihilistic movement born of despair. Despite its initial setback, the movement achieved its aim by gaining independence for Kenya. After years in prison, a distinguished revolutionary Kikuyu was released and brought to power; this was Jomo Kenyatta, "the fiery javelin of Kenya," who pledged himself "to rebuild the fallen sanctuaries." (See also *Adornment; Blacksmiths; Cattle; Education; Royalty.*)   G.B.

KINSHIP. If consanguinity were viewed in its true biological sense, every person would have an enormous number of kin (going back into the past, the number of one's ascendants would double in each generation, and all those descended from the many pairs of ancestors would be one's collateral relatives). In order for kinship to be a workable system of social organization, peoples throughout the world give precedence to only one line of ascendance: either the female line (which is traced through a person's mother and her female forebears) or through the male line (which is traced back through one's father and his male forebears). Kinship systems that give precedence to the female line are known as matrilineal systems, while those favoring the male line are patrilineal systems. In both types of kinship systems, only one individual in each generation is considered to be a person's ancestor in that generation, and all other forebears are excluded. In Africa, the choice of male or female line is often rationalized by theories of conception. The Yao, for instance, who are matrilineal, believe that the sperm merely awakens the embryo, which lies in the woman's womb before intercourse. The patrilineal Rwanda, on the other hand, believe that the sperm forms the child and repeated supplies of sperm are indispensable during pregnancy to develop the fetus.

The network of relationships between descendants of the same ancestor is a universal phenomenon and is familiar in our own society, but the overwhelming im-

Wakerewe ancestor statue. Tanzania. Wood. Museum für Völkerkunde, Berlin. *Museum photo, Karl H. Paulmann.*

portance of bonds of kinship in the life of individuals is peculiar to traditional Africa. The principle of kinship—in other words, the fact that he is the son of a particular man (or woman, in a matrilineal system) and, through this first link, the descendant of a particular ancestor—is sometimes the only reference that can situate an individual. In societies where production is very near subsistence level and the population is consequently sparse, the landmarks that usually define the individual's place in the society as a whole—profession, social class, standard of education, income group, religion—do not exist. The bonds of kinship alone can distinguish him from others, and his line of descent determines his relationship with them.

Socially identified in the first place as the

descendant of an ancestor, the individual identifies others within the same framework. It is by knowing their respective places in a network of consanguinity that two people between whom a social relationship is beginning know how to behave toward each other. The pattern of their behavior is already decided; there is no need to invent it. The Bahamba, for instance, allow and expect a boy or man to take considerable liberties with his mother's brother, which can go as far as taking some of his uncle's goods. The uncle's reactions are prescribed just as clearly; he cannot object to being deprived of his possessions, so he can only resort to hurling abuse and mockery at his nephew. In every African society, boys and girls are gradually taught during their childhood the rights and obligations attached to each relationship that they will have to assume: the younger brother toward the elder, the daughter toward her father, the grandson toward his grandparents, etc.

Naturally, the African comes into contact with other people besides his relatives in his day-to-day life. However, the assimilation of various kinds of relationships with each other greatly enlarges the kinship network. A horizontal extension allows an African to behave in the same way toward relations who are all fairly close, belong to the same generation and who are about the same age, and to address them in the same terms: thus, one's father and one's father's brothers and parallel (male) cousins are classed in the same category and referred to by the same term; and, similarly, one's mother, her sisters and her parallel (female) cousins. A vertical extension draws him back toward ancestors who are more or less distant or even mythical, which increases the number of living persons whom he can consider as collaterals. In the broadest type of vertical extensions, all the members of a single society are reputed to be descendants of the same ancestor. Thus, the African lives in a world in which kinship is much more extensive than in ours.

Consanguinity is the basis for some kinds of "fellowship" groups. Membership in such a group means that the individual does not have to face hostility, difficulties and misfortunes alone; he belongs to a community of "brothers" who help and protect each other.

While the principle of blood relationship (descent through one line or another and collaterality) has an immense importance in Africa and defines a vast field of relationships, kinship through marriage doubles it. Let us first consider how the principle works on the side of Ego's wife (we shall adopt the practice of anthropologists and apply the term Ego to the individual whom we are taking as the central point of the bonds of kinship). The consanguineal relations of Ego's wife are the affinal relations (relations by marriage) of Ego, and here again the behavior patterns are carefully prescribed. In several African societies, for example, the sexual relations that Ego may enjoy with the sisters or cousins of his wife are not considered adulterous, even though they may be frowned upon, but he has to be very circumspect in his treatment of another relation by marriage, his wife's mother. In so far as Ego's consanguineal relations are concerned, affinity extends his kinship with these to the wives of his consanguineal relations; for instance, Ego's uncle by marriage (the husband of his father's sister) is not a stranger to him, and in Rwanda this affinal uncle is treated with the same respect that is due his consanguineal uncle. (See also *Clans; Genealogy; Incest; Industry; Lineage; Markets; Marriage; Royalty; Tribes; Uncles; Widows.*)   J.M.

KIRDI. The term "Kirdi" is used throughout northern Cameroun by Muslims, particularly by the Fulani, to describe non-Muslim peoples among whom they live. This word may be of Bagirmi origin; the corresponding Fulani word is "Kado" (plural "Habe"). The term "Kirdi" has been adopted by the administrative services, which use it to refer to all the non-Muslims of northern Cameroun and the southwestern frontier areas of Chad; that is to say, it describes nearly 1 million individuals from a variety of tribes, often with nothing in common except the fact that at different periods they suffered the incursions of the Fulani, Mandara, Bornu and Bagirmi. The area occupied by the Kirdi is roughly bounded on the north by the twelfth parallel, on the west by the Mandara Mountains, on the east by the Chari River and on the south by the Benue River and the foothills of the Adamawa Mountains. In political terms, the Kirdi straddle the borders of Nigeria, Cameroun and Chad. They occupy the Sudanese climatic zone, where differences in altitude result in wide variations in climate. Three regions can be distinguished: the mountains (the Mandara); the plains that are broken up by inselbergs, which are characteristic of northern Cameroun; and the flat plains, in some places liable to flooding by the Mayo-Kebbi, Logone and Chari Rivers. The groups in the mountainous region include, from south to north, the Fali (42,000), the Gidder (44,000), the Njei (25,000), the Gude (38,000), the Daba (22,000), the Hina

Fali village. Kirdi. Cameroun.
Photo: Jean-Paul Lebeuf.

(10,000), the Djimi (2,500), the Kapsiki (30,000), the Mofu (42,000), the Matakam (100,000) and the Margi (60,000). The groups occupying the Mora Massif total 60,000 people, including the Podokwo (10,000), the Muktale (10,000), the Mada (10,000), the Molkwa (4,000) and several smaller groups. The groups situated between the mountains and the plains are the Gidder, the Mundang (95,000) and the Gisiga (55,000). The plains groups are, from north to south, the Musgu (40,000), the Massa (125,000), the Kun (10,000), the Gaberi (10,000) and the Marba (17,000) who occupy an area that is not subject to flooding. The Tuburi (100,000), the Kare (6,000), the Kado (15,000), the Peve (10,000), the Mussoi (80,000) and the Mesme (12,000) are spread throughout the treed savanna zone. Some writers add to these ethnic groups non-Islamized Adamawa peoples—the Namshi (15,000), the Demsa (5,000), the Duru (16,000) and the Mbum (28,000)—as well as two groups situated further north, the Kotoko (31,000) and the Mandara (17,000), whose Islamization is relatively recent.

Of the heterogeneous tribes that make up the Kirdi, only the Fali, the Massa, the Tuburi, the Mussoi, and the Mundang have been studied systematically. The nomenclature of the different ethnic groups designated by the term "Kirdi" is fluid, particularly since it refers to fragmented societies that only rarely are organized into groups consisting of more than members of a common lineage. For example, the people called "Kapsiki" in Cameroun are called "Higi" in Nigeria; under the term "Banana" there are grouped nearly 300,000 people who in reality belong to four distinct ethnic groups: the Musgu, the Massa, the Tuburi and the Mussoi. Moreover, these groups hardly ever refer to themselves by these names. Demographically, the Matakam, Gisiga, Tuburi, Mussoi and Massa are increasing (1.5 to 2.5 percent annually); among the Mofu, Daba and Mundang the growth is .5 to 2.5 percent annually; the populations of the Gidder, Hina, Gude, Musgu, Kapsiki and Fali are stationary or declining. Anthropological data about their physique is scanty, but it seems that most of the Kirdi belong to the Sudanese race. They tend mainly to be dolichocephalic and of average height or tall (five and a half feet among the Mofu, nearly six feet among the Musgu). They are distinguishable from the brachycephalic Sara living to the east of them and from the populations living in the forest clearings, who are generally shorter.

Labrets are worn by women of all the Kirdi groups. The Podokwo distend their earlobes by inserting disks. Tattooing and scarification are discreet and fairly rare. On the other hand, filing of the teeth is common among both sexes. Men and women wear clothing that is scanty and traditional. Among the tribes in the plains young girls go naked, married women wear loincloths of bark, cotton, leather or plant fibers. Mountain people (such as the Mofu, Kapsiki and Matakam) also wear loincloths deco-

Above: Mundang huts. Kirdi. Chad. *Photo: Pierre Ichac.*
Right: Young Mundang woman. Kirdi. Chad. *Photo: Pierre Ichac.*

rated with pieces of metal. Men wear a piece of kidskin attached to their buttocks. Penis shields are traditionally worn by the Mundang, Gisiga, Namshi, and Gidder. Excision is not practiced by any of the Kirdi, and only the Namshi, Demsa and Mundang practice circumcision, perhaps under Fulani influence.

Linguists have taken little interest in this part of Africa, and classification of its languages is still vague. The majority of the languages spoken in this area probably belong to the Chad-Hamitic group, within which several ill-defined subgroups are distinguishable (such as the Logone-Mandara and the Kabi-Benue families). There appear to be certain parallels among the languages of the Demsa, Njei, Fali, Kapsiki, Podokwo and Matakam. The vocabularies of the Musgu, Massa, Mussoi, Marba and Mesme are very similar. The Mundang, Tuburi, Duru, Fali, Mbum and Peve languages also show some resemblances.

The mountain people use primitive blast furnaces to smelt iron ore, and their blacksmiths form an endogamous caste. Copper-casting by the lost-wax method is common among all the Kirdi. The people in the mountainous and the hilly regions use bows and arrows. The plainsmen have only throwing knives and clubs. Among the latter, basketry and ropework have reached a high level of technical excellence.

The mountain people terrace slopes for agriculture and raise a few cattle, including dwarf oxen among the Namshi and Kapsiki. Every four years, on a feast day (the Marey), the Matakam and the people who live on the Mora Massif make a sacrifice of cattle that have been fattened without ever leaving their stalls. The people in the intermediate zone between the plains and the mountains (such as the Mundang, Gidder and Gisiga) cultivate sorghum that requires transplanting, cotton and peanuts and raise livestock. The Mundang fish a little. Fulani influence is noticeable in these intermediate zone groups. All the people of the plains (Musgu, Massa, Tuburi, Mussoi and Marba) are farmers, fishermen and animal husbanders. The relative importance of these activities varies according to the group. The zebu has an important economic and social significance for the first three groups, among whom it is the most important part of the bride-price. Among the Mussoi and Marba a small horse (the *laka*), which used to be common in northern Cameroun, takes the place of the zebu.

In all these societies descent is patrilineal,

and the married couple live with the husband's family. Marriage is limited only by the prohibition against a man taking a wife of the same lineage as his mother or father. The established political structure, with divisions into canton, village and district, is modern. Traditionally, politicoreligious authority was held by the descendants of the first ancestor to settle there, and even today the descendants of this ancestor designate a chief of the land or the mountain, who retains the land rights and is responsible for agrarian ceremonies. Diviners play an essential role in politicoreligious life, for they prescribe the form of sacrifices necessary to restore order after a temporary disturbance. Initiation may exist among the Mundang, Gidder and Fali, whose initiators may wear a kind of fiber cowl. Among the many peoples in the plains, initiation is less than eighty years old; it is most common among the Musgu, Massa and Tuburi.

Despite profound cultural differences, the Kirdi share a common psychological attitude toward their neighbors who have adopted Islam. Until recently, they implicitly admitted its superiority by trying to adopt practices that were a mixture of Fulani, Hausa, Arab, Bornu and Bagirmi cultures in preference to black-urban examples. This process of adopting Islamic culture has gone very far among the Kotoko, Mandara and Musgu, who are hardly distinguishable today from the Muslim tribes who surround them. (See also *Clothing; Migrations; Palaeonegrids; Posture; Sao.*)   I.G.

KISSI. The Kissi, who may number about 220,000, straddle the nations of Guinea, Sierra Leone and Liberia. Their neighbors to the north are the Malinke, a savanna people, and to the east and south are the forest peoples. The Kissi are border-dwellers, and this factor, which is discernible in the landscape itself, is reflected in their material, social and religious life. Their villages are hidden in woods which also conceal both their places of worship—specific springs, sacred rocks or trees—and the clearing where adolescents undergo a period of retreat before initiation. Their rice fields are spread over denuded hillsides or lie in the depths of valleys that are both humid and sunny. No transplanting and no irrigation is carried out; the rice fields are on low-lying ground and are simply submerged in the rainy season. Today, kola trees and coffee plantations provide trade with the outside world, and this should increase when communications improve.

The Kissi have no masks or large statues, but their stone sculptures, generally small in size, are appreciated by art connoisseurs. Ten years ago it was still possible to find these stone sculptures, known as "*pomdo*," on nearly all family altars. Most often they portrayed human figures, but sometimes they were cylinders or shaped like small pestles with square bases, axes of polished stone or simply pebbles worn smooth by river water. The statuettes, which are always carved in soapstone that can be scratched with a fingernail, are of uncertain date—the most that can be said is that some details of their costume are reminiscent of Portuguese armor of the sixteenth century. The diversity of styles displayed in a moderate sized collection indicates a wide range of dates. The modern pieces, of very inferior craftsmanship, are regarded as bogus even by the Kissi themselves. *Pomdo* are popular far beyond Kissi country—they are found throughout Sierra Leone, especially in Mande country, and also as far away as Sherbro Island. As the name indicates (*pom* = death), a *pomdo* is an image of a dead person. Not all *pomdo* are of equal value: the stones seen on family altars are regarded merely as heirlooms, and the owners sometimes agree to give them away; but to give up a "real" *pomdo* is still unthinkable; each one is named after the ancestor whom it portrays. Swathed in bands of cotton that are black with the blood of sacrifices, the statuette is preserved by its guardian, usually the son or grandson of the ancestor who has "returned" from the land of the dead. The Kissi say that sometime after the death of an important man (or woman), the *pomdo* "emerges." It is unearthed either by a farmer digging in the rice fields or in the village or the immediate vicinity. The identity of the statue is revealed, often even before its discovery, in a dream had by one of his descendants in which the ancestor appears and orders him to go and dig up the stone at a particular spot. The name of the ancestor may also be disclosed during a feast, when the other statues in the neighborhood are questioned according to the usual procedure for the interrogation of the deceased: the stone is firmly attached to a stretcher, which is carried on the head of one or two bearers, and inclines to the right or left in response to the questions. When it leans to the right the answer is affirmative, denoting truth and health; when it leans to the left the answer is negative, implying illness and death. The ancestor does not always reside in the statue; his presence there becomes manifest only after he has been invoked by means of vigorous oscillation of the stretcher. An ancestor is approached in order to ask him

Kissi statuette. Guinea. Stone. Pierre Guerre Collection, Marseille. *Photo: Jacques Verroust.*

for advice and also to demand punishment of a guilty party who has escaped punishment. Oaths are sworn on some statues; perjury is punished by lightning or madness, and, in order to be cured, the perjurer must confess his crime and be purified by the guardian, who will cleanse him with water in which leaves of a plant that grows near the altar of the ancestors have been soaked. There are statues of every important Kissi person. The most famous perhaps is Kissi Kaba, who welcomed the French when they came, then rebelled and was executed in 1898. His memory is perpetuated by a conical package of blackened cotton, shining with dried blood, topped by porcupine quills surmounted by a ring of cotton; the porcupine quills make the *pomdo* slightly resemble a bird of prey. (See also *Body Painting; Rattles; Rice; Sculpture, Stone; Sistra.*)

D.P.

KITARA. Africans who inhabit the regions of the Great Lakes pronounce the word "Kitara" with great reverence and pride. It evokes an empire which rose mysteriously out of a distant past and vanished just as mysteriously. It lay between Lake Albert and Lake Victoria and was powerful, rich and civilized. It was governed by a dynasty of the Bachwezi clan, a light-skinned people. Its inhabitants had the skills that go with prosperity: they planted coffee, raised thoroughbred cattle, wove materials of bark, built large huts in wickerwork and, by techniques that have since been lost, dug wells through layers of rock and made terraced fortifications. The Bachwezi also developed a sophisticated social life, including court etiquette and a game of checkers known as *igisoro*. This brilliant period lasted for only a few reigns; then the natural world began to fail them. Rivers dried up, cows gave less milk, disquieting portents appeared. The diviners told the king that he would continue to rule, but in another land. The last Bachwezi sovereign, Wamara, still undefeated, decided to leave his land and plunged into the waters of Lake Victoria, where he entered into the land of spirits whom he continues to rule. And ever since, the living render to the Bachwezi the worship due the masters of the kingdom of the dead.

The kingdom of Kitara is not just a figment of the imagination. Archeologists have found the remains of its townships surrounded by defensive trenches. Historians, by comparing the oral traditions concerning dynasties of the states that succeeded Kitara, have been able to establish a tentative but well-founded chronology.

The Bachwezi were a clan of Ethiopid shepherds who dominated the northern part of the Great Lakes region between the thirteenth and fifteenth centuries A.D. After a period of resistance to the Nilotic Luo invaders, who crossed the Victoria Nile at about this time (the Swazi fortifications at the Bigo and Mubende Hill sites face north), they were forced to abandon the region. The newcomers were strong but not well governed, and Kitara, which had been replaced by the Banyoro ruled by the Bito clan, survived only as a glorious memory of a golden age. (See also *Migrations.*)   J.M.

KONGO. The kingdom of Kongo was one of the earliest to be discovered by Europeans (1482) and one of the most celebrated. In the following century its praises were being sung by the Portuguese poet Camoëns in his *Lusiads.* At the time of its discovery, the kingdom and its dependencies covered the lower basin of the Congo River and formed a political unit comprising about 116,000 square miles. Its inhabitants numbered between 2 million and 3 million. Mbanza Kongo, the capital, was a populous city built around the royal precinct. A state was established, urban civilization developed and arts and crafts flourished. The founding of Kongo took place between 1350 and the last decades of the fourteenth century. Its royal founder, Ntinu Wéné, remains alive in myths and legends, more in the guise of a civilized hero than of a historical king. There are two aspects to his character: the powerful, conquering warrior and the dispenser of justice and blacksmith who gave his people weapons for war and tools for agriculture. His civilizing role is reflected in his title of *Ngangula a Kongo,* Blacksmith of the Kongo.

The kingdom was opened to the Portuguese at the end of the fifteenth century. They established themselves there, and missionaries tried to convert it to Christianity. The first Christian king was baptized in 1491, and in the following century the name of the capital was changed to São Salvador. This union between authority and the new faith remained brittle, but it nevertheless brought a transformation of religion and art in its wake, and an opening for foreign culture and modern trends. King Affonso I (born Nzinga Bemba), who reigned in the kingdom of Kongo from 1506 to 1543, was the principal author of these changes and the most efficient organizer of the state. A priest described him as a man of great faith, wisdom and justice. It is quite true that the king helped to establish Christianity, built the first schools and extracted a sort of

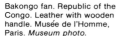

Mbanza Kongo, capital of Kongo. Illustration from *Description of Africa*, by O. Dapper (Amsterdam, 1686).

Bakongo fan. Republic of the Congo. Leather with wooden handle. Musée de l'Homme, Paris. *Museum photo.*

technical assistance program from his Portuguese protectors. Nevertheless, before the end of his reign, his relations with the Portuguese deteriorated for economic reasons (the slave trade was already provoking rivalries) and political reasons (relations with the king of Portugal took on a more colonial character). Unrest broke out again after Affonso's death. The frontiers were threatened, and clashes between the Kongolese and Portuguese grew more frequent. The Portuguese finally defeated the Kongolese in the Battle of Amboila in 1665, after which the kingdom slowly decayed, despite an attempt to restore it to its former glory at the beginning of the eighteenth century.

The vicissitudes of history were unable to destroy a civilization which had been brilliant for nearly three centuries. A number of techniques continued to develop, and craftsmen have always been highly respected people. Today the most important craft is ironwork. The blacksmith is the custodian of

a power that has ranked him with chiefs as well as with priests and magicians. He is the subject of many taboos. He can dispel insidious threats, just as the weapons made by his skill disperse the enemy. Besides iron, the Bakongo, as the present inhabitants are called, work copper and cast lead. Their special products are rings and anklets which are used simultaneously for adornment, as clan treasure and as marks of social status.

Historians were first attracted to Bakongo products and arts by the quality of their basketry and their highly skilled weaving. Mats are widely used in daily life for sleeping and are also employed in decorating the houses of the nobility, in order to "enhance their appearance." Weaving is done with vegetable fibers—particularly those of the raffia palm—on a vertical loom. The results vary, both in size and quality. The most beautiful, owned only by the wealthy, remind one of brocades, velvets, damasks, taffetas and sarcenets. According to one observer, "these materials are in no way inferior to silk." Some fine materials were used as currency in competition with the shell money that was put into circulation and controlled by the royal administrators.

Kongo art, which rose out of religious needs, was threatened by the iconoclastic fervor that destroyed "idols," "works of the devil" and masks. As early as the reign of Affonso I, Christianity tried to make progress by recourse to *autos-da-fé*. Nevertheless, pieces of proscribed artwork have survived the onslaughts of men and time, notably the statuettes of soft stone known as *mintadi* (guardians), which have been found mainly in burial places reserved

Left: Bakongo statue, probably of an ancestor. Republic of the Congo. Wood. Princess Gourielli Collection, Paris. *Photo: Jacques Verroust.* *Right:* Bakongo ancestor statue. Zaire. Wood. Musée royal de l'Afrique centrale, Tervuren. *Photo: Eliot Elisofon.*

for high-ranking nobles. The majority were substitutes for a living chief who was temporarily absent or doubles of a chief who had died. They were primarily symbolic portraits. The expression on the face was more important than the faithful portrayal of its features, and the meaning of the gestures mattered more than copying the exact proportions of the body. Symbolic attributes, such as stylized headdresses, necklaces and knives that were marks of rank, were not simple accessories; they were portrayed because of their significance and not for the sake of realism. This sculpture, which aimed at expressiveness through economy by dispensing with useless detail and overrefinement, possesses an undeniable power. Some statues of chiefs meditating have been described as "the first images of the Thinker produced by the black world." Statuettes in the same style and the same stone as the *mintadi,* but portraying moth-

erhood or a mother holding a child or giving him her breast, were invocations for fruitfulness and protection against sterility. Their sculptors were the precursors of modern woodcarvers who use similar themes, such as a mother and child or an old woman. Christianity inspired the destruction of idols carved in wood and masks, but it gave birth, at the beginning of the sixteenth century, to a new form of sacred art in which the Crucifixion, the Virgin and various saints became the favorite subjects of metal-workers. They were not imitators; they adapted and transformed Portuguese originals. Christ is Africanized in the modeling of his face and various details. The arms of the cross are often decorated with motifs that suggest mythical tales, linking Christian and traditional themes. In fact, Christian symbols were quickly diverted to serve other purposes. Crucifixes (called *nkangi*) and sacred statuettes were converted into beneficent charms or into instruments to assist fecundity and fertility. The crosses (*kuluzu*) are used in magic rites. In fact, Kongo tradition has always been able to revive in new guises and has displayed more vigor than the fallen kingdom. (See also *Armies; Bateke; Bayaka; Blacksmiths; Christianity; Congo River; Granaries; Sculpture, Stone; Slave Trade; Towns and Cities.*) G.B.

LAKES. See *Chad, Lake; Great Lakes.*

LANGUAGES, SECRET. In a number of tribes, there are, in addition to the common language understood by everyone, languages that can be understood only by members of particular groups. Such languages, known as "secret languages," may be either sacred or profane. Sacred languages are used mainly by societies of initiates or by officiating priests in the course of certain magical ceremonies. Profane languages are used by certain groups within the community— young men (in the presence of girls), parents (in front of their children) or members of a particular profession or even a particular lineage (among themselves). Secret languages can be divided linguistically into four main types: those which use archaic or dialectic forms of the common language; those which are distortions of the common language by the transposition of syllables and phonemes (Loucherbem type); those which employ the interpolation of redundant sounds or the systematic distortion of vowels ("Javanese" type); those which give words of the common language obscure meanings. The first type is common in religious rites and ceremonies; the second is mainly put to profane use; the third is used particularly in women's societies or among social subgroups who are asserting themselves against the community as a whole (the *rara* of the Yoruba lineages and the mottoes of the Sudanese clans are examples of such languages); and the fourth chiefly occurs when contact is made with strange milieus, particularly modern towns, where it results in private slang. Quite often, the so-called secret languages are, in reality, understood by most of the community, but they are only spoken by those who belong to particular subgroups: this is the case with many of the languages of initiates, the "secret" character of which is a sort of social fiction. A more peculiar type of secret language is that which involves glossolalia of certain kinds and is used by modern syncretic sects: formulas which are supposed to be in "Latin," or in "tongues," even in "Russian," are in fact meaningless. Similar to this is the "genii language" employed in cults of possession (such as the Hausa and Songhai *bori*) and for some rites of divination. (See also *Drum Language; Elephants; Mottoes; Myths; Names; Prayer; Riddles; Societies, Secret; Writing.*) P.A.

LAW. It is easy to understand why legal systems vary so greatly from one part of black Africa to another: differences in legal systems parallel the differences in kinship systems, political structure, economic systems, ways of life and external influences —such as the Malikite (in the Sudan) and the Shafi'ite (on the east coast) schools of Muslim law and the legal codes and traditions inherited from different colonists —found in various parts of black Africa. The customary laws of Africa, however, have some general characteristics in common, the most important of which is undoubtedly the precedence of group responsibility over individual responsibility; not that individual responsibility does not exist, but it is generally a factor only within a group of fairly limited size. In dealings with the outside world, the responsibility of the group is substituted for that of its individual members in order that actions be to the advantage or the disadvantage of another group rather than to the advantage or disadvantage of one or more individuals as such. Furthermore, the legal status of each member within the context of the group is almost entirely defined in terms of his position within one or more social categories —such as sex, age group, caste or filiation— rather than in terms of personal characteristics. The law takes little account of the individual. It follows from this essentially social character of African law that determination of responsibility is only partially based on the idea of free will, since the predominant criterion for judging an action is also social and is basically objective rather than subjective. Another consequence of this social approach to law is the general failure to distinguish between public and private law, or between penal and civil law. An offense against an individual's inheritance or his person is the concern of his entire group and of the guilty person's as well, and the penalty for such an offense is a compensation as much as a punishment.

Distinctions between penal and civil law, however, are not completely unknown. They are found, in varying degrees, wherever judicial systems have been developed that tend to remove the direct means of settlement from the participants in a dispute. The complexity and maturation of the legal system are usually in proportion to that of the political structure. In primitive societies without chiefs, individual behavior is forced to conform to customary norms by collective pressure, which may take the form of moral persuasion, magic or physical coercion. Disputes between groups are settled either by friendly negotiations or by war. A legal structure comes into being when a person or, more frequently, a social group (elders, for example) is able to make decisions and enforce them, either acting as a body or through a specialized organization. In societies where political power is dispersed, the decision-making bodies and the bodies that execute the decisions are often special societies (among the Igbo and Yako of Nigeria and the Mande of Sierra Leone, for example). Real tribunals begin to appear when political power is concentrated at the level of a chieftain; and in fully formed states and protostates one ends up with a true legal hierarchy, either of a feudal type, in which at each level of authority the chief holds his judicial power on a personal basis (e.g., among the Ashanti and the Kotokoli of Togo), or of a centralized type, in which each judge derives his authority by delegation from the central power (e.g., among the Baganda, in Dahomey and in the old Zulu system). It should be noted, however, that even in centralized societies each chief or collective local authority is competent to judge, at least prior to appeal, cases involving members of his group.

It seems that the distinction between public and private law tends to be introduced indirectly by the magico-religious system: the earliest violations of public law in a society generally concern ritual, infraction of taboos or witchcraft, which endanger the whole community. Later, when the society is more complexly developed, one finds offenses that may be considered to be lese majesty or lese society. But not until a later stage of the society's development does one find offenses that, although primarily harmful to the interests of an individual, are regarded as endangering social order and hence become cardinal sins of sorts. At this stage, homicide, premeditated or not, theft, even adultery no longer result in compensation to the group to which the victim belongs but are penalized regularly by death, banishment, slavery or the like, and only then one can speak of a valid distinction between civil and penal law.

The introduction of European law destroyed the customary laws by imposing the notion of individual responsibility based on motive, which was a universal phenomenon even where colonists pretended to respect the customary law. The French, even more than the British, separated civil and criminal law and imposed penal laws relevant to a social system based on concepts of kinship, property, etc., that bore no relation to Africa. As a result, clandestine legal systems often emerged parallel to the official courts and filled the gaps in colonial law or corrected its decisions. On the whole, independence has not seriously affected this situation, and colonial legal systems continue to be enforced. Some countries have undertaken, or attempted to undertake, the codification and, in some cases, the standardization, of the common laws. But one wonders whether this kind of effort does not risk ending up as an artificial preservative for institutions that are either obsolescent and on the point of being abandoned or else are in the process of being transformed and adapted to a drastic social and economic upheaval, which has not been forced to slow down by national emancipation. (See also *Bamum; Family; Initiation; Kikuyu; Lineage; Proverbs; Societies, Secret; Wisdom; Women.*)   P.A.

LEGENDS. Legends may be defined as creations of the collective imagination which are based on fact. In Africa, legends are closely linked to tribal epics, poems and myths about the cosmos, particularly myths about the origin of man. It is therefore often very difficult to decide whether a particular event or character in these stories is legendary in the strict sense of the word or purely mythical—that is to say, representing an archetype or symbol. After attaching more importance to myths than to legends in interpreting these tales, experts in African ethnology now tend to attribute a legendary origin to certain characters who, not long ago, were regarded as mythical; for example, the Baule queen Aura Poka, who was the leader of the great migration in the eighteenth century; the ancestor-hero of the Shilluk, Nyikang; and the hunter Ouidiraogo, founder of the Mossi kingdom. On the other hand, tales of much more probable events, particularly the overcoming of geographical obstacles such as mountains and especially rivers, are given a symbolic explanation today. These changes are justified by improved methods of ethnohistory and by the study of oral traditions about men and events concerning which there is independent evidence. Even today we can witness the birth of legends about contemporary events and people; for example, in Basaland in Cameroun about the nationalist leader Um Nyobe, who was killed in 1958; in Zaire about the messianic prophet Simon Kimbangu; and among the Laadi of

The Legend of Kabrin Kabrat.
A performance given by the
Tropical Ballet. Ivory Coast.
*Photo: Service d'Information
de la Côte d'Ivoire.*

the Republic of Congo about another prophet, André Matswa. Legends are created by a process of reinterpreting genuine facts and rumors and by attributing to an individual stereotyped characteristics such as miraculous powers, which are borrowed from local traditions or even from a foreign cultural source such as Christianity. (See also *Agriculture; Balunda; Bambara; Bapende; Blacksmiths; Divination; Epics; Fang; Kikuyu; Kongo; Literature, Oral; Mossi; Myths; Poetry; Taboos.*)   P.A.

LEOPARD MEN. See *Lion Men and Leopard Men.*

LINEAGE. In all traditional societies of Africa, without exception it seems, there are closely knit groups made up of people descended from the same ancestor. In every African language, these groups are designated by a particular name, but anthropologists translate many different names with the term "lineage." This application of a single term to so many concrete units is legitimate, since these groups really are part of the same institution, which is common to all sub-Saharan Africa. A lineage is based on kinship by consanguinity. An individual traces back his descent to a common ancestor through the links of the paternal line (patrilineal descent) or through the maternal line (matrilineal descent), according to whichever principle is adopted by the society to which he belongs. The ancestor

who founded the line was an outstanding figure during his lifetime either for his wealth or for some remarkable deed; his descendants are proud to be able to call themselves his "sons" and participate in the stream of life that began with him. The members of a lineage consider the bond uniting them as a profound and essential basis for communion. This concept of communion is expressed in the religious sphere by the ritual offerings with which the members of a lineage celebrate the memory of their ancestor. The bond of lineage is even more pregnant with this meaning at crucial moments in the life of an individual—marriage, the cultivating of a field for the first time, personal crises or succession. This is the reason why belonging to a lineage dominates the existence of Africans.

A group whose bonds of loyalty are strong, the lineage will collectively protect a "brother" who is threatened by a stranger. If he is wronged, the lineage will exact reparation; if he is killed, he will be avenged; if he himself is the aggressor, he will still be protected. If disagreement develops between two descendants of the common ancestor, everything will be done to reconcile them so that harmony will again reign between blood relations.

Apart from intervening in such crises in human relationships, the lineage exercises a permanent function. When a man chooses a wife—and this directly concerns the lineage because the children of the new couple will perpetuate the life of the ancestor—the descent group excludes from his choice anyone who is his lineal "sister" (exogamy); but then it helps him to pay the bride-price if he cannot bear the burden alone. The lineage gives him a field so that the new household can be sure of a livelihood, and a band of "brothers" helps him clear the field and build his dwelling. If his crops are poor, he will be given all he requires to feed his family and to replant. If he dies, his wives and children will be looked after by his blood relations, and their standard of living will in no way be affected by the death of their husband and father, even if they are young. This is the meaning of the statement that there are no widows and orphans in Africa.

In order that the lineage may efficiently fulfill these functions—which social systems in industrial nations have not yet been completely successful at fulfilling—it has to be organized. The elders of a lineage, who are nearest to the ancestor, usually exercise the authority within the group; the patriarch is the most revered of these elders. Group decisions are not authoritarian, nor imposed by physical coercion. All the married men can give their opinions, but the patriarch's wishes are generally respected. The dependence of the individual on the lineage, which provides him with everything, is so great that he adheres to its decisions without being constrained by force.

A lineage, which is like a triangle with the ancestor at the apex and a base that broadens with every generation, cannot be a permanent group. As the number of descendants is continually growing, there comes a time when it must split. Migrations and quarrels offer opportunities to descendants of an eminent man, who is of the same lineage but less remote than the common ancestor, to adopt him as their founder in the future. In this way, a new lineage originates. (See also *Ancestors; Blood; Clans; Family; Genealogy; Incest; Jewelry; Kinship; Kirdi; Languages, Secret; Markets; Marriage; Person; Polygamy; Royalty; Uncles.*)   J.M.

LION MEN and LEOPARD MEN. The belief that certain initiates possess the power to change themselves bodily into wild beasts and killers is not exclusively African. The lion men of Tanzania and Chad, the leopard men of the Congolese and Ubangi forests and of Gabon, Liberia and Sierra Leone, and the crocodile men of the banks of the Congo River, to cite only the best known, are not fundamentally different from the werewolves of Europe or the tiger men of southern Asia. Ancient Germany had its wolf warriors who dressed themselves in wolfskins, fought in a state of trance and, it is said, gnawed their shields when in a state of anger. It would take few additions (except perhaps an intoxicating drink, which would not be incongruous in this context) to make these Germans seem like relatives of the lion men who were hunters and warriors and who, at the beginning of this century, still dominated the territory of the Sara in Chad.

Unfortunately, very little is known about the secret societies to which lion, leopard and crocodile men belonged, even though their history, rituals and psychological impact on both actors and victims would be of the utmost interest to us. The secrecy surrounding them was protected by fearful taboos and was later reinforced by the repressive legislation imposed upon them by European administrations. In fact, almost our only sources of information about them are criminal-court records, from the colonial period, of murders, mutilation, torture and, on occasion, cannibalism. The accounts of the inquests and hearings represent so many one-way dialogues between magistrates applying European laws, terrorized witnesses and accused individuals who remained silent but stubbornly convinced that they were in the right. To these accounts were added incriminating evidence: iron claws and hooks, animal skins and sometimes wooden sandals carved in the shape of the paws of wild beasts.

There is an important distinction to be made between lion men and leopard men. Although leopards are common throughout almost the whole of Africa, confraternities of leopard men were apparently confined to the forest areas. Their activities generally included cannibalism. A candidate for initiation could be accepted only if he sacrificed a member of his family—wife, child or relative—to the community. The victim was dragged along some lonely path and his throat cut with an iron claw. Some parts of his body were then set aside for a communal feast. Animal footprints around the remains of the body made it appear as though a panther had attacked the victim, and the terror spread by the sect effectively silenced the uninitiated. This was the practice of the Congolese *Anioto* societies, which caused considerable trouble to the Belgian authorities. In Sierra Leone, a little human fat was included in the "medicine bag" known as *borfima*. In 1913, a report by the governor of Sierra Leone defined leopard men as "a very large and powerful secret organization to which all, or almost all, the authorities in some districts belong." There, as elsewhere, virtual epidemics of murder led to hundreds of arrests and numerous death

sentences. In reality, we have never been in a position to know the underlying reasons for such conduct, which horrifies us today. Possibly, the murder of a parent, like the cannibalistic meal itself, was a means of deliberately defying the most sacred human laws in order to rise above simple humanity or of confirming, through criminal action, the solidarity of the sect. Going further back, these confraternities may originally have performed the social and political tasks of law enforcement.

In contrast to the leopard men, whose presence has been attested to in the greater part of the forest zones, the lion men occupy only small areas of the savanna. Lion men also display wider variation in their characteristic activities than do leopard men. In southeastern Angola, their function was probably to ensure social harmony, by restraining the abuse of authority by the chiefs, a function similar to that of the *Ngil* (from the word for gorilla?) society among the Fang in Gabon. On the other hand, the *Mboyo* of the high plateau in Tanzania have committed, right up to modern times, a substantial record of murders followed by cannibalism, which makes them similar to the leopard men of the forests. The deaths were sometimes attributed to attacks by real lions, but lion hunts in the regions of Singuida and Dodoma, during which 8 lions were killed in 1920 and 38 in 1947-1948, have been less effective than the arrest of the sorcerers responsible. The *Mboyo* members themselves did not kill, which made them radically different from their "colleagues" in other sects. Their activities were limited to buying unfortunate girls and boys, breaking down their resistance and drugging them until they became docile instruments of

murder and, disguised as lions, were hired out to anyone who required their services. The really typical lion men come from the territory of the Sara in Chad. Their name alone—*Ngue tel bogue* ("those who change into lions")—describes them clearly enough. Even though it is thought that traces of more ancient practices are discernible among them (some, it was said, could turn themselves into lions, buffalo or wild dogs) or of practices imported from subequatorial regions (they make use of two varieties of yam, one bitter and one edible, of the species *Dioscorea latifolia*, traditionally associated with the leopard men of the Ubangi forest), it seems that the original organized brotherhoods came into being south of Koumra, near Bediondo, during the first third of the nineteenth century. Their expansion, accompanied by hunting, war and robbery, coincided with the great period of anarchy resulting from the pressure on the Sara lands by slave-trading Muslim empires: the Fulani of the Adamawa in the west; the Bagirmi and the Wadai in the east. The *Ngue tel bogue* appears to have originated among the Nar and, thanks to two related groups, has gained members mainly from among the Nar, the Mbai and the Day, spreading as far as the banks of the Bahr Sara. Some segments of the Sara people, for example those in Bedaya, have never had lion men. The initiated, who normally worked only for themselves, with the object of procuring game or slaves, could also be mobilized as soldiers for distant campaigns. They were paid for their services with bundles of throwing knives (the Sara currency of this period). In this capacity, they intervened on several occasions either for or against the sultans of Bagirmi. Before putting on lion-

Left: Wooden sole of a lion man from the Sara country. *Center:* One of the impressions, like a lion's pawprint, left by the sole. *Right:* Claw, made of forged iron, belonging to a lion man from the Sara country. Evidence from the court records of Fort Archambault, Chad. *Photos: Pierre Ichac.*

Tame lions of the emperor of
Ethiopia. Folk painting.
Photo: Rapho, R. Michaud.

men took part, which is hard to imagine, they might well be regarded as a public menace. (See also *Fang; Fauna; Ibibio; Initiation; Masks; Societies, Secret; Sorcery; Weapons.*) P.I.

LIONS. In Mediterranean Europe, Asia and Africa, in both ancient and modern times, the lion has been regarded as an exceptional animal. In the world of the bush, the wild counterpart of the village, he is regarded as man's equal. He is king of animals and often the initial owner of the soil. Like a king, he has the power to destroy as well as to protect. He is just and kills only for good reason; if he has to attack men or their domestic animals, it is never wantonly. Several African clans, such as the Bambara Diara, bear his name and claim kinship with him. Dead chiefs are believed to live on as lions. Two complementary attitudes can be detected in this conception of the animal, and only a few ancient civilizations, Egypt in particular, succeeded in combining them: the first of these attitudes seems to be associated with pastoral and warrior tribes, especially the neo-Sudanese royal houses; the second with several groups of Palaeonegrid farmers in the savanna.

To the former group, the lion appears as a warrior worthy of combat. He might be an adversary or ally, or even the embodiment of a chief. It is significant how often a hero—be he Hercules, Samson, Antar or Chaka—acquires renown with his first victory over a lion. The Fulani *silatigui* views a similar combat with a lion as the culmination of his initiation. And the same sort of confrontation, at least in symbolic form, was part of the coronation ceremonies of pharaohs—but this did not prevent them from later keeping a favorite lion at their sides. Similarly, young Masai *elmorane*, in order to qualify in their social hierarchy for the men's age group, had to defeat a lion or man. In Ethiopia, soldiers who were honored by the emperor received a lion's mane as a headdress from him. Even today, some officers of the Ethiopian imperial guard wear imitation lionskins made of printed material over their uniforms. Tame lions, traditionally fed in the *guebi* in Addis Ababa and even in the imperial antechamber, symbolize the power of African royalty as much as the official title of the emperor "Conquering Lion of Judah." Rameses II, whose lion Anta-m-Nekht ("the goddess Anta loves me") accompanied him constantly in peace and war, based his actions on the same concept.

The latter group views the lion as ally and kin. Among some Palaeonegrid farmers,

skins, arming themselves with iron claws or hunting harpoons and roaring into their calabash resonators, they had to eat dog meat. An intoxicating drink helped to make them unrecognizable and turned them, in their own and everyone else's estimation, into wild beasts. Some had an additional power, which was acquired by undergoing a more strenuous initiation than that demanded of other lion men: with the aid of a magic bracelet (and presumably by spreading some vegetable ingredients on the ground, as some Ubangi tribes do), they were able to control real lions at long range or even cause them to be born. Thus, *bol-ninga,* the lion bracelet, supplemented the action of *bol-tel,* the person "changed" into a lion. This ability was quite similar to that of the land chiefs, who were the masters and allies of their village lions, and it is tempting to recognize in them the distant origin of the lion men. Ever since the first years of the French occupation, lion men have been subjected to ruthless suppression, including the death penalty. Today, apart from some isolated and doubtful instances, which are probably due to local quarrels, the activities of lion men appear to be limited to a little hunting, an annual dance in a sacred wood and funerals of dead members. The so-called lion men, whose frolics have for some years past enlivened the displays of folklore at Fort Lamy and Fort Archambault, can deceive only tourists and photographers. If real lion relations between men and lions are unexpectedly peaceful. They take the form of a contract of alliance and kinship between a village community, represented by its land priest (or chief), and a family of lions (or rather a male lion followed by his family). The animals often wander around the village, and the children tending their goats, like the women working in the fields, feel protected anywhere on the hunting ground of "their" lions. Lions allow men who are friendly to them to take away the carcasses of antelopes that they have killed. During the annual harvesting and sowing feasts, the lions come to the village and "communicate," in the true sense of the word, with the villagers by drinking their share of the sacramental millet beer. The priests also have the power to summon them by praying before the altars of lions or those of the earth. Whoever addresses the altar addresses the lions. Whoever pours a libation or makes a sacrifice on it does so for their benefit. Lions can intervene in ordeals and, in a conflict with an alien village, can be used as remote-controlled weapons of war and vengeance. This may perhaps be the key to some unexplained attacks by "man-eating" lions. Finally, the death of an old lion heralds or follows the death of his priest.

This ritual bond with lions and, in some mountain regions, with equally friendly but less docile leopards is little more than a survival in modern Africa. Until recently it could be observed in certain regions of Chad that are rich in game, but it disappeared with the advent of safaris, tourists, livestock raising, and religious and social change. In the rest of Africa it seems to hardly have been studied. However, traces of it in various forms have been discovered in local traditions and, better still, in the evidence of European travelers of the past. They tended to regard these tales as inventions and were almost ashamed to record them. But it is disquieting to consider the profound similarities, including just the details that they reticently recorded, among these stories. In the lower Zambezi region, the area south of Lake Tanganyika, Uganda, the Sudanese region of the upper Nile and the savannas of Ubangi, Upper Volta and Chad, they found lions taking part in rural festivities, "giving meat," and capable, when so ordered by their priests, of attacking their enemies and their enemies' herds.

These African village lions, representing the earth from which men draw their subsistence, make us think of other ancient civilizations and their divinities. There was an old land chief (personally known to this writer) whose aged and almost toothless lion drank his last millet beer of the new harvest in February 1957, exactly one month before being killed by a hunter from Paris. He was like a humble and distant successor of the famous Mother Goddess of Asia Minor, Rhea or Cybele, Mistress of the Earth and Wild Beasts—whom tradition represented, like him, with lions at her side—or of the Egyptian priests of the Late Period, keepers in the temple of Leontopolis of the sacred lions to whom the pharaoh still offers, on the steles in museums, the hieroglyphic sign of a cultivated field. The difference between them was that the lion of the African land chief was not kept in captivity, but was wild and free. Ethno-zoology is yet in its infancy, and Africa probably has much to teach us.

The consumption of lion meat is common, except among clans for whom the lion is a totem or ally. But the meat is far less important than the entrails and other parts of the body where it is popularly believed his strength is concentrated: the heart, the seat of courage; the liver and gall, which are used in some poisons; the precious mass of hair which is found in the stomach (aegagropila); and the fat, a sovereign remedy for rheumatism; the claws and the teeth; and even the urine. (See also *Fauna; Hunting; Lion Men and Leopard Men; Stories; Totemism.*) P.I.

LITERATURE, ORAL. Until recently, the literary wealth of black Africa was found outside of books; it was stored in people's memories and was given expression in specific circumstances. Its content was made up of what we term "oral tradition." The works included in this body of literature are the creations of cultures in which spoken words and significant gestures are more important than graphic signs. Words are never treated lightly, and the body of knowledge of a people is often associated with a theory of the spoken word. This conception of language explains the power of solemn or ritual formulas, mottoes and proverbial sayings, and the importance given to the denomination of things. All oral expression by Africans, apart from ordinary conversation, shows some degree of literary intent. Every palaver is the occasion for an outpouring of eloquence, every amorous approach requires fine language and every public event is the setting for a display of good speechmaking. In traditional Africa there are professional verbalizers who perform recognized social functions: actor-narrators, who provide entertainment for village social evenings; skilled speakers, who are called "masters of the word" or "hoaxers of the ear"; griots, who celebrate the glorious deeds of the powerful and wield the intimidating weapon of mockery; keepers of knowledge; and spokesmen attending kings. Oral literature, which is created by everyone and preserved by everyone, is not only kept alive but is increased; a specialist has estimated the number of individual stories in African literature to be about a quarter of a million.

Oral literature can be divided into categories. Among the Yoruba of Nigeria, for example, there are eight genres that can be recognized and named: myths, legends, stories, enigmas, proverbs, songs, incantations and "couplets" which accompany divination sessions. The classification of oral literature into types is often precisely defined by the literary men who are the guardians of the oral tradition. The Dogon of Mali make a clear distinction between "ordinary speech" and "poetic speech" which is governed by the desire to create a "fine composition." They apply a generic term, *elume,* to all prose narrative of a fictional nature—excluding myths, which should be believed, and revered legends pertaining to ancestors. They include in this class animal fables that come to etiological conclusions, stories about people that can be interpreted in an esoteric or psychological way, cosmic tales that seem like myths with a moral, popularized mythic stories and poetic prose that, in order to achieve a certain stylistic effect, is composed of riddles, proverbs and enigmas. The Dogon also distinguish poetry, but do not give it a precise name; it is constituted by songs and mottoes. Songs manifest a great deal of variety and lend themselves to revision, for they accompany every life situation. Mottoes are linked to the individual and make his identity and social connections clear. But both kinds of poetry have certain definite characteristics in common: archaism, enigmatic images or formulas, a strong rhythm produced by repetition, a refrain, assonance and alliteration.

All studies devoted to black African poetry have stressed its remarkable imagery, form, rhythm and song, which are the essence of black African genius and the product of deeply felt experience. Ethnological works have shown that court poets often enjoyed considerable prestige in highly civilized countries. The ancient kingdom of Rwanda is an example of one such country. There, the "dynastic poets" had the responsibility of composing and preserving, unchanged, the texts of poems in praise of royalty and kings. Their families were exempt from all civil jurisdiction and had no other duties than to preserve the works, which they transmitted from generation to generation under the supervision of a special official. African oral literature is a rich and varied panorama ranging from learned and esoteric poetry to stories and popular legends. It has preserved its wealth and vigor because it was an inherent part of the community's life and movement. It came into being in the most diverse circumstances; it often found itself on the borders of dramatic creation—and when the theater took shape, as it did among the Malinke of Mali, it crossed these borders. It suggests the possibility of a literature in action: a lesson that "book civilizations" might well learn. (See also *Birds; Diet; Griots; Heroes; Kikuyu; Legends; Love; Mottoes; Mussoi; Myths; Poetry; Proverbs; Riddles; Rwanda; Song; Stories; Theater.*)   G.B.

LITERATURE, WRITTEN. The literary wealth of black Africa is being stored less and less in men's memories and more and more in libraries. Oral tradition is weakening, while written language is exalting new ideas and assuring the preservation of ancient dreams. There is a revolution in ways of seeing and feeling; the meanings of the legends change as the means of communication change. There are two landmarks in the history of modern African literature: 1921, when Blaise Cendrars published his *Anthologie nègre,* a selection of traditional stories and legends; and 1948, when Léopold Senghor introduced a surprised and fascinated public to black African and Madagascan poetry. The beginnings of this literature were modest, as if the written transcription had dried up the sources of folklore and epic by taming them. *Chaka,* by Thomas Mofolo, who wrote in his native Basuto, however, immortalized some of the legends about the Zulu state. Other works, too, remained close to their African roots; for example, Paul Hazoumé's *Doguicimi* (1926), a sort of historic gest glorifying the kings and the ancient kingdom of Dahomey.

One literary effort had no posterity; this was the gentle, moving story of a shepherd and former Senegalese infantryman, Bakary Diallo, that was a tribute to colonization. It was entitled *Force-Bonté* (*Benevolent Force,* 1926) and was written by a "son of the government." It was reassuring after the scandal caused by the awarding of the 1921 Goncourt prize to *Batouala, véritable roman nègre,* by René Maran, a West Indian novelist and administrator of the Republic of Central Africa. The hero of the latter book, a tribal chief called Batoula, gave virulent expression to the popular discontent with the white colonists. It was the first of a long series of protest novels.

Until 1945 there were hardly a dozen African written literary works of any value. The number has increased since then, and there are now more than a hundred. This phenomenon can be explained as part of the social and cultural stirrings of black Africa. It is a renaissance that was produced by the maturation of several influences. The West Indians writing in French were preponderant among these. In June 1932, some young Martiniquans published an inflammatory review with a bright red cover called *Légitime Défense*. In it they attacked the established order, particularly in its colonial form, and its accepted ideas. Inspired by the surrealist movement, their rejection of current values constituted the first step toward discovering and asserting their negritude. The poet Aimé Césaire followed in their wake and founded the review *Tropiques* in 1941, which was an exploration and recognition of Africa.

In Paris, West Indians and Africans, including Césaire, Senghor, the novelist Ousmane Socé and the storyteller Birago Diop, got together and published a small, unpretentious review, *L'Étudiant noir,* as a platform for their ideas. The main topic of discussion was the major question of whether the political revolution should precede the cultural revolution or whether politics was only an aspect of culture. The Africans tended to favor the second point of view. They explored the wealth of traditional literature, subjected Western values to searching criticism and confronted them with the values of negritude. The term "negritude" itself was the subject of endless controversy; it was raised to the level of a philosophical idea by Jean-Paul Sartre in "Orphée noir," the preface to an anthology of poetry compiled by Senghor, and it colored the ideology of the first black intellectuals grouped round Alioune Diop, who founded the review *Présence africaine* in 1947. Thus, the beginning was promising; African literature had writers to create it and theorists to give it direction. Poetical works were more numerous at first, and their brilliance commanded attention. It was a brilliance that depended on typically African qualities: rhythm and ideas expressed through symbolic imagery. Senghor was the most distinguished of the African poets (*Chants d'ombre,* 1945; *Hosties noires,* 1948; *Éthiopiques,* 1956, followed by *Nocturnes*). A return to Mother Africa and to the ancestral sources was the driving force of his work. He evoked the "kingdom of childhood" and the past of his people, the symbols with which the myths and rituals were filled, the piety felt toward ancestors and the

mysteries of revealed knowledge. He sang paeans to the black woman: "Naked woman, somber woman, ripe fruit with firm flesh...." Then he demanded liberty for Africa and a just society for all men: "the transparent dawn of a new day." Senghor's work is dominated by the beat of an "inner music," by an insistent rhythm: "a poem is a failure unless it makes you want to sing both words and music at the same time." Other, younger poets have added and are adding to the heritage of African poetry. They do not reject the themes drawn from traditional civilizations, but they are more open to violence and more sympathetic to the poetry of revolt (David Diop, Bernard Dadié, Keita Fodéba). It is significant that an *Anthology of Black Poetry Written in Portuguese* (1958) should have been compiled by Mario de Andrade, one of the leaders of the nationalist movement in Angola. Tchikaya U'Tamsi, a rising Zaire poet who writes in French, has won considerable acclaim.

The black African novel, which is second in importance only to poetry, is vigorous today. Its initial aim was to testify for Africa against the disturbing effects of Westernization, whether the form of expression was a "novel of manners" (like the novels of Abdoulaye Sadji), idealized memories of childhood (*L'Enfant noir,* 1953, by Camara Laye), racy criticism of colonial society (*Une Vie de boy,* 1956, by Ferdinand Oyona; *Le Pauvre Christ de Bomba,* 1956, by Mongo Beti) or an autobiographical novel showing the inadaptability of the African intellectual when he returns to his traditional setting. Although the first novels were more concerned with communicating a message than with creating a literary form, some of the later novels show greater interest in the problems of their genre. One example is the Guinean Camara Laye's *Regard du roi* (1955), in which the symbols and their meanings fuse and suggest surrealist techniques. Similarly, the narrative of Cheikh Kane entitled *L'Aventure ambiguë* (1961) is a masterly account of the conflict between the Muslim faith and modern ideas. Kane has molded his style into a flexible instrument; the encounters between the colonist and the colonized are transcended, the feelings are controlled and the only violence is in the mind, which is consonant with the theme of the book.

A microcosm of the novel, the short story restores a part of the rich African folklore of the past, and often the only discrepancy that exists is between the transcription and its translation. Black writers excel in this genre, where the genuine voice of Africa is never masked by literary artifice. It fuses wisdom, humor, social criticism and popular beliefs into a definite mixture of the different African civilizations. Some works have enduring qualities; among these are *Contes d'Amadou Koumba,* published by Birago Diop in 1947, and *Légende de M'Foumou ma mazono* by Jean Malonga, published in 1954. One exceptional work must be mentioned here: *Palm-wine Drunkard* (1952) by Amos Tutuola, a Yoruba from Nigeria, who was an orderly by profession. Written in English, it describes the adventures of the narrator in "The Bush and the World of Strange and Terrible Beings" in a rough, unpolished style, which is disturbingly unconcerned with avoiding inconsistencies and contradictions. An excellent anthology compiled by Leonard Sainville, *Anthologie I* (1963), reflects the creative wealth of "black African novelists and storytellers." It gives, however, only an incomplete picture. The literary movement is growing, the "schools" are increasing in the English-speaking countries of Africa, and the work is becoming more varied, notably with the development of theatrical literature.

Important studies are now being written that have considerable literary merit. These are scholarly works by writers such as Abdoulaye Ly, Hampaté Ba, J.E. Danquah and A. Kagame. These works do not always conceal their militant attitudes, as is the case with the study by Cheikh Anta Diop, *Nations nègres et culture* (1954), which presents black Africa as the cradle of the Egyptian and classical civilizations. They are a means by which the writer can express his commitment and fundamental beliefs and can almost be classified as topical literature of conflict. African literature is becoming more complex as it increases in quantity. There is no mistaking its originality as it pursues its ambition to "help found a universal humanism" (Aimé Césaire). (See also *Arab Chroniclers; Negritude; Poetry; Stories; Theater.*)   G.B.

LIVESTOCK. See *Animal Husbandry; Cattle.*

LOST-WAX PROCESS. The lost-wax technique of casting bronze and other metals such as gold, silver and copper has been employed in much of Africa probably since very ancient times. At one time it was suggested that it was introduced by Europeans in the fifteenth century or later, but this is not a tenable theory, and it is more likely that the art is of ancient Mediterranean or Middle Eastern origin, by way of Egypt and Nubia rather than a local invention. The main area where it was developed, some-times with a striking degree of refinement, was West Africa, from the Ivory Coast to Cameroun, from the Gulf of Guinea as far inland as the Sudanese savannas. The most delicate and varied examples of lost-wax castings were produced in ancient Ife, the kingdom of Benin, and the lands of the Ashanti and Baule.

Casting by the lost-wax process involves several steps. First, the sculpture to be cast is modeled in wax. For small objects and basreliefs all the details of the finished work are included in the wax model. But for large works and works in high relief one begins by modeling a core of fireproof clay, which is worked roughly and with details sometimes omitted; a thin layer of wax—a few millimeters thick for the large bronze heads of Ife —is then applied to this core and worked more delicately. Next, the finished model is covered with a fireproof clay mold that fits the original shape exactly; extending through the clay mold from the finished wax model is a kind of funnel that is joined to it by one or more ducts. The core and the mold are attached to one another, so that the core cannot move. Then, molten metal is poured from a crucible into the funnel; this fills the space occupied by the wax, which the metal expels if it has not been previously melted. Once the work is cool, the mold is carefully broken and eventually the clay core, if there is one, is extracted. Finally, the metal that has accumulated in the ducts leading into the mold is removed, and sometimes the details have to be retouched.

This long and delicate work was often accompanied by rituals, which were supposed to assure its success. In Benin, the king himself supervised the making of the bronze head which represented his predecessor and would be put on his altar. He himself would begin the pouring of the metal: it was part of the ceremony of his accession to the throne. (See also *Ashanti; Bamum; Baule; Benin; Bobo; Bronze; Dahomey; Gold; Ife; Kirdi; Yoruba.*)   P.M.

LOVE. Marriage for love does not exist in traditional African societies. There is no place for love in what is primarily an alliance between two social groups, and not the union between two individuals who have chosen each other freely. The couple share the same bed, produce children and constitute an economic unit within a large family, but they hardly have any private life, nor any intimacy apart from their sexual relations. They remain strangers to each other because they belong to different lineages and because many social activities, beginning with the partaking of meals, separate men from women—from strangers. It is inconceivable that confidences would be exchanged between them, as would be natural between relations. Conversation and the expression of feelings are supposed to be reduced to a minimum. A betrothed couple among the Fulani of Niger are supposed to behave with the greatest reserve in public, neither speaking nor touching one another, and marriage only brings a slight relaxation of this rule. In some tribes, a married couple does not have the right to be seen together; in others, they cannot call each other by name. In any case, they are seldom allowed to express the least external sign of affection. Marriage probably does not completely exclude affectionate relationships between married couples; such relationships can develop in time. But the Wolof of Senegal, for instance, say that they cannot show affection before a third person without feeling ashamed.

Love, or at least mutual attraction, and exclusive preference are elements of social disorder; they only exist in adulterous relationships, which are revolts against marriages prescribed for the good of society. But oral literature, particularly songs and poems, to compensate for their proscription gives them an important place and glorifies the beloved woman. Her charms and qualities are minutely described in stereotyped phrases, and she is addressed in impassioned, sometimes desperate terms. In some societies, especially among the Palaeonegrid tribes, the free choice of a sexual partner, intimacy and the expression of affection between man and woman are permitted, but only before marriage and on condition that they do not compromise an engagement. Love has its hour, but when the time comes for the young woman to join her husband, love has to be forgotten and social order takes its place. Suicide is the only means of escape, and it is sometimes chosen by young women. (See also *Calabashes; Lineage; Magic; Marriage; Women.*) P.M.

LYCANTHROPY. See *Lion Men and Leopard Men.*

MAGIC. Magic is considered here as being a particular segment of a society's system of rituals and beliefs—the segment that includes maneuvers and manipulations deemed effective for the relatively direct attainment of concrete results. In these terms, it constitutes what may be termed "the materialistic sector of religion." One hesitates to speak of the "supernatural," because magical practices are, in fact, conditioned by a particular conception of nature: it is not a

Fon statuette. Dahomey. Bronze cast by the lost-wax process. Le Corneur Collection, Paris. *Photo: Giraudon.*

Statuette used for healing illness. Montol. Nigeria. Wood. Raymond Wielgus Collection, Chicago. *Photo: Walter Dräyer.*

matter of a "prelogical," "alogical," or "illogical" way of seeing things, but rather of a logic that is usually coherent once its premises are admitted. Now, these premises nearly always postulate the existence of a universal cosmic energy (called the "life force" by some writers and simply "force" in African languages) which the magician knows now to capture and manipulate more easily than ordinary mortals. In this sense, Sir James Frazer was correct in seeing in magic the first embryo of scientific thought. Magical acts and activities cover the whole gamut from the simple recitation of a ready-made formula, which is close to prayer, to the making of charms and talismans (known as "gri-gri" or "medicine"), which borders on the technical domain. In fact, many technical activities require magical accessories, which are reputed to increase the effectiveness of certain processes. There is total confusion between magical and technical skills in the field of medicine; here, magic and technique are inseparable and, moreover, form an effective combination. This is also true of all *ad nominem* magic, whether it is a matter of aggressive or protective magic, of love charms, of trials by ordeal, or of any other kind of magic designed to induce certain behavior in a human being, provided only that the subject knows that he is being subjected to magic. Magic is evidently less effective when the magical act is aimed not at men but at things, animals or natural phenomena. Meteorological magic—especially by the masters of rain or thunder—is nevertheless widespread and given credence by many (not only by Africans). Mention is often made of magicians who refuse to perform their rainmaking ritual, or who at least prolong it, until natural signs tell them that the barometer is falling. Similarly, "sorcerer hunters" have been accused of "uncovering" as evil sorcerers only people who are already unpopular or suspect for other reasons. One should not conclude, however, that these magicians are charlatans who trade on public credulity and who do not believe in their own art. Magicians, at least those found in traditional milieux, are specialists who are both respected and feared, who can protect and also be dangerous. Their function consists largely of crystallizing and expressing the feelings of the community about important difficult and dangerous subjects, and of manipulating the forces that are in constant danger of escaping from their control and turning against them or their kin.

Magical object. Baluba. Zaire. Wood and calabash filled with various materials. Paul Tishman Collection, New York. *Photo: Musée de l'Homme.*

Most societies make a distinction between sorcerers and magicians. In contrast, the distinction between magicians, healers, priests, diviners, servants of spirits and persons possessed by spirits is less easy to make (and is only justifiable in some societies). Furthermore, one has to make a distinction between amateurs and professionals, which is also not always easy to do. Indeed, everyone employs certain magical practices, and he can be taught (notably during initiation) or can buy other methods and formulas. However, professionals usually belong to more or less secret, but definitely closed, societies, which were often regarded with suspicion and opposed by colonial and post-colonial authorities.

The European distinction between white and black magic is not exactly comparable to the African distinction between magic and sorcery. African magic is always a delicate and dangerous art, but morally it is neutral or ambiguous; it may be regarded as good or evil, depending upon the use to which it is put by the practitioner. The same spell may be used to defeat a sorcerer or to bring suffering to an innocent person; or a laudable end may be attained through morally repellent or unconventional procedures; or again, the magician may only be successful by knowingly and deliberately violating certain taboos (especially sexual taboos). In the latter case, the gap between sorcerer and magician diminishes and may completely disappear if the magician loses control of the dangerous forces he employs and allows himself to be possessed by them. He then turns into an enemy of society who is all the more dangerous since his magic powers and knowledge protect him from all restraints. (See also *Armies; Blacksmiths; Calabashes; Fetishes; Flora; Jewelry; Languages, Secret; Numeration; Pharmacopoeia; Philosophy; Priests; Royalty; Song; Sorcery; Spirits and Genii; Weapons; Zulus.*)   P.A.

MALI. Mali, whose name was adopted by the inhabitants of the former colony of French Sudan, was once one of the powerful medieval empires of West Africa. (The name *Mali* means "where the king lives"; *Malinke* and *Mandingo* designate the "men, or subjects, of Mali.") The ancient kingdom covered a vast territory stretching from the Atlantic to beyond Niamey. Its early beginnings are obscure. In the middle of the eleventh century, the rulers of the little state of Kangaba on the upper Niger River were converted to Islam. At the end of the twelfth century, after a struggle between the Taraore and Konate clans, the Keita won the upper

Timbuktu, Mali. *Photo: Documentation française.*

hand, but suffered reverses. At this point, the hero Sundiata Keita—whose legend is still sung—appeared on the scene. Sundiata created a permanent army and challenged and killed (c. 1235) Sumanguru, the king of Susu. Around 1240, he destroyed Ghana, which was the capital of a rival whom he now replaced. His successive conquests transformed the kingdom of Kangaba into the empire which has been known by the name Mali ever since. Mali took over Ghana's control of the gold-bearing provinces of Senegal and Bouré and with them the trade in gold dust, which was carried by caravans from Morocco, Tripoli and Egypt and exchanged in the towns bordering on the Sahara for salt, fabrics, copper and glassware; but no foreigner could get near the gold placers, whose location remains a secret. In 1324, the greatest of Mali's rulers, Mansa Musa, went on a famous pilgrimage to Mecca. The splendor of his retinue, including thousands of slaves, each bearing a rod of gold, dazzled the Arabs. The sovereign himself distributed hundreds of kilos of gold in alms and presents. He took back with him several well-known Muslims, among them the architect and poet es-Saheli, who has been wrongly credited with introducing into Mali a style of architecture that, in fact, he only revived, building a mosque and a palace for Mansa Musa in his capital at Niani. After establishing diplomatic relations with the rulers of Morocco and Egypt, the Emperor Mansa Musa

invited to Mali several Arab scholars and traders from the Maghrib, and it was through them that Timbuktu's reputation as a town of learned men reached Europe, where it outlasted the empire of Mali. The great Arab traveler ibn-Batuta, whose previous wanderings had taken him as far as China, left a valuable account of his visit to Mali in 1352, twenty years after the death of Mansa Musa. "Acts of injustice are rare among them," he wrote, "and they are less liable to commit them than any other people. The sultan never pardons anyone who is guilty. A perfect order exists throughout the country, and the traveller has no fear of robbery or violence anywhere in it." Ibn-Batuta often comments on the prosperous state of agriculture and trade and the ease with which travelers could find good food and lodging for the night.

In the fifteenth century, the weakness of its princes and extortionate practices of its governors brought the decline of Mali. The Tuareg took Timbuktu in 1435, and the Mossi conducted raids even on the far side of the Niger River; but Europe was ill-informed of the events in West Africa and still thought Mali was a powerful state. As the situation deteriorated, the reigning emperor asked for help from the Portuguese governor of the settlements along the Gulf of Guinea, but he only sent a diplomatic mission. After this, the defeats increased; the leadership passed to the Songhai, former subjects of Mali living along the middle reaches of the Niger

River, who gained independence and established a capital at Gao. By the middle of the seventeenth century, Mali had shrunk to its modest beginnings and only controlled the country around Kangaba. (See also *Bow, Musical; Epics; Gold; Harps; Hausa; Sudan; Xylophones.*) D.P.

MARKETS. It is paradoxical that the market scene should be one of the most typical subjects of picturesque Africa, because the traditional economy was self-supporting and most important products required for subsistence did not pass through markets. Every rural family unit produced nearly everything it needed to feed itself, and the surplus it could have bartered was greatly reduced after payment in kind to the chief or king. The volume of bartered merchandise was therefore not very large. There are two limitations to this generalization: it only applies to the village markets that served an immediate locality and not to the great international markets of the towns; furthermore, there were parts of Africa where production was great enough for there to be an appreciable surplus that was used for barter. Taking into account these exceptions, it is true that the market was not the most important channel for circulating goods.

A distinction must be made here between the market as a place and as an economic system. For example, we live in a market economy, even though we may never go to a market. The traditional African economy was only partly a market economy; many goods circulated through a network of political relations (a portion of the taxes levied on the people by the governing authorities was redistributed during feasts given for the people by the governing authorities) and through a network of kinship relations (land was given to a young household by the patriarch of the lineage and help was given to the patriarch by lineage members when the harvest was poor) rather than through a market. A similar type of redistribution applied to services: an individual would work for the chief, for the patriarch or in the work crew of other members of one's lineage. The market sector of the economy did exist—there was an exchange of goods (millet for goats) and of services (people worked so that they would be fed)—but it was of subsidiary importance, and only part of this market economy operated in the marketplace itself. For example, the supply and demand of work generally had nothing to do with the market. Although village markets attracted large crowds, this was not primarily due to the economic importance of the transactions that were carried on there. The village market was a pleasant meetingplace; it was where one found old friends, where one made the acquaintance of foreign itinerant merchants and learned the latest news and domestic scandals, where political intrigues could be plotted and romantic relationships begun. In some parts of central Africa, the market was a peaceful refuge where the chief guaranteed everyone's safety.

The international markets of the city-states of the Sudanese region had quite a different political and economic significance. They were the termini of the caravan routes from the Maghrib across the Sahara and the points where precious merchandise from the north (salt, weapons, fabrics, Mediterranean products) converged with the riches from the south (gold, ivory, skins, kola nuts). The rulers of Ghana, Mali and the kingdom of the Songhai levied taxes on the import and export of these various goods or reserved for themselves the exclusive sale abroad of their countries' products. The revenues, and consequently the power, of these governments depended on the international trade represented by these urban markets.

In Africa today, the market economy system has acquired primary importance. Non-economic networks no doubt continue to maintain the circulation of goods and services to a certain extent, but the factors of modern development are integrated into a system of economic relationships. The marketplaces themselves still preserve some features from traditional days. They have remained the centers of intense community life, and there is a busier exchange of greetings, information and gossip than of merchandise or money. Only small quantities of things are purchased (cigarettes are sometimes sold singly), and merchants generally only have minimal stocks. The urban markets are naturally better supplied, but the gold, ebony and ivory of yore have been replaced by mass-produced, imported objects. There is a gay din of talk and laughter, a brilliant mixture of loud but exquisite colors of clothing, and a warm smell of fruit and spices in the sun. The markets of modern Africa lack nothing to match the picturesque markets of yesterday. (See also *Arabs in East Africa; Beads; Gold; Salt; Towns and Cities; Villages.*)   J.M.

MARRIAGE. The continuity of the ancestral line depends on marriage. In the West, only people with prestigious surnames and extensive hereditary wealth are anxious to prevent the extinction of their family name. But in traditional Africa the lineage is important to everyone because it protects, helps and supports the individual member all through his life. In order to fulfill its functions efficiently, the lineage has to be strong and its members numerous. The marriage of one of its members not only concerns that member and his future partner, but also all their "fathers and mothers," "brothers and sisters." The future partner is an outsider; a union between

Wedding of a Dogorda girl.
Chad. *Photo: Hoa-Qui.*

Carrying a Bahutu bride. Rwanda. *Photo: Jacques Maquet.*

descendants of the same ancestor would be incestuous. In a patrilineal system, which is the common kinship system in Africa, this means that a girl belonging to one lineage will benefit another lineage with her fertility, since her children will be attached to her husband's line. Under the difficult conditions of life that prevailed throughout most of traditional Africa (high infant mortality, serious endemic diseases, frequent epidemics), the potential fertility of a girl was an invaluable asset, and very naturally the lineage that was going to lose this asset wanted adequate compensation.

The most direct way of achieving this was by *exchange marriage*. Exchange marriage is still practiced in some hunting and agricultural communities in the equatorial forest, like those of the Bambuti of the Ituri area and the Bahamba of the Ruwenzori region, but it is a relic of former days and .is becoming rare. It involves a double marriage: the lineage that requests a wife for one of its men offers one of its own women in exchange; the woman who has been offered will marry a "brother" (male member of the lineage) of the woman who has been requested. Consequently, neither lineage is the poorer. But a double marriage has disadvantages: it is not always possible to find partners for the second marriage at the required moment, and if one of the marriages

breaks down, it is difficult to maintain the other because it is based on reciprocity. Marriage accompanied by matrimonial compensation, which exists all over black Africa, mitigates these inconveniences. The lineage that requests the wife offers goods to the lineage supplying her. These goods (hoes, for example, in a farming community, cattle in a pastoral society) allow the group that gives up the girl to obtain another when one of its men wants to marry. This avoids the constraints of simultaneous marriages and narrow reciprocity. Africans are justified in feeling offended when we regard matrimonial compensation as the cost-price of a wife. They say that this interpretation is just as false as considering the European dowry the price a father pays to procure a husband for his daughter. The payment of the "African dowry," as the marriage goods are sometimes mistakenly called, is proof that one group has surrendered its rights over the fertility of one of its girls to another group. It is the essence of a marriage: until the compensation is completely paid the offspring of the young household belong to the kin group of the mother.

The African marriage has been considered an alliance between lineages rather than a union between two individuals who like one another. This is probably true, but it seldom involves a heart-rending alternative. Although the initial steps are taken by the parents of the young man, he has already made his wishes known. On the other hand, the girl's parents are sounded on the question so that they have time to consult her, and if she refuses, no one loses face. When personal preference conflicts with the choice of the lineage, there are customary procedures that generally allow the boy or girl to get his or her own way, provided he or she has sufficient energy to resist family pressures.

Once the marriage has been concluded to the satisfaction of both lineages, it is in their interest to preserve its stability, and they do their best to persuade incompatible couples not to separate. If, however, the wife returns to her own home and repeated attempts to smooth over the differences meet with failure, the lineages resign themselves to a final breakdown. The wife returns to her family with her young children. When they are old enough to be independent of their mother, they go back to their father, unless the matrimonial compensation has not been paid or has been returned, in which case they become members of the maternal lineage which, contrary to what sometimes happens in Europe, will always be delighted to receive them. (See also *Castes; Cattle; Emancipation of Women; Excision; Family; Guro; Ibibio; Incest; Lineage; Love; Polygamy; Pygmies; Widows; Women.*) J.M.

MASKS. African masks in the form that they are known in the West are quite different from what they were in traditional Africa. Not only have they been taken out of their normal settings—as have been African statues, drums and weapons—but they have also been mutilated and perverted. They are mutilated in the sense that we have only the part of the mask that covers the face or even just the crest that is set on top of the head (like the famous Bambara antelope masks or the Senufo helmets); the complete mask, however, also comprises elements made of woven fibers—some for attaching the mask firmly to the wearer and some for completely hiding the rest of his body. They are perverted in the sense that we treat these sections of masks like statues and display them under the cunning lighting of museums, although the masks were intended to be seen in movement at communal ceremonies as a part of the dancing and music.

Masks are very common in Africa—just as they were in the Greco-Roman world, in classical Asia, in pre-Columbian America and in Melanesia—while in Europe they are hardly more than folk survivals. This is why African masks are so difficult for us to understand, although they fascinate us and appeal to something in the depths of our consciousness. We cannot react with indifference to the ambiguity of this object which masks one face while unmasking another.

Left: Baluba mask. Zaire. Painted wood. Musée royal de l'Afrique centrale, Tervuren. *Museum photo.*
Below: Dan mask. Ivory Coast. Painted wood, feathers and horsehair. *Photo: Hugo Zemp.*

Bakwele mask. Republic of
the Congo. Painted wood.
Christophe Tzara Collection,
Paris. *Photo: Ciccione.*

Baloumbo mask. Republic of
the Congo. Painted wood.
Princess Gourielli Collection,
Paris. *Photo: Ciccione.*

Senufo mask. Ivory Coast.
Wood. Webster Plass
Collection, British Museum.
Photo: Eliot Elisofon.

An African mask obviously has more than
one significance and more than one function.
Its prime purpose, however, is to act as a
temporary dwelling place for a god—the
term "god" here meaning any being or force
that is invisible because it is not permanently
united with a body. The mask is a theophany,
the visible manifestation of a god. The
dwelling place is not only the object of wood
and fiber but also the man it envelops; and
the spirit takes possession of them both. So
long as the divine presence lasts, the mask
(the wearer and the thing worn) belongs to
the world of the sacred. Even when there is
no crisis of "possession" in the strict sense of
the word (which, to us, denotes a pathological
state), the man is no longer himself; it is
the god who acts through him. In the context
of a philosophy in which all beings share the
same life, invisible beings are invested with
enormous strength. Thus, the "vital charge"
of the mask is dangerous, and certain
precautions have to be taken for the wearer's
return to the profane life. Once the wearer
becomes a simple villager again, his costume
is put away, and the mask does not exist until
the next incarnation of the god.

The African mask is not a disguise that the
wearer uses to hide his identity by borrowing
another's appearance; it is not a man
pretending to be a god, but a god who
becomes visible in his real form. The sculptor
who makes a mask does not try to imitate a
human face or an animal head, but aims to
fashion the most expressive part of the
ephemeral body of a force more powerful
than man. There is no deception; even
though women and children are not supposed to know that it is their own men-folk
who are acting as interpreters for invisible
beings, the wearers themselves believe that
the gods are manifesting themselves through
them.

Besides this fundamental significance of
the mask, which we believe is common to
many traditional black African societies,
masks may have a number of secondary
meanings that are either derived from this
primary significance or are even perversions
of it. Initiation masks, which force young
men to undergo the ordeals marking their
entry into adult life, have such a secondary
significance. It is, incidentally, during
initiation that the part played by human
beings in the appearance of masks is revealed
to young men. The masks of the confraternities or groups that are often referred
to as "secret societies" in books on eth-
nography because their members never
appear in public with their faces uncovered
also have a significance other than the
primary one. Although they claim to derive

their authority from the sacred world, these confraternities act as pressure groups in the profane affairs of the village. When a villager is not behaving as he should, in the opinion of the confraternity, the masks surround his dwelling during the night and threaten or maltreat him until he conforms. The fear of invisible beings and the anonymity of the masks are useful means of coercion. The greatest perversion and greatest debasement of the mask occurs in its use as an accessory of the terrorist activities of bands of criminals like the famous *Anioto* society, the leopard men of the Belgian Congo. The hood masks of the *Anioto* members, made out of leopardskin, had no religious significance; their purpose was simply to terrify the victim while hiding the identity of the wearer.

Functioning at its highest level, the mask expresses the myths of a society or is even an element of those myths. This close relationship between mask and myth has been thoroughly investigated among the Dogon by Marcel Griaule and his followers. The Dogon *kanaga* mask is surmounted by a sort of cross of Lorraine consisting of very simple forms, with one horizontal element representing the creator god, heaven and earth, and the other, the helicoidal movement of the god stirring from his immobility; at the same time, the cross symbolizes man, who is himself associated with the creation. Another Dogon mask, the *sirige,* which is sometimes over fifteen feet high, symbolizes, with its eighty niches, the eighty original ancestors; the wearer swings it from east to west to imitate the course of the sun. The oldest Dogon mask, called *iminana,* is associated with the myth that recounts how it was carved to commemorate the first man who died.

The mask can also be a work of art. Masks and statues of ancestors represent the essence of Negro art for us and also for Africans. The aesthetic intentions of the artist are forcefully expressed in the various forms of the mask; in making a face for a god, African artists enjoy even greater freedom from imitation of nature than when they are carving a statue. When creating a statue, they never aim to reproduce faithfully what they see, although they are required to make a representation of a man or a woman. When making a mask, though, they are freed from even this minor limitation.

The human face, as one might expect, is a common subject for the maskmaker, and it is interpreted in innumerable ways: among the Bateke, it is represented by an absolutely plane surface decorated with geometric patterns in which the features of the human face are unrecognizable at first glance;

Basonge mask. Zaire. Painted wood. Vonder Heydt Collection, Rietberg Museum, Zurich. *Photo: Bernhard Moosbrugger.*

Baham (Bamileke group) mask. Cameroun. Wood. Rietberg Museum, Zurich. *Photo: Ernest Hahn.*

Bakuba mask. Zaire. Wood, basketry, skins, beads and cowries. Smithsonian Institution. *Photo: Eliot Elisofon.*

Fang mask. Gabon. Painted wood. Paul Tishman Collection, New York. *Photo: Musée de l'Homme.*

among the Dan, it is modeled with an idealized realism; it is expressed in a slight concavity in the heart-shaped masks of the Bakwele; Bamum figures have very inflated cheeks; Gere-Wobe masks are cut in deep relief; and concave volumes are characteristic of the Fang and Bajokwe masks. Animal masks are equally varied: the Kurumba antelopes and the hyenas and baboons of the Senufo are only a few among many examples. The variety of styles is also extremely wide. Some writers distinguish them by using terms that have been evolved to describe currents in Western painting and sculpture: "cubist," "surrealist," "art nouveau," etc. The validity of this approach may well be questioned; if it is merely based on a simple analogy of lines, volumes and decoration, it is certainly not valid. Such an approach can only be applied legitimately to African masks if the labels of Western art history can be shown to have a universal bearing because they represent permanent tendencies in all stylistic tradition. This can be done with some terms ("classical," "baroque," "expressionist," "impressionist," for example), but it cannot, or at least not yet, be done with most of them. (See also *Antelopes; Art, African; Art, Styles of; Basketry; Birds; Body Painting; Bullroarers; Calabashes; Dance; Flora; Societies, Secret;* individual tribes.)   J.M.

MASSA. The Massa, who are often improperly called "Banana," live on the flood plains bordering the middle course of

the Logone River, about 155 miles south of Fort Lamy. There are 50,000 Massa in the Republic of Chad and 75,000 in Cameroun. They build their enclosures on land above the flood line and keep their cattle near their huts only during the dry season.

The Massa live by farming, fishing and raising livestock. They have a balanced diet, which is rare in the center of the savanna. The principal agricultural product is quick-growing red sorghum, which is grown on level ground during the rainy season. Millet, sorghum requiring transplanting, peanuts, rice, beans and peas are subsidiary products. Fishing is carried on all year round in the Logone and its tributaries. When the floods subside, the men organize fishing expeditions in the lower courses of the Logone and Chari Rivers. In addition, they raise goats, sheep and small zebus. The latter are an important part of the economic and community life of the Massa. Owners of zebus enjoy high social status: first, because a man is required to give ten fertile cows to the family of his future wife before he can marry her, and second, heads of families extend the network of their social and commercial relations by building up a complex system of lending cattle. The taking of a milk treatment by oneself or one's children is also considered to be a sign of wealth. When a person goes in for such a treatment, he stops working and drinks large quantities of milk and sorghum gruel to get fat. He spends the best part of the day attending to his appearance and physique in preparation for the wrestling,

Fishing in the Tandjile River in Massa country. Chad. *Photo: Pierre Ichac.*

Massa village: Kolong, Chad.
Photo: Pierre Ichac.

singing and dancing which are part of the festivals of the dry season.

The Massa are skillful basketmakers who use the reeds in the flood areas. The lack of trees and stones has caused them to master the art of making cob (a mixture of clay and straw), which they use for the walls of their huts and furniture. They know how to work iron and copper, which the blacksmiths make into bracelets and pipes by means of the lost-wax process. They do not use bows but employ assegais and throwing knives. The most common weapon is the cudgel, and a man is never without one. Formerly, it was used for what may truly be called "fencing," practiced with heads protected by padded helmets.

The political organization of the Massa hardly goes beyond the framework of patrilineal lineages. Preferential marriage—marriage to someone of a particular parentage—does not exist. Rather marriage is exogamous and people are required to marry outside their patrilineage and communal residence. The Massa follow the practice of levirate—marrying the widow of one's brother. The administrative division of the country into cantons, villages and districts masks the former division into lands occupied by members of the same patrilineage. Within the lineage, the elders and the land chief, elected by descendants of the founder-ancestor, wield the highest authority. The land chief supervises the division of the fields and decides when the main agricultural operations should begin. It is

also incumbent on him to perform the rites and sacrifices on which the prosperity of the community depends, and to win the favor of the ancestors and the different genii. The powers of the other world include: Laona, a beneficent god who lives in the sky and sends the rains; Nagata, Mother Earth; Matna, the genius of death; and Mununta, the genius of water. Soothsayers are constantly required to decide the nature and purpose of the sacrifices that must be performed to appease the powers above. Their systems of divination consist in arranging several hundred signs in spirals on the ground. For hundreds of years, the Massa have used an initiation similar to that of the Yondo, one of the neighboring Sara tribes. In their general development, though, the Massa tend to follow the example of the Muslim societies (Fulani and Bagirmi) with whom they live. (See also *Basketry; Birds; Breasts; Household Furnishings; Kirdi; Millet; Mussoi; Rain; Rice; Traps; Weapons.*)   I.G.

MEALS. The eating hours and composition of meals are similar all over Africa. A meal consists of a single dish made from the staple food of the area: a cereal or leguminous plant in the tropical zone, a tuber or plantains in the equatorial zone. It is eaten with a sauce that is cooked separately and which varies according to the tribe and the time of year. The staple food is monotonous, and variety is provided by countless sauces, which contain most of the proteins, fats and vitamins in the diet. Meals with several dishes are only to be found in towns. In traditional rural communities, eating two different dishes at the same meal is often considered harmful and the cause of intestinal disorders.

The main meal is eaten in the evening. It is served hot, and there is plenty of it. Very often, a portion of this meal is kept for the next morning and eaten with a different sauce. The midday meal frequently consists of a boiled cereal with milk added or a small portion of the staple food accompanied by a light sauce. This meal varies with the season's work and the food available. In the Sudan region, one or two meals a day are omitted during the dry season in order to save the food resources for the rainy season, when most of the agricultural work—which demands a considerable expenditure of energy—is done. Like anywhere else, the meals offered to visitors are exceptional: the best is offered to them, and it is prepared with more than the usual care. The vulnerable groups in the community (pregnant women, nursing mothers and young children) are almost always treated with special consideration.

Preparing meals occupies most of a housewife's day because the steps in making the staple food edible are so complex; in fact, it takes five to eight hours a day. In African households, which are often polygynous, the preparation and eating of meals are organized very carefully. A wife knows exactly what she ought to prepare each day for herself and her children, for the married men

of the family, the unmarried members and any guests who may come.

Most traditional dishes are eaten with one's hands and, to a certain extent, their consistency and temperature are affected by this. Ladles and spoons are nearly always used in the preparation and serving of food. The division into groups at meals depends on social customs and magico-religious beliefs. It is unusual for men and women, young and old, initiated and uninitiated, nobles and commoners to eat out of the same plate. A son-in-law is often not allowed to eat in the presence of his mother-in-law. Vulnerable individuals (old men, convalescent children, invalids) and those in a state of impurity (menstruating and sterile women, and persons who have broken a taboo) eat separately so as not to contaminate other people. Obeying the rules of hospitality is compulsory in African societies, with a guest generally being given deferential treatment aimed at honoring him and proving to him that the food is neither poisoned nor under a spell. Meals are seldom eaten lightheartedly, because in societies whose subsistence is precarious, food seems like a gift from the supernatural powers whose nature men share. Each meal is to some degree a form of communion through which the eater incorporates a portion of his ancestors into himself. Most sacrifices end with a feast of communion, and sharing in such a feast sometimes establishes bonds between individuals as close as filiation, which can even entail a prohibition against marriage, as among the Mussoi of Chad. (See also *Diet; Millet; Poisons; Spoons.*)   I.G.

MEAT. All African languages contain terms for expressing the concepts of "hunger for meat," "a gift of meat," "finding meat in the bush." Meat is the most valued item in the African diet simply because of its rarity. Livestock is plentiful on the African continent; there is one sheep or goat per capita and one cow to every two people. Yet the average annual per capita consumption of meat is 12 pounds in western Africa and 26 pounds in eastern and central Africa against a minimum of 88 pounds per capita in Europe. In traditional societies meat is used in very small quantities unless a sacrifice is made or a wild animal is captured. Then, vast amounts are eaten to satisfy the "hunger for meat," which is so common in Africa. The deficiency of animal proteins, which is common in the traditional diet, is the result of the inadequate use of the available livestock: livestock supplies only 1,000,600 tons of meat annually, although, in theory, 12 million tons are needed to satisfy the

Ajukru preparing cassava. Ivory Coast. *Photo: Denise Paulme.*

dietary requirements of Africa. There are several reasons for this inadequate use of livestock. First, livestock raising areas are clearly defined geographically, and meat, even on the hoof, is difficult to transport. Second, the pastoral tribes set a high value on the numerical increase of their herds; their animals are intended for exchange in a closed society, to procure prestige and wives rather than to be sold outside the group and, for very good reasons, killed for human consumption. Only meat obtained in hunting is eaten willingly and without any reservations, but there is seldom a regular supply of it. In traditional communities, a domestic animal is generally killed for a special social or religious occasion. Its throat is cut according to a prescribed ritual and the celebrant often belongs to a special caste. Meat is an expensive commodity. Butcher's meat normally comes from small cattle, because the poverty of the people is such that the meat of an ox cannot be disposed of except in a well-patronized market. With the exception of the famous *biltong* (narrow strips of meat, dried in the sun) of South Africa, few traditional societies have developed satisfactory techniques for preserving meat. Throughout rural Africa, the most recently introduced breeds of domestic animals (Barbary ducks and new varieties of sheep and goats) are the animals most readily killed for meat, because they are not a traditional part of life, as are the older kinds of livestock. (See also *Cattle; Diet; Hunger; Hunting.*)

I.G.

MEROE. In the ninth century B.C., a local power rose in Nubia out of the disintegration of the New Kingdom of Egypt. Its center was Napata, a little downstream from the Fourth Cataract of the Nile. This young power, known as Cush, grew until it inherited the succession and kingdom of the pharaohs (becoming the Twenty-fifth Dynasty, which ruled from the end of the eighth to the first half of the seventh century B.C.), but its supremacy was brief, and it soon lost all but its Sudanese lands. Some time during the sixth or fifth century B.C., it transferred its capital to Meroe, much further to the south, between the Fifth and Sixth Cataracts. From there its kings and queens, called *candaces,* ruled a powerful and prosperous empire until about A.D. 200. It spread from Egypt (ruled by the Lagides, then the Romans) and probably included Kordofan and might have reached to the marshes of the Bahr el Ghazal, the Abyssinian plateau and the Red Sea. Archeological researches have shown that it declined in the third century and finally collapsed in the first half of the fourth. The events leading to its fall are obscure. The empire was probably invaded by the Nobades and then destroyed by the armies of Aksum, if in fact it was not already dead. Meroe—the name applies to both the kingdom and its civilization—disappeared as if it had fallen through a trapdoor.

The heart of the empire was the "island of Meroe," between the lower reaches of the Blue Nile and the Atbara, which was then a fertile region and the area in which the

Tombs of the pharaohs and candaces of Meroe. *Photo: Museum of Fine Arts, Boston.*

A king of Meroe. Fragment of a pillar from the temple of Isis at Meroe. About 100 B.C. Sandstone. Ny Carlsberg Glyptotek, Copenhagen.

tropical rains began. Timber and minerals were the basis of a highly developed iron metallurgy during the last centuries before the Christian era. There are innumerable archeological sites. That of Meroe proper, perhaps only a tenth of which has been excavated, lies quite near the river, some of it under hillocks filled with the treasures of the past: royal cemeteries and their pyramids, the ruins of palaces (the old Temple of the Sun, described by Herodotus, and the large Temple of Amun, once approached by an avenue of curly stone rams) and enormous slag heaps which have earned it the name of the "Birmingham of ancient Africa." There are other sites nearby: Wadban-Naga, for example, with the ruins of the residence of the *candaces*—a vast palace whose first floor, above a number of shops, included large living rooms and a comfortable, splendid, brightly colored state room; and also Naga, with its four temples, one of which is a piquant mixture of styles. Jewelry, pottery and sculpture are witnesses to a vital and varied native artistic life as well as to an appetite for luxury that was fed by imports from distant lands.

The culture of Meroe was very largely the product of Egypt, and Egyptologists find its religion, architecture and royal panoply familiar. But the long association of its Cushite sovereigns with the cults, aristocracy and conventions of Egypt cannot obscure the fact that the heritage of Meroe was maintained by an African people whose character brought innovations and changes to it: newcomers to the pantheon (an elephant-god and above all a lion-god, Apademak, who was considered to be a deity of the highest rank); the concept of transmission of power from brother to brother before it was handed on to the following generation; the evolution of Egyptian hieroglyphics into a form of writing specially adapted to the language of the country (still undeciphered today); and an original native decorative style, embellished with foreign techniques. These innovations came from a variety of sources. To its Egyptian heritage Meroe added many other influences, largely Hellenistic and Roman, but also Arab and particularly Indian (such as cotton growing and Indian stylistic elements). There are even some indications that a chain of contacts stretched from Meroe to China. Meroe ranks among the great ancient civilizations. The present state of our sources and our knowledge about Meroe are inadequate to distinguish the precise nature of its African basis or the nature and extent of its influence over the rest of the continent, but they are still sufficient to anticipate that arche-

ological research will throw fresh light on this aspect of African history. (See also *Camels; Christianity; Egypt; Gold; Iron; Nile; Sudan.*) H.M.

MIGRATIONS. Some African peoples claim to be autochthonous—that is, to have sprung from the earth or descended from heaven at the creation of the world—but most Africans take into account the migrations that brought them to the country where they are now living. The oral traditions are not always precise and often recount only the last stage of a migration or only the migration of the ruling class. They have frequently been transformed into myths in which the interest is focused on the crossing of a river, because this was a trial imposed on an ancestor which the ancestor successfully overcame, or on a marsh, because this was visible evidence of the power of a clan of blacksmiths who were able to dry it with their bellows. Traditions are sometimes altered in the course of history. For example, when the Yoruba came into contact with Islam, they discovered that their ancestor was an Arab by birth, and they made him come to the Niger, pursued by the troops of the Prophet. The historical facts have to be patiently sifted out from the oral traditions that preserve them. Comparisons with the traditions of a neighboring tribe are often enlightening. Also, the facts preserved by oral traditions can often be added to or tested by paleontological, archeological, ethnological or linguistic evidence. But this may still not lead to convincing or consistent conclusions in tracing migrations. It is not always possible to see clearly and deduce one fact from another in the distribution of objects, beliefs, institutions and the movements of peoples. After Delafosse had noticed resemblances between the Baule and Egyptian cultures, he suggested that a group of Egyptians had emigrated toward the present Ivory Coast, but the resemblances, if they are confirmed, can be explained even if no migration took place.

The inhabitation of Africa took place much earlier than was thought thirty-five years ago. Paleontological discoveries have increased, and some scholars have even suggested that Africa was the cradle of humanity. But we still cannot establish a continuous line of migratory movements from the very early inhabitation, which took place several millions of years ago, to the historical movements of the last few millenniums. The exact origins of the black peoples is still the subject of controversy, since in many places they were preceded by people of a different race and culture. The Bushmen and Hottentots seem to have occupied a large part of eastern Africa before they were driven toward the south and southwest in the course of a long migration under pressure from newcomers. Their itinerary can be traced by the rock paintings scattered along their path. This withdrawal coincided with the expansion of the Bantu in at least one direction. In western Africa, the Pygmies may have been the first inhabitants, before they were pushed into the forests of central Africa. This is indicated by the frequency of oral traditions about little men who became genii of the bush and forest, and the references to them in the stories gathered by Herodotus. The movements of the black peoples were complex: a descent toward the south during the desiccation of the Sahara (we know that it was thickly populated during the last rainy period); movements along a line from east to west in the Sudanese zone (the direction varied in different periods) and along a line running north and south in eastern Africa (the cultivators were succeeded by the pastoral people who had taken their place in the region of the Great Lakes of the Rift Valley); and the penetration of the forests toward the south, west and northwest. The characteristic pattern of these migrations is a first wave of refugees that is followed by a wave of a people who are expanding and who are creating a more vigorous culture in their place. In the course of these great movements, small groups settled in safe zones where they could defend themselves.

These were the main lines of migrations. But regional histories show more detailed segments, and in some cases the causes of migrations can be traced. An example in point is the technical and political development of the medieval Sudan. This brought a rise in the population, which in turn probably produced a similar rise in the Guinean zone immediately to the south. The expansion of this part of the country was made easier by the introduction of new cultivable plants from Asia. The movement is well illustrated in several oral traditions. The best-known migrations are those of conquering minorities who had more effective techniques for harnessing nature and organizing society than the peoples they displaced or absorbed. The Alur of Uganda, for example, have absorbed a whole series of peoples in the course of the last centuries by organizing them into technical military districts having a ritual character. Several kingdoms between Lake Chad and northern Dahomey are associated with the same conquering group, which must have founded all of them and is represented by the figure of

Kisira in traditional stories. The collapse of a center of power and the dispersal of its people is a frequent theme in these stories. Examples of such collapsed empires are the kingdom of Kitara, which was the origin of the states in the Great Lakes region; the kingdom of Dagomba, which supplied most of the states in Volta with their rulers and their aristocracies; Allada, which gave birth to the kingdoms of the Yoruba, Tado and Ife, which in turn produced the kingdoms of southern Dahomey; the Mande country, which is linked in stories to many different tribes of the Sudan (this dispersion is connected historically with the fall of the empire of Ghana, which appears in myths as an explanation for complex kinship groupings and common religious beliefs); the empire of Monomotapa, from which so many kingdoms of the Zambezi and Congo River regions were derived, may never have existed as an empire, but only as a cultural area from which a style of architecture, modeled on that of Zimbabwe, was disseminated.

When struggles of succession broke out in kingdoms, the vanquished were always led further afield after each confrontation; thus, the Ashanti came to found the kingdoms of the Anyi and Baule toward the west. The creation of new states forced the peoples who would not submit to flee or to withdraw beyond their borders; a circle of refractory tribes, for instance, surrounds the land of the Mossi. The movements were sometimes considerable, and the repercussions were widespread. The holy war of the Muslim Fulani began in northern Nigeria at the end of the eighteenth century and ended fifty years later in Cameroun; not only did it drive the Kirdi peoples into the mountains, but it also gradually pushed back other groups, who in turn struggled with one another, and the repercussions were felt as far away as Gabon and the Ubangi River region. The activities of the coastal states, in their work as intermediaries in the slave trade, had similar consequences. In the end, the violent shocks drove tribes in all directions like leaves scurrying in a wind. The creation of the Zulu kingdom by Chaka, the "Black Napoleon," at the beginning of the nineteenth century is a good illustration of this line of shock waves because it is comparatively recent and well known. Bands of people emigrated, driving back others; famines, following on the pillaging, led to other displacements; dissidents founded new states, like the Ndebele, to the north of the Zambezi River, and the Ngoni, near Lake Nyasa, after wanderings that had taken them very much further north; heterogeneous groups of refugees, having come together under unified leadership, formed themselves into a new group of people and organized a defensive position, like the Swazi and the Basuto in the south.

Not all migrations are as dramatic as this. The great migrations have often been made up of an infinite number of small movements. A group would leave in search of new lands when their own was exhausted, the pressure of population became too great or the village unit grew too large and they were forced to cultivate land too far away. Villages divided, hamlets were formed, and then new independent villages came into being. The tribal unit was organized in this way; but no sooner was it organized than an expansive front might grow and move toward a free zone or toward zones that were already inhabited, and whose people it would gradually drive out. The picture of the population was therefore constantly changing: only a persistent external danger forced a people to remain within a limited area. Adventuring toward new lands is a common theme in African oral traditions: a group is displaced, a hunter discovers a promising region and returns with the news, the group pushes on still further, living by hunting and a rudimentary agriculture until it settles down permanently. These were dangerous ventures during which the ancestor encountered obstacles and was often helped by a god or an animal, such as a crocodile, which took him across a river on its back, so that the descendants are forbidden to eat its flesh.

Ear of millet. *Photo: Viollet, Roger.*

Modern Africa has known vast migrations of a different nature. Young men go to work for a season on plantations, down mines or on building sites. If they are not actually forced to do this, the need for money draws them there. There is a population drift toward the towns. The aspect of adventure still remains, adventure in new surroundings which may be difficult and hostile. The seasonal migrations are considered in several regions as a substitute or a complement of initiation into adult responsibilities. (See also *Bambara; Bapende; Chad, Lake; Great Lakes; Hottentots; Mossi; Race; Rock Art; Sao; Slave Trade; Villages.*)   P.M.

MILLET. Millet of one kind or another is the staple food of the peoples who live in the Sahel and the savanna. The total millet production of the African continent is about 125 million tons annually. The term "millet" is used loosely to refer to several species of *Gramineae* (grasses): the sorghums or coarse millets, pearl (or bulrush) millets, the eleusines, *digitaria* and *paspalum*. The last three are generally called "fonios" in French-speaking Africa, although this term should really only be applied to *digitaria* and *paspalum*. There are other millets (panicum, setaria, echinochloa), but they are less common in Africa.

The sorghums, which are mainly African in origin, are characterized by full, more or less loosely growing panicles (ears) with coarse grain. They are rather like maize, and there are several species (*Sorghum guineense, durra, caudatum*, etc.). They require a fairly high amount of rainfall (between 20 and 47 inches) and comparatively rich clay soil. Traditional methods of farming produce a yield of more than 350 to 700 lbs. of sorghum per acre. The Massa and the Tuburi of the Logone River region, who are good examples of sorghum cultivators, grow three principal types of sorghums: the quick growing varieties, sown in June and harvested in mid-August; the semi-quick growing kinds, which are sown at the same time and harvested in October; and sorghums for transplanting, which are late— they are harvested in February and get no rain. The farmers can differentiate among about fifty different varieties, distinguished by the length of the stem and the color and shape of the panicle. Some of these are cultivated specially for the sweet pith in the stem. Some varieties are eaten raw when the grain is still soft, and they are also sometimes toasted over a fire. The most usual way of eating millet is as a cake—the "ball" that is served as a main course—accompanied by a sauce. Sorghum gruel is eaten with water or milk added. Millet beer, which is drunk at most rites of savanna peoples, generally has a sorghum base.

Pearl millets also probably originated in Africa. There are about twenty species: *Pennisetum typhoides, gambiense, pycnostachyum,* etc. The panicles are stiff, cylindrical and tight; the stems never have sweet pith. Pearl millets can be grown where the annual rainfall is only 16 to 32 inches and flourish in sandy, light or well-drained soils. Traditional methods of farming produce a yield of approximately 175 to 450 lbs. per acre. Pearl millet is the staple food for countless tribes of the dry savanna, such as the Wolof and Serer in Senegal and the Hausa of Niger. It is eaten as a cake or in a gruel but never raw or toasted. When sorghums and pearl millets are grown in the same area, they never compete for space because they require different types of soil.

Eleusine (*Eleusine coracana*) is a secondary cereal that can be grown in poor soil and where there is low rainfall. It is cultivated in the savanna areas in central and eastern Africa. Despite its low yield it is valued because it can be harvested early.

The fonios (*digitaria* and *paspalum*), with their tiny grain, are favored for the same reason. They have an important place in the rites of the Dogon and Bambara of the central Sudan area.

Millets supply most of the calories in the diets of the savanna populations. They have a carbohydrate content of about 60 percent. The sorghums and pearl millets have a protein value of about 11 percent; the eleusines and fonios about 6 percent. Millets contain vitamins B_1, the PP factor and iron, and although they are poor in vitamins A and C, their protein content makes them more satisfactory as staple foods than tubers. (See also *Agriculture; Bambara; Beverages; Birds; Diet; Dogon; Dreams; Granaries; Massa; Mussoi.*)   I.G.

MONOMOTAPA. When the Portuguese rounded the Cape of Good Hope in 1498, they tried to gain control of the trade in gold, ivory and slaves, which had attracted Oriental merchants to the east coast of Africa since time immemorial. After taking possession of Sofala at the beginning of the sixteenth century, they heard of a vast empire in the interior, the *regnum Monomotapae,* stretching, if the most enthusiastic accounts are to be believed, from the Cape to the Zambezi River, and whose sovereign, the *monomotapa,* possessed fabulous riches. The extent of the kingdom has never been ascertained precisely, and in different accounts its area has varied so much that

some modern historians have relegated the *monomotapas,* their land and subjects to the realm of fantasy. But nothing justifies this scepticism. The word "monomotapa" has been variously interpreted. Sometimes it is translated "Master of the water elephants"; the hippopotamus is still considered a sacred animal by the Vakaranga of Rhodesia, whose ruler is known as a *mwenemutapa.* When the Portuguese arrived, the capital of the kingdom was situated in the far north of the Rhodesian plateau, whose escarpment towers more than 3,000 feet above the Zambezi Valley. It was about 220 miles north of the great gold-bearing region of the plateau and 310 miles from the stone ruins of Zimbabwe. According to the oral traditions of the Vakaranga, the tribe came from the south around the middle of the fifteenth century, during the dynasty of the Monomotapas, in search of salt. It seems likely then that the Monomotapas were the successors to the dynasty of the kings of Zimbabwe, whose first buildings are now dated by the archeologists as being from the eleventh century. From their new residence, the Monomotapas dominated the Zambezi Valley over an area extending more than 600 miles from the mouth of the river. Their authority, exercised either directly or indirectly, extended over the northern and eastern part of the Rhodesian plateau and the southern part of Mozambique between the Zambezi and Limpopo Rivers. All control of the region that they had abandoned passed out of their hands. Nevertheless, the Portuguese did not gain access to it; rather, a new dynasty took possession of it and traded with the foreigners, not directly but through the markets established on the lands of the Monomotapas.

The first contacts of the Portuguese were with the vassals of the Monomotapa in the hinterland of Sofala. Next, they took possession, or took over from the Arab or Swahili merchants, the river ports of Sena and Tete in the territory of the Monomotapas. With Tete occupied in 1560, the Portuguese were only five days' march from the capital. The first of them to reach it was a missionary, who baptized the Monomotapa but was immediately put to death at the instigation of the king's Muslim counsellors. In the following years, the power of the Monomotapa gradually disintegrated with a series of rebellions, which led the ruler to recognize the king of Portugal as his overlord, a step that precipitated the decline of his kingdom. On the one hand, his power over the lower reaches of the Zambezi River was destroyed by the erection of Portuguese forts, which acted as storage places for gold

Mossi. Upper Volta. *Photo: Hoa-Qui.*

and slaves, and he became hardly more than a puppet baptized with a Portuguese name by the Dominicans; and, on the other hand, his vassals in the interior ceased, one after the other, to recognize his authority. By the end of the sixteenth century, the Vakaranga and their Portuguese masters had been chased from the plateau and only controlled a strip of valley between Tete and Zumbo. But the conquerors of the Monomotapas were vanquished themselves by the great invasion of Zulu warriors, who appeared at the beginning of the nineteenth century, occupied all the country and established themselves as masters. (See also *Gold, Migrations; Sacrifice; Savanna.*)   D.P.

MOSSI. According to native traditions, at the beginning of the eleventh century, the king of Gambaga, in the north of present-day Ghana, came back victorious from several raiding expeditions on his neighbors and advanced toward the north as far as the region of Tenkodogo. His daughter, who commanded a corps in the army, wandered away from the camp one day and into the thick forest, where she met a hunter. From their union a child was born; he was called Ouidiraogo, meaning "stallion" in Mossi, in memory of the steed who had led his mother to the hunter. Later on, Ouidiraogo subdued the country of Tenkodogo and then the

neighboring territories, whose inhabitants were either driven out or absorbed.

These were the legendary beginnings of the huge Mossi group, made up of the union of native river dwellers in the upper reaches of the Black and White Volta Rivers with the "Reds" who had ridden their horses from the east and northeast, from the environs of Lake Chad. These newcomers may have fled from the Berber invasions of the tenth century, from which the Hausa states arose. Much more numerous than the original inhabitants, the newcomers mixed with them, eventually spoke their language and were converted to their religion. Only a few groups managed to escape from the domination of the conquering horsemen and took refuge in the marshes and escarpments, like the Dogon in the Bandiagara Escarpment. The raids continued, and in the fourteenth and fifteenth centuries the rich cities of the Niger River region were plundered several times by bands of horsemen from the south; the chronicles record the sack of Timbuktu in 1333. About 1480, an expedition advanced as far as Oualata on the border of the desert, but it was repulsed by the Songhai, who prevented further penetration northward. The peoples and territories, which had been subjugated and immediately brought into the central organization, formed the three large Mossi states of Ouagadougou, Yatenga and Fada-n-Gourma. The Mossi kings never controlled the great markets of the north, but they certainly took their share of the traffic in slaves, gold and kola nuts. Each state comprised tributary provinces administered by relatives of the emperor, who allowed them complete freedom of action and only demanded an annual tribute and military contingents if the need arose. The Mossi states, which were well governed and hostile to Islam escaped the general chaos following the Moroccan invasion. When the Europeans arrived at the end of the nineteenth century, they were still governed by the same dynasty and occupied almost the same territories as when they were founded five centuries earlier.

This remarkable continuity was mainly owing to the cult of ancestors. The *Mogho naba* is the direct descendant of the first rulers and their living image. Because of this, he is treated as a demi-god: his bare feet are never permitted to touch the ground, for they would burn it like the sun, and he is isolated by strict social rules. His subjects are also incarnations of their ancestors, and they accept their master in the same way as the first inhabitants accepted the newcomers and the government they imposed. All the descendants of the *Mogho naba* enjoy considerable privileges on account of their birth. To this day, the *Mogho naba* lives in the capital of Ouagadougou. Five high-ranking officials attend him: the chief of the eunuchs, the chief of the cavalry, the chief of the infantry, the chief of the royal tombs and the palace steward, each of whom governs a province. At the death of the *Mogho naba,* there is an interregnum and complete anarchy, but it only lasts a short time. An electoral college, comprised of four high-ranking officials, selects a successor fairly quickly. The electoral college's freedom of choice is limited by the obligation to choose the new king from among the direct descendants of the first *Mogho naba.* As soon as the college is unanimous in its choice of a name, it summons the warriors, who range themselves around the new master.

This strongly established state control is a contrast to the anarchy of the western savanna, just as the sparse population is a contrast to the density of the Mossi territories. Mossi workers are common in the Ivory Coast and Ghana, where they are to be found on the plantations, the mines and in the towns. They stay long enough to save the indispensable money for a marriage compensation, sometimes longer, but they seldom give up all idea of returning to their native land. Their political organization and the density of their population isolate the Mossi from their immediate neighbors but give them an affinity with an eastern bloc of organized civilization extending to northern Nigeria. This, as well as other features, would explain the armor of matelassé cotton worn by the king's honor guard, which is like that which Barth originally pointed out at the court of the sultan of Kano; it is probably the final transformation of the armor of the late Roman Empire. (See also *Birds; Clothing; Eunuchs; Household Furnishings; Mali; Royalty; Scarification; Sudan; Weapons.*) D.P.

MOTTOES. A motto is a stereotyped phrase—often elliptical, poetic or enigmatic—that is intended to furnish the essential identification of an individual, a group, a supernatural being or even an object and to assert its qualities to the world. An African often has several mottoes: one that is hereditary and indicates his clan or lineage; one given at his birth or when he was named (it may have a connection with the meaning of his name); sometimes one or several others given during the course of initiations or to mark an outstanding event or notable feat (for example, the *isibongo*—literally "motto" or "praise name"—given to Zulu military regiments). In form, these mottoes resemble proverbs or riddles. However, they should not be confused with war-cries, which often borrow elements from true mottoes. Most mottoes correspond to characteristic musical themes, which are sorts of signature tunes of the owners of the mottoes; in the Hausa and Songhai cults of possession by spirits (*bori*) and in those of the Benin coast, for example, the mottoes of the genii are played on drums to summon them to a ceremony. In bush telegraph, the "address" and "signature" of the recipient and sender are communicated in drum language, which reproduces the characteristic tones of their spoken or sung mottoes. Mottoes are sometimes symbolized graphically or in the form of a drawing or sculpture; for example, in the frescoes, tapestries and bas-reliefs of Abomey (the inland capital of Dahomey), the *recados* of the Benin coast, the *mindem* (engraved marks) of the Fang, and some details of the royal sculptures of the Bakuba and Baluba of Zaire. They may also be symbolized by an ordinary object or an animal, especially one connected with a taboo suggested in the motto. The ceremonial recital of mottoes plays an important role in social etiquette and in some rites, particularly royal rites. The purpose of the recital is to praise the bearer of the motto and increase his power. A motto can also be used as a means of respecting the prohibition against mentioning the royal name. (See also *Appliqué Work; Calabashes; Languages, Secret; Literature, Oral; Names; Proverbs; Rattles; Recados.*) P.A.

MPONGWE. The strange white-faced masks of the Mpongwe have spread the name of the tribe far beyond the limited circle of African ethnologists. These masks appeal to Westerners as do the bronze heads from Ife, and for the same reasons: the vision of the artist is fundamentally realistic (the natural proportions are preserved) and they idealize facial features (the faces are smooth and the expressions serene). They do not make us feel that we are in the presence of the unfamiliar; they could be placed in the artistic tradition that was generally accepted in the West from the Renaissance to the nineteenth century. The hair arranged in a symmetrical crest and painted black, the small mouth with red lips, the slit eyes and the coating of white over the face in the Mpongwe masks bear a very close resemblance to some masks of the Japanese theater, to the "classical" type that appeals to Westerners. A theory has even been put forward that the Mpongwe imitated a specimen from the Far East that may have arrived accidentally in the Gabon forests.

Mpongwe mask. Gabon.
Painted wood. *Photo:
Sougez.*

This is obviously not impossible, but a hypothesis corresponding so closely to a constant assumption of Western thought has to be treated with the greatest caution; it assumes, in fact, that there is an external origin for every element of African culture that does not seem to conform to the notion it has formed of African civilizations. Far from being an alien importation, these masks are an integral part of traditional institutions and beliefs; they are worn by the members of a secret society and are invested by the spirits of the dead. The Mpongwe are farmers who live in clearings of the equatorial forests, not far from the Atlantic coast, in Gabon. Although the first white masks were found among this tribe, we now realize that the area of their distribution is far more extensive than the territory of the Mpongwe. Masks of the Mpongwe style are made by other tribes in the forest: the Masango, Eshira and Baloumbo. The name "Baloumbo" is sometimes also applied to the Mpongwe and Eshira. J.M.

MUSIC. Music and dance were the first, and for a long time the only, African arts to attract the attention of travelers and historians. While Negro sculpture was not discovered, or at any rate not appreciated, before the end of the nineteenth century, Arab, European and even Chinese chroniclers mentioned African musical instruments as early as the Middle Ages and remarked that slaves of African origin were well known for their musical talents. The first muezzin designated by the Prophet to call the faithful to prayer was said to be a former Abyssinian slave called Bilal. But much earlier, in the classical period, blacks were employed as musicians and, according to an emblem on a Greek shield, one of them was a trumpet player. In more recent times we know that blacks were used in the seventeenth and eighteenth centuries as kettle drummers in military bands in Germany, France and England. By this time there were an increasing number of descriptions of music of Africa, the islands off America and the American coast. Even before the nineteenth century, some forty travel books in which the subject of black African music was mentioned had been published, and some of their information about types and names of instruments, styles of singing and dance forms has since been confirmed. Undoubtedly, this interest in African music was related to the contemporary popularity of exotic things and ideas, which was evident in French ballet and opera. However, treatises by travelers in Africa, who were surprised by such intense passion for music and dancing, do not abound in picturesque descriptions and mainly concentrate on the order of events at the few ceremonies they attended.

Whatever faults were ascribed to black Africans by early visitors, one quality was appreciated, namely the "trouble" they took to "learn" to sing and dance. Savage though it seemed, black African music evidently obeyed rules that required training. Early writers referred to a course of instruction of some kind. In the seventeenth century, they mentioned houses set apart or lonely places in the forest serving as training schools that were attended by children of either sex. These are probably allusions to initiation rituals, some of which still include, in addition to physical ordeals, long exercises in memorizing music, dances and even part songs. No one was surprised by the absence of notation. Music had been printed for more than a century, and no one could imagine that any system of notation other than the European one could exist, especially since no writing of any kind was known to exist in black Africa. Nevertheless, it was said that musical instruments might be capable of transmitting and receiving messages. These are the first allusions to language based on differences of pitch or length of notes. At a time when the manufacture of instruments was making such progress in Europe, the ingenuity that Africans employed in making theirs aroused interest. Of all African objects, they are about the only ones described in detail by travelers and reproduced in their works. The xylophone particularly fascinated them, if

Court musicians. Gao, Niger.
Photo: Hoa-Qui.

only because it bore a resemblance in looks and sound to the clavichord or organ.

In the nineteenth and twentieth centuries, the great expeditions into the interior, world's fairs and the invention of the gramophone extended the knowledge of African music. The exploration, for example, of the area around Lake Chad, the upper Congo basin and, further east, the Great Lakes (the journeys of Clapperton, Burton, Schweinfurth, Dybowski, Decorse, Csekanowski, etc.) brought to light hitherto unknown instruments as well as the most primitive sounds or noises. Schweinfurth's description of immense choirs accompanied by trumpets, drums, rattles, and bells, which he heard among the Bongo about 1870, will always remain one of the most vivid passages in Africanist literature. The songs of boatmen are mentioned several times, and some were even noted down. They acquired such renown that a group of Fang were sent to Paris for the exposition of 1889, so that they could perform them on the Seine and musicologists could satisfy themselves of the existence of vocal polyphony, which travelers had been reporting from black Africa for almost a century. For the next exposition, in 1900, the Anthropological Society of Paris made recordings of non-European music, and more than fifty Senegalese, Fulani, Dahoman and Madagascan songs were transferred to its cylinders. In 1906 recordings began to be made in Africa itself (in Madagascar, Tanganyika, Rwanda, Cameroun), and the cylinders were deposited in

Trumpet player from Benin. Nigeria. Bronze. *Photo: Louis Carré.*

Mussoi woman and child.
Chad. *Photo: Pierre Ichac.*

matter how limited they may be. Similarly, in devising musical variations, the African is outstanding among all "primitive" peoples for the endless tiny changes he can make on a melodic line or a rhythmic pattern. His ear is exceptionally sensitive to the subtlest harmonies, and he draws a greater variety of tones from combinations of instruments and voices than does the European or Asian musician. (See also *Bells; Bows, Musical; Bull-roarers; Dance; Drum Language; Drums; Flutes and Whistles; Griots; Harps; Horns and Trumpets; Poetry; Rattles; Sistra; Song; Theater; Thumb Pianos; Xylophones; Zithers.*)   A.S.

MUSSOI. The Mussoi, often called "Banana Hoho," live about 185 miles south of Fort Lamy, in an area bordered by the Fianga Lakes in the north, the Logone River in the east and 9° North Latitude in the south. Their population is 97,000, if the 17,000 Marba, who are closely associated with them, are counted. Apart from a small canton of 6,000 people in Cameroun, the whole group lives in the Republic of Chad. Their language differs little from that spoken by the Massa. They are called "Hoho" because every man has a signature tune and mottoes that can be sung and be played on a whistle.

The Mussoi are excellent farmers and produce 10 percent of the cotton in Chad. Most crops are grown along ridges. The most common are sorghum, including some varieties that call for transplanting, millet, eleusine and rice. Peanuts, peas, beans, sesame and cucumbers cover vast areas. Fishing is of only minor interest to the Mussoi. They do a great deal of raising of small animals, but have hardly any cattle. They breed small horses (with withers of only 4 feet), called Kirdi horses or *lakas,* which are very sturdy and were to be found, prior to the Fulani invasions, even in the mountains of northern Cameroun. Marriage compensation is calculated in horses. Hunting horses are bred carefully. The way in which they are mounted and ridden (without saddle or stirrups), their harnesses, their painted accessories for special occasions and the weapons used by their riders are all unique features of Mussoi culture. The most famous horses are buried and mourned like men. Cotton growing has hastened the changeover of the economy into a monetary system, and money has tended to replace goats, horses, packets of small hoes and balls of iron, which were traditionally used for marriage compensations.

Patrilineal lineages live on clearly marked out territorial areas and form the main

the phonographic archives that Carl Stumpf had founded in Berlin. In 1908, some of the songs (Madagascan, Wanyamwezi, Wassukuma, Bahutu, Batusi, and Batwa) were transcribed and analyzed by Erich von Hornbestel, which were the first studies ever made of African music. Subsequently, direct recordings on records and later on tape made possible the much clearer reproduction of voices and truer tonal quality.

Research on and documentation of African music have gone on steadily ever since an ivory trumpet from Benin, an iron double bell and a multiple bow were reproduced in Michael Praetorius's *Syntagma Musicum,* published in the seventeenth century. Modern studies have demonstrated the musical capabilities of black Africans, which cannot be measured by the quality of the materials used, the degree of refinement of their instruments or the complexity of the sounds employed. The mistake made by some theoreticians, both musicologists and sociologists, has been to try to compare the resources available to African music with those of the more sophisticated cultures of Europe and Asia without taking into consideration the effects that are produced with the available resources. The black musician makes the most of the resources of his instrument no traditional socio-political units. Filiation is patrilineal and residence patrilocal. The rules for marrying are simple. A man is forbidden to marry a woman from his own lineage or from the extended family to which his mother belongs. When the head of a family dies, his wives marry his younger brothers, his sons who have a different mother or the sons of his brothers.

A traditional politico-religious authority coexists with that which is conferred on the chiefs of cantons and villages by the central government. The traditional authority is vested in the land chief, who is responsible for the soil and is in charge of performing sacrifices to the supernatural powers on behalf of the individuals living on the land he controls. He is generally helped by the elders who belong to the lineage of the founder-ancestor of the first village. Sacrificers, generally recruited from among his uterine nephews, help him with his duties. The technical operations connected with the main crops and with communal hunting and fishing are celebrated with complicated rituals. The Mussoi use a technique of divination that is rather similar to that of the Massa. Possession by spirits plays an important role in the social and religious life of the community. Possessed persons, rigged out with jewelry, finery and weapons, are organized into societies under the authority of a chief, who is an important figure in traditional communities. Young people undergo an initiation that is less secret than that of their Massa and Sara neighbors. Warrior qualities are admired, and vendettas stained the country with blood only fifty years ago. Even today, revenge and suicide are not uncommon.

Mussoi dancers wear feather headdresses and crests decorated with animal horns and the beaks of birds, belts decorated with cowrie shells, and play calabash rattles, which are also used at funerals. The funerals of eminent figures are accompanied by elaborate feasts. Animals and other riches change hands while the tomb, which is covered with dozens of tree trunks painted red, is being constructed. The Mussoi have an extensive oral literature. The most characteristic forms are stories, which are often gargantuan, and songs accompanied by guitar. (See also *Birds; Diet; Kirdi; Meals; Rain.*)   I.G.

MYTHS. Myths are the language of tradition; according to black African conceptions, they give speech its content and effectiveness. In the body of knowledge transmitted orally, they are the principal elements, along with stories, legends and pseudo-historical lore, from which myths cannot always be clearly distinguished. In the hierarchy of indigenous theories, they hold a position of supreme importance, for they contribute to the order of things and men. They constitute a sort of inviolable code, connected with the origins of the world and the beginnings of human endeavor, that preserves societies and their works from the constant threat of a return to chaos. Their invocation and recital require ritual and ceremony, which are observed with strict discipline by everyone who contributes to or is present at their performance.

Mythical thought and knowledge do not lend themselves to summary analysis. The body of myths can be understood on different levels, and each level requires a very different degree of knowledge. The most esoteric "speech" is possessed by only a minority of the very privileged, for whom it is the foundation of their power and status. At another level, myths are a composite of very universal knowledge. They generally embrace a theory of the universe and the creation (a cosmogony and a cosmology), manipulated history, knowledge gained from experience and ideological themes that justify accepted ideas and the existing order. In so-called "archaic" societies, myths are intellectual tools and also stimulators of religious and artistic activity.

The importance of the mythical and symbolic world has been recognized by ethnologists; some of them go so far as to regard African societies and cultures as the material expression of mythical and symbolic concepts. This approach often confers on indigenous theory expressed in myths the ability to explain everything that occurred in the past; it provides constant inducement to discover other kinds of knowledge contained in myths.

The myths of the Dogon of Mali have been studied more thoroughly than those of any other African people. For the Dogon, myths are "words of wisdom" and articles of faith. They can only be revealed gradually and are taught mainly during the process of initiation by means of a secret language. These esoteric versions of the myths, which are known only by initiates, have poetic form; their aim is not so much to explain as to arouse emotion and impart strength. In contrast, the versions of myths told in the common language for general information, provide only very superficial knowledge. They are very well known and constitute a sort of minimum fund of knowledge.

Dogon mythology is mainly concerned with the drama of creation. The principal figures are: the god of creation and father of creatures, Amma; the mother, made pregnant by the "word" of Amma and symbolized by the "egg of the world"; the first created beings, androgynous twins, one of whom revolted against the authority of his father while the other was a savior who restored the order disturbed by the behavior of his brother. The appearance of men, animals and plants in the universe was connected with this restoration of order. The narrative then explains how speech and techniques were acquired, how death came into the world, how the first national ritual was established, and so on. It offers a general conception of the world and a dynamic interpretation of social order, laying due importance on the conflict of opposing forces. Dogon theory does not make a clearcut distinction between mythical knowledge, retained in the memories of people who might be called men-books, and other expressions of oral tradition. The latter are regarded as translations of some myths, which are simplified and use different symbolism. Every fictional element in the prose narratives of the Dogon has, in some way, its correspondence in the mythical corpus.

Myths never remain in a fixed form. They are subjected to historical vicissitudes, which produce variations in the plot and commentary around the immutable themes. Fresh material can be added from the experiences of the social group, and, to a certain extent, it reflects that experience. This is why mythographers try to classify myths or sequences having a cosmological, divine, heroic, semi-historical or technological character; considered in this way, myths are a breakdown of knowledge as a whole into its constitutive elements. Mythical stories are all stories of beginnings: the creation of the universe, the separation of the creator god from his creatures, the appearance of death and disease, the invention of techniques and tools, the birth of the founder-heroes of kingdoms and empires and the establishment of the great rites. Social practices were justified and "sanctified" by this reference to primordial times.

Myths are also vehicles for conveying knowledge concerning human destiny and an implicit philosophy. The figure of death appears in black African mythologies in various guises. It is sometimes identified with the moon, condemned to disappear gradually each time it appears again, like the generations of man (in Hottentot mythology); or with a chameleon which became a divine messenger (in the mythology of the Bakamba of Kenya); or with a monstrous giant which a young hero fights in vain (in the mythology of the Krachi of Ghana); or with a woman considered as essentially ambiguous, "giver of life and giver of death" (in Dogon mythology). All these "explanations" of death are associated with the interaction of the forces of change and disorder. They prescribe the procedures for the renewal of the society and for the attainment of real life (the "life everlasting" as the Bakongo call it) by individuals.

In traditional societies with a political organization, myths help to reinforce the ruler's power and guarantee the union of political power and the sacred by binding authority to royal rituals. The founder-kings belong to the periods of the origins of their peoples—prior to chronology—and are culture-heroes. According to the Baganda of Uganda, Kintu had to accomplish a number of celestial exploits before he could marry the daughter of the "King of the Heavens" and qualify as the first king and builder of Buganda. According to the ancient Rwanda myth of the origins of the world, Kigwa was born in the heavens and fell onto the earth; his name means "the fallen." Kigwa's descent among men was accompanied by that of his brother and his sister, whose incestuous union was the source of the royal line and the aristocrat clans. The newcomers brought the first elements of civilization with them: fire, iron, a forge and domestic animals, notably horned cattle. They established their authority, drew up the rules for personal dependence and began the royal genealogy with names of symbolic figures who preceded the historical kings. Myth and historical tradition overlap in a narrative centered on three kings with symbolic traits: the culture-hero, the founder and the conqueror. Thus, one can see that mythical narrative, by means of certain sequences, can be allied with political ideology; it justifies, legitimizes and makes holy the powers and privileges of their possessors. To do this, it turns back to the early days of the group, plunges into the depths of history and becomes homologous with what it sets up in the domain of personal destinies. (See also *Blacksmiths; Chad, Lake; Circumcision; Death; Divination; Divinities; Dogon; Gods; Heaven; Heroes; Incest; Legends; Literature, Oral; Masks; Religion; Senufo; Stories; Work; Yoruba.*)　　　　G.B.

NAMES. The similarity between the Latin words for "name" and "divinity" (*nomen* and *numen*) can be paralleled in a number of African languages (Fang: *jwi* and *ijwi,* for example). In Africa, a name is much more than a simple device to distinguish and identify an individual; it is a primordial element of his individuality and often its mainstay. In various languages, the word for "name" may also mean "personality," "authority," "character" or "social reputation." The selection of a child's name is very rarely left to his parents. A number of factors can affect the choice: an event concomitant with the child's birth or conception, such as an accident, omen, or dream; recourse to divination, especially when the child is believed to be a reincarnation of an ancestor; or the social position and family of the individual. The Akan and Ewe (of Ghana and Togo) have extremely complex names that indicate their sex, day of birth, rank in the family, lineage and dedication to a genius or the spirit of an ancestor, as well as, in many cases, nicknames and "greeting names," which are used mainly in summonses delivered by drum. Throughout the western Sudan, the following combination is often found: Arab (Muslim) or European (lay or Christian) name, rank name, clan name (Bambara: *dyamu*), surname. Among the eastern Bantu a common combination is: a personal name, the personal name of the head of the family and a complimentary name.

There is space here to give only a brief idea of the variety and significance of names. A provisional name is given to a child and is used until he receives his proper name, which may not be until he is initiated as an adolescent. There is a distinction between public names, which are known to everyone, and secret "real names," which are only known to a few intimates or to the co-initiates of a secret or ritual society. Pejorative names (Mary-lie-down-there; Little Swine) are given to avert misfortune or the hostility of supernatural enemies. Names are changed during the rites of passage from one age group to another or at the time of a change in social status (the title names of the Yoruba and of the dignitaries of the Kotokoli, for example); they are also changed to avert evil after a continuous series of misfortunes. Curious taboos concerning African names include the prohibition against a sovereign's name being pronounced by his subjects (the southern Bantu practice of *hlonipha*) or the name of parents-in-law being pronounced by a woman (eastern Bantu, Basa of Cameroun). Among some tribes, there is a relationship resembling kinship between bearers of the same name. There is nothing exceptional about the fact that considerable magical importance is attached to names, since many other African words are treated in the same way. For example, popular etymology is frequently used to explain the world and describe esoteric relationships between various forces in its creation. (See also *Drum Language; Fauna; Fulani; Griots; Mottoes; Twins.*)   P.A.

NEGRILLOS. See *Pygmies.*

NEGRITUDE. The poet Aimé Césaire coined the word "negritude" sometime during the years 1932-34, using it in his work to proudly affirm that he was a member of the black race: "Negritude is not a tower or a cathedral. It strikes deep into the red flesh of the soil. . . ." Léopold Sédar Senghor also coined the word at about the same time. He defined it in the following terms: "Negritude is the sum total of cultural, economic, social and political values that characterize black people." Jean-Paul Sartre gave the concept of negritude philosophical status in a study entitled "Orphée noir" ("Black Orpheus," 1948), pointing out that negritude has political significance—it is a weapon against colonial domination—and literary bearing —it infects the African poet so that he identifies himself with his people. Negritude has its exegetists (Thomas Melone, L.-V. Thomas) and its critics who denounce it as "ideological charlatanry." Its most tireless advocate is still Senghor (see his work *Liberté I*). He explains it, justifies and tries to communicate it as if it were a religious faith. For him, negritude is not simply a tool for creating a cultural revival and turning Africans into producers rather than just "consumers of civilization." Rather, it has a permanent value as an expression of the inner being of the black man and gives him an aim in the world today. It is an ontology, in so far as it is a way of thinking, and a millennialism, in so far as it is a way of behaving. The first World Festival of Black Arts, held at Dakar in April 1966, was an expression of negritude, of shared black African values. (See also *Literature, Written; Pan-Africanism.*)   G.B.

NGERE. The Ngere (Kra in Liberia), Wobe and Niabua are tribes living along or near the Cavally River in the southwestern part of the Ivory Coast. They are the southern neighbors of the Dan, whose social institutions and way of life appear at first sight to be almost identical. However, the Dan come from the savanna, whereas the Ngere are forest people. The difference becomes clear in the masks of the two groups, whose styles are diametrically opposed. The Dan mask tends to display a purified realism, whereas the Ngere sculptor distorts the natural features: hemispheric forehead, prominent cheeks protruding from a vertical surface

beneath which there may be curved boar tusks, dilated nostrils, a mouth that is either "cubist" or "realistic" in style. The artist, in his search for a particular expression, stresses what he thinks is the most typical feature and does not hesitate to exaggerate it, even to the extent of repeating the same part of a face two or three times, whether forehead, eyes, mouth, nose or cheeks. Contrasting volumes and the interplay of light and shadow on the salient features increase the impression of terror. The grotesque and extravagant Ngere mask is the intimation of another world. The expression of the Ngere mask is in striking contrast with the classicism of the Dan. However, as a result of contacts between these neighboring tribes, some of the differences of style within the two groups can be classed as local variations. Experts have succeeded in identifying certain regional subdivisions of the basic Dan and Ngere styles, which blend elements derived from both basic styles. But geography is not the only explanation for similarities and differences of style. No matter what his tribal origin, an artist is free to follow his inspiration, and each of his works is an original creation. There is at least one known sculptor whose output included as many "Dan" as "Ngere" masks. (See also *Dan; Societies, Secret.*)　　　D.P.

NILE. Among the marvelous relics from the tomb of Tutankhamen now in the Cairo Museum is a fine carved ivory headrest that presents a geographical and metaphysical picture of Egypt. In the center is a kneeling god who supports the curved rest, representing the sky, with his head and raised hands. This is the primordial gesture of the creation of the world; it was made by Shu, the divine incarnation of the atmosphere, when he finally separated the closely united couple Nut (the Sky) and Geb (the Earth). On either side of the kneeling god are stretched-out lions, which are guardians and symbols of the "two horizons": on the right, guarding the East, is the symbol of the Arabian desert, where the sun rises each morning: this is Day, Tomorrow, Good; on the left, guarding the West, is its opposite, the lion of the Libyan desert, who devours the sun every evening and represents Night, Yesterday, Evil. Between the knees of the god and, like him, turned toward the south—the source of the Nile—is the "Black Earth" of the Nile Valley, the axis of the world.

It is nearly 2,500 years since Herodotus described Egypt as "a gift of the Nile." The phrase has become a commonplace with the passing of time. It expresses the unquestionable truth that no other river in the world has so just a claim as the Nile to be the creator of a civilization—not even its rivals in Mesopotamia, the Euphrates and the Tigris, which throughout their history were in close proximity to the turbulent arena of nomadic conquerors. The Nile, flowing through the desert, brought down, along with water from the water reserves of equatorial Africa and Ethiopia, not only the incentive and the means for building a civilization, but also the ingredients needed to make it endure. Once the Old Kingdom had been established, Egypt remained unchanged for 3,500 years, from the time of the beginning of writing to the decline of Rome—it is, in fact, a world record. And today we are uncovering traces of its prodigious discoveries, the offspring of the harsh climate and human ingenuity, which form the bases for our knowledge, our technical skills, our morality and our arts.

The history of Egyptian civilization began in the Sahara, when the area was still habitable and the home of hunters armed with weapons of chipped stone. A Nile River that flowed more swiftly than the one we know today swept over and later hollowed out the valley, giving it its present shape. Whenever the country went through a particularly dry period, human life returned to the marshy lands bordering the river. The Faiyum Depression, the valley and the newly formed Nile Delta were like a marvelously placed trap, situated at the point of convergence of human currents from the upper Nile, Libya, Palestinian Asia and, perhaps, Mesopotamia, since roads were also open in that direction. Once men, with their varying aptitudes, were gathered in this trap, the desert closed in on them, and they were condemned to a settled life and to progress. A major revolution had already taken place among them, in that the gathering of wild grasses (*Gramineae*) was replaced by the cultivation of wheat. Animal husbandry techniques had been added to hunting and had been developed so far during the Old Kingdom that the wildest and least tractable of herbivora, like the oryx and ibex, were treated as domesticated animals. These early Egyptians also developed a virtuosity in working stone that remained unrivaled, except perhaps in China and pre-Columbian America. As a result, in later years, even in the midst of the Age of Metals and until the beginning of the Christian era, Egyptian civilization seemed like a glorification of the Neolithic Age. In Tutankhamen's tomb, daggers of bronze, gold and iron lay side by side with flint knives; and arrowheads of bronze, ivory and glass lay beside sickles with flint teeth. Around 2,000 B.C., the Egyptians produced a profusion of

Map of the Nile from the French edition of *Description de l'Afrique, Tierce Partie du Monde,* by Leo Africanus (Lyon, 1556).

elegantly shaped vases of polished stone—perfectly fashioned in a variety of materials ranging from alabaster to porphyry, from basalt to rock crystal—that were the luxurious counterparts of ordinary pottery. It was with stone tools, too, that the Egyptians excavated limestone from the quarries at Tura, granite from the First Cataract and diorite from Nubia (already worked in the time of Cheops), sculpted temples and statues, polished sarcophagi until they looked like sheets of steel, trimmed the faces of obelisks and engraved them with hieroglyphics as perfectly incised as medals, thus posing, for future generations, technical problems which are still far from having been solved.

From the beginning, Egyptian culture presented a dual personality in which archaic attitudes were coupled with a remarkable concern for perfection and progress. Their religious and funerary practices belonged to the realm of totemism and magic. Animal worship was combined with incantatory formulas. The pharaoh, who was the first divine king in the history of Africa (which has seen many since and even knows them today), had to divest himself of the old man in him and renew his vital forces several times during the course of his reign, during the festival of Sed. This festival was probably a rite substituted for an older form of ritual killing which is known to have lasted into the last century among the Shilluk of the upper Nile. The innumerable centers of civilization scattered along the banks of the Nile during the predynastic period endowed Egypt with countless divinities and a multitude of cosmogonies. Bas-reliefs and papyrus illustrations suggest that masked priests acted the parts of the gods. The coronation ceremonies preserved traces of rites whose meanings may have been lost by the time of the Old Kingdom. Yet it was this need to preserve the legacy of Africa and Asia from the earliest times that was the justification for every kind of progress. For thousands of years on end, Egypt strove to regain the original perfection, both material and spiritual, that existed in the "time of the gods." The goddess Maat, whose weight was balanced in the scales of Judgment against the hearts of the dead, was not only the dispenser of Truth and Justice but also of Exactitude and Perfection. Although popular superstitions were rife in the Late Period, Pythagorus and, it is said, Plato visited the temples to learn their wisdom, and it was the Egyptians of this period who spread the conceptions of immortality of the soul and moral purity throughout the Mediterranean world, thereby preparing it for Christianity. It was in Egypt, at the beginning of the third millennium B.C., that a genius, the Vizier Imhotep, was the first person in the world to develop the techniques of stone architecture, employing it for the famous Step Pyramid of Zoser and his funerary temple. Three-quarters of a century later, the unknown builders of the Great Pyramid of Cheops, which was called "the Dazzling" because of its polished limestone facing, showed that they had acquired an even greater architectural mastery. The mass of straight-edged stones was a celestial stairway glinting in the sun's rays and rising higher than the second platform of the Eiffel Tower. There is only an error of 2 to 5 minutes (1/30 to 1/12 of a degree) in the orientation of the sides of the square base toward the four cardinal points of the compass; the greatest discrepancy between the shortest and longest of these sides is not more than 8 inches on a measurement of 70 feet; and the most accurate right angle only diverges by 2 seconds from 90 degrees, that is, an error of 1/800 of a degree. We have already entered the modern world.

The Egyptians were molded by the beneficent Nile; it provided them with the framework and rhythm of their lives. From the beginning of time, they only knew three seasons: winter, summer and the Nile. (It would be impossible to underestimate the revolution brought about by the Aswan High Dam, which controls the river so that it flows constantly, thus making the Nile season last all year round.) The Nile was also the source of a political unity that is still very marked in our day. It was indirectly responsible 5,000 years ago for the building of a centralized state and one of the oldest administrative organizations in history. The scribe, the bureaucrat and the tax-collector, who are elements of the modern state, came into existence under the divine kings as a result of the need to control flooding, to make a property boundary survey, to channel the water and to maintain the first irrigation canals. The same requirements led to the invention of the calendar (a day and a night of 12 hours, a year of 365¼ days—but the Egyptians forgot to invent the leap year). The Egyptian word for "year" was written exactly like the word for "census," because the pharaoh's clerks had to re-assess the taxable part of the wheat and the number of taxpayers before each harvest. The need for surveying and architecture led to the development of geometry and the preservation of written records.

The Nile provided the long Egyptian oasis with an incomparable means of communication with access to the Mediterranean and the Middle East in the north, and to black Africa in the south. All through history, it was the great highway of ideas, trade, imperialism and sometimes of hostile attack. For 5,000 years, the "black African" and the "Asiatic" were the two traditional constant anxieties of Egyptian policy. And today, the pan-Arab ambitions of the U.A.R., its interminable conflict with Israel, even the decision to build the gigantic High Dam at Aswan (which is the key to future development of the country, but which is equally capable of drowning 300 miles of Nubia beneath the waters of its reservoir, 125 of which are in Sudanese territory) are only modern equivalents of these millennial obsessions. The pharaohs began their penetration of Nubia as early as the First Dynasty. Trading posts and fortresses and then temples—some of which, like the one at Soleb, were in no way inferior to those in Egypt—were built along the Nile. Boats and caravans returned carrying gold, cattle, skins, ivory and ebony (*heben* in Egyptian). Twice under the Old Kingdom, the heads of missions brought back a marvelous "dancing dwarf," a Pygmy, to the pharaoh's court. Black soldiers served in the army and continued to do so in modern Egypt until the independence of the Sudan in 1956. Nubian princes held high administrative posts. Gradually, Nubia found itself equipped with the same techniques, the same gods and the same culture as Egypt. The penetration was so thorough that in 751 B.C., when the

Nubian sovereigns of Napata, near the Fourth Cataract, came to take over power in Thebes and founded the Twenty-fifth Dynasty, it was done in the name of legitimacy and the god Amun. Later, Egyptian influence infiltrated further south, reaching as far upstream as the Fifth Cataract at the time of the founding of the famous kingdom of Meroe, which seems to have been the first great center to spread the use of iron metallurgy in black Africa. Later still, beginning in the sixth century A.D., the whole of Nubia was converted to Christianity, from Aswan to beyond Khartoum, and remained Christian until the Arabs destroyed its last churches and its last kingdom in the fifteenth century.

One of the most important contributions made to the West by the civilization of the Nile was the profound mysticism that it infused into early Christianity. This mysticism was the source of the Gnostic heresy and also of the great flame of faith that caught up the Desert Fathers—Macarius, Pachoumius, Paul of Thebes—among whom St. Benedict found inspiration for the principles of Western monasticism. Mahdism, which exploded into a violent religious war in 1881, and left an ineradicable mark on the Sudanese regions of the Nile, should be added to the ideologies and wars that have stirred the Nile Valley in the course of centuries. (See also *Cattle; Egypt; Great Lakes; Ivory; Meroe; Sudan.*) P.I.

NOK. Excavated archeological finds are rare in black Africa, where most of the evidence from past eras has been collected on the surface of the earth. The unique exception to date is the pottery discovered in the same stratum as the tin extracted from the mines on the Bauchi plateau of central Nigeria, which enabled the British archeologist Bernard Fagg to identify the Nok civilization in 1943. Radiocarbon dating has placed it between 500 B.C. and A.D. 200. According to the latest research, it covered an area of 311 miles from east to west and 186 miles from north to south. In the second half of the first millennium B.C., the whole of central Africa from the Atlantic to the Indian Ocean went through a "rain age," and a vast network of rivers, which have now disappeared, swept the rain water toward the Benue Valley and, from there, via the Niger River to the Bight of Benin. Several riverside villages must have been hastily abandoned, because, besides polished stone axes and a few iron axes of the same shape, fragments of terracotta statues, which must have rolled into the river during the flood, have also been discovered embedded in the alluvium. The

hill tribes were still extracting tin from the alluvium during the last century, and it was the appearance of this metal in the markets south of the Benue River that led to the discovery and development of the rich deposits situated further north.

There is no reason to suppose that the Nok potters were the first; it is very likely that

Nok head. Nigeria. Terracotta. Nigerian Museum, Lagos. *Photo: Walter Dräyer.*

Nok head. Nigeria. Terracotta. Nigerian Museum, Lagos. *Photo: Eliot Elisofon.*

earlier terracottas, which may never be found, exist elsewhere, and it is equally conceivable that the earlier work was made of unbaked clay or wood. Whatever happened in those remote times, the few hundreds of surviving fragments show no trace of the tentativeness characteristic of an incipient artistic tradition. There is a profound stylistic unity in the whole collection exhibited at the local museum of Jos. Its broad characteristics are simple: the pupils, nostrils, ears, and sometimes the mouth, are pierced; the eyes are triangular or semicircular in shape; but the final effect was not monotonous because the Nok artists varied the shape of the human head, sometimes shaping it like a sphere, sometimes like a cone or a cylinder. Many later styles drew their original inspiration from these. The Nok terracotta heads vary in size from 1 inch to life-size, and it seems that all these heads originally belonged to statues that are now broken. In every instance where it has been possible to draw a conclusion, the head seems to have been enormous in proportion to the rest of the body, as in nearly all African sculpture, in order to emphasize its importance as the seat of the vital force.

The way of life of the Nok people was probably similar to that of the central Nigerian tribes today, who are both farmers and hunters. It appears, however, that the former inhabitants lived in the lowlands as well as the hills, but that the Muslim expansion confined the "infidels" to the hills where they live today. Statues are a feature of their tribal ancestor cults, in which the ancestors are mediators between the living members of the tribe and a distant creator. The Nok potters may have made their statues with the same purpose in view.

We do not know whether it was a cataclysm or slow decline that brought the Nok civilization to an end. We are equally ignorant of the beginning of the Yoruba civilization, whose art reached its zenith in the terracottas and bronzes of Ife, which may date from the thirteenth century. A comparison of the pottery of the two cultures makes one fundamental difference clear: the Nok heads are much more stylized, while the Ife terracottas are naturalistic in manner. There are, however, similarities in the treatment of the human body, which the Ife sculptors modeled less carefully than the head. The similarity in the beads and other adornments is so close that fragments from one collection would not look out of place in the other. A major technical distinction is that the Ife artists were masters of bronze casting, while those of Nok, who may have

lived a thousand years earlier, knew nothing about casting metals. The evidence of these civilizations points to the fact that the development of agriculture, pottery and metalwork in the area southwest of Lake Chad was more advanced than in any other region anywhere south of the Sahara. (See also *Iron; Pottery.*) D.P.

NUBIA. See *Meroe; Nile; Sudan.*

NUMERATION. Linguistics indicate that all black African systems of numeration must have used 5 as a base (1, 2, . . . 5, 5+1, 5+2, 2x5, (2x5)+1, etc.). The terms for 3, 4 and 5 often seem to be connected with the same original root (*Tat, Nan, Tan*). The Africans subsequently went on to a system that used 10 as a base (1, 2, . . . 10, 10+1, . . . 2x10, (2x10)+1, etc.), which is now the most widespread system. In the Kwa language group (Akan, Ewe, Yoruba), it is combined with a base 20 system. Some observers have suggested that there are traces among the Pygmies and the Khoisan group (Bushmen and Hottentots) of a system that used 2 as a base, but this has been questioned. All the strictly black African systems reach at least 100, a few extend to 1,000 and some very exceptional ones go as far as 5,000 or 10,000. Arabic numeration is used side by side with a native system among the Hausa, the Swahili and the Fulani.

Besides mathematical numeration, used for the practical purpose of counting, there is a sort of magical and mystical arithmetic, an esoteric numerology, which is related to the Jewish cabbala in Islamized areas but seems purely African elsewhere (it would not be idle to speculate that the cabbala may originally have been African and was later passed on to Egypt). This esoteric numerology is only taught as knowledge required for initiation; little is known about it, and it is rapidly disappearing. Although it varies from one region to another, the importance of the number 4 in many different areas is striking. Four is a vital, often feminine symbol (equal numbers often seem to be feminine) and forms a basis for reference and for analysis of other numbers. The number 3 is next in importance. Among many Bantu peoples, 9 is important because it seems mystically equivalent to 7 according to the following kind of reasoning (Ntumu tribe of Cameroun): 4+3=7 (single bisexual) and "single bisexual" = 1, but furthermore (4)+(3) = 2 (the single, or only, couple) and "the single couple" = 1; 5+4 = 9 (double bisexual [?]); 9 is beneficent, while 7 is probably, or could be, evil. Sexual polarity seems to be the basis of systems of this kind; the numbers

1 to 5 represent pairs or couples as well as an isolated and complementary element, and each of them can be taken either as a single complex element or as the sum total of such elements. It bears an odd resemblance to a sort of theory of sets. (See also *Weights.*)
P.A.

OLDUVAI GORGE. Olduvai Gorge is a prehistoric site in western Tanzania where the archeologist L.S.B. Leakey and his family made some extremely important discoveries. It is rather like a mound of flaked pastry, about 328 feet high, in which the layers occupied by prehistoric man alternate with layers of sediment. It offers evidence of cultures stretching from the dawn of mankind to the present day. The first and oldest layer contained a large number of the most primitive tools known to us—roughly hewn stones, the total collection of which is known as the Oldowan Culture. In 1959, the remains of a primate, which was first called *Zinjanthropus boisei,* were also discovered in this mound. Subsequently, it was realized that this hominid fossil was similar to the *Paranthropus,* one of the South African Australopithecinae which was at a stage of development half way between man and ape. The conclusion deduced from this was that the *Zinjanthropus* was the earliest of the toolmakers and was therefore the first man. But later on the remains of a more human primate were uncovered in the same layer. He walked on feet similar to those of present-day man, but had less developed hands, a rather short stature and a less evolved brain than our own. Anatomically, he could be placed between the *Australopithecus* and the *Homo erectus* of Asia and Africa. This seems to have been the creature who trimmed the Oldowan stones, and Leakey called him *Homo habilis.* Oldowan man and *Homo habilis* have so far been found only in Africa, where it seems humanity emerged nearly two million years ago. (See also *Fossils, Human.*)
J.H.

ORDEALS. In addition to rational enquiry consisting of examining the evidence and hearing witnesses, judicial and semi-judicial processes in most African societies have recourse to methods that are based on the supernatural: divination, imprecatory oaths and ordeals. An ordeal consists of subjecting litigants, initiation candidates or persons suspected of committing an offense or impure action to a sort of test. Failure or a negative result is the sign of guilt, bad faith, impurity, etc. Among the Bwaka of the Congo, for instance, candidates for the

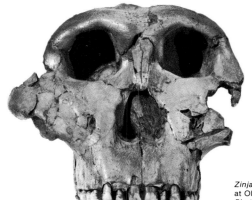

Zinjanthropus boisei found at Olduvai Gorge, Tanzania. Photo: *Musée de l'Homme.*

wama initiation must, in addition to other trials, hit the iron part of an assegai with a stone thrown from a distance in order to prove that they are not sorcerers. The widows of Bamileke chiefs have to cross a river without dropping a stick placed between their thighs to prove that they have been faithful to the dead, etc.

The most common ordeal is the judicial ordeal, and its most usual form is ordeal by poison, which is known throughout Africa. The innocent reject the poison by natural means (vomiting, urination, perspiration, etc.) or do not react, while the guilty die or are very ill. The poison is often given to an animal (chicken, sometimes a dog or a kid) that represents the suspect, particularly in less serious cases, and sometimes, too, from fear of the police. Another common form of ordeal is by burning. The subject walks barefooted across glowing embers (Chad), or picks a jewel out of a pot of boiling water or oil (Slave Coast, Gabon, southern Cameroun), or carries burning-hot stones (East Africa, Great Lakes) or touches the red-hot blade of a knife with his tongue (Ghana, Togo). Livingstone pointed out the resemblance between ordeal by submersion in modern Zambezi and in medieval Scotland.

The African explanation of the working of ordeals is based on a variety of supernatural factors: the intervention of ancestors or spirits, the peculiar power of the poison itself, etc. In fact, the unquestionable social efficacity of the process can be explained psychologically: the suspect is convicted and at the same time convinced; it seems that certain psycho-physiological phenomena, such as hot sweating or the inhibition of reflexes, can in some cases actually separate those who feel themselves guilty from the others. (See also *Azande; Divination; Initiation; Lions; Magic; Masks; Poisons; Societies, Secret.*)
P.A.

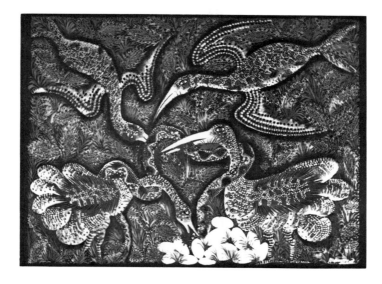

Painting by Joseph Kabongo of the Elisabethville Academy. Jacques Maquet Collection. *Photo: Jacques Maquet.*

Gouache by Gotène. Poto-Poto School, Brazzaville. Lucien Demesse Collection. *Photo: Lucien Demesse.*

Gouache by Ossieté. Brazzaville School. Jacques Maquet Collection. *Photo: Jacques Maquet.*

PAINTING, MODERN. The painting that is being done today in Africa is of great interest to art historians and sociologists because it shows how new art is born, but it is of little interest to collectors. Indeed, easel painting is new for Africans. Rock painting was traditional, but this tradition, which went back to prehistoric times, died out at the end of the nineteenth century with the last Bushman painter: it was the expression of a civilization of hunters, and it disappeared with them. The practice of rock painting is now limited to a few remote parts of southern Africa, and very few of our contemporaries in Africa are aware that it is done. In some parts of traditional Africa, decorative or ideographic paintings covered the walls of dwellings, shields and masks, but

nowhere do modern works show any continuity with these traditional paintings. Unlike contemporary African sculptors, African painters today are beginning from nothing and are not the inheritors of any African tradition.

Western European traditions have, on the other hand, greatly influenced African painting. There are two currents in modern African painting. One is directly inspired by European painting; this is the art that is taught by the arts and crafts schools founded during the colonial period, which offer instruction that has the many shortcomings and the few advantages of academicism, and that is produced in commercial studios, which employ young people who have a gift for drawing and who execute genre scenes (market women, canoes and sunsets). The other current has its source in the few European and African masters who have tried to leave their students alone to reinvent painting and have sometimes not even given them a course in the history of art. Among these students are to be found some of the best modern African artists. Some of them have studied in Europe or the United States, where they have encountered all the tendencies of visual art today.

Since painters do, indeed, exist in Africa, the question will inevitably be asked whether their work has a specifically African character. Before replying in the affirmative, one would have to be able to detect in the structure of the painting—in its lines, composition and colors—a style that was common to the best African-born painters. This has not yet been discovered. The productions of the same studio certainly have certain features in common, but they derive from a common technique (the dark, uniform background of the Brazzaville studio or the colored lines and dots separating the main forms that are characteristic of the Elisabethville painters) and are limited to a single art center. This absence of a specifically African character in painting is not surprising; it reflects the general state of the plastic and graphic arts today in all urban and industrialized societies. On the one hand, similar basic material goods in these societies and, on the other, the rapid diffusion of photographic reproductions of works of art and the increase in contacts between artists from different places have put an end to national and regional traditions in painting. There is no School of Paris or of New York now; it is impossible to determine by merely looking at a picture whether the artist is French or Japanese, American or Tunisian. African painters have been swept into this world movement. Ignorance of this fact explains the disappointing impression made on many people interested in art when they are confronted by "African painting." They compare a collection of paintings that have been gathered into an exhibition simply because their creators are African-born with a collection of traditional African sculptures. The comparison is obviously shattering, because they are contrasting statues and masks which, in spite of their variety, constitute *a whole art form* and were sculpted by several generations of artists in a fairly large number of workshops, with a few paintings executed by a few individuals who belong to a single generation and work in a smaller number of centers. (See also *Ethiopia; Painting, Mural.*)   J.M.

PAINTING, MURAL. "Hut" paintings, unlike rock paintings, often have no purpose other than to be decorative. In the forests of Guinea and nearby in the Ivory Coast, the puddled clay walls of the huts are patched and whitewashed every three or four years by the women. When the mistress of a hut has finished, she will, if she has the time and the inclination, decorate the outside walls, which are protected by the overhanging thatch roof. Sometimes, too, all the houses in a village must be repainted for an important festival; the most common event for which this is done is the celebration at the end of initiation, when the boys who have just spent several months in the forest away from the village return and make their solemn entry in the presence of all their relatives and friends. Hut decorations are painted with a mixture of soot and cow-dung dissolved in water. The artist may also use ochre, which provides a reddish-brown color, a dash of indigo or a ball of bluing; however, blue and ochre fade quickly in the rain. Having no brushes, the woman dips her finger into the liquid or uses her broom, made from the frayed stem of a coconut palm. The sureness of the line is therefore all the more remarkable. Some motifs are quite obvious—birds, snakes, mortars or winnowing-baskets—others are more enigmatic. The traditional subjects are related to household activities: carrying

The sultan's house. Tessaoua, Niger. *Photo: Musée de l'Homme.*

Painting outside a hut, with portrait of King Albert on the left. Manono, Zaire. *Photo: Musée de l'Homme, Lebied.*

Mural painting of a mask on stilts. Dan. Ivory Coast. *Photo: Hugo Zemp.*

Painting on the wall of a hut. *Photo: Rapho, R. Merle.*

Tura girl painting on the wall of a hut. Ivory Coast. *Photo: Hugo Zemp.*

water, crushing or winnowing grain. Occasionally, a young man returning to the village after a temporary sojourn elsewhere, during which he has worked to save a marriage compensation (which fathers of marriageable girls never find sufficient), will paint the inside walls of a dwelling. The young man decorates the house to which he will welcome his wife with pictures connected with his travels. One of the favorite motifs at one time was a siren with long, flowing hair, and a body ending in a fish's tail —the *femme fatale* whose whims lure boys to the bottom of the waters. A very popular theme at the moment is means of transportation: bicycles, trucks, ships, airplanes, singly or forming a frieze on the outside walls of dwellings, have replaced caravans and chiefs being carried in their hammocks. A new style has appeared with the spread of schools. The master of the house now not only wants to inscribe his name at the entrance to his house but also wants to add his portrait, either profile or full face. Paintings of the same kind can be seen in the towns; for example, on the signboards of hairdressers, garment-cutting schools and secretarial colleges. (See also *Architecture; Painting, Modern; Rock Art.*) D.P.

PALAEONEGRIDS. The word "Palaeonegrid" was coined by German ethnologists, who considered the Palaeonegrid civilization to be not only the oldest, but also the most characteristic of black civilizations. It left "traces everywhere," but has been preserved "with little change" only in "isolated places, notably in the mountainous districts of the Sudan" (H. Baumann). Numerous small ethnic groups, which are the fragments of other groups, occupy the hilly regions from Senegal to the Nile, including the escarpments of the curving Niger River, the low northern mountain masses of Ghana, Togo and Dahomey, the Bauchi plateau of Nigeria, the hills of Kordofan and also, in eastern Africa, part of the Great Lakes region. The Palaeonegrid peoples were all refugees from the aggressions of warrior states. At first sight, they have several characteristics in common, but a closer examination reveals that there are as many differences as there are similarities among them. It is doubtful whether these remaining groups can be easily identified with a single, homogeneous civilization, which is supposed to have covered a large part of Africa at one time. The mountain enclaves were not only preservers of culture, they were also crucibles in which successive waves of refugees, sometimes with very diverse backgrounds, were mixed and fused to form a number of new cultural units in the course of the centuries. The fact that many of them claim descent from the same ancestor should not mislead us; this is only the mythical expression of a unity acquired with the passing of time.

The physical characteristics and languages of the Palaeonegrids vary. A more important fact is that their institutions and beliefs show great diversity. S.F. Nadel's description of the Fanyan of Kordofan clearly shows how, in the same area of refuge, each hill may support a completely separate society. Their descent systems, like their forms of marriage, vary, although descent through the paternal line is the system that is most common. Well-organized age groups are not found everywhere. The range of religions is fairly extensive: a supreme deity is worshiped by some peoples and not by others; the worship of ancestors is often the dominant form of religion, but sometimes the worship of the earth takes precedence; rites of possession by spirits are of major importance among some tribes, while they are unknown to others. Similarly there are considerable differences in skills and techniques—apart from farming methods, which do not vary much. In architecture, for example, the only thing the Palaeonegrids have in common is their remarkable ingenuity. The same holds true for metalwork: the Fanyan know nothing about it, while some of the most skilled

metalworkers of Africa have developed their craft in northern Dahomey. The absence of weaving is almost general: women cover themselves with loin-coverings made of bark and bunches of leaves; men often go naked, although some wear scanty garments made of skins and bark and penis shields made of basketwork or calabashes. Of course, all these differences can be explained by the influences of other cultures: the penis shield, for instance, may have been taken over from a civilization of hunters. Nevertheless, the concept of an early common civilization, in the absence of any precise historical evidence, still appears to be an arbitrary reconstruction.

The unquestionable similarities may be, at least partly, the result of an identical situation. The areas occupied by the so-called Palaeonegrids, who were crowded into a mountainous region and deprived of all possibility of expansion for a long time, are very densely populated—and now that they have the opportunity to expand, they are slow to do so. Their farming techniques are among the most thorough and efficient: intensive farming, complex fertilizers, very little fallow land, and terrace cultivation or at least the dividing of hill slopes into squares with stone walls to reduce soil erosion. This is really horticulture; the soil is so poor and the humus is so precious that they sometimes gather it up from the foot of the hills after each rainy season. It is easy, in the face of new agricultural techniques, to forget exactly how societies have responded to the challenges of difficult environments and historical situations. Such difficulties may well explain a certain austerity in those civilizations which, with a few brilliant exceptions, have not produced any great art. Like their skills and techniques, the current social systems of the Palaeonegrids, despite a great number of variations, share certain basic characteristics. Wherever the place of habitation is not continually being broken up, large family units are practically autonomous and the elders retain authority, for neither states nor complex hierarchies have been formed. These are "egalitarian" societies (the term "anarchic," in the strictly etymological sense of the word, has even been applied to them) which have, nevertheless, been drawn together by common religious beliefs and institutions and clearly evolved forms of ritual cooperation. The so-called Palaeonegrid peoples are not the only ones to be organized in this way, and in many cases the limited size of the population provides a sufficient explanation for such organization; there is no need to postulate that a single civilization that existed in the past is perpetuated by them. (See also *Agriculture; Bobo; Clothing; Genealogy; Goats; Lions; Love; Possession by Spirits; Sports; Villages*.) P.M.

PAN-AFRICANISM. Pan-Africanism is comparable with Pan-Slavism; it is a mixture of myth and utopianism, political fact and cultural attitudes, and a means of defining elements of solidarity within the black world and of demarcating the limits of that world. The origins of Pan-Africanism were American rather than African, and the earliest demands of American blacks sprang from it. In its broad sense, Pan-Africanism postulates the unity of black people. The founder of the movement was W.E.B. Du Bois (1869-1963), a United States-born sociologist and a militant advocate of racial equality since the beginning of this century; he was the first to call for a return to African sources. Marcus Garvey, a visionary born in 1885 in Jamaica, evolved a sort of millennial Pan-Africanism and published the "Declaration of the Rights of the Negro Peoples of the World." He preached emigration back to the "motherland," Africa, in order to found an independent nation. In Haiti, during the same period, Dr. Price-Mars was writing enthusiastically about the contributions of black cultures to world civilization. It was Dr. Du Bois who organized the first of the Pan-African congresses. In 1923, in London, he remarked: "Pan-Africanism is an idea rather than a fact." It was an idea that added power to their demands for freedom. The Fifth Pan-African Congress, held at Manchester in 1945, following the end of the Second World War, brought into prominence two figures, Nkwame Nkrumah and Jomo Kenyatta, who rose to power soon after. The modern theorist of Pan-Africanism is George Padmore, who is a writer and militant advocate from the West Indies. He has given the movement a political aim: "government of Africans, by Africans, for Africans." Pan-Africanism soon went beyond the demands for independence; its supporters began to aim for a "United States of Africa." This theme of unity has been taken up by a variety of organs, including the review *Pan African Age,* and for a time

Accra, Ghana, became the capital of Pan-Africanism. Ghana even set up a learned foundation with plans for a monumental *African Encyclopedia.* Negritude is the cultural counterpart of Pan-Africanism, which is a political ideology. (See also *Negritude; Press; Third World.*) G.B.

PEANUTS. The peanut, which is American in origin, is now commonly found in most parts of tropical and equatorial Africa. It is the most extensively cultivated of all edible plants and is grown for commercial purposes. In West Africa, it has for a long time been the main form of cultivation imposed on rural inhabitants by administrative groups so that the poll-tax can be paid in peanuts. The Senegalese economy is based on peanuts, which take up half the cultivated land; annual production is around 1 million tons, of which 900,000 are made into oil and 100,000 are used for family consumption. This leguminous plant forms part of the traditional agricultural cycle in most savanna societies. It is much appreciated because it is one of the first edible plants to be harvested after the end of the rainy season, when food supplies are always difficult to obtain. During the peanut season, peasants begin to pick the pods while the seeds are still green; they then know that the time for the cereal harvest is not far off.

In traditional cooking, peanuts are either roasted in their shells, or shelled and boiled in water. They are often used to bind sauces. Peanut butter, which keeps for several months, is sold in all African markets. But very few traditional societies know how to extract peanut oil, and most of them are content with a mash that is rich in fat. Peanuts are an important element of the African diet because they contain 45 percent oil and 27 percent vegetable proteins, both of which nutrients are otherwise rare in the diets of villagers. Some international organizations and firms have tried to develop peanut flours which would have no oil in order to make up for the protein deficiency of some vulnerable groups of Africans, such as pregnant women, nursing mothers and infants. Peanuts keep well when stored by traditional methods, but are damaged by parasites that infest granaries. The leaves make choice fodder and are carefully preserved by settled tribes who raise cattle and other animals. (See also *Agriculture; Diet; Hunger; Mussoi; Songhai; Vegetables.*) I.G.

PERSON. Africans believe that every adult man and woman is a single, permanent ego. This concept, which is obviously not peculiar to Africa, merely reflects the universal

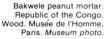

Bakwele peanut mortar. Republic of the Congo. Wood. Musée de l'Homme, Paris. *Museum photo.*

psychological experience of the normal man, who views himself directly as a conscious entity, existing unchanged throughout his life. It differs from the Christian idea of man in that no distinction is made between body and soul, and there is no belief that the soul alone constitutes the essential person or that it alone is immortal while the body is only its temporary sheath. Although the body-soul dichotomy is alien to African thought, there is, nonetheless, an ontological division in man. The Rwanda, whose beliefs are representative of African ideology, think that each person has three components: the body, which becomes a corpse after death; the shadow (visible in sunlight), which is metamorphosed into a spirit after death (a corpse has no shadow); and the vital force, which is liberated by a person at the moment of death and is not entirely recuperated by the spirit. This explains why it can be said that a dead person has been reincarnated in a particular child while his spirit is still languishing in the kingdom of the dead. The vital force of an ascendant of the child penetrates the child when he is in his mother's womb. Because of this, the child will not become that ancestor; he will bear his ancestor's name, but he will never be identified with that ancestor. This penetration by the life force—which is somewhat impersonal, since it does not lead to identification with the ancestor, yet is also somewhat individualized, since it is the reason for the transmission of his name— shows quite clearly that belonging to a lineage is at the very core of personality. In the most intimate part of his self, a man is a link between one of his ascendants and one of his descendants. The individual person is as clearly defined a unit for Africans as for Westerners; ego and nonego are never confused. But for Africans, the individual is not isolated and cut off from the rest of humanity: one network of ligaments binds him to the past and the future; and another binds him to the living beings of the present from whom he awaits an increase of vitality. (See also *Ashanti; Blood; Body; Death; Dogon; Heads; Names; Religion; Spirits and Genii; Wisdom.*)   J.M.

PEUL. See *Fulani.*

PHARMACOPOEIA. The study of the traditional African pharmacopoeia has long been neglected. Until recently, ethnologists were primarily interested in the magical aspects of medicine because they did not have the necessary qualifications to study the physiological effects of the drugs used. But during the past decade botanists, doctors and chemists trained in the West have begun

A healer's stall in Mwanza, Tanzania. *Photo: Musée de l'Homme.*

to be interested in this question. However, the gradual disappearance of traditional education and the application of colonial regulations to the practice of medicine have led to a marked lowering of the quality, if not the quantity, of practitioners of traditional medicine in recent years. In many African languages, as in the most common Euro-African lingoes, the use of a single term (pidgin English: *ju-ju;* colonial French: *gri-gri*) to refer to magical objects (and sometimes complex magical processes) having a curative purpose and to pharmaceutical preparations that may be associated with them clearly indicates that there is no clear-cut distinction between curative magic and drugs. The whole cure is conceived as a totality, and this has often led observers to underestimate the empirical realism that can enter into it. Modern investigations have shown, however, that the traditional pharmacopoeia is based on a fairly thorough knowledge of the properties of certain substances derived from animals, minerals and especially plants.

The plant pharmacopoeia is the most extensive. It is comprised of ashes; crushed extracts, either fresh or dried; decoctions; infusions of leaves, flowers, bark, roots, etc.; and sap, applied both externally (with plasters, in baths or rubbed on the skin) and

Condiments and other medicinal products in a market in Ibadan, Nigeria. *Photo: Jacques Maquet.*

internally (by instillation, by injection, or orally). The remedies often combine different extracts from the same plant, extracts from different plants or a mixture of plant and animal extracts. The plant pharmacopoeia is, obviously, particularly complex in the forest belts, but even in the areas bordering the steppe there is very extensive use of all available plant resources.

The animal pharmacopoeia consists of portions of the animal or human anatomy, which are eaten, often in connection with sympathetic magic; ashes; boiled elements; and putrid extracts. For example, the Baji of southern Cameroun use the ashes of touraco feathers (kunduk or *Corythacola cristala*) as a cure for arthritis of the fingers, and these ashes have recently been discovered to contain a measurable proportion of copper salts and traces of gold salts. In Togo, scorpion bites are tended with crushed extracts from these insects combined with extracts from unidentified plants in the form of an ointment in which the fat of monitor lizards is used as an excipient; the ointment is rubbed into cuts made near the bite. The arrow poison of the Gabon Pygmies seems to contain extracts from the cadavers of mammals, a powder made from the heads of snakes and venomous caterpillars and extracts from strophanthus shrubs, all mixed in an excipient of latex taken from poisonous euphorbiaceous plants.

The mineral pharmacopoeia is probably the poorest, but some products, like natron (hydrated sodium carbonate), are very widely used and are traded on a large scale. Geophagy, which is practiced in nearly all parts of Africa, often has a medical aspect; swallowing kaolin, earth from ant hills or flies' nests are common means of soothing the digestive system.

The preparation of certain complicated and rare medicines is handled by specialists, who buy the formulas from their elders, sometimes for large sums. These specialists sometimes belong to medical societies of initiates, often connected with religious cults that are associated with snakes (in Dahomey and West Africa, and among the eastern and northwestern Bantu). Besides the nostrums of the specialists, there is a whole family pharmacopoeia, which is learned at home and may vary according to the sex of the "pharmacist," because women do not prepare the same remedies as men. A common feature of all these medicines is that they do not acquire their *vix medicatrix* without some kind of magical operation, generally incantatory or sacrificial, or both. Traditional African medicine forms a complete spectrum ranging from the local equivalent of an aspirin to an act of pure magic, which can perhaps be compared to a psychoanalytic or psychosomatic cure. The power of the active agent used in a treatment does not depend on the composition of the product but is imparted to it by an act of will on the part of the person preparing it; in certain cases, the material preparation of pharmaceutical products is absent and only the emanation of the healing power remains. (See also *Hunting; Lions; Poisons; Priests; Salt; Spiders.*)   P.A.

PHILOSOPHY. Every people has a "philosophy," in the broadest sense of the word—that is, every ethnic group holds some body of ideas concerning nature, man and his place in the world; what the relations between individuals are and should be; and the values that give meaning to life. These conceptions, related coherently to each other, satisfy an apparently universal need among men to understand each other and define their position in relation to the other human beings whom they know. Only a negligible part of a person's ideas on these subjects is contributed by the individual himself; like the rest of culture, some kind of philosophy—whether it is concerned with the techniques of economic production or with ways of dressing, eating and speaking—is offered by every society to its members and forms part of the social heritage transmitted from generation to generation.

In traditional African societies, such philosophy takes two quite distinct forms: expressed knowledge, which is esoteric, and implicit themes underlying this esoteric knowledge. In the first, which is perfectly illustrated by the Dogon cosmology that was explained to Marcel Griaule by an old initiate, a vision of the world is contained in secret narratives, which are memorized and transmitted by certain men who have reached the highest rank of a society of initiates. These esoteric traditions are expressed, like all sacred lore, in a compact language that is full of images requiring an exegesis to make them clear. But, although this lore may be difficult to interpret, it does supply an explicit foundation. This cannot be said of the second form taken by traditional African philosophy: the ideas are not expressed in the texts; they are inferred by the observer from behavior, customs, beliefs and rites. Placide Tempels reconstructed what he called the "Bantu philosophy" by this kind of logical deduction. The philosophy itself consists of a number of principles of an ontological nature, since they are concerned with the nature of reality, which lies beyond phenomena and serves as their foundation. It is, in fact, an explanatory hypothesis; the Baluba, among whom Tempels worked as a missionary, behave as if they believed that the final

reality, which is also an absolute value, is the vital force. Expressed conceptions and explicit principles are substantially the same. It would be useless to try to describe them with the conceptual precision common to a scholarly tradition that sets a high value on philosophical discussion. But, although these notions are barely elaborated, they are nonetheless deeply rooted and therefore effective.

The few traditional African philosophies we know are all dynamist—that is, they do not regard the world as a stable entity, fixed in being, but as a becoming in perpetual state of growth. For the Dogon, for example, sowing fonio, which symbolizes the original seed of life, causes it to burst out of its husk and be enlarged in a movement that has no limits. The image of sowing seed is often used in African cosmological conceptions; the form of the spiral, which is a universally understood sign for organic growth, is found in the sculpture of several African societies. The vision of the universe as a group of forces in constant movement is completely consistent with the existential experience of Africans in the traditional period. Nearly all of them lived in small communities whose existence and perpetuation were closely tied to two processes of vital growth: the germination of plants and the fecundation of women. Harvests and the birth of children, without which villages and lineages were doomed to extinction, came at the end of a period of mysterious seminal growth. It is not surprising that Africans from different regions should very naturally give primary importance in their conceptions of the world to the creative evolution of their fundamental values. Nor is it surprising that these philosophies should have in common the conception that all beings—men and animals, trees and grass—partake of the same life force, which causes growth of leaves, when the rains return, as well as of the young of men and animals. As they share the same life, all beings, including man, are strongly bound in a brotherhood. When a hunter has been forced to kill an elephant for its meat, he has to purify himself and ask pardon of the animal's spirit. A sculptor cannot cut down a tree until he has accomplished certain rites that will compensate for the disorder he has created in the forest. According to this conception of existence, man's place in the world does not depend on his asserting himself against everything that is not himself or his works, as it does according to Western ideologies, but on his ability to see himself as a part of nature and on his continuity with it. This involvement is also rooted in the daily experience of rural

Africans, who know that, if their activities are to produce results, they have to be in harmony with their environment—associated with it and not antagonistic to it.

The acquisition of this energy, this life force, which courses through the unique network embracing all living things, is the supreme goal. Everyone tries to possess it in its greatest intensity. It is, in fact, variable; when it diminishes, men fall sick, women are sterile, cattle waste away and the fields are arid. Various measures are taken to strengthen this vitality, particularly prayers to ancestors and magical practices. Ancestors, whose vigor is proved by their numerous offspring, can benefit their descendants by imparting it to them. Magic and the use of special words, movements and objects enable men to appropriate some of the force flowing through the universe and use it to their own ends. The importance placed on prayer and magic does not in any way mean that Africans neglected rational means to cure their sick, cultivate their fields and breed their animals, but the limited efficacity of the rational techniques at their disposal left a large area in which they had to resign themselves passively to failure or try to act directly on the forces of the universe.

Beside the ultimate goal of a full and intense life, there are a number of secondary or intermediate goals which are the concrete aims of human action in every society: for warriors, military feats; for shepherds, the multiplication of herds; for farmers, plentiful reserves in their granaries; and for chiefs, lavish feasts, which add to their prestige. These goals, which are greatly desired and sought after, cannot be reached by just any kind of means. African philosophies include ethics. But their ethics are not based on a divine command forbidding certain acts and, in consequence, turning them into sins; evil is what harms others and what endangers the

peace and survival of the community. This morality is not absolute; the acts it prohibits are only proscribed in relation to particular people. Killing and robbing the members of one's society are forbidden, but there is generally no interdict against attacking the life and property of a stranger. Sexual relations with a neighbor's wife are not allowed, but they are permitted with a brother's wife, to whom a man is closely bound by lineal links. Although the supreme and remote god is not concerned with the moral order, the ancestors are its guardians, and they punish those of their descendants who do not respect it. (See also *Africanism; Bantu; Death; Dogon; Dwellings; Person; Religion; Sacrifice; Sorcery; Wisdom.*) J.M.

PIPES. Indian hemp (marijuana) in one form or another—hashish, *bang, dagga* or *kef*—was probably smoked in Africa for several centuries before tobacco, which was introduced into Africa from America at about the same time that it was introduced into Europe. Both Indian hemp and tobacco were smoked in pipes until cigarettes appeared at the end of the nineteenth century. Pipe-smoking is still the most usual form of smoking in rural areas, where pipes are smoked by both men and women. African pipes are made of wood, terracotta, soft stone, metal, calabash or horn; the range of pipes includes all the kinds of pipes used in Europe and America plus the water-pipe, which came from India or Arabia and is used in East Africa and the Sudan. The shapes of African pipes are even more varied than the materials from which they are made: from the Moro pipe, made of calabash and shaped like a cigarette-holder, with the bowl in a line with the stem, to the Bamum royal pipes, sculpted with realistic or stylized masks, leopard heads or entwined snakes, to the bobbin pipes of the northwestern Bantu and

Pipe. Mbangala. Angola. Iron and wood. Musée de l'Homme, Paris. *Museum photo.*

Pipe with a cover. Mbangala. Angola. Wood. Musée de l'Homme, Paris. *Museum photo.*

the corncob pipes of the Slave Coast (similar to corncob pipes used in the American South). The local tobaccos are so strong that they generally have to be smoked in long pipes whose stems are merely touched to the lips rather than sucked; however, short clay pipes with small bowls are to be found in Africa. Pipes are usually fairly wide so that they draw easily, and the tobaccos, which are almost incombustible, although they give out smoke, often have to be kept alight with a burning coal. A briar from Saint-Claude or Bond Street would not last long with such treatment. But the rhythm of life is quickening even in the bush; people have less time to idle away and, consequently, less chance to devote to a worthy pipe the measured calm that is the hallmark of the real pipe-lover.

Clay pipes discovered in West Africa by archeologists indicate that pipe-smoking began there no earlier than 1600, tobacco having been introduced into the Sudan in 1595 and no pipes having been discovered in excavated medieval sites in that part of Africa—indicating that other plants that can be smoked, such as Indian hemp (*Cannabis indica*) and *Datura metel,* were also not smoked prior to that time. (See also *Baluba; Granaries; Massa; Sao.*)   P.A.

POETRY. All oral African literature—that is, all African speech that is formally elaborated in order to be distinguished from the ordinary communication of raw information, meaning virtually all African literature, including oratory—is, in the final analysis, poetical. It is "poetical" in the broadest sense of the word, that is to say, if one takes into account the emotive content

and the use, nature, frequency, ingeniousness and richness of images and metaphors. These images are often expressed by means of words that are known as "ideophones," and have no equivalents outside Africa. The Oxford Concise Dictionary defines poetry as "elevated expression of elevated thought or feeling in metrical form." This is where the difficulty begins, for we do not know enough about black African languages to be able to distinguish prose from verse in most of their productions with any certainty. European researchers have been aided in their studies by the fact that Fulani, Swahili and Hausa writers have been influenced by Arabic poetic meters and genres, particularly lyric and epic poetry, and have adapted them equally successfully to the structure of their languages and to the

Hunters preparing poison for their arrows. *Photo: Rapho, Williams.*

arrival of the Europeans. Poetry written in the vernacular language has grown up mainly in the English-speaking states, notably among the Yoruba of Nigeria and in South Africa. European-style poetry has given rise to a literary school in French-speaking parts of Africa (Léopold Senghor, Tchikaya U'Tamsi, M. Sinda, M. Sy, etc.). It is difficult to speak of a school in the English-speaking parts of West Africa, although some outstanding poets have written in English there; but there is a South African school, which is very similar in tone and subject matter to the modern Afro-American school. (See also *Epics; Legends; Literature, Oral; Love; Sahara; Song.*)   P.A.

POISONS. Mysterious African poisons are frequent ingredients of cheap detective novels. However, there is nothing mysterious about many African poisons. Ouabain, strophanthin and the essences of various euphorbiaceae are as well known in our own pharmacopoeia as they are in that of the African *nganga;* in fact, they are better known here because the art of poison is disappearing in Africa. Poison is not necessarily connected with foul murder; its use may be perfectly legitimate and socially acceptable. In Africa, its most common and best-known legitimate use was as an effective substance administered directly to the suspect or to an animal that took his place as part of an ordeal. It has been said that direct administration gave a better chance to the innocent because his clear conscience made him vomit. It has also been said that investigating judges administered the doses of poison in accordance with their personal antipathies. Hallucinogenic poisons are mainly used in the forest belt by both traditional and modern cults, especially among the central and western Bantu. The most common hallucinogenic poisons are *alan* (*Alchornea floribunda*) and *iboga* (*Tabernanthe iboja*), which are used by *bwiti* devotees in Gabon to induce visions. In East Africa, Indian hemp, or hashish (*Cannabis sativa*), is used for the same purpose. Another legitimate use was as a warning poison to induce someone who had wandered from the path of duty to return to it. Along the Guinea Coast, it was used by ritual societies and by chiefs; elsewhere (in Cameroun and among the Sudanese Mande and the southeastern Bantu), it was employed by women to bring back their erring husbands. Murder for reasons of state should be added to these legitimate uses.

Criminal poisoning was, and still is, practiced by a large number of tribes. In

spirit of their peoples. Similarly, in western and equatorial Africa, there are poems scanned and rhymed in imitation of French poetry. Elsewhere, the only general rules that seem fairly certain are that verse is distinguished from prose by a more marked periodic rhythm (but sustained prose is also rhythmic) and often by the regular repetition of certain tonic patterns, which form a sort of tonal rhyme, sometimes supported by alliteration. Consequently, verse is melodic and very similar to song; a large part, if not the greater part of poetry is actually sung, either with or without instrumental accompaniment.

African poetic genres differ in content and form. Lyric poetry is not very common, while the elegy, particularly the erotic elegy, satire and occasional verse are to be found nearly everywhere. Epics are the characteristic poetry of politically organized societies and those with well-established hierarchies. Good examples of epics are the laudatory songs of the Zulus and the dynastic poetry of Rwanda. Well-developed national epics, however, are also composed by loosely organized tribes; in such cases, they are generally preserved by societies of initiates. Religious songs that are sung during rites and ceremonies are found everywhere, even in Islamized areas. There are also professional poets, who may be either attached to courts or independent; most of them are itinerant and travel alone or accompanied by a small band of musicians. Written poetry, which has existed for a long time among the Muslim black Africans, developed among other groups after the some regions (the Slave Coast and the Congo Basin), the fear of poisoning verges on group neurosis, but in the Islamized savanna areas it seems relatively rare. This fear of poison has often been crystallized in a code of hospitality rituals for dining together; these include such conventions as the tasting of the food by the host or one of his children before the guest eats and the serving of only bottles with unbroken seals or unpeeled fruit. In spite of this fear, genuine cases of poisoning appear to be much rarer than is supposed, and many alleged poisonings are really psychosomatic or psychotic symptoms, notably in urban areas. (See also *Buffalo; Bushmen; Lions; Meals; Ordeals; Pharmacopoeia; Societies, Secret; Weapons; Women.*) P.A.

POLITICAL ORGANIZATION. See *Lineage; Royalty; Villages.*

POLYGAMY. For obvious reasons, men and women who have always lived in a society in which monogamy is the only kind of marriage that is permitted have always been keenly interested in polygamy and have often been surprised by it. Yet, monogamous marriage is the exception rather than the rule among the various societies of the world. A large proportion of the societies of the world —probably about 80 percent—practice polygamy. All black African societies are included in this majority. The African variety of polygamy is polygyny (the marriage of one man to several women). Polyandry (the marriage of one woman to several men) is unknown south of the Sahara. Africa is polygynous in the sense that this form of marriage is recognized everywhere and enjoys greater prestige than monogamy. But not all Africans are polygamous. The approximately equal balance of male and female births in a population group, even though it may be modified by a high mortality rate among young men in places where they are engaged in dangerous occupations, is an obstacle to every man's marrying several girls. Furthermore, in polygynous African societies, many unions are, in fact, monogamous, and very few plural unions comprise more than two or three wives. Only the great chiefs can afford dozens of wives—and sometimes even hundreds of them, as the king of the Bakuba is supposed to have had.

The erotic significance of polygamy, which is particularly attractive to the Western imagination, is the least important aspect of this institution. A plurality of wives naturally brings variety into the sexual life of a man, but this is only a subsidiary, although agreeable, consequence. African wives are never cloistered in a harem to await the convenience of their lord. Each one lives with her children in her own dwelling and cultivates her own field. This activity reveals the most obvious purpose of polygamy in a farming community; it is economic. The nuclear family (a couple and their children) is

The king of Abomey and his wives. Dahomey. *Photo: Hoa-Qui.*

the agricultural production unit of traditional Africa. The man who contracts a second marriage becomes the head of a second economic unit, with the result that he has more consumer products at his disposal than the monogamous man. The plural marriage is the means and the sign of prosperity. For kings and chiefs, it is also a means of governing. On the purely political plane, it is a way of procuring the alliance, or at least the neutrality, of groups whose daughters the ruler has married. On the ritual plane, the sexual union of the king with a woman from each of the great lineages symbolizes the unity of the society as a whole and induces fertility in the different groups occupying the territory that is under the authority of the king.

Polygyny also ensures a high birth rate while safeguarding the health of the women by spacing the pregnancies at reasonable intervals. Although some Christian missionaries have denied that polygyny encourages a high birth rate, it is only because their religious beliefs have made them attribute to the system what can only be imputed to distortions of it. Where there was great inequality of riches, which was rare in traditional Africa, some wealthy old men could possess so many young wives that many young men were forced to remain bachelors. This obviously created a serious

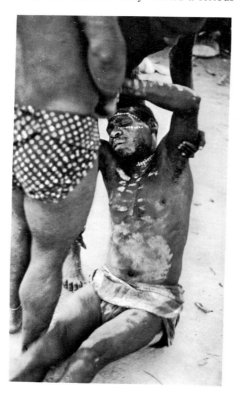

Trance at the end of a divination dance. Babinga. Republic of the Congo. *Photo: Lucien Demesse.*

social disequilibrium. It would be interesting to know whether, in regions where this occurred, it happened often or lasted a long time and what its precise effect on the birth rate was, because an old, polygamous husband would hardly inspire unswerving loyalty among his young wives. (See also *Family; Industry; Pygmies; Women.*) J.M.

POSSESSION BY SPIRITS. Divinities and all the other powers of nature that religion tries to affect manifest their presence in the world of men in many ways. The most spectacular is probably by possessing men— by dwelling inside them for a while, by "entering their heads," as the Dahomans put it, and by seizing their whole being so that they fall into a trance in which they lose consciousness. Once the shock is absorbed and the trance controlled with the appropriate treatment—prayers, gesticulations and the drinking of suitable decoctions—the man becomes, for the duration of the ceremony, the visible and animate substantiation of the divinity, his dwelling, his wife, the horse he rides; the human being is absorbed by the divinity and behaves exactly as the divinity would in every way. This contract with the world of the gods without an intermediary is an elementary form of mystical life. Divinities may choose their human substantiations haphazardly, but generally the men who are chosen have been prepared, by means of initiation, to receive them. The men are carefully conditioned so that they will be more responsive to a divinity's movements and receptive to the signals, such as drummed rhythms, announcing his presence and desire to possess them.

Sometimes ancestors who are not content to be partially reincarnated in their descendants manifest their presence by possessing people; this occurs, for example, among the Mashona and Bavenda of southeastern Africa, the Ila of the Zambezi River area, the Nuba of eastern Sudan and a number of the Palaeonegrid tribes. But more frequently, it is the major gods of the great polytheistic religions or the minor divinities and the genii who are the focal points of possession cults; on the Benin Coast, these cults actually serve as the basis of religious activity.

The devotee of a god (*vodun* in Dahomey; *orisha* among the Yoruba)—who approaches the god voluntarily, at a sign from a diviner or at the direct invitation of the god —must always be ready to receive him. When, after a long initiation, the devotee enters, "resuscitated," into a new life, he has assimilated, partly unconsciously, everything associated with the god on whom he depends: his way of dancing, the songs and rhythms devoted to him, his way of expressing himself and behaving. The man becomes himself in daily life, but a ceremony in honor of his god can bring the god back into his head. He oscillates between two lives, between two often different personalities and even between two languages, one spoken by men, the other by the god. Possession rituals have sometimes been equated with psychoanalytical treatment.

The possession cults associated with minor divinities and genii are of a similar nature, but their mythical basis is less elaborate and less well organized and the initiation is often less thorough. Typical examples of such cults are those of the *tour,* among the Serer of Senegal, and the *bori,* among the Hausa of Nigeria and Niger, which neighboring tribes like the Zerma have adopted. Several genii—grouped in order of rank and each one having a particular sex, a specific color, a bond with a part of the universe, its own animal or other kind of symbols, a personality with both virtues and faults and a certain amount of prestige—are summoned among men in the course of extraordinarily intense ceremonies. Cults like these may be the last remaining traces of traditional religions that have been undermined by Islam. They are sometimes revived in the most surprising ways; for example, among the immigrant Zerma in Ghana such cults are the basis of a religious response to the difficulties and problems of the world today. During the colonial period, the traditional genii were joined by other genii representing technical power, such as the railway engine, and political authority, such as the governor; this is an indication of how the concept of these spirits satisfies a continuing psychological need by adapting itself to the modern world. The exalted feeling resulting from possession by these genii offers devotees a brief escape from the daily round of a precarious and rootless life. (See also *Divinities; Drums; Languages, Secret; Magic; Masks; Mottoes; Mussoi; Palaeonegrids; Prayer; Priests; Religion; Songhai; Sorcery; Spirits and Genii; Symbols; Voodoo; Yoruba; Zar.*)   P.M.

POSTURE. The variations among African civilizations show up in the many different ways in which people are in the habit of using their bodies. The kinds of posture adopted for relaxation depend on the furniture and clothes of the society in question. They also depend on nonmaterial factors, such as conventions governing the relations between the individuals and the groups who compose the society and how one is expected to

Stance for resting on one foot. Rwanda. *Photo: Jacques Maquet.*

behave toward the powers of the world beyond. Habitual movements are not innate; they are inculcated at a very early age by the community and determine what a person considers to be a comfortable reclining position as well as how he sits when he is visiting someone.

The Nilotic tribes and most of the herdsmen of the Sahel zone can rest standing up; they assume what is called the "stiltbird stance," one leg bent up with the foot resting against the knee of the other leg. Africans enjoy squatting as much as sitting and can stay in a squatting position for hours without feeling the need for a chair. Since most domestic work is done at ground level, the African housewife is far more supple than a woman who is used to tables and chairs. For sleeping, Africans generally adopt a "leaping dog position," with the head resting flat on the bed. African beds are seldom more than 5 feet long and are often extremely hard. Flowing garments are largely responsible for the slow movements and dignified posture of Muslims in the subdesert belt. Another consequence of this clothing is that the men have to squat to urinate. Modesty is the most elementary form of etiquette, and nudity does not in any way exclude it; when the Kirdi men of northern Cameroun are

Kaoko woman grinding corn.
Republic of South Africa.
*Photo: South African
Information Service, Pretoria.*

Topoke potter. Zaire. *Photo:
Musée de l'Homme.*

standing up in public, they stand so that their penis is hidden between their closely pressed thighs. They are able to walk and run in this position, which eventually produces a deformation of the penis.

Techniques of love-making are also part of a cultural legacy. Africans rarely kiss; instead, they often mingle their breath. Among the Tallensi, for example, the man squats between the legs of the woman during sexual intercourse, and this precarious position requires the use of a hard bed. It is considered a serious offense, which can lead to divorce, for a wife to throw her husband off balance.

The position adopted by a woman in labor varies from tribe to tribe. Among the Mandja in the Republic of Central Africa, the woman sits on the ground, with her knees drawn up, to give birth; an assistant sits in front of her to support her and lift her up when the child appears. Among the Tuburi of Chad, the woman sits on a chair; an assistant stands behind her, pressing hard on her shoulders and exhorting her to make the necessary efforts; and a midwife, positioned in front of the mother, receives the child in a bed of leaves, because it must not touch the ground.

Etiquette and courtesy are manifested by means of a multitude of postures and gestures that are based on a whole system of conventions and beliefs. The Mussoi of Chad consider that pointing at someone with a finger or staring hard at him is an attempt to cast a spell, and an apology has to be made for this kind of behavior. In most traditional societies, the right hand is reserved for noble purposes, such as eating food or greeting someone. Members of a society indicate their status by the postures they adopt in public and by the tokens of respect they proffer to others. These are prescribed by etiquette, which is often very complex in societies having a strong hierarchical structure (among the Hausa and the Mossi, for example). Among the Nupe of Nigeria, two men of the same rank greet each other with a light bow, then touch each other's right hand several times with the tips of the fingers. An inferior bows low and kneels but does not offer his hand to a superior. Visitors, in the presence of members of a royal family, squat with their arms folded on their laps because it would show lack of respect to let them rest on the ground of a royal dwelling. (See also *Dance; Prayer.*)
I.G.

POTTERY. Pottery is one of the ancient arts of Africa. Modern dating methods have shown that the oldest pieces of African pottery were made several thousands of years before the Christian era. The terracottas of Nok, in central Nigeria, belonging to a period prior to the Christian era, and the superb mastery of terracotta-making of Ife, in the same region, are evidence of a tradition that probably began before the thirteenth century B.C. There are very few regions in Africa today where pottery is not made. Agriculturalists, especially those in regions with ancient cultural traditions, primarily in the Sudanese area and in the southeast, are the main producers of pottery. The former area is said to have a "clay civilization" because so many things produced by it besides pottery in the narrow sense of the word—houses and their furniture, granaries, hives, drums and forge bellows—are modeled in clay. However, some food-gathering and hunting groups, such as the Pygmies and Bushmen, make little or no pottery.

Nearly everywhere it is the women who make the pottery. Northeastern Ethiopia is a notable exception, but not the only one; in Niger, around Maradi, for example, the mass production of water pitchers is carried out by men when it is off season for agricultural work. In the Sudan area as a whole, where there are women who specialize in pottery-making, it is often connected with iron-forging, even when the potters are not the wives of blacksmiths. Elsewhere, it is either a nonspecialized female activity or the occasional occupation of particular families.

Pottery vessels are formed using various combinations of the principal manual methods (excluding those requiring a potter's wheel). The bowl part is often prepared first, and the other parts are mounted separately on it afterward. A common method, employed from the western coast to the Nile, is to mold the bowl either on the base of an inverted pot or by lining a concave mold—bowl, calabash or hollowed-out heavy wooden block (the latter method is used by the Kapsiki potters of northern Cameroun)—with clay. Elsewhere, the bowl, and sometimes the whole vessel, is modeled by gradually hollowing out a lump of clay. The Dogon use a large, rounded stone to support the wall, which is gradually stretched and thinned by tapping it with a pebble. In Nubia, the support is a large bowl filled with ashes, and the clay is stretched over it with both hands. In the Ubangi region, the Mandja potters turn the lump of clay with one hand while hollowing it out gradually with the other. In the area stretching from the shores of Lake Victoria to Rhodesia, a unique process is used, with the base being closed last: the clay is first modeled around an open cylinder; only when it begins to dry and the rough, baseless model is inverted is the base closed. The technique of building up the entire pot with rings of clay is found in its purest form near the Guinea Coast and in Zaire, but more often,

the coiling technique is used as a method of adding extra pieces of clay in order to make deep vessels. The stretching, shaping and smoothing of the clay are sometimes done with the potter's bare hands and sometimes with a beater.

Firing methods are less varied. The most usual is to arrange the pots in a heap and place the fuel (wood, bark, dried dung) around it, in regular layers at the bottom and in continuous layers of greater or less thickness on top. Sometimes branches and straw, which produce a bright flame, are added in the course of firing. In addition to this fundamental method of direct firing, various devices are used to regulate the heat. In several regions of central and eastern Africa, the base of the fuel pile is kept in place by a circle of bricks and broken pots; in Ethiopia, it is maintained by covering it with large potsherds. Genuine kilns have been found in at least two parts of the Sudan region: Mali and Niger. They are constructed in the shape of cylinders and are sometimes divided into a hearth and a firing chamber in which the pots are stacked and covered with fragments that form a dome for the duration of the firing.

The final appearance of the pottery depends on the surface decoration of the clay prior to firing, on the conditions that affect the clay during baking and sometimes on how the pottery is treated after it is baked. The technical means at the disposal of African potters gives them a choice of several kinds of decorative effects, including relief, polished surface and brilliant color. One of

Baya jar. Cameroun. Terracotta blackened in firing. Musée de l'Homme, Paris. *Museum photo.*

these three effects is generally chosen as the main means of decoration. If our knowledge of African pottery were sufficiently accurate, it would be interesting to draw up a map to see how pottery styles have differed from area to area and which styles have been combined, and then compare them with the distribution of other forms of aesthetic expression. Relief effects, obtained by making deep impressions or by modeling the clay (and sometimes producing very high relief), are found mainly in the area stretching from the Ivory Coast to Cameroun. Pottery is polished nearly everywhere; polishing can give a very brilliant look, either to the whole surface or to certain parts that are alternated with sections that are left with a mat finish or shaded with hatchings or impressions. The polishing is rarely done on the clay itself, but on a coating of slip that has a warm ochre color. It is generally these surfaces, which are at least partially polished, that are treated with the smoking process to produce the fine, glossy black finish that is as popular in Niger as in Ethiopia and is liked from the Sudan to southern Africa; it is especially admired in central Africa, in the Ubangi and the Congo River regions. Besides such monochrome decorations, there are two other kinds of color effects: decorations produced either by contrasting the colors of the clays used, a method rarely found outside the northern Sudan and southern Rhodesia, and those made by applying vegetable juices after firing, either as geometric figures, which are then outlined with incised lines, or as marbling, which is obtained by sprinkling the juice over just the shoulder or over the whole surface. (See also *Architecture; Household Furnishings; Kikuyu; Nok; Pipes; Sanga; Sao; Zimbabwe*.)   H.B.

Cephalomorphic pottery. Bena Kanioka. Zaire. Terracotta. Musée royal de l'Afrique centrale, Tervuren. *Photo: Hoa-Qui.*

Mangbetu pitcher. Zaire. Terracotta. Tropen Museum, Amsterdam. *Museum photo.*

PRAYER. Prayer, either alone or accompanied by sacrifices and libations, has an important place in African religions, both as a group act and as an individual act. Prayers, including those said by individuals, are often stereotyped. This formalism links prayer with the religion of the society, and its effectiveness depends on conformation with accepted patterns. There are, however, ejaculatory prayers or spontaneous outpourings on a particular subject, whose form is free or merely outlined. Besides doxologies and rogatory prayers that make either a general or private request, there are also occasional imprecatory prayers in which the suppliant rails against the divinity and even goes so far as to insult him. The latter resembles rough joking between familiars. As many or even more prayers are addressed to intermediary divinities, specialized gods, demi-gods, genii and spirits of ancestors as are directed to the supreme god himself. Not only are the contents of prayers prescribed but also the way they have to be uttered— ranging from a murmur to singing or shouting—the position of the body while

Praying at the conclusion of
Ramadan. Bamako, Mali.
Photo: Hoa-Qui.

saying them and the place, day, hour and circumstances for uttering them. Rogatory prayers are often accompanied by a vow that has to be fulfilled either immediately or when the prayer is answered. Facial incisions, mutilations of the body, certain hairstyles, clothes or makeup are typical consequences of such vows.

Some African Muslim confraternities have modified the compulsory Muslim prayers, either by changing the direction in which the worshipers face, their body position ("folded-arm prayers"), the style of recitation (shouted prayers) or the number of repetitions. Similarly, several schismatic or syncretic sects which originated in Christianity practice individual or group praying that is auto-hypnotic or hallucinatory and leads to a crisis of possession with glossolalia and sometimes cataleptic fits. Many prayers are like poetry in their style and content, and are worthy of translation; others are so elliptical that they resemble riddles or proverbs. (See also *Funerals; Gods; Magic; Philosophy; Possession by Spirits; Priests; Religion; Sculpture, Wood.*)   P.A.

PRESS. The first newspapers printed in black Africa were printed in Cape Colony at the beginning of the nineteenth century.

However, their readers were mainly Europeans, and they should not be classified as black African newspapers. It was not until the middle of the nineteenth century that a newspaper appeared in Sierra Leone, although still in English, that was aimed at an African public. The first newspaper in French, the highly official *Moniteur du Sénégal,* appeared during the same period, and the first missionary periodicals in the vernacular appeared a little later. During the colonial era, a press for the European public and another for the African public existed side by side. The latter included African-language papers, the most common mastheads being those of missionary or official periodicals and newspapers in French and English. French- and English-language newspapers fell into two categories: those belonging to European chains, which had technical means and often large financial assets, and those owned by Africans, whose means were far inferior and whose publication was made all the more precarious and risky by frequent judicial proceedings and ruinous fines resulting from their political content.

After independence, the press for the European public became smaller and, in some places, disappeared altogether. The

African press enjoyed a brief and somewhat anarchic orgy of freedom, but it ran into financial difficulties and soon found itself once again subjected to pressures for political conformity that were often harsher than before emancipation. The market is dominated by organs of the parties in power, which are rather provincial in character because they are mainly concerned with local interests, and by magazines belonging either to the big European chains (in French, *Bingo, Vie africaine;* in English, *Drum, West Africa*) or to the missions (*Afrique nouvelle, Les Flambeaux*), which tend to be more pan-African in character than the political organs. Once decolonization was over, freedom of the press did not seem to be as indispensable to African opinion as it did during the struggle for independence. Most of the African representatives at the international congress of journalists at Dakar (September 1962) maintained that their primary function was the education and intellectual guidance of their readers rather than the presentation of politically objective information. Consequently, the African press remains a press of opinions and may even be militant. This position has been forced on it by the requisites of new states that are in the process of being built up and which have social and economic foundations that are still weak. (See also *Literature, Written; Pan-Africanism.*)   P.A.

PRIESTS. Any man who offers a sacrifice is on that occasion fulfilling the function of a priest, but the term "priest" can correctly be applied only to a man who is qualified to preside over a ceremony, pray to a divinity or other powers in the name of the community and celebrate the rites of an established religion. It is not always easy to distinguish the priest from the magician, the healer and the diviner. The religious knowledge required of a priest can range from a thorough acquaintance with myths to the simple ability to perform rituals along with a great familiarity with the god of the cult. Generally, people don't bother to acquire this knowledge until or unless they are chosen to be priests. The priestly vocation may be taken on in answer to insistent summonses from the divinity, but more often, a priest is designated by heredity or because he occupies a position in the society that carries priestly duties with it. Sometimes a person becomes a priest by "buying" an altar and knowledge of a ritual; such a priest is very much like a magician. A priest rarely devotes all his time to his ministry and usually does not depend on the gifts and services of the faithful for his livelihood. Most priests

exercise their priestly functions only during certain periods and on certain occasions, and their privileges, if they have any, are derived from another source. The injunctions constraining the activities of priests are often light and temporary—for example, sexual abstention and a particular diet in preparation for a ceremony—but they sometimes take the form of permanent taboos or fairly strict reclusion. The priests affected by such stringent injunctions are not only performers of ritual functions but are also men whose every gesture affects the world, not just because of what they do but also because of what they are.

There are many kinds of priests. The humblest is the head of the family who, in this capacity, takes charge of the worship of its ancestors; he is the oldest man in the family and thus the closest to the ancestors, for he will soon join them. Sometimes he is also responsible for the worship of a local power that dwells in a stone or a tree on his land. If he is the head of an extended family or clan, his function is more important, and he often has additional responsibilities; for example, he may be the land priest, heir to the founder who made a pact with the earth. In still a larger sphere, the priest-chief of the tribe sometimes officiates in the name of the whole society. He has no highly specialized political power and is as much a divine figure, by virtue of his own nature, as a priest who acts according to ritual. The Hogon of the Dogon is an example of such a priest; he may not touch the ground because he is the sun and may not perspire because the sweat would drain away his strength; he helps the sun to rise and the plants to grow and, as the guarantor of the order of the world, is bound by obligations that regulate his whole life to the last detail. Although a figure like this does not really belong to the political order, he influences the life of his society by means of the religious sanctions he is entitled to apply. There is every shade of difference between this type of priest and a political chief or king. The chief of the Alur of Uganda possesses special powers; he is a rainmaker, and his temporal power depends on this. The king of the Jukun of Nigeria was priest and god, responsible for keeping the universe in good order, and each of his movements had mythical significance; any weakening of his powers brought ritual death on him.

In some regions there existed an actual clergy whose members were organized into a hierarchy related to the importance of the divinities they worshiped, with each of the great divinities having its own minister. The members of the clergy could be troublesome, and kings exerted a great deal of effort to control them. In Dahomey, for example, the king exerted control by creating a sort of religious ministry. Even today, the *voduno*, or minister of the god, is in charge of a temple, supervises the prayers and sacrifices and organizes the initiation of the faithful; after initiation, the faithful become *vodunsi*, wives of the god, and the god can then enter them and take possession of them. A man who is designated for the Dahomey priesthood, either by heredity or by a direct call from the god, is prepared for his task by an initiation and by instruction that lasts several years, during which time he must abstain from alcohol and sexual intercourse. He remains subordinate to the priest who has trained him. Although he often takes on other duties, "the *vodun* feeds him"—in other words, he lives partly on gifts from the faithful. (See also *Altars; Diet; Divination; Dogon; Dreams; Gods; Ibo; Jewelry; Kirdi; Languages, Secret; Lions; Magic; Rain; Religion; Royalty; Senufo; Songhai; Villages; Voodoo; Zulus*.)   P.M.

PROVERBS. Although we are far from having a complete knowledge of African proverbs, we do know that the proverb is the richest literary genre of black Africa; collections containing two or three thousand proverbs put together from individual cultural groups have been made without exhausting their resources. This wealth is in itself an indication of the social importance of the proverb; the phrase "wisdom of the people" can be justly applied to it. The African proverb is, in fact, much more than a sort of epigram on the nature or the behavior of man and his weaknesses and inclinations; it is rather a sort of social axiom, an expression, in mnemonic form, of rules and principles peculiar to each culture. It is connected with the juridical jibe; among the Yoruba of Nigeria, trials often consist of battles of proverbs between the parties. Furthermore, each proverb is quoted in an allusive form, sometimes reduced to just a single word, and the exchange of proverbs can be followed only by the initiated. Quite understandably, the teaching of tribal proverbs is a basic function of traditional education. Strictly speaking, a proverb is an expression of information of a social nature in concise, stylized, often enigmatic form and therefore requires a commentary before it can be understood and used appropriately. The same precept is often expressed in various forms—humorous, dramatic, noble, familiar, etc.—and the way in which it can or should be quoted varies with the situation, the context in which the precept is supposed

Weight for weighing gold dust representing the proverb "Birds of a feather flock together." Anyi. Ivory Coast. Musée de l'Homme, Paris. *Museum photo.*

to be recalled, the person who recalls it and the person to whom the reminder is addressed. The same concept can often be expressed proverbially in both insulting and laudatory form. At one extreme are proverbs resembling mottoes and at the other those akin to enigmas or riddles.

Other proverbs constitute formulas for magical protection or mild curses. Like mottoes, proverbs sometimes are expressed in graphic or plastic form by certain ethnic groups; for example, some of the motifs on Baule and Ashanti weights and the counter disks used for the *abia* game played by the Ewodi, Baji and Fang represent proverbs. A thorough knowledge of proverbs is a great asset for political orators in both modern and traditional societies. (See also *Calabashes; Literature, Oral; Mottoes; Riddles*.)   P.A.

PYGMIES. The Pygmies (also called Negrillos, Twa, Batwa and Twides) pose a number of unanswered questions for us. Their physical type—height not exceeding 4 feet 6 inches, reddish skin, male facial hair and hair on their heads that is not kinky—is found elsewhere only among the Negritos of the Pacific (Andaman Islanders, Semang, Aeta, etc.) and is clearly distinct from that of their black neighbors, although it has some affinities with the Bushmen physique. They speak no language that is distinct only to their group, and many speak archaic forms of black African tongues that are only spoken far away from their present homes. They are scattered unevenly throughout the forest belt stretching from the Congo Basin through the Republic of Central Africa and Gabon to southern Cameroun, with isolated groups remaining in the savanna in Cameroun and among the Azande (Akoa), and there are some racially mixed groups (Batwa) living in the province of Kivu in Zaire and in Rwanda. They seem to have inhabited a much larger area at one time:

Pygmy encampment.
Republic of Central Africa.
Photo: Hoa-Qui.

they were definitely known in dynastic Egypt —an expedition into Nubia brought one back to the court of the pharaoh Pepi II— and there are countless legends about red dwarves who were good dancers and archers and were once the masters of west African as well as east African territory. No archeological or paleontological discoveries have provided evidence for this theory, and the hypothesis that some forest tribes, such as the Gagu of the Ivory Coast, have Pygmy ancestors has not been confirmed by an examination of the blood groups found among the Pygmies and the Gagu.

The Pygmies live mainly from hunting and food-gathering and lead nomadic lives while pursuing game within fairly well-defined districts. Their material culture is very poor; they show no knowledge of metallurgy, pottery-making or weaving, and their artifacts are made exclusively of animal and plant materials (horn, bone, skins) that are scarcely altered in any way. They live in symbiosis with neighboring black groups, who provide them with iron tools, pottery, fabrics and cultivated plants in exchange for

game, skins, ivory and the products of food-gathering. This symbiosis varies from a simple alliance among the groups in the Ituri Forest to actual exploitation of the northern groups by the Bantu. Among the northern groups there is a marked tendency toward intermarriage, a settled agricultural life and assimilation into the dominant Bantu tribes (such as the Bakoko of Cameroun).

The nonmaterial culture of the Pygmies is quite rich: fairly varied music (the flute is an important instrument), dances, legends and myths, mainly concerned with hunting, the most important activity of Pygmy life. The social unit is the band, which contains several small divisions; a number of bands constitute a patrilineal clan, which leads a nomadic life within a particular area and gathers together from time to time for important hunts and the rites connected with them. There are no chiefs except those ruling the small divisions, but the most experienced hunters of each band wield authority based on their ritual efficacy. Sometimes, elders of the clan also enjoy ritual authority. The rare instances of polygamy existing among the

Babinga starting a fire.
Republic of the Congo.
Photo: Lucien Demesse.

Babinga drummers. Republic
of the Congo. *Photo:
Hoa-Qui.*

Pygmies are to be found among these elders; most of the chiefs of small divisions are monogynous, although a kind of polyandry may exist among some groups in Zaire. Marriages are made by exchanging women, probably between clans. The relations between the sexes are much more egalitarian than they are among their black neighbors.

Their religion is based largely on hunting. The totemism described by missionaries of the Anthropos school seems to be only an inexact interpretation of Pygmy hunting rites. Their single, supreme god has the character of a forest and hunting divinity, and his bow is represented by the rainbow. On the whole, the little we know of Pygmy religion often bears a striking resemblance to the religious system of the Bushmen.

The total number of Pygmies has been calculated as being between 20,000 and 250,000, depending on whether some tribes of more or less mixed race are included. Natural selection acts as a harsh force in the forest, and their population has probably remained stationary. In regions where they are living at close quarters with blacks, the Pygmies seem to be disappearing more through intermarriage and assimilation than extinction. (See also *Architecture; Basketry; Buffalo; Bushmen; Death; Diet; Fauna; Great Lakes; Hottentots; Hunting; Migrations; Pharmacopoeia; Race; Rwanda; Song; Vegetables.*)   P.A.

RACE. The terms "Negroes," "Negroid peoples" and "black race" are used to designate dark-skinned peoples of African origin. In addition to dark skin, other distinguishing characteristics of these peoples are kinky hair and a very high incidence of the blood group R_0 (a subgroup of the Rh system). These last two features are unique, whereas dark skin is found in other parts of the world, caused apparently by the same selective impact of exposure to the sun on different hereditary traits. Physically, the populations of black Africa vary greatly: the lowest average height in the world is found among the Pygmies of the Ituri rain forest and a very high one is found among the Dinka of the upper Nile; there are ethnic groups with thin noses, like the Batusi, and others with very broad noses, like the tribes of the equatorial forests; peoples with slender build, long thin legs and narrow shoulders, like the Dinka, Batusi, Bahima and Masai, and others with massive bone structures and well-developed muscles, like the Balega of Zaire.

On the basis of certain physical traits, early anthropologists divided the peoples of the world into races. Today, however, we realize that these "races" are not biological entities, but somewhat arbitrary creations of the classifiers, and that there are no definite boundaries between them. The aim of modern ethnologists is not to classify, but to

Mangbetu woman. Zaire.
Photo: Musée de l'Homme.

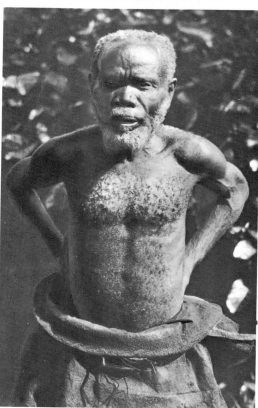

Bambuti Pygmy. Zaire.
Photo: Musée de l'Homme.

interpret the observed variations in terms of the correct differentiating factors.

Natural selection, one of the most important of these factors, helps the population to adapt itself genetically to its living conditions. For example, there is a close connection between the humidity of the atmosphere and the size of the nose. It seems, too, that climatic factors, operating over many generations, have gradually caused the variations in inherited characteristics. Populations living in the steppes or savanna tend to be tall and slender, with very dark skin and little hair; these characteristics are pronounced among such groups as the Shilluk and the Dinka of the upper Nile. Conversely, populations of the equatorial forest tend to be shorter, with lighter skin and more hair; these tendencies are found in an extreme form among the Pygmies, who appear to have lived for a long time in the equatorial forests. Quite different environmental factors affect other hereditary characteristics. For example, the frequency of sickle-cell anemia—a hemoglobin disease common among blacks in Africa and America today—results from a balance between people who suffer from sickle-cell anemia (if they inherit a sickle-cell gene from each parent—the homozygous condition) and people who have a relative immunity to malaria (if they inherit a sickle-cell gene from only one parent—the heterozygous condition). There seem to be very few characteristics that can escape the selective pressure exercised by various environmental factors such as climate, pathology, food and possibly even certain cultural elements.

A second differentiating factor that is important in Africa is genetic deviation, the random alteration in specific inherited characteristics which may occur within a small community. It is frequent among hunters and food-gathering peoples (an uncommon way of life today, but the usual way a few thousand years ago) and can occur in agricultural communities. It is also noticeable when a small group breaks off from a larger one, an event that is recorded in a number of traditions about the origins of African ethnic groups.

A third factor, mutation, may have a considerable effect in conjunction with natural selection. The latter can only modify the frequency of existing hereditary characteristics, while the former may create new ones. Thus, hemoglobin C, which originated in West Africa, has spread over a small area of the continent and produced distinctive genetic characteristics.

The last of the factors that influence heredity is intermarriage, or a mixture of genetically different populations—as all peoples are. A major factor in Africa as elsewhere, it disseminates new characteristics produced by mutations and reduces the differences between the various parts of Africa which were caused by the interplay of natural selection and genetic deviation.

At a given time, the inherited characteristics of any people are the result of different factors and forces. Every modification or occurrence of these forces— migrations to other climates, changes in living conditions through agriculture, variation in food resources and eating habits, the fight against disease, demographic fluctuations, the integration of foreigners— will upset the equilibrium and the population will evolve into a new genetic state. Massive migrations and geographical expansion, such as that of the Bantu-speaking peoples, have often recast the anthropological map of Africa. Besides its impact upon the human genetic inheritance, environment affects the capacity of the individual to realize his inherited potentialities. Food and hygiene are contributing factors, as is education, particularly in developing intellectual efficiency.

Although foreign groups, such as the Yemenite element in Somaliland and Ethiopia, can be distinguished in some regions, it seems that the present populations of Africa originated from various elements in Africa itself. Some, living in complete isolation, have developed peculiarities that distinguish them sharply from others. This is particularly true of the Khoisan group, composed of Bushmen and Hottentots, who have characteristically yellowish-brown skin, iron-gray hair, flat faces and steatopygia, or the accumulation of excessive fat on the buttocks, a common characteristic among Hottentot women. Some of these characteristics formerly led people to believe that there was a racial affinity between the Khoisans and Asiatics. Today such resemblances seem fortuitous, and the Khoisans appear to be a special group of Africans. A completely different evolutionary trend has led to populations who are dark-skinned, tall and slender, with narrow noses in long, thin faces that are not prognathous, such as the Batusi of Rwanda and Burundi, the Bahima in Uganda and the Masai in Kenya. Some people have thought they could trace in this development an important non-African component, but it now seems more in conformity with anthropological data to view it as an evolutionary tendency peculiar to black Africa.

The theory that there exist superior and

Above: Masai. Tanzania.
Photo: Hoa-Qui.
Left: Afar woman. French Territory of Afars and Issas.
Photo: Rapho, R. Michaud.

inferior races, which is often advanced by racists to maintain the privileged position of people of European origin in relation to the blacks of Africa and America, has been categorically refuted by science. No evidence has ever been found of any difference in inherited capacity for intellectual development between different peoples of the world.

The realization of these potentialities is entirely dependent on cultural factors. (See also *Baule; Bushmen; Egypt; Fossils, Human; Great Lakes; Hottentots; Hunting; Kirdi; Negritude; Pygmies; Rock Art; Rwanda.*)   J.H.

RAIN. The low rainfall over most of Africa limits the development of animal husbandry and agriculture. Crops require an annual rainfall of more than 15 inches in regions where irrigation is impossible. Throughout the savanna, farmers wait anxiously for the first showers, which signal that they can begin plowing the ground that has been hardened by seven months of no rain. Rain is indispensable for sowing, and, if the crops are to flourish, it has to rain fairly continuously during the first part of their growth cycle. Sudanese farmers often suffer from a lack of rain after a premature sowing. Long experience with the rhythm of the seasons and an instinct for forecasting the weather are required before one can judge the right moment for sowing. The function of forecasting rain is generally carried out by a specialist, such as a land chief, rainmaker or priest-king, who is responsible for bringing rain, thanking the powers who dispense it and sending it back to the sky when it is no longer needed.

Rain is deified everywhere and is very often considered the manifestation of a great god. It is not an accident that among the Massa, the Mussoi and the Kerre of Chad the word for rain is the same as that for the vault of heaven and the name of the great creator genius. A close analogy can be observed among the Churi, the Ewe and the Masai. When it rains, they often say that "God is falling" or "God is weeping." For the Bambara of Mali, rain, like most other atmospheric phenomena, is produced by Faro, the genius who reorganized the universe. Rain and other water are his domain, but only the rain water is pure and purifying. It is the rain that really sows the seed because it brings the soul (*Ni*) to the grain. This distinction between the purifying water of rain and the water of rivers, which often belong to maleficent spirits, is a common one. The Bathonga and many other peoples believe that a lack of rain is brought about by a broken taboo (incest) or certain magical practices (among the Mussoi, for example, rain can be walled up by closing the hole of a tree with a stone), and the perpetrator must be found and punished or appeased. With rare exceptions, such as the Ekoi, most people consider a celestial divinity maleficent when he sends too much rain to the earth. (See also *Agriculture; Hunger; Millet; Religion; Savanna.*)   I.G.

RATTLES. The rattle is the most common resonant instrument employed in black Africa, where it is found in a wider variety of forms than anywhere else. Its continuous rustling sound is frequently mingled with the sounds of other musical instruments, although it may accompany singing or be heard on its own. Seldom used as a plaything, it is associated with different rites and is used during initiation to direct the dancing. When a tribe has several different kinds of rattles, the function of each is strictly defined: one may be used exclusively by men, another by women and different ones are reserved for particular rites. Rattles are usually spherical, ovoid, conical or cylindrical. They may be made of calabashes, husks of the baobab fruit, wickerwork baskets or cornets, leaves that have been sewn together or bamboo or basketry tubing, and they may contain seeds, nuts, shells or pebbles, or occasionally scraps of iron. The narrowest part of the fruit or a small rod piercing the rind serves as a handle. Rattles made of basketry and played in pairs have handles or are mounted on the tops of long sticks. If the instrument consists of a bamboo pipe, it is held horizontally between both hands or, as in Madagascar, is rested on the knees and struck with the fist. Rattles can also be hung from the players' wrists or from the ankles or calves of dancers; small fruit husks or bags made of palm leaves are strung on a thread and tied to the knees. Women play a game whose object is to knock together, with a flick of the wrist, two seed-

Massa divination to forecast rain. Chad. *Photo: Pierre Ichac.*

filled husks that are secured by a short string; each of the different resulting sounds corresponds to a different motto.

The bell-rattle, which is peculiar to West Africa, does not contain any granular filling. Instead, a calabash is covered with a loosely meshed net in which nuts, snake vertebrae or beads are knotted or entwined. They are struck against the rind when the calabash is shaken or swung to and fro within the tautly held net. A rattle of this kind, with external percussive elements, first pointed out in the early eighteenth century in the Benin region, is played in Mali by the Bambara and Dogon and along the Atlantic coast from Guinea to Nigeria. Among the Kissi and the Toma of Guinea, it is connected with the ritual of excision and accompanies the dancing and singing of the girls. It is also found in the West Indies and Brazil in cults of African origin, such as voodoo. (See also *Bow, Musical; Calabashes; Drum Language; Music; Mussoi.*)   A.S.

RECADOS. The staff of office, or *recado* in Portuguese, was occasionally unadorned, but more often it was decorated. It was found in many African states, where it was one of the symbols of authority and of the legitimacy of royal rule, but most of our information about its significance and function comes from the kingdoms of the Benin coast, particularly from Dahomey. In Dahomey, the *recado* in its simplest form was a wooden crook, resembling the handle of a hoe or the curved club that, according to tradition, was carried by warriors in the early days of the kingdom. We do not know when this object became a royal emblem, but early travelers saw it used for this purpose in Dahomey. Many *recados* have been preserved. Some are of polished wood, like the original model, but on most of them the short arm of the crook is carved or is decorated with metalwork that is either inlaid in the wood, cut out or cast by the lost-wax process. Some are completely covered with silver leaf that fits closely over the outlines of the sculpture. The sculptures and decorations of the *recados* convey the mottoes, or "strong names," of the kings more simply than do the bas-reliefs and appliqué materials. One *recado*, sculpted in the shape of a lion's head covered with silver and having eyes of coral, brings to mind one of the mottoes of Glele, the penultimate king of independent Dahomey: "The lion's teeth have grown, he is the terror of all."

The *recado*, like the throne, not only represented the king but also was the king. He carried one of his *recados* in his hand or hung over his shoulder. He had as many

Baule rattles. Ivory Coast.
Photo: Hugo Zemp.

Recado of King Glele. Abomey, Dahomey. Wood and ivory. Musée de l'Homme, Paris *Photo: Giraudon.*

recados as he had mottoes, although in certain ceremonies he carried the *recado* of his predecessor, with whom he temporarily identified himself. Where the *recado* was, the king was. When carried by a messenger, it gave validity to the command that he brought. It was given the same honors as the king himself. European merchants and ambassadors who sought an audience with the king waited at the port of Ouidah for "the road to be opened" by a *recado* sent by the king. It was carried in front of their transport and served as their safe conduct to the capital. (See also *Dahomey; Mottoes*.) P.M.

RELIGION. Prior to the spread of Islam and Christianity, revealed religion with a universal mission was unknown in Africa. There were, rather, as many independent religious systems as there were autonomous societies, and it is difficult to find a term that will cover all of them and epitomize what they had in common. Several terms have been used and suggested: "fetishism," which is pejorative and is the result of a misunderstanding of the purpose of fetishes, should be excluded; "paganism" would be better, but it is stretching the original meaning of the word, which was "a religion of peasants"; "polytheism" can only be applied to some African religions; "animism" does not raise the same objection, but it is an inadequate description of actual belief and practice; "vitalism," which places a justified emphasis on the omnipresent notion of the vital force, has been used for too many other things. We are forced to fall back on the vague term "traditional religions," a simple label that does not epitomize the common features that are so striking in spite of the variety of myths, pantheons, rites and aims comprised by African religious activity. This variety reflects the diversity of ways of life and types of social and political organization found in Africa: among hunters, the propitiation of the powers of the bush and the spirits of animals, as well as the acceptance of pacts and kinship bonds with them, are fundamental; among pastoral peoples, the principal beliefs are focused on the sky gods, founder-heroes of clans or kingdoms and ancestors; among agricultural peoples, land worship, ancestor cults and myths about culture-heroes predominate; in organized states, myths and cults associated with the person of the king are added to these. These various religious systems have influenced each other or have been intermingled as a result of conquests, migrations and economic changes. They appear all the more clearly to draw, each in its own way, on a common source and to share the same kind of attitude toward man's position in the world.

Traditional religions are all nature religions, not in the sense that nature is worshiped in them, but in the sense that man is deeply implanted in nature; he is a microcosm in which the whole world appears in a reduced form, and he has an allotted place in a hierarchy of forces and beings that embraces everything—gods, animals, plants, minerals, everything "from the creator god to the village dung heap" (Marcel Griaule). Men live not only *from* nature but *with* nature; they do not dominate it, but are allied with it; and they cannot survive and perpetuate themselves without knowing how to maneuver correctly the forces animating it. There is no supernatural world that is separate from nature; nature and the supernatural world form a continuity that is life itself. A religion cannot be independent of a particular place—a piece of land, the sky above it and the society that is essentially bound to it. The world and the people described in the myths of creation of a people are precisely that place and that society; the myths are strictly limited to them except when, in unusual cases, a few neighboring tribes are included. Proselytism and conversion have no meaning for religions that are so localized and concrete; attachment to a religion as distinct from a locality and a people is unthinkable; at most, in the great polytheisms of the Guinea Coast, a particular god could become the object of an exceptionally close attachment. It was always possible, of course, to take over gods and complementary myths from other societies and to quickly merge them into the tradition. There was no place for intolerance, and even Africans who have been converted to one of the great world religions have kept some of this heritage.

African religion attaches a man irretrievably to his society, and it should be understood by this, not only to the living but also to the dead—his ancestors—to the gods and to all the forces linked to his land, which together form an inseparable unit. Religion maintains the cohesion, justifies the institutions and penetrates all the activities of the society. These activities, ranging from those concerned with individual material gain to those involving the good of the community, always have some ritual aspect, and the most important activities involve complicated ceremonies. African religions are profoundly ritualistic; they require the correct performance of the rites—and even the technical movements of everyday life have ritual overtones—that ensure the success of hunting, the fertility of the earth and cattle, rain, the perpetuation of the tribe and the preservation of order in the society and in the world. Disorder, personified in mythological figures, is a constant threat and has to be contained. Good and happiness, which are identical, are conceived of as being simply full participation in the life of the society and the world; they are the fruits of conformity, which may seem like conformism to us. Sin does not exist; there are only offenses against ancestors or gods and broken taboos, which are not always deliberate; amends can be made by performing the appropriate rituals. In this type of religion, a division between good and evil after death is rare; furthermore, conceptions of the world beyond are fluid because the dead live primarily among the living. At most, the dead who have been struck down by gods or who are suspected of sorcery have a different fate after death, and this is anticipated in their funerals.

A religion is primarily a conception of the world, its creation and the way it functions, and these concepts are often described in a complex cosmogony. It is usually difficult to collect all the ideas associated with a particular cosmogony, and as a result few cosmogonies are known in such detail as those of the Dogon and Bambara of Mali, the Yoruba of Nigeria and the Fali of Cameroun. The same fundamental themes appear in all of them: the world is created and organized from chaos; it is sometimes restored after a first outbreak of disorder; man is established on earth and receives the revelation of speech and techniques; death appears. These cosmogonies provide a classification of the elements of nature, which correspond to each other with countless symbolic overtones; the classification supplies the meaning of the external aspects of rites—that is, the material used and the movements made, which at first sight seem so arbitrary. These complex, varied interpretations of the world all depend on the same basic notion: the vital force. This unique, impersonal force, which originates in the supreme god, impregnates the whole universe. Among the Dogon, the *nyama* "tends to make the support to which it is temporarily (a mortal being) or eternally (an immortal being) attached persevere in its being" (Griaule). The *elima* of the Bakundu of the Republic of Congo is similar. On the other hand, the *kele* of the Lobi of the Ivory Coast and the *evur* of the Fang of Gabon are among the innumerable variants in which the concept of the vital force has been more or less weakened. The amount of vital force in a being depends on its position in the hierarchy. The greatest degree of concentration of vital force is found in divinities, men (both dead and alive) and some animals. The vital force is an essential part of the human individual, who has multiple "souls." It circulates in the blood and is concentrated in the head, heart and liver. It is increased in

all living beings during the course of their lives by means of the intake of food. But only gods, ancestors and men who carry out certain rituals can regulate its distribution and control it. A man can strengthen it in himself by sacrificing and rendering to the gods and ancestors what he has received from them. He can also accumulate it on artificial structures—such as altars, masks and statues—where he can draw upon it at a later time. It must always be attached to a particular spot because when it is free and uncontrolled, it is dangerous, like an electric current without a conductor. Some peoples seem to have retained only this "harmful fluid" concept of the vital force; in hunting rites, for example, they avert the vengeance of the animal they have killed by imprisoning its life force.

From the supreme god to the recent dead, there stretches a hierarchy of divine or semi-divine figures who possess the vital force preeminently and whose cooperation must be sought. Each religious system has its own method of selecting from among this massive assembly; a divine being may be of supreme importance in one place and occupy a secondary rank elsewhere. The supreme creator god, who is generally associated with the sky, is more or less personalized and remote. In some places he has temples; in others he is invoked only at the opening of a rite; more often he is neglected in preference to more accessible powers. In some systems, he is a vague being behind the first ancestor or the founder-hero, who acquires some of his attributes, while in polytheisms, he is a more distant figure than the other gods. The major divinities, who sometimes are bound very closely to the supreme god and at other times are independent or opposed to him, vary greatly. In agricultural societies, it is the earth with whom men make a pact, guaranteeing their right to occupy and work a piece of land. Among pastoral communities, the divinities of the atmosphere are the most important. And in the complex polytheistic systems, each of the specialized divinities governs a particular sphere of the universe. The founder- or culture-hero may resemble these divinities very closely if he is endowed with cosmic functions; however, he may also be only the most important figure in a hierarchy of ancestors—who are the protectors of the living, the guarantors of order in the society and its perpetuation and the ideal intermediaries between men and the gods—and worship of them may eclipse that of all the others. Finally, there is a multitude of lesser divinities located at various levels in the hierarchy. These include divinities associated with fertility, with the fight against disease and with divination; supernatural powers who are connected with particular places and are jealous of their prerogatives; spirits and genii of the bush or of the waters, which may be beneficent or maleficent, are sometimes former proprietors of the land and are often hideous to look at; and the characters in the many tales that resemble stories more than do the great, solemn myths that explain the world.

Religious knowledge is not shared equally by everyone. Superficial descriptions of African religions cover only the external and most commonplace features of the religions, which are known to everyone in the societies in which they are practiced. The progression from this type of knowledge to a slight understanding and then to profound knowledge is achieved only by a few; it can only be acquired slowly and through an initiation that may last a lifetime. Most men join in rites or celebrate them without understanding them completely, but their ignorance does not bar them from religious activity; moreover, they may unwittingly make movements that have profound mythical significance, such as the movements connected with certain techniques. Any man can act as a sacrificer or priest in certain circumstances. There are also more or less specialized priests whose position in the society or whose possession of particular knowledge gives them special competence: the heads of family groups, who are

Sherbro statuette connected with rice growing. Sierra Leone. Stone. British Museum. *Museum photo.*

responsible for the worship of ancestors; members of lineages who are in charge of a local cult; chiefs and kings whom a complicated enthronement has made both priests and gods and who are responsible for the order of the world and capable of bringing rain and ensuring the fertility of the earth. In some cases, as in the polytheistic religions of the Benin Coast, a real clergy that is well organized into a hierarchy around each divinity exists. The high priests, surrounded by assistants, are in charge of worship and supervise the initiation of the faithful.

Religious observances are extraordinarily varied, but whether or not they form a part of daily life or are fulfilled in a time and place specially set aside for them, they permeate every aspect and every phase of individual and community life. Prayer, possession by spirits, offerings, sacrifices and the making of a work of art are all means of having definite contact with divinities. Whoever the powers may be who are invoked, all African religions are based on three fundamental preoccupations. First, subsistence: rites concerned with hunting, animal husbandry, agriculture, which are sometimes linked with the great ceremonies for restoring the life of the world and inaugurating the new year and which are guarantees for maintaining essential fertility and the vital sources of life. Second, the order and fecundity of the society: propitiation of the ancestors of all families and of the gods who may assist them; sometimes worship of royal ancestors, who represent the unity of the country and its people, may also be included. Third, the course of human life: from rites for becoming a member of the society, starting with the selection of a name, through countless initiations, which may be open to everyone or only to the few who desire it or are called to it by the gods, to the funeral rites and the establishment of ancestors in the world. There is no act or event that is not magnified by a cult and that does not depend more or less directly on a mythical model for its significance. The cohesion of each society depends on the communal observance of rites. (See also *Agriculture; Ancestors; Art, African; Christianity; Death; Divination; Divinities; Fetishes; Gods; Islam; Myths; Philosophy; Prayer; Royalty; Sacrifice; Spirits and Genii; Totemism; Voodoo; Zar.*)

P.M.

RICE. The consumption of rice is tending to increase among traditional African peoples. About 2 million tons of rice a year are produced on the continent. The most common varieties grown today come from Asia; however, a native species, *Oryza* *glaberrima,* originated in the Niger Delta and the Casamance Island region of Senegal. Wild rice (*Oryza barthii* and *breviligulata*) grows in flood areas and is still gathered for food by, for example, the Songhai of the middle Niger and the Musgu and the Massa, who live along the Logone River. The cultivation of Asiatic rice (*Oryza sativa*) probably began in the sixteenth century along the coast of West Africa. But before the cultivation of Asiatic rice became widespread, the Ashanti and the Ewe probably cultivated African rice, which they must have acquired from the Mande tribes.

There are two methods of growing rice in Africa: on cultivable soil above flood level in the mountains, and on marshland near permanent stretches of water that can be used for irrigation. The Kissi of Guinea, who have been aptly called the "rice people," practice both methods of cultivation simultaneously. They classify rice into nine varieties according to the characteristics of the grain and the requirements for cultivation. Irrigated rice can be grown without crop rotation and can provide more food per acre than any other cereal. In Africa, from 900 pounds to 2,500 pounds can be grown per acre, and its cultivation has been encouraged by a number of governments. The yield of mountain rice, which demands less work, is only 450 pounds to 600 pounds per acre. It is widely cultivated in Guinea, Sierra Leone, Liberia and the Ivory Coast.

Rice is energy-giving and also contains proteins of good quality, but it is deficient in calcium and vitamin B_1. Traditional ways of cooking rice in Africa preserve this vitamin fairly well, but the growing popularity of polished rice is increasing the risk of beriberi, which has been unknown in Africa until now. (See also *Agriculture; Baga; Diet; Granaries; Kissi; Mussoi.*) I.G.

RIDDLES. A riddle, or enigma, is a "statement or question that is worded so as to make the person to whom it is directed exercise his ingenuity in answering it or finding out what it means." In Africa, riddling consists of a ritual exchange of conventional phrases that starts with a declaration or challenge—the statement of a riddle. This is followed by the acceptance of the challenge by the person to whom the declaration is put. Next, the challenger asks a question—which may be a paradoxical or allusive description of a person, a thing or a situation—and this is answered by the challenged person. Finally, a set formula, which varies according to whether the answer was right or wrong, ends the game. To the outsider, the subjects of riddles often

Bushmen playing riddles.
Photo: South African Information Service, Pretoria.

appear blindingly obvious or absurdly far-fetched. The fact is that the formula exchange of the ritual phrases is of much greater importance than the effort expended to find an answer. Riddling is a kind of game or verbal dance performed in a strictly defined social context. Usually, if not always, the person being questioned knows the answer in advance; not to know it would show a lack of education. It is almost an exchange of passwords or recognition signals. Riddles often have double meanings: one is quite obvious; the other, which is symbolic and hidden, is revealed only at a certain stage of traditional education or initiation and consequently eludes anyone outside the group, even if he knows the language. Riddles are both forms of conversation and means of teaching certain subjects. They are taught first for their simple meanings and later for their esoteric content. Riddles are used as codes of formal relations between social groups and particularly between the sexes, rather like friendly insults. For example, riddling is a means of starting ritual courting sessions between young men and girls, with a clear-cut distinction between a boy's question and a girl's answer, and vice versa. These sessions may last entire evenings. Riddles, like certain stories, are nearly always "night phrases" that may be pronounced only after sunset. Riddling has been studied thoroughly by Marcel Griaule's team among the Dogon and Bambara. It is found all over Africa, and some basically identical riddles recur throughout widely differing tribes, while others, obviously including those based on word play, belong to much more limited linguistic zones. (See also *Games; Mottoes; Proverbs; Song*.)   P.A.

RITES OF PASSAGE. See *Age Groups; Circumcision; Excision; Initiation*.

ROCK ART. The painting and chiseling of designs on cave walls and overhanging rocks date back in Europe to the Upper Paleolithic Age. In Africa, the same type of art is spread over vast but fairly clearly defined areas. The Sahara and the whole of the southern part of the continent are particularly rich in this art, but rock paintings do exist elsewhere, such as among the Dogon of Mali, where they are still connected with male initiation rites; even today old men draw the different Dogon masks on rocks as they explain the mythical origin of each to the young men. In some of the hunting and dancing scenes discovered on rocks in the Sahara, one finds masks that have no modern counterparts anywhere except in West Africa, which is probably a sign of early migrations.

Rock painting of a masked figure at Tintazarift, Tassili, Algeria. Illustration from *Merveilles du Tassili N'Ajjer* (Editions du Chêne, Paris). Photo: Rapho, Lajoux.

The wealth of rock paintings and engravings in southern Africa attracted the attention of travelers and scholars at a very early date. Until recently, the Bushmen of the Kalahari Desert painted hunting scenes on the inner walls of their shelters; these scenes, in which the prey was pierced by arrows, expressed their hopes of a successful hunt. But only the latest examples of South African rock art are likely to be the work of the Bushmen. The figures are usually pricked in outline on the rock, but some are real engravings. The animals include extinct species, and some combine the body of a rhinoceros with the head of an elephant. The numerous paintings have been divided into many geographical groups: those of South-West Africa and southeastern Rhodesia on one side; those of Lesotho and South Africa (the Orange Free State and the eastern part of the Cape) on the other. There is a marked contrast in patina, state of preservation, subjects, colors and style between the works of each group. Some shelters were decorated at one period only, others were used continuously or at varying times, so that the superimposition of paintings left by successive settlers makes the deciphering of walls as difficult as reading a palimpsest. In the region to the east of the Orange River, the Abbé Breuil, by correlating the data of four corresponding regions, was able to single out at least sixteen series of paintings, of which only the most recent demonstrate the successive presence of various pastoral peoples, first Hottentots, then Bantu. The pictures on the Christol shelter show tall blacks in battle with a horde of small Bushmen who are attacking their cattle. In the most recent pictures, Europeans are quite recognizable in their nineteenth-century dress.

The oldest engravings and paintings may well be contemporary with the Upper Paleolithic Age of Europe and actually related to the cave frescoes found in eastern Spain, to which they bear a close resemblance. Southern Africa shows definite similarities with Western Europe of the Paleolithic Age both in its rock art and in the technical developments of its Stone Age. Besides its affinities with Iberian painting, the rock art of southern Africa shows a close resemblance to the frescoes of the southeastern Sahara and Libya. They show the same interest in the incidents of everyday life, as, for example, in the rock paintings of Tassili N'Ajjer. We know, too, that the Egyptians themselves probably derived their naturalistic animal art from a prehistoric Libyan source. This Libyan civilization may date back to the thawing of the last glacial age and would therefore be several thousands of years old. Naturalistic paintings were discovered a few years ago in the immediate vicinity of the copper-bearing Katanga Massif. The level at which the artists worked has been excavated from under thick strata of wind-blown sand below the paintings. Carbon-14 dating has placed them as belonging to the years 4600-4100 B.C.—that is, the period during which Paleolithic civilization still survived in the Sahara, the Maghrib and as far as Western Europe, while Neolithic civilization, which had first appeared in the Near East, reached Greece, Crete and the Nile Valley. Experts have been able to deduce from these facts that there were large migrations of peoples who fled from the desert and from northeastern Africa at about the same time and who gradually reached Spain, the Maghrib and southern Africa. It may be objected at first that there was a considerable time-lag between the time they left the desert and northern Africa and their arrival in southern Africa. This delay is considered insignificant by both geologists and specialists in the area of prehistory, accustomed as they are to counting in thousands of years. The Bantu, who only arrived there in the seventeenth century, could be the last wave of these immigrants who were always heading southward, passing between the equatorial forests and the western shores of the Great Lakes. Intermarriage, which began while they were on their way and continued when they reached the land of their choice, gradually integrated the newcomers with the original inhabitants.

The most famous of all rock paintings in southern Africa is that of the *White Lady* in the Brandberg Mountains, whose peaks rise in a desolate area of South-West Africa and separate the Kalahari from the coastal desert. Above a group of figures, which could belong to any of about ten earlier pictorial techniques, appear the astonishing figures of the eleventh layer. A ceremonial procession passes in profile between two rows of oryx (antelopes) and moves toward a group of musicians, two of whom are playing the musical bow. In the middle, the "White Lady" walks lightly, dressed in an ornate garment, rather like those of the girls pictured in Cretan bullfights. She carries an offering in her right hand and an archer's gauntlet covers her left. Of the twenty-five figures in the procession, seventeen have red hair trimmed like a wig, six are Mediterranean types, six others are certainly blacks, and not one is a Bushman or a Hottentot. All are shod and some appear to be helmeted. There are no quivers, no

Rock painting. Tanzoumaitak, Tassili, Algeria. *Photo: Rapho, Lajoux.*

shields, no assegais and no domestic animals. The Abbé Breuil concluded: "It shows a mixed population, including white elements and blacks with a strong Egyptian strain." But the specialists are more reserved on the subject today, especially on the figure of the "White Lady" (is it even a woman?) and the age of the painting.

During the course of its long history, Egyptian civilization certainly reached the limits of the rain forest on several occasions. Centers, earlier than this civilization, existed at least as far south as Khartoum, where

Rock painting known as the *White Lady*. Brandberg Mountains, South-West Africa. Copied by the Abbé Breuil. *Photo: Musée de l'Homme.*

archeologists have discovered the remains of a Mesolithic settlement, which may date back to the seventh millennium B.C. Isolated elements that go back even further and that did not evolve comparable civilizations left distinct traces of their presence in the otherwise persistently Paleolithic setting. (See also *Buffalo; Bushmen; Cattle; Dance; Elephants; Horses; Migrations; Painting, Modern; Sahara.*) D.P.

ROYALTY. Africa has evolved a great variety of ways of governing people; we are only just beginning to realize the wealth of its traditional political experience. African political systems form a complex series ranging from the Pygmy or Negrillo "band" to the military state organized among the Zulu by Chaka.

A number of societies are organized within the framework of clan or lineage groups; power is based on genealogical order and kinship (in the broadest sense of the term), while alliances resulting from matrimonial exchange and common ritual obligations weave a network of interdependence. In other societies, particularly in East Africa, age groups, which can be joined only by participating in specific initiation rites, are the instruments of government, as is the case among the Masai and the Kikuyu of Kenya.

Chieftainships constitute a more clearly defined political unit, and they exist in Africa in several different forms. One of the most elaborate has been developed by the Bamileke of Cameroun. It has political machinery, is centered in a capital, employs "civil servants" and uses the services of specialized societies and age groups, which participate mainly in work of communal interest. The leading figures of the Bamileke chieftainship are the chief (*fo*) and the first dignitary (*kwipu*), who was once mainly a war chief. The first acts as a unifying force, the guardian of the established order, a conciliator and intercessor before the ancestors and the most important divinities. The second official is more concerned with external affairs; he is responsible for guarding against threats to the state from outside and supervising its military strength. They are rival powers to a certain extent, counterbalancing each other in their activities. This example indicates the quality of the political mechanisms that can operate within the most developed types of chieftainships. It also illustrates certain characteristics of the African political phenomenon: the relationship with the sacred and the polarization of power, which is supposed to ensure internal peace and safe frontiers. The African chieftainships anticipated the traditional state, but they were not the same as states, even when they united in a confederation like that of the Ashanti of Ghana. Several of them seem like political systems that resulted from the disintegration of a state—for example, those found on the borders of the ancient empire of Mali in the western Sudan or on the fringes of the ancient empire of Balunda in central Africa.

The monarchical and imperial states that continued to exist for several eras left their marks on African history and filled its pages with illustrious names: the empires of Ghana, Mali and the Songhai succeeded each other in the west during the Middle Ages; the kingdoms of the interlacustrine region in East Africa were rebuilt between the seventeenth and the nineteenth centuries; the great central states, such as Kongo, and southeastern states, such as the famous Monomotapa, were known at a very early date as a result of contacts established with the interior. Until recently, new states were created and older states were undone with great frequency: the new Hausa sultanates of Nigeria and the Zulu kingdom were formed during the first two decades of the nineteenth century, but the monarchy of Rwanda collapsed once it regained independence. In contrast, there are states that have lasted an exceptionally long time: the Mossi state in Upper Volta, which arose at the turn of the twelfth and thirteenth centuries, survived the vicissitudes of colonization and the establishment of a Voltaic government at the end of the colonial period; the kingdom of the

Baganda, in Uganda, by modernizing its governmental machinery, has continued to have a place in history; and the Hausa states still exercise fairly strong pressure on Nigerian politics. The kings of Africa did not all succumb under the weight of colonialism or the attacks of modernity.

The traditional African states can be divided into types according to a number of criteria. The kind of social inequality characteristic of the state structure is one of the most relevant types of criteria: Is the society divided into a hierarchy of groups differentiated according to ethnic origins (the interlacustrine kingdoms), organized in a system of "orders" and castes (the Wolof kingdoms of Senegal), or stratified into social proto-classes (modern Buganda)? The nature of relations with the sacred, which largely determines the personality of the ruler and the style of government, offers another basis for classification. Some states can be said to have a divine royalty, as in the Benin region, where the royal genealogies are extensions of those of the gods. The Yoruba believe that Odudua, "born from the lord of the heavens," is the root of humanity and the father of all their rulers. The kings of the

King Kata Mbula. Bakuba. Zaire. Wood. Musée royal de l'Afrique centrale, Tervuren. *Museum photo.*

Sacred drums of Rwanda, symbols of the royal power. They are given the same respect as the king himself. *Photo: Jacques Maquet.*

Sacred precinct in the royal
palace of the Banyoro.
Uganda. *Photo: Magnum,
George Rodger.*

reinforced by the authority he exercised over
the believers. The theocracy set up by the
Tukulor in Senegal toward the end of the
eighteenth century is a perfect illustration of
this type of state.

The symbolic systems and rituals, the
obligations and taboos that govern the
behavior of African kings contain elements
from which theories of royalty can be
deduced. An illustration of this kind of
theoretical reconstruction is the deduction of
a "political philosophy" from the treatment
of the king of the Banyoro of Uganda. The
ruler (*mukama*) is the embodiment of the
country. The sacred characteristics of his
power and person are exalted. The king is the
source of life for his country and people; he is
the instigator and protector of a civilizing
force that is primarily concerned with the
fight against death. He has to be protected
against evil, separated from everything that
is a sign of disease or death and maintained
in a state of ritual purity. These obligations
can be explained by the need for the correct
handling of his power, called *mahano*, which
has sacred origins—a power that arranges all
things in proper order, but that can be the
source of disorder if its ritual treatment is not
correct. The ceremonial associated with the
king also reflects the position of the ruler,
who is both separate (he is "unique") and
superior; it provides him with specific names
and honorific titles, and demands the use of a
special vocabulary exclusively concerned
with his person and activities. When the king
is invested with his authority, behavior is
prescribed for him and various symbols
attached to him express his functions on the
strictly political plane; he ordains, protects,
dispenses justice and maintains the peace of
the realm. At this time, he is also given
instruction in all his duties toward his
people. Political theory is solemnly set forth,
analyzed and explained in countless ways.

The traditional African states were not
only instruments for effective government
and makers of history, they were also stimuli
for the creating of the products of civilization. The borders of these states coincide
to some extent with the lines enclosing the
great regions of black art in western and
central Africa. Benin and Ife, the Bateke and
Kongo kingdoms, the realms of the Baluba
and Bakuba were creators of works that now
belong to the treasury of world civilization.
The royal figures of Ife and the sculpted
portraits of the Bakuba kings dominate
exhibitions in museums just as they once
dominated the scene of African history. (See
also *Architecture; Armies; Art, African;
Castes; Elephants; Feudalism; Granaries;
Incest; Lions; Myths; Recados; Religion;*

Yoruba were considered to be gods; the
layouts of their palaces were symbolic of
celestial royalty; they themselves were
thought to be above the trivial necessities of
eating, drinking and sleeping, and were
immune from disease and death; a mastery
over the forces of life and fertility was
attributed to them. In other traditional
states, royalty had a magical emphasis: the
rulers were not assimilated with the gods, but
they possessed exceptional powers that
revealed their tacit connection with the
sacred. The ancient kingdom of Kongo
exemplifies this type of state. The person of
the king of Kongo and the country were one,
bound in a mystic union that was held
together by a set of forces that govern life and
prosperity. The ruler had to give proof of his
vigor by triumphing over his rivals and
seizing his royal status—an obligation that is
expressed in a well-known Kongolese
proverb. The domination of the king over
men (he was the "absolute lord") was also a
domination over the cosmos; he controlled
the mechanisms that ensured social order
and the order of the world. Finally, there
were the theocratic states that were created
by the expansion of black Islam, where the
ruler wielded political power that was

Tribute; Widows; individual tribes, kingdoms and empires.) G.B.

RWANDA. The bibliography of recent works on Rwanda is probably longer than that on any other country in Africa. It is small and densely populated; the area is just a little larger than Maryland and has a population of nearly 4 million—that is, a density of 245 inhabitants per square mile. There are many reasons for the interest roused in this attractive country. The landscape has a gentle, human appeal, with its hills scattered with houses surrounded by banana plantations, green valleys, fields and pastures. The physical types of its people are very varied: the Batusi (Tutsi or Watutsi) are slender and tall, the Bahutu (Hutu) vigorous and thick-set, while the Batwa have Pygmoid traits. Its traditional ceremonies are particularly picturesque: the solemn display of the long-horned cattle to the notables and the often-filmed war dances, for example. There are other and more serious reasons for the number and importance of the historical, anthropological and sociological studies devoted to traditional and modern Rwanda. The texts of its oral traditions have been fixed for generations, and this is a rare gift for historians of Africa because they can establish landmarks in a dynastic chronology that goes back about four centuries. The social institutions and ancient cultural structures have lasted for a long time too. The first European did not cross the country until 1894, and it was not until 1925 that the first far-reaching reforms imposed from outside were put through. In about the middle of the twentieth century it was still possible for anthropologists to question several survivors from the old regime. A violent social revolt by the mass of Bahutu peasants against the traditional Batusi aristocracy broke out in 1959. This liberation movement succeeded in overthrowing the monarchy and eliminating all the influence of the old privileged governing caste in the new independent republic, which succeeded the Belgian protectorate in 1962. Rwanda, in fact, richly deserves all the attention it has attracted.

Rwanda was one of the interlacustrine kingdoms that escaped the invasion of the Nilotic Luo in the fifteenth century. Consequently, the Batusi, who were pastoral warriors of Ethiopid origin and descendants of conquerors themselves, were able to maintain their domination over agriculturists five or six times more numerous than they. This supremacy was at first political. Physical coercion, the ultimate sanction of power, was the prerogative of the Batusi alone; in the armies, the Bahutu were put in charge of only administration and supplies. Furthermore, the hierarchy that wielded the authority, the king (*mwami*), his councillors, the chiefs of provinces and hills, the masters of the land and herds, were all Batusi. This monopoly of the privileges of public office continued under Belgian colonization. In 1957, for example, the Batusi, who represented 17 percent of the Rwanda population, occupied 97 percent of the seats in the upper council of the country.

Although all the governors were Batusi, not all the Batusi were administrators, but they all did enjoy a social position superior to that of any peasant. The mere fact of belonging to the upper caste enabled a Batusi to bring effective pressure to bear on a peasant. The diffuse, overall power was crystalized in the feudal institution of *Ubuhake,* which was a means by which a peasant obtained the protection of one noble against the abuses of the others. He bound himself to the noble who became his lord and, in exchange for his protection, gave him the produce of his fields and the service of his labor. The Batusi safeguarded their rank by erecting barriers that segregated them from the peasants; they ate, pursued their recreations, married and raised their children within their caste. The barriers were not abolished during the colonial period; in fact, they even succeeded in raising them in new spheres of activity; schools, professions and careers became Batusi preserves.

While the Rwanda monarchy was strengthening its iron grip on the mass of

Lake Bulera, Rwanda. *Photo: Hoa-Qui.*

Batusi dancer. Rwanda.
Photo: Jacques Maquet.

peasants to the benefit of the Batusi aristocracy, it was also extending its territory by subjugating its neighboring kingdoms by conquest and intrigue. The gradual territorial expansion has been compared to the same kind of historical movements that preceded the stabilization of the frontiers of Western nations. The German occupation of Rwanda in 1899 halted this development. With the exception of a few disputed regions, traditional Rwanda, colonial Rwanda and independent Rwanda have had the same frontiers. The republic of Rwanda is consequently one of the only two young states of black Africa (the other is its neighbor Burundi) to be constituted on the base of a single, integrated traditional society. Although the Batusi monarchy did not manage to survive in independent Rwanda (it was rejected by 80 percent of the voters during the referendum of 1961), its work, the national unity of Rwanda, endures. It was, like so many other nations, forged by interest and compulsion. (See also *Armies; Basketry; Castes; Cows; Epics; Family; Feudalism; Incest; Kinship; Literature, Oral; Myths; Person; Pygmies; Race; Totemism.*) J.M.

SACRIFICE. The blood sacrifice is the culminating point of most rites and is a feature of all complex religious ceremonies. The immolation of the sacrificial victim frees the vital force that is contained in its blood so that it can then be used for a specific purpose. The blood is generally poured over an altar, to which it gives additional strength, and nourishes the divinity that is attached to the altar. Satisfied and often lured by the blood,

which has also been poured over the sacrificer, the suppliant and the participating group, the god will impart some of his strength to them in answer to their prayers. A sacrifice, then, is an exchange of friendly services between men and gods who need each other. Men and gods communicate in the body of the victim; secondary participants get small portions—of the heart and liver as well as the blood—while the most important members of the group receive carefully prescribed portions according to their age and position in the kin group or any other hierarchy.

The occasions for offering sacrifices are innumerable: when a man is weakened by illness, by breaking a taboo, by offending his ancestors or one of the gods; when a group is faced with a difficult undertaking, such as the inauguration of a new year of work or settling in a new spot, or is threatened with danger; when a new altar has to be consecrated; or when a person is on the verge of rising through initiation to a new status. The sacrifice is minutely regulated according to the purpose of the offering; the nature of the victim, its sex, its color, the conditions for its immolation, the way in which its blood is poured and the disposal of its remains are all carefully prescribed. There are countless secondary aspects to a sacrifice; among other things, it is often an act of divination. In such instances, the victim must die slowly so that its final movements can be carefully interpreted.

Most of the victims are domesticated animals, such as hens, goats, sheep or cattle —the choice depends on the importance of the ceremony and how extensively the vital force has to be distributed. Hunters sometimes sacrifice wild animals. But in a number of African societies, special circumstances and certain cults required human victims. When a serious danger threatened the whole country, the Bambara of Mali sacrificed an albino because his physical characteristics, according to myth, were associated with the powers of the waters; the different parts of his body were disposed of according to precise rules and some of them were eaten. The ancient Malinke, like the ancient Dahomans, offered human sacrifices when the foundation of a town or palace was laid or when a rampart was constructed so as to ensure that it would last. But it was primarily the royal cults that made routine use of human sacrifice. In the Zambezi region, the Mashona and other tribes that constituted the Monomotapa empire during the Middle Ages sacrificed men on the tombs of the king's ancestors. In the kingdoms of the Benin region, not only did the wives and servants of the king accompany him in his death, but, in addition, the immolation of a large number of human victims, generally prisoners of war or condemned men, was required by the cult of royal ancestors so that they could carry the messages of the reigning king to the eminent dead. The immolation of the king himself should be distinguished from this type of sacrifice. This was performed among tribes who thought that the weakening or loss of the king's powers through illness or old age would endanger the equilibrium and fecundity of the world and the community, and his ritual death and replacement by a more vigorous man was necessary to reestablish them. (See also *Altars; Cattle; Diet; Divination; Funerals; Heads; Meals; Meat; Mussoi; Pharmacopoeia; Priests; Religion; Sculpture, Stone; Sculpture, Wood; Zar.*) **P.M.**

SAHARA. *"God is white, and so is milk; lead balls are black, and so is the thirst of summer."* The three constants of nomadic Sahara civilization—milk from their herds, war and thirst—could not be better defined in so few images as in this Tuareg proverb from the Hoggar region of Algeria. Life was probably not always this hard. The engravings and paintings on the rocks of the Sahara reflect pleasanter living conditions, which gradually disintegrated. A Sahara of large wild animals is attested to by the engravings of the Fezzan, the Hoggar and the borderlands between Algeria and Morocco. A Sahara with the first black cultivators and their masked dancers is represented in the oldest frescoes of Tassili N'Ajjer. A Sahara of pastoral people of the "bovidian" period, which all the evidence suggests was a forgotten phase in the first Fulani migrations, is also depicted. More recent rock art, scattered between the Fezzan and the Sudanese Sahara, contains pictures of a Sahara with chariots, three millennia before cars drove across it. Herodotus, writing 2,500 years ago, described the Fezzan Garamantes pursuing the Ethiopian troglodytes (probably ancestors of the present-day Teda) "in four-horse chariots." But in the time of Herodotus, the eastern Sahara had already been invaded by Persians from Egypt who had a new means of transport, the camel.

The camel brought a far-reaching revolution to these almost barren lands. The people who adapted themselves to its paradoxical feeding habits used it as a means of surviving in the desert and of dominating the desert politically. In their endless search for pasture lands, it was the camel that governed the nomads' way of life. When the pastures were

Sacrifice of a kid at Ouidah, Dahomey. *Photo: Hoa-Qui.*

far from any wells, the herdsman lived for months on the milk of his camels. This alliance with the desert and the camel created a strange race of men who were both indolent and indefatigable, pillagers yet hospitable, who based their lives on a unique combination of livestock raising, trade, armed robbery and poetry. The Sahara has had the power to attract some of the most outstanding foreigners, to hold them and bind them all with the spell of its bareness and to make mystics of them. Examples range from the Desert Fathers to Duveyrier, from Foucauld to Psichari, and include countless soldiers and geologists.

The southern edge of the Sahara bordering on the Sudan and commonly referred to as the Sahel (from the Arabic word *sahil,* meaning "border" or "coast") was once a flourishing region of great markets. In recent years, however, it has become an area of widespread famine due to drought and the encroachment of the desert into the once fertile lands to the south of it.

The economic and social stability of the western and southern Sahara, which are now undergoing radical change, once depended on the duality of white desert nomads and black cultivators of the oases, the former of whom both protected and exploited the

Rock painting at Tassili N'Ajjer in the Sahara. Illustration from *Merveilles du Tassili N'Ajjer* (Editions du Chêne, Paris). *Photo: Rapho, Lajoux.*

The Sahara and the Niger; to the right is King Mansa Musa. Detail from the *Catalan Atlas* of Charles V by the Majorcan Abraham Cresque (1375). Bibliothèque nationale, Paris.

latter. The whole society, from top to bottom, was based on a feudal structure. At the top were the noble Tuareg and Mauri; beneath them were the nomadic groups (called "goat people" in Tuareg country) who paid them an annual tribute; and still lower were the cultivators or slaves, who had a great deal of black African blood in their veins. Another vertical cleavage made a clear division between the Tuareg, who are close to their Berber origins, and the neighboring Mauri and Arabs. The culture of the former is based on leather; their tents, shields, saddle-bags to hold their provisions and possessions and, at one time, even their clothes were all made of skins. The latter,

who are strongly influenced by Arabic customs, have tents and bags woven of wool.

Innumerable accounts have exhausted the subject of life on the oases and its dual nature, rural and urban. Stopping places with artificially made greenery are scattered along the caravan routes and are an example of the ingenuity developed by the desert dwellers long ago in their search for and distribution and use of underground water-supplies. But these stop-overs seem like prisons to the outside observer. Modern times are bringing the oases dwellers a chance to escape for the first time. Many in Algeria and Libya abandoned their date palms and wheat for oil-prospecting work, but once this came to an end, most of them settled on the outskirts of towns and helped to swell the ranks of unemployed. (See also *Almoravids; Arab Chroniclers; Bornu; Camels; Goats; Gold; Hunger; Ivory; Migrations; Nile; Rock Art; Salt; Songhai; Sudan; Weaving.*)　　　　P.A.

SAHEL. See *Sahara.*

SALT. Africa is a very old continent, largely constituted by land that emerged at the beginning of the earth's development and consequently without any large sedimentary basins. Nearly all its coastline is rectilinear, with very sheer drops and narrow beaches, so that the tide does not spread far over the land. A consequence of this is the rarity of certain mineral salts: calcium and especially sodium chloride. There are no rich salt deposits except in the Sahara and on the coasts of Senegal, Somaliland and Eritrea, where the formation of the shore, the course of the tides and, in particular, the general dryness and hot sun make collecting salt fairly easy.

Lack of salt has pathological results: it decreases resistance to certain infections and leaves the body vulnerable to certain forms of anemia. The cannibalism that was once known to exist in the center of the continent and in the remote parts of the forest belt was one way of winning the battle against this deficiency. There are other, less radical ways of winning: the most common is to use an ersatz form of salt—potassium salt, which is obtained by burning certain plants and leaching the ashes. Natron (hydrated sodium carbonate) is quite commonly found in wells used by animals in the central and eastern Sudan. By far the largest source is the importation of salt from abroad, coming by sea today and by land across the Sahara in early times. Salt was for a long time the main article of barter used by the whites of the Maghrib and the desert. According to Arab

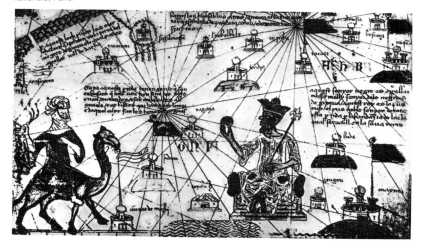

Duel between Tuareg of the Hoggar region. *Photo: Pierre Ichac.*

Detail of a burial urn of the Kisalean culture (seventh-eighth centuries). Sanga excavations. Zaire. *Photo: Jacques Maquet.*

chroniclers, it was bartered for its weight in gold dust and the negotiations were carried on with gestures.

Saharan salt was of prime political importance in the history of the Sudan states; political and economic supremacy depended on controlling the import routes and even, at times, the salt mines themselves. The quarrel between the Songhai and Morocco, which eventually led to the Moroccan invasion of 1959, concerned the ownership of the Taodenni deposits. Walata, Timbuktu, Gao, Agades and Bilma were originally salt trading centers. The *azalai*, the "great caravan" from Taodenni, with its thousands of *mehara* loaded with salt in slabs and bars, was still flourishing at the end of the Second World War, but at that time, rather than bartering slaves for a half-quintal slab (approximately 500 pounds), skins and cattle were exchanged for the salt. The slabs and bars were cut up in the trading centers and then exported south toward the forests by river or by such modern means as trucks, which brought kola nuts from the forest back to the savanna. In spite of imported sea salt and the installation of salt pans along the Atlantic coast, Saharan salt and "herb salt" (potassium salt extracted from ashes) are still used as luxury condiments and in the traditional pharmacopoeia. The caravan trade in rock salt is still thriving in the center of the continent (around Wadai and Darfur), where the competition of imported salt is restricted by the prohibitive cost of transport. (See also *Camels; Chad, Lake; Ghana; Gold; Markets; Songhai.*)   P.A.

SANGA. Sanga is a prehistoric site in the Republic of Zaire, on the west bank of Lake Kisale, which is drained by the Lualaba River. It is a vast cemetery dating from about 1000 B.C. Each skeleton in it is surrounded by an oval of pots made specially for this purpose: none shows any sign of having been used; many are too small for domestic use, and some are very tiny and roughly modeled. Elegant, simple decorations, which follow the lines of the vessels, give the pots a classical, balanced look. Nenquin hás distinguished three cultures at Sanga and has designated the principal one as "the Kisalean culture." The pottery of all three is quite different from that of the Baluba, who now live in the region. The collection includes some small vessels whose bodies are decorated with friezes of human figures and whose long necks end in flattened lips on each of which is drawn, beneath a row of scallops, a figure that may be that of a man or a bull. In several tombs, a piece of a goat's or antelope's hoof is arranged beside the corpse. In one tomb, there are the remains of a morsel of food pushed into the mouth of the dead man. Several metal objects have been found, mainly of copper and iron: spear- and arrowheads, knives, razors, small crosses, hooks, needles and nails. There is also a profusion of ornaments: belts made of copper chains or twisted wire, metal necklaces, breastplates of copper leaf, bracelets of metal or carved ivory, copper rings and other objects. The Sanga collection, which was discovered only recently, appears to be unrelated culturally to any other known collection, either past or present. The skeletons are still being examined.   J.H.

SAO. The name Sao has been applied to several different black non-Muslim peoples, no longer extant, who lived south of Lake Chad (in Nigeria, Cameroun and Chad) from the fifth century B.C. until the

Ancestor statue of the Sao. Chad. Pottery. *Photo: Dominique Darbois.*

introduction of Islam. Among the many names that had been given to them—*So, Soo, Soy, Sau, Saw, Tso, Nssoh* and *Sao*—the last was finally adopted because it corresponded to the usual pronunciation of the word used in their former territory to mean "men" and implying "men of former times."

The Sao people were constituted by a regrouping of people of diverse origins. From the north, from Bilma and Fachi, came hunters armed with spears and clothed in skins who worked their way down along the northwest tip of Lake Chad. From the south, from the Mandara Mountains, hunters had come armed with bows and arrows. Added to these were fishermen from the east, from the area round Lake Fitri, and other hunters. The Sao were distinct from the Muslim peoples of the Chad country (the term "Chad" being used in its broadest sense); they had an obvious affinity with the animist Kirdi groups in northern Cameroun, and some institutions of a number of tribes in central Chad and northern Nigeria can be compared with those of these vanished people.

The remains of their former settlements can be located accurately between the Yoobé River and Lake Chad, in the west and north,

and Lake Fitri, which is east of the Chari River. The lower course of the Chari, south of Mandjafa, the Logone River as far north as Sarasara and their branches constituted the principal axes of their country, although oral tradition, gathered over a vast area, claims that it covered a larger territory. They have even been credited with building Kano and drilling wells between Tanout and Agades, as well as living at Kanem before they settled south of Lake Chad.

At a later date, obviously Islamic characteristics were added to the legends which made them into giants whose achievements were colossal and which attributed to them the construction of most of the walled cities in this part of Africa. This explains why followers of Muhammed believed that they were of eastern origin. The historical truth seems to be that they were connected with the kingdom of Kanem-Bornu. Nevertheless, they were a well-organized group of tribes, composed of variously armed hunters and fishermen who were not only able to preserve their independence but also to maintain their supremacy over the country for several hundreds of years, from the eleventh to the fourteenth centuries. Little is known about them before the eighth century, the period before the first dynasty of Kanem, when the Sao occupied an area stretching to the north and east of Lake Chad. In 930, they were also established south of the lake, where they founded Minntour forty years later. They lived on good terms with the rulers of Kanem until the fourteenth century, when they had to fight to keep their independence. The struggle went on for more than two centuries, notably against Idris Alaoma, king of Bornu and successor to the Kanembu rulers. At the end of the sixteenth century, most of the Sao towns were conquered by the Bornuans, and large numbers of inhabitants were massacred or led into slavery. Those who succeeded in escaping were scattered and sought refuge in the islands in Lake Chad or emigrated to the Mandara Mountains and as far as the middle reaches of the Benue River, where recently discovered remains have been attributed to them. Several tribes of this region still claim a Sao origin: the Mobber on the banks of the Yoobé, the Manga and Dogara of the Gouré, the Kuri and Buduma of Lake Chad, the Gamergu and Mandara of the Mandara Mountains, the Gueue, Njei and Holma of the Benue. The Sao who remained along the lower reaches of the Chari and Logone Rivers were forced to abjure their ancient faith and accept Islam, although this conversion was not completed in the south until the eighteenth century. Their most direct descendants intermarried with the invaders and are known as the Kotoko, whose institutions, while strongly influenced by those of the Kanuri (or Bornuans), bear traces of those of their Sao ancestors, with whom they are often confused both in oral literature and written texts. But it should be noted that a number of present-day tribes with similar names, the So of the Congo Basin and the Saho (also called Sao) among others, have no connection with the Sao of the Chad region.

Several hundreds of hillocks mark the sites of their former settlements, some of which are still occupied by the Kotoko. Most of them are situated beside rivers or temporary water-courses, in particular the Chari, the Logone, the Serbéouel and El Obéit. They are easily recognizable because they constitute the only high ground that is not submerged during the annual floods. A wealth of material has been excavated from them, mainly made of terracotta and metal (copper, bronze and iron). Although the collection is heterogeneous, there is no doubt about its cultural unity. It has been divided for the moment into two principal periods, Sao I and Sao II, followed by a more recent and shorter period, Sao III. It is thought that the hunters occupied the smallest hillocks (Sao I) because long graves, which have been found only in the deepest layers of the other sites, have been uncovered in them. These graves contained fine, delicately ornamented pottery—some pieces of which resemble the potsherds found in the Bahr el Ghazal of Chad—metal objects and the oldest human figurines of baked clay.

The most extensive hillocks (Sao II), which are surrounded by walls and were occupied more recently (some of them are still lived on by the Kotoko), are far more numerous than the Sao I sites. Two kinds of graves have been excavated in them: tombs in which the body is stretched out, like those in the small hillocks, and urn burials, which are found above the tombs. A probable explanation is that the hunters living there were overrun by a large group of fishermen who transformed their vulnerable settlements into clusters of dwellings that were protected by wooden ramparts. These were soon replaced by imposing enclosures of dried mud in which the builders buried human victims. The art of pottery-making flourished with this wave of immigrants. They modeled large burial urns, human and animal figurines (statuettes and masks in various styles) and diverse objects, including domestic and ritual vessels, toys, money, jewelry, tools, chairs and pipes. They may also have introduced spinning and cotton

Head from a Sao statue. Chad. Pottery. *Photo: Dominique Darbois.*

weaving into the region and a refined metallurgy in which bronze was cast by the lost-wax process to make heavy ritual rings, libation bowls and delicate jewels, sometimes decorated with finely modeled faces. Their other artifacts included axes of Neolithic appearance, which were used for religious ceremonies, ivory and mother-of-pearl jewels and bone harpoons. (See also *Chad, Lake.*)   J.-P.L.

SAVANNA. The term "savanna" is applied to tropical grassland regions where rainfall is seasonal and there is one long, dry season. Various kinds of grasses form the main vegetation along with trees and shrubs that vary in kind and number according to the climate and soil but that never grow densely enough to hinder the growth of a thick carpet of grass. Herbivorous ungulates and animals living off them are the principal fauna of the savanna. The character of the savanna is both natural and artificial. The practice of lighting bush fires and shifting agricultural land to burn ground tends to enlarge the savanna area by destroying trees and even forests in places where they exist in precarious equilibrium with the grassland.

The savanna landscape varies greatly. The Guinean savannas skirt the equatorial forest and then continue along the water-courses (in the Baule country in the Ivory Coast and in the Ashanti country in Ghana, for example). The annual rainfall of the savannas in the southern Sudan is more than 40 inches; several varieties of large trees grow there, and butter trees are to be found. It is possible to raise livestock in the Basari country in Senegal and in the Bobo and Lobi country in Upper Volta because the tsetse fly is rare. The rainfall of the northern Sudanese savanna is only 23 to 39 inches. Here, baobab, tamarind and acacia trees are

Gao, Mali. *Photo: Documentation française.*

common. Most of the Sudanese empires grew up in this area. In the savanna of the Sahel, the butter tree disappears and acacias become the most common variety of tree. Palm trees and *Cenchrus biflorus,* the characteristic grass of this zone, are also found there. It is the country of nomadic herdsmen (the Fulani and Bororo). In the lagoon areas along the Gulf of Guinea, the coastal savannas are veritable clearings in the forest and fostered an environment in which the civilizations of Benin and Ife were able to develop.

In eastern and southern Africa, the higher altitude of the land and the higher rainfall modify the distribution of the savanna regions. The eastern equatorial part of the savanna belt occupies most of Kenya, Tanzania and Uganda. The coastal area on the east is a mosaic of forest and wooded savanna. In the Great Lakes region and on the eastern and central plateaus, dense forest and savanna often coexist. A comparison has often been drawn between the "temperate, human" savanna and the forest "full of fears." Most of the African kingdoms and empires whose names are familiar to us arose in the savanna: the realms of Fouta Toro, Segou and Adamawa; the empires of Mali, Yatenga and Bornu; and, in the south, the kingdoms of Loango and Buganda and the empire of Monomotapa.

The balanced, energy-giving food resources of the savanna belt have bred strong, tall peoples. Livestock, fish and millet, which is easy to store and transport, are plentiful. Easy communications over open, flat country and flourishing trade probably contributed to the rise of the African empires. But the savanna countries were also open to influences from the Mediterranean lands of North Africa, and the ease of communications across the grasslands was partly responsible for the rapid disintegration of the empires that were built on them. (See also *Agriculture; Bajokwe; Bakuba; Balunda; Bamum; Bapende; Baule; Calendars; Cassava; Cattle; Dwellings;*

Herd of gazelles in the savanna. *Photo: Hoa-Qui.*

Fauna; Flora; Granaries; Guro; Hunger;
Ivory; Massa; Peanuts; Stories; Sudan;
Traps.)   I.G.

SCARIFICATION. In Africa, tattooing
(an unsuitable word hallowed by use) does
not only consist in injecting an indelible ink
beneath the skin with a needle (as among the
ancient Polynesians and in Europe and
America), it also takes the form of linear
scars cut in grooves or in relief. The grooved
scarifications of the Hausa are made up of
short, fine lines that are either isolated or
grouped more or less densely. Among other
tribes, such as the Bateke, the scar grooves
are spread over a large area and the lines are
long and fine. Grooved scarifications are
particularly common in West Africa. Here,
they are much broader than those just

described, and they vary in length among the
Bargu, the Bambara and the Mossi. Salient,
or relief, scarifications range from single
points to graphic configurations whose
composition and execution are obviously
products of great artistic skill; this is the case
with the scarifications of the Bamileke, for
example. Finally, in contrast to grooved
facial slashes, there are equally prominent
salient slashes—for example, those of the
Sara in Chad. Whether the operation takes a
short or long time, it is always painful. In the
Bamileke country, in southern Cameroun,
the artist uses three instruments: a long iron
needle, a knife with a wooden handle and a
curved blade, and a triangularly shaped
native razor. The design is first traced lightly
with the knife, then touched up with the
razor or needle; the needle is inserted into the
marked area of the skin to raise it, and the
necessary amount of flesh is then cut away
with the razor. Many of these scars are tribal
marks: during the initiation retreats that take
place during adolescence, children have the
signs of their new dignity and responsibilities
incised into their flesh—the signs that they
have become men. The operation may
spread over several years. Among the Kabre
of Togo, boys become *efalu* when they are
fourteen and are then marked with their first

Scarifications. Dengese royal
statue. Zaire. Wood.
Sammlung für Völkerkunde,
University of Zurich. *Photo:*
Jacques Verroust.

Scarifications. Dar es
Salaam, Tanzania. *Photo:*
Jacques Maquet.

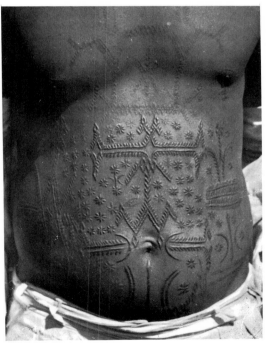

scars; at about the age of seventeen, the *efalu* become *espa* and their heads are shaved in public; but it is not until they are twenty that they are promoted to the rank of *kondo* and receive all the marks that prove they have become active members of the community. In Dahomey, men and women dedicated to the cult of a *vodun* are marked for life with the signs of their dedication. Elsewhere, tattooing, especially most female tattooing, has only an aesthetic purpose. The scarifications of the Tiv of Nigeria vary according to tribe and also according to age; those scars known as *abaji* are made only on men over forty-five years old, while the young only have a right to have marks scratched with a fingernail. The Bushmen hunters still preserve a prehistoric custom that consists in incising the back and arms of a young boy and rubbing the wounds with burnt meat to instill in him the energy and agility of game animals. Quite often, the designs incised on faces and bodies are copied by local sculptors and used as decorative elements. This kind of decoration can help to fix the exact provenance of a statue when it is otherwise uncertain. (See also *Art, African; Bena Lulua; Body; Ife; Societies, Secret.*) D.P.

SCULPTURE, STONE. African artists apparently considered stone more as a substitute for wood than as a distinct material associated with its own carving techniques and particular forms. Stone sculptures are small—statuettes rather than statues. The material used is nearly always a

Mintadi figurine. Zaire. Steatite. Musée royal de l'Afrique centrale, Tervuren. *Museum photo.*

soft stone, like steatite, that can be cut with a knife without crumbling.

In the Kissi country in upper Guinea, *pomdo* statuettes, which are representations of dead people, are found on the family cult altars in nearly every village. These works, which can be uncovered a little below the surface of the ground, are not products of the present inhabitants or of their immediate ancestors. Most of them are anthropomorphic—a human head or a complete standing figure. Animals are rarer; there are also cylinders and small pestles with square bases, some of them hewn from polished stone. It is not certain how old they are. The only bases for judgment are a few details of their costumes—breast-plates, helmets with rear peaks and rondaches—which suggest Portuguese armor of the sixteenth century. Modern imitations made of stone and pottery are of no interest. "Real" *pomdos* differ from these anonymous imitations in that each bears the name of an ancestor and is supposed to be his portrait. The identity of the statue, when this has not been revealed in a dream, is determined by the common practice of questioning it: the stone, laid on a litter suspended between the heads of two porters, leans to the right or left in answer to the questions. A "real" *pomdo* looks like a shapeless parcel covered with a black crust of sacrificial blood. It is questioned about the future and is asked to punish the guilty who remain undiscovered. The *nomoli* of Sierra Leone are made of steatite and are small, like the Kissi stone sculptures, but are quite different in style; often the figure is in a crouching position and has a hooked, prominent nose and parted lips that show its teeth. They received offerings after a plentiful harvest, but were sometimes beaten by owners of fields if the rains held off too long after the seeds were sown.

The largest group of African stone statues is found near the village of Esie in western Nigeria, in the Yoruba country, and contains nearly 800 pieces. The statues are probably contemporary with the "classical period," when the Ife artists were working in both bronze and terracotta. The Esie sculptures bear little resemblance to the modern Yoruba wooden sculptures. They may be the work of Nupe artists, the Nupe being a people who were converted to Islam around 1830 by force of arms and whose descendants are now living north of the Yoruba. Very few examples of Nupe statuary are known, and we do not know whether there was an earlier Nupe style. In Ife itself and in the surrounding area, artists sculpted steatite men and animals in a naturalistic style. They also erected granite monoliths, nearly twenty feet high, and carved elaborate chairs for ritual use out of enormous blocks of quartz. This is the sole example of the true mastery of stone-cutting techniques to be found in Africa.

A few years ago, 300 blocks of basalt were discovered in the Ekoi country along the upper reaches of the Cross River, on the frontiers of eastern Nigeria and Cameroun; they were engraved rather than sculpted. The tradition of adding a new block at the death of every clan chief continued until about 1900. Until recent times, the Bakongo on the south bank of the Congo River, on the Angola border, carved stone statuettes of their dead chiefs that hardly differ in style from their wooden statues of ancestors. This is probably a survival from the kingdom of Kongo, which the Portuguese said was extremely prosperous when they first arrived at the mouth of the Congo River. (See also *Kissi; Kongo; Zimbabwe*.)   D.P.

SCULPTURE, WOOD. Some characteristics are common to all African sculpture. With few exceptions, the form is governed by two equally important factors: first, the dominant tradition of the region or of the artist's village or tribe; second, the personal genius of the artist and his own powers of expression. The African sculptor does not imitate nature; he interprets, amplifies, sometimes simplifies the forms that he considers significant and treats casually or even ignores the details that he thinks are unimportant. Tradition governs the decorative motifs and the forms to a great extent, but a gifted artist who has the necessary technical means at his disposal can leave his personal mark on his work.

Wood is the most usual material, and the human figure is the most common subject. The starting point of the artist is a tree, which he cuts down in the forest, or a forked branch. The form of the trunk remains apparent in the large cylindrical drums and also in certain elongated ancestor figures, most of which are a little less than life-size. The general impression left by a work also depends on the accessories attached to the basic wood sculpture: the fiber skirt or loincloth in bark, clay, inlaid shells, beads, metal jewelry, feathers, pieces of leather. Statues of ancestors, both masculine and feminine, are sometimes carved as temporary refuges for the dead and sometimes just as commemorative images. Statues of ancestors are kept by the oldest member of the lineage, whose dwelling is the center of the family cult. Statues of this kind should be distinguished from "fetishes" (Africans have adopted the same word today), which seldom have such care lavished on them.

Stone sculpture; one of 800 found in the bush near Esie in the north of the Yoruba country. Nigeria. *Photo: Walter Dräyer.*

Shaft of a stone column. Kissi. Musée de l'Homme, Paris. *Museum photo, R. Pasquin.*

Some fetishes are kept by specialists, either magicians or diviners who, as "fetishists," know how to make them effective. Others are owned by individuals who have paid a high price for them. They serve to avert evil influences and defend their owner; they are dangerous to his enemies and, in a general way, to everyone they do not know; in fact, it is better to keep away from them. An anthropomorphic statue may also be the traditional image of a god to whom prayers and sacrifices are offered. It is often impossible to tell the difference between the statue of an ancestor and the image of a minor diety in the absence of precise information. The supreme god is present in every religion, but his image is never carved because prayers are not offered to him directly, just as a prince is not addressed directly but through an intermediary.

The pillars of houses, doors and locks, headrests, chairs, shells for loom pulleys and bowls are often decorated with motifs that are incised or carved in either high or low relief and that are inspired by the human figure or by animal forms. Such motifs are sometimes combined with others connected with weaving or basketry, which we would tend to describe as simply geometric but which have names that indicate otherwise. All ceremonial accessories, including the apparatus of a diviner, musical instruments

Bangwa (Bamileke) statue.
Cameroun. Wood. Princess
Gourielli Collection, Paris.
Photo: Ciccione.

Detail of a pulley for a Baule
weaving loom. Ivory Coast.
Wood. Pierre Vérité
Collection, Paris. *Photo:
Eliot Elisofon.*

Temne statue. Sierra Leone.
Wood. University Museum,
Philadelphia. *Museum photo.*

Baluba sculpture known as
"The Beggar Woman." Zaire.
Wood. Musée royal de
l'Afrique centrale, Tervuren.

and weapons are similarly decorated with motifs that nearly always have symbolic meaning; the decoration is the vehicle of a message whose meaning may have been lost or is, inevitably, not understood by everyone.

The geographical area or tribe that has produced a piece of sculpture can be deduced at least partially from its formal characteristics. But there are considerable stylistic variations in the work of a single tribe. Several factors contribute to the making of a style. First, the proportions of the different parts and the way they balance each other express certain relationships as well as convey a sense of overall volume; for example, a huge head, combined with an elongated bust in proportion to insignificant legs. Second, there is the treatment of the surfaces and the handling of detail; for example, the "concave" faces of Fang statues, in which the stylization of the eyes may sometimes be a single slit, sometimes an empty circle or a projecting cylinder. Within the same society, each tribe, sometimes each village, has its own style or substyle. Analogies can be made between some styles, but it would be impossible to speak of African sculpture as a whole or a unique style for the whole continent. The number and variety of styles reflect the vast range of African sculpture. Furthermore, the depredations of termites and the climate, which is often humid, have meant that no style could ever be fixed by the presence of authoritative models; the average life of a wooden sculpture is between twenty and twenty-five years. Thus, every sculptor could give free rein to his inspiration within the limits of fixed canons.

The African artist was nearly always a professional, trained craftsman, and he may have been a priest, a diviner or a magician as well. There are societies in which each man had to carve the mask that he would wear for a particular ceremony, perhaps only once in his life. In others, sculpture is a hereditary craft: the blacksmith may carve wood as well as work metal. Elsewhere, it is a matter of the preference or talent of an individual. But everywhere, the artist works within the framework of his tribal traditions. He enjoys social prestige and might fulfill a political or religious function. The presence of a professional artist and the work expected of him imply a certain amount of economic security and a more or less sedentary type of life; the Pygmies, for instance, who are continually on the move in search of game and food to be gathered in the forest, could never have the leisure to maintain professional sculptors.

The tools of wood sculptors are made of iron, the most important being an adz and perhaps a knife, a scraper and a chisel. When the sculptor has finished his training, he not only knows how to use his tools, he can make them. A master passes on to his pupil all the experience he has acquired as well as the secrets of his craft and the way to render traditional motifs.

Whether his medium is wood, metal or stone, the African artist gives his work three

Bajokwe "Young Girl" mask. Angola. Wood and plant fibers. Kinshasa Museum. *Photo: Eliot Elisofon.*

dimensions; a statue can only be fully appreciated if you walk around and, if possible, feel it. Although the forms have their points of departure in nature, they are not slavishly bound to realism. Each sculpture has its use, which is seldom for the benefit of an individual, but nearly always for at least part of a tribe—that is, for a village, a lineage, secret society, or age group. The work, then, is not only the expression of an individual, but emanates from the whole society.

The age of an African wood carving is always difficult to determine. The only sure date is that of its acquisition by its native locality; its date of purchase from a dealer indicates nothing. But the place of acquisition is not necessarily where it originated; works move around, and so do their sculptors. Few wooden pieces are more than 50 years old when acquired. Most of the

sculptures and masks preserved in museums and private collections are less than 150 years old. In some regions, statuary has disappeared; elsewhere, a falling off in the quality corresponds to a neglect of the traditional cults. Sculptors who formerly worked for sanctuaries or for special rites in which each detail had a purpose and whose work bore meaning related to the purpose for which it was created now try to sell works to strangers who cannot understand their meaning. These modern pieces, which have the same provenance as former works, are of interest only as copies, and generally mediocre ones at that. In some more fortunate regions, the institutions that controlled the sculptor have survived, and he continues the tradition of his fathers with renewed inspiration. (See also *Ancestors; Antelopes; Art, African; Art, Styles of; Bells; Dolls; Headrests; Horns; Household Furnishings; Masks; Spoons;* individual tribes.)

D.P.

SECRET SOCIETIES. See *Societies, Secret.*

SENUFO. The Senufo, who number about 1 million, live in an area divided today between the republics of the Ivory Coast, Mali and Upper Volta. They have not always occupied this territory; most of them came from the north two or three centuries ago. They manage to live off poor soil which they cultivate with the simplest implements. Their social structures are equally simple: the villagers lead closed existences and are unconcerned about the world outside; preferably, marriages unite different lineages of the same village. In another form of union, the married woman continues to live with her own people and her husband joins her two or three evenings a week; the children of such unions belong to the mother's lineage. Besides the village chief, there is a "master of the land," who is a representative of the first inhabitants and primarily a priest serving as an intermediary between the visible and invisible worlds; the earth is a divinity, not an object that can be owned.

The institution known as *Lo* cuts across kinship lines. All the adult men of the community belong to it, but young men have to undergo certain trials before they are given the esoteric knowledge that the society imparts to its sons from generation to generation but withholds from its daughters. There are three stages in the *Lo* organization, each of which lasts seven years; the first covers childhood, the second adolescence and the third adult life. An initiation rite marks the passage from one to the other, and

Mende statue. Sierra Leone. Wood. British Museum. *Museum photo.*

the final stage cannot be entered before the age of thirty. Once the initiation is completed, the Senufo is no longer bound to perform agricultural tasks; at this point, he joins the ranks of the "elders," whom the chief consults before making important decisions.

Each village has a sacred wood with a clearing that only the initiated may penetrate and where the attributes of the *Lo* are kept. These are masks and sculptures that invade the village when the society holds its festivals, initiations, funerals, rites marking the end of mourning and agrarian festivals. The ancestors preside over all these activities. The masks have several functions. Those representing ancestors barely cover the face. They are naturalistic in style, but do not attempt to be reproductions of human faces and cannot be considered portraits. A heraldic symbol—bird, chameleon or bunch of palm nuts—crowns each mask and indicates the caste or group to which the wearer belongs. The best known of the great composite masks is a combination of antelope horns, the muzzle of a carnivore

and the jaw of a crocodile. The sorcerer hunter puts it on for his nocturnal expeditions. Armed with a whip and spitting flames of burning hemp fibers, he leaps about to the sound of horns and spreads terror around him.

The large Senufo statues are among the masterpieces of African art. They are ancestor figures, and the newly initiated, during their nocturnal processions, pound them against the ground as they pray to the Great Mother of the village, Ka Tyeleo, to grant them her gifts of abundant harvests and numerous children.

Their use explains the elongated form of these statues, which are midway between the

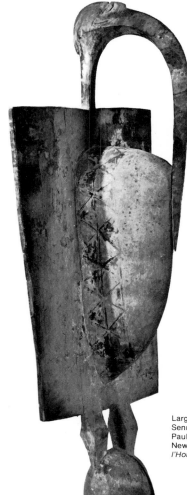

Large sculpture of a calao. Senufo. Ivory Coast. Wood. Paul Tishman Collection, New York. *Photo: Musée de l'Homme.*

Detail of a Senufo statue. Ivory Coast. Wood. Rietberg Museum, Zurich. *Photo: W. Dräyer.*

Senufo door. Ivory Coast. Wood. Abidjan Museum. *Photo: Ciné-Publicité.*

Calabash sistrum used at Dogon circumcision ceremony. Mali. Musée de l'Homme, Paris. *Museum photo.*

extended forms of the Sudan and the more compact statues of Guinea. Smaller sculptures are used for divination and fertility rites. The styles vary considerably from region to region, and the subjects include mother and child, horsemen, seated and standing couples and hornbills, with their long beaks curved onto their protruding bellies and outstretched wings, which are carved in the form of two long rectangles. According to Senufo mythology, the hornbill was one of the first five animals to appear on the earth, along with the chameleon, the tortoise, the snake and the crocodile; it was the first, too, to be killed for food; and it is the hornbill who carries the souls of the dead to the other world. In spite of their weight, the large hornbill statues (some are more than four feet high) were carried on the heads of the novices at the *Lo* ceremonies, during which they represented the living forces of the universe. (See also *Art, Styles of; Birds; Masks.*) D.P.

SISTRA. The sistrum is a musical instrument that was known to several ancient civilizations—Sumer, Egypt and Crete among them—and an almost identical form of the instrument is still played in the Ethiopian Church. Except for its wooden handle, the Ethiopian sistrum is completely made of metal; small wires attached to two upright rods are threaded with disks that clash against each other when the slightest movement is made. Two primitive types of sistra, made entirely of wood, were reported nearly a century ago in Mali and Guinea. Both types are fashioned from a bough of a tree, with the bough stripped of all but one smaller branch. The larger branch serves as a handle, and disks, made from whole calabashes or from the ends of fruit rinds cut in the form of roundels, are slipped over the smaller one. The instrument is held upright and shaken so that the pile of disks bangs up against the top end of the small branch and then drops down to the bottom end. Only sistra with roundels can be used to beat an exact rhythm. Sistra are associated with the rites of circumcision or excision, depending on the region. In Mali, the instrument is played by the newly circumcised to herald their presence and ward off women. In Guinea, members of both sexes use it during the dances that are part of initiation ceremony celebrations. The sistrum is generally made in the place of retreat and is sometimes destroyed after initiation. Among the Bozo and Bambara, where the top of the handle is sometimes sculpted with the image of a mask, it is reserved for use by the men. The sistra of the circumcised and excised

among the Malinke and Kissi are decorated between the handle and the rod with a network of multicolored cotton threads, called "thread crosses," that are considered to be apotropaic. (See also *Dance; Music.*)
A.S.

SKY. See *Heaven.*

SLAVERY. The term "slavery" evokes, simultaneously, the idea of the social condition that made people dependent and deprived of political rights as well as the idea of the shameful traffic that was carried on by slave traders. Within Africa, slavery, which was sometimes referred to as "captivity," entailed loss of personal liberty and complete dependence upon a social group or a man of means. Among the Wolof and Serer of Senegal, for instance, captives were quite distinct from free men, whether the latter were aristocrats or commoners, and from craftsmen, who constituted the castes. They were either slaves of the crown and dependents of the king, who conferred certain clearly defined duties upon them, or domestic slaves, in which case they were under the authority of the chief of a lineage or the head of a family. The slave did not enjoy full citizenship, but he could contribute toward running the machinery of government, as in the Hausa sultanates of Nigeria, and he could become the trusted advisor of a nobleman, which was sometimes dangerous. He generally had the advantage of material living conditions comparable to those of free men and was less deprived of the comforts of life than of rights and social status. René Caillé, commenting on this after his visit to Timbuktu, said, "Men of this class are well dressed and fed, and seldom beaten." However, in moments of crisis, when someone had to take the blame, the slave was often made a scapegoat. (See also *Bambara; Eunuchs; Mali; Sao; Slave Trade; Tribute.*)
G.B.

SLAVE TRADE. The export of black slaves goes back to early classical times; the Greeks, the Egyptians, the Romans and especially the Phoenicians set a high value on the "Nubians," "Ethiopians" and "Cushites." Islam revived the trade on its own account over the trans-Saharan routes and across the Red Sea and Indian Ocean. In the ninth and tenth centuries, the Zanj, the black slaves of Iraq, rebelled, took Bassorah and held out for fifteen years against the Abbasid caliphs. The European slave trade, which began in the sixteenth century, following the Portuguese discoveries, was the next landmark in the history of the export of black slaves. In

Slave captured in a net to be sold. Nineteenth century.
Photo: Musée de l'Homme.

the beginning it was negligible and only involved condemned men and supernumerary domestic slaves sold by the coastal rulers. American colonization quickened the pace as soon as the Portuguese and especially the Spaniards realized that the American Indians could not stand up to the work in the mines and on the plantations. Paradoxically, the humanitarian campaigns waged on their behalf by Bishop Bartholomé de Las Casas brought blood-stained disaster to West Africa. Nearly 1 million Africans were disembarked in America from 1510 to 1600, nearly 3 million from 1600 to 1700, more than 7 million in the eighteenth century and about 4 million between 1800 and 1870; 15 million in all, according to the most likely assessments. Added to these, who arrived alive, were those who died on the voyage or in the *baracons* and slave ships along the African coast and those who were killed during the resupplying expeditions made along the coasts by the slavers. On top of all this, there were the adverse demographic effects.

During the sixteenth century, the slave trade was almost a Portuguese monopoly. The main areas of supply were the Gold Coast and the Slave Coast as far east as the mouth of the Niger River. In the seventeenth century, the Dutch drove the Portuguese to the mouth of the Congo and Angola, but

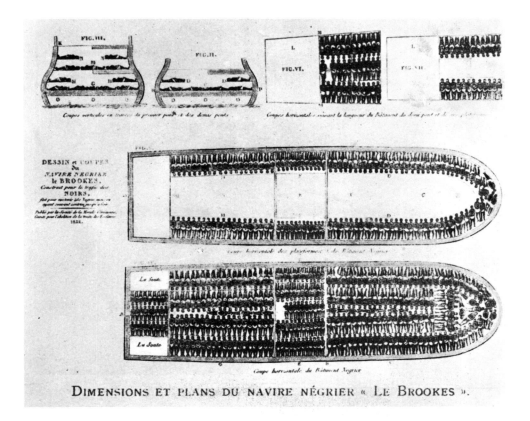

DIMENSIONS ET PLANS DU NAVIRE NÉGRIER « LE BROOKES ».

Plans and dimensions of the slave ship "Le Brookes."
Photo: Viollet, Roger.

they soon came up against the rivalry of the French and especially of the British. British naval superiority was able to clear their rivals from all the best slave-trading spots and seize more than 50 percent of a three-way trade: departure from Europe supplied with merchandise for barter—weapons, powder, alcohol, cotton goods and copper in bars or made into goods; the middle passage from Africa to America ladened with "ebony" slaves; the return journey bearing sugar and other American products. Yet, it was the British who made the greatest efforts after 1815 to suppress the slave trade which, although it was now illegal, flourished all the same, with conditions that were probably worse than before, until slavery was completely abolished, which did not take effect in Brazil until 1888.

The slave trade in East Africa had been disrupted by the conflict between the Arabs and Portuguese at the end of the fifteenth century but was revived at the end of the seventeenth century. The two main routes of the Arab slave traders were by sea via the Indian Ocean, with Zanzibar as the principal center in the nineteenth century, and by land through Khartoum and the Nile Valley toward Egypt. The Egyptian slave trade was based on organized military expeditions, and

the Khedive government conceded an area of supply to each trader. The Arab maritime slave trade closely resembled the European trade; the traders preferred to buy slaves from certain warrior tribes, for example, the Yao of Nyasa, the Wanyamwezi of Tanganyika and Katanga Province and the Baganda. Some of them also organized raids against weaker tribes. One way or another, Arab slave trading in the eighteenth and nineteenth centuries must have had about the same number of victims as the Atlantic trade; it was probably responsible for the low population of Chad and the Central African Republic today.

There is no lack of information about the slave trade in Africa; ethno-geographic descriptions abound, beginning with Arabic writings in the ninth century and continuing with European writings that first appeared in the fifteenth century and were especially abundant from the second half of the seventeenth century. A *Memoir* of a man from Nantes, written in 1760, distinguishes seven slave-trading regions on the west coast of Africa—from Senegal, where the island of Gorée was a "sort of warehouse," to the mouth of the Congo and northern Angola. The Slave Coast was scattered with forts and trading posts. Treatises for the "perfect trader" point out the areas where "the finest pieces of India"—blacks who are "gentle, submissive and adaptable to slavery"—could be found. It is impossible to give definite statistics for the deportation of these people. P. Rinchon has estimated that 13,250,000 human beings were "exported" to America from the Congolese region alone. Although the figures can be disputed, neither the intensity of the traffic nor the consequences of the slave trade can be. It exacerbated national and individual greed; there was even a priest in the Congo who went so far as to sell the furnishings of his church in order to buy slaves. And it caused rivalries and wars between the people who participated in it.

Besides its demographic consequences, which were hardly compensated by the introduction of edible American plants (maize and especially cassava), the slave trade had political and cultural repercussions. On the political plane, it caused the decline of the coastal slave states (Kongo and Angola) in the beginning, and later, in the seventeenth century, it caused new states (Dahomey and Ashanti) determined to break the coastal monopoly of the profitable business to arise in the immediate hinterland. On the economic plane, the slave trade was partly responsible for drawing the trans-Saharan trade to the Guinea Coast, which weakened the ties between Mediterranean and Sudanese Islam. On the ethnological plane, it created a demographic vacuum in some areas of the hinterland of equatorial Africa, which partly explains the migrations from the interior at the end of the eighteenth century. Finally—and this may prove to be the principal consequence—it created a large Afro-American population on the other side of the Atlantic. (See also *Arabs in East Africa; Ashanti; Bajokwe; Bapende; Bateke; Bayaka; Bena Lulua; Benin; Beverages; Bronze; Dahomey; Guinea; Hausa; Ibo; Ivory; Kongo; Migrations; Monomotapa; Mossi; Salt; Slavery; Songhai; Towns and Cities.*)   P.A.

SOCIETIES, SECRET. Traditionally, all African societies had a religious basis, and almost all required some sort of initiation ceremony for admission. Their cohesion, influence or power over nonmembers naturally depended on special knowledge which was jealously guarded and shrouded in deep secrecy. They all, therefore, had some of the attributes of secret societies. But the term "secret society" is generally applied only to those societies that exploited the fear they inspired in the noninitiated as a weapon to seize power, exercise or influence authority, or help maintain law and order. Many of

these secret societies were official and helped in the administration of justice and police duties, the execution of the guilty and the punishment of law-breakers. Others were clandestine, perhaps even evil, and devoted to particular interests or to exacting vengeance. Their outward, visible activities were, therefore, either performed in precise circumstances and regulated down to the minutest detail or, as in the case of those involving vengeance, were unpredictable and consequently more alarming.

The more reassuring of these secret societies were the "societies of men," the trustees of traditions and legends, whose knowledge was forbidden to women and children. The *Awa* of the Dogon is a union of all circumcised men, except for slaves and men of caste. They learn to make, consecrate and use the masks that are brought out for the great ceremonies during which the members act, among other things, as the village police. The *Komo* of the Bambara and Malinke was formed in the same way. It directed religious life and other village activities as well. It was pitiless for those who betrayed its secrets, and the Great Mask killed them with its poisoned fangs. Among the Sara in the Republic of Central Africa,

Ceremonial costume of a Bamileke secret society. Cameroun. *Photo: Hoa-Qui.*

Mask of the *Ekpo* society. Ibibio. Nigeria. Wood and plant fibers. Linden Museum, Stuttgart. *Museum photo.*

all young men were initiated into a society called *Hyondo.* The initiation took place in a camp in the bush and sometimes lasted several years. There, the men received their scarifications and learned a secret language, dances, ceremonial and the use of poisons. They were subjected to harsh ordeals, such as flagellations and absolute immobility for long periods. All these societies, through their impressive public displays and the respect and fear they inspired in women and children, enabled the men to assert their dominance in the community. In the *Hyondo* there are traces of the more spectacular and mysterious features of the secret societies, to which admission may be voluntary or decided by rules, vocation or co-option.

The more specialized of these exclusive secret societies, several of which could exist in the same community, were particularly common in the forest belt of Guinea and central Africa. They often met at night or wore masks and clothes that completely covered their bodies. The meeting was heralded by the sound of the bull-roarer, and they disguised their voices with reed pipes. Others, like the *Oro* society of the Yoruba, allowed themselves to be heard but not seen, and, formerly, the noninitiated who inadvertently or for curiosity's sake set eyes on them were put to death. They left symbolic signs, such as a lopped-off tree, to show that

they had passed through a place. *Oro* members were the executors of death sentences. Other societies had political functions, for example the *Ogboni* of the Yoruba, who discreetly managed most of the administration of the towns. Several had judicial functions and carried out their own sentences, like the *Mau* of the Ibo and the *Ekpo* of the Ibibio, who represented ancestors and punished the guilty and the troublemakers by ransacking their belongings. These representatives of the dead were sometimes only their messengers, as were the *Egungun* of the Yoruba, whose activities were extended to entertainments and mimes. Several secret societies that have not turned into pressure groups or to freemasonry have diverted their aims to activities that are partly recreational or simply impressive displays. The *Ekon,* the former Ibibio society of headhunters, has become the society of the rich. Many secret societies, though, were too closely tied to the terrors they inspired and the bloody rites that they performed to develop in this fashion. An exception is the society of lion men of the Sara in Chad, whose members, wearing lionskins and sandals that left the paw-marks of lions, used to tear their human victims apart with iron claws; it survives today by devoting itself to hunting ceremonies. The societies of leopard men, which once existed from Guinea to the northern part of the Congo Basin, have had to disappear or take refuge in even deeper secrecy. Their members, also clothed in skins and armed with long iron claws, ambushed and killed men who walked alone, tore their hearts out for ritual purposes and would sometimes make a communal meal of their flesh. The blood was offered at the societies' altars.

Secret societies have often spread from one tribe to another, as among the Azande, despite resistance from the traditional authorities. They sometimes became multiracial and forged solid links between small autonomous tribes. The *Simo* society spread all over lower Guinea, among the Susu, Baga and Nalu, and the *Poro* spread through upper Guinea and Sierra Leone, among the Mande, Temne, Ngere, Toma and other tribes. Today, anyone can join by paying an admission fee. In earlier times, the initiation was very long and took up to four years, comprising mythical, ritual and moral teaching. The *Poro* played an important political role and, in some circumstances, could take the place of the king or chief. The *Poro* brotherhood helped to better relations between communities, and modern political parties have sometimes been glad to avail themselves of its services. (See also *Baga;*

Bakota; Balega; Bambara; Bamileke; Bobo; Dogon; Education; Ekoi; Fang; Funerals; Games; Guro; Hunting; Ibibio; Ibo; Initiation; Islam; Languages, Secret; Lion Men and Leopard Men; Magic; Masks; Mpongwe; Mussoi; Sculpture, Wood; Senufo; Symbols; Women; Yoruba.) P.M.

SONG. The African, who has often been called "a man with a drum," could be called, even more appropriately, "a man with a song." Even the rhythms he beats on drums have a lively expression or a linear movement that makes them resemble spoken or sung phrases. Many black African languages have words to express the idea that a drum "speaks," but ethnologists seem to be unaware that the terms are equivalent to expressions in European languages indicating that a musical instrument "sings."

Almost every kind of vocal music is to be found in Africa, but choral singing is by far the most widespread. Choirs are sometimes mixed, but they are generally composed exclusively of members of one sex and are used to accompany the rites and work that are the particular responsibility of individuals of that sex. The most common form of choral music is responsive singing, with the body of the choir answering, at intervals, a leader or, as in Guinea and the Malagasy Republic, a small group of soloists. The mode of alternation differs from one tribe to another, and Africans have probably explored every possible combination. Sometimes the soloist's part is fairly long, sometimes the choir has the principal part. In one instance, the choir's part is limited to repeating the last words of the soloist or intoning a brief refrain, which may be reduced to a single note, like a sharp interjection. Elsewhere, the choir develops a phrase first sung by the soloist or sings a completely independent strophe, repeated endlessly, or two different strophes, which alternate regularly or irregularly. The choir sometimes intervenes before the leader has finished his phrase and the overlapping produces true polyphony. The choir can also produce this by dividing and singing in two or three parts. Strictly speaking, this choral part singing produces heterophony because the lines either remain rigorously parallel, at intervals of a third, a fourth and so on, or they draw together or away from each other for a short while, so that a third succeeds a series of fourths, or a second interrupts a chain of thirds, or the singers jump from thirds to a fourth. In view of the number of these irregularities, the intention is, very clearly, to play on the differences in timbre of the intervals. The general effect of such compositions is like that of a tiled floor made with unequally cut tiles, not through clumsiness, but from a very sure instinct for the value of the slightest irregularities, and this can be seen in the dissymmetry or unevenness of certain rhythms.

Individual singing is rarer than might be supposed from the accounts of some travelers. Its main place is in choral music, where it intervenes, as explained above, and leads the song. A number of rituals require that the celebrant should sing. His singing is generally close to speaking and is even interrupted with sentences that are actually spoken. Some magicians have special songs for invoking rain or, inversely, for suspending it, for healing, for exorcism, and so on. There are songs for women: cradle songs, work songs, plaints and funeral laments. There are countless children's songs which are, on rare occasions, executed by boy soloists. Usually they are intoned in unison and divided into parts which answer each other and are full of onomatopoeia; they are sung very rapidly, and there is evidently a connection with oral games such as riddling.

One further kind of secular singing must be mentioned; this is the singing done by the professional or semiprofessional male singers called griots in West Africa. Griots have often been compared to medieval jongleurs or troubadours and are only to be found in regions that are Muslim or influenced to some degree by Islam. Some are attached to the court of a chief, most are itinerant musicians. Their repertoire consists of laudatory, historical and legendary, humorous and satirical songs. They usually accompany themselves on plucked instruments, such as harps or lute harps, or on small drums that can be tucked under the arm. Griots have often been confused with musicians who play in the instrumental ensembles of chiefs, in which women and girls may also play and sing, as in the Malinke country. Semiprofessional singers are simply farmers who are known for their good voices and who are summoned to perform on special occasions, in the same way as drummers, harpists and trumpeters are.

There is nothing to distinguish most black African singing from what we consider "natural" singing. Its general tone is very different from Arab singing. The register of women's voices can be extraordinarily high. Ritual and magical songs are often distinguished by the peculiar use of vocal noises: sounds made with a closed mouth, falsetto singing, yodeling (especially among the Pygmies and neighboring tribes), whistling and imitations of animal cries.

Portamenti, long *glissandi* and chromaticisms sometimes break the regularity of pentatonic or heptatonic scales, of which the first are the most common in the forest belt and the second in the savanna region. (See also *Bells; Bushmen; Games; Griots; Literature, Oral; Love; Massa; Music; Poetry; Rattles; Theater; Zithers.*)   A.S.

SONGHAI. The Songhai, or Sonhrai, occupy the middle reaches of the Niger River —from Lake Debo to the confluence of the Kebbi River in Nigeria. They are divided among five countries: Mali, Upper Volta, Dahomey, Niger and Nigeria. There are probably more than 300,000 actual Songhai and an additional 650,000 members of tribes that they have assimilated (Zerma, Azna, Kurfei, etc.). The river is closely woven into Songhai history. The Sorko, who may have come from Chad via the Benue River, took control of the Niger River at a remote period, while the Gow occupied the bush. Delafosse places the arrival of a group of Berbers, who were descendants of the Lemta of Libya, at about the seventh century. Their chief, Kukya, the first ruler of the Za dynasty, drove out the Sorko, who ascended the Niger River, founded Gao and spread as far as Mopti. The fifteenth Za ruler was converted to Islam and transferred his capital to Gao, which by that time had become an important market. Toward the end of the thirteenth century, Gao came under the rule of Mali, but it regained its independence a century later. The real founder of the Songhai empire

was Sonni Ali, who reigned from 1464 to 1492 and fought against the Fulani, the Malinke and the Mossi. His descendants still enjoy a reputation for being magicians. The greatest successor of Sonni Ali, Askia Mohammed (Askia the Great), went on a pilgrimage to Mecca in 1495-1497 and returned with the support of the Abbasid caliph of Egypt, who had designated him his lieutenant for all West Africa. With this alliance, Askia Mohammed organized the vast territory conquered by Sonni Ali and extended his power as far south as the country around Abomey and as far east as Agades. After reigning for twenty-six years, the old ruler, who had gone blind, was exiled by his sons to an island in the river, but his sons and grandsons exhausted their resources in fratricidal warfare. The sultan of Marrakesh did not remain indifferent to this spectacle. He coveted the riches that he believed would be found in the "empire of gold" and attacked it with a column of 3,000 Moroccans and Spanish mercenaries commanded by a renegade, the pasha Djuder. On April 12, 1591, near the hill of Tondibi, the Moroccan musketeers put to flight a Songhai army of 30,000 to 40,000 men who had never seen firearms before. This was the end of the Songhai empire; the ruler was crushed, his states pillaged, and Moroccan supremacy established along the middle Niger. The rule of the mercenaries, who were disappointed by the poverty of the country, did not go beyond severe exploitation and did not lead to further conquests. It collapsed about 1660. The most lasting consequence was the organization of a real slave trade, which till then had been confined to local needs. After the defeat of the Songhai, caravans left each year for victorious Morocco, where the slaves and their sons formed the nucleus of the black Moroccan troops. In 1825, when René Caillé arrived there, Timbuktu was still drawing its wealth from the trade in salt and slaves. The caravan of 400 camels that he joined for his journey to Morocco was composed mainly of slaves. The Songhai, torn by rivalries between their princes, were easy prey to the greed of their neighbors, who had been dependents of the Gao empire. At the beginning of the nineteenth century, the Fulani from the whole Sudan, encouraged by Osman dan Fodio, who had seized hold of Sokoto, declared a "holy war" on them. After the Fulani, the Tuareg fell upon the disintegrated empire; but the advancing French troops took Timbuktu in 1894, Gao in 1898, and in 1900 the Tuareg were routed and peace was established.

Early travelers described the Niger Valley

Tomb of the Askia dynasty near Gao, Mali. *Photo: Documentation française.*

as a new Egypt, but this visible prosperity, limited to a narrow strip along the river that was located in a tropical climate and on the borders of the desert, soon proved to be a deception. Today, agriculture engages the whole population, but the soil, threatened by sands from the north and impoverished by laterite in the south, is hardly sufficient to feed it. Work in the fields lasts from May (sowing) to October (harvest). The rest of the year, the men rest or hire their services out to nearby construction works. Many of them emigrate temporarily to Ghana, whose large cities—Accra and Kumasi—seem like legendary cities, the source of fabulous riches and also holy places where new religions are forged and whose devotees are possessed, "ridden," by powerful genii.

The traditional game hunted by the Sorko is the hippopotamus, but they also hunt crocodile and manatee (a kind of aquatic mammal). Their way of stalking has not altered since ibn-Batuta watched them in 1352, when he traveled from Timbuktu to Gao. The animal is harpooned, tires itself out by towing a heavy canoe and is then finished off with a spear. The Sorko are proud of their hunting technique, which they consider to be a mark of nobility, and they refuse to fish with nets. Net-fishing is in the hands of the river-dwellers of Kebbi and Dendi, who canoe up the river each year. The fish caught during the expedition are dried or smoked and gradually sold as far away as 65 miles downstream in Nigeria.

One of the advantages that the Songhai had was their position on the border between black and white Africa, at the crossroads of the trade routes leading from Mali to the Maghrib and Egypt. Today, the roads from the north, in spite of the automobile routes traversing the Sahara, do not have the same importance except for the transport of salt from Taodenni, which is still brought by caravan as far as Timbuktu before being distributed throughout Mali. Most other merchandise comes from the coast. Although the northern part of the Songhai country can trade easily with the town of Bamako by traveling along the river, the lack of navigation on the Gao-Niamey section of the Niger River, especially the barrage of rapids at Boussa, limits transport to the east; the products imported by the south come from Dahomey, from Nigeria via Kano and the Hausa hawkers, and from Ghana. Peanuts and herds of oxen follow the same routes in the other direction. Only dried fish are taken down the river toward Nigeria.

At first glance, the Songhai seem entirely Islamized. Actually, since the eleventh century, the probable date of their first "conversion," Islam has come up against the Songhai's ability to assimilate while remaining faithful to traditional customs, which is so evident throughout Africa. Rather than obliterating the old beliefs, the new religion brought them new elements. Local cults of genii, masters of the earth or the waters, whose priests are the descendants of the first arrivals, and ancestor cults, often combined with the former, have survived: fishermen, hunters and heads of families also have their altars, while the stones and trees that shelter the altars are used for magical practices. Alongside these, a cult of genii (*holley*) developed and is very popular today. Marked by dances of possession in which the genii "ride" their devotees and speak through their mouths, it has revived the preceding cults and arrived at a sort of tacit coexistence with Islam. Its pantheon comprises divinities of water, heaven, thunder, wind and rain, villages and the bush, who have been joined in recent years by a new family, the *hawka,* or genii of power, whose hierarchy seems modeled on that of the administration or army. At first badly received by the authorities, these modern gods have triumphed today, and they are particularly popular among young men who have worked for some time as unskilled laborers in urban centers far from their homeland. (See also *Fishing; Fulani; Funerals; Games; Gold; Griots; Hausa; Hunting; Languages, Secret; Mali; Markets; Mossi; Mottoes; Rice; Royalty; Salt; Spirits and Genii; Sudan; Towns and Cities.*) D.P.

SORCERY. Belief in sorcery is largely explained by the predominance of "why" over "how" in the African conception of the world; where a Westerner would normally ask "how" something happened, an African would want to know "why" it had happened, especially when it concerned any of a variety of accidents, fortunate or unfortunate, affecting human life. A man is killed by a wild beast; this is the "how," and it hardly begs the question. But why him and not another? It could be that it was his own fault, because he broke a taboo or neglected a rite. It could be that he was the victim of someone else, and it is this other person who will often be accused of sorcery. Conversely, an accusation of sorcery will also be brought against a man who draws attention to himself by an outstanding success that has no apparent technical basis (a technical basis, in Africa, includes magic).

While magic is, in fact, an art and a technique, sorcery is primarily a state, often an unconscious one. It can happen that a magician is a sorcerer (although the initiation process often includes tests that are deliberately intended to prevent a sorcerer from becoming a magician), but a sorcerer has no need at all to be a magician; he often acts without any visible special methods, sometimes even unwittingly, particularly in his sleep. His discovery requires specialists—diviners, witch doctors or witch smellers—who may also have the responsibility of curing him or eliminating him physically. In one sense, sorcery is like a disease; the sorcerer is inhabited or possessed—again often without his knowledge—by a material or nonmaterial maleficent entity which, acting at a distance, draws off the vital energy, the cosmic force, of the victim. (The term "stealer of vital force" would be better than the more commonly used "soul eater.") But even though he may be unaware of his powers, the sorcerer is always responsible. It is extraordinary to see that the unhappy persons who are detected by diviners after an epidemic or an epizooty, for example, almost always confess their guilt, even though this may lead to their execution; they are impaled through the anus among the Ngoni, drowned among the Ewe, Duala and Bete, slowly strangled by the Tem, buried alive in the western Sudan and burned alive by the interlacustrine Bantu. Sorcery is often considered contagious and hereditary; the Fang, for example, believe that an individual who, in order to grow rich, has contracted the *evu,* a maleficent animal that takes refuge in human entrails and increases the person's power, may transmit it involuntarily to his relations and children.

Sorcerers are deemed to act in various ways: by telekinesis or bilocation, by using men changed into animals, or by employing poisons or immaterial effluvia. If a sorcerer attacks either another sorcerer who is more powerful than he or a well-protected nonsorcerer, he runs the risk of seeing his sorcery turned against him and of suffering a dangerous repercussion. A sorcerer's motives are considered to be immoral and antisocial; they include spite, jealousy, lust, avarice and the desire for political or economic power. Once a sorcerer is convicted, he is, depending on the tribe and also on the circumstances, obliged to make reparation or eliminated either by death or banishment, unless his power is so great that he is safe from direct reprisals. Sorcery generally breaks out in areas of social tension: among underprivileged groups (slaves, old women), groups that make up a political opposition (witch-hunting offers an opportunity to get rid of them), nonconformists (sexual perverts, followers of new religions) and economic rivals. The

searching out and elimination of sorcerers are both signs of these tensions and means of releasing them; many new religions, "fetishes" and syncretist churches (for example, the Atagara of the Slave Coast, the *bwiti* of Gabon and the *lumpa* of Zambia) indulge in them frequently.

Paradoxically, sorcery becomes almost a norm in some extreme cases. Among the Azande and their neighbors, relations among commoners took the form of a network of reciprocal acts of sorcery which were arbitrated by the chiefs who, by their nature, could not be sorcerers themselves. Among the Baji of Cameroun, possession by the *evu* was an indispensable element of personal success for a man, on condition that he got rid of it before his death by means of costly purification ceremonies, which left him materially the poorer but with his reputation enhanced. Sorcery may verge on magic, and sometimes is closely associated with it in one of two ways. First, a magician who had undertaken to fight against sorcerers might allow himself to be contaminated accidentally by sorcery; for example, by allowing himself to be possessed by the maleficent entity that had been forced to abandon a convicted sorcerer. Second, in some ethnic groups, it is possible to become a sorcerer with the help of appropriate rites or magical operations. In the latter case, it would be correct to speak of black magic, which is illicit, the provenance of sorcerers and different from white magic; this black magic tends to act as a form of social protection. Some societies of lycanthropes, like the Congolese leopard men and the cayman men of the Douala region—dear to adventure-story writers—fall into this category. (See also *Azande; Death; Funerals; Initiation; Kikuyu; Lion Men and Leopard Men; Magic; Religion; Senufo; Spirits and Genii; Women; Zulus.*)   P.A.

SPIDERS. Two species of spiders are common in folklore and divination: the large spotted Arachnomorphae and the Mygalomorphae, or trap-door spiders. The Arachnomorpha, which can often be seen hanging at the end of its thread in forest clearings, is said to have been the messenger of the gods at the creation of the world and also their clown. It is called *Anansi* by the Ashanti—which became Aunt Nancy in the Afro-American folklore of the southern United States—*Nden-Bobo* by the Ewondo, and *Bibi Buibui* in East Africa. It is associated with solar and celestial myths and, as would be expected, with the invention of spinning and weaving. The spider is generally considered a harbinger of good luck, and there are legends in which it does not hesitate to betray its divine masters to help human beings who have won its favor.

The trap-door spider, which is associated with earth cults, has a more sinister character (its bite is very dangerous). The Basa of Cameroun use it for divination. Sixty-four different kinds and shapes of leaves are laid in front of its hole, and the nature of future events is deduced from the disturbance in their arrangement during the night. Other tribes around the Gulf of Guinea use straws, small seeds or a layer of fine sand in the same way.

The spider is a royal creature for the Bamum of the mountains of western Cameroun and is frequently represented in their art, especially in bronzes made by the lost-wax process, which remind one of Benin bronzes. The spider and its web are common remedies in the African pharmacopoeia. (See also *Fauna*.)   P.A.

SPIRITS and GENII. The rather vague term "spirit" refers to a whole group of incorporeal entities, generally possessing some, but not all, attributes of human beings and lacking, especially, a tangible body. The absence of human attributes, rather than the possession of special additional faculties, often explains the superhuman powers of some kinds of spirits. It is impossible to give an exhaustive list here of the different varieties of spirits, if only because the beliefs concerning them vary so much from one cultural group to another. Some types of spirits, however, are fairly widely accepted.

First, there are the spirits of the dead. Their exact nature depends on conceptions of the human person or, to be more precise, of the elements of a person that are considered imperishable, like his name, intellect, vital force or energy. A distinction is commonly made between the spirits of good men, who become benevolent protectors, and those of the other dead, who become dangerous phantoms. The first reveal themselves in dreams and oracles and willingly come to the assistance of their pious descendants. The second kind—less dead, so to speak—reappear in their corporeal form, although sometimes in a different color, and can easily turn malevolent. One of the purposes of scrupulously observing funeral and commemorative rites is to win the favor or neutrality of the spirits of the dead and prevent them from becoming dangerous phantoms. Rites to invoke these spirits are rather uncommon and are found most frequently in East Africa.

Another common group comprises the

Mask for dances in honor of the bush spirits. Chamba. Nigeria. Wood and plant fibers. Museum für Völkerkunde und Vorgeschichte, Hamburg. *Photo: Jacques Verroust.*

spirits of the bush, who are often personifications of nature. Although they are not human—which differentiates them from phantoms—they can have human attributes, including names. According to some ethnic groups, they cannot be apprehended by the senses and can only communicate directly with certain clairvoyants. Others believe that they can take on a visible or audible form, which is sometimes familiar and at other times strange and frightening. Most of the time they are dangerous, hostile or, at least, disagreeable, but they can be useful to someone who knows how to conciliate or coerce them through the appropriate magical rites. They often have special dwelling places, such as rivers, trees or rocks, where they can or should be given offerings.

Genii are related to spirits both of the dead and of the bush; a dead man can become a genius. Genii have more clearly defined personalities than nature spirits. In the *bori* cult, which is widespread in Hausa, Songhai (where it is called *holley*) and Bargu country and among the Nigerian migrants from Ghana, the *hawka* genii have very marked personalities that are borrowed from figures and objects in the contemporary world, such as highly placed civil servants, politicians and airplanes.

Cynocephalous agrarian divinity or genius of the bush. Baule. Ivory Coast. Wood. Musée de l'Homme, Paris. *Museum photo.*

The *vodoos* and *orisha* of the Slave Coast are spirits that are midway between genii and the divinities above. In contrast, in much of West Africa it is thought that the genii and chthonian spirits look like red dwarves (this may be the last, legendary trace of a pre-Negro Pygmoid race) and are similar to phantoms.

Phantoms, genii and nature spirits can often be incarnated. They can possess men, a phenomenon that has been feared, desired and sometimes both feared and desired. The possession can take various forms: an ancestor can be reincarnated in a descendant bearing his name; a medium, often a woman, can lend her voice to a dead man; a spirit of the bush can madden a solitary traveler or a hunter who has strayed. The best examples are found in the cults of possession, some of which, especially in Ghana, seem to be efficacious forms of therapy for neuroses arising from cultural maladjustment. Spirits can also be incarnated in animals; such spirits are generally harmful and impossible to capture by normal methods, but they sometimes protect crops and herds against "natural" predatory animals. Here, we are on the borderline of sorcery. Spirits can penetrate inanimate objects, particularly masks and statues, as well as other objects; such inhabited objects can be called "fetishes," and this is probably the only valid application of the word. The objects may be

Tiv spoon. Northern Nigeria. Paul Tishman Collection, New York. *Photo: Musée de l'Homme.*

inhabited permanently or only during ceremonies, when it is dangerous for some classes of people to touch them or even to look at them. Ecumenical religions have added spirits of their own (angels, *jinn, ifrit,* demons) to the list of African spirits without reducing the number of indigenous varieties. While Islam and several syncretic religions have been comparatively tolerant toward these beliefs, Christian missionaries have often simply changed the label, declaring them to be diabolical spirits without denying their existence. (See also *Birds; Bull-Roarers; Dan; Death; Divinities; Dreams; Fauna; Islam; Languages, Secret; Magic; Ordeals; Person; Possession by Spirits; Rain; Religion; Songhai; Stories; Zar.*) P.A.

SPOONS. Spoons with large bowls, which are actually ladles, are used by the housewife to dip into pots and serve out food to her family. Individual members of the family use smaller spoons for eating sauces, boiled cereals or vegetable soup while holding solid foods in their left hands. Spoons are also employed to draw water and measure out oil to be sold. Sometimes, the technical functions of this simple utensil are sublimated, and the spoon becomes a symbol that is used only on the occasion of important ceremonies. Spoons, like all objects found in the home, are, if they are finely crafted, signs of the wealth and social rank of their owner. The two parts of the spoon that lend themselves to artistic variation are the handle and the bowl. Generally, the designs are simple, but often they are true plastic creations that take every advantage of the formal requirements of the bowl and its extension and transform them, for example, into a head and a body. The variations in designs are as closely associated with the material of which the spoon is made—calabash, wood, bone, horn, ivory or metal—as they are with the meanings contained in the traditional allegorical repertoire, which includes geometric motifs and naturalistic representations.

Calabash spoons are commonly used for cooking in Senegal, Niger, Dahomey and northern Cameroun, and, like all objects made from this gourd, are products of a long process. First, the calabash is soaked in a pool until it is completely rotted; then it is opened, emptied and dried in the sun. When the skin becomes as hard as wood, it can be decorated with pyrogravure or simply carved with a knife and, finally, colored with natural dyes.

Wooden spoons which are no longer used as domestic utensils but as sculptures with symbolic significance can be found in West

Africa, Zaire, and South Africa. The size of the extraordinary spoons of the Baule and the Dan in the Ivory Coast and Liberia indicates that they were sculpted for display or for the solemn serving of food on special occasions.

A fine spoon that is sculpted in the form of a woman is an essentially feminine object and is an attempt to express what the woman represents to society: an almost sacred figure who is above all a mother—mother of men, mother of chiefs, mother of the king—but who is also the giver of food on whom the family depends for its subsistence. Upon the death of a woman who was head of the Ubangi village of Nzakara, a spoon with a fine, sensitive head on a long neck ending in a generous bowl was carved in her honor. Spoons belonging to the society of notables of the Balega of northeastern Zaire are similarly symbolic and extremely varied. They are made of ivory having a yellow or orange patina and are precious objects of a very distinct style of art. Although these Balega ivories seldom deviate from the basic form of the smallest, most banal spoon, they reveal a plastic inventiveness that never falters and that is always classically pure. On the flat handle of a spoon made of some attractive material there might be carved, in low relief, a mask abstracted into two eyelids, a nose and delicate lips; it is characteristic of the restrained style of the Balega. (See also *Calabashes; Meals.*) J.D.

SPORTS. Competitive sports in Africa probably date back to ancient times. Wrestling was universal, as were various kinds of racing (running and walking, horseback riding and boating). There were also local types of team games which often had very complicated rules, as did *anjek,* a sort of rugby played in Cameroun with a latex ball and assegais. There was a markedly ritual character to these games; they had social value in that they were a means of releasing tensions between groups and sometimes resembled the Panathenaic games of ancient Greece. From this point of view, some forms of periodic war having a strictly regulated pattern (for example, the battles of the Palaeonegrids of West Africa and of the non-Bantu peoples of Kenya and Tanzania) can be considered as sports.

The kinds of sports played now depend mainly on the habits of the former colonizers; soccer is a common denominator between tennis and cricket, which are played in some parts of Africa, and cycling and pétanque (a form of bowls), which are the main sports in other parts. The new sports are greatly influenced by old community traditions, and the matches often rouse the most violent reactions in the public that is watching tribal, regional or national games. In contrast to this, individual exploits are often more important in playing the game than cooperation among members of the team.

Professional sports began when boxers were sent first to England in the eighteenth century and then to France in the twentieth; some of these boxers became stars. In Africa itself, professional sports are not very important, mainly for economic reasons, although there has been a notable increase lately in pseudo-amateurism. The skimming off of African clubs by European teams and managers continues. Performance sports, especially athletics, developed rather late but became more common after the Second World War, with their growth often related to the development of secondary and advanced education. Africa has produced jumpers, runners and throwers of international stature. Her sportsmen would probably excel in other fields, notably swimming and rowing, but at the moment these sports have no chance to develop because of the lack of organization and financial means. (See also *Games.*) P.A.

STORIES. The story is probably the most common and most popular literary genre in black Africa and also one that remains the most vital today. Generally, its satiric and socially didactic character gives it a certain similarity to the European fable or moral tale of the Middle Ages. The mythological story, whose contents are symbolic and often esoteric, has failed to resist European, particularly missionary, influence perhaps more than any other form; although this type of story is fairly widespread, the underlying meanings have often been lost and can be recovered only through learned interpretation (this is also the case with numerous European folk tales). There is a Pan-African cycle of fables that have animals as characters. These fables relate the adventures of a weak but cunning animal to a number of other animal characters who are strong but inflexible and tell how he overcomes them with his cunning. The hero is the hare in the savanna regions, the tortoise in the forest belt and the jackal in the Kalahari and among the Berbers of North Africa. Pitted against him are either cruel, stupid animals, like the hyena and leopard, or the kings of the bush, like the lion and the elephant. The English linguist Alice Werner thinks these stories were the sources of Aesop's *Fables* (Aesop = Ethiop, "black African") and, via them, of the *Roman de Renart* and La

Griot. Dosso, Niger. *Photo: Documentation française.*

Fontaine's *Fables.* There is no doubt that these stories crossed the Atlantic in the slave ships and were the original versions of the Afro-American cycles of *Ol' Br'er Rabbit* and *Ol' Br'er Terrapin.* Another category of story that can be recognized as a part of universal folklore is the Cinderella-type story based on the tensions and conflicts resulting from family structure and telling of a series of threatened orphans, unjust stepfathers and stepmothers and hostile half-brothers and half-sisters. The fables about married couples can also be included in this category, although they are more complex than their European counterparts because of the institution of polygamy. Finally there is a type of story that covers implicit versions of the great myths of cosmic creation (stories about the creation, the conflict of the sun and the moon, etc.), the supernatural world (ghosts and genii, ogres and bush spirits), the origins of social institutions and relations with foreign societies, including white men.

In spite of specialized storytellers, both professional and amateur, narrative has become public property. However, it still observes strict rules of social etiquette which lay down who can relate what to whom and when. Traditional stories, especially fables with animal characters, have been adapted to the social changes of the colonial and post-colonial periods; in doing so, they have retained their satiric flavor, which eludes the authorities who are the butt of the teller. Some contemporary African writers, like the Senegalese Birago Diop, have produced literary versions of traditional stories or have used them as a base for writing new ones. Similarly, political speakers often use them directly or indirectly to put over their ideas to the masses in a form that is familiar to them. (See also *Hares; Heroes; Legends; Literature, Oral; Literature, Written; Mussoi; Myths; Riddles; Theater.*)   P.A.

SUDAN. The *Bilad as-Sudan* of Arab writers literally means "land of the blacks"— that is, Africa south of the Sahara— although neither the word "Sudan" nor its compound was used exclusively to denote the blacks and their country. In fact, the name "Sudan" was applied, first in Arabic and then in European usage, only to the vast area of the savanna and its borderlands stretching from the Atlantic to the Red Sea which were then known to Islam. The Sudan owes its special character and history to the ease of communication from earliest times because of the nature of its landscape and to the ambiguous nature of its northern and southern limits, which acted either as formidable barriers or offered easy means of access through all the vicissitudes of its history. On one side was the immense desert, which had been a redoubtable obstacle since the Neolithic desiccation, separating two physical and human worlds and yet constantly crossed by camel. On the other side, there was the forest and the tsetse fly (which stopped marauding cavalry), a world hostile to the endeavors of man and relations with distant places, an area where another Africa began, but also one where the contrasts were often not very sharp because of the close proximity of communities, the gradual transition from savanna to forest where the two interpenetrated and regions in which the forest was thin and gave men an opportunity to tame it and break their isolation. In the east, the valleys of the Nile downstream and the Blue Nile and the Atbara upstream provided communication with the exterior. The double barrier encouraged the peculiar character of the Sudan, and the double opening to the world outside brought it new life. On the one side, the Sudan was intimately united with the black bloc, of which it is an integral part and whose genius it shares; on the other, it opened in the north on a distant world of rich civilizations, especially since the appearance of Islam, which was for so long a dynamic element at the crossroads of the Old World. Giving and receiving from both sides, the Sudan lay at the intersection of two historical roads: that of the heart of Africa and that of the Mediterranean world and the Middle East. Heavy traffic has always crossed it: trade routes leading from the south (carrying gold from its borders, kola nuts from the forest, etc.) and from the Sahel and the desert (bringing salt, dates, teachers of Arabic and Islamic learning); the great transverse line, which brought so many human and cultural contributions from the east and along which pilgrims journeyed to Mecca; the continuations of trans-Saharan routes bearing slaves and gold and merchandise to be distributed; and everywhere the great movements of groups of peoples.

The Sudan is a land of empires and kingdoms. There were many others in Africa, but those in the Sudan were revived more frequently and many of them have remained under forms of organizations in which the political structure has greater homogeneity. After Meroe, the Nilotic Sudan saw the rise of the Christian kingdoms of Nubia in the Middle Ages and then of the sultanate of the Fung, which appeared in the sixteenth century, achieved its brilliant zenith in the seventeenth century and did not finally collapse until the beginning of the nineteenth century. In the west, the powerful and splendid empires of Ghana, Mali and the Songhai succeeded each other, but their histories overlap. Around Lake Chad there was the millennial empire of Kanem-Bornu, which was flanked on the west by the city-states of the Hausa. The sultanates of Darfur and Wadai appeared in the seventeenth century. There were pagan states, too, like those of the Bambara in the seventeenth and eighteenth centuries and the more stable Mossi bloc. The dawn of the nineteenth century saw the flowering of the new Muslim Fulani states, which were already budding at Fouta Djallon and Fouta Toro and which

bloomed in Macina, in Hausa territory and in northern Cameroun. El-Hadj Umar, who rose to power in the middle of the century, Samory Touré, who appeared at its end, and the Mahdists, who came to power along the Nile, conclude this summary list.

The Sudan is also a land of cities and towns, of large and small capitals and trading towns especially in the middle of the region and on the edge of the desert (Djenne and Timbuktu, Kano, etc.). This feature is not unique, but it was fairly rare in Africa in former times. The nature of the towns and an appreciation of their real historic weight must, of course, be considered in relation to the basically agricultural societies in which they existed and to their dependence on external factors if they were trading towns.

It is an Islamic land, but the depth and extent of its conversion varied with different societies. In some parts of the country, Islam was a thin veneer; in others, it was outstandingly pure and intellectually brilliant. The Nile Valley in the seventeenth century, Timbuktu and Djenne in the fourteenth to sixteenth centuries and several centers between the Sahara, Lake Chad and Niger at the turn of the eighteenth and nineteenth centuries were distinguished centers of learning and devotion. (See also *Architecture; Bambara; Bornu; Camels; Cattle; Chad, Lake; Clothing; Divination; Eunuchs; European Discovery; Games; Ghana; Goats; Gold; Hausa; Hunger; Islam; Kirdi; Mali; Markets; Meroe; Migrations; Nile; Salt; Savanna; Songhai; Towns and Cities; Tribute.*) H.M.

Mosque at Djenne, Mali, in the Sudan. *Photo: Musée de l'Homme.*

SYMBOLS. External, immediately apparent cultural symbolism varies from one African society to another and ranges from an almost superabundant richness in the states and city-states of West Africa (Akan, Yoruba, Ewe, Fon, Mossi, etc.) and the Bantu kingdoms of the Great Lakes region and the Zambezi-Congo corridor to the bareness of the Palaeonegrid rural tribes of the 10th parallel and the nomadic animal husbanders of the savanna and steppe. The opulent symbolism of societies organized into states shows up both in the material trappings and in the elaboration of religious ceremonies; these things are also features of some peoples that are not organized into states, but whose ritual societies, with their masks, statues, altars, etc., also proliferate visible symbols. It is not surprising that the first explorers to encounter African societies of this type referred to their idolatry and accused the blacks of an extravagant love of external appearances and signs, although this reproach could equally well be made against all European countries, where outward social symbolism (Trooping the Colors, May Day, military pomp, etc.) is developed to an advanced degree.

The uniqueness of and reason for ethnographical interest in African cultures lies less in this external and immediately visible symbolism than in the symbolism that can be called internal and which only a thorough study can lay bare. This does not mean that the study of internal African symbols requires methods akin to psychoanalysis; the peculiarity of these African symbols is that, although they resemble the universal, psychoanalytic symbols, they are expressed mainly at the conscious levels of the personality. In other words, each object, every concrete or abstract element of such cultures possesses, in addition to its immediate and proper value as a weapon, tool, piece of technical apparatus, etc., a symbolic value that is generally related to an image that is both cosmic and part of the social environment. Marcel Griaule and his school have shown how every tool, gesture and word of members of various societies in West Africa (Dogon, Bambara, Fali) symbolizes an element in the cosmic system or social institution.

It is possible to conceive of this universal symbolism as a means not only of explaining but also of perpetuating and making an entire autonomous social system work on both communal and individual levels. In fact, symbolism in general may be a means of formulating and resolving some social tensions and contradictions on a plane that does not endanger the cohesion of the

Abia game counters carved out of coconuts. Fang. Musée de l'Homme, Paris. *Museum photo.*

community. All individual or community action, even if it appears at first sight to be purely technical or economic, may at the same time be a symbolic action concerned with social adaptation and integration. It is understandable how a profound attack on the symbolism of a community, such as religious conversion or the suppression of a sacred chieftainship, has the effect, to some extent, of "demonetizing" conduct that seems to be completely profane. Some forms of mental disorder that are prevalent in Africa today may be explained by the disintegration of old symbolic systems. There is little doubt that the psychotherapeutic aspect of religious neo-paganism and syncretism (notably, in cults of possession) consists in the elaboration of a new symbolism and the re-integration, by means of re-interpretation, of some of the old *sacramenta*. On the plane of individual psychology, the observer is often struck by the fact that some unconscious European symbols, particularly sexual ones, have the same significance in Africa—but on the conscious level, as was noted before. One of the conclusions to be drawn from this observation is that many of the psychotherapeutic techniques that are valid in Europe should not be used in Africa. (See also *Art, African; Possession by Spirits.*)

P.A.

TABOOS. A taboo is a prohibition against performing certain acts and is motivated by magical or social sanction. There are taboos that forbid sexual relations with certain people or in certain places or circumstances; certain products, hunting certain animals or using certain instruments; fulfilling particular everyday acts in a particular way; watching some things; pronouncing special words; etc.

The phenomenon is common to all civilizations, including industrial civilizations, but it is particularly developed and systemized in some African societies. The taboos vary considerably from one society to another. The taboo of incest applies to a larger range of people in Africa than in the West; it applies not only to the immediate kin but also to all the members of the lineage or clan. A distinction should be made between the taboos concerning marriage and those concerning copulation, as the first are always much stricter and more extensive than the latter. The rules of exogamy, which result from these taboos, have an important bearing on the structure of family systems. They control the more or less complicated circulation and exchange of women and marriage compensations, which are appreciable factors in maintaining the cohesion of societies, particularly those that are not organized as states. The ceremonial violation of sexual taboos is often the privilege or obligation of some eminent figures; for example, royal incest in the Bantu states of the Great Lakes region.

The list of taboos is a long one. They can be classified under permanent taboos and temporary ones which apply only at certain times, such as during mourning, in the planting season, before departure for hunting and war, during pregnancy or while mining ore. Some taboos affect individuals while others are laid on a whole community, clan, lineage or age group, or on all the men and women of a particular occupation. The justification given for a taboo depends on legend or on ideas concerning associative or sympathetic magic; one Kotokoli clan is forbidden to hunt rabbits because a rabbit helped their ancestor to escape his enemy; a pregnant woman of the Ewondo tribe is forbidden to knot string because this will cause a difficult birth, and so on. The sanction can be precise (for example, if a Baji woman who has not reached menopause eats duck, her children will have web fingers) or vague (if an uninitiated Bete eats Caston bushbuck, he will have bad luck). The consequences are always automatic and unavoidable except if one performs the appropriate reparation rites. In some instances, breaking a taboo will be baneful not only to the guilty person but also to the whole community. The reparation can then take on a repressive and punitive character and, often after an enquiry, is administered by the judicial or political authority.

In many instances, the taboos form a sort of symbolic system, distinguishing or emphasizing the various relationships within a community while, at the same time, helping to perpetuate them and ensuring that the different individual or community rules are respected. This is particularly striking in the case of taboos involving age, sex, caste, occupation and the royal person. Examples of the power of the last kind can be seen in the way revolutionaries like Chaka and, more recently, the Mau Mau leaders in Kenya forced those whom they dominated to break the traditional taboos while imposing new ones on them. There is no doubt about the effectiveness of taboos, because the voluntary breach of a taboo sets off a violent psychological crisis, which may even cause the death of the transgressor. The spread of Islam and Christianity seems primarily to have superimposed new taboos (eating pork and drinking alcohol, fast days, etc.) on those already existing. Taboos applied to some sectors of traditional social systems—relations between young people and adults, political institutions and premonetary labor and economic organizations—have been weakened or have disappeared altogether as a result of modern cultural upheavals. In these sectors, taboos do survive, but they are deprived of their social justification and hardly differ from Western superstitions. (See also *Beverages; Blacksmiths; Blood; Clans; Death; Diet; Griots; Hens; Incest; Magic; Meals; Names; Priests; Rain; Religion; Widows; Work.*) P.A.

THEATER. In precolonial Africa, the type of performance that resembled theater most closely was the mixture of mime, dance, music and choral singing that accompanied hunting, war and fertility rites or the recital of myths. The scene as a whole was sometimes like a ballet or opera and sometimes like an oratorio. The art of storytelling, in so far as its strictly oral character required a public, also had a theatrical and dramatic side to it; this theatricalism included the gestures and facial expressions of the narrator as well as being evident in the musical and vocal accompaniment that was often part of the storytelling performance.

European-type theater appeared with colonization, first in institutions of advanced education (at the William Ponty School in Dakar and at Achimota College in Ghana, for example) and then in presentations by youth groups such as the scouts. At the moment, it is still run mainly by amateurs who are associated with cultural organizations and educational establishments. For economic reasons, professional companies have to be subsidized by the state. The performances of these groups are also planned as cultural propaganda primarily geared for foreign tours; this is the case with the national companies that participate in the Théâtre des Nations festival in Paris and with Keita Fodéba's Guinean Ballet. There are also professional or semiprofessional companies working in Europe, like the company of Les Griots in France, as well as individual African artists who have made careers for themselves abroad. The repertoires of the earliest companies were taken from European sources, and the works, with no revisions, were performed either in French or English. Later on, these European plays were adapted for local conditions and were performed either in the original language or in translation. Several of Molière's plays were adapted in this way; for instance, there are versions of *Le Bourgeois Gentilhomme* and *Le Malade Imaginaire* in

Swahili. One should also mention the translations—without any adaptation or with only very minor changes—of Shakespeare's plays, such as the translation of *Julius Caesar* by the President of Tanzania Julius K. Nyerere.

Alongside these adapted and translated European plays, there arose an African drama, first with plays in French and English, then in some native languages. In the beginning, it took the form of satirical comedy, which is still popular, and plays with historical subjects; later on, there were works with social subjects and contemporary plots and settings. At the outset, the style and construction of these plays were fairly close imitations of their European models. They soon developed away from these by introducing a good deal of singing and especially by audience participation, first almost casually, then regularly following the playwright's stage directions; in the Krio translation of *Julius Caesar,* for instance, the audience "plays" the crowd. Curiously, the playwrights of French-speaking Africa are practically all amateurs whose works seem less influenced by modern tendencies in drama than are the writings of their colleagues in English-speaking Africa. Their plays are seldom published, while the works of Ghaneans, South Africans, Nigerians, etc. —such as J. C. De Graft, L. Nkosi, W. Soyinka, R. Njau and several others who have been influenced by Becket, Ionesco and the Angry Young Men—are to be found in bookstores. One likely reason is that the tradition of amateur theater is more solidly implanted and more advanced in countries with an English culture, where public and private financial assistance is more generous. Modern opera also hardly exists except in English-speaking Africa; an opera adapted from Amos Tutuola's *Palm-wine Drunkard* is very popular in Nigeria, and *King Kong,* a South African jazz-opera, had a successful run in London. On the other hand, music hall and variety seem more developed in French-speaking Africa. (See also *Literature, Written.*) P.A.

THIRD WORLD. A few decades ago it was common to distinguish between "primitive" peoples and "civilized" nations. But the end of the colonial era brought with it a change in vocabulary. The concepts "primitive mentality" and "archaism of primitive peoples" are now challenged, and a new terminology has been formulated. Labels such as "underdeveloped countries" have replaced the old pejorative references. The expression "Tiers-Monde" was coined in 1956 as a book title for a work of multiple authorship compiled by Georges Balandier, *Le Tiers-Monde, sous-developpement et developpement.* It caught on rapidly and was finally adopted, with a slight change of nuance, as "Third World" by English-speaking countries. The term aimed at drawing attention to the major problem of the twentieth century and at arousing concern about it.

The widespread use of the term makes it desirable to explain its meaning. Actually, it has two meanings. First, it indicates a class of nations that, like the Third Estate (the commoners) in the ancient regime of France, "is nothing" but has the advantage of numbers and potential power, which are beginning to alter the course of history. Second, it points to the position, in the front ranks of the international political scene, of the new nations that are unattached to either of the two blocs. The expression was well received because it appeared shortly after the Bandung Conference (1955), which was a kind of General Assembly of Asian and African countries. In Africa, the eminent politicians and intelligentsia declared their unity with the group of underprivileged peoples at an early stage and refused to be black replicas of the West (neocapitalists) or of the East (socialists). They focused attention on the nature of black African civilization and societies; the theory of negritude, the African personality and African socialist doctrine reflect this. The cultural and humanist intentions of the Pan-African movement have not excluded the political aims; when the conception of the Third World was put forward, a Senegalese writer, Abdoulaye Ly, declared, "A belt of fire is flaming all round the Tropics." (See also *Pan-Africanism.*) G.B.

THUMB PIANOS. The thumb piano is a musical instrument of strictly African invention; it is played only by blacks, and it was they who brought it to the West Indies and to some parts of South America. It was first reported in Guiana by a European traveler at the beginning of the nineteenth century (*Narrative of a Five Years' Expedition against the Negroes of Surinam* by I. G. Stedman). The name by which it was first known, *loango-bania,* indicates that the instrument originated in equatorial Africa and that it spread elsewhere from there. It is found in parts of West Africa (Guinea, Liberia, Togo, Nigeria, Cameroun) where former slaves returning from America could have introduced it. The instrument is often referred to as a *sanza,* from the word *sansi,* a term borrowed from a language spoken in Malawi and also used in the Congo and Angola. The thumb piano consists of a row of blades or flexible stems made from plants (rattan, palm, bamboo) or metal that are attached to a small board or a small, rectangular box. The ends of the blades are struck with the fingers, mainly the thumbs of both hands, and the board or box amplifies the sound. The number of blades (or keys) varies from four to about twenty. The sounds they make are rather like those of plucked strings. A bell-like tinkle may be added to this if rings of white metal are put around metallic blades or if beads threaded on thorns are tapped against blades made of plant fiber. The thumb piano is ideal for free compositions of pure music, comparable to sonata movements, in which the development consists of rhythmic variations. The thumb piano and the drum are the two instruments that lend themselves to the African musician's greatest displays of virtuosity.   A.S.

TOTEMISM. The burning controversies roused by totemism during the first quarter of this century have now died down completely. Prior to passing into the common vocabulary of anthropologists, the word "totem," like the terms "taboo," "mana," and "potlatch," denoted, in the language of a specific preliterate society, an institution peculiar to that society. "Totem," a word in a North American Indian language, originally described the relation that the Ojibwa Indians recognized between a kinship group and a species of animal. Ethnologists established that a belief in this relationship was widespread among the peoples they studied; they considered it to be a fundamental conception of preliterate societies and tried to elucidate its meaning.

In traditional Africa, the relationship between men and animals takes different forms. The classic type of totemic relationship is a bond between a species of animal or plant and a clan; in Rwanda, for instance, one finds a bond between the leopard and the Abazigaba clan, the frog and the Abega clan, and the wagtail and the Abagesera clan. The members of the clan are forbidden to kill an animal of their totemic species. A mystical bond has often been sought between the totem and the human group, but the Rwandan clans did not believe that they were descended from a mythical animal, nor that their human ancestors were reincarnated in animals of their totemic species; the totem was only the living emblem of their clan. A much closer relationship between the individual animal and the human individual has been institutionalized among the Longarim of the Sudan; when a boy reaches puberty, he must

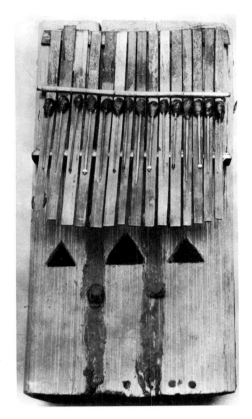

Thumb piano. Cameroun.
Musée de l'Homme, Paris.
Museum photo.

choose a calf which will be his favorite animal, and he can have only one such favorite bull during his lifetime; if his bull and another man's attack each other, he has to fight the man associated with the other bull; at the death of his bull, he mourns it as he would a close relative; men have even been known to commit suicide when their bulls died. It may well be asked whether this type of relationship—which is rare in Africa—between two individuals instead of between a species and a group can accurately be described as totemic. Whatever the answer, this extreme case of the identification of a man with an animal is most revealing about the African view of the continuity of the world of the living. (See also *Clans; Diet; Dogon; Elephants; Fauna; Lions; Pygmies.*)
                                                J.M.

TOWNS and CITIES. Africa is, on the whole, a land of villages. In most regions, technical and economic specialization were not sufficiently developed, commercial exchanges were too irregular and political organization was too modest for towns and cities to grow up. In many cases, the capitals of kingdoms were just large villages that expanded or stagnated with the success or failure of a dynasty and that could disappear

View of Kano, Nigeria.
Photo: Magnum,
Marc Riboud.

almost without leaving a trace, particularly since the buildings were constructed with impermanent materials. Once a famous capital disintegrated, it often lived on in legends and represented for its scattered people a place of sacred origin where their ancestors still lived. This is true of Mbanza Kongo, capital of the kingdom of Kongo, which was destroyed in the seventeenth century.

In some parts of Africa, however, towns came into being with a character all their own and survived for many centuries; some of them lasted until modern times. The stone buildings of the Zambezi region appear to have been constructed in towns or, at least, in the centers of towns in which most of the houses were built of lighter materials; Zimbabwe is an example of such a town center. These towns, which were destroyed in the sixteenth century, may have lasted a thousand years. They were certainly political centers, perhaps mining centers, and also centers of trade with the Middle and Far East, as archeological discoveries have proved. In two other regions on the fringe of the black subcontinent—on the eastern coast and on the borders of the Sahara—towns and cities flourished in the Middle Ages or were founded during that period. Whether or not they had political importance, the main function of the towns on the eastern coast, from Somaliland to Mozambique, was to serve as the ports, while those near the borders of the Sahara served the heavy commercial caravan traffic that crossed the

desert. Most of these towns declined during recent centuries. At a later date, a unique urban civilization developed in the Benin area, among the Yoruba. Its origin remains an enigma that conjectures about Ife, which was the prototype of the urban centers of Benin, have failed to solve.

The principal cities and towns of the eastern coast—Mogadishu, Mombasa, Zanzibar, Kilwa, Masoko and Sofala, to name only the most important ones—were founded after the end of the seventh century; the earliest ones by Arabs, later ones by Persians who gradually settled there. They were commercial towns, first trading iron for ivory and then dealing in gold and copper until the slave trade became their main business. These towns were colonies at first, but gradually became small, independent and very wealthy states. Kilwa, from the fourteenth to the sixteenth century, and Zanzibar, from the eighteenth century onward, established their hegemony over a great part of the coast. They remained alien to Africa, although they sometimes subdued the neighboring peoples or formed alliances with them, thus spreading their influence to a certain extent. They introduced Islam, Islamic laws and some techniques, such as masonry, the nailed timber framework, cotton weaving, sewing and plant cultivation. Very few monuments (funeral columns, mosques, palaces and houses) dating from earlier than the seventeenth century have survived, and the cities themselves have either fallen into ruin or were completely transformed during the colonial period. It should be remembered that they went through a very difficult period after the arrival of the Portuguese in the sixteenth century.

In the western Sudan, the growth of urban centers was associated with the creation and development of the empires that furnished the lands of the Maghrib with gold. The most ancient site known is Koumbi Saleh, possibly the ruins of the capital of Ghana, which began to decline in the twelfth century. Some towns, including Djenne, Timbuktu, Gao and Kano, have survived until today. Apart from Kano, their decadence in the fifteenth century began with the development of commerce along the coastal regions. The splendid image of Timbuktu, which still lingered in the European imagination at the beginning of the nineteenth century, corresponded to a reality that had vanished 200 years before; by the nineteenth century it was only a sleepy village. It had been the perfect example of a Sudanese town, with its fine architecture, its specialized districts, its thriving trade and a hinterland that provided it with food or manufactured goods from other centers such as Djenne. There were mosques and schools with high reputations, where Muslims from the Maghrib and the East sometimes came to listen to famous teachers. All this collapsed under the blows of the Moroccans at the end of the sixteenth century, at the same time that the Songhai empire fell; with the decline in trade across

the Sahara, it never regained its former luster.

In Yoruba country, towns, or at least large concentrations of people, were not the exception, but the rule. Today, there are half a dozen towns with more than 100,000 inhabitants, including the large city of Ibadan. They are not, as elsewhere, the products of colonization. One could call

Timbuktu, Mali. Drawing by René Caillé. *Photo: Musée de l'Homme.*

Capital of the kingdom of Benin. Illustration from *Description of Africa* by O. Dapper (Amsterdam, 1686).

them rural towns. The family homes are in the towns, but, if the fields are far away, the members of the family live in agricultural hamlets for part of the year. These towns are also commercial centers, with huge markets open day and night, as well as craft centers where, in former times, specialized groups such as blacksmiths, iron founders, sculptors, weavers and shoemakers devoted themselves to their work under the direction of the king or town authorities. The towns were, in fact, always capitals or actual states, self-governing and sometimes independent. They included ramparts, gates and the palace, which in the large capitals was a town within a town. The towns were not planned as such; they were jumbles of houses and networks of small streets with open spaces only for the great palace square and the marketplaces. It was only in the town of Benin, although this was under Yoruba influence, that systematic town-planning with long streets intersecting at right angles and houses built in straight rows existed. A remarkable style of architecture was developed in several regions: huge houses with a central court and compluvium surrounded by a covered gallery leading into the rooms. Its origin poses as many questions as that of the towns themselves. (See also *Arabs in East Africa; Architecture; Benin; Colonization; Ibadan; Industry; Islam; Markets; Sahara; Sudan; Yoruba; Zimbabwe*.)   P.M.

TRAPS. It is more common for traditional African societies to capture animals by means of traps than by hunting and fishing.

Trap with trigger release. Toma. Guinea. Musée de l'Homme, Paris. *Museum photo.*

Besides true traps—that is, devices that function on their own and immobilize the animal—Africans often use other types of traps which require direct action on the part of the hunter or fisherman. During the battues that accompany the annual savanna fires, the hunters have to kill the antelopes before they are disengaged from the nets into which they have been driven.

The Massa of Chad put baskets filled with branches into water courses because the fish take shelter from the sun in the baskets; at a suitable time, the Massa pull the baskets onto the bank and take out their booty. The simplest traps have nooses that the animals pull tight around their necks with their own weight. Some hunting nets used in northern Cameroun are made with a series of running knots that are held open by a small piece of grass; the grass tie snaps and releases the loop under the impact of an animal throwing itself against the net. Nooses that tighten with the action of a primitive spring are common in Africa. They range from tiny bow traps which are used for catching rats to antelope traps employed in the forest areas. In the latter, a supporting frame equipped with a noose springs up and hangs the animal above the ground. Traps with radical spikes are peculiar to Africa. Such a trap consists of a noose that is placed horizontally on the ground and is surrounded by a contraption of bamboo spikes. This contraption consists of two disks separated by a circle of slivers of bamboo. The outside ends of the slivers are attached to one or the other of the disks, and the ends pointing toward the center are free. The whole device—noose and spikes—is laid over a pit so that when an animal puts its foot on top of it, the flexible bamboo splinters spread out under the pressure and imprison

Hunters setting a trap. Yoruba mask. Dahomey. Wood. Paul Tishman Collection, New York. *Photo: Musée de l'Homme.*

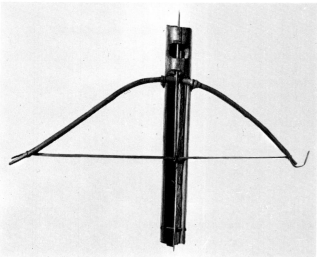

the limb, while the animal tightens the noose round its neck by struggling. Many other kinds of traps are used in Africa. There are trenches covered and camouflaged with branches and brushwood and having sharpened stakes, which are sometimes poisoned, underneath. Leopard labyrinths used in Gabon are designed in such a way that the animal can neither turn around nor back its way out. In some devices, the animal, as it tugs at the bait, brings down a trap-door and imprisons itself. The traps used in the Guinean region for catching leopards and hyenas are elaborate constructions of mud or stone and are of this type. Deadfalls and breakbacks are traps in which the animal releases a heavy object that kills it. They are often found in the forest regions, where some are armed with poisoned iron spikes for killing elephants. Lime twigs are used for catching birds, with resins, fig tree latex and wild euphorbia being used to make the birdlime. Hooks, often unbaited, have long been used for fishing. Spoon nets, baskets, bow nets and fish mazes are to be found almost everywhere in Africa. In Chad, the Kotoko along the Chari River use enormous square dipping nets which are thrown in from a canoe. Dragnets seem to be used more commonly in Africa than fixed nets. Traps are sometimes combined with the use of a lure. The Lobi and the Dagari of Upper Volta play flutes to attract bushbuck. The Bozo along the Niger River keep a piece of bait in constant movement under water to attract some kinds of fish.

Techniques for diminishing the agility of game and fish serve as subsidiary forms of traps. Smoke and fire are used for this purpose on land, toxins in water. Under the influence of industrialized civilizations, hunting with a gun is beginning to take the place of trapping. Traps with iron plates, fish-hooks and imported nylon nets are tending to replace the traditional devices. (See also *Basketry; Birds; Buffalo; Elephants; Fauna; Fishing; Hunting.*) I.G.

TRIBES. Originally, tribes were societal groups whose members considered themselves to be descended from the same ancestor; there were countless numbers of these groups in traditional Africa. Each societal group had a word in its language for clearly distinguishing those who were members from outsiders. The activities of the members were organized so that they complemented each other and assured the survival and development of the group as a whole and of the individuals composing it. Observing the same customs, speaking the same language, sharing the same world view

Fishing net. Pomo. Republic of the Congo. *Photo: Lucien Demesse.*

and consciously wanting to live together, members of the same societal group felt themselves to be part of a closely knit community. It is not surprising that in most cases they attributed this community spirit to common descent. Indeed, the principle of kinship, on which the lineage and clan were also based, dominated the experience and, consequently, the conscience of Africans. They tended to use kinship as an explanation for a large number of social relationships that appeared to have some analogy with it. Not until a single, strong network of political relationships united everyone living on the same territory so that everyone depended on the same government could Africans conceive a societal group that was not based on kinship. The unifying principle that was then recognized was a common allegiance to the same ruler.

Tribal units survived to a greater or lesser extent during three-quarters of a century of colonial rule. In the young independent states of today, some tribal groups are showing renewed vitality, expressing it by means of political parties. This tribalism, also known as regionalism, is a serious threat to the recently formed national entities, which are still not firmly established; the attempts at secession of Katanga and Biafra

are excellent illustrations of this. Several African governments have tried to combat these centrifugal tendencies by encouraging the formation of parties with a national scope that will include men whose fathers and grandfathers belonged to different and often antagonistic tribes. (See also *Clans; Ethnic Groups; Kinship; Migrations; Race.*)
J.M.

TRIBUTE. In societies in which some sort of tax system existed, the system was essentially communal in nature; the tax assessment never applied below the level of the extended family, even in most of the Islamized societies, where legal alms were supposed to be contributed by individuals. It should be noted that fiscal systems did not exist in societies that had not attained a certain level of political organization, that level being, at a minimum, the chieftainship. At that level, a system of multilateral and reciprocal communal prestations (obligatory payments in kind or in service) was replaced by a system of converging prestations in which counterprestations were no longer reciprocal. This type of system is particularly well developed in multiracial states, for example in the Hausa emirates of northern Nigeria, where it is combined with the Koranic financial system, and in the Bantu kingdoms of the Great Lakes region. Here, the internal tax system seems to be based on a tax system that could be termed international: a militarily dominant ethnic group would require its weaker neighbors to provide prestations which, in turn, would help to strengthen and maintain its initial military supremacy. Thus, the internal tax system, generally applied to groups alien to the lineage or ethnic group of the ruler, provided the ruler with the means to keep up his court and, eventually, his army, and thereby to establish his authority and that of his people.

In powerful states both types of systems existed side by side; the *kabaka* of Buganda collected taxes from his own subjects as well as levying a tax on neighboring kingdoms. Similarly, in the central Sudan, the Muslim rulers, while collecting legal alms from their subjects and even redemption money—to which Muslim law, in principle, subjected only pagans—also tried to levy a tax on neighboring kingdoms and added periodic levies on pagan tribes that were not under their direct authority. In Chad and Adamawa, rulers who were devout Muslims have been known to prevent pagan tribes from being converted to Islam so that they could continue to levy a redemption tax on

them. Sometimes the positions were reversed, with the representative or chief of a governing ethnic group periodically offering a tribute—which was generally financially negligible but symbolically of great value—to a representative of the subject ethnic group. In most cases, this tribute represented a historic rent for the use of the land or the waters, whose fertility remained under the magical dominion of the original proprietors.

Tributes in the strict sense of the word and taxes of tributary origin were seldom paid in currency or protocurrency, which was generally reserved for indirect taxes or customs payments. The usual form of payment was in kind: grain, cattle, loincloths, various artifacts or, in former times, slaves. Even today, tributary lineages send to the *uro eso* of the Tem in Togo and to the *na* of the Dagomba of Ghana unattached girls whom the chief himself marries without paying marriage compensation. He may also give them in marriage to his dignitaries or young men whose position at court is rather like that of pages or grooms. These special wives and page-hostages lived in courts from the eastern and southern Bantu kingdoms to Senegal, where they gave Faidherbe the idea for his "hostage school" and, later on, his "school for the sons of chieftains." The institution was also a special prestation that was intended simultaneously to symbolize and to perpetuate a bond of vassalage. (See also *Baluba; Cattle; Weights.*)
P.A.

TRUMPETS. See *Horns and Trumpets.*

TWINS. Every abnormal or unusual birth can be thought of as being either beneficent or maleficent, depending on whether it is viewed as a sign of a great destiny and special power or a sign of disorder. This is true, for example, of twin births. Sometimes, both twins were killed at birth, as was done among some of the Ibo of Nigeria, and sometimes only one of them was killed, as was the rule among the Bushmen. Other tribes regarded the twin birth as the ideal example of fertility, and the children were then endowed with appropriate powers and made the objects of a cult. But in many cases there was a certain degree of ambiguity: the twin birth, while being beneficent, could at the same time present dangers that had to be guarded against, especially if one of the twins or both died young. This was a common view in West Africa.

The beneficent character of twins has a mythical basis; the principle of gemination has an important position in a number of cosmogonies. In Dahomey, for example, the great divinities are always double. They are either conceived of as a single, androgynous person or as twins of different sex; the creation, for instance, was the work of the Mawu-Lissa couple, and the god Dan, who helped them, is also double—in the rainbow, which is his manifestation, the colors red and blue reflect the two sexual aspects of his person. And when new gods were adopted, they were cast in the same mold. The Bambara and Dogon consider every single birth to be an abortive twin birth; a man has twin souls of different sex, and it is circumcision that gives the male soul its primacy. In the creation myth, the single birth of the first son of the God of Heaven and Earth produced a being of disorder; it was the following birth of twins that produced the powers generative of order, which act as guides in the organization of the world and society.

In societies in which the appearance of human twins is considered an evocation of equilibrium as well as fertility, twins receive special treatment; sometimes their mother does too, but she is less honored. In the Bamileke country of Cameroun, an honorary title is conferred on her, she occasionally assumes certain priestly functions and she and her husband change their names. In Dahomey, the particular celestial horizon where the twins originated is discovered by divination; the newborn twins are then exhibited in the marketplace, and their mother receives everyone's congratulations. In Dahomey and in several other regions, a double altar, which remains the center of a cult even after their death, is consecrated to them. It is invoked in cases of sterility, and sometimes offerings of seeds and the first fruits are made to it, as to ancestors. The Yoruba make statues of dead twins that are about ten inches high, more or less realistic, sexless and often have elaborate hairstyles. The surviving twin or the mother, if both are dead, treats the statuette like a child: pretends to feed it, washes it and dresses it. Here, the cult of twins borders on the great myths and rites involving the major divinities. In any case, it has resulted in an art that, although of minor importance, has produced a large number of beautiful carvings. Specialists in Yoruban art consider these statuettes extremely important because they "serve as a basis for the study of local and individual variations in the treatment of the human body" in wood sculpture. They are also valuable because they are often preserved for a long time and, consequently, can be ascribed to a particular family and

often dated. The features of old pieces are softened, sometimes almost smoothed away, with long handling. (See also *Circumcision; Dogon; Dolls; Incest; Myths; Yoruba.*)
P.M.

UNCLES. Although most people in the Western world follow a fundamentally patrilineal system of kinship—that is, the legal line of descent and family name is traced through the father rather than through both parents—they apply the term "uncle" to both their mother's and their father's brothers; in fact, in many parts of the Western world, the term is also applied to the husband of the father's or mother's sister. African languages are more precise; most of them have different words for the four kinds of relationships, which actually are different. It is not awkward for us to use one word for these four relationships because American and European children behave the same toward all the men of their parents' generation, whether they are related by blood or marriage. Young Africans, on the other hand, are taught to vary their behavior according to whether they are with their paternal or maternal uncle. In a patrilineal system, the young African (let us call him "Ego," as anthropologists do in discussions of kinship) owes respect and obedience to his father's brother. If Ego becomes an orphan, his paternal uncle takes his father's place and exercises familial authority over him. The daughters of this uncle, Ego's cousins on his father's side, are virtually his sisters, and his behavior toward them has to be very circumspect; the most innocent friendship could give rise to suspicions of incest. On the other hand, Ego can and even ought to maintain a familiar attitude toward his mother's brother, and his actions can verge on insolence. For instance, among the Bahamba of the equatorial forest, Ego is allowed to take away openly and without permission the belongings of his maternal uncle. The uncle has to put up with these exasperating impertinences without being able to stop them. He cannot even prevent his daughters and Ego from indulging in any games and taking any liberties with each other that they might fancy. If Ego marries one of his cousins on his mother's side, the matrimonial compensation paid to the uncle is very low. The reason why the maternal uncle has to adopt this permissive attitude is quite simple: when Ego's father married, the goods that were given to his wife's lineage (Ego's mother's lineage) were later used to obtain a wife for her brother (Ego's maternal uncle), with the result that he is perpetually in debt to Ego's lineage, and the rules of the society allow Ego to take advantage of it.

All this, or nearly all of it, is reversed where the matrilineal principle is accepted. In matrilineal societies, Ego's maternal uncle acts as his foremost and immediate familial authority because the role of disciplinarian, played by the father in a patrilineal system, is not assumed by the mother in a matrilineal society, but rather by her brother, Ego's maternal uncle. In a matrilineal family, the authority remains masculine. As soon as Ego is old enough to do without his mother's protection, he goes to live with his uncle; he gets him to pay the matrimonial compensation when he wants to marry; and he inherits his uncle's possessions and responsibilities (and not those of his father). The father, however, is not merely a progenitor; Ego lives in his home for the first few years of his life and later on maintains a connection with his father, who is consulted notably when Ego is on the point of marrying. It is very rare for the two influences not to clash; in matrilineal societies, relationships are generally strained between a man and his brother-in-law. But the position of the paternal uncle in matrilineal societies is extremely weak because he is only a substitute for the father. In the machinery of African kinship, each cog is too precisely defined for the very general term "uncle" to be applied without confusion. (See also *Family; Ghana; Guro; Kinship; Lineage; Wisdom.*)   J.M.

VEGETABLES. All African agricultural societies raise vegetables—that, is, herbaceous plants whose fruit, seeds, roots, tubers, bulbs, stems, leaves or flower parts are used for food. Near the family enclosure there is almost always a garden which is tended by the wife. It provides most of the condiments for her sauces. In the tropical zone, leguminous plants are often grown together with cereals, although in some communities whole fields of beans and peas can be seen. Peanuts are very widely cultivated for industrial purposes in tropical regions. Tubers of one kind or another—cassava, yams, taro, coleus, sweet potatoes or chufa—are the staple food for most of the forest dwellers. Of these tubers, only the yam and the coleus are of African origin. Tubers are generally cultivated by transplanting cuttings. Their yield is fairly high, and they can be grown in nearly all seasons, which explains why they are so common in spite of their low nutritional value. The rhizomes of lotus and other water plants, of yams and of wild onions are often gathered for food. The

shoots of most of the cultivated tubers and hibiscus (okra, Guinean sorrel) are boiled in sauces. Africans often eat the leaves of wild plants, especially when other food is scarce. The Serer of Senegal eat the leaves of the amaranth (*Amaranthus spinosus*), *Moringa pterigosperma, Leptadenia hastata, Cassia obtusifolia* and *Crateva adansoni* by the pound. The vitamin content of these leaves is considerably reduced by prolonged boiling. The terminal buds of several varieties of palm are eaten all over the equatorial zone. The flowers of the silk-cotton tree (*Ceiba pentandra*) are often incorporated in sauces.

A wide variety of gourds, cucumbers and melons, including watermelons, are found in Africa, many of them native to the continent. Some of them are grown only for their seeds, which are rich in fats. Tomatoes, eggplants and pimentos are often raised, but tend to be small. They are dried and then stored so that they can be eaten later during the year. There are two principal varieties of bananas: the small banana, which is the kind most familiar to people in Europe and the United States, and the plantain, which is boiled, powdered and eaten as a staple food by many forest dwellers. The plantain can grow to a foot in length.

The term "legumes," or "leguminous plants," refers to plants whose seeds grow in pods or husks. These plants are less important in Africa than the plants discussed above, but they are essential because they contain nutritional elements that are deficient in the diets of country dwellers (proteins of good quality, calcium, iron and riboflavin). Peanuts are the most common of the leguminous plants, followed by beans, peas and lentils, which are grown over vast areas and are ready for harvesting when other foods are scarce. Some varieties of beans are cultivated for their fibers only. Leguminous plants can be stored easily but are subject to deterioration from granary parasites. The daily amount of leguminous vegetables consumed in Africa as a whole is 1.4 ounces per person. Far more legumes are eaten in some regions, such as in the Moba country in Togo, where consumption reaches 5 ounces (beans and peanuts), and in some parts of Rwanda, where it is as high as 14 ounces. The list of wild legumes consumed in Africa is long: the most common are cassia (Chinese cinnamon), tamarind, bauhinia and nerine. Forest peoples (for example, the Pygmies in Zaire, the Eton and Ewondo of the Cameroun) eat huge quantities of many different kinds of mushrooms. (See also *Cassava; Diet; Granaries; Meals; Peanuts.*)
          I.G.

Liberian village. *Photo: Pierre Ichac.*

VILLAGES. In Africa a village is, first of all, the territory of a particular group of people. Long occupation results in every part of the territory being known, named and used to its utmost by the inhabitants. The area is changed to suit the needs of the inhabitants; it is cleared of stones, some trees are cut down and others preserved, and the wood supply area and the hunting ground are demarcated. Depending on the size of the territory and the density of the population of the region, the village will either use its territory to its full potential—this is the case, for example, among the Palaeonegrid refugees—or will float in excessive space and the territory will be wasted over a long period by exploitation with careless techniques because it would take generations or centuries to inhabit, cultivate and domesticate the whole area. The members of the village have absolute and imprescriptible rights over this land; furthermore, they have an alliance with it. Settling on new land is a religious act; a pact has to be concluded with all the powers of the place and with the earth itself, which is the primary force. Lengthy ceremonies culminate in the establishment of an altar to the earth. At a suitable time, worship of the founder-ancestor will be added to the earth cult; the African village is primarily a "parish" (H. Labouret). The members of the village comprise all the descendants of the founder and may preserve links with the village from which they came. Other people may join the village group later, but the original occupants will retain their ritual authority and supply the land priest, whether the new arrivals have come with the permission of the first occupants or have seized political power by force or other means. Consequently, villages are more or less homogeneous, although they sometimes include several clan, ethnic group or caste districts or adjoin districts of foreign traders.

Every village, nevertheless, has its own character, which is preserved by its inhabitants, however diverse and unequal they may be, and which is perceived by its neighbors. It is based on common history, on common religious background and on political autonomy. Traditionally, even though the village might be subordinate to a state or kingdom, the chief was hardly ever nominated by the central power; rather, he was chosen by the village council from a particular family and could not be deprived of his office. The village was a real community that could, under extreme circumstances, be self-sufficient. However, this was rare because the search for wives and the need for certain products forced it to turn to the world outside its boundaries. In-

Dogon cliff village in
Mali. *Photo: Rapho,
Philippe Billère.*

desultory conversations in which the wisdom of the oldest was imparted to the youngest—all of which were a significant part of the village or had a proper place in it.

The village was neither immortal nor immutable: sometimes it had to be moved elsewhere because the soil was exhausted or because too many illnesses or deaths indicated the activity of evilly disposed powers. This departure could not take place without duly informing the gods with whom an alliance had been made formerly and the ancestors whose altars would have to be moved; their consent was required. A deserted site was not always completely abandoned; periodic rites were performed there to ward off the unforeseeable ill will of the supernatural. A village could also split apart. As soon as a village reached a certain size, small groups migrated toward the periphery of the territory and formed cultural hamlets, which gradually established themselves as new villages without completely breaking their bonds with the original village. Sometimes the authorities of the latter came solemnly to inaugurate the new community. In some cases, the unity of the whole complex was gradually strengthened, and the group of villages—the canton or township—continued to have important social, political and religious ties. (See also *Age Groups; Bobo; Colonization; Dahomey; Divinities; Dogon; Ekoi; Granaries; Ibibio; Kissi; Massa; Migrations; Mussoi; Senufo; Work; Zulus.*) P.M.

VOODOO. The term "voodoo" is derived from the Fon word *vodu.* The equivalent Yoruba term is *orisha.* (Fon is spoken in Dahomey, Yoruba in Nigeria and Dahomey.) The black slaves who were bought on the shores of the Bight of Benin brought the voodoo cult with them to the West Indies and Brazil, where the religious ideas connected with it captured the interest of Western observers. Most of the blacks from the Slave Coast—which corresponds to the coast of eastern Nigeria, Dahomey and Togo—were settled on plantations in the New World, and it was on these plantations that Westerners first had extended contact with the tenets of this religion. For a long time, the Europeans who could have studied the voodoo rites and beliefs in the country where they originated saw them only as part of an idolatrous "fetish" cult and confused the divinities with their material manifestations. Admittedly, they were slave-dealers, who were hardly attracted by the study of metaphysical systems and were inclined to deny any speculative powers in the men they treated like salable cattle.

volvement in the life of the kingdom or in regional secret societies often created links with several other villages. But each village included every, or almost every, social category found in the society: craftsmen, priests, magicians, diviners, healers. Most of the important social events—agrarian rites, initiations and the acquisition of honorary titles—could take place in totum within the village. Kin groups and often age groups formed a framework for organizing work and carrying out major exchanges of goods. The common activities and interests were expressed materially in the village, especially when it was compactly built, by the rampart or moat, the temples or altars of the common cults, the bush camp for initiations, the men's shelter or hut where their palavers were carried on—the arbitration of conflicts, decisions, the discussion of plans or the

It is difficult to give a concise account of this complex of religious ideas because the conception of the voodoo varies so much from one region to another. The voodoos of each ethnic subgroup form a pantheon, but the relations between them are imprecise and there is no real hierarchy. A voodoo who presides as the principal divinity in one sanctuary is only a secondary divinity in a neighboring temple, which is dedicated to another voodoo who is only an assistant in the first. The whole concept of voodoo is variable: in East Africa, where these cults originated, voodoo is both a nature force and a deified ancestor, but in West Africa, it is essentially a nature force, and the positions of the lineage divinities are occupied by the *yehwe.* Even the sex of the divinities can vary. For instance, Mawu—the feminine member of a creator couple of which the male member is Lissa in Dahomey—becomes a hermaphroditic divinity in Togo, where its cult is practically nonexistent but where it is invoked in circumstances of extreme gravity, with the ceremony itself taking place in the sanctuary of a voodoo who is especially feared. An explanation of these extreme differences is that the part of the continent where voodoo cults are practiced was never completely unified by the empires of West Africa, and its history has been one of considerable political fragmentation.

An alliance contracted with a voodoo is represented by a specific object, which is kept by the priest: a "thunder axe" (Neolithic axe) for the god Xevioso or pieces of iron for the war god Gu, for example. The purpose of the ceremonies with offerings, the baths with infusions of special leaves, the blood sacrifices, the dances and the recital of *oriki* (set invocations that are a mixture of mottoes and praises) is to revitalize the sacred force of the voodoo. He requires the performance of these rites, and in return he confers his divine favors on those who perform them. Each sanctuary is in the charge of a priest—*voduno* or *hubono*—who is virtually the proprietor of the temple and of the objects that are proof of alliances. In principle, he is a descendant of the first "keeper of the sacred force." This priest is assisted by a group of *vodunsi* or *husi* ("wives of the voodoo"), whom the god himself has chosen. He indicates this choice in a variety of ways: for instance, by revealing that he is the source of an uncured illness from which the person suffers or, often, by causing a crisis of possession. It is by "descending onto the head" of the chosen, outwardly manifested by a state of trance, that the voodoo reveals himself and can then speak through

The Fali village of Ngoutchoumi, Cameroun.
Photo: Jean-Paul Lebeuf.

the mouth of the person he possesses. The chosen one undergoes an initiation, during the course of which he is confined in the temple, where he becomes dead to his previous life and is born again as a *vodunsi.* These *vodunsi*—whose scarifications, dress and emblems are peculiar to the divinity to whom they are dedicated—dance during the ceremonies that take place on ground adjacent to the temple. It is mainly during these spectacular ceremonies that the divinity is incarnated in one or several of his "wives," who can be men as well as women. The sacred college is completed by the acolytes, the *hunovi,* the "brothers of the voodoo," who, unlike the *vodunsi,* have themselves made the decision to serve the god. Although during the ceremonies (when the simplicity of their dress is striking) they appear in public as attendants of the "wives of the voodoo," in the temple they are responsible for seeing that the *vodunsi* observe the rules.

There are a number of important voodoos besides Mawu and the Mawu-Lissa couple, who have already been mentioned (the name of the Yoruba *orisha* is given in parentheses after the name of the Fon voodoo to which it corresponds): Sakpata (Sopona), the voodoo of smallpox; Da (Oshumare), the python god, whose cult struck the imaginations of the first travelers in the Ouidah region; Gu (Ogun), god of iron and war; So (Shango), better known by the name of Xevioso (from the village of Xevié in

Dahomey), the god of thunder, whose cult is the most important in the western part of the Bight of Benin. Another of these voodoos, Legba (Eshu, or Elegbara), occupies a special place simply because there are so many of his images about. These images are found at the entrances to and in the open spaces and courts of villages, temples and private huts. They are massive anthropomorphic clay figures with enormous erect phalluses, and are almost always accompanied by smaller statues of Legba. Early travelers assumed they were statues of Satan because of their indecency and the occasional presence of horns on their heads; missionaries translated "devil" as "Legba." In fact, Legba does not in any way correspond to Evil. Like the other voodoos, he cannot be integrated into a Christian system, with its opposition between good and evil. It is true that his sensitive and facetious character may make him do something bad, either because he considers that he has been insulted by neglect or simply because he has been carried away by his love of farce, which is rather vulgar and, at times, dangerous. But he has his good side, which is evidenced in his most important function: to act as a protector; Legba is the guardian of villages and temples as well as simple huts. He is also the messenger of the other voodoos, whose wishes he translates into human language. This function gives him the privilege of receiving the first offerings during all ceremonies, no matter to which voodoo they are dedicated. Neglect of this rule ruffles his sensibilities, and experienced devotees always benefit from observing it. Finally, there is Fa or Afa (Ifa), the spokesman of the

voodoos. He presides over divination and is consulted at all the important junctures of life through the intermediary of his priest, the *bokono (babalawa)*, who interprets the signs given by the coconuts used in this rite. (See also *Divination; Possession by Spirits; Priest; Rattles; Scarification; Spirits and Genii; Zar*.) G.C.

WEAPONS. Weapons, as instruments for wounding or terrifying, as ornaments or emblems, as real or symbolic instruments of death, are the most difficult of all the material components of culture to classify. They have nevertheless been the subjects of systematic study since the latter part of the last century, when writers who were exponents of the concept of "cultural zones" drew maps to show the distribution of weapons according to basic characteristics and functions.

Weapons can be characterized according to whether they are thrown or not thrown. Both throwing weapons and nonthrowing weapons are used for war, fishing and hunting. Nonthrowing weapons that don't have blades are comparatively rare. Martial jewelry is one kind of bladeless nonthrowing weapon; strange bracelets with points or claws and the related rings fitted with spikes are used mainly by the peoples of the Nile and the Great Lakes regions, although they are also found in northwestern Cameroun. This type of jewelry is worn as a sign of martial prowess, but often only on special occasions: for example, during the ceremonies that accompany initiation into an adult age group, which, as among the Bari, may include fighting. Iron weapons ending in

Fang knife. Republic of the Congo. Wood and iron. Musée de l'Homme, Paris. *Museum photo.*

Kuya throwing knife. Republic of Central Africa. Iron and basketry. Musée de l'Homme, Paris. *Museum photo.*

Zande throwing knife. Zaire. Iron and plant fibers. Musée royal de l'Afrique centrale, Tervuren. *Museum photo.*

Baule ceremonial saber.
Ivory Coast. Iron and gold
leaf. Musée de l'Homme,
Paris. *Photo: R. Pasquino.*

Fon saber. Dahomey. Iron.
Musée de l'Homme, Paris.
Museum photo.

Mangbetu knife. Zaire.
Iron and ivory. Musée
de l'Homme, Paris.
Museum photo.

sharp hooks, resembling the claws of a wild animal, are only used by lion men and leopard men for executions ordered by their societies.

Clubs, either of solid wood or with a head of plain or decorated iron, are found in many regions. The handles are sometimes decorated in the middle with a coil of metal, leather thongs, wire or copper, and the knobs are sometimes sculpted in one of a variety of ways. The typical Zulu club is a good example of this kind of bladeless weapon. It is made from a gracefully curving rhinoceros horn; the end is decorated with a thick spiral of iron; and the spherical head is flattened on top. Some East African peoples have a long, heavy truncheon whose head and handle are in one piece; it is grooved throughout its length and is tapered at either end.

The most common, the most varied and the deadliest weapons are those with blades. The number of different kinds of knives and daggers found in Chad, Gabon and the regions of the Congo and the Ubangi is proverbial. The blacksmiths modified the basic shape of the hilt and the blade so much that the importance, if not the regal character, of these weapons is obvious: broad, thin blades of glittering steel or red copper; blades shaped like trapeziums, leaves, triangles; tips like half moons or a pair of back-to-back crescents; open-work decoration and incredible engraving of the metal parts that is impossible to describe; hilts of leather or ivory; sheaths of leather or wood decorated with a wealth of inventiveness like the blades. The great ceremonial swords of the Ivory Coast and

Dahomey have iron blades decorated with filigree and engraving and hilts covered with copper foil (gold foil among aristocratic Akan families) that is connected to the hilt by means of clasps. The symbolic value of many weapons and the power they represent tend to outweigh their utilitarian functions. The axe in particular, both as a weapon and a tool, has become, in black Africa, a ceremonial or ritual object or an accessory for dances and processions. Blacksmiths often shape the handle of the axe into a human figure and attach the blade at the mouth of the figure; such axes can be found among the Bateke in Congo, for example.

Throwing weapons are the most typical arms found in Africa south of the Sahara. Besides curved throwing sticks, which are common in much of black Africa, there are throwing knives whose distribution includes a large, irregular area in the middle of Africa going from Chad to the Republic of Congo and central Zaire. There are two distinct types of throwing knives: the knives with single blades shaped like hornbills' heads (typical of those of the Fang) and knives with several blades and shafts of about equal size or with a single curved shaft (typical of those of the Azande and Mangbetu). Great skill in the art of blade-making has resulted in the creation of certain examples whose shapes are so cleverly varied, while retaining the original purpose of the knives (to be used as lethal weapons), that they exhibit a remarkable compromise between imagination and efficiency. Among the Bakuba, in the Kasai-Sankuru region, the name Shango, which was applied exclusively to the royal

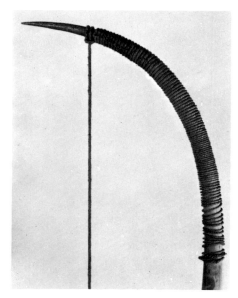

Detail of the string wound around a bow. Zaire. Musée de l'Homme, Paris. *Museum photo.*

Basonge ceremonial ax. Zaire. Iron and copper. Musée de l'Homme, Paris. *Museum photo.*

Fang crossbow Republic of the Congo. Wood, with leather quiver. Musée de l'Homme, Paris. *Museum photo.*

clan, meant "four-bladed throwing knife," a weapon which had been banned by one of their great kings who was deeply concerned with culture and the maintenance of peace. Spears, as weapons both for throwing and for thrusting, are widely used in Africa. Like knives, spears can have several blades: they may have double or triple blades, or a ring of small blades around a large central one. The blades—which may be curved, or shaped like arrows, willow leaves or half moons, or serrated—are mounted on decorated shafts. Spears are common in an area that extends

from Senegal to Cameroun and reaches as far as East Africa.

There are several different types of arrows which can be categorized according to the kind of feathering—for instance, the feathering may be a trimmed leaf or a guinea-fowl's feather—whether the tip is tanged or socketed, whether or not the tip is poisoned and, if it is poisoned, whether it is poisoned with vegetable juices or with cobra or other snake venom. The size of the area in which bows and arrows are found is gradually diminishing. Children's miniature bows and arrows are often the only reminders of weapons that have been replaced by fire-arms. The crossbow, which came to Africa from Europe, has, unlike the simple bow, only a very limited distribution.

Shields and armor, which are used only in war, evolved from various methods of protection. From Niger to the kingdom of Bornu, sultans have had guards of armored lancers. Their padded armor provided complete protection against arrows for both man and horse. Soft armor is used from the land of the Mossi as far as eastern Cameroun. Coats of mail made of metal and helmets of the same material, which are worn by the Fulani and the Hausa, are probably of more ancient origin than soft armor. In Cameroun, Massa warriors in the south wear leather corselets and helmets, and those in the north wear a type of armor that is similar but made of basketry. Several kinds of shields are used. Some cover the body of the warrior entirely, while others, like the basketry shoulder-shields in central Africa, are less cumbersome and give ample freedom of movement. The very beautiful ox-skin shields of the Zulu in southeastern Africa, which evolved from stick-shields, also allow maximum mobility. The oval wooden shields of the Masai are decorated with painted geometrical designs which are virtually coats of arms; the warriors can recognize the social group (clan and age group) to which each shield-bearer belongs.

It is impossible to catalog all the different kinds of weapons: arms that are carried for self-defense, military and ceremonial weapons, executioners' implements, equipment for hunting and fishing and even magical weapons whose effectiveness depends less upon the keenness of the blade or the weight of the club than upon their supernatural power. The importance of weapons is evident from the number of works of art in which they appear. A standard feature of the bronze plaques that covered the wooden pillars of the royal palace in the old city of Benin was depictions of chiefs and their warriors brandishing their arms. The horseman with his spear is a common subject of Dogon, Bambara and Senufo statuary. The clearest illustration of the menace and prestige of weapons is the astounding forest of metal knives, spearheads, nails and rusty blades of every shape and size that cover the bodies of Bakongo fetish figures. The Bakongo say that the name of a future victim is mirrored in the eyes of a statue and that its arm, holding a weapon, is already anticipating the fatal blow. (See also *Bakuba; Basketry; Benin; Blacksmiths; Buffalo; Bushmen; Dance; Elephants; Fauna; Gold; Hunting; Kikuyu; Kongo; Lion Men; Massa; Sao; Sculpture, Wood; Songhai; Traps; Voodoo; Zimbabwe.)* J.D.

WEAVING. Not all African peoples weave. Weaving is done mainly in the Sudanese zone, from the Atlantic to Ethiopia, and is unknown south of the equator outside an east-central arc stretching from Rhodesia to the Congo River through the Great Lakes region. The preliminary operations of preparing the fibers are carried out by either men or women, depending on the region, but the actual weaving is done by men, almost without exception, in Africa. It is quite frequently the province of specialized craftsmen, some of whom are itinerant weavers who go from village to village to hire out their services. Before discussing the

Bambara weaving loom. Mali.
Photo: Musée de l'Homme.

techniques of weaving, it is interesting to note the distribution of weaving materials. Except along the fringe of the Sahara, where processes of working wool and goat and camel hair common to nomads from the Maghrib to central Asia are dying out, the weaving domain is shared unequally by two types of materials: cotton in the north and southeast and palm fibers, especially raffia, in the central zone; the two materials overlap in the west along the Gulf of Guinea. The distribution of weaving processes and loom types can be divided into four zones, which are related to the areas in which particular materials are used but do not coincide with them. In both the northwest and northeast regions, cotton-weaving is done on looms of the "double-heddle" type, of which there are two main kinds with slight local differences. From the central Sudan to Rhodesia, cotton is woven on horizontal looms with a single row of heddles, which are related to one of the Madagascan types and the wool looms of the nomads. The region where palm fibers are used coincides closely with an unusual loom, which has a vertical warp and a single row of heddles.

In the western, double-heddle loom, the warp is made from a large ball of thread that is gradually unwound as the woven strip is rolled onto the breast-beam, which is equipped with a catch and in front of which the weaver sits. A frame supports the harness —that is, all the working parts of the loom: the heddle bars and the reed. As the threads of the warp are engaged alternately by one or the other of the two rows of heddles, a shed (opening) is formed for the passage of the weft by the ascending and descending movements of the heddle bars. Each row of heddles is connected to a pulley system and is moved in turn by a treadle. The movements of the heddles are controlled by pulleys. The threads of the weft are wound around small spools that act as bobbins; the bobbins are unwound by rotating on axes in the cavities of shuttles. After each pick (throw of the weft thread), the work is pressed down by a reed, generally weighted with a heavy piece of wood that forms the lower beam and acts as a batten. In the west, strips, sometimes as narrow as four inches, are woven. The looms offer a striking contrast between the roughness of the frame, made of a few barely trimmed poles, and the individual components—heddles and heddle bars, shuttles and especially the reeds and pulleys—which have the careful finish of objects made for personal use; the outsides of the pulleys are exquisitely decorated and are often enlarged by means of some kind of anthropomorphic sculpture. The loom components are the essential equipment of the weaver; the rest is often only a temporary construction, especially when the weaver is an itinerant worker. The sign that one of these looms, which are quite small, is in use is a long skein

of weft thread stretching several feet behind the loom and wound onto a stake or rolled into a large ball kept taut by a stone.

The eastern loom (employed in Ethiopia and Somalia) is much larger than the western, double-heddle loom. The warp is raised above the top of the frame and then attached behind the weaver, who can relieve the tension at will by rolling a length of fabric onto the heavy beam that constitutes the breast-beam. He generally sits on the edge of a trench, over which the loom is built, while his feet rest on the treadles—an arrangement that allows the heddles to move more freely. The heddle bars are wider than in the western loom and are held horizontally by a hanging unit that is independent of both ends. Instead of a single pulley, there are two little balances (or rudder-like flaps). In this aspect, the East African loom is comparable to those of Asia rather than those of the West (Europe and West Africa), which tend to use pulleys.

The two other types of looms work by the combined action of heddles and a separating bar. The separating bar slips between the two sets of warp threads (even and uneven) and lifts one of them, while each of the threads of the other is engaged by the single row of heddles, which are attached to a rod (the heddle bar). The shed is formed by the lifting of each set of threads in turn. And here end the similarities between central and eastern looms, which, in fact, are limited to features coimon to all single-heddle looms.

In the loom of the east-central region (from Sudan to Rhodesia), the entire warp (whose length is consequently limited) is

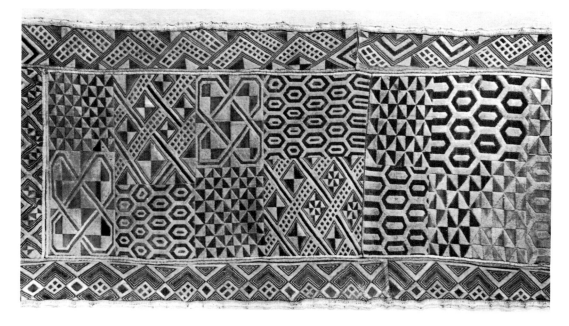

Bakuba fabric of plant fibers embroidered on raffia, called "Kasai velvet." Zaire. Paul Tishman Collection, New York. *Photo: Musée de l'Homme.*

stretched horizontally between two rollers attached to four posts and is generally just high enough from the ground for the craftsman to work seated in front of the breast-beam with his legs stretched out beneath the loom. In the north, he (or she) sits on the part already woven, and his weight keeps the warp in place in spite of the repeated movements of the pressing blade, which are particularly strong when coarse wool is being closely woven. The heddle shaft is always held up high, either by two brackets on which its two ends rest or by a frame from which it is suspended and which is like that on the double-heddle looms with treadles. The separating bar, situated behind the loom, controls the alternation of the shed: it lifts the set of unengaged threads when it is pushed right up against the heddles or is raised on its edge. Then it is drawn away or laid flat, allowing the tension of the heddles to lift the engaged threads. A wooden blade, inserted into the barely opened shed, prepares the passage of the shuttle which, pulled hard with both hands by the weaver, serves to press down the weft threads.

The vertical raffia loom works quite differently because it is based on the mobility of the heddle shaft. The weaver pulls the engaged threads forward with one hand while the other inserts the blade, which draws a piece of the weft with it into the open space. When he releases the rod, the separating bar causes the unengaged set of threads to return to their initial position. The warp threads are tied with cord to two cylinders, one attached either to the upper beam of the frame or to some sort of support, the other held at the base of the frame or directly on the ground by two pegs. The weft is always inserted in the same direction because the strands, which are short, are left free at both ends. The work is finished off by other means: knotting (if it is fringed) or sewing.

The looms described above can produce only plain cloth weaves (the 1/1 type), unless the weaver raises a few threads with his fingers and thereby creates a decorative effect. There are, however, some instances of figured woven cloth. On the raffia fabrics of the Congo region, a cross weave with a chevron effect seems an imitation of basketry decorations, which are very elaborate in this part of Africa. In the weaving of cotton strips, various relief and open-work effects are produced by lifting certain threads, by pressing or spacing the threads unequally or by including some threads that are of finer quality than the rest of the thread. Everywhere in Africa and on every kind of loom, multicolored decorations in bands, stripes,

Girls spinning. Abéché, Chad. *Photo: Rapho, L. Herschtriff.*

checks and squares are produced by using colored threads in the warp, weft or both. However, the most varied and richest decorative effects are produced by other methods, including printing, dyeing (with a wide range of resist processes) and embroidery (true embroidery on cotton and raffia, velvet raffia, appliqué work, etc.), but they are only mentioned here in passing because they are carried out by other craftsmen after the weaving has been completed. (See also *Basketry; Flora; Guro; Kitara; Kongo; Sao; Sculpture, Wood; Spiders; Towns and Cities; Work.*)   H.B.

WEIGHTS. Small figurines made of brass and sometimes of gold were among the first African works of art to be valued by Europeans. They were made by the delicate lost-wax process and were used for measuring the weight of gold dust and nuggets, assessing the rate of tribute due to a chief and the fines to be exacted from subjects who had not shown proper respect to a political or religious dignitary. Their use was common among all the Akan tribes living in the southern part of present-day Ghana (formerly the Gold Coast) and the area around the Ivory Coast (the lands of the Anyi and the Baule). In Africa, as in most of the archaic civilizations of the Mediterranean basin and the shores of the Indian Ocean, the first units of measure were seeds. The smallest unit was the *pesewa,* a tiny black papilionaceous bean that weighed the same as a grain of wheat—equivalent to 0.04 gram, or a little less than an English grain. The *damba,* a red seed with a black tip (*Abrus precartorius*) weighed twice as much—that is, 0.08 to 0.09 gram. The *abrus* appears from India to Batavia under different names, both as a measure of weight and as a monetary unit, and we do not know if its use as a weight

Weaving loom pulley. Baule. Ivory Coast. Wood. Pierre Vérité Collection, Paris. *Photo: Eliot Elisofon.*

originated on the west coast of Africa. On the basis of these three units, the Akan developed a complex system about which we do not know all the details. They added new measures when they learned about them from foreigners, like the Portuguese, without worrying about the correct proportions between the various units they were using. The Akan system was influenced to some extent by the Islamic system in which the most common unit of weight was the mitkal (4.5 grams), equivalent to 24 carats or seeds of the carob tree. In the Akan scale, the mitkal was a unit that was equal to 48 *damba*, or 96 *pesewa*. In order to make the weight of a figurative sculpture equivalent to the weight assigned to it—the weight of a particular seed or its multiple—its weight was increased by adding an excrescence of metal or decreased by paring away some of the metal.

The variety of shapes of these weights is endless: geometric forms, discs, squares, rectangles, pyramids, lozenges, trapeziums. The weights are decorated with motifs that are scarcely understood today; a common design is the swastika, called the "monkey's foot" in this part of Africa. The subjects of the figurative weights are equally inexhaustible: fish, reptiles, birds, weapons, musical instruments, seats, scenes from everyday life. Whether the artist made casts of natural objects, such as insects or seeds (especially peanuts), or whether he molded the figurines, the idiom of the figurative creation is always subtle, expressing its significance indirectly, by allusion; each weight illustrates a saying whose meaning

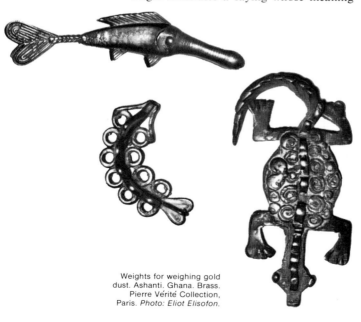

Weights for weighing gold dust. Ashanti. Ghana. Brass. Pierre Vérité Collection, Paris. *Photo: Eliot Elisofon.*

could not fail to be understood by the recipient. For example, the saying, "Birds of a feather flock together" is illustrated by birds perched on a tree; two entwined crocodiles correspond to the proverb, "Stomachs joined, crocodiles joined, what we eat passes down our respective throats, but we only have one stomach," which was often quoted when a relation showed little inclination to share. Two birds facing each other on a stylized base are interpreted as, "Scarab fallen into the farmyard and all the birds flutter excitedly." A creditor could remind a debtor of a sum due by sending a weight corresponding to the amount of money in question.

In addition to weights themselves, there are tiny, flawless scales, minute cylindrical or cubic boxes in which the gold dust was kept, shovels for gathering it up and little sieves for removing the impurities. The gold dust trade gradually declined until it ceased altogether in the nineteenth century, but new figurative weights were cast to attract tourists and curio hunters; however, they lack the interest of the earlier ones. (See also *Ashanti; Baule; Bronze; Lost-Wax Process; Proverbs; Writing.*)   D.P.

WIDOWS. Widows sometimes followed their husbands in death, but this fate was generally reserved for the wives of chiefs and kings, or for only some of them. During the funeral of a chief, the Walamba of Zambia used to kill two of his wives with spears, cut their bodies in pieces and give them to birds of prey. In the kingdoms of the Benin region, some of the wives of the king were shut up alive in his tomb along with a few of his servants, sometimes with their legs broken; it is said that until the last few reigns there was no lack of volunteers. In most cases, however, widows only had to submit to rituals and constricting taboos. In the land of the Fang, they were shut up in the hut of the dead man for a month, shaved, covered with ashes and forbidden to wash until the end of the month. The latter customs and the purification rites concluding the period of mourning were very common in Africa. The mourning period could last a long time; the Swazi of South Africa continued it for three years. During the ceremonies marking the end of mourning—among the Bakongo, for example—the widow was sometimes handed over to her new husband or was given permission to return to her people in exchange for repayment of the marriage compensation that had been given for her. The death of the husband did not, in fact, break the alliance concluded between the two family groups, one of whom had given up a potentially fertile woman in exchange for various compensations. On occasions when the widow's right to end the alliance was recognized, these compensations had to be returned to the donors, unless she was too old to bear any more children. In principle, the younger brother of the deceased "inherited" his widow. If there was no younger brother, sons could be the heirs—but, since a son obviously could not inherit his own mother, this could only affect the widows of polygamous marriages. Wives of a polygamous marriage were sometimes portioned out in the husband's will, as among the Basuto of South Africa. Sometimes a widow had the right to choose her new husband from among the relatives of the deceased— this was the custom of the Tiv of Nigeria. Whoever the heir might be, he was either a substitute for the deceased—and the widow's children were attributed posthumously to him—or a husband in his own right or simply a guardian and protector, if the widow was old. No matter what, widows were not abandoned by their husband's kin group unless they chose to exclude themselves. They remained attached to it through their children, who belonged to him, at least in patrilineal systems. In some tribes—the Tiv, for example—the members of the dead man's age group were always ready to help her in everyday tasks, such as cultivating her field, or in any serious difficulty. (See also *Adornment; Funerals.*)   P.M.

WISDOM. When nature provides a dry season or a rainy season, barren laterite or fertile soil, tasty antelope or dangerous buffalo, it is necessary to be in harmony with nature; when nature causes a person to have the will to power or the need for security, an attraction to or a fear of someone else, the desire to possess or the dissatisfaction of being deprived, it is wise to conform with nature. Traditional African wisdom has succeeded in bringing some sort of order to the inner life of the individual, which is reflected in his outer life—in relations between individuals. The first precept of African wisdom is that in human relations as little as possible should be left to individual choice. In the course of his education, a child learns gradually, but very accurately, the different social roles he will have to fulfill in his adult life. The African has a complex network of rights and duties toward each of his relatives (father, mother, father's wives, maternal uncles, cross and parallel cousins, etc.), his wives, his neighbors and strangers. An understanding of his role enables him to behave properly in most of his encounters with other people.

During the period of preparation for initiation, which in most African societies marks the entry of girls and boys who have reached puberty into the world of adult responsibilities, the initiation masters try to make them into socially well-adjusted individuals. Their aim is not to develop strong, unique personalities; they encourage conformity, not competition, which is considered a source of tension in the life of the community. In spite of this cautious conditioning, conflicts do arise, but African wisdom makes hardly any use of abstract principles to settle them. It attempts not to establish an ideal and lawful order, but to find a solution acceptable to both parties, which will grant each of them part of what he claims. What matters is restoring sufficient harmony for everyone to be able to live and work together. This approach excludes extreme solutions, rigid positions and absolute norms. A marriage alliance between two kinship groups is an affair decided by the lineages, not the future married couple. If one of the lineages objects to the union, the marriage will usually not take place; however, if a girl and boy want to marry each other against the wishes of their lineages, they can have their own way. Another example is that of a couple who want to end their marriage, but whose respective lineages are against breaking the alliance; here again, the principle of the primacy of group interests over individual interests is ignored if the two are sufficiently insistent and energetic in their desire to separate. The social norms are observed in most cases, and the community brings pressure to bear to see that they are, but they are not absolute; when their strict application creates a risk of serious discontent, and consequently a hindrance to the proper functioning of the group, an alternative solution is found.

Institutions based on an equilibrium of apparently contradictory obligations shows the African genius for a working compromise. The principle of the authority of the elders and notables, on the one hand, and the principle that everyone should share in decisions affecting the whole village on the other, are combined in the actual workings of the assemblies: everyone is invited to give his opinion, but not everyone's opinion bears the same weight; at the end of the discussion, it is the opinion of the men in authority that generally prevails, and the rest of the people rally unanimously. Both heredity and popular support frequently affect the selection of a new king. To become the successor to a ruler who has just died, a person must be one of his descendants born during his reign (thus, there is a group of individuals designated by heredity). Furthermore, the candidate has either to be chosen by a council consisting of some of the important notables, who represent the interests of the great lineages, or to overcome the other pretenders in a struggle that can be violent. The strength of the forces supporting the different candidates is the decisive factor, and in this way the people intervene, to a certain extent, in the choice of their ruler.

"African wisdom" is not merely a convenient expression; it is something that exists. It is a collection of unique precepts that enable the people of traditional Africa to settle as harmoniously as possible the disputes that mar human relationships. (See also *Education; Law; Person; Philosophy; Villages.*)   J.M.

WITCHCRAFT. See *Sorcery.*

WOMEN.
The social status of African women has been defined by several writers as a condition of alienation and unbridled exploitation by men. There is a good deal of truth in these charges, but they describe a situation that has grown up fairly recently, owing notably to economic consequences of colonization, and one that, furthermore, is

Lelapa, or women's quarters. Ndebele. Republic of South Africa. *Photo: Hoa-Qui.*

rapidly changing. Although women generally lived in a state of dependence in traditional societies, they benefited on the whole from fairly effective social mechanisms. The very clear-cut sexual division (the rites of excision and circumcision often accentuated this division symbolically) resulted, in effect, in separating tribes into two societies, each with its own customs, privileges and guarantees, a tendency that was further accentuated by the obligation to marry outside the clan (exogamy). The effect this had on the married couple was that husband and wife were legally strangers to each other; the married woman often continued to depend on her father—not her husband—for anything that involved important ritual or juridical obligations. It was not unusual for a woman, as a person with a certain intimate feminine physiology, to be regarded as magically dangerous. At the same time, her social importance depended entirely on her fertility, which was indispensable for the survival of the group to which she belonged. Consequently, it was in the role of mother that she most achieved fulfillment. According to the novelist Mongo Beti, Africa is matricentric; this is apparent in the ritual importance of the queen-mother in societies organized as states or protostates and in the quasi-mystical castigation attached to feminine sterility. On the other hand, queens are very rarely rulers; an authentic example, that of the Queen of the Rains of the Balovedu of South Africa, seems a recent historical phenomenon. The mother's curse is far more feared than the father's (positive female attribute), but women are more often accused of sorcery (negative female attribute). There is always a certain ambiguity that marks the feminine personality, in contrast to steadiness of the male personality.

In a subsistence economy, the division of labor between the sexes gave the woman, who contributed equally with her husband to feeding the family, a certain economic autonomy; she very often benefited from a sort of separation of goods. On the religious plane, women have their own cults, which are forbidden to men, and they continue to be animists in societies in which the men have been converted to Islam (among the Lebu of Dakar and the Hausa, for example). The feminine ritual societies, which have often been weakened in our day by missionary proselytism, tended to create a substitute bond between women who were strangers to one another and to their husbands (as a consequence of exogamy and patrilocal and all-male residence). They also acted as sorts of feminine unions that used charms or mild poisons to protect their members against ill-treatment from their husbands.

On the whole, although masculine dominance remained undisputed, the organization of traditional societies gave women a certain amount of independence as a group, which assured them of fairly effective protection. Colonization upset this state of affairs in several ways. The propagation of universal religions—Islam and Christianity—sapped the ritual sanctions of feminine societies to a large extent. Furthermore, the new monetary economy benefited men first and foremost (salaried posts, plantation jobs). It changed the very essence of the marriage compensation by giving it the character of a payment for something sold, and consequently modified the distribution of women; the new forms of polygamy in the plantation regions have taken on the character of capitalist accumulations of the means of production (women, in this case), resulting in a sort of unisexual proletariat. Women have become the sources of legal action to a far greater extent than they were in traditional societies. (See also *Adornment; Amazons; Bells; Blood; Body Painting; Breasts; Clothing; Dance; Diet; Dolls; Emancipation of Women; Family; Incest; Love; Marriage; Philosophy; Polygamy; Societies, Secret; Taboos; Twins; Widows; Work; Zar.*) P.A.

WORK. Work in Africa is never totally profane. It is closely connected with rites and is doomed to failure unless these are performed correctly. Work itself can be a rite as much as a physical activity. It is often supported by a myth: work causes or reproduces the movements or other manifestations of a divinity. This divinity is nearly always a culture-divinity or hero who taught the people the techniques that they use for whatever kind of work they do, and initiations place a certain amount of stress, which is more or less symbolic, on the apprenticeship of the initiates to the culture-divinity. Work not only has to follow the rhythm of the seasons; it also has to be in close harmony with the order of the world and contribute to its maintenance. Man cannot act on nature without discretion. He cannot force nature to do anything; he can obtain from her only what she chooses to give him, in acknowledgment of the alliance he has made with her, and he can only do so with the aid of suitable tools and at propitious times, which have a religious as well as a technical bearing. The most important work is that which results in the production of food and is connected with control over the fertility of the land, livestock

Left: Hollowing a cassava mortar. Dzem. Cameroun. *Photo: Pierre Ichac.*
Below: Team work in a field to the beat of a drum. Senufo. Ivory Coast. *Photo: Hugo Zemp.*

Little girls pounding cassava.
Bahutu. Itombwe, Zaire.
Photo: Jacques Maquet.

or wild animals, depending upon whether one is a farmer, herdsman or hunter. Craftsmanship also has a sacred aspect. The blacksmith is everywhere as much a man of ritual as of technique. He neither smelts ore nor forges metal without setting in motion the divinities who support him; his tools, from blast-furnace to the bellows, are altars, and their shapes, which often reveal a sexual identity, personify various powers. The act of weaving is made into a ritual by some tribes; for the Dogon, the loom and the movement of the threads evoke the primordial organization of the world.

The division of labor is often simple, as in all societies that have poorly developed technologies. In some states the craftsmen devoted all their time to their specialized work and were organized into large, cooperative families, generally in the service of the king or under his control. But in most cases, craftsmen worked only part-time or seasonally. Consequently, the division of labor was based mainly on sex and age. Among hunting peoples, the men pursued game, while the women did the food-gathering. In predominantly pastoral cultures, the men occupied themselves with the raising of livestock and the women with related activities, although they were subjected to severe taboos: they were forbidden to milk cows and sometimes even to touch them. Some writers have suggested that agriculture was originally an exclusively female occupation—derived from food-gathering as a

generally female occupation. Admittedly, in the Republic of Congo and Zaire, for example, after the men clear the ground, when this demands strength, the women alone till, sow, weed and gather the crops. But in most African societies, men and women share the work at every stage, and some of it can be done by either. Even sowing the seed, which is often reserved for the women because they impart their fecundity to the earth, is sometimes performed by men. Besides these agricultural tasks, the women, helped by the girls and children, naturally do the housework, see to the wood and water, do the cooking and look after the children. Although the picture of the African woman ground down by work at the side of her half-idle husband is not wholly justified, a woman's tasks are more numerous and more time-consuming—especially the preparation of food—than her husband's, and keep her more continuously busy.

Agricultural work, more than any other kind of work, is a collective, communal activity; it is based on cooperation and exchange. The members of an extended family produce together what they will consume together—under the strict control of the head of the family. Work on individual plots is not scorned, but it is secondary and is referred to by a different name; in some places, people were forbidden to grow any noble grains (the staple food) on them. Related families generally cultivate neighboring fields and often get together to help each other in countless ways. Work is a service that is often exchanged between relatives according to precise rules, depending, among other things, on the closeness of kinship. Mutual aid goes beyond family groups. A group of relatives and friends may get together to clear a piece of ground and turn it over. Sometimes it is the whole village, but more often the group consists of one or several age groups who offer their services whenever a job needs to be done quickly, or in order to help out a family head who is sick, and also to do work that affects the whole village community, such as the upkeep of trails and the repair of public buildings. The work done by these groups is often filled with a spirit of competition; the laborers advance in a line or teams move toward each other. Group work is performed to the rhythm of drums and in the form of a dance, not only for pleasure, which is increased by the distribution of food and drink to the laborers, but, in some cases, as an expression of a complex symbolism. Sometimes a temporary title is bestowed on the best worker. In the past, an African worked not for personal profit but for prestige—to have the honor of being a man who correctly performed the movements required by his work, as if it were a dance or a rite, and thus showing that he was worthy and fitted harmoniously into the family and village that benefited from his activity. Michel Leiris has remarked that in the Dogon initiation language, "there are two more or less synonymous terms whose meanings include both the idea of work, of movement in its broadest sense, and a concept related to moral and aesthetic value: the beneficent nature of a thing. The common denominator of these ideas, which have little connection, seems to be the notion of a useful, well performed activity...." (See also *Age Groups; Agriculture; Blacksmiths; Calendars; Colonization; Dwellings; Fishing; Hunting; Taboos; Villages; Weaving; Wisdom.*)   P.M.

WRITING. "Black Africa, land without a written language," is a phrase as false as it is hackneyed. To begin with, two world-wide systems—the Arabic and the Roman alphabets—penetrated Africa, one in the tenth and eleventh centuries and the other in the sixteenth century. The Roman alphabet, used by missionaries and colonists and also in international trade, is the more widely used of the two systems; it is employed as the medium for writing French, English, Portuguese and Afrikaans and also, with the addition of extra letters (alphabet of the International African Institute) or of superscript and subscript diacritical signs (Lepsius alphabet), for transcribing African languages. About a hundred such transcription systems are in more or less common use. However, only recently have the Roman alphabet and its derivatives gained an importance comparable with that of the Arabic alphabet. The Arabic alphabet is common mainly in the cursive *Nashki* type of Maghribi script, which was variously adapted to the phonetics of black African languages by the addition of dots to some characters. The best known of these variants is the Hausa *aljamia*. Kufic script is less widely used and is to be found mainly on the east coast. The Arabic alphabet has generally been used to write Fulani, Hausa, Kanuri, Swahili and Malinke. In recent years, the Roman alphabet has begun to replace it in transcriptions of these languages, but very orthodox Muslims still use it and are even trying to introduce it into the regions that are being converted to Islam (the lands of the Songhai and the Tem). On the borders of the Sudan, secret alphabets derived from the Arabic one are also used for inscribing

First Bamum alphabet (1895-1896). Illustration from *Ecriture des Bamum* by I. Dugast and M.D.W. Jeffreys (Report of the Institut français d'Afrique noire, 1950).

amulets and talismans. *Tifinagh,* a writing of Libyan origin, is still used by the Tuareg, but it is disappearing in the face of the advance of Arabic.

Besides these foreign systems, there exist a few purely black African alphabets, most of which were invented fairly recently. The most famous is the Bamum writing, evolved about 1900 by the king of Foumban, Njoya the Great. At first it was ideographic, but within a generation it developed a syllabic form and then an alphabetic form, while the number of signs fell from over 300 to about 40. Unfortunately, it is being abandoned by the younger generations, who prefer either the Roman or Arabic alphabet. The Vai writing of Sierra Leone and Liberia is more commonly used. It was evolved about 1835 by Momolu Duwalu Bukele and is a syllabic system of about 200 signs, which may have been derived from an older, pictographic system. A similar system, the Nsidibi, is still used in Calabar, eastern Nigeria, by a society of initiates of the Efik tribe. In Liberia and Sierra Leone there is also a Basa alphabet, dating from the beginning of the century, as well as a Mande alphabet, which is probably derived from Vai and which may itself have been imitated by the Toma and the Guerze of Liberia and upper Guinea.

An examination of how these different alphabets came into existence leads to the conclusion that the graphic expression of ideas (as distinct from language), in the form of proto-writing, either pictographic or ideographic, was much more widespread in traditional Africa than is commonly supposed. Africanists have recognized, or rather surmised, the existence of more or less precise systems of ideograms in the decorations on Dogon huts, the motifs on Bambara blankets, the weights for measuring gold among the Akan and the counters for the *abia* game played by the Fang. These proto-writings were only understood and used by high-ranking initiates. Few of them are still alive today, and too often they died without transmitting their knowledge. (See also *Bamum; Calabashes; Islam; Meroe; Music.*) P.A.

XYLOPHONES. The xylophone was more frequently described by travelers and illustrated in old prints than any other musical instrument of black Africa or black America. It was compared to the organ, the spinet and, later, the piano ("the piano of the blacks"), and was known as a *balafo,* a Malinke word that really referred to the musician, the player of the *bala.* Another name, *marimba,* borrowed from the Bantu languages, accompanied the instrument to Central America (Guatemala and Nicaragua); from there it was brought to Europe and applied to the modern xylophone. The instrument was first mentioned in the fourteenth century by the Arab traveler ibn-Batuta, who had seen it at the court of Mali. By that time, the African marimba was already constructed with a calabash under each wooden strip (or key), a feature that distinguished it from other types of xylophones used in Oceania and the Far East, whose strips were hung over an open case. The calabashes acted as resonators and also modified the timbre of the wood that was struck. They were pierced, and the hole, covered with a bit of an insect's cocoon or a cobweb, acted like a kazoo. The addition of the kazoos is an African invention and is found on two common types of xylophones: one where the strips are attached to a trapezoidal case that stands on the ground (sub-equatorial Africa); the other, a unique, portable instrument that is hung from the neck of the player, has strips attached to a frame that is flat or deeply curved (central and southern Africa). The number of blades

Fifth Bamum alphabet, "a ka u ku" (1910). Illustration from *Ecriture des Bamum* by I. Dugast and M.D.W. Jeffreys (Report of the Institut français d'Afrique noire, 1950).

varies between 14 and 20. They are struck with two batons or even four—a pair in each hand—with felt or, more often, rubber covering the ends. In the Malinke country, where there are real xylophone orchestras, the players wear bracelets from which copper bells dangle.

More primitive forms of xylophones, without calabash resonators, are found in various parts of Africa. One type, brought to Madagascar by Indonesians, consists of between six and a dozen wooden bars that are laid on the legs of a woman who is seated on the ground; the instrument is played by this woman and another person, who sits beside her. This is the origin of xylophone-on-the-legs, a game still played by children in West Africa. Another type of primitive xylophone that is African in origin was discovered in the seventeenth or eighteenth century in Barbados and on the coast of Guinea, and since then it has been found south of the equator. Its bars or strips are attached to two cross-bars placed on the ground, and a fairly deep ditch is sometimes dug between the cross-bars. At times, the strips are carried around in a bag and then attached to two banana tree trunks that are cut down on the spot. In Zaire, there are instruments consisting of a few strips attached to the edges of a boat-shaped case, which is the only example in Africa of a xylophone with a case. (See also *Calabashes; Dreams; Drums; Iron; Music.*)   A.S.

YORUBA. The Yoruba, numbering about 8 million, live in southwestern Nigeria and in southeastern and central Dahomey. All evidence indicates that they came from Ife, which is the center of the inhabited world in their mythology. It was there, in any case, that the first kingdom in this part of Africa was established, and the other Yoruba kingdoms were modeled after it. According to their oral tradition, their founders were the sons or grandsons of Odudua—all the Yoruba call themselves the "children of Odudua"—who gave firmness to the earth and built the town of Ife at its center. When he died, his possessions and domains were divided among his sons. The youngest, Oranyan, was cunning enough to keep the throne of Ife, which he entrusted to a regent, for himself. After a long period of adventurous wars, he founded the kingdom of Oyo, which dominated a large area of the country from the seventeenth to the nineteenth century. Besides the king of Ife, there were seven "crowned kings." The crowns were actually headdresses enlarged by tight networks of pearls which veiled the sacred faces of the rulers. The descendants of these

Playing curved xylophones. Balunda. Zaire. *Photo: Hoa-Qui.*

kings retained the privilege of wearing the crowns, although many of them played only minor roles while the uncrowned chiefs carved out powerful states for themselves. In spite of their strong feeling of a common origin, religion and culture, the Yoruba were never unified into a single political organization.

In a country where a curious urban civilization developed, each town had a large measure of autonomy. When an empire or a political hegemony which had included some of these towns collapsed, each town could form an independent state with the land surrounding it. This is what happened when Oyo fell under the attacks of the Fulani in the first half of the nineteenth century. When the British conquered the territory, nothing remained of these ancient suzerainties which had built up the vast, peaceful areas that had so impressed the first explorers, Clapperton and the Lander brothers. A king or land chief —a *bale*—ruled the town and territory that it sometimes controlled. The king was considered a sacred person, priest and god in human form. His enthronement identified him with a divinity. He lived apart from ordinary men, who were not permitted to see his face or speak to him directly. He did not eat or drink—that is to say, he never did in public. Nor did he die: the divinity simply passed from one human sheath to another. However, it seems that originally the king was killed after seven years' reign; in later years, if his subjects were discontented they could force him to commit suicide. The contradiction here is only apparent; it was

Yoruba statuette. Dahomey. Bronze. Josef Müller Collection, Solothurn. *Photo: Walter Dräyer.*

indispensable that the god-king should have a visible form that was strong and beyond criticism. The political organization was complex; besides the officials, who bore titles and more or less acted as ministers, the *Ogboni* secret society shared the power in a number of towns.

The Yoruba mythology, with its "201 gods," is one of the richest in West Africa. There is a continuity between the divinities, the kings and the ancestors. Odudua reigned

Worshiper of Shango. Yoruba. Dahomey. Wood. Museum of Primitive Art, New York. *Photo: Eliot Elisofon.*

at Ife and Shango at Oyo; several of the divinities are ancestors who specialize in a particular task and the control of a section of the universe. Except for the great organizing powers of the world, the same divinity can be either major or secondary, depending upon the place. The outstanding figures in the pantheon are: Shango, thunder; Olokun, the sea; Shokpona, the earth; Oko, agriculture; and Ogun, war and the forge. Around each of these gods or around clusters of them, cult groups are organized which can be joined through initiation; the gods "mount" their devotees during a ritual of possession. Both Eshu—the messenger of the gods, who is less a spirit of disorder than of accidents, of imagination and, through this, of liberty, the "hidden companion" of all gods and men— and Fa—the fate that is questioned in divination—have a special place in the pantheon.

The Yoruba land was one of the most extraordinary centers of art in all Africa. Stone, terracotta and bronze sculpture, which flourished at Ife before the thirteenth century, are all astonishingly classical in style. Religious, court and popular art existed side by side. Stone sculpture continued for a long time, and is indicated by the hundreds of heads discovered at Esié, which are thought to have been saved from the sack of the ancient town of Oyo. Metalwork by the lost-wax process declined more quickly, and eventually only jewelry and the *edan*, brass figurines that indicated membership in the *Ogboni* society, were produced. Sculpture in wood remained vital until modern times; "their doors, drums, everything of wood is carved," remarked Clapperton, who was the first European to visit the Yoruba country. The work is, in fact, very varied. The mask is the summit of a costume that hides the dancer. The masks of the *Guelede* society are simple heads with elongated skulls, but their faces are realistic and present a whole gallery of portrait types: the young man, the coquette, the seducer, the trader, the servant, the Shango initiate. *Epa* society masks are sometimes surmounted by carved objects and figures or may even be little more than pediments for a complex group of statues arranged around a central figure. These masks are generally painted in bright colors. The most remarkable drums are those belonging to the *Ogboni* society; these drums feature a sculpture of a man with fish-legs that curl their tails up to his hands. The divination trays are surrounded by carvings that include the face of Eshu. The great entrance doors to the family precincts were often covered with carved panels of scenes from everyday life, history or myth.

Yoruba mask of the *Guelede* society. Dahomey. Wood. Paul Tishman Collection, New York. *Photo: Musée de l'Homme.*

Yoruba mask of the *Epa* society. Dahomey. Wood. Museum of Primitive Art, New York.

The veranda posts were also carved with tiers of figures. And finally, the carving of statuettes of twins was a minor art of astonishing variety within rigid conventions. (See also *Agriculture; Allada; Amazons; Architecture; Benin; Bronze; Dahomey; Divination; Divinities; Dolls; Fetishes; Hausa; Heaven; Heroes; Ibadan; Ife; Ijo; Initiation; Ivory; Literature, Oral; Literature, Written; Numeration; Poetry; Possession by Spirits; Proverbs; Sculpture, Stone; Societies, Secret; Towns and Cities; Twins; Voodoo.*) P.M.

ZAR. In Ethiopia (among Monophysite Christians, Muslims and Falasha Jews), Somalia, Sudan, Egypt, Arabia and Turkey, there is a cult that is devoted to *zar,* invisible creatures whose name, according to Enrico Cerulli, is derived from the supreme god in the old religions of various Cushitic people. In spite of condemnation by the church and derision from the enlightened, a large body of faithful in Ethiopia attribute most evils, both physical and psychic, and all kinds of accidents in life to the interference of these male and female genii, who are divided into several categories. The cult is particularly

Yoruba mask. Dahomey. Wood. Musée des Arts africains et océaniens, Paris. *Photo: Réunion des Musées nationaux.*

popular among women. It takes a dual form: in the country, it is a family affair; in the towns, it has given rise to confraternities of sorts, each of which has a healer. The healer, who can be either a man or a woman, is someone who was once struck by *zar* and, after recovering, has remained the medium for some of them.

Since the harmful effect of the genius is due to its discontent, the essence of the treatment consists in ascertaining the source of discontent in the patient. This is accomplished during gatherings of devotees by means of singing and dancing to the accompaniment of a drum and crises of possession during which the patient is the "mount," the material habitation of the genius. After a while (usually quite a long while), the *zar*—speaking through the mouth of the patient, who is in a trance—reveals its identity and, eventually, yields to the objurgations of the great *zar*, represented by the healer, and consents to pardon the patient in return for sacrifices and offerings that will be donated to the "mount" of the great *zar*. Finally, the healer assigns a particular *zar* to the patient; this *zar* will watch over him and will periodically receive further sacrifices and offerings from him. In theory, the treatment is simple, but in practice it is very complicated and onerous because there is never just one genius involved but rather several genii who exercise their influence, and peace has to be made with each one. This provides a

convenient explanation in the not uncommon event that the treatment proves ineffective, since another dissatisfied genius, which did not declare itself, can always be incriminated. Since most of the sacrifices and offerings are made at the house of the healer, they are a source of income for him and provide a comfortable basis for his style of living; furthermore, since many of the oblations are means of communion and their purpose is to honor the *zar* of the individual donor, these offerings are often substantial. It is said that the most reputable of the healers are not directly paid, but the system obviously lends itself to abuse.

The *zar* play an important part in the private life of Ethiopians. The healer or the devotee concerned acts as an intermediary for the *zar* and often takes a definite point of view in family affairs (divorces and conflicting interests, for example), and wives often use them as a means of getting their own way with their husbands. Since the healer is really a *zar* incarnate, he can act as an adviser to his followers and, in so far as the general public is concerned, can make predictions, warn people and make himself feared by the curses he is in a position to utter. His house is visited by an extremely mixed clientele, especially since all kinds of people are sure of being received hospitably. A further attraction is the spectacular nature of the meetings that are held there; the crises of possession offer an opportunity to the actors to be centers of attention. Highly

Ruins of Zimbabwe. Rhodesia. *Photo: Magnum, Marc Riboud.*

similar institutions exist elsewhere in black Africa; in Nigeria, there is the *bori* of the Hausa, for example, and in Niger, the *holley* of the Songhai. Syncretic cults that originated in Africa, like Haitian voodoo and Brazilian *kandomble,* bear a strong resemblance to the *zar* cult. (See also *Ethiopia; Possession by Spirits; Spirits and Genii.*)
M.L.

ZIMBABWE. Zimbabwe, the largest archeological site in Rhodesia, is located about 18½ miles southeast of Fort Victoria. Approximately a hundred similar ruins, scattered over the territory formerly occupied by the Mashona, are known. In each of the chieftainships, the Mashona built a *dzimbahwe,* or "stone house," which was a venerated place where representatives of the tribe assembled to invoke the ancestors. The Zimbabwe ruins are divided mainly between the Valley and the Acropolis. The ground of the "Valley" is covered with a labyrinth of stone walls about 8 feet high. The "Temple"

is an oval enclosure, 31 feet high and, in some parts, more than 16 feet thick. Its walls, like those of all the Zimbabwe buildings, are constructed of uncemented stones; there are no foundations, but the ground must have been leveled before building began. Inside the Temple is a "Tower" that is apparently a solid, truncated cone; the Tower is more than 29 feet high and about 18 feet in diameter at the base. Less than a mile away, the ruins of the Acropolis occupy the summit of a hill whose slope determines the form of the enclosures stretching along its axis. The enclosure before the last one to the east, at the foot of a mass of fallen earth and stone, forms a small natural theater. It was here that the famous steatite birds were found, which may have been the relics of chiefs and are now in the museums of Capetown, Bulawayo, Salisbury and Berlin.

The Zulu invasions at the beginning of the nineteenth century destroyed the Mashona confederation, and the present inhabitants cannot offer any information about the

Half-man, half-bird figure from the Zimbabwe culture. Serpentine rock. Paul Tishman Collection, New York. *Photo: Musée de l'Homme.*

Ruins of Zimbabwe. Passage between two walls. Rhodesia. *Photo: Viollet, Roger.*

previous occupants, nor about the age or purpose of the structures. Portuguese writers of the sixteenth and seventeenth centuries mention a number of "Zimbaboe," but we are not sure that they were referring to the buildings of Zimbabwe. Its ruins were discovered in 1868 by Karl Mauch and described for the first time by J. T. Bent in 1891. The first serious archeological researches began in 1905 and were carried out by D. Randall MacIver, who established the African origin of the ruins. In 1929, the British archeologist G. Caton-Thompson directed systematic excavations, and since 1947 these excavations have been continued methodically on all the archeological sites of Rhodesia. Zimbabwe itself was excavated again in 1958. We are now sure that the stone walls were often used as the outer walls of dwellings made of puddled clay. In the western enclosure of the Acropolis, the 1958 excavations laid bare several superimposed layers: houses were gradually rebuilt on sites that had previously been occupied. The Acropolis precinct probably had a religious purpose.

Most of the objects unearthed were made locally: pottery, copper wire ornaments (of a type still worn in the region), iron weapons and tools, some gold jewelry and the stone birds of prey, some of them crowning a pedestal or column, which may have been connected with the cult of the thunder-bird that is still venerated in the region. But the finds also included fragments of pottery whose provenance was identified as Asiatic:

Chinese porcelain, Persian pottery, glass from Arabia and many imported glass beads. The most recent excavations have been followed by carbon-14 studies which have shown that there were several periods of occupation, the earliest of which was during the fourth century B.C. The walls date from the mid-fifteenth century, which is confirmed by historical traditions. Some of the later structures may have been the work of the Barotse, a tribe that dominated the Mashona confederation in the eighteenth century. (See also *Migrations; Monomotapa; Towns and Cities.*)   D.P.

ZITHERS. The term "zither" refers to a stringed instrument that has no neck. The strings are stretched the length of the body and attached to it at either end. The body is usually a flat or convex board, although a cylindrical surface such as a piece of bamboo can be used instead; but no matter what the curve, the strings remain equidistant from the body surface. This equidistance, which is a feature of the most highly developed types of zithers in Asia and Europe, is a result of the nature of the strings that have been used in black Africa and in the lands around the Indian Ocean from the earliest times until the present. The strings are thin strips that are partially detached from a piece of rattan or bamboo bark, which forms the body of the instrument. The finest example of this type of zither is the valiha of Madagascar; to make the strings, ten to twenty slivers are made in the bark of a shoot of bamboo and

Batusi zither player. Rwanda.
Photo: Jacques Maquet.

Zither player. Cameroun.
Photo: Hoa-Qui.

then pulled away from it with small wedges that act as bridges. This primitive way of creating tension, which leaves the two ends of the strip still attached to the stem, is also used in West Africa. It is most common in Dahomey, where about a dozen plant stems are attached side by side, like a raft, and two rods, placed transversally, raise the fibers. This kind of zither, called a raft zither, is played by scraping or plucking the strings and striking the back of the raft with the hand. Zithers made of single bamboo poles are only plucked. The music composed for the Madagascan valiha, in spite of the variety of influences it reflects, is very individual and offers the player considerable opportunities for displaying his virtuosity.

An unusual kind of instrument that is related to the zither has four or five strings, made from strips of raffia palm bark, that are stretched—unlike the strings of any other type of zither—on the same plane, perpendicular to the stem, like the strings of a harp. A long, thin bridge, attached to the body, lifts them in the middle to varying heights. One or two calabashes are attached under the stem to act as soundboxes. The instrument is a model of designing down to the ingenious construction of the least detail. It has been classed as a development of the musical bow and also as a combination of harp and zither, but this no more explains how it came into existence than the fact that it is found only in Gabon and around the middle reaches of the Congo River, side by side with highly dissimilar types.

An equally unusual instrument of central Africa poses another problem. Like the musical bow, it has only one string made of the usual plant fiber. It is stretched from one end of an oblong wooden board to the other; the board is generally concave and resembles a basin or trough. The six to ten parallel strands of the same string look like separate strings and, in fact, produce different notes. This instrument, too, could be considered as a development of the musical bow; it contains a primitive version of a sounding-board, which became an essential element in the final development of the zither. The instrument is found in the region between the Great Lakes and the upper courses of the Congo and the Ubangi Rivers, in an area of the continent where a number of influences seem to have converged. It is played mainly as an accompaniment for singing and dancing.

The final type of zither found in Africa is common in Madagascar, along the east coast of the continent and in various parts of Zaire, which may indicate influence from southeast Asia and Indonesia. It has from one to three strings stretched over a plank of wood with several projections that are used for frets. At one end, the strings are rolled around a transversal peg or simply knotted to one end of the bridge, which is pointed or fork-shaped. These instruments have one or two calabash soundboxes. The aboriginal inhabitants of India, Indo-China and the Celebes use the same kind of zither. Some are made of a plank of wood, but most are made from a bamboo pole, which may have been the original material for making the instrument. (See also *Bows, Musical; Harps; Music*.) A.S.

ZULUS. The Zulus, who were the most powerful of the South African tribes, fought against European domination until 1906. They were an amalgamation of the various Nguni clans of Natal and the Transvaal and were united by the conqueror Chaka at the beginning of the nineteenth century. The Nguni were Bantu who appeared on the coast of Mozambique toward the end of the fifteenth century and probably originated in the region round the source of the Congo River. The Nguni are divided into three branches: the Tembu, Batonga and Ndebele, who have to varying degrees been influenced by the Hottentots; this is recognizable in linguistic features, such as the click. The Zulus belong to the western branch—the Ndebele—who arrived in the Natal region at the beginning of the eighteenth century. Two great clans—the Mtetwa, under Chief Dingiswayo, and the Ndwandwe, under Chief Zwide—rose to prominence at the end of the eighteenth century. Each one tried to federate the Nguni clans of Natal under his authority. Eventually Chaka succeeded by beating Zwide after the latter had killed Dingiswayo in 1818. He himself was killed

and replaced by his half-brother Dingaan. Dingaan, beaten by the Boers on the Blood River in 1837, tried in vain to extend his authority northward; he was overcome and killed by the Swazi in 1840. His successor Mpande left practically all the power in the hands of his son Cetywayo, who succeeded him in 1872 and was beaten by the British in 1879 after a campaign during which the Prince Imperial, son of Napoleon III, was killed. At the death of Cetywayo in 1884, Zululand was occupied by the Boers and the British and finally lost its independence in spite of uprisings in 1886-1889 and 1906.

Zulu customs resemble those of other Nguni (Xosa, Mpondo, etc.). The main differences resulted from Chaka's reforms: political centralization and a strong military organization. Kinship is patrilineal, and each clan (*isibongo*, literally "motto") is theoretically descended from an ancestor in the male line; but this is in theory only, because, since Chaka's time, the clans have been amalgamated and mixed together. At the head of the political and territorial organization was the king; at the base was the *umuzi*, or patriarchal kraal; in between were the district, or *isigodi*, generally corresponding to the clan, and the province, or *isifunda* —both commanded by *induna*, who were local chiefs and counsellors of the king. The king was primarily a priest-king, responsible

Zulu village. Republic of South Africa. *Photo: South African Information Service, Pretoria.*

Zulu statue. Republic of South Africa. Wood. British Museum. *Museum photo.*

Zulu warriors. English engraving from the Transvaal War period, 1876.

for a whole series of rites on which depended the fertility of women, cattle and the land, the strength of the army and the good will of the ancestors. Secondly, he was a high judge. Finally, he was a legislator, and in this sphere, as in the judicial sphere, he could not act against the advice of his *induna* (although Chaka and his successor, Dingaan, did not respect this rule).

Military organization was based on age groups. Each regiment, or *impi,* corresponded to a group, and a new regiment was formed every six or seven years. The women, like the men, were divided into age groups, but there were only regiments of women under Chaka. Boys joined a military camp, *ikhanda,* a few months or even some years after puberty ceremonies. They could not marry or wear a head ring, *khehla,* until the regiment passed into the reserves (a period of six months or a year for the last regiments formed in the twentieth century). Each *impi* had its own uniform and mottoes, *isibongo,* which were reminders of its outstanding achievements. The primary military tactics consisted of a crescent formation: the wings would close in on the enemy, who was already engaged by the center, formed by the royal guard. A warrior who killed an enemy remained impure until

he had fornicated with a woman or, failing to do this, with an adolescent outside his clan.

Zulu women raised cereals, but the main economic activity was animal husbandry, which was reserved exclusively for the men and was particularly rich in magical and religious associations. The heart of the village was, topographically and spiritually, the livestock enclosure, around which the dwellings were built and which the women could not enter. Royal power was symbolized by the royal herds, which were divided according to the colors of their coats. Nearly 300 terms in Zulu describe the different varieties of livestock.

Religious and magical practices were centered in the cult of the ancestors, fertility rites and the fight against sorcerers. This fight was confined to a corporation of magicians exempt from military service and taxes who sniffed out the sorcerers during the course of impressive ritual ceremonies (see Rider Haggard's *King Solomon's Mines* for a vivid description of these). When sorcerers were discovered, they were impaled, their whole family was massacred and their goods were confiscated. The power of the college of magicians was so great that it even threatened the royal authority, although the king was, by his very nature, free from sorcery. Chaka had to resort to a purificatory slaughter of sorcerers, and Cetywayo established an asylum for chiefs accused of sorcery.

The Zulus have impressed all European observers by their courage and dignity. Romantic literature and even the contemporary cinema reflect this admiration. They were the most unyielding opponents of the *voortrekkers* and are proud of this record, which explains why they are found in the front rank of the fight against apartheid. (See also *Armies; Chaka; Initiation; Law; Migrations; Monomotapa; Mottoes; Poetry; Royalty; Weapons; Zimbabwe.*)   P.A.

Zulu divination sculpture.
Republic of South Africa.
Photo: Eliot Elisofon.

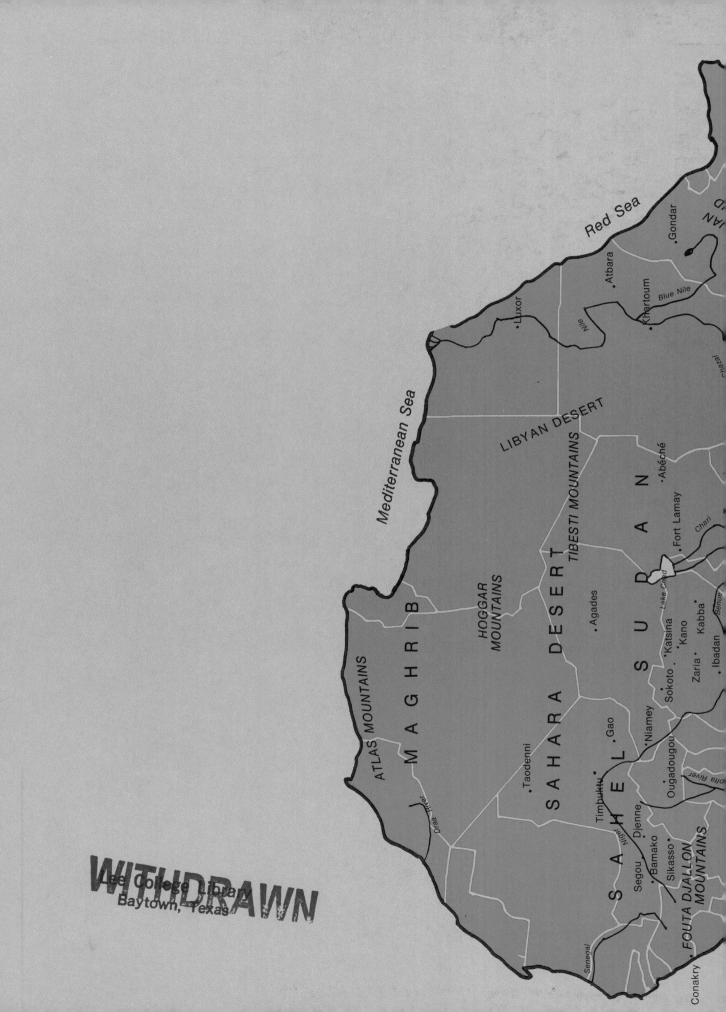

85520

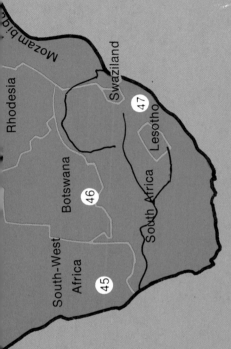

Madaga

Mozambique

Mozambique

Rhodesia

Swaziland

Lesotho

Botswana

South Africa

South-West
Africa

(47)
(46)
(45)

12	Ashanti	36	Bayaka
30	Azande	40	Bena Lulua
1	Baga	9	Bobo
39	Bajokwe	46	Bushmen
35	Bakongo	3	Dan
32	Bakota	10	Dogon
38	Bakuba	18	Edo
41	Balega	23	Ekoi
43	Baluba	31	Fang
44	Balunda	14	Fon
4	Bambara	7	Guro
25	Bamileke	16	Hausa
24	Bamum	45	Hottentots
37	Bapende	21	Ibibio
34	Bateke	20	Ibo
8	Baule	17	Ife

19	Ijo	33	Mpongwe
42	Kikuyu	28	Mussoi
27	Kirdi	5	Ngere
2	Kissi	22	Nok
29	Massa	26	Sao
11	Mossi	6	Senufo
		13	Songhai
		15	Yoruba
		47	Zulu

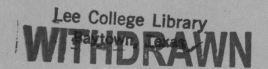